PUBLIC COMPANIES AND EQUITY FINANCE

PUBLIC COMPANIES AND EQUITY FINANCE

Alexis Mavrikakis MA (Cantab), Solicitor

Published by

College of Law Publishing,
Braboeuf Manor, Portsmouth Road, St Catherines, Guildford GU3 1HA

British Library Cataloguing-in-Publication Data

A catalogue record for this book is available from the British Library.

ISBN 978 1 910019 08 5

Typeset by Style Photosetting Ltd, Mayfield, East Sussex

Printed in Great Britain by Polestar Wheatons, Exeter

Preface

This book traces the life of a public company from birth (and its planned conception too), through adolescence and its growth into maturity until its demise, or at least the possibility of its demise, for immortality of course may beckon for this legal form of person. In doing so it concentrates on the public company listed on the London Stock Exchange. It is the mightiest of all companies, the biggest and the most high-profile. As such it operates subject to a whole raft of additional rules and regulations (advice on which provides many a fat cheque for lawyers and other advisers), and is required to expose itself to unparalled public scrutiny (providing rich pickings for newspaper and television journalists with unending column inches or minutes to fill).

This book has been written to explain the issues a lawyer may encounter when advising a public company. It seeks in particular to explain the principles behind the rules and to decipher the jargon which lawyers like to use in relation to those rules.

This book should be useful to law students and trainees in corporate seats, as an overview of public company work and as a guide to using the primary sources more effectively. It may also be of interest to the other professionals who work alongside public company lawyers, such as lawyers who undertake corporate support work, accountants and stockbrokers, as an insight into just what public company lawyers do.

To achieve an overview of public company issues, the best way to read this book is to start at Chapter 1 and read through to Chapter 24. This will guide you in a logical manner through the issues which face a public company, from registration, through flotation, to complying with continuing obligations, raising funds and entering into transactions. However, the book is also suitably cross-referenced to enable it to be used in practice as a reference book.

As a result of tremendous regulatory activity in the field of public companies over the past few years, primarily provoked by a raft of EU legislation and the global financial crisis, there have been plenty of significant amendments to primary sources. More significant changes will continue to occur in the coming years, not least because both the UK Government and the EU are fundamentally overhauling the system of regulation affecting public companies, but also since the economic outlook threatens to be decidely choppy for the foreseeable future.

I am most grateful to Alastair MacQueen, Robert Nisbet-Smith, Catherine Shephard, David Stott and Peter Watson for variously their bequest, forbearance in the face of deadlines stretched, scrupulous attention to detail and lawyerly insight.

This book should not be relied upon for the provision of or as a substitute for legal advice.

Please free to e-mail any comments to alexis.mavrikakis@law.ac.uk.

The law is stated as 1 October 2013.

Alexis Mavrikakis
The University of Law
Brussels

For Robert
and in memoriam
Alistair MacQueen
Suzanne Lowe
and Daisy

Contents

Table of Cases

Table of Statutes

Table of Secondary Legislation

Glossary

ABI	Association of British Insurers (which represents the interests of the UK's insurance industry)
ABI Guidelines	See **14.5.7**. Reproduced in **Appendix 2**
accounting reference date	The date on which the financial year of a company ends
Admission and Disclosure Standards	Rules made by the Stock Exchange in relation to admission to trading and disclosure of information (see **2.9**). Reproduced in **Appendix 1**
ADS	Admission and Disclosure Standard
AGM	An Annual General Meeting of shareholders and directors held pursuant to s 336 of the CA 2006
AIM	The Alternative Investment Market of the London Stock Exchange: a global market for smaller and growing companies
AIM Rules	Rules published by the Stock Exchange for AIM-quoted companies. Reproduced in **Appendix 4**
AIM Rules for Nominated Advisers	Rules published by the Stock Exchange for Nomads of AIM-quoted companies
analyst	Person employed by an investment bank or stockbroking firm to study a company or sector's performance
analyst's report	Report produced by an analyst, rating a company's shares as a buy, sell or hold. Often the report will coincide with the release of the company's results, and can influence the decision of investors as to whether to buy or sell shares in that company
audit committee	A committee of the board of directors, concerned with matters relating to the company's accounts and auditing (see **8.3.7.3**)
BIS	Department for Business, Innovation and Skills
bonus issue	See capitalisation of reserves
bookbuilding	See **4.4.2.1**
BVCA	British Private Equity and Venture Capital Association (the industry body for the private equity and venture capital industry in the UK)
CA 1985	Companies Act 1985 (which ceased to be in force on 1 October 2009)
CA 2006	Companies Act 2006
Cadbury Report	The 1992 report of the Committee on the Financial Aspects of Corporate Governance under the chairmanship of Sir Adrian Cadbury (see **8.3.2.1**)
capitalisation of reserves	An issue of securities, credited as fully paid, out of the issuer's reserves, to existing shareholders in proportion to their existing shareholdings (also known as a 'bonus' or 'scrip' issue) (see **13.5.5**)
CARD	Consolidated Admissions and Reporting Directive 2001/34/EC

CBI	The Confederation of British Industry (the UK's leading employers organisation)
certificate of approval	See **6.11**
CJA 1993	Criminal Justice Act 1993
CMA	Competition and Markets Authority (see **23.5.1**)
Combined Code	The Combined Code on Corporate Governance (see **8.3**)
CoMC	Code of Market Conduct. A code produced by the FCA, pursuant to s 119 of the FSMA 2000, to assist on the question whether particular behaviour is market abuse (see **10.1.2**). Contained in MAR1 of the Market Conduct (MAR) part of the FCA Handbook of Rules and Guidance
Company Reporting Directive	Directive 2006/46/EC (on accounts and the need for a corporate governance statement)
Conduct of Business Sourcebook	An FCA sourcebook which forms part of the FCA Handbook
continuing obligations	Obligations set out primarily in the Prospectus Rules, the Listing Rules, the Disclosure Rules, the Transparency Rules and the Corporate Governance Rules to which a company becomes subject when its securities are admitted to the Official List (see **Chapter 7**)
contract for differences	See **21.8.10.5**
Corporate Governance Rules	Rules published by the FCA relating to the establishment of an audit committee and the inclusion of a corporate governance statement in a listed company's annual report
CREST	The electronic settlement system for uncertificated securities trading (see **2.5.3.1**)
dematerialisation	The process of replacing paper share certificates and stock transfer forms with an electronic system (see **2.10.1**)
derivative	A financial instrument the value of which depends on the performance of an underlying asset or security. Examples include futures, options and swaps (see **21.8.10.5**)
Disclosure Rules	Rules published by the FCA relating to the disclosure of inside information and transactions by PDMRs and their connected persons
DTR	Disclosure and Transparency Rule
EA 2002	Enterprise Act 2002
EC Merger Regulation	Council Regulation 139/2004/EC
EEA	European Economic Area, a trading area comprising the Member States and Iceland, Liechtenstein and Norway
EFTA	European Free Trade Association: a free trade area established in 1960. Its current members are Iceland, Liechtenstein, Norway and Switzerland
equity securities	As defined in s 560 of the CA 2006, ordinary shares in a company or rights to subscribe for or to convert securities into, ordinary shares in the company

equity shares	As defined in s 548 of the CA 2006 and the Listing Rules, shares comprised in a company's equity share capital, that is, the issued share capital excluding any part of that capital which, neither as respects dividends nor as respects capital, carries any right to participate beyond a specified amount in a distribution
ESA	European Supervisory Authority, of which ESMA is one
ESMA	European Securities and Markets Authority, the EU regulatory body overseeing the financial markets including stock exchanges in the EU
Euroclear UK & Ireland Limited	The operator of CREST, owned by Euroclear plc
European Union (EU)	An economic and political union of European Member States created on 1 November 1993 by the Treaty on European Union (the 'Maastricht Treaty')
FCA	Financial Conduct Authority
FCA Handbook	A handbook published by the FCA, and updated monthly, of the rules and guidance issued by the FCA under the FSMA 2000, including the Part 6 Rules and the Code of Market Conduct
flotation	See IPO
FPO 2005	Financial Services and Markets Act 2000 (Financial Promotion) Order 2005 (SI 2005/1529)
FRC	Financial Reporting Council. An independent regulator which has responsibility for accounting standards in the UK and promotes high standards of corporate governance. Produces the UK Corporate Governance Code and The Stewardship Code
financial year	The period for which a company must prepare statutory accounts pursuant to the CA 2006
FSA	Financial Services Authority
FSA 2012	Financial Services Act 2012
FSAP	The European Commission's Financial Services Action Plan
FSMA 2000	Financial Services and Markets Act 2000
FTSE 100	A Stock Exchange index of the largest (by market capitalisation) 100 companies admitted to trading on the Stock Exchange
GAP	general accounting practice
GC100	The Association of General Counsel and Company Secretaries of the FTSE 100, which produces guidelines to assist its members in complying with the Part 6 Rules
gearing	The ratio of a company's debt to its equity (see **18.9.1**)
GM	General Meeting of the company
Greenbury Report	The 1995 report of the Committee on Directors' Remuneration under the chairmanship of Sir Richard Greenbury (see **8.3.2.1**)
Hampel Report	The 1998 report of the Committee on Corporate Governance under the chairmanship of Sir Ronald Hampel (see **8.3.2.1**)
Higgs Review	The 2003 review of the role and effectiveness of non-executive directors made by Derek Higgs

ICSA	Institute of Chartered Secretaries and Administrators (the leading professional body for company secretaries)
IIC	Institutional Investor Committee (a group of trade associations that represent institutional investors, and which comprises ABI, IMA and NAPF)
IMA	Investment Management Association (the trade body for the UK's asset management industry)
inside information	See **7.5.2.1**
International Accounting Standards	Accounting standards adopted for use in the EU in accordance with art 3 of the IAS Regulation (EC) No 1606/2001
IPCs	Investment Protection Committees (representative bodies of major institutional investors)
IPO	Initial public offering (of shares), also known as flotation. This refers to the company's first offer of shares on a stock market
irrevocable undertaking	See **21.10**
leverage	The opportunity to create profit by financing a business through debt which is entitled to only a finite return (see **18.2.2**)
liquidity	The ease with which a security can be traded on a market
listing particulars	A marketing document published, in terms acceptable to the FCA, as a condition of admission of certain specialist securities to listing (see **6.3**)
Listing Regulations 2001	Financial Services and Markets Act 2000 (Official Listing of Securities) Regulations 2001 (SI 2001/2956)
Listing Rules	Rules published by the FCA, relating to the admission of securities to listing on the Official List and the continuing obligations of listed companies
long-form articles	See **1.9.3.1**
LR	Listing Rule
MAD	Market Abuse Directive 2003/6/EC
MAD Regulations 2005	Financial Services and Markets Act 2000 (Market Abuse) Regulations 2005 (SI 2005/381)
Main Market	The Stock Exchange's principal market for listed securities
Market Abuse Directive	Directive 2003/6/EC (to tackle market manipulation and update the insider dealing regime)
market capitalisation	See **13.3.6**
Markets in Financial Instruments Directive	Directive 2004/39/EC (sets the legislative framework for investment firms and securities markets in the EU)
market-makers	A member of the Stock Exchange offering the market a two-way price (ie, buying and selling) in particular securities (see **2.5.2**)
member firms	See **2.5.1**

Member States	The 28 Member States of the European Union, namely Austria, Belgium, Bulgaria, Croatia, Cyprus, Czech Republic, Denmark, Estonia, Finland, France, Germany, Greece, Hungary, Ireland, Italy, Latvia, Lithuania, Luxembourg, Malta, the Netherlands, Poland, Portugal, Romania, Slovak Republic, Slovenia, Spain, Sweden and the UK. Currently applications for membership from the Former Yugoslav Republic of Macedonia (FYROM), Iceland, Montenegro, Serbia and Turkey are under consideration
MiFID	See Markets in Financial Instruments Directive
Misleading Statements Order 2001	Financial Services and Markets Act 2000 (Misleading Statements and Practices) Order 2001 (SI 2001/3645)
Model Code	A code regulating dealings by directors and certain others in the shares of their own companies. Premium listed companies must comply with this code or some other no less exacting in its terms (see **7.8**)
NAPF	National Association of Pension Funds (the UK representative body for organisations providing pensions)
NASDAQ	A stock market based in New York
NED	non-executive director
Nomad	The nominated adviser of an AIM Company (see **24.4.1**)
NSM	National Storage Mechanism (the UK's online facility for storing regulated information as required by the Transparency Directive)
offer period	See **22.3.4**
Official List	The list of securities which have been admitted to listing, maintained by the FCA under s 74(1) of the FSMA 2000
OFT	Office of Fair Trading
PAL	Provisional allotment letter, which is a negotiable document issued by a company which notifies the recipient that securities have been allotted to him on a provisional basis (see **17.7.3.1**)
Panel	Panel on Takeovers and Mergers (which regulates public company takeovers in the UK and issues the Takeover Code)
Part 6 Rules	The Listing Rules, the Prospectus Rules, the Disclosure Rules, the Transparency Rules and the Corporate Governance Rules
Perimeter Guidance Manual	A regulatory guide, forming part of the FCA Handbook, about the circumstances in which authorisation is required under FSMA 2000
PDMR	Person discharging managerial responsibility. See **7.8.2.1**
PD Regulation	EC Regulation 809/2004
PERG	Perimeter Guidance Manual
PIP	Primary Information Provider
PIRC	Pensions & Investment Research Consultants (the UK's leading independent research and advisory consultancy, providing services to institutional investors on corporate governance)
PMQI Order 2001	Financial Services and Markets Act (Prescribed Markets and Qualifying Investments) Order 2001 (SI 2001/1996)

poison pills	See **22.4.9**
PRA	Prudential Regulation Authority
Practice Statements	Informal guidance issued by the Panel Executive (see **20.5.6.1**)
Pre-emption Group Statement of Principles	See **14.6.16**
premium listing	A listing on the premium segment of the Official List
Primary Information Provider	See **7.5.2.7**
private equity house	See venture capital company
Professional Securities Market	The Stock Exchange's market for listing debt, convertibles and depositary receipts. Debt securities can be listed on either the Main Market or on the Professional Securities Market
profit forecast	See **22.4.5.1**
prospectus	A marketing document, published in terms acceptable to the FCA. See **Chapter 6**
Prospectus Directive	Directive 2003/71/EC (sets out the need for a prospectus for the issuers of securities on regulated markets across the EU)
PR	Prospectus Rule
Prospectus Regulations	SI 2005/1433
Prospectus Rules	Rules published by the FCA setting out the form, content and approval requirements for a prospectus
QCA	The Quoted Companies Alliance (a UK representative body established to protect the interests of the smaller quoted company (that is, outside the FTSE 350))
QCA Code	The corporate governance guidelines for Small and Mid-sized Quoted companies by the Quoted Companies Alliance (see **24.7**)
Regulated Activities Order 2001	Financial Services and Markets Act 2000 (Regulated Activities) Order 2001 (SI 2001/544)
Regulatory Information Service	See **7.5.2.6**
remuneration committee	A committee of the board of directors with responsibility primarily for determining or recommending the remuneration of the executive directors (see **8.3.7.4**)
responsibility statement	See **6.5.2.1** and **22.4.5.2**
RIE	Recognised Investment Exchange (includes the Stock Exchange)
rights issue	An issue to existing holders of securities of rights to subscribe or purchase further securities pro rata their existing holdings made by means of the issue of a PAL or other negotiable document (see **17.7.1**)
RIS	Regulatory Information Service (includes RNS)
RNS	Company news service of the Stock Exchange (an RIS)

rump	Those shares not taken up by the shareholders on a rights issue which it is sought to place in the market (see **17.7.5**)
scrip issue	See capitalisation of reserves
SEAQ	The Stock Exchange Automated Quotations System, a computer screen system enabling Stock Exchange members to advertise share prices for AIM-quoted securities that are not traded on SETS (see **2.5.2**)
Secondary Information Provider	See **7.4.2.2**
Second Company Law Directive	Directive 77/91/EC
settlement	See **2.5.3**
SETS	The Stock Exchange Electronic Trading Service, an order-driven electronic trading system for FTSE 100 securities and for the most traded AIM-quoted securities (see **2.5.2**)
SETSqx	The Stock Exchange Electronic Trading Service – quotes and crosses. A trading system for securities less liquid than those traded on SETS
short-form articles	See **1.9.3.1**
SIP	Secondary Information Provider
SLC	substantial lessening of competition
SMEs	small and medium-sized enterprises
Smith Report	The report of an independent group, chaired by Sir Robert Smith, to clarify the role and responsibility of audit committees (see **8.3.2.2**)
Societas Europaea (SE)	A European public limited liability company, which must be registered in a Member State with a share capital of at least €120,000
sponsor	A person approved by the FCA to sponsor an application for a premium listing of securities and to assist the issuer in fulfilling its continuing obligations
stamp duty reserve tax	A tax introduced by the Finance Act 1986 to cover paperless share transactions (which fall outside the ambit of stamp duty)
standard listing	A listing on the standard segment of the Official List
Statutory Audit Directive	Directive 2006/43/EC (on statutory audits of annual accounts)
stick	Those shares not taken up by shareholders on a rights issue, nor subsequently placed in the market, and which, therefore, fall to the underwriters or sub-underwriters (see **17.7.5**)
Stock Exchange	The London Stock Exchange Group plc
sub-underwriter	A person to whom the underwriters have laid off some or all of the underwriting risk on a marketing of securities
Takeover Code	City Code on Takeovers and Mergers, issued by the Panel (see above)
Takeovers Directive	Directive 2004/25/EC (regulating the takeovers of companies trading on a regulated market in the EU)

Transparency Directive	Directive 2004/109/EC (to enhance transparency on EU financial markets by requiring disclosure of periodic financial reports and of major shareholdings for companies trading on a regulated market in the EU)
Transparency Rules	Rules published by the FCA setting out the requirements for periodic financial reporting for listed companies and the disclosure of major shareholdings
Turnbull Report	Guidance, published by the FRC, for directors of listed companies regarding internal controls (see **8.3.5.1**)
UK Corporate Governance Code	A set of corporate governance standards for premium listed companies drawn up by the FRC.
UK GAAP	Generally Accepted Accounting Principles in the UK
UK Stewardship Code	A good practice guide for institutional investors when engaging with listed companies in which they invest, drawn up by the FRC.
UKLA	The UK Listing Authority, being a division of the FCA acting in its capacity as the competent authority for the purposes of Pt VI of the FSMA 2000
underwriter	In insurance terms, a person who takes on an insurance risk; in terms of the marketing of securities, a person who agrees to take up shares not purchased or subscribed for
venture capital company	A company which specialises in investing, typically, in unlisted, high risk businesses. The venture capital company helps to develop the business, often with a view to listing, with the aim of achieving significant return on its investment
Walker Review	An independent review by Sir David Walker of corporate governance in the UK banking industry carried out in 2009

PART I

BECOMING A LISTED COMPANY

CHAPTER 1

PUBLIC COMPANIES

1.1 INTRODUCTION

There are more than two million companies registered in England and Wales. Fewer than 15,000 are public companies. Of those public companies, approximately 2,400 have floated on the London Stock Exchange. Around 1,300 are listed on the London Stock Exchange's principal market for larger, more established companies (the 'Main Market'), with approximately a further 1,100 quoted on the Stock Exchange's international market for smaller, growing companies (the Alternative Investment Market or 'AIM').

This book is concerned with the small minority of companies which are public, and with that even smaller minority of public companies which have floated on the London Stock Exchange.

1.2 WHAT IS A PUBLIC COMPANY?

A public company is defined by s 4(2) of the Companies Act 2006 (CA 2006). It is a company limited by shares or by guarantee and having a share capital, which has complied with the requirements of the CA 2006 (or former Companies Acts) to enable it to be registered or re-registered as such.

How a company can achieve public company status is explained at **1.9**.

1.3 WHAT IS A LISTED COMPANY?

There are several specific definitions of a listed company in company law legislation, some of which are explored in more depth elsewhere in this book. However, broadly, a listed company is a public company any of the shares in which are officially listed and trade on a stock market.

The stock market which is the focus of this book is the London Stock Exchange's 'Main Market' which is the largest market in the UK. The London Stock Exchange's other market, AIM, is considered in more detail at **2.4** and in **Chapter 24**. In the UK there are two smaller competitor stock markets to the Main Market, ISDX and NYSE Euronext London. Companies may also be listed on stock markets based overseas, such as the Deutsche Börse in Germany, NASDAQ and the New York Stock Exchange in the USA, NYSE Euronext in Amsterdam, Brussels, Lisbon and Paris, NASDAQ OMX Nordic covering Denmark, Finland, Iceland and Sweden, and NASDAQ OMX Baltic covering the Baltic countries.

Obviously, when working with specific legislation, care must be taken to analyse the specific definition of 'listed'. For example, under some legislation a company which has its shares quoted on AIM rather than the Main Market will be a listed company, while under other legislation the same company will fall outside the definition of a listed company.

The words 'quoted' and 'listed' are usually used interchangeably, both by the layperson and by the practitioner. However, again, care should be taken to use appropriate terminology in relation to specific markets; the London Stock Exchange, for example, defines shares listed on the Main Market as listed (but not quoted) and shares listed on AIM as quoted but unlisted. Furthermore, the CA 2006 definition of 'quoted company' in s 385 refers to companies listed on 'regulated markets' including the Main Market but not AIM!

This can, of course lead to confusion. The key is to not take for granted the meaning of the terms 'listed' and 'quoted', but to examine (if interpreting such terms) or explain (if using such terms) the context in which they are used, taking account of the differing definitions.

For the purposes of this book, 'listed' is used to mean ordinary shares of an English company admitted to listing on the Official List of the Financial Conduct Authority (FCA) and admitted to trading on the Main Market of the London Stock Exchange.

1.4   THE DISTINCTION BETWEEN 'PUBLIC' AND 'LISTED'

❋ important

Just because a company is a *public* company, it does not automatically follow that it is a *listed* company. There is some correlation between public companies and listed companies, in that a company must be a public company to become a listed company (private companies cannot become listed companies). However, we already know that only about 10% of public companies are listed.

The distinction between the terms is important, because a company's status will determine how that company is regulated. Public companies are more heavily regulated than private companies; listed public companies are significantly more heavily regulated than unlisted public companies. The question therefore arises, why would investors wish to put their money in a company which is subject to additional restrictions and cost, imposed as a result of greater regulation? The answer rests on a consideration of the advantages (**1.5** and **1.7** below) and disadvantages (**1.6** and **1.8** below) of becoming a public company and a listed company.

1.5   ADVANTAGES OF PUBLIC COMPANY STATUS

WS1 ①
CD extra

1.5.1   Ability to offer shares to the public

It is prohibited for a private company to offer its shares to the public under s 755 of the CA 2006. The main reason for registering or re-registering as a public company, therefore, is to enable a company to offer its shares to the public. The ability to offer shares to the public is an advantage, as it provides a company with a new source of finance (the consideration received for the shares) and opens up new opportunities for raising finance which otherwise may be unavailable to the company.

If s 755 is breached the court has the power to re-register the offending private company as a public one under s 758 of the CA 2006. If, though, the company does not meet the requirements to become a public company then the court either may order that the company is wound up (s 758), or it may make a remedial order under s 759 of the CA 2006. The remedial order seeks to put a person affected by a breach of s 755 back in the position he was in before the breach. The court has wide-ranging powers to achieve this. The application to court for a s 758 or s 759 order can be made by a shareholder or creditor of the offending company, or by the Secretary of State for Business, Innovation and Skills (BIS).

1.5.2 Prestige

A secondary reason for a company to register or re-register as a public company is to benefit from the prestige conferred by the letters 'plc' ('public limited company'). Some companies therefore opt for public company status even if they have no immediate plans to offer shares to the public. Subsidiaries of public companies are often public companies too, for this reason.

1.6 POTENTIAL DISADVANTAGES OF PUBLIC COMPANY STATUS

As noted at **1.5.1** and **1.5.2** above, public company status brings with it the financial advantage of being able to offer shares to the public, and a certain element of commercial respectability. However, these advantages mean (in theory at least) that any public company, even if unlisted, can be owned by members of the public who have little day to day involvement in the company's business, and who therefore require greater statutory protection than the owners of a private company, who typically are more involved in the running of their companies, often as directors. For this reason, public companies are much more strictly regulated than private companies. This will add to the cost of running the company, and may restrict what it wishes to do and how it seeks to operate. **Table 1.1** below summarises the main differences between the regulation of public companies and private companies.

Table 1.1: Public companies compared to private companies

	Public company	Private company
Accounts	Must file with Companies House within 6 months after end of accounting reference period (CA 2006, s 442(2)(b)).	Must file within 9 months after end of accounting reference period (CA 2006, s 442(2)(a)).
	Must file full accounts with Companies House (CA 2006, ss 446 and 447 and ss 384 and 467).	Requirements to file full accounts can be relaxed for small and medium-sized companies (CA 2006, ss 444 and 445).
	Accounts must be laid before a General Meeting no later than 6 months after end of accounting reference period (CA 2006, s 437).	No requirement to do so.
Administration	Must hold an Annual General Meeting (AGM) (CA 2006, s 336).	No requirement to hold an AGM unless articles require it (SI 2007/ 2194, Sch 3, para 32(11)).
	The requisite percentage for holding a General Meeting on short notice is 95% (CA 2006, s 307(6)(b)).	The requisite percentage for holding a General Meeting on short notice is 90% (CA 2006, s 307(6)(a)).
	Cannot use the written resolution procedure (CA 2006, s 288).	Can use the written resolution procedure (CA 2006, s 288).
Directors	Minimum of 2 (CA 2006, s 154(2)).	Minimum of 1 (CA 2006, s 154(1)).

	Public company	Private company
	Restrictions apply on voting for the appointment of more than one director in just one resolution (CA 2006, s 160).	No equivalent restriction applies.
	A public company can only make a quasi-loan and a credit transaction with one of its directors provided prior shareholder approval has been obtained (CA 2006, ss 198 and 201).	The need for shareholder approval for quasi-loans and credit transactions with a director will be required only if the private company is 'associated with a public company', as defined in CA 2006, s 256 (CA 2006, ss 198(1) and 201(1)).
Financial assistance	Prohibited (CA 2006, s 678), subject to CA 2006, ss 681 and 682. See **Chapter 16**.	Generally permitted. Restrictions apply to private companies which are subsidiaries of public companies.
Secretary	A secretary is required (CA 2006, s 271). Section 273 sets out qualifications required.	A secretary is not compulsory (CA 2006, s 270(1)). If a company chooses to have one, there are no qualification requirements.
Share capital	The company must have allotted share capital at least up to the value of the authorised minimum (currently £50,000 – CA 2006, s 763 permits a euro equivalent to this amount, set at €57,100 (SI 2009/ 2425)) to register (CA 2006, s 761) or re-register (CA 2006, s 91(1)). The company must maintain this as its minimum share capital (CA 2006, ss 650 and 662).	No restriction on allotted share capital.
	Each share allotted must be paid up to at least one-quarter of its nominal value together with the whole of any premium on it (CA 2006, s 586).	No equivalent restriction applies. Can allot shares nil paid, partly paid or fully paid.
	Section 561 pre-emption rights on allotment can be disapplied under s 570 or 571 by special resolution or excluded and replaced by articles conferring a corresponding right under s 568.	Section 561 pre-emption rights on allotment can be disapplied under s 569 (by special resolution or provision in the articles), under s 570 or 571 by special resolution or excluded under s 567 (by provision in the articles).
	Restrictions apply on consideration for allotment of shares (ss 585, 587 and 598).	These sections do not apply.

	Public company	Private company
	Valuer's report required to value non-cash consideration for the allotment of shares (s 593).	No equivalent requirement applies.
	GM required in the event of a serious loss of capital (s 656).	No equivalent requirement applies.
	Charges on own shares are void, subject to certain exceptions (s 670).	Subject to certain requirements in s 670(2), charges on own shares are permitted.
	Can redeem and purchase shares out of distributable profits or the proceeds of a fresh issue, but not out of capital (ss 687 and 692).	Can redeem and purchase shares out of distributable profits, the proceeds of a fresh issue, or out of capital (ss 687 and 692).
Shareholders	Has disclosure obligations under DTR 5 and CA 2006, Pt 22 (see **Chapter 15**).	No equivalent restrictions apply.
Takeovers	Subject to the City Code on Takeovers and Mergers.	Typically not subject to the City Code on Takeovers and Mergers (but see exceptions at **20.5**).

1.7 ADVANTAGES OF LISTING

If obtaining public company status enables a company to offer shares to the public, what further advantage is there in listing?

1.7.1 Providing a market for the company's shares

A listing will provide access to a market on which members of the public and financial institutions can buy and sell shares in the company. As the shares can be bought at a pre-agreed price and sold relatively easily (the shares are said to be 'liquid'), they will be an attractive investment, particularly for members of the public who may not be familiar with the (usually more complicated) methods of buying and selling shares off the stock market. This market also enables the original owners of the company or private equity or venture capitalist investors to sell their shares and exit from the company, thereby reaping the rewards of their investment (although they may be restricted from exiting for a period of time immediately following the listing, to promote confidence in the company).

An extract from a newspaper article (below) gives an example of what this can mean in practice (whilst at the same time making you question your choice of career ...).

Flotation makes Sports Direct founder a billionaire

Julia Finch

SPORTSWEAR entrepreneur Mike Ashley joined the ranks of the super-rich yesterday after his Sports Direct retail empire floated on the Stock Exchange.

Mr Ashley sold 43% of his wholly-owned business – which includes 465 Sports World discount stores, Lilly-whites in London and brands like Dunlop, Donnay and Slazenger – to institutional investors, netting £929m in cash. He retains a 57% stake worth more than £1bn.

Source: *Guardian*, 28 February 2007

In October 2013 Mike Ashley sold a further 2.7% shareholding for £106 million, still leaving him 61.7% of the company, worth a tidy £2.5 billion at the the time of writing.

As we know from **1.5** above, those same members of the public and financial institutions can buy and sell shares in an unlisted public company if that company chooses to offer them its shares. Although both unlisted and listed companies need to take account of the same rules regarding how the shares are offered to the public (see **Chapter 6**), the shares in an unlisted company will not be listed or trading on a stock market. Therefore, the process of buying the shares, and subsequently finding people to sell them to, will not be as easy (the shares are not as 'liquid') and so members of the public, in particular, will be less inclined to invest in them.

1.7.2 Easier access to capital

A listing enables the company to raise finance through issuing new shares ('equity finance'), both at the same time as the initial listing and afterwards, from the huge supply of capital available through the stock market. See **4.4** and **Chapter 17**. A large number of listed companies are taking advantage of this equity finance to raise money in light of the much more restricted access to debt finance (ie, lending) as a result of the ongoing fallout from the global 'credit crunch'.

1.7.3 Access to acquisition opportunities

As a result of its access to the stock market and to its ready supply of capital, a listed company can often more easily raise cash or offer new shares in itself as consideration, thereby generally affording it the opportunity to expand through acquisition of other companies or businesses. Unlisted companies do not have the same access to this capital, not being part of a stock market, and, as explained in **1.7.1** above, unlisted company shares are not as attractive a form of consideration from a seller's perspective.

1.7.4 Prestige

The prestige attached to public company status (see **1.5.2**) can be enhanced further if the company lists successfully. In order to list, a company has to receive regulatory approval following considerable investigation into the company's suitability for listing. As listed companies have had their affairs scrutinised yet still obtained this approval, potential customers and suppliers may perceive listed companies to have greater financial standing than unlisted companies. This may help a listed company to negotiate better terms on which to conduct its business.

1.7.5 Profile

The press usually focuses its coverage on listed rather than unlisted companies, and listed companies will also be the subject of analysts' reports (produced by investment banks which rate a company's shares as a buy, sell or hold in order to assist investors with their investment decisions), so the profile of the company and its products will be raised. This can help create and sustain demand for, and therefore liquidity in, its shares.

1.7.6 Employee incentives

Listed companies can offer share ownership schemes to employees. While share ownership schemes are available to private companies, and are commonly used to motivate senior staff, listed companies have the additional advantage of being able to offer employees shares which have an identifiable value (as they are listed on a stock market). If employees own part of the company, the hope is that their commitment to the business will increase. The company should, therefore, benefit from being able to recruit and retain key employees.

1.7.7 Increased efficiency

Listed companies are strictly regulated (see **1.8.1** below). To comply with regulatory requirements, listed companies often have to improve their existing internal regulatory checks and controls. These improvements can, in turn, improve the operating efficiency of the company as a whole.

1.8 POTENTIAL DISADVANTAGES OF LISTING

1.8.1 Increased regulatory regime

As **Table 1.1** above shows, even an unlisted public company's regulatory regime is much stricter than that of a private company, to reflect the fact that any public company can offer shares to the public at large. However, once a public company is listed, the regime becomes even stricter than that set out in **Table 1.1**. This is because, as noted in **1.7.1** above, the ready market in listed company shares means that, in practice, members of the public tend to invest in listed companies, rather than in unlisted public companies, and therefore it is the shareholders of listed companies who require the most protection. The increased level of regulation involves higher costs for the company, a greater administrative burden, and places restrictions on what the company and its directors can do and how they do it. So what extra rules, over and above those summarised in **Table 1.1**, are imposed on a listed company?

1.8.1.1 Prospectus Rules, Listing Rules, Disclosure Rules, Transparency Rules and Corporate Governance Rules

The Prospectus Rules, the Listing Rules, the Disclosure Rules, the Transparency Rules and the Corporate Governance Rules, introduced in response to EU legislation, apply to any listed company. Such companies must consider the Prospectus Rules and the Listing Rules when first seeking a listing and subsequently when raising equity finance, and the Prospectus Rules, the Listing Rules, the Disclosure Rules, the Transparency Rules and the Corporate Governance Rules for their continuing obligations while listed on the Stock Exchange. **Chapters 5** and **6** consider the listing process; **Chapter 17** examines equity finance. **Chapter 7** looks at continuing obligations in more detail.

1.8.1.2 Statutory provisions

Certain statutory provisions apply to listed companies only:

(a) *The CA 2006*. For example, pursuant to s 420, the directors of a listed company are required to prepare a remuneration report on their pay, bonuses, share options and other related matters for inclusion in the company's Annual Report. It is a criminal offence for a director to fail to do so.

(b) *The FSMA 2000*. The market abuse provisions in Pt VIII of the Financial Services and Markets Act 2000 (FSMA 2000) apply to shares listed on various markets, including the Main Market. **Chapter 10** explores the market abuse provisions in more detail.

(c) *The CJA 1993*. Part V of the Criminal Justice Act 1993 (CJA 1993) provides that it is a criminal offence for a person who holds knowledge as an insider to deal, or encourage someone else to deal, in shares listed on a regulated market (which includes the Main Market). This is known as 'insider dealing'. **Chapter 11** considers insider dealing in more detail.

1.8.2 External forces

External forces beyond the control of a listed company, such as market conditions, rumour or developments in a certain market sector, can affect the company's value. Sometimes external forces can have a positive effect on share price, such as a cut in interest rates which may push up the share price of a heavily indebted company if its interest payments are reduced as a result; but on other occasions external forces work to depress the share price (consider, for example, the effect of the increased restrictions on carbon emissions on the share price of companies in the power generation industry). The fact that the value of the company can be so affected by forces outside its control can be a source of frustration to management.

1.8.3   Increased shareholder power

A large number of outsiders will become shareholders in the company when it lists. An extreme example is BT plc, which has approximately 1 million shareholders. Not only will any equity held by management be diluted by the influx of these shareholders, but listed companies are required to obtain shareholder approval of certain transactions and decisions which, in unlisted companies, would fall to management alone. The inevitable consequence is a decrease in management's level of control over the company. Furthermore, the pressure to keep shareholders happy with, for example, continually increasing dividend payments can cause management to focus on short-term rather than long-term performance. There is also the risk that shareholders will sell to unwelcome buyers seeking to take over the company.

1.8.4   Loss of privacy

The listing process under the Prospectus Rules and the Listing Rules, and the continuing obligations of the Prospectus Rules, the Listing Rules, the Disclosure Rules, the Transparency Rules and the Corporate Governance Rules (referred to at **1.8.1.1** above), the higher profile of the company (referred to at **1.7.5** above), and the greater accountability to shareholders (referred to at **1.8.3** above) mean that decisions of the management of a listed company are subject to much greater scrutiny than an unlisted company. If the company is underperforming, this loss of privacy can be very unwelcome.

1.8.5   Cost and time

The cost and time spent on the listing process, raising equity finance, complying with the continuing obligations of a listed company and maintaining good relations with investors can be onerous, and the company must decide before listing whether this time and money would be better directed towards running the business. The former co-founder and chairman of Betfair plc, which floated in 2010, in discussing mistakes which ultimately led to him resigning as chairman, said that the IPO 'was more of a distraction than we realised at the time. It took us 12 months at least to fully digest the process and that knocked us out of our stride for a bit.'

1.8.6   De-listing

These factors may equally apply to companies already trading on the Stock Exchange. Mainly because of the recession, a number of companies have decided to de-list from the Stock Exchange. In other words they are leaving the Stock Exchange and reverting to being unlisted public companies. An example is Parkwood Holdings plc which announced its intention to de-list in April 2011. Its board of directors argued that the costs (including lawyers' fees) and regulation of a listing, the management time that had to be expended as a listed company, the low share price and the low trading volume in the company's shares outweighed the benefits.

1.9   ACHIEVING PUBLIC COMPANY STATUS

A company can achieve public company status in three ways:

(a)   registering as a public company on original incorporation;

(b)   registering as a private company on original incorporation then re-registering as a public company; or

(c)   registering as a Societas Europaea (SE), a European public limited company.

The procedures under (a) and (b) ensure that the resulting public company complies with the CA 2006 requirements relating to a public company's articles, name and share capital.

The SE must comply with EC Regulation 2157/2001 on the Statute for a European Company and related legislation.

1.9.1 Incorporation of a company

Under s 9 of the CA 2006, the following must be sent to the Registrar of Companies to incorporate any company, private or public:

(a) memorandum of association (in the form set out in Sch 1 to the Companies (Registration) Regulations 2008 (SI 2008/3014));

(b) an application for registration (Form INO1) containing:

    (i) a statement of share capital and initial shareholding (content requirements set out in s 10);

    (ii) a statement of the proposed first officers of the company (content requirements set out in s 12);

    (iii) a statement of the intended registered office;

    (iv) copy articles of association (unless the new model articles are adopted unamended); and

    (v) a statement of compliance that all requirements of the CA 2006 have been met (further requirements set out in s 13); and

(c) a registration fee.

1.9.2 Registration as a public company on original incorporation

In addition to sending the documents referred to at **1.9.1** above to the Registrar, there are the following extra requirements to register as a public company on original incorporation:

(a) *Articles.* The articles must be in a form suitable for a public company. Under s 20 of the CA 2006, on registration of a public company a default set of model articles will apply, save to the extent that they are excluded or modified. These public company model articles can be found in Sch 3 to the Companies (Model Articles) Regulations 2008 (SI 2008/3229).

(b) *Name.* The company name must end with 'public limited company' or the Welsh equivalent (CA 2006, s 58), or with the abbreviation 'plc' or its Welsh equivalent 'ccc' (CA 2006, s 58(2)).

(c) *Allotted share capital.* The allotted share capital of the company must be not less than the 'authorised minimum' (CA 2006, s 761(2)). Currently the authorised minimum is £50,000 (CA 2006, s 763). In addition, each share allotted must be paid up to at least one-quarter of its nominal value together with the whole of any premium on it (CA 2006, s 586).

1.9.2.1 Certificate of incorporation

If the company meets all the requirements set out at **1.9.1** and **1.9.2** above, then it will be able to obtain a certificate from the Registrar that the company has been registered as a public company on original incorporation. However, although this certificate of incorporation will prove that the public company exists (CA 2006, s 15(1)), and details of the company will now be recorded at Companies House, the public company needs to obtain one other certificate before it can commence business – a trading certificate.

1.9.2.2 Trading certificate

A company which has been registered as a public company on original incorporation must not begin business or exercise any borrowing powers until it has a trading certificate, issued under s 761 of the CA 2006, confirming that the company has met the *allotted* share capital requirements of the CA 2006 (see **1.9.2** above). The certificate is proof that the company can trade and borrow. To obtain this certificate, an application must be made (accompanied by a statement of compliance) to the Registrar under s 762 of the CA 2006.

The allotted share capital requirements are that the company must have allotted shares at least up to the value of the authorised minimum (CA 2006, s 761), which, as stated in **1.9.2** above, is currently £50,000 (s 763) or the euro equivalent – currently €57,100 (Companies (Authorised Minimum) Regulations 2009 (SI 2009/2425)). Each allotted share must be paid up to at least one-quarter of its nominal value together with the whole of any premium on it (CA 2006, s 568).

What does this mean in practice? Well, if 50,000 shares with a nominal value of £1 each are allotted at nominal value with no premium, the minimum consideration which must be paid to the company is one-quarter of the nominal value of each share, that is 0.25p per share, making a total minimum payment of £12,500 for 50,000 shares.

If, however, the shares are allotted for, say, £3 each, then each share has a premium (the amount by which the price exceeds the nominal value) of £2. This premium must be paid to the company together with a minimum of a quarter of the nominal value of each share, which is £2 plus 0.25p, that is £2.25 per share, making a total minimum payment of £112,500 for 50,000 shares.

1.9.3 Re-registration as a public company

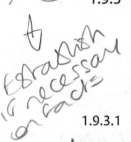

A company which has registered as a private company on original incorporation (by complying with the requirements detailed at **1.9.1** above) can re-register as a public company pursuant to ss 90–96 of the CA 2006. The company must pass a special (or written) resolution, meet the specified conditions and submit an application in a prescribed form to the Registrar (s 90(1)).

1.9.3.1 Resolution

The special (or written) resolution must:

(a) approve the re-registration of the company (CA 2006, s 90(1)(a));

(b) alter the company's name so it is in a form suitable for a public company. Section 58(1) of the CA 2006 requires that the name must end with 'public limited company' or 'plc' (or the Welsh equivalent – s 58(2)); and

(c) alter the articles so that they are in a form suitable for a public company. It is probable that the existing private company articles will require substantial amendment; it is often easier to adopt an entirely new set of articles rather than to amend the existing articles. If the company is re-registering as a public company as a preliminary step to listing in the immediate future, it may be appropriate to adopt a set of articles suitable not only for a public company but also for a public company which is listed. In this case the articles will probably disapply the model articles in their entirety and will be bespoke. These are known as long-form articles (as opposed to articles which apply the model articles either in their entirety or with some amendment, which are referred to as short-form articles).

1.9.3.2 Share capital requirements

The resolution deals with the requirements as to a public company's articles and name. What about the share capital requirements of a public company? This is dealt with by s 90(2). At the time the shareholders pass the special resolution (see **1.9.3.1**) the company must have satisfied certain conditions as to its share capital, namely that the company must have allotted shares at least up to the value of the authorised minimum (s 91(1)(a)), which is currently £50,000 (CA 2006, s 763) or the euro equivalent, currently €57,100, and that each allotted share must be paid up to at least one-quarter of its nominal value together with the whole of any premium on it (s 91(1)(b)).

(These requirements reflect the requirements which must be satisfied when a company originally incorporated as a public company applies for a trading certificate, set out at **1.9.2.2** above. A trading certificate therefore is not required for a private company which re-registers as a public company; the certificate of incorporation is all the company requires.)

Note that s 91(1)(c) and (d) provide some further requirements as to shares which have been allotted in consideration of an undertaking. Note also that some shares can be disregarded for the purposes of satisfying the share capital requirements (see s 91(2), (3) and (4)).

1.9.3.3 Application for re-registration

The special resolution must be delivered to the Registrar together with an application for re-registration on Form RR01, which has been signed by a director, the company secretary or a person authorised by the directors under s 270 or s 274 of the CA 2006. If the existing private company does not have a company secretary, one must be appointed and details included in the application. This is because under s 271 of the CA 2006, a public company must have a company secretary, whereas this is not a requirement for a private company. The application must be accompanied by the fee for re-registration (currently £20, together with £10 for any change of name – this change of name fee is not required if the company simply changes from 'ltd' to 'plc'; there is a same-day service available for £50) and the following documents:

(a) the revised articles (s 94(2)(b));

(b) a balance sheet prepared not more than seven months before the application, containing an unqualified report by the company's auditors (s 94(2)(c), s 92(1)). If the company's accounting reference date is within this seven-month period, this requirement can be met by the end of year balance sheet; if not, then an interim balance sheet must be prepared and must be audited, which can prove time-consuming and expensive. The auditors must also provide a written statement regarding the level of the company's net assets (as revealed by the balance sheet) in comparison to the company's called-up share capital and undistributable reserves (s 92(1)(c));

(c) a valuation report on any shares which have been allotted for non-cash consideration between the date of the balance sheet (referred to at (b) above) and the date the special resolution was passed (s 93(1)(a), s 93(2)(a)). This ensures that a private company seeking to re-register is brought into line with the general requirement under s 593 that public companies seeking to allot shares for non-cash consideration must have such consideration valued before allotting the shares; and

(d) a statement of compliance in the prescribed form (s 90(1)(c)(ii)).

1.9.3.4 Certificate of re-registration on incorporation as a public company

If the Registrar is satisfied with the application, he will issue the company with a certificate of re-registration on incorporation as a public company (CA 2006, s 96). The private company becomes a public company, and the revised articles and change of name will take effect on the issue of this certificate, which is proof of public company status.

1.9.3.5 Trading disclosures

The Companies (Trading Disclosures) Regulations 2008 (SI 2008/495) made under s 82 of the CA 2006 set out the requirements for a company to identify itself, at certain locations (including any place of business), on certain documents (including letters and order forms) and on its websites. The company must state its registered name and certain other registration details depending on the circumstances. Breach of these requirements can result in a fine for the company and any officer of the company who is in default. The company must update its websites and order new signs and company documentation, which will reflect its new identity, in advance of re-registration to ensure that it can meet these requirements with effect from the date the certificate of incorporation on re-registration is issued.

1.9.4 Registration as a Societas Europaea

The SE, the European public company, can be formed in any EEA Member State in accordance with EC Regulation 2157/2001 on the Statute for a European Company. In the UK this is supplemented by the European Public Limited Liability Company Regulations 2004 (SI 2004/2326). An SE can be formed in one of five ways, but only by existing companies.

Since their introduction in October 2004, very few SEs have been formed in the EEA (the German insurance giant, Allianz, being a notable exception in 2005). This is partly because an SE is subject not just to EU law but also to the domestic company law of the Member States in which it is registered and operates. Another reason is the need for the SE's operations to have been subject to the laws of at least two Member States before it became an SE. For example, an English public company can transform into an SE provided it has for two years had a subsidiary company governed by the laws of another Member State. An example is Scotty Group plc, which converted to an SE in September 2011 and was subject to English and Austrian company law.

An SE registered in England would be subject to the rules of formation, dissolution, reporting and management under the EC Regulation but also to much of the law which applies to English plcs.

We shall not consider the SE any further in this book, but it should be noted that the European Commission completed a review in July 2010 of the SE, and changes to the regime may be introduced in the future as a result. Also, proposals presented by the European Commission in 2008 for the creation of a European private company are likely to result in an increase in popularity in the SE should the European private company become a reality. The proposed legislation is currently on hold after a failure to reach agreement among Member States.

1.10 ACHIEVING LISTED COMPANY STATUS

When a company which does not have any shares listed on the stock market decides to list shares for the first time, the listing process is known as flotation or an IPO. There are different methods of flotation, the main methods for a company new to listing being by a public offer, placing or an introduction. Deciding to float is a serious step for a public company; the process is much more complex (and expensive) than that required for a private company to achieve public company status. **Chapters 4, 5** and **6** examine the complexities of flotation in more detail.

CHAPTER 2

THE LONDON STOCK EXCHANGE

2.1 WHAT IS THE LONDON STOCK EXCHANGE?

London Stock Exchange plc (the Stock Exchange) is a listed company. It has four principal areas of business:

(a) a market place for trading in company securities;

(b) a provider of trading platforms on which brokers can buy and sell securities;

(c) a supplier of market information to the financial community, and

(d) a market place for trading in equity derivatives.

The focus of this book is on the Stock Exchange's role as a market place for trading in a specific type of company securities – shares.

The Stock Exchange is at the centre of one of the world's three main financial centres – London, New York and Tokyo – with over 2,400 companies listed on it worth an estimated £4,000 billion, and is the most international stock market in the world, with companies from over 80 countries and territories, from the USA and China to Malawi, Bangladesh, Papua New Guinea and the Marshall Islands, listed on it. It also has one of the world's largest pools (and Europe's largest pool) of capital, with an estimated £2,500 billion available from UK-based sources, such as pension and insurance funds.

2.2 THE MARKET PLACE

The Stock Exchange has two markets for shares, the Main Market and the Alternative Investment Market (AIM). Both markets serve two main functions. First, they enable companies to raise funds by issuing new shares to the public. This is referred to as the primary market for shares. Secondly, they allow those issued shares to be traded (bought and sold) by the public. This is referred to as the secondary market for shares. The Main Market has both a primary and secondary market, therefore, as does AIM.

2.3 THE MAIN MARKET

The Main Market is the Stock Exchange's principal market for listed companies and is what the layman will think of as 'the stock market'. This is the market on which the shares of many household-name companies, such as Vodafone, BP, HSBC and Marks & Spencer (as well as a host of lesser-known companies), are listed. Within the Main Market, there are specific groupings for certain sectors: techMARK for innovative technology companies; landMARK for UK regional companies. There is also a High Growth Segment (HGS), established in 2013 for companies which may grow in size very quickly, such as internet-based companies. Note, however, that companies on the HGS, although part of the Main Market, do not have to join the Official List. They are therefore treated differently from listed companies. There are currently about 1,300 companies listed on the Main Market, which includes not only UK companies but also approximately 420 overseas companies.

The 100 largest companies make up the FTSE 100, which is used as a measure for judging the market value of these Main Market companies at any one given time. It is this FTSE 100 value which is used in the press to describe the current market, for example when a newspaper headline states, 'The FTSE 100 has dropped below 5,000'. The 100 largest companies are selected every three months.

2.4 AIM

The AIM is the Stock Exchange's Alternative Investment Market. It is a global market for smaller and growing companies. The AIM is a separate market from the Main Market, and while some companies may choose to move from AIM onto the Main Market at some point (such as Sportingbet plc, the online betting company in May 2010), there is no obligation to do so. In fact, lately, the trend has been for Main Market companies to move to AIM (such as Pinewood Shepperton plc in June 2012), where the regulatory burden can be lower than on the Main Market, or to leave it altogether to avoid the regulatory burden and costs.

There are currently approximately 1,100 companies listed on AIM (such as Mulberry, Glasgow Rangers FC, Prezzo and Majestic Wine), which includes over 350 overseas companies. The AIM has been a rapidly expanding market, but over the last couple of years the number of new admissions has slumped as a result of the global recession.

As stated at **1.3** above, the focus of this book is on companies which are listed on the Main Market. However, **Chapter 24** provides a brief overview of the regulation of AIM companies, compares AIM with the Main Market, and considers the advantages and disadvantages of joining AIM.

2.5 DEALING ON THE MARKETS

Dealing (ie, buying and selling shares) is not an area in which a corporate lawyer typically will have much involvement. The focus of the lawyer's role is to help to bring a client company to the market successfully, and then ensure that the company is advised of the regulatory regime it must follow in order to maintain its listing. However, the corporate lawyer's clients may well have an in-depth knowledge of dealing and the markets, and those clients may be unsettled if the lawyer helping to bring the company to market has no comprehension of how that market works. The following, therefore, is intended to provide some basic information on the mechanics of dealing.

There are two elements to buying and selling shares. The first is usually referred to as 'trading', and this is the process by which a seller is matched with a buyer. The second element is 'settlement', which is the process of paying the purchase price and transferring the shares.

2.5.1 Member firms

Member firms carry out most of the trading on the Stock Exchange's markets. They are investment firms (banks, stockbrokers and fund managers) which trade either on behalf of clients, or on behalf of their firms. Examples of current member firms are Barclays Bank plc, Citigroup Global Markets, Crédit Suisse Securities, Deutsche Bank AG, Goldman Sachs International, Merrill Lynch International and UBS.

2.5.2 Mechanics of trading

The Stock Exchange has fully automated trading systems. This means that any pictures you may see of people shouting and waving on a trading floor are either very out-of-date (this was discontinued in London in 1986 after the 'Big Bang'), or show one of the stock exchanges abroad (eg NYSE) which retains that system.

The Stock Exchange has devised various electronic systems for trading shares. These apply regardless of whether the shares are held in paper form (with a share certificate) or electronically (via CREST, see **2.5.3.1**). For the large Main Market-listed companies, including those on the FTSE 100 index, and for the most highly traded AIM-quoted companies, there is the Stock Exchange Electronic Trading Service (SETS), which is known as the order book. This electronic system matches 'buy' and 'sell' orders for the same shares and executes the trade automatically. A further system, SETSqx, supports the trading of shares in companies with turnover which is insufficient for the SETS system (such as the least liquid Main Market companies and most AIM companies). Finally, there is the Stock Exchange Automated Quotations (SEAQ) system for AIM securities not traded on SETS or SETSqx. With this system certain member firms act as competing 'market makers' in relation to certain shares. They will set the 'buy' and 'sell' prices for these shares, using current news about the company, the market sector and the strength of demand for shares as a guide. Member firms acting as 'brokers' will then buy and sell the shares when they think the price set by the market makers is right.

On average, over half a million trades a day in shares are executed on the Stock Exchange's markets.

2.5.3 Settlement

Once a share has been traded on the market, it needs to be transferred from the seller to the buyer, and the consideration monies need to be transferred from the buyer to the seller. This process is known as 'settlement'. There is a risk during the time between the trade being struck and settlement being made that the transaction will fail (for example, if one of the parties is declared bankrupt).

The settlement system discussed in **2.5.3.1** covers shares held in uncertificated form only, as these represent the vast majority of shares traded on the Stock Exchange.

2.5.3.1 CREST

CREST was introduced in 1996 and is a paperless (that is, the shares are held in electronic form and no share certificates exist, ie they are uncertificated) share settlement system through which trades on the Stock Exchange's markets can be settled. The system has legal backing under the Uncertificated Securities Regulations 2001 (SI 2001/3755). Euroclear UK and Ireland Limited operates this system. As the system is electronic and paperless, settlement can be made swiftly (within three business days of any trade), so the risk period between trade and settlement is reduced. Approximately 85% of the UK share market's value is voluntarily traded through CREST. There are various options for a shareholder wishing to hold shares through CREST.

CREST member

A CREST member must be linked up to CREST by computer network, so typically it is the member firms of the Stock Exchange (see **2.5.1** above) who have this type of membership. CREST members hold shares as nominees for individual clients (institutional or private investors), so the name of the CREST member, rather than the client, will be entered into the company's register of members as legal owner. The client will be the beneficial owner of the shares.

Each CREST member has an identification number for itself ('participant ID') and at least one other identification number for specific accounts it holds, such as an account for shares beneficially held on behalf of a specific institution ('member account ID').

CREST 'sponsored member'

This type of membership is designed to attract private investors (institutions and individuals). The benefit to the private investor is that its name will appear on the company's register of members (in contrast to the position if it holds shares through a CREST member, where the CREST member's name will feature on the register). Sponsored members who are individuals are known as 'personal members' to distinguish them from sponsored members which are corporate bodies. However, one drawback is that the CREST personal member does not have the required computer link-up to CREST. A CREST sponsor, who will be a CREST member, will provide this for the sponsored member, and will charge for the service.

Nominee shareholder

Other investors who are not CREST members or sponsored members, who hold their shares in electronic form, will hold them as nominees. This means that the shareholder will be the beneficial owner of their shares rather than the legal owner, and the name of the nominee (usually a CREST member) will appear on the share register.

The corporate lawyer and CREST

In practice, the impact of CREST for the corporate lawyer is not dramatic. For example it may involve ensuring that some standard wording is drafted into certain documents, such as how CREST shareholders can accept an offer and receive consideration (in a takeover) or take up shares (when raising equity finance), or being aware of CREST shareholders when considering the mechanics of an AGM. Some standard wording is available on the Euroclear website. The lawyer should be aware that Stamp Duty Reserve Tax is collected on paperless share transactions such as the transfer of shares within CREST. CREST itself, however, is responsible for collecting this tax.

2.6 INVESTORS IN THE MARKETS

2.6.1 Members of the public

Members of the public have significant involvement with the Stock Exchange. They can invest directly in shares listed on the Main Market or on AIM, either in the primary market (by subscribing for new shares issued by a company on flotation) or in the secondary market (by buying or selling shares which are already in issue). They can also invest indirectly (because, for example, their pensions, other savings schemes or employment incentive schemes are tied up in the Stock Exchange's markets). Obviously, the aim of the member of the public who invests is to realise a healthy profit on the sale of the investment but, as has been seen all too clearly in the current recession, what is intended and what is achieved can be very different.

2.6.2 Institutional investors

Institutional investors (also known as institutional shareholders), such as pension funds and investment funds, have sizeable funds available for investment. The amount they have available to invest means that institutional investors have considerable influence over the companies in which they invest. By way of example, BT plc has approximately 12,723 institutional investors who own around 89.12% of its issued share capital. One hundred and seventy-seven of them hold over 5 million shares each. By contrast, the remaining 968,889 shareholders (mainly members of the public) own 10.88%.

The main institutional investors have formed their own representative bodies called Investment Protection Committees (IPCs). Well known IPCs include the Association of

British Insurers (ABI) and the National Association of Pension Funds (NAPF). The IPCs have also joined together to form one representative body, the Institutional Shareholders' Committee (ISC). The IPCs issue guidelines as to how members should exercise their shareholder vote. While these guidelines do not have the force of law, listed companies do generally treat them as binding, such is the influence of the institutional shareholders.

Chapter 14 looks at some of these guidelines in more detail. **Chapter 8** also considers the role of institutional investors in relation to corporate governance.

2.7 REGULATION OF THE STOCK EXCHANGE

Section 19 of the FSMA 2000 prohibits any person from carrying on any regulated activity in the UK unless that person is either authorised or exempt. This is known as the general prohibition (see **9.4**). The Financial Conduct Authority (FCA) has granted a recognition order to the Stock Exchange under s 290 of the FSMA 2000. This means that the Stock Exchange is a 'recognised investment exchange' and, therefore, under s 285(2) of the 2000 Act, is exempt from the general prohibition. To remain a recognised investment exchange, the Stock Exchange must continue to satisfy various requirements drafted pursuant to s 286 of the FSMA 2000, including the Financial Services and Markets Act 2000 (Recognition Requirements for Investment Exchanges and Clearing Houses) Regulations 2001 (SI 2001/995), as amended, and the rules in the specialist sourcebook, 'Recognised Investment Exchanges', which form part of the FCA Handbook of Rules and Guidance. These requirements include that the Stock Exchange must:

(a) ensure that business conducted by means of its facilities is conducted in an orderly manner and so as to afford proper protection to investors;

(b) make arrangements for the provision of pre-trade and post-trade information about share trading;

(c) make clear and transparent rules concerning the admission of securities to trading on its financial markets; and

(d) be able to promote and maintain high standards of integrity and fair dealing in the carrying on of regulated activities by persons using facilities provided by the Stock Exchange.

2.8 THE ROLE OF THE STOCK EXCHANGE IN THE FLOTATION PROCESS

The Stock Exchange shares responsibility with the FCA for regulating IPOs. The FCA has responsibility for the official listing of securities in the UK. **Chapter 3** considers this role more closely. The Stock Exchange has responsibility for admitting shares to trading on its markets. Any company seeking to be a listed company (as defined in **1.3** above) must seek to have its shares:

(a) admitted to listing on the Official List (for which it must liaise with the FCA); and

(b) admitted to trading on the Main Market (for which it must liaise with the Stock Exchange).

Chapter 5 considers this process in more detail.

2.9 ADMISSION AND DISCLOSURE STANDARDS

The Stock Exchange has its own set of rules for companies joining the Main Market (they do not apply to companies joining AIM). These rules are called the Admission and Disclosure Standards, and they set out the requirements for companies seeking admission to trading, as well as the continuing obligations for companies already admitted to trading. They apply to both companies incorporated in the UK and overseas. Extracts from the Admission and Disclosure Standards as at 16 April 2013 are reproduced in **Appendix 1**. The full set of Standards is available on the Stock Exchange's website.

2.10 FUTURE DEVELOPMENTS

2.10.1 Trading

Under ss 783 to 790 of the CA 2006, there is the power for BIS to make regulations to enable shares to be owned or transferred without written documentation. At the time of writing, no such regulations exist. Replacing paper share certificates and stock transfer forms with an electronic system is known as 'dematerialisation'.

The EU is currently in the process of agreeing a new regulation, the CSD (Central Securities Depositories) Regulation. This will standardise the procedure for the settlement of securities in the EU (see **2.5.3** above for what settlement entails). As part of this new Regulation all shares in listed companies would have to be dematerialised and their shareholders would no longer be able to hold shares in paper form. The European Commission is aiming to have the CSD Regulation come into force by 2015. Current proposals suggest the Regulation will include a final deadline for dematerialisation of 2025.

CHAPTER 3

THE EU AND THE FINANCIAL CONDUCT AUTHORITY

3.1 EU REGULATION ⇒D in resource folder

The regulatory framework governing the listing of companies on the Stock Exchange in the UK has its basis in EU law. In 1999 the European Commission adopted a Financial Services Action Plan (FSAP), with the aims of creating a single market in financial services across all Member States of the EU by the end of 2005 and strengthening regulatory supervision. Over 40 measures have been implemented to achieve the FSAP, mostly in the form of directives (requiring implementing national legislation) and regulations (not requiring further national legislation).

The original regime regulating the listing of companies was established by the Consolidated Admissions and Reporting Directive (CARD) in 2001. This has been radically overhauled by four more recent directives, namely the Prospectus Directive, the Market Abuse Directive (deliciously abbreviated to MAD), the Transparency Directive, and the Markets in Financial Instruments Directive (MiFID). MiFID, although important in practice, is very technical in its subject matter and is of only limited relevance to this book.

The implementation of these EU Directives in the UK has fundamentally shaped the UK's listing regime. The FSMA 2000, as amended, is the primary piece of UK implementing legislation and the FCA Handbook sets out many of the key rules. The most important for our purposes are three 'sourcebooks' which are grouped together in the Handbook under the heading, 'Listing, Prospectus and Disclosure'. These three sourcebooks contain five sets of rules: the Listing Rules, the Prospectus Rules, the Disclosure Rules, the Transparency Rules and the Corporate Governance Rules. The last three are found in the Disclosure sourcebook and are known collectively as the Disclosure and Transparency Rules or DTRs.

The Listing Rules, Prospectus Rules, Disclosure Rules, Transparency Rules and Corporate Governance Rules are collectively referred to as the 'Part 6 Rules' by s 73A of the FSMA 2000.

In response to the 2007/08 global financial crisis and the complete failure of the various regulatory bodies to prevent the near collapse of the financial markets, the EU introduced a completely new regulatory system to oversee its financial markets including stock exchanges. The major development affecting listed companies is that the EU has established the European Securities Markets Authority (ESMA) which is based in Paris. The ESMA joins a European Banking Authority (EBA) and a European Insurance and Occupational Pension Authority (EIOPA), each being known as a European Supervisory Authority (ESA). This regulatory triumvirate has joined national regulatory authorities (such as the FCA in the UK) to form the European System of Financial Supervisors (ESFS). The intention is that this alphabet soup of acronyms (joined by the European Systemic Risk Board (ESRB)) will provide a more robust and effective regulatory and supervisory system for the financial services industry in the EU than was previously the case, with the aim of heading off the next financial crisis before its effects become as damaging as in 2007/08.

Whilst the European Commission still has executive responsibility for setting policy and proposing legislation regarding the financial markets, the ESMA has overarching responsibility for regulating and supervising financial markets, including the Main Market of the Stock Exchange in the UK. The ESMA issues draft technical standards and guidelines applicable across the EU which become binding when adopted by the Commission, or in certain cases where no objection has been raised by the Council or Parliament. It also makes recommendations and guidelines on the application of EU law, issues opinions to the EU institutions, encourages a common regulatory approach among all Member States, has powers to take emergency action when instructed by the Council, and has the power to ban or restrict temporarily certain financial activities which threaten the stability or orderly functioning of the EU's financial markets. It also has certain enforcement powers should national authorities (such as the FCA) not follow its recommendations. The ESMA intends

> to improve the functioning of the internal market, including in particular by ensuring a high, effective and consistent level of regulation and supervision ... to protect investors, to promote the integrity, efficiency and orderly functioning of financial markets, to safeguard the stability of the financial system, and to strengthen international supervisory co-ordination for the benefit of the economy at large ...

The ESMA website is http://esma.europa.eu. The ESMA is governed by EU Regulation 1095/2010 (the ESMA Regulation).

3.2   THE COMPETENT AUTHORITY FOR LISTING IN THE UK

The Directives referred to at **3.1** require each Member State to nominate an authority which is competent (the 'competent authority') to undertake the tasks which are set out in the Directives. The competent authority for listing in the UK is the FCA (see for example the glossary of the FCA Handbook). The former competent authority and the regulatory body for the entire financial services market in the UK, the Financial Services Authority (FSA), was replaced by the FCA, the Prudential Regulation Authority (PRA) and the Financial Policy Committee (FPC) on 1 April 2013. These changes were introduced by the UK Government, once again in response to the global financial crisis in 2007/08 which hit the UK particularly hard and resulted in a number of major banks being nationalised and a deep recession.

The FCA has a number of roles including that of markets regulator. This includes the regulation of issuers of securities subject to listing, and oversight of trading platforms and Recognised Investment Exchanges (RIEs) such as the Stock Exchange. It is therefore the regulator which dominates this book. You should, however, be aware that certain listed companies will also fall under the regulation of the PRA. The PRA authorises, regulates and supervises institutions such as banks, building societies, insurance companies and systemically important investment companies. In other words Barclays Bank plc, which is listed on the Main Market of the Stock Exchange, will be subject to regulation by both the FCA and the PRA, whereas Ocado plc, the supermarket delivery firm, will only be regulated by the FCA. The financial services companies are subject to extra scrutiny due to their special importance to the UK's economy and, frankly, because it was not the non-financial services companies such as Tesco plc, easyJet plc and Marks and Spencer plc which caused the 2007/08 financial crisis, and nor are they likely to cause the next one. You can find out more about the PRA on its website www.bankofengland.co.uk/PRA.

The FCA has a separate division to perform the specific role of competent authority for listing in the UK, and this is called the UK Listing Authority (UKLA).

Neither the FSMA 2000 nor the Listing Rules refer to the term 'UK Listing Authority' or 'UKLA'; they both refer to the FCA. Note, however, that in practice the FCA does still operate through its UKLA division in relation to all things to do with listing, and the FCA website has a separate section for UKLA matters. The FCA Handbook online also describes the Listing Rules as the UKLA listing rules on its contents page (similarly, it adds 'UKLA' for the Prospectus Rules and DTRs). In this book, to avoid confusion, the UKLA is not referred to when describing these rules.

3.3 WHAT DOES THE FCA (IN ITS CAPACITY AS THE UKLA) DO?

The FCA (in its capacity as the UKLA) has responsibility for the official listing of securities under Pt VI of the FSMA 2000. This includes:

(a)   maintaining the Official List (s 74(1));

(b)   drafting the Prospectus Rules, the Listing Rules, the Disclosure Rules, the Transparency Rules and the Corporate Governance Rules (s 73A);

(c)   determining applications for admission to listing, which includes reviewing the documentation which a company must produce to have its shares listed (s 75);

(d)   ensuring that listed companies comply with their continuing obligations under the Listing Rules, the Disclosure Rules, the Transparency Rules, the Corporate Governance Rules and the Prospectus Rules, which includes approving documentation prepared by listed companies, such as circulars (s 73); and

(e)   having the power to sanction any listed company which does not comply with the Prospectus Rules, the Listing Rules, the Disclosure Rules, the Transparency Rules and the Corporate Governance Rules (or any director of such a company) (eg s 91).

Chapter 5 looks at the listing process in more detail and considers how the FCA is involved in that process in practice.

3.4 RELATIONSHIP BETWEEN THE FCA AND THE STOCK EXCHANGE

In its capacity as markets regulator under the FSMA 2000, the FCA regulates the Stock Exchange. In an IPO, as stated at **2.8** above, both the FCA and the Stock Exchange are involved in the flotation process and have different roles to play. The FCA oversees the admission of shares to *listing* and the Stock Exchange oversees the admission of shares to *trading*. A listed company needs to have its shares admitted both to listing and to trading. **Chapters 4, 5** and **6** consider how a company can do this.

3.5 PROSPECTUS, LISTING, DISCLOSURE, TRANSPARENCY AND CORPORATE GOVERNANCE RULES

As referred to at **3.3**, the FCA has responsibility for five sets of rules, discussed at **3.5.1** to **3.5.3** below.

References to the Prospectus Rules and Listing Rules are prefaced with 'PR' and 'LR', and the Disclosure, Transparency and Corporate Governance Rules with 'DTR'. The paragraph number is suffixed with 'R' to indicate if this is a rule (and so binding), or 'G' to indicate if this is guidance (non-binding but generally if followed will be acceptable conduct).

3.5.1 The Prospectus Rules

The Prospectus Rules (together with the PD Regulation and the Prospectus Regulations 2005, 2011, 2012 and 2013 – see **3.5.1.1** and **3.5.1.2**) implement the Prospectus Directive in the UK. They contain provisions about the content of, and approval process for, a marketing document for an IPO called a prospectus.

These Rules apply to companies:

(a)   seeking to *offer* shares to *the public in the UK*. This includes offers of shares by companies seeking admission to AIM or the Main Market for the first time, or which are already admitted; and/or

(b)   seeking to *admit* shares to *trading on a regulated market in the* UK (which includes the Main Market but not AIM) (even where there is no offer to the public referred to at (a) above).

The fact that the Prospectus Rules apply both to companies which are quoted on AIM and companies listed on the Main Market is a break with the tradition of having separate regulatory regimes for AIM companies and Main Market companies. The Prospectus Rules apply to companies where the UK is the Home State under the Prospectus Directive, in other words companies incorporated in the UK and non-EEA companies which have offered their shares to the public in the UK or whose shares are admitted to AIM or the Main Market. They also apply where the securities regulator in another EEA Member State transfers responsibility to the FCA. Companies incorporated in other EEA Member States will generally comply with their own national law which is equivalent to the Prospectus Rules as the Prospectus Directive is law across all Member States. In addition the Prospectus Rules apply to an offer of depositary receipts by overseas companies rather than shares. The focus of this book, however, remains with listed companies as defined at **1.3** above.

The Prospectus Directive was drafted as a 'maximum harmonisation' measure, meaning that the UK was unable to set higher standards (known as 'super-equivalent' measures) for the issues covered by the Directive.

Chapters 5 and **6** consider the Prospectus Rules in more detail.

3.5.1.1   The Prospectus Directive Regulation (PD Regulation)

The Prospectus Directive takes the form of a framework directive. Much of the detail required for implementation is contained in an EC Regulation, the PD Regulation. Its articles and annexes specify in detail the form and content requirements of a prospectus. Helpfully for the practitioner, the Prospectus Rules, which, as explained above, implement the Prospectus Directive in the UK, replicate the contents of the Regulation (the articles are set out at PR 2.3.1EU and the annexes at Appendix 3). This means that the lawyer needs to be aware of the existence of the PD Regulation (it is referred to in the Prospectus Rules), but he will have all he requires in the Prospectus Rules.

3.5.1.2   The Prospectus Regulations 2005

The Prospectus Regulations (SI 2005/1433) are UK legislation which effected necessary changes to existing UK legislation in order to implement the Prospectus Directive.

3.5.1.3   The Prospectus Regulations 2011, 2012 and 2013

The Prospectus Regulations 2011 (SI 2011/1668), the Prospectus Regulations 2012 (SI 2012/1538) and the Prospectus Regulations 2013 (SI 2013/1125) implement the Directive amending the Prospectus Directive (Directive 2010/73/EU) by amending the FSMA 2000. The amending Directive seeks to reduce the administrative burden on companies raising money from the financial markets and to clarify a number of uncertainties which had arisen under the original Directive.

3.5.2   The Listing Rules

The Listing Rules contain the following key provisions:

(a)   six Listing Principles (see **3.5.2.1** below);

(b)   the eligibility criteria for listing;

(c)   the listing application process;

(d)   rules regarding sponsors;

(e)   the cancellation and suspension of listing; and

(f)   the continuing obligations of a listed company (supplemented by some continuing obligations in the DTRs and one continuing obligation in the Prospectus Rules).

The Listing Rules apply to companies whose shares trade on a regulated market, so they will apply to companies whose shares trade on the Main Market but not to companies whose shares trade on AIM. They apply both to companies incorporated in the UK and those incorporated overseas. The Listing Rules also apply to companies which are the subject of an application for listing but whose shares are not yet trading on a regulated market. This means that a company seeking to float on the Main Market of the Stock Exchange will have to take account of the Listing Rules even before its listing has successfully completed.

The Listing Rules also apply to other types of security listed on the Main Market such as depositary receipts, which are sometimes listed by companies registered in overseas countries instead of shares.

The Listing Rules are divided into 20 chapters. Chapters 1 to 3 and 5 apply to all securities; Chapters 6 to 14 apply to equity securities; and Chapters 4 and 15 to 20 apply to investment funds, investment companies, debt securities, depositary receipts (Chapter 18), derivatives and miscellaneous securities respectively (and so are not the focus of this book).

3.5.2.1   The Listing Principles

The six Principles, set out at 7.2.1R of the Listing Rules, are as follows:

Principle 1   A listed company must take reasonable steps to enable its directors to understand their responsibilities and obligations as directors.

Principle 2   A listed company must take reasonable steps to establish and maintain adequate procedures, systems and controls to enable it to comply with its obligations.

Principle 3   A listed company must act with integrity towards holders and potential holders of its listed equity securities.

Principle 4   A listed company must communicate information to holders and potential holders of its listed equity securities in such a way as to avoid the creation or continuation of a false market in such listed equity securities.

Principle 5   A listed company must ensure that it treats all holders of the same class of its listed equity securities that are in the same position equally in respect of the rights attaching to such listed equity securities.

Principle 6   A listed company must deal with the FCA in an open and co-operative manner.

The Principles are intended to ensure adherence to the spirit as well as the letter of the Listing Rules, and it is intended that they will work much like the general principles of the Takeover Code (see 20.5.5 below). The Listing Rules must be interpreted in line with the Listing Principles. The FCA has provided guidance on the application of the Principles (in its Technical Note UKLA/TN/203.1 Compliance with the Listing Principles, available in the UKLA section of the FCA's website) and has stated that it does not intend that they will apply any different standards to companies than are expected under the Listing Rules. The Principles are, however, enforceable like any other Listing Rule, and breach can lead to sanction by the FCA (see **3.6** below). For example, Prudential plc was fined £14 million in January 2011 for breaching Listing Principle 6 and other rules. In its Technical Note UKLA/TN/203.1 Compliance with the Listing Principles, the FCA has confirmed that it is prepared to take enforcement action on the basis of breach of the Listing Principles alone. It is important to note that these Principles only apply to companies which have a premium listing on the Main Market of the Stock Exchange and not to companies which have a standard listing (see **4.3.1.1**).

3.5.3   The Disclosure, Transparency and Corporate Governance Rules

These three sets of rules are contained in one FCA sourcebook, the Disclosure and Transparency Rules (DTRs). DTRs 1–3 contain the Disclosure Rules and DTRs 1A and 4–6 set out the Transparency Rules. DTRs 1B, 4.1.7R and 7 contain the Corporate Governance Rules.

The Disclosure Rules (together with amendments made to the FSMA 2000) implement the Market Abuse Directive in the UK and seek to prevent insider dealing and market manipulation.

These Rules contain rules and guidance about a listed company's continuing obligation to:

(a)   inform the market about new developments and its financial condition and performance (that is, to disclose 'inside information'); and

(b)   disclose transactions in shares by directors and senior executives and persons connected to them.

They are examined in detail in **Chapter 7**. The Code of Market Conduct (see **10.1.2**) and the Model Code (see **7.6**) should also be considered in addition to the Disclosure Rules and the FSMA 2000.

The Transparency Rules (together with amendments made to the FSMA 2000) implement the Transparency Directive in the UK. They seek principally to improve investors' access to information about companies trading on the UK financial markets, to enable them to invest more efficiently.

The Transparency Rules require more financial information to be revealed publicly about companies listed on the Stock Exchange more regularly than before. They also require the disclosure of significant shareholdings in listed companies, to ensure that these companies are aware of who is building up a significant stake in them, which may be a precursor to a takeover. They are considered in greater detail in **Chapters 7 and 15**.

As with the Listing Rules, DTRs 1–4 and 6–7 apply to companies whose shares trade on a regulated market, so they will apply to companies whose shares trade on the Main Market but not to companies which are quoted on AIM. Note, however, that DTR 5 applies to both types of company. The Disclosure Rules (DTRs 1–3) also apply to companies which are the subject of an application for trading but whose shares are not yet trading on a regulated market. Once again this means that a company seeking to float on the Main Market of the Stock Exchange will have to take account of the Disclosure Rules even before its flotation has successfully completed. The Disclosure Rules apply in most cases to overseas listed companies, and for the Transparency Rules it is necessary to read each particular rule to determine its application to overseas listed companies.

The Corporate Governance Rules were made under s 89(O) of the FSMA 2000. The Rules implement part of the Statutory Audit Directive and the Company Reporting Directive in the UK. Among other provisions, the Statutory Audit Directive requires listed companies to establish an audit committee in compliance with the Directive's terms. Rules relating to the establishment of an audit committee were already in existence for listed companies in the UK but on a non-statutory basis (see **8.3**). The Statutory Audit Directive requires harmonisation of the rules across the EU and, in the UK, for the existing rules to be put on a statutory basis. The Company Reporting Directive, in order to help promote credible company financial reporting and to prevent financial malpractice, requires listed companies to include a corporate governance statement in their annual reports. The Corporate Governance Rules are considered in greater detail in **Chapters 7 and 8**.

3.6   SANCTIONS FOR BREACH OF THE PART 6 RULES

The FCA can impose a variety of sanctions under powers granted by the FSMA 2000, depending on the particular set of Part 6 Rules breached. The sanctions may apply to securities other than just shares, such as debt securities, but as these are beyond the scope of this textbook they are not discussed. If necessary, reference should be made to the FSMA 2000 and the relevant definitions.

For breaches of *any of the Part 6 Rules* (Listing Rules, Prospectus Rules, Disclosure Rules, Transparency Rules and Corporate Governance Rules) the FCA can:

(a)   privately or publicly censure:

   (i)   the listed company (FSMA 2000, s 91(3)), and/or

   (ii)   a director or former director of the listed company knowingly concerned in the breach (FSMA 2000, s 91(3));

(b)   impose an unlimited fine on:

   (i)   the listed company (FSMA 2000, s 91(1), (1ZA), (1A) and (1B)), and/or

   (ii)   a director or former director of the listed company knowingly concerned in the breach (FSMA 2000, s 91(2)).

The FCA tends to censure a listed company rather than fine it when it is in severe financial difficulty (eg Cattles Limited in March 2012). Note that Cattles was a plc and a listed company but had left the market and reverted to a private company by the time proceedings were instituted against it.

In addition the FCA can:

(a)   suspend the *listing* on the Official List of a listed company's shares (FSMA 2000, s 77(2) and LR 5.1.1R and LR 5.1.2G);

(b)   cancel the *listing* on the Official List of a listed company's shares (FSMA 2000, s 77(1) and LR 5.2.1G);

(c)   impose an unlimited fine, publicly censure, impose conditions on or suspend the sponsor for a breach of its responsibilities (FSMA 2000, s 88A). The FSA, the forerunner to the FCA, used this last power for the first time in June 2011, censuring BDO LLP for breach of LR 8.3.3R and LR 8.3.5R (see **4.2.2** below) in relation to its acting as a sponsor for Shore Group plc.

Further, for a breach of the *Prospectus Rules* the FCA can:

(a)   suspend or require the withdrawal of the offer of shares to the public (FSMA 2000, s 87K(2) and (3));

(b)   suspend *trading* or prohibit *trading* in the listed company's shares (FSMA 2000, s 87L).

In addition, for a breach of the *Disclosure Rules* the FCA can:

(a)   privately or publicly censure (FSMA 2000, s 91(3) and DTR 1.5.3(1)R):

   (i)   Persons Discharging Managerial Responsibility (PDMRs) as defined in s 96B of the FSMA 2000; and/or

   (ii)   a connected person of a PDMR as defined in s 96B of the FSMA 2000 (DTR 1.5.3(1)R);

(b)   impose an unlimited fine on (FSMA 2000, s 91(1ZA) and DTR 1.5.3(2)R):

   (i)   PDMRs, and/or

   (ii)   a connected person of a PDMR;

(c)   suspend *trading* in the listed company's shares (FSMA 2000, s 96C and DTR1.4.1(R)).

In addition, for a breach of the *Transparency Rules* the FCA can:

(a)   suspend or prohibit the *trading* on the Main Market of a listed company's shares (FSMA 2000, s 89L);

(b)   impose an unlimited fine on a person subject to the Transparency Rules (FSMA 2000, s 91(1B)). For example, in August 2011 the FSA, forerunner to the FCA, imposed a fine of £210,000 on Sir Ken Morrison (formerly Chairman and director of Wm Morrison Supermarkets Plc) for his failure to comply with the Transparency Rules.

In addition, for a breach of the *Corporate Governance Rules* the FCA can suspend or prohibit the trading on the Main Market of a listed company's shares (FSMA 2000, s 87L).

Breaches of the Part 6 Rules may also give rise to the civil liability set out at **6.7.1** and the criminal liability set out at **6.7.2**.

The FCA has prepared the Enforcement Guide (EG) and a Decision Procedure and Penalties Manual (DPPM), which can be found in the Regulatory Guides and Regulatory Processes sections respectively of the FCA Handbook on the FCA's website. They provide useful guidance on the approach the FCA will take regarding enforcement of breaches of the Part 6 (and other) Rules.

3.7 FUTURE DEVELOPMENTS

3.7.1 Transparency Directive review

On 26 November 2013, a Directive to amend the Transparency Directive in order to make its application more effective and equal across Member States became law, with the new Directive having to be implemented by Member States within two years afterwards. Key changes to the law are highlighted where relevant in this book.

3.7.2 Market Abuse Directive review

The European Commission published in October 2011 proposals to update MAD to reduce the burdens imposed on business and to make it operate more effectively in light of perceived deficiencies which came to light during the global financial crisis. The Commission's proposals (known as MAD II) are to replace MAD with a new Market Abuse Regulation (known as MAR) and a new Directive on Criminal Sanctions for insider dealing and market manipulation (known as CSMAD). The proposals will have to be agreed by both the European Parliament and the Council of the EU. At the time of writing, agreement had been reached on the text of MAR and CSMAD. The text of MAR, however, cannot be finalised until the text of MiFID II (see **6.7.3** below) has been agreed as this will affect the scope of MAR. It therefore seems likely that the new rules will not come into force until 2016 at the earliest. The UK Government has announced that it does not currently intend to adopt the new Directive on Criminal Sanctions when it comes into force (it has the right to 'opt out' under the Lisbon Treaty). You can find out details of the latest position on http://ec. europa.eu.

3.7.3 Markets in Financial Instruments Directive (MiFID) review

In October 2011 the European Commission published proposals to replace MiFID with a new Directive, MiFID II, and a new Regulation on Markets in Financial Instruments (MiFIR) in order to improve investor protection in light of the financial crisis and to keep up with changing technology and market practice. It is hoped to finalise agreement on the proposals before the European Parliament elections in May 2014. It therefore seems likely that the new rules will not come into force until 2016 at the earliest. You can find out details of the latest position on http://ec/europa.eu.

3.7.4 FCA Handbook: Listing Principles

At the time of writing, the FCA is consulting on extending Listing Principles 2 and 6 (see **3.5.2.1** above) to standard listed companies as well as to premium listed ones. The remaining principles will be renamed Premium Listing Principles. In addition, it is proposed that two further Premium Listing Principles be added, one that each voting share in a class of listed shares has equal voting power, and the second that where more than one class of shares is listed, the aggregate voting rights should be broadly proportionate to their respective interests in the equity of the company. Both of these Principles aim to prevent a small group of shareholders exercising disproportionate control. These changes form part of a package of measures to restore confidence in the Main Market following problems with controlling shareholders in two foreign-owned companies, Bumi plc and ENRC. The consultation finishes in February 2014 and any changes to the Listing Rules are likely to come into force in mid-2014. The latest developments will be available on the FCA website.

CHAPTER 4

INITIAL PUBLIC OFFERINGS: PREPARATION

4.1 WHAT IS AN INITIAL PUBLIC OFFERING?

An initial public offering (IPO), also known as a flotation, is the process by which a company becomes a listed company (for our purposes as defined at **1.3** above). The terms 'IPO' and 'flotation' are used interchangeably. As **Chapters 2** and **3** established, any company seeking to become such a listed company must undergo a parallel admission procedure to have its shares:

(a) admitted to *listing* on the Official List (for which it must liaise with the FCA and comply with the Prospectus Rules and the Listing Rules); and

(b) admitted to *trading* on the Main Market (for which it must liaise with the Stock Exchange and comply with the Admission and Disclosure Standards).

While lawyers and other advisers need to be aware of the distinction between admission to listing and admission to trading, in practice the FCA and the Stock Exchange co-operate to ensure that the process is seamless. In fact, the layman would probably not be aware that, technically, an IPO involves two admission procedures. **Chapter 5** considers the actual IPO process in more detail. This chapter looks at the preparatory steps a company should take in the year (or two) preceding the IPO.

4.2 APPOINTING A TEAM OF ADVISERS

An IPO is a very complex transaction and good corporate advisers are vital to a successful outcome. In the year before the IPO the company must consider carefully who to appoint as its advisers. Usually it will seek preliminary advice on this matter from its current advisers (typically its lawyers and accountants). These advisers may not have the necessary expertise to advise in relation to the IPO itself, but they should be able to recommend suitable advisers who can provide guidance to the company. The company will sign engagement letters with some of the key advisers to govern the terms and conditions of their appointment specifically in relation to the IPO.

Any company seeking to float requires professional advice in relation to a wide range of issues. Lawyers advising on the legal aspects of the IPO form just part of a considerably larger team of advisers, who each take responsibility for various aspects of the float. Lawyers advising on an IPO cannot expect to work in isolation. They need excellent communication and project management skills. They also need a good understanding of the roles and responsibilities of the rest of the team. So who does what?

4.2.1 The company and the directors

As set out in **Chapter 6** below, the main marketing document for a float is the prospectus, and this must contain a substantial amount of information about the company. It is the directors who have primary responsibility for the accuracy of this information. While the directors cannot delegate this responsibility, practically they cannot supply all the information required in the time provided. Instead they enlist the help of the company secretary and key managers to locate, and provide to the advisers drafting the prospectus, accurate information about the company. Obviously this diverts many of the company's senior employees and directors from their usual role of day-to-day management and ensuring that the company is profitable. Companies need to be made aware of this hidden cost and distraction from their usual roles.

4.2.2 Sponsor/financial adviser

A company seeking an IPO to become a listed company must decide whether to have a premium listing or a standard listing on the Main Market of the Stock Exchange (see **4.3.1.1** below). Listing Rule 8.2.1R provides that any company applying for a *premium listing only* which requires the publication of a prospectus must have a sponsor (see **4.3.1.2** below). A sponsor is therefore not required if the company seeks a standard listing of its shares. Chapter 8 of the Listing Rules contains the rules relating to the sponsor. Listing Rule 8.3 sets out the responsibilities and principles for a sponsor, including the duty to act with due care and skill (LR 8.3.3R). With the exception of LR 8.3.5 (requiring sponsors to deal with the FCA in an open and co-operative manner and to deal promptly with FCA enquiries), which applies to sponsors at all times, LR 8.3 only applies to sponsors in connection with the provision of 'sponsor services', that is when they have to act under LR 8.2. Advice given by a sponsor outside of this definition is not within the Listing Rules and subject to other legal rules.

Listing Rules 8.4.1R to 8.4.4G set out the specific duties of the sponsor in relation to a float. The sponsor owes duties to the FCA, and a firm must take up an appointment as sponsor only once it is satisfied of the company's suitability for listing. Of course, no sponsor would want to be associated with an unsuccessful float in any event.

The sponsor has a crucial role in guiding the company and its management through the flotation process and advising the company on the interpretation of the Listing Rules. It will liaise with the FCA and, to a lesser extent, the Stock Exchange on behalf of the company, and will relay any comments back to the company. The sponsor also co-ordinates the team of advisers and will advise them on the timetable for the IPO. The lawyers in particular will have day-to-day contact with the sponsor as the flotation process progresses.

Usually an investment bank, a stockbroker or an accountancy firm will adopt the role of sponsor, but it must be approved by the FCA. Listing Rule 8.6 sets out the criteria for sponsor approval. A list of approved sponsors is on the FCA website, accessible via the UKLA section (LR 8.6.1G). The sponsor must abide by rules in LR 8.3 to ensure that conflicts of interest which may arise do not adversely affect its ability to perform its functions properly.

4.2.3 Broker

The broker advises the company with a view to ensuring that there is sufficient demand for the company's shares once the company has floated. The broker will analyse market conditions, liaise with potential investors to market the shares and advise the company on the best method of flotation (see **4.4** below) and other tactical issues, such the price of the shares to be marketed and the timing of the IPO. If the firm appointed as sponsor (see **4.2.2**) has stockbroking capability then it may also take on the role of broker.

4.2.4   Financial adviser

The financial adviser will advise on a wide range of tactical issues, such as the timing of the IPO, how the offer should be structured (see **4.4** below) and the offer price. Again, this role is usually adopted by the firm acting as sponsor on a premium listing. If a company is proposing to seek a standard listing on the Main Market of the Stock Exchange, it will of course still require expert financial advice and guidance through the listing process. A financial adviser (who will be drawn from the same pool of investment banks, etc which act as sponsors) will therefore be an essential appointment. However, the difference from a premium listing is that this adviser will not be treated as a sponsor under the Listing Rules and does not need to comply with Chapter 8 of the Listing Rules. The financial adviser will, though, have to ensure that the company complies with the other Listing Rules applicable to a standard listing, as well as with its own onerous responsibilities under the FSMA 2000 as an authorised person and other legal rules.

4.2.5   Reporting accountants

The reporting accountants review the company's finances. This is an important role, because whatever the company states in the prospectus about its financial situation will influence potential investors as to whether the company is an attractive investment. The company will want to present as positive a financial picture as possible, but the reporting accountants must ensure that this picture is accurate.

The reporting accountants will produce three main reports. The lawyers will have little involvement in the production of these, but they do need to know what they are (there will be frequent references to them in meetings). The first report is the 'long form' report, which is not published but forms the basis of the financial information required to draft the prospectus. The second report is the 'short form' report. This is based on the long form report, but it is published; it forms part of the prospectus. The third report is the 'working capital' report. The reporting accountants prepare this so that the sponsor can ascertain the company's anticipated working capital position for a period following the IPO (see **4.3.1.2**, Chapter 6(c)).

The reporting accountants may also provide 'comfort letters' to the directors, to enable the directors to make certain statements in the prospectus about the financial status of the company which are required by the Listing Rules (the directors cannot, however, delegate responsibility for making such statements to the accountants). The reporting accountants may also advise on taxation issues.

Note that the role of reporting accountants is separate from the role of the company's existing auditors. Often the same accountancy firm does adopt both roles, but allocates a different team to each. The sponsor, however, may prefer that the role of reporting accountant is adopted by an entirely different firm, so that it is seen to be independent.

4.2.6   Lawyers

There are usually two teams of lawyers, from different firms, involved in a flotation. They will be specialists in corporate finance. One team advises the company and one team advises the sponsor/financial adviser. Both teams must work closely together to provide a seamless service. The requirement for two teams reflects the fact that, while both the sponsor/financial adviser and the company have the common aim of a successful IPO, there are issues on which their needs conflict. For example, with a premium listing the sponsor owes certain duties to the FCA (see **4.2.2**) which the company does not owe. The sponsor will be highly sensitive about the risks of being involved with an unsuccessful IPO, or one which generates bad publicity, and the impact this will have on its ability to obtain work in the future. It may, therefore, wish to exercise a more cautious approach than the company in certain areas. The company and the sponsor/financial adviser are also likely to have conflicting interests regarding underwriting (see **4.2.7** below).

In addition to the company's lawyers and the sponsor's/financial adviser's lawyers, there may also be other lawyers representing any selling shareholders, if there is a conflict of interest between the company and such shareholders. If there is no conflict, the company's lawyers may also act for any selling shareholders.

4.2.6.1   The company's lawyers

The company's lawyers draft all the documentation relating to the IPO. This includes not only the prospectus but also any ancillary documents, including any preparatory documentation required to restructure the company (see **4.5** below), such as changing the articles of association, drafting new service contracts for the directors and re-registering the company as a public company (see **1.9.3** above). The company's lawyers are also responsible for the verification process (see **5.3.5** and **6.8** below) and ensure that the directors are fully aware of their responsibilities in relation to the content of the key marketing document for the IPO, the prospectus. The workload of the lawyers is examined in more detail at **5.3**.

4.2.6.2   The sponsor's/financial adviser's lawyers

These lawyers work with the company's lawyers to negotiate the agreements between the sponsor/financial adviser and the company and its shareholders (for example, the underwriting agreement). While the company's lawyers will have primary responsibility for processing the IPO documentation, the sponsor's/financial adviser's lawyers will also contribute towards drafting. They will keep a close eye on the company lawyers' progress regarding the legal documentation and the verification exercise (see **5.3.5** and **6.8**), and advise their client accordingly. Remember, the sponsor/financial adviser will not wish to be involved with a failure; if anything is not progressing as planned, the sponsor's/financial adviser's lawyers must alert their client.

4.2.7   Underwriters

The underwriters take up any shares left over after the IPO (in the event that the float is 'undersubscribed') in return for a negotiated fee, which is typically around 3 to 4% of the amount underwritten. If the IPO is 'fully subscribed' and there are no shares left over, the underwriter has no liability to take any shares. This arrangement is recorded in an underwriting agreement. The underwriter will usually allocate some or all of the risk of the offer being undersubscribed to sub-underwriters, by way of a sub-underwriting agreement (the company will not be party to any sub-underwriting agreement). Often the sponsor/ financial adviser will adopt the role of underwriter. Occasionally the broker (if different from the sponsor/financial adviser) will be the underwriter. Usually the sub-underwriters will be other banks and brokers, and the large institutional investors.

4.2.8   Receiving bank

If the IPO is by way of an offer for sale and/or subscription (see **4.4.1.1** below), the receiving bank deals with the application forms (see **5.4.2.2**) and consideration for shares. Often the company's clearing bank fulfils this role.

4.2.9   Registrars

The registrars manage the company's share register. They send the share certificates to the successful applicants. This can be a considerable task if the offer is sizeable. Often the company's clearing bank takes this role in addition to the role of receiving bank.

4.2.10   Financial public relations consultants

It is important for a company to have a positive public profile before, during and after the IPO. Financial PR consultants liaise with the media and analysts to heighten the profile of the company. They also ensure that the company's communications are effective.

For reasons explained in **Chapter 6**, it is important from a legal perspective that the company's communications are not misleading and can be verified by the company (see **5.3.5** and **6.8** below). The lawyers, therefore, have a role in ensuring that the financial PR consultants take into account these legal requirements. There can, in a process which is ultimately about selling a company and its management to investors, be a tendency towards emphasising exuberant unqualified statements, such as 'we are the biggest/the fastest/the best'; these, while being excellent selling messages, rarely survive the lawyers' red pens.

Good financial PR consultants will be aware of the legal limitations on the company's sales pitch from the outset, and can manage the company's expectations in this regard. It is not just pre-prepared communications which need to be handled cautiously, though. The consultants and the lawyers may also provide the directors with media training, so that when the directors are marketing the IPO they do not say anything ('we are the biggest/the fastest/the best') which might have adverse legal implications because it cannot be verified.

4.2.11 Printers

The IPO documentation will be created initially by word processor, but ultimately the final version will be professionally printed. Once each document is in substantially final draft form, it will be taken to print. Thereafter, each draft will be printed rather than take the form of a word-processed document. The printers need to turn around the documentation quickly, accurately and securely. Towards the end of the IPO the lawyers will spend some time, often well into the night, at the printers, checking *in situ* the final amendments to the draft.

4.3 IS THE COMPANY READY TO FLOAT?

The company may consider that it is ready to float, but the advisers, and particularly the sponsor/financial adviser, will need to ensure that the company has taken account of all relevant factors in reaching this conclusion. There are two main considerations, namely:

(a) Will the company meet the regulatory requirements for an IPO laid down by the FCA (in relation to listing) and the Stock Exchange (in relation to trading) (see **4.3.1** below)?

(b) Will investors perceive the company to be an attractive investment opportunity (see **4.3.2** below)?

4.3.1 Regulatory requirements

The company may not have considered any regulatory requirements at the time it appoints its advisers. However, as soon as the advisers are on board they will go through the regulatory requirements with the company and discuss the extent to which the company fulfils them. The company can then take action to remedy any problems.

4.3.1.1 Regulatory requirements for admission to listing

Under s 75(4) of the FSMA 2000, the FCA cannot grant an application for listing unless it is satisfied that the requirements of the Listing Rules have been complied with.

There is a two-tier system for companies seeking a listing on the Main Market of the Stock Exchange. Companies can seek to be admitted to either the premium or standard listing segment of the Official List. A premium listing requires compliance with the full set of conditions for listing as set out in the Listing Rules and elsewhere. A standard listing requires compliance only with those listing conditions required under relevant EU law. A premium listing therefore requires a company to observe so-called 'super-equivalent' provisions not necessary under EU law but imposed under English law by the FCA. This system was introduced to encourage companies to seek a listing on the Main Market in light of the collapse in the IPO market following the global financial crisis. By introducing a less regulated EU law-minimum listing option, the Stock Exchange hoped that more companies would list on the Main Market than would be the case with just the enhanced regulation listing option.

The factors for deciding which option to choose in essence come down to the level of regulation with which the company is capable of complying and prepared to bear, and the ease with which the company is likely to raise finance from investors. So far virtually all companies joining the Main Market, both UK and overseas companies, have done as Royal Mail plc, the UK's formerly nationalised postal service, which in October 2013 chose a premium listing. The reason is that, by complying with a higher level of regulation than required, the company is showing to investors that it is adhering to the highest possible standards and is likely to be a safer investment as the controls placed on it are more stringent. In February 2010, Horizon Acquisition Company plc sought a standard rather than a premium listing as it did not meet the requirements for the minimum period of existence as a trading company needed for a premium listing. It eventually bought another company with a sufficient trading record, changed its name and now has a premium listing as APR Energy plc.

Within each of the premium and standard listing options there is more than one category of listing, as set out in LR 1.6.1G. For a premium listing the three categories are dependent on the type of company. For most companies the 'commercial company' category will apply, and as such this is all we shall consider in this book. The five categories of standard listing depend on the type of security being listed, and so for our purposes it will be the 'shares' category that is relevant.

You should be aware that a company which has a premium listing of equity shares will be able to switch to a standard listing and vice versa under LR 5.4A. In July 2010, Phoenix Group plc was the first company to undertake such a transfer, moving from a standard to a premium listing. Certain changes between the various categories of premium listing are also permitted. There are a number of requirements which will need to be met in each case and which are set out in LR 5.4A.

4.3.1.2   Premium listing of equity securities

The FCA has the following requirements which a company must meet before its shares can be admitted to a premium listing on the Main Market of the Stock Exchange. The IPO team must be aware of these requirements and ensure that by the time the FCA hears the listing application, the company is capable of meeting all of them.

Sponsor

Listing Rule 8.2.1R provides that any company seeking a premium listing must appoint a sponsor. The sponsor's role is discussed in more detail at **4.2.2** above; however, the key role of the sponsor from the FCA's point of view is to ensure that the company is suitable for listing, to act as a link between the FCA and the company, and to advise the company in relation to the application for admission to listing and in relation to the Listing Rules.

Eligibility criteria (or 'conditions for listing')

Chapter 2 of the Listing Rules sets out the conditions which a company must satisfy before it can admit any type of security to the Official List, be these equity shares (such as ordinary shares) or depositary receipts for certain overseas-incorporated companies. Chapter 6 of the Listing Rules sets out additional conditions which must be satisfied by commercial companies seeking a premium listing of their equity shares, such as ordinary shares. A commercial company seeking a premium listing of its shares on the Official List therefore must fulfil the conditions for listing in both Chapter 2 and Chapter 6 of the Listing Rules. In addition, the FCA may impose additional requirements if it thinks it is necessary to protect investors (LR 2.1.4R(1)). By contrast an overseas company seeking to list its depositary receipts must comply with Chapters 2 and 18.

The conditions in Chapters 2 and 6 are discussed below, although the Rules, and particularly the Guidance to the Rules, should be consulted for further detail.

Chapter 2

(a) *Incorporation (LR 2.2.1R).* The company must be duly incorporated and operate in conformity with its constitution. For UK companies this means being a public company (as referred to at **1.5.1**, a private company cannot offer shares to the public). The methods by which a company can achieve public company status are discussed at **1.9** above.

(b) *Validity of securities (LR 2.2.2R).* The securities (for our purposes, shares) of the company must comply with all legal requirements and be authorised under the company's memorandum and articles. This means that the company must comply with all the provisions of the CA 2006 relating to the issue of shares, such as ss 551 and 561 (see **14.3** and **Chapters 13** and **14** generally).

(c) *Admission to trading (LR 2.2.3R).* Shares must be admitted to trading in order to be admitted to listing. As explained at **4.1**, companies seeking to float must not only apply to have their shares listed on the Official List, they must also apply to have their shares admitted to trading (for our purposes, on the Main Market). It is this condition to listing which links the two requirements and ensures a company cannot have shares which are admitted to listing but not to trading.

(d) *Transferability (LR 2.2.4R).* In order to list successfully, shares must be marketable. Therefore they must be freely transferable. This means that rights attaching to shares which are common in private companies, such as rights of pre-emption on transfer and the right of directors to refuse to register share transfers, generally are not permitted in the articles of any company seeking to list. (Note, for the avoidance of confusion, that s 561 of the CA 2006 provides a right of pre-emption on the *allotment*, not *transfer*, of shares, and so does not affect this condition in any way.)

(e) *Market capitalisation (LR 2.2.7R).* Market capitalisation refers to the number of issued shares in a company multiplied by the current market value of each share. In other words, it represents how much the company is worth. It is a condition to listing that the expected aggregate market capitalisation of the shares to be listed should be at least £700,000. In practice, given the amount of time and costs a company must invest in an IPO, the market capitalisation of shares to be issued on flotation is usually considerably in excess of this figure (for example, the Royal Mail plc IPO in October 2013 valued the company's shares at over £3.3 billion). Nevertheless, the FCA has discretion to accept a lower threshold if it is satisfied that there will be an adequate market for the shares (LR 2.2.8G).

(f) *Whole class to be listed (LR 2.2.9R).* If a company has different classes of share (eg, ordinary shares and preference shares), it can choose to list one class and not another (eg, list only the ordinary shares), but it cannot choose to list only part of one class (eg, half of the ordinary shares); all shares of that class must be listed.

(g) *Prospectus (LR 2.2.10R).* A marketing document, known as a prospectus, must be approved by the FCA and published if s 85 of the FSMA 2000 applies to the listing (see Chapter 6). (Note that LR 2.2.11R refers to the need for listing particulars, rather than a prospectus, if LR 4 applies. This concerns the issue of specialist securities which are not the focus of this book.)

Chapter 6

(a) *Historical financial information (LR 6.1.3R).* The company must have published or filed independently audited historical financial information for at least three years ending not more than six months before the date of the prospectus and not more than nine months before admission of the shares. The accounts must be consolidated for the company and all of its subsidiaries. The historical financial information must represent at least 75% of the company's business and put prospective investors in a position to make an informed assessment of the business for which admission is sought (LR 6.1.3BR). Listing Rule 6.1.3EG explains that the purpose of this rule is to ensure that the company has representative financial information for the three-year period before the IPO, and to assist the investor in making an assessment of the future prospects of the company's business.

Listing Rule 6.1.3BR sets out some of the circumstances in which the FCA may deem that the financial information may not be sufficient for the company to be eligible for a premium listing, for example if the value of the business on admission will be determined, to a significant degree, by reference to future developments rather than on past performance.

The FCA has discretion to accept accounts for a period of less than three years if satisfied that it is desirable in the interests of investors and that investors have the necessary information to make an informed judgement about the company and its listed shares (LR 6.1.13G).

(b)   *Control of assets and independence* (LR 6.1.4R). The company must carry on an independent business as its main activity, and the company must have controlled (and must still control, at the time of application for listing, and for at least the time period mentioned in (a) above) the majority of its assets.

The FCA has discretion to accept a trading record shorter than three years on the basis outlined at (a) above (desirability and investors having necessary information), but it must be satisfied that there is an overriding reason for the company seeking a listing on the Official List as opposed to seeking admission for a standard listing or to a market more suited to a company with a trading record of less than three years (such as AIM) (LR 6.1.13G to LR 6.1.15G).

(c)   *Working capital* (LR 6.1.16R). The company and its subsidiaries must have sufficient working capital for the group's requirements for at least 12 months from the date on which the prospectus is published.

(d)   *Shares in public hands* (LR 6.1.19R). Following the flotation, at least 25% of the class of shares to be listed should be 'in public hands' across the European Economic Area (EEA). This is to ensure there is a sufficient market in the shares. Listing Rule 6.1.19(4)R explains what are *not* considered to be 'public hands', including directors, anyone connected with a director (again, as defined by the Listing Rules) and anyone interested in shares which represent 5% or more of that class of share. The current EEA States are named in the definitions section of the Listing Rules at Appendix 1.

The FCA has discretion to accept a percentage below 25% if it considers the market will nevertheless operate properly in view of the large number of shares of the same class and the extent of their distribution to the public (LR 6.1.20G). If sufficient shares are not in public hands even after the IPO, then the FCA has the power to cancel the company's listing. An example of this was the cancellation of Simon Group plc's listing on 22 August 2007 because only 5% of its shares were in public hands.

(e)   *Electronic settlement* (LR 6.1.23R). All shares listed must be compatible with electronic settlement (see **2.5.3.1** above).

4.3.1.3   Standard listing of equity securities

A company seeking a standard listing of its shares must similarly comply with all of the requirements in Chapter 2 as set out at **4.3.1.2** above (LR 14.2.1R). However, as a standard listing represents compliance only with the applicable EU law requirements, such a company will not have to comply with Chapter 6, as these requirements represent 'super-equivalent' provisions imposed solely on a national level in the UK by the FCA. Listing Rule 14.2.2R does, however, go on to require that at least 25% of the class of shares to be listed should be in 'public hands' across the EEA. This mirrors the requirement in LR 6.1.19R and is a condition of listing for the same reason, to ensure a sufficient market in the company's shares once it has listed. There is an identical provision to LR 6.1.20G in LR 14.2.3G, enabling the FCA to accept a lower percentage than 25%.

It does mean, though, that for a standard listing there is, for example, no need to show a trading history and accounts for three years, as with a premium listing, which may therefore be attractive to newly-established companies.

4.3.1.4 Listing non-equity securities

Chapter 2 also applies to all other types of security which can be listed on the Main Market, such as debt securities. Chapters 17 to 20, rather than Chapter 6, set out the additional conditions if the securities to be listed are other than equity securities. As the focus of this book is on equity securities, and in particular shares, these chapters are not considered further.

4.3.1.5 Application procedure

Chapter 3 of the Listing Rules sets out a detailed application procedure, to which the company must adhere in order to have its shares admitted to listing, be it a premium or standard listing. In particular, the company and its advisers must publish an important marketing document which gives potential investors information about the company so that they can make an informed decision about whether to invest. This document must comply with the requirements of the Prospectus Rules and be submitted to the FCA in accordance with the Listing Rules. Before the document can be published, the FCA must approve it. The marketing document required for a share issue is called a prospectus (where the issue is of specialist securities – encountered rarely in practice – it is called 'listing particulars'). **Chapter 6** below examines the prospectus further.

4.3.1.6 Regulatory requirements for admission to trading

As noted at **4.3.1.2**, LR 2.2.3R provides that shares cannot be admitted to listing without also being admitted to trading. There is a parallel provision in the Guidance to ADS 1.1 of the Stock Exchange's Admission and Disclosure Standards (see **Appendix 1**), which provides that shares cannot be admitted to trading unless they are listed or proposed to be listed. As the two processes are tied together in this way, there is no need for the Stock Exchange to duplicate the onerous regulatory requirements for listing. Instead, the Stock Exchange can 'piggy-back' onto the requirements for listing, and can proceed safe in the knowledge that any company seeking to have its shares admitted to trading will have to fulfil the regulatory requirements for listing set out in the Listing Rules, and comply with the Prospectus Rules, before its application for admission to trading can succeed.

For this reason there are few formal regulatory requirements for admission to trading. Instead, the Stock Exchange's Admission and Disclosure Standards set out a very straightforward set of conditions (ADS 1), which state that the company must be in compliance with the Stock Exchange's requirements and that the Stock Exchange has discretion to refuse admission in certain circumstances (including the inability to comply with any bespoke condition the Stock Exchange imposes for admission). In effect, therefore, these conditions simply give the Stock Exchange the flexibility to supplement the requirements for listing should it wish. The Admission and Disclosure Standards also set out a basic admission procedure which is detailed at **5.3.7** and **5.4.3** below.

4.3.2 Commercial requirements

The regulatory requirements detailed in **4.3.1** above obviously exist to ensure that the company is in good shape for the IPO. However, just because a company meets these criteria does not necessarily mean that investors will think the company is an attractive investment. As part of its preparation, the company needs to take an objective view of its business and consider whether, commercially, it is good enough to meet the expectations of potential investors. The sponsor and broker will be able to guide the company through the relevant considerations, but matters to consider include:

(a)   Does the company have a good track record?

(b)   Where is the company headed? Does it have a viable business plan?

(c)   Does the company have an effective board and management team?

(d)   Is there anything about the company which could put off investors? Is the company open to any criticism over corporate governance issues (see **Chapter 8**)? Is there an influential substantial shareholder? Have there been any accounting issues? Will the company be able to withstand the intense scrutiny of the IPO process?

(e)   Are the market conditions right for an IPO?

(f)   Is this the right time in the company's development for an IPO, or would it be better to wait a couple of years?

(g)   Is the Main Market the right market for the company, or would AIM be more suitable (see **Chapter 24**)?

Initial public offerings ceased in the turmoil of the global financial crisis in 2007/08. Companies which dipped their toes into the IPO market even in 2010 found the water still freezing. One example was Ocado plc's IPO in July 2010 which raised much less money than was initially hoped and the share price plummeted when the company joined the Main Market; but the much larger £3.3 billion IPO of Royal Mail plc in October 2013 was a notable success, with the share price doubling on the first day of trading. Indeed, after several years of subdued IPO activity due to the global financial and eurozone crises and the severe austerity measures and deep recession which resulted from them, the IPO market has recovered. This is now reflected in the fact that the UK economy in 2013 finally seems to have turned the corner and returned to sustained growth. Twenty-seven UK companies joined the Main Market in the first 10 months of 2013, raising £6.9 billion from the market. This compares with 20 IPOs by UK companies raising £2.3 billion in the same period in 2012. But as the article below explains, the recovery has not always been a smooth process.

Hands' wind power venture Infinis head trio of flotation flops

Jamie Dunkley

Companies planning to list on the London Stock Exchange were handed a reality check yesterday as investors turned their backs on three of the newest entrants to the market.

Guy Hands' wind power company Infinis made a disappointing start to life as a listed company after being floated at the bottom end of its price range.

Shares in the company crept above the 260p float price, closing at 270p during its first day of conditional trading.

Mr Hands' private equity firm Terra Firma picked up £234m from the listing, which valued Infinis at £780m, but held on to 69 per cent of the group. The flotation is the latest step on the long road to redemption for Mr Hands, whose reputation was severely damaged by Terra Firma's disastrous £4bn takeover of the music retailer EMI at the height of the private equity bubble in 2007.

Meanwhile, Just Retirement, another private equity-backed listing, suffered during its first day of unconditional trading on the market. The shares tumbled 2p to 195p, significantly below its 225p float price, raising fears that it had been overpriced by bankers. The group, which provides pensions to people with health problems, was sold off by private equity firm Permira for £1.12bn.

Shares in the online Russian lender TCS also tanked 4.1p to 11.5p – or 27 per cent – on reports that Russia's parliament is considering proposals to make it harder for banks that do not have branches to issue credit cards. TCS was founded in 2007 by Oleg Tinkov, who is best known for developing a successful brewing business in the country before he branched out into financial services.

"The currently proposed new clause has been misinterpreted by some commentators and has been read as meaning that credit cards can only be collected by customers at a fixed location (ie branch)," the group said.

"Our understanding from conversations with the authors of this legislation is that the legislators intend to target unsolicited, blanket mailings of credit cards which gives us a good reason to believe that this clause will be amended."

On a more positive note, Bonmarche, the over-50s fashion retailer, is also set to go public after pricing its shares at 200p ahead of its debut on Wednesday. The group hopes to raise £40m on London's junior AIM market.

Ahead of more expected listings over the coming months, including Poundland and Zoopla, David Vaughan, EY's IPO leader for UK & Ireland, said: "It's not perhaps surprising that after a spate of new issues, investors may just be pausing a little.

"However, there are still some very good companies in the pipeline which, if priced correctly, will attract support."

Source: *Independent*, 16 November 2013

4.4   CHOOSING HOW TO FLOAT

The company must choose the most suitable way to float on the Stock Exchange. There are a number of different ways in which a company seeking to float can list its shares, namely by:

(a)   a public offer;

(b)   a placing;

(c)   an intermediaries offer; or

(d)   an introduction.

The method, or methods, chosen will depend on a number of factors, including how much money the company is prepared to spend on the float (some methods are generally cheaper than others), how well-known the company seeking to float is (some methods are less suitable for relatively unknown companies), how much money the company wishes to raise both on flotation and afterwards (some methods favour a certain type of investor who may have deeper and more open pockets than others), what type of investor the company wishes to have initially (some methods will result in mainly institutional shareholders, others will involve the general public), how wide the company wishes its shareholder base to be after the float (some methods will result in a wider spread of shareholders than others, which may affect how easy it is to trade in the shares).

In the first 10 months of 2013 there were 27 IPOs, of which two were public offers, 21 were placings and three were introductions. It is also important to note that the methods of flotation are not mutually exclusive: a combination of methods (usually a public offer and a placing) can be used to effect an IPO, and one of these was carried out in the same period of 2013.

The rules for listing used to contain a list of specific methods by which a company could float. That is no longer the case. Although some of the methods above are referred to in the definitions section (Appendix 1) to the Listing Rules, the Listing Rules now only concentrate on special features of certain methods of flotation rather setting out a definitive list of how companies can float. As a consequence, you will find that IPOs are frequently described in terms different from those above. These alternative terms are discussed at **4.4.2** below. It should also be noted that there are further ways to list shares once the company has been through the IPO process and is listed on the Stock Exchange (see **17.6**).

4.4.1   Methods of flotation

4.4.1.1   Public offer

A public offer involves an invitation being made to members of the public to buy shares in the company seeking to float. It is usually structured in one of three different ways: as an offer for subscription; as an offer for sale; or as a combination of the two.

An offer for subscription (defined in Appendix 1 to the Listing Rules) is an invitation to the public to subscribe for (ie buy) shares not yet in issue. In other words, on flotation the company will issue new shares and raise new money for the company. This is one of the key advantages to obtaining a listing (see **1.7.2**).

An offer for sale (defined in Appendix 1 to the Listing Rules) is an invitation to the public to subscribe for (ie buy) shares already in issue. In other words, shareholders currently owning a part of the company before the IPO are using the opportunity afforded by the IPO to sell their shares. No new money is raised for the company in this case – all the money goes to the selling shareholders. This allows shareholders (such as venture capitalists or founder shareholders) to realise their investment in the company and is another common reason for a company seeking an IPO.

As mentioned above, it is perfectly – in fact it is very common – both for existing shareholders to want to offload some of their shares and for the company to issue new shares at the same time as part of the IPO. This would mean that the public offer would entail both an offer for subscription and an offer for sale.

Although an essential element of a public offer is that it involves private investors buying shares in the company, it does not preclude institutional investors (such as pension funds, insurance companies and investment banks) from participating in the IPO and buying shares in the company at the same time. In fact, in light of the huge resources available to them, the involvement of institutional investors will be essential. The key distinguishing feature of a public offer then is that it involves private investors, but not exclusively so.

The advantages of a public offer are:

(a)   This is usually the most appropriate method to raise large amounts of capital.

(b)   Private investors can purchase shares, rather than just institutional investors. This means that the shareholder base will be broader (there will be more investors, holding fewer shares), which in turn facilitates the trading of the shares on the market (that is, the shares are more 'liquid').

The disadvantages are:

(a)   This is the most expensive method of flotation, partly because it involves underwriting (see **4.2.7** above).

(b)   Due to the involvement of the public, the regulatory burden is more onerous.

A recent example of a public offer is Merlin Entertainment plc's (the owner of Madame Tussauds, etc) £3.2 billion IPO in November 2013.

4.4.1.2   Placing

A placing (defined in Appendix 1 to the Listing Rules) involves the marketing of shares either already in issue or not yet in issue to specified persons, or clients of the sponsor or other securities house assisting the placing. Typically this involves the sponsor offering the shares in the company seeking to float to institutional investors. Those shares may be new (raising more money for the company), or existing ones being sold by the current shareholders (raising money for the selling shareholders). The definition of a placing in the Listing Rules goes on to state that it does not involve an offer to the public. Great care must be taken here. All this definition seeks to do is to distinguish a placing from a public offer in **4.4.1.1** above for the purposes of the Listing Rules. It will not, therefore, involve a general offer to private investors at large. It has no impact on the separate definition of offer to the public under s 85(1) of the FSMA 2000 regarding the need to prepare a prospectus (see **6.4.1.3**).

The advantages of a placing are:

(a)   This is usually cheaper than a public offer.

(b)   The company has greater discretion to choose its shareholders.

(c)   The company can raise large amounts of capital.

The key disadvantage is that the shareholder base will be narrower (there will be fewer shareholders, holding more shares), which can impede trading in the company's shares (the shares have less 'liquidity').

A recent example of a placing is the estate agent, Foxtons Group plc's £650 million IPO in September 2013.

4.4.1.3   Intermediaries offer

An intermediaries offer (defined in Appendix 1 to the Listing Rules) is similar to a placing (see **4.4.1.2** above). However, the shares can be marketed only to firms who comply with the definition of an intermediary in the FCA Handbook, which broadly means they are offered to stockbrokers independent of the sponsor and any securities house assisting with the IPO. On receipt of the shares, the stockbroker then acts as intermediary and sells them to clients in exchange for a commission.

The advantage of an intermediaries offer is that this method can achieve a wider spread of professional investors than a placing alone.

The disadvantage of an intermediaries offer is that it involves considerable administration and tends to be suitable only in very large IPOs. For this reason, intermediaries offers are quite rare. Royal Mail plc's £3.3 billion IPO in October 2013 partially involved an intermediaries offer.

4.4.1.4 Introduction

An introduction is not defined in the Listing Rules. It involves a company with shares already held by the public or institutional investors being admitted to listing on the Stock Exchange without offering any further shares. As we have seen, most companies seek to use an IPO to raise money which can be put towards acquisitions of other companies or businesses, paying off debt or investment in the current business. The question therefore arises as to why a company would wish to float on the Stock Exchange and not raise more money. When is an introduction useful? It is used mainly in three situations:

(a) By overseas companies which already have a wide spread of shareholders. For example, a company may already be listed on the Shanghai Stock Exchange and now wishes to list in London to bring it closer to one of the biggest sources of equity investment in the world.

(b) Companies quoted on AIM may wish to transfer to the Main Market and take advantage of the higher profile and greater liquidity in shares that this offers. For example, Avocet Mining plc, a gold mining and exploration company operating in West Africa, was introduced to the Main Market from AIM in July 2013.

(c) An existing listed company may decide to 'demerge' part or all of its business. Carphone Warehouse Group plc decided to demerge (ie split) its business into two new companies which were both floated separately on the Stock Exchange, a new Carphone Warehouse Group plc plc (the retail operation) and Talk Talk Telecom Group plc (the home phone and broadband internet operations). Both companies were introduced to the Main Market in March 2010.

Generally such a company will have to show a sufficiently wide spread of shareholders, with usually at least 25% being held in public hands as defined under the Listing Rules (see **4.3.1.2**). The theory is that, as the company's shares are already widely held and in public hands, the company has already demonstrated the marketability of its shares.

The advantages of an introduction are:

(a) this is usually the cheapest method of flotation;

(b) as it does not usually involve the issue or marketing of any shares, there is no need for underwriting (as underwriting covers the risk that shares offered are not taken up); and

(c) there is little need for advertising.

The disadvantages of an introduction are:

(a) it does not of itself afford an opportunity to raise capital (as no shares are being issued, the company receives no consideration); and

(b) it does not afford the company the same opportunities for publicity as a public offer or placing. This could affect the marketability of the shares after flotation (although as the shares are already widely held in public hands, and are therefore clearly marketable, often this is not an issue).

4.4.2 Other methods

As stated at **4.4** above, you will often see IPOs described in terms different from those set out in **4.4.1**, and these tend to focus on who the offer is aimed at. These include:

(a)   an institutional offer;

(b)   a retail offer;

(c)   a global or international offer;

(d)   an employee offer; or

(e)   a 'friends and family' offer.

Frequently the word 'offering' is used in place of 'offer' here.

It is important to note that usually one or other of the terms above overlaps with the methods of floating a company described in **4.4.1**. This often causes unnecessary confusion. The key really is to remember that these are all simply different ways of explaining the same thing, namely how a company floats on the Stock Exchange. The fact that there is more than one way to describe an offer of shares involving the public (public offer, offer for subscription, offer for sale and retail offer (see **4.4.2.2**)) does not change the practical reality common to them all, that the shares of the company seeking to list on the Main Market will be offered to private investors at large rather than just to institutional investors. Some of the terms may be more specific: for example, public offer and retail offer are wide terms (focusing on the fact that shares are offered to private investors), whereas an offer for sale (being both a public offer and a retail offer) provides additional information in that it highlights that some of the shares being offered to the public will be coming from existing shareholders (and therefore the money raised will not be of benefit to the company). An offer for sale is also specifically addressed in the Listing Rules.

4.4.2.1   Institutional offer

An institutional offer describes an offering of shares on flotation to institutional investors such as investment banks, pension funds and insurance companies. Typically the offer is made by way of a placing, but this is not essential. The key element is the participation of institutional investors in the offer. The institutional offer can be made on a bookbuilt basis or a fixed price basis.

Bookbuilding

The sponsor sends potential investors an invitation to bid for shares before it sets the share price and the size of the offer. Usually the invitation to bid will set out a range of prices. The institutional investor will then bid, stating the number of shares it is willing to buy and at what price, or range of prices. The bids are not binding. The bank will keep a record ('book') of the bids it receives, which helps it to assess the appropriate share price and the likely level of demand for the shares. The thinking is that this process will ensure the highest possible value for the company's shares.

As the offer is not underwritten until all bids have been received, the underwriting risk is reduced to some extent, as the demand for the shares has already been tested among institutional investors, and the period of risk tends to be shorter. This means that usually the offer can be underwritten at a much lower commission rate than with a fixed price institutional offer, thereby saving the company money.

Fixed price

The sponsor and broker use their knowledge of the market to advise on a suitable fixed price per share, which should be attractive to potential investors but which is not too low. Typically the offer will be fully underwritten.

It is currently much more common for such offers to be made on a bookbuilt basis.

4.4.2.2   Retail offer

A retail offer is when the shares are offered to members of the public. This can increase demand for the shares and can raise the profile of the company, because the media will market the IPO to the public. A retail offer is made by way of offer for subscription and/or sale. It is suitable for larger IPOs.

As the public need more protection than institutional investors, a retail offer is more heavily regulated than an institutional offer. Usually a retail offer is made together with an institutional offer.

4.4.2.3 Employee offer

This is when the shares are offered to employees of the company (and often to employees of other group companies). The employees may be given preferential allocation rights for new shares being issued in the company. As referred to at **1.7.6** above, an employee offer allows the company to reward its employees. It also encourages employees to invest in the company, which then ensures they have a vested interest in the ongoing success of the company.

As with a retail offer, an employee offer can increase demand for the shares. The company will set eligibility criteria, such as length of service, to determine which employees can take up the offer. Usually an employee offer is made together with a retail offer, and will mirror its terms.

4.4.2.4 Friends and family offer

This is when the shares are offered to certain individuals. 'Friends and family' captures the essence of the nature of these individuals, but in practice other people, such as suppliers, customers and initial backers, can be offered shares as part of a friends and family offer.

4.4.2.5 Global or international offer

As the name suggests, this is when the offer of shares in the company seeking to float is made to investors not just in the UK but also abroad. Typically it will comprise an offer for subscription and an offer for sale, but the key element is the involvement of overseas investors. A global offer suits larger companies and those with a significant international presence or aspirations to expand internationally.

Depending on how this offer is structured it may require full compliance with local securities laws, which will make the offer even more costly and time-consuming than a pure UK offer. It is usual, though, to set up the offer to take advantage of exemptions under those local laws, for example by limiting the offer overseas to qualifying institutional investors and thereby reducing the foreign regulatory burden.

4.4.3 Combination of different methods

As explained at **4.4** above, it is possible to combine the different methods when a company floats on the Stock Exchange. You will see in the extract from the announcement by Royal Mail, set out below, how it describes its then forthcoming IPO in October 2013. Note how the IPO is described as an 'Offer', which consists of an 'Institutional Offer' (ie to institutional investors) both in the UK and overseas, and as a 'Retail Offer' (for private investors). There is also a reference to intermediaries becoming involved. Furthermore, the announcement states that the Offer will just consist of existing shares. Although not expressly stated, this of course means that the offer will take the form of an offer for sale to private and institutional investors. Because this was a privatisation of a company with already sufficient resources, there was no need to raise further cash for the company by way of an offer for subscription. Note that there was also an Employee Free Shares Offer and an Employee Priority Offer.

Royal Mail

Announcement of Intention to Float

Her Majesty's Government ("HM Government") today announces its intention to proceed with an initial public offering (the "IPO" or the "Offer") of Royal Mail.

...

HM Government intends to dispose of a majority of the existing Shares, taking into account shares sold and the 10 per cent. of Royal Mail to be made available for free to around 150,000 eligible UK-based Royal Mail employees at the time of listing under an employee free shares offer (the "Employee Free Shares Offer"), which is separate and in addition to the Employee Priority Offer referred to below.

...

Offer to comprise an offer to institutional investors in qualifying jurisdictions (in the UK and elsewhere outside the United States under Regulation S and to QIBs in the United States in reliance on Rule 144A) (the "Institutional Offer") and an offer to members of the public located in the UK (the "Retail Offer"), which includes a priority offer to eligible Royal Mail employees located in the UK (the "Employee Priority Offer").

Members of the public located in the UK will be able to apply for Royal Mail shares in the Retail Offer:

– through participating Intermediaries, who will apply for Royal Mail shares on behalf of their clients; or

– through a direct online or postal application to HM Government.

In addition, eligible Royal Mail employees located in the UK will be able to apply to HM Government online or through postal application with priority under the Employee Priority Offer (which is part of the Retail Offer).

Minimum application size in the Retail Offer will be £750 for members of the public and £500 for Royal Mail employees eligible under the Employee Priority Offer.

4.5   RESTRUCTURING THE COMPANY

It is not always necessary to restructure a company before its IPO. The company seeking to float may be in perfect shape. However, it is important that the company is in good order when it floats, and so in the year or so prior to the IPO the company must consider whether it needs to implement any changes. The following are some of the common areas of concern.

4.5.1   Group structure

In all likelihood the company seeking to float will form part of a wider group of companies. Before the company floats, the lawyers must make sure that this group has a rational structure. The most common structure is for the company seeking the IPO to be the holding company of the group. The other companies will then be subsidiaries, organised in a logical manner. A supermarket chain, for example, might group the companies in its supermarket business together, its banking related companies together and its companies for its mobile phone operations together, as in **Figure 4.1** below.

Figure 4.1: Group structure

While this seems straightforward, in fact many businesses have grown in an unwieldy fashion through acquisitions and organic growth, with little thought paid to group structure. The company seeking the IPO might be a subsidiary company. Subsidiaries may exist which are now dormant (for example, because all the assets were transferred out of a subsidiary by a previous business sale) and may need to be dissolved. It may be that the company is planning to acquire or dispose of a business or company. If this is the case, the transaction should be completed as soon as possible so that the company structure is stable in the run up to completion. The lawyers need to examine the group structure well in advance of the IPO and effect any necessary changes, possibly by way of share and/or asset sales or purchases, company incorporation and/or dissolution, so that the company forms part of a logical group of companies.

4.5.2 Capital structure

It is of course very important that the offer price of the shares is fixed at the correct level. The share capital of the company may need to be altered to take account of this. For example, imagine that the advisers have stated that the offer price should be between £1.75 and £2.25 per share. However, the company has a current issued share capital of 2,000,000 shares of £1 each (nominal value) and is currently worth £20,000,000. This means that each share has a current value of £10. How could the shares be offered at the advised offer price without the company suffering a huge loss?

There are various solutions which the lawyers can effect. The simplest here would be to subdivide each share of £1 into 5 shares of 20p. This would mean that the company is still worth £20,000,000, but now has an issued share capital of 10,000,000 shares of 20p each, so each share has a current value of £2.00, which is within the acceptable price range.

4.5.3 Company constitution

If the company has not been incorporated as a public company, the lawyers will need to re-register the company as detailed at **1.9.3**. The company's constitution will comprise the articles of association and the memorandum of association. In advance of the IPO, the lawyers need to check these documents to make sure there is nothing in them which is inconsistent with *listed* company status. Usually the company will adopt a completely new set of articles which comply with the requirements for a listed company. Two notable requirements with which the company's existing articles may not comply are:

(a)   there should be no restrictions on the transfer of shares (see **4.3.1.2**, 'Eligibility critera (or "conditions for listing")' above); and

(b)   each class of shares should have the same voting rights (often unlisted companies attach enhanced rights to some, but not all, shares in a certain class).

4.5.4 The board of directors

As explained in **Chapter 8**, the board of directors of a listed company needs to comply with various principles of corporate governance (best practice). The lawyers need to consider whether any changes should be made to the board well in advance of the IPO, so that the company can make the required appointments and/or dismissals. In addition, it may be that the boards of subsidiary companies could be rationalised further (taking the example in **Figure 4.1** above, it may be logical for Ms Y, a key manager in the Supermarkets Division, to sit on the board of each of the companies in the Supermarkets Division), or perhaps the records of board appointments at Companies House need to be updated.

4.5.5 Legal issues

As **Chapter 6** explores further, the IPO process involves considerable disclosure about the company. Any negative news may discourage potential investors. The lawyers will examine the company's history to identify any breaches of the law and, to the extent possible, remedy them (for example, ensure that all filings at Companies House are up to date). However, when the structure of the IPO is being planned, the lawyer also needs to be alert to any issues which may give rise to legal problems. Two potential problems lawyers need to bear in mind at this stage are:

(a)   Might the IPO arrangements give rise to any financial assistance issues (see **Chapter 16**)?

(b)   Section 580 of the CA 2006 provides that no share should be issued at a discount to its nominal value (see **13.3.1**).

4.6 FUTURE DEVELOPMENTS

In order to avoid a repeat of problems which arose with listed companies such as Bumi and ENRC, where controlling shareholders ignored the wishes of independent shareholders (a quick Google search will reveal the full horrors), the FCA is at the time of writing consulting on changes to the Listing Rules for premium listed companies which are deemed to have a controlling shareholder (that is where a person and his associates control 30% or more of the votes).

Among the changes being proposed is a requirement for there to be a relationship agreement between the listed company and the controlling shareholder setting out obligations, including the need to carry out all transactions at arm's length and a commitment to abide by the Listing Rules. A failure to comply with the agreement may result in a requirement for prior independent shareholder approval of all transactions between the company and the controlling shareholder, whatever their size, and a breach of the Listing Rules.

A further change would require any appointment of a new independent director to the board of such a company to be approved by a vote of not only all the company's shareholders but by a second vote of just the independent shareholders. This is to ensure that the director meets with the independent shareholders' approval and is not imposed on them by the controlling shareholder.

These changes therefore seek to ensure the smooth functioning of the Main Market and fairness for all shareholders. They will currently affect companies such as Sports Direct International plc (where Mike Ashley owns over 60% of the company's shares) and easyJet plc (where Stelios Haji-Ioannou's family owns over 37% of the company's shares).

There will be changes to various provisions including to LR Chapters 6 and 14. You can find details of the consultation CP13/15 on the FCA's website. The final version of the changes is expected to be available on the FCA's website in the second half of 2014.

4.7   WHAT NEXT?

This chapter has outlined the preliminary steps a company can take in advance of the IPO process. While it can take a year (or longer) for the company to prepare for an IPO, the actual IPO process itself is much shorter (usually between three to six months). **Chapter 5** considers the IPO process.

CHAPTER 5

Initial Public Offerings: The Process

5.1 INTRODUCTION

This chapter must be read in conjunction with **Chapter 4**, which explains what an IPO is and the preliminary steps a company seeking to float must take, and **Chapter 6**, which examines the content of the vital marketing document, the prospectus. This chapter considers the IPO process itself, that is, the period of between 12 and 24 weeks before flotation when the company applies to the FCA for admission to listing and to the Stock Exchange for admission to trading. The preparation referred to in **Chapter 4**, which takes place in the year or two before the IPO, is generally referred to as 'pre-IPO preparation' rather than as part of the IPO process itself. (Remember, when reading references to the FCA in this chapter, that it is expected to be replaced by the FCA in 2013 – see **3.7** above.)

5.2 THE IPO PROCESS

A simplified version of the IPO process (other than by way of a bookbuilt offer – see **4.4.2.1**) is set out in **Table 5.1** below. Please note that this sets out the procedure for a premium listing. The procedure for a standard listing is very similar but there is no sponsor involved. The timing of the process is by reference to what is known as 'impact day'. This is the day when the IPO is announced to the market, the offer price is made known and the marketing document, the prospectus (see **Chapter 6**), is advertised. Impact day is not the day the company actually floats. The company floats when the FCA makes an Official List announcement (see **5.4.3.1** below) and the Stock Exchange publishes a London Stock Exchange Notice (see **5.4.3.2** below). Dealing in the company's shares can then begin. This day is known as 'admission day'.

5.3 THE LAWYERS' PERSPECTIVE

Table 5.1 provides an overview of the IPO process. It includes not just the dual applications for listing and trading but also the advisers' roles. As mentioned previously, it is important that the lawyers appreciate not only who the company's other advisers are, but also what they do and when. Of course, there are some areas where the lawyers will have little or no involvement, and other areas where the lawyers' role will be vital. So where does the lawyers' work lie?

5.3.1 Agreeing the timetable and the list of documents

At the beginning of the IPO process the sponsors will draw up a draft timetable for the IPO. Several factors drive the timetable. The FCA and the Stock Exchange have their own rules about timing, which cannot be changed. The company may have particular requirements as to timing, which may be inflexible (such as a desire to dovetail the IPO with a particular point in the company's financial year) or subject to change (for example, if the company's IPO is dependent on the occurrence of a certain event which has no fixed deadline). There are also practicalities to be taken into account, such as the prevailing movement on the stock market and the fact that it is virtually impossible to reduce the IPO procedure to anything less than three months (even on the premise that the advisers require very little sleep). The lawyers will be asked to comment on the draft timetable and agree it. The sponsor will have the task of ensuring that the agreed timetable does not slip. The lawyers need to ensure that:

(a)   there are no omissions in the timetable; and

(b)   the timetable is viable.

The lawyers will also be involved early in the IPO process in commenting on the list of documents drawn up by the sponsor. The list sets out all the documents required, the parties and who has primary responsibility for producing them. Like the timetable, this will be used as a reference point by all advisers, and so needs to be detailed and accurate.

Table 5.1: The IPO process

24–52 weeks (6–12 months) before impact day	**Pre-IPO preparation.** Company chooses advisers, considers its suitability for an IPO and the most appropriate method of listing its shares, and effects any necessary restructuring (see **Chapter 4**). Company takes decision to proceed with IPO.
12–24 weeks (3–6 months) before impact day	**The IPO process begins.** Company appoints advisers and meets sponsor. Sponsor drafts and advisers agree a timetable. Sponsor informs FCA about intended IPO. First marketing meetings with sponsor and broker. Initial planning meetings with advisers take place. Legal and financial due diligence begins (see **5.3.4**).
6–12 weeks (1.5–3 months) before impact day	**The process gathers momentum.** Key managers of the company work full-time on the IPO. Accountants produce long-form and draft short-form report (see **4.2.5**). Lawyers produce draft prospectus and begin the verification process (see **5.3.5** and **6.8**). Initial drafting meetings with advisers. Sponsor submits draft documentation relating to the approval of the prospectus (including 2 drafts of the prospectus) to the FCA (see **5.3.6.1** and **5.3.6.2**). Pay FCA fee for approval of the prospectus (see **5.3.6.2**). Sponsor and company have first meeting with the Stock Exchange. Initial pricing meetings with sponsor, broker, and any underwriters and sub-underwriters. Valuation of any key assets. Meetings with Financial PR consultants (sponsors, brokers and lawyers present).

2–6 weeks (one month) before impact day	**The process becomes intense.** Detailed drafting meetings, incorporating FCA's comments. Lawyers complete verification. Publish any pathfinder prospectus. Accountants and sponsors review cash-flow statements and any profit forecasts. Convene completion GM of company. Further PR meetings. Ensure any ancillary documentation (re-registering the company, new memorandum and articles) is prepared. First meeting with registrars. Deadline for submitting draft prospectus to the FCA is 20 days before impact day (see **5.3.6.1**). Submit draft application for listing to FCA and draft application for trading to LSE.
The week before impact day	**The preparation peaks.** Completion GM held. Directors' marketing roadshows.
The day before impact day	**All documentation must be signed off:** (a) Verification meeting. (b) Completion board meeting (sometimes known as a pricing meeting). (c) Underwriting agreement signed and held in escrow. (d) Any other agreements (placing, offer for sale) signed and held in escrow. Submit final version of prospectus (and any ancillary documentation referred to in the prospectus) to the FCA. Pricing meeting to agree offer price.
Impact day	**IPO announced.** FCA approves prospectus. Offer price is made public. Put prospectus on website and print copies. File prospectus with National Storage Mechanism. Advertise prospectus. Release underwriting agreement from escrow.
The week after impact day	**Attend to formalities.** Continue to publish prospectus and advertise the IPO. Directors' roadshows continue. Submit '48 hour' documents to the FCA (see **5.3.6.3**) and 'Two day' documents to the Stock Exchange (see **5.3.7.2**) to apply for admission to listing and to trading. Pay FCA admission fee (see **5.3.6.3**). **Day of admissions hearings.** Submit 'on the day' documents to the FCA (see **5.3.6.4**). The FCA hears application for admission to listing. The Stock Exchange hears application for admission to trading. Open application lists and receive applications from investors (see **5.4.2.2**). Close application lists (see **5.4.2.2**).

2 weeks after impact day	**Admission week.** Announce basis of allotment of shares. Despatch letters of acceptance/regret to investors. **Admission day.** The FCA makes an Official List announcement that shares have been admitted to listing (see **5.4.3.1**) and the Stock Exchange publishes a London Stock Exchange Notice that shares have been admitted to listing (see **5.4.3.2**). Dealing in shares commences. Stock Exchange invoice raised (see **5.3.7.3**).
3–5 weeks after impact day	**Formalities.** Receive letters of acceptance. Issue share certificates. Lodge information with the FCA (see **5.3.6.5**) and the Stock Exchange (see **5.3.7.4**). Pay Stock Exchange fee (see **5.3.7.3**).

5.3.2 Drafting documentation

The majority of the lawyers' time will be divided between drafting, meetings (see **5.3.3**) and due diligence (see **5.3.4**). The most important document the lawyers will draft is the prospectus. This is a lengthy, detailed document and **Chapter 6** considers it in more detail.

There will also be ancillary documentation for the lawyers to draft. This could include documents to effect any restructuring (see **4.5** above). It will certainly include board minutes which record the board's progress through the IPO process, and the board's approval of the process and related documentation.

There will also be documentation relating to the method of listing the shares. If it is a public offer by way of an offer for subscription and/or sale (see **4.4.1**), an agreement (between the company, its directors, any selling shareholders and the sponsor) will be required. For a placing (see **4.4.1.2**), a placing agreement is needed (the parties are the same as for an offer for subscription and/or sale agreement).

The lawyers will also produce a sizeable document called a verification note (see **5.3.5** below).

5.3.3 Attending meetings

5.3.3.1 Drafting meetings

So many advisers, as well as the company, need to feed information into the prospectus that it becomes impossible for the adviser with responsibility for the document (the sponsor or the lawyers) to collate and incorporate comments on the draft by e-mail or telephone. Once the draft prospectus is reasonably progressed, there will be numerous drafting meetings, where all the parties can contribute and discuss their comments on the draft. If more than one party has comments on a certain point, those parties can agree revised wording. The meetings are productive, but can be very time-consuming.

5.3.3.2 Completion GM

The completion GM takes place a few days before impact day. The IPO itself does not require shareholder approval, but some matters which are vital to the preparation of the company for the IPO often do require such approval. The completion GM is the forum to obtain this consent. Usually, the lawyers will draft the notice to convene this meeting and ensure that it is sent out within the required time limits in the CA 2006 (at least 21 clear days' notice for all resolutions of a public company unless approval is obtained by the shareholders at an AGM to shorten the notice period to 14 clear days – see **8.6.1**). The company's articles of association may extend this notice period. The lawyers will then draft the necessary resolutions and usually will attend the GM to deal with any issues which may arise on the day. There is little scope for error.

The resolutions which may be necessary depend on the particular requirements of the company, but they may include:

(a) if the IPO involves an offer of shares by way of subscription (ie, it involves the company issuing new shares):

    (i) granting authority to allot under s 551 of the CA 2006,

    (ii) disapplying pre-emption rights under s 561 of the CA 2006 on allotment (see **Chapter 14**);

(b) reorganising the share capital (see **4.5.2** above); and/or

(c) adopting new articles of association (see **4.5.3** above).

5.3.3.3 Verification meeting

The verification meeting takes place just before the completion board meeting. The board sign the verification note at this meeting (see **5.3.5** and **6.8** below).

5.3.3.4 Completion board meeting

The completion board meeting takes place the day before impact day. The directors will approve all the IPO documentation and the steps required to float the company. In particular, the board will resolve to:

(a) approve the terms of the prospectus;

(b) approve the terms of any ancillary documentation; and

(c) proceed with the IPO, and in particular the application for admission to listing and the application for admission to trading.

After the completion board meeting the prospectus is submitted to the FCA for final approval.

5.3.4 Due diligence

Due diligence, often referred to as 'DD' or 'due dil', or sometimes called 'legal review', is a time-consuming exercise that begins early on in the IPO process. The aim of due diligence is to investigate the company thoroughly and collate comprehensive information about it, which can then be used in the prospectus, the financial reports and other IPO documentation. The process also helps the advisers to identify the value of the company (and therefore fix the offer price) and any steps which are necessary to prepare the company for the IPO, such as those outlined at **4.5** above.

Due diligence falls into three main categories:

(a) business due diligence;

(b) financial due diligence; and

(c) legal due diligence.

5.3.4.1 Business due diligence

This is an investigation into the commercial aspects of the company, such as its performance, competitors and strategy. The lawyers do not lead this due diligence, but they do need some of the results of it for the legal due diligence exercise (see **5.3.4.3**).

5.3.4.2 Financial due diligence

This is the investigation carried out by the reporting accountants so that they can produce the long form report, the short form report and the working capital report to which **4.2.5** above refers.

5.3.4.3   Legal due diligence

The lawyers have responsibility for the legal due diligence exercise. Trainees are heavily involved in this process. Basic information about the company will be obtained from public registries, such as Companies House, Land Registry and the Land Charges department, the Patent Office, the Trade Mark Registry and the Designs Registry, and the lawyers will also request copies of the company's statutory books. However, the scope of the legal due diligence exercise is very broad, and the lawyers really need access to the company's management to obtain the level of information required.

As should be clear from the timetable in **Table 5.1** above, the company's management are not time-rich during this stage of the IPO process, and so the lawyers need to make the most of the time that management makes available to them. The usual procedure is for the lawyers to draw up a document called a due diligence questionnaire, which has a heading for each area to be investigated and then lists questions requesting information and documentation relating to each area. The usual areas for investigation are:

(a)   corporate – structure and constitution of the company;

(b)   business and trading – including requests for all material agreements;

(c)   assets;

(d)   property;

(e)   environmental matters;

(f)   insurance;

(g)   basic financial information – for example, requests for report and accounts, details of charges and insolvency events (the accountants will request more detailed information as part of the financial due diligence process referred to at **5.3.4.2**);

(h)   intellectual property and information technology;

(i)   employees;

(j)   pensions;

(k)   disputes; and

(l)   any market-specific regulatory issues.

Each question will be given a number, as will each document requested, so that when the deluge of responses arrive, the lawyers can identify the question to which each response relates. It also means that the responses can be filed in an orderly and logical manner. The company can respond to the due diligence questionnaire in a variety of ways. Some responses can be e-mailed, some need to be discussed face to face. The company may be advised to set up a data room, where all the information provided in response to the questionnaire is kept. This has some advantages for the trainee responsible for due diligence; if there is no data room, often the trainee's office will become the storage place for all the due diligence files. Increasingly, for larger, cross-border transactions, a secure electronic data room may be set up so that the necessary documents can be accessed and reviewed more easily.

The lawyers must review all the responses very carefully. This involves disseminating the information to specialist teams of lawyers within the firm (for example, all the information will be received by the corporate lawyer who sent out the questionnaire, but when he or she receives a response relating to pensions, that response will be copied to the pensions department for their comment, and similarly information about employees will be copied to the employment department and so on). The corporate lawyer who co-ordinates the due diligence process must have excellent project management skills.

Once all the information has been reviewed by the appropriate specialists, the corporate lawyer must compile the product of the review into a due diligence report. The level of detail in the report can vary. Some reports focus solely on any problematic issues revealed by the due diligence process, others report in detail on all areas which were reviewed, even if they were problem-free. Either way, the most important part of the due diligence report from the company's point of view is what is known as the 'executive summary'. This is a chapter at the beginning of the report which states succinctly, and in layman's terms, the key issues revealed by due diligence and advises of any steps which are required before or after the IPO in relation to such issues. It is the executive summary which the directors will actually read and act upon. The detail in the rest of the report is still important, however, both for the lawyers (to record that the process was carried out thoroughly and diligently) and for the directors (to record the efforts they have made to ensure that the information in the prospectus complies with the requirements of the Prospectus Rules, the Listing Rules and the FSMA 2000 (see **Chapter 6**)).

5.3.5 Verification

While due diligence is undertaken early in the IPO process, to provide the information which goes into the prospectus, verification does not begin until the first draft of the prospectus is reasonably progressed. Verification is actually part of the due diligence process, but it has evolved into a discrete exercise. Again, trainees are heavily involved in verification. So what is it? Essentially it is a process which produces a written record (called a 'verification note') so that the company can support what it has said in the prospectus. The purpose of verification is to protect those who have responsibility for the prospectus (particularly the directors) from legal liability arising out of its publication (see **6.6** and **6.8** below).

Verification can involve a painstaking line-by-line examination of the prospectus. In the verification note, each statement in the prospectus is phrased as a question, to test that it is true, accurate and not misleading. For example, if there is a line in the prospectus which states, 'We, Cheap as Chips plc, are the largest chain of supermarkets in the world', the verification note would contain a question along the lines of, 'Please confirm that Cheap as Chips plc is the largest chain of supermarkets in the world'. The answer to this question would then be recorded and copies of any supporting documentation would be annexed to the verification note. It may be, of course, that the answer to the question has already been provided as a response to the due diligence questionnaire. If so, management will not appreciate the lawyers asking the same question again. By the time the lawyers carry out verification, therefore, they must be familiar with the responses to the due diligence questionnaire. If the verification process raises questions not dealt with in the due diligence process (which is often not as detailed as the verification process) then the lawyer will send this new list of questions to the company, so management can collate the necessary information before meeting with the lawyers to provide the responses.

Alternatively, the verification process may be limited to ensuring the key selling messages in the prospectus are adequately supported and may ignore the more obvious statements.

The directors and anyone else who has formal responsibility for the prospectus (see **6.5**) cannot be available to all advisers at all times, so in practice they delegate responsibility for answering verification questions to key management (however, they cannot delegate ultimate legal responsibility for the content of the prospectus).

The lawyers must be vigilant in ensuring that the responses the company provides to the due diligence or verification questionnaire really do answer the questions posed. For example, in the example above, a full answer would detail the basis of this pivotal statement: What is the measure of 'largest' – is the company referring to turnover, profits, number of outlets, number of employees? What constitutes a 'chain' – just two shops, or more? How is 'supermarket' defined – is it just a shop that sells predominantly food, or does it include those that sell clothes, books, DVDs, personal financial products and petrol? What is meant by 'world'? Think of the Baseball World Series involving teams from just the USA and Canada! And so on. The verifier must bear in mind all the elements of the statement and ensure that she covers them adequately when drafting her response.

If the lawyers are not satisfied that the company can support the statement sufficiently, they will feed this information into the drafting meetings and the statement in the prospectus will be amended until the lawyers are satisfied that the statement can be supported. For example, the reference in the statement above to the 'largest' might be amended to 'one of the largest'.

As you might imagine, although this process is ultimately for the benefit of those responsible for the prospectus, including the directors, it is often a source of great frustration to those who have to provide the information, and each lawyer involved in the process (often a junior lawyer or a trainee) must have well-developed social skills, a good sense of humour and a thick skin to survive the process. Each director, and any other person bearing responsibility for the prospectus (see **6.5**), will sign the verification note in the verification meeting (just before the completion board meeting), and it, together with the due diligence report, will provide reassurance to the directors as they accept responsibility for the prospectus in the completion board meeting itself.

5.3.6   Submission of documentation to the FCA

The sponsor will have the responsibility of ensuring that the documents listed below are submitted to the FCA, and that the documents listed at **5.3.7** below are submitted to the Stock Exchange, in a timely manner. However, each adviser, including the lawyers, needs to be aware of the deadlines.

The documents referred to at **5.3.6.1** (prospectus) and **5.3.6.2** (documents to be submitted with the prospectus) are required by Chapter 3 of the Prospectus Rules as part of the prospectus approval process. The documents referred to at **5.3.6.3** to **5.3.6.5** ('48 hour' documents, 'on the day' documents and information to be lodged after admission day) are required by Chapter 3 of the Listing Rules as part of the listing application procedure.

The Transparency Directive requires each Member State to appoint a mechanism to store all regulated information regarding listed companies. One copy of all finalised documents must be sent electronically or uploaded onto an online facility, the National Storage Mechanism (NSM). The purpose is to ensure that investors and members of the public can easily access the information and print it off if need be. The website can be found at www.morningstar. co.uk/uk/NSM and is run by the private company, Morningstar plc. It should be noted that submission of the documents to the NSM does not replace the obligation on companies to make certain information public as set out in the Part 6 Rules.

Under the Directive amending the Transparency Directive (see **3.7.3** above), the ESMA will have to set up a single web portal by 1 January 2018 where all regulated information from all EU Member States, including the NSM, can be accessed.

5.3.6.1   Prospectus

The FCA must approve the prospectus, pursuant to the procedure set out in the Prospectus Rules, before it can be published (PR 3.1.10R and FSMA 2000, s 85(7)) (remember that the FCA is expected to be replaced by the FCA in 2013). The company must submit two copies of the draft prospectus to the FCA, in hard copy or an agreed electronic format, at least 20 working (ie business) days before impact day (PR 3.1.3R and PR 3.1.4R). The draft must be annotated in the margin to indicate compliance with all applicable requirements of Pt VI of the FSMA 2000 and the Prospectus Rules (this is a common trainee task) (PR 3.1.4R) (see **6.5.2.4**).

The FCA will provide its comments on the draft and return the draft to the company's advisers. In practice, 20 working days would not allow much time to deal with any comments the FCA might make. The earlier the draft is submitted the better, and the sponsor will aim to submit the draft some two to three months before impact day. On receipt of the FCA's comments, the document will be redrafted and resubmitted to the FCA. This process will continue until the FCA confirms it has no further comments. At this point, the prospectus can be printed and submitted in final form to the FCA for approval.

The FCA can approve the prospectus only when it is satisfied that it meets certain criteria set out in s 87A of the FSMA 2000, PR 3.1.7UK and PR 3.1.8G. In practice, the FCA will not give formal approval until impact day itself. Once the prospectus has been approved it must be filed with the FCA (PR 3.2.1R). This is done by submitting it to the NSM (see **5.3.6** above) (PR 3.2.1AR).

Further information can be obtained from UKLA Technical Note UKLA/PN/904.1 Public offer prospectus – drafting and approval (available on the FCA website).

5.3.6.2   Documents to be submitted with the prospectus

The FCA requires that a Risk Information Sheet (available from the UKLA section of the FCA's website) is submitted with the first draft of the prospectus sent to it. As part of the process set out in the Prospectus Rules for approving the prospectus, the draft prospectus, referred to at **5.3.6.1** above, must also be accompanied by the following (PR 3.1.3R):

(a)   completed Form A (available from the UKLA section of the FCA website) in final form;

(b)   the relevant fee (set out in the Fees Manual in the High Level Standards section of the FCA Handbook); and

(c)   drafts of the documents set out at PR 3.1.1R, namely:

   (i)   a cross-referenced list identifying where each item in the PD Regulation (set out, for information, in Appendix 3 of the Prospectus Rules; see **3.5.1.1** and **6.5.2**) can be found in the prospectus (if the order of items in the prospectus does not coincide with the order set out in the PD Regulation – see PR 2.2.10EU, para 4),

   (ii)   a letter identifying any items from the PD Regulation (set out in Appendix 3 of the Prospectus Rules) which are not applicable and so have not been included,

   (iii)   a copy of any document incorporated into the prospectus by reference (annotated to indicate which item of the schedules and building blocks in the PD Regulation it relates to) (see **6.5.2.2**),

   (iv)   information required by PR 2.5.3R (if requesting permission to omit information from the prospectus – see **6.5.2.3**),

   (v)   contact details of individuals, sufficiently knowledgeable about the documents submitted, who can answer queries from the FCA between the hours of 7 am and 6 pm, and

   (vi)   any other information the FCA specifically requires.

5.3.6.3   '48 hour' documents

No later than midday, at least two business days before the FCA hears the company's application for the admission to listing, the company must submit to the FCA, in final form, the documents set out at LR 3.3.2R. These include:

(a)   the Application for Admission of Securities to the Official List;

(b)   the FCA-approved prospectus;

(c)   any circular published in connection with the application;

(d)   any FCA-approved supplementary prospectus; and

(e)   written confirmation of the number of shares to be allotted pursuant to a board resolution allotting the shares (or, if this is not possible, the written confirmation must be provided to the FCA at least one hour before the admission to listing is to become effective).

In addition, LR 3.2.2R provides that a fee becomes payable on the date the company makes its application for listing (set out in the Fees Manual in the High Level Standards section of the FCA Handbook).

5.3.6.4   'On the day' documents

By 9 am on the day the FCA hears the company's application for admission to listing (see **5.4.3**), the company must lodge with the FCA a completed Shareholder Statement, signed by the sponsor (LR 3.3.3R). The form is available from the UKLA section of the FCA website.

5.3.6.5   Information to be lodged after admission day

The company must provide to the FCA written confirmation of the number of shares that were allotted if the actual number was lower than that originally announced, as soon as practicable following the hearing of the application for admission to listing (LR 3.3.5R).

5.3.6.6   Information to be kept after admission day

The company must keep copies of a number of documents used in the IPO for six years after the date of the IPO and make these available to the FCA at its request. A full list is set out in LR 3.3.6R which includes all letters, valuations, contracts, reports and other documents referred to in the prospectus, and the annual report and accounts for the period covered in the prospectus (usually the three prior years).

5.3.7   Submission of documents to the Stock Exchange

5.3.7.1   Provisional application for admission to trading

New applicants (that is, all companies seeking to float) must complete an application form (Form 1, available on the Stock Exchange's website) and submit it, together with a draft copy of the prospectus, to the Stock Exchange no later than 12.00 pm at least 10 business days before the requested date for the hearing of the company's application for admission to trading (ADS 2.1, **Appendix 1**). This is treated as a provisional application. A formal application can only be made once the prospectus has been approved by the FCA (see **5.3.7.2**).

5.3.7.2   'Two day' documents

By 12.00 pm on the day which is at least two business days before the Stock Exchange hears the company's application for admission to trading, the company must submit to the Stock Exchange a copy of the documents listed at ADS 2.4.1, **Appendix 1**, namely:

(a)   an application for admission to trading on the finalised Form 1;

(b)   an electronic copy of the prospectus;

(c)   an electronic copy of any circular, announcement or other document relating to the issue of shares;

(d)   an electronic copy of any notice of meeting referred to in any of the documents mentioned above;

(e)   written confirmation of the number of shares to be allotted pursuant to the board resolution (or, if this is not possible, it must be provided to the Stock Exchange by 7.00 am on the expected day of admission); and

(f)   a copy of the Regulatory Information Service announcement relating to the admission.

This deadline will correspond with that for the submission of the '48 hour' documents to the FCA (see **5.3.6.3**).

5.3.7.3   Fee payable on the day of the application hearing

The Stock Exchange will raise an invoice on admission, which the company must pay within 30 days (Guidance to ADS 2.1, **Appendix 1**).

5.3.7.4   Information to be lodged after admission day

The company must lodge a statement of the number of shares which were issued (and, where different, the total number of issued shares of that class) as soon as this information is available (ADS 2.5, **Appendix 1**). This corresponds with the requirement of the FCA referred to at **5.3.6.5** above.

5.4   KEY DATES

5.4.1   Impact day

By the time of impact day all paperwork will have been finalised and the offer price will have been set (at the previous day's completion or pricing board meeting). The prospectus will have been submitted to the FCA at least 20 working days (probably more) before impact day (see **5.3.6.1** above). Section 87C of the FSMA 2000 provides that the FCA must notify the company whether it has decided to approve the prospectus before the end of the period of 20 working days beginning with the date the application is received. In practice, while the FCA will indicate that is has no further comments on the prospectus, actually it will formally approve the prospectus on impact day itself. Once it is approved, the prospectus must then be filed with the FCA under PR 3.2.1R.

Other ancillary agreements, such as the offer for sale agreement, placing agreement and underwriting agreement, will be dated.

The IPO is 'live' with effect from impact day. Investors can apply to invest in the company. However, the company has not yet floated. Flotation is still conditional upon the FCA admitting the shares to listing and the Stock Exchange admitting the shares to trading, and this will not be done until admission day (see **5.4.3**). The shares in the company are not yet being traded.

5.4.2   Between impact day and admission day

5.4.2.1   Publishing the prospectus

Having been approved by and filed with the FCA (by submitting it to the NSM), the prospectus can be published. The company must publish the prospectus at least six working days before the end of the offer period (PR 3.2.3R). Prospectus Rule 3.2 governs the publication process.

There are four different ways to publish the prospectus, set out in PR 3.2.4R:

(a)   insert it into one or more newspapers widely circulated in the UK;

(b)   make it available to the public, in printed form, free of charge, at the offices of the Stock Exchange or the company's registered office and at the office of any intermediary placing or selling the shares;

(c)   make it available in electronic form on the company's website and on the website of any intermediary placing or selling the shares; or

(d)   make it available in electronic form on the Stock Exchange website.

If the prospectus is published by method (a) or (b) above then it must also be published in accordance with method (c) above on a website; and if the company chooses to publish in electronic form, pursuant to (c) or (d) above, it should be aware that, nevertheless, any investor is entitled to demand a free hard copy under PR 3.2.6R.

5.4.2.2   Applications for shares

Investors who have been impressed by the prospectus and wish to invest in the company will complete the application form attached to the prospectus and send it to the receiving bank (see **4.2.8**). The application form states the deadline by which the form must reach the receiving bank. This is usually 10.00 am on the day following the FCA's admission hearing. This deadline is known as the time the 'lists open'.

If the offer is popular and over-subscribed, the lists will close at 10.01 am. The board, advised by the sponsor, will then decide on the basis of allotment. If the offer is over-subscribed, clearly not all applicants will receive all the shares they applied for. The basis of allotment is a formula which decides the proportion of shares each applicant will receive. It varies according to the circumstances of the IPO, but it could be, for example, that each applicant receives, say, two-thirds of the number of shares applied for. On the other hand, it could be that the two-thirds ratio is applied only to those investors applying for significant numbers of shares, and those investors applying for small numbers of shares simply enter into a ballot system where they may be allotted their full quota, or none at all. Once the board has decided the basis of allotment, the company will make a formal announcement of the decision to investors.

The £3.3 billion Royal Mail plc IPO in October 2013 comprised a retail offer and an intitutional offer. In the retail offer, applicants for up to £10,000 worth of shares all received £750 worth of shares (the minimum allocation) and applicants for over £10,000 received nothing. The retail offer was over-subscribed 7 times. Such was the demand for shares under the institutional offer that it was over-subscribed 20 times.

If the offer is under-subscribed, the lists will remain open longer. The company will then inform the underwriters how many shares they need to take up.

The receiving bank will cash the applicants' cheques and account to the company, and any shareholders who sold existing shares, for the proceeds. The company will then send share certificates, or letters of acceptance (see **5.4.3.4** below), to the successful investors, and (in the event that the IPO is over-subscribed) will send letters of regret to the investors who applied but have not been successful in buying any or all of the shares for which they applied.

5.4.2.3   Admission hearings

The FCA will hear the application for admission to listing on the same day that the Stock Exchange hears the application for admission to trading. The Listing Rules provide that the FCA can refuse admission to listing in certain circumstances, such as if it considers that admission would be detrimental to investors' interests (LR 2.1.3G and FSMA 2000, s 75(5)). The Admission and Disclosure Standards (ADS 1.5(a), **Appendix 1**) also reserve the right for the Stock Exchange to refuse admission to trading if admission might be detrimental to the orderly operation or integrity of the market. However, by the time the hearings take place, all the hard work on the IPO has been completed. The company and its advisers will have been in regular contact with the FCA and the Stock Exchange throughout the IPO process. It is very rare, therefore, for the FCA or the Stock Exchange to refuse admission at this stage.

5.4.3   Admission day

5.4.3.1   The Official List announcement

When the FCA is satisfied that it is prepared to admit the shares to listing, it must announce the admission through a Regulatory Information Service (LR 3.2.7G). In practice, the Official List issues an announcement, referred to as an Official List announcement or notice, to the Regulatory News Service (RNS) each day at 8am. This announcement refers to all companies which will list securities that day (both new applicants and companies which are already listed but which are listing further securities). The list does not distinguish the new applicants from the applicants which are already listed but which are listing further shares. Once the announcement is made (often referred to as 'going down the wire') the listing is effective, and dealing in the company's shares can begin. The company has floated.

An excerpt from the Official List announcement dated 13 November 2013 (the date Merlin Entertainments plc, a new applicant, floated) follows:

NOTICE OF ADMISSION TO THE OFFICIAL LIST

13/11/2013 08:00 AM

The Financial Conduct Authority ("FCA") hereby admits the following securities to the Official List with effect from the time and date of this notice:–

CARACAL ENERGY INC.

| 5,782,880 | Common Shares of No Par Value fully paid | Premium Equity Commercial Companies | (CA1407561077) |

MERLIN ENTERTAINMENTS PLC

| 1,013,746,032 | Ordinary shares of 1p each fully paid | Premium Equity Commercial Companies | (GB00BDZT6P94) |

ULTRA ELECTRONICS HOLDINGS PLC

| | | | Block Listing |
| 85,000 | Ordinary shares of 1p each fully paid | Premium Equity Commercial Companies | (GB0009123323) |

5.4.3.2 The London Stock Exchange Notice

Similarly, when the Stock Exchange is satisfied that it wishes to admit the shares to trading, it must announce the admission using its website (Guidance to ADS 2.1). In practice, this will go down the wire at the same time as the Official List announcement.

An excerpt from the London Stock Exchange Notice dated 13 November 2013 is set out below:

NOTICE OF ADMISSION TO TRADING ON THE LONDON STOCK EXCHANGE

13/11/2013 - 8:00AM

The following securities are admitted to trading on the LSE with effect from the time and date of this notice

CARACAL ENERGY INC.

| 5,782,880 | Common Shares of No Par Value fully paid | (BB97882)(CA1407561077) |

| MERLIN ENTERTAINMENTS PLC | | (BDZT6P9)(GB00BDZT6P94) |
| 1,013,746,032 | Ordinary shares of 1p each fully paid | |

ULTRA ELECTRONICS HOLDINGS PLC		BLOCK ADMISSION
		(0912332)(GB0009123323)
85,000	Ordinary Shares of 5p each fully paid	

5.4.3.3 Dealings in shares

The company and its advisers will watch the market with bated breath on the first day of dealings. Ideally, the market price will rise a little above the offer price, meaning that the shares are trading at a small premium. This can suggest that the company pitched the offer price correctly. If the market price rises significantly, this may suggest that the offer price was something of a giveaway. The shares in Royal Mail plc, which was privatised by the UK Government in October 2013, rose by over 40% on the company's first day's trading on the Main Market. Inevitably this led to commentators complaining that the family silver had been sold on the cheap. Such was the outcry, representatives from investment banks involved in the IPO (such as Goldman Sachs and UBS) were called to give evidence before the House of Commons BIS Select Committee to explain the decisions they took.

If the market price drops below the offer price, the shares are trading at a discount, which may evidence a lack of demand for the shares. Ocado's shares dropped 10% on their first day's trading on the Stock Exchange in July 2010, reflecting ongoing concerns from investors that the shares had been overpriced, particularly since Ocado had not made a profit in the 10 years of its existence.

5.4.3.4   Letters of acceptance

Sometimes the offer is structured so that initially successful applicants do not receive a share certificate, but a renounceable letter of acceptance. This is a bearer document, and the recipient can transfer title in the shares to someone else simply by handing them the letter (rather than by stock transfer form which is the usual method of transferring shares). Shares can be traded by way of renounceable letter for six weeks from admission day. The company's registrars will enter into the company's register of members whoever holds the letter at the end of that six-week period, and will send them a share certificate.

Letters of acceptance can be a useful method by which shares can be transferred easily at time when there tends to be substantial trading in shares. This also saves the registrars from issuing several new certificates in respect of the same shares.

5.4.4   After admission day

Admission day should not be seen as the end of a process but as the beginning of one. The company is now a listed company. The directors, key managers and the advisers will take the opportunity to celebrate the IPO together, and will then attempt to catch up on the many hours of sleep lost in the previous weeks. Then the company has to get back to business. The directors and management will return to their day-to-day business of running the company. However, life cannot simply return to how it was pre-IPO. There is now a whole new set of rules and regulations for the company to comply with. **Parts II, III** and **IV** of this book consider what life is like for a public company. Before we leave behind the IPO process, however, **Chapter 6** takes a detailed look at the main marketing document for any IPO: the prospectus.

CHAPTER 6

INITIAL PUBLIC OFFERINGS: THE PROSPECTUS

6.1 INTRODUCTION

The lawyer must refer to the Prospectus Rules and Pt VI of the FSMA 2000 (Official Listing) in order to advise whether a prospectus is required and, if so, what information the document must contain. Assistance is available on interpreting parts of the legislation from the FCA (through the UKLA's technical and procedural notes, available on its website) and from the ESMA (see **3.1** above) (FAQs regarding prospectuses are available on its website: http://esma.europa.eu).

6.2 PURPOSE

The prospectus is the main marketing document for the IPO process. Potential investors will read the document and, it is hoped, the information it contains will encourage them to invest in the company. However, the company cannot be selective about what information to include in the document. The Prospectus Rules and the FSMA 2000 prescribe its contents. The lawyers must make sure that the document complies with all of the legal requirements as to content, but that it also retains the style of a marketing document which will attract investors. The prospectus is vital to the success of the IPO and, as is evident from **Chapter 5**, the drafting of this document takes up a large proportion of the IPO process.

6.3 PROSPECTUS OR LISTING PARTICULARS?

The main marketing document for an IPO on the Main Market is called a prospectus. You will see references in the Listing Rules to another listing document called listing particulars. There is no room for confusion here. Listing particulars are required only for the issue of certain specialist securities, such as debt securities (eg bonds) or depositary receipts (certificates which represent ownership of shares – these are one method by which it is possible to trade in overseas companies). As the focus of this book is on the listing of shares, it makes no further reference to listing particulars and considers only the most important document, the prospectus.

6.4   THE REQUIREMENT FOR A PROSPECTUS

Prospectus Rule 1.2.1UK and s 85 of the FSMA 2000 provide that a prospectus, approved by the FCA, is required if the company wishes to do either or both of the following events:

(a)   *offer* transferable securities *to the public* in the UK (s 85(1)); or

(b)   request *admission* of transferable securities to *trading* on a regulated market situated or operating in the UK (even if there is no offer to the public) (s 85(2)).

This book focuses on IPOs which involve the issue and/or sale of ordinary shares which will be listed on the Official List and admitted to trading on the Main Market. This type of IPO involves both (a) and (b) above; both s 85(1) and s 85(2) apply, and, subject to any exemptions, a prospectus will be required (one prospectus will suffice). Note that even if the circumstances of an IPO meant that it involved only (a) or (b) above, then, subject to any exemptions, a prospectus would still be required.

The FSMA 2000 includes exemptions to s 85(1) and s 85(2). If these exemptions apply, a prospectus is not required, so the lawyer must be ready to advise how the float might be structured to avoid the need for this time-consuming and costly document.

It is important to recognise that the exemptions are drafted to apply specifically either to s 85(1) (offer to the public) or to s 85(2) (admission to trading). To take the example of our IPO, which involves both an offer to the public and admission to trading, even if it benefits from one of the 'offer to the public' exemptions, it will still require a prospectus unless one of the 'admission to trading' exemptions also applies.

Paragraphs **6.4.1** and **6.4.2** below examine the criteria of s 85(1) and s 85(2), and consider the different exemptions which apply to them.

6.4.1   Section 85(1): offering transferable securities to the public in the UK

Section 85(1) refers to all public offers of shares, including shares not listed on the Official List (such as shares admitted to the AIM).

Section 103 of the FSMA 2000 states that 'offer of transferable securities to the public' has the meaning in s 102B of the FSMA 2000. This in turn provides guidance on the interpretation of some of the key terms used in s 85(1).

6.4.1.1   Offer

There will be an offer if there is a communication to any person which presents sufficient information, on the shares to be offered and the terms on which they are offered, to enable an investor to decide to buy or subscribe for those shares (s 102B(1)). The communication may be made in any form and by any means (s 102B(3)).

A flotation by way of an offer for subscription and/or sale, placing or intermediaries offer will fulfil this criterion.

6.4.1.2   Transferable securities

Section 102A(3) defines 'transferable security' by reference to the Markets in Financial Instruments Directive (MiFID). For our purposes it is enough to note that this term includes ordinary shares. Therefore our example of an IPO involving the issue or sale of ordinary shares will fulfil this criterion.

6.4.1.3   To the public

Section 102B(2) of the FSMA 2000 provides that if the offer is made to 'a person in the United Kingdom' it is made to the public in the UK.

It is likely that an offer for sale or subscription will fulfil this criterion, but that a placing and intermediaries offer will be structured to fall within one of the exemptions, such as the 'qualified investors' or '150 persons' exemption, so that they do not fulfil this criterion. Note that LR Appendix 1.1 defines a placing as not constituting a public offer. However, this is unconnected to the definition of a public offer under the FSMA 2000 and so s 85 must still be considered.

6.4.1.4   In the UK

As referred to at **6.4.1.3** above, s 102B(2) of the FSMA 2000 makes clear that this criterion is satisfied if any recipient of the offer is in the UK.

The list of recipients of any offer for subscription and/or sale, placing or intermediaries offer must be analysed to see if this criterion is fulfilled.

6.4.1.5   Exemptions

The exemptions to s 85(1) of the FSMA 2000 (requiring a prospectus for offers to the public) are set out in s 85(5) (which in turn refers to Sch 11A to the FSMA 2000 and PR 1.2.2R) and s 86 of the FSMA 2000. The principal exemptions are as follows:

(a)   *Offers to qualified investors (FSMA 2000, s 86(1)(a))*. A qualified investor is defined in s 86(7) of the FSMA 2000 and includes 'professional clients' as defined in MiFID. Institutional investors, such as insurance companies, investment firms and pension funds, will fall within this definition.

(b)   *Offers to fewer than 150 persons (who are not qualified investors) in each EEA State (FSMA 2000, s 86(1)(b))*. The Treasury has confirmed that there is no need to include the clients of discretionary brokers in calculating the number of persons to whom the offer is made.

(c)   *Offers involving significant investment by each investor (FSMA 2000, s 86(1)(c) and (d))*. This will apply where each investor invests a minimum total consideration of €100,000 or where the shares being offered are denominated in amounts of at least €100,000 (or equivalent).

(d)   *Small offers*. There are two exemptions relating to small offers. First, s 86(1)(e) of the FSMA 2000 exempts offers where the total consideration for the *transferable securities* cannot exceed €100,000. Secondly, s 85(5)(a) of and para 9 of Sch 11A to the FSMA 2000 exempt offers where the total consideration for the *offer* is less than €5 million. The second exemption was inserted into the Directive at a very late stage and there has been little commentary on the interaction between the apparently contradictory two small offer exemptions. One possible interpretation is that the €5 million exemption across the EEA takes the offer outside of the Prospectus Directive altogether and therefore would allow Member States to apply national legislation to such an offer requiring a prospectus or similar document, whereas offers for less than €100,000 are still within the Prospectus Directive and so national legislation cannot require a prospectus. In any event, in the UK this does not create any problems as no prospectus is required for any amount under €5 million.

(e)   *Share swaps (PR 1.2.2R(1))*. The issue of shares must not involve any increase in the company's issued share capital.

(f)   *Offers in conjunction with takeovers (by way of share for share exchange) or mergers (PR 1.2.2R(2) and (3))*. However, a document must be available which contains information which the FCA regards as equivalent to that of a prospectus (referred to as an 'equivalent document').

(g)   *Bonus issues and scrip dividends of a class of shares already listed (PR 1.2.2R(4))*. However, a document must be available which contains basic information about the number and type of shares offered, and the reasons for and the detail of the offer.

(h)   *Offers by listed companies to employees and/or directors (PR 1.2.2R(5))*.

6.4.2   Section 85(2): admitting transferable securities to trading on a regulated market

6.4.2.1   Transferable securities

The definition of transferable securities is discussed at **6.4.1.2** above. Ordinary shares are transferable securities, so our IPO will fulfil this criterion.

6.4.2.2   Admit to trading

The type of IPO which is the focus of this book involves the admission of shares to trading (on the Main Market) and so fulfils this criterion.

6.4.2.3   Regulated market

This is defined in s 103(1) of the FSMA 2000. This refers to the definition contained in Art 4.1(14) of MiFID. It will probably pay to be seated before attempting to read it.

> 'Regulated market' means a multilateral system operated and/or managed by a market operator, which brings together or facilitates the bringing together of multiple third-party buying and selling interests in financial instruments – in the system and in accordance with its non-discretionary rules – in a way that results in a contract, in respect of the financial instruments admitted to trading under its rules and/or systems, and which is authorised and functions regularly and in accordance with the provisions of Title III.

Under the Title III referred to, it is up to the FCA to oversee the regulation of such regulated markets, and Art 47 of MiFID requires a list of regulated markets to be produced. Note that the ECJ has decided that it is not a precondition of being a regulated market that the market be included on the Art 47 list (*Nilas and Others* (Case C-248/11)).

A list of regulated markets can be found on the FCA's and the European Commission's websites. It is far from easy navigating either website to locate this information (it is much easier to Google, particularly for the FCA), and when finally you reach the list it merely refers to 'London Stock Exchange – regulated market'.

What is not apparent from this is that the Main Market of the Stock Exchange is a regulated market under MiFID but AIM is not. The other two regulated markets in the UK are ISDX Main Board and NYSE Euronext London.

Our IPO, being on the Main Market, will therefore involve a regulated market. (Note, however, that an AIM float will require a prospectus only if s 85(1) applies, ie that shares are being offered to the public as defined and no exemptions apply.)

6.4.2.4   Exemptions

The exemptions to s 85(2) of the FSMA 2000 (requiring a prospectus for shares to be admitted to trading on a regulated market) are set out in s 85(6) (which in turn refers to Pt 1 of Sch 11A to the FSMA 2000 and PR 1.2.3R). The principal exemptions are as follows:

(a)   *Admission of shares representing less than 10% of shares of the same class already admitted to trading on the same market (PR 1.2.3R(1)).* This is a 'de minimis' provision. The FCA's Technical Note UKLA/TN/602.1 Exemptions from the requirement to produce a prospectus (available in the UKLA section of the FCA's website) confirms that the 10% limit is applied over a rolling 12-month period. This means that any shares admitted over the previous 12 months, which have not benefited from any *other* exemption, would count towards the 10%.

> **EXAMPLE**
>
> Imagine a company has 1,000 shares in issue on 28 April 2014. On 5 July 2015 it issued 50 shares to employees under the admission to trading exemption referred to at (e) below. On 5 January 2016 it issues a further 50 shares which are placed with institutions, under the offer to the public exemption referred to at (a) in **6.4.1.5** above. The calculation to work out whether the 10% admission to trading exemption applies to this issue of 50 shares is as follows:
>
> $$\frac{\text{Number of shares to be issued (including shares admitted over last 12 mths which have not benefited from any other exemption)}}{\text{Number of shares of the same class already admitted to trading on the same market}}$$
>
> that is,
>
> $$\frac{50 \text{ (other issue within the last 12 months benefited from another exemption)}}{1{,}050}$$
>
> that is, 4.7%. This issue of 50 shares would therefore be covered by the 10% exemption.
>
> One month later, the company issues a further 50 shares. The calculation is now:
>
> $$\frac{50 \text{ (this was covered by the 10\% exemption, not any other exemption, so counts)} + 50}{1{,}100}$$
>
> that is, 9.09%, so this issue is covered by the 10% exemption.
>
> One month later, the company issues a further 50 shares. The calculation is:
>
> $$\frac{50 + 50 + 50}{1{,}150}$$
>
> that is, 13%, so this issue is outside the 10% exemption and will therefore require a prospectus.

(b)   *Share swaps (PR 1.2.3R(2)). As **6.4.1.5(e)** above.*

(c)   *Offers in conjunction with takeovers (by way of share for share exchange) or mergers (PR 1.2.3R(3) and (4)). As at **6.4.1.5(f)** an equivalent document must be available.*

(d)   *Bonus issues and scrip dividends of a class of shares already listed (PR 1.2.3R(5)). As **6.4.1.5(g)** above.*

(e)   *Offers to employees and/or directors of a class already listed (PR 1.2.3R(6)).*

(f)   *Shares of a class already listed resulting from the exercise of exchange or conversion rights (PR 1.2.3R(7)).*

(g)   *Shares already admitted to trading on another regulated market (subject to conditions) (PR 1.2.3R(8)).*

6.4.3   Conclusion

Having analysed the criteria, we can conclude that:

(a)   an IPO;

(b)   involving the offer or sale of ordinary shares;

(c)   which will be listed on the Official List and admitted to trading on the Main Market,

will require a prospectus, *unless* it benefits from *both*:

(d)   an 'offer to the public' exemption; and

(e)   an 'admission to trading' exemption.

In practice, as **Table 6.1** below shows, it is unlikely that an IPO can be structured to benefit from the required combination of exemptions.

Table 6.1

Method of flotation	Public offer under s 85(1)?	Admission to trading under s 85(2)?	Prospectus required?
Public offer	Yes. '150 persons' exemption possible but highly unlikely, given size of most retail offers.	Yes. '10%' exemption irrelevant in context of IPO, as no shares currently admitted to trading.	Yes (s 85(1) and s 85(2)).
Placing	Yes – however, likely to benefit from 'qualified investor' or '150 persons' exemption.	Yes. '10%' exemption irrelevant in context of IPO, as no shares currently admitted to trading.	Yes (s 85(2)).
Intermediaries offer	Yes. Likely to benefit from 'qualified investor' or '150 persons' exemption.	Yes. '10%' exemption irrelevant in context of IPO, as no shares currently admitted to trading.	Yes (s 85(2)).
Introduction	No. No offer involved.	Yes. '10%' exemption irrelevant in context of IPO, as no shares currently admitted to trading.	Yes (s 85(2)).

6.5   CONTENT

The FSMA 2000 and the Prospectus Rules prescribe the content of a prospectus.

Reading about the content requirements of a prospectus is essential, but there is no substitute for having a look at the real thing. I would recommend checking the websites of companies which have recently floated as companies post the prospectus and other documents, such as RNS announcements, on the area of their website aimed at shareholders (usually entitled 'investor relations') or via the NSM.

6.5.1   General content requirements

As set out in PR 2.1.1UK, s 87A(2), (3) and (4) of the FSMA 2000 provide for the general content requirements of a prospectus. These provisions require that any prospectus must:

(a)   contain information necessary to enable investors to make an informed assessment of the assets and liabilities, financial position, profits and losses and prospects of the company, and the rights attaching to any securities (for our purposes, shares) (s 87A(2)); and

(b)   present the information referred to at (a) above in a form which is comprehensible and easy to analyse (s 87A(3)).

The information must be prepared having regard to the particular nature of the shares and the company (there is not an identical format of prospectus for all companies) (s 87A(4)). The FCA must not approve a prospectus unless it is satisfied that such general content requirements have been met (s 87A(1)).

6.5.2 Specific content requirements

As explained at **3.5.1.1**, the requirements regarding the content of a prospectus are set out in the articles and annexes of the PD Regulation, the aim being that prospectuses issued by companies across the EU contain the same information in the same circumstances. These requirements are duplicated in the Prospectus Rules (the articles are set out at PR 2.3.1EU and the annexes are replicated at Appendix 3 of the Prospectus Rules).

Prospectus Rule 2.3 sets out the minimum information to be included in a prospectus. This rule refers to the 'schedules' and 'building blocks' of the annexes of the PD Regulation (and therefore of Appendix 3 of the Prospectus Rules), which are defined as follows:

> *Schedule* a list of minimum information requirements adapted to the particular nature of the different types of issuers and/or the different securities involved.
>
> *Building block* a list of additional information requirements, not included in one of the schedules, to be added to one or more schedules, as the case may be, depending on the type of instrument and/or transaction for which a prospectus ... is drawn up.

In other words, the Prospectus Rules contain various minimum content requirements which may apply, depending on the type of company issuing shares and the nature of the shares. Not all of the information will be required in every prospectus. It is the lawyer's job to select which minimum content requirements are relevant for the particular transaction.

How can the lawyer find the content requirements required specifically for an IPO? In Annex XVIII of the PD Regulation there are tables which summarise which schedules and building blocks are required, depending on the circumstances of the issue (PR 2.3.1EU, citing PD Regulation, art 21). You can view the tables online by going to Annex XVIII in Appendix 3 to the Prospectus Rules and following the link to Commission Delegated Regulation EU 759/2013. They are on pages 4–9 of the pdf.

Do not worry if you are flummoxed after having looked at these tables. They are, like much financial services legislation, not easy to make sense of. For a straightforward IPO of ordinary shares, the appropriate schedules will be the share schedules (Annexes I and III) of the PD Regulation which you can find back in Appendix 3 of the Prospectus Rules, and the pro forma financial information building block (Annex II). (The other annexes are relevant, for example, for the issue of debt securities, derivatives, depositary receipts or guarantees, or if the issuer falls within a certain category, for example it is a Member State.) Note that under PR 2.3.1A EU it is possible to produce an abbreviated prospectus for small and medium-sized enterprises (SMEs) and companies with reduced market capitalisation (Small Cap) (in other words for certain smaller companies).

A SME is defined in art 2(1)(f) of the Prospectus Directive 2003/71/EC as:

> a company which, according to their last annual or consolidated accounts, meet at least two of the following three criteria:
>
> 1.   an average number of employees during the financial year of less than 250;
>
> 2.   a total balance sheet not exceeding €43 000 000;
>
> 3.   an annual net turnover not exceeding €50 000 000.

A Small Cap is defined in art 2(1)(t) of the Prospectus Directive 2003/71/EC as 'a company listed on a regulated market and having had an average market capitalisation of less than €100 000 000 on the basis of end-year quotes during the last three calendar years'.

Such companies need only provide the lesser information in Annex XXV (set out in Appendix 3 to the Prospectus Rules). It is worth noting that in practice a company which could produce an abbreviated prospectus may still choose to issue a full prospectus if it wishes. Indeed it may have to in order to satisfy overseas securities laws, such as in the US. It is still too early to tell how successful the introduction of the PD Regulation has been and how many SMEs and Small Caps will be able to use this regime in practice.

6.5.2.1   Format of the prospectus

The company has a choice of how it draws up the prospectus. Either it prepares a single document, or the prospectus may comprise three separate documents (PR 2.2.1R):

(a)   a summary (PR 2.1.2UK);

(b)   a registration document (PR 2.2.2R); and

(c)   a securities note (PR 2.2.2R).

Prospectus Rule 2.2.10EU sets out requirements as to the basic format of the prospectus.

It was intended that the option to draw up three separate documents would assist companies who are regular issuers of shares in circumstances which require a prospectus (see **6.4** above), as PR 5.1.4 provides that any approved registration document remains valid for up to 12 months from the date of approval (subject to the requirement to update). This means that once a registration document has been approved, any further issue of shares will require only a new summary and securities note. However, as explained at **6.10**, the new securities note must also update the registration document as to any material changes. This means that due diligence is still required each time the company wishes to use its registration document. As a result of this, and the fact that a bespoke prospectus tends to have advantages from a marketing perspective, to date companies have used the single document format. A very rare exception to this was the prospectus for Royal Mail plc's £3.3 billion IPO in October 2013. It was divided into the three constituent parts. Each part makes it clear that the other two parts should also be read.

The summary, registration document and securities note are considered in more detail below. Note that even if the company chooses the single document format, the document must include an identifiable summary and the information required by the registration document and securities note.

The summary

Prospectus Rule 2.1.2UK provides that in the UK, whichever format of prospectus is selected, the prospectus must include a self-contained summary. This must set out, briefly and in non-technical language and in an appropriate structure, the key information relevant to the securities to which the prospectus relates, and when read with the rest of the prospectus must be an aid to investors considering whether to invest in the shares. 'Key information' is defined in outline in s 87A(9) and (10) of the FSMA 2000 and in detail in the PD Regulation, and seeks to aid investors in deciding whether to invest.

Prospectus Rules 2.1.4EU to 2.1.7R explain how the content of the summary will be determined. The following are the key requirements (PR 2.1.4EU):

(a)   The summary must contain the key information set out in Annex XXII of the PD Regulation. This is reproduced in Appendix 3 to Chapter 3 of the Prospectus Rules. It comprises five sections, each made up of a table with various elements, covering an investor warning, the shares being offered, the risks of investing, the shares themselves and the offer of shares.

(b)   The order of the sections and elements are mandatory as set out in the Annex. In other words, all summaries will follow the same format. This is to enable easier comparison with prospectuses for other securities.

(c)   If an item in the Annex is not relevant to the prospectus then 'not applicable' must be entered alongside that element of the summary.

(d)   The summary must not cross-refer to other parts of the prospectus. It must therefore be self-contained.

(e)   The summary cannot exceed 15 pages or 7% of the total of the prospectus, whichever is the longer.

Note that the summary has particular importance under the passporting procedure (see **6.11** below) as it is the only part of the prospectus which another Member State can request to be translated.

The registration document

The registration document must provide information about the company. Prospectus Rule 2.3.1EU provides that it should contain the information set out in Annex I of the PD Regulation (set out at Appendix 3 of the Prospectus Rules). The main content requirements of Annex I are summarised below, but this is intended to provide only a flavour of the content of the prospectus. For comprehensive details of the content requirements, reference must be made to the Prospectus Rules themselves. The numerical paragraph references below correspond to the paragraph numbers of Annex I:

1.   *Persons responsible.* The document must identify all persons responsible for the information given in the registration document, and those persons must declare in the document that:

    having taken all reasonable care to ensure that such is the case, the information contained in the registration document is, to the best of their knowledge, in accordance with the facts and contains no omission likely to affect its import.

    This is referred to as the 'responsibility statement'. (Paragraphs **6.6** and **6.7** below discuss further the issues of responsibility and liability for the document.)

2.   *Statutory auditors.* The document must identify the company's auditors.

3.   *Selected financial information.* Certain financial information must be provided.

4.   *Risk factors.* A section headed 'risk factors' must include prominent disclosure of any and all risk factors which are specific to the company or its industry.

    This is one of the most important disclosures regarding the company for potential investors. For example, the prospectus issued for Ocado plc's July 2010 IPO contained 49 separate risk factors, including the fact that it is dependent on the specialist skills of its current executive directors, it had never made a profit in its 10 years of existence and anticipates making further losses, its online ordering system may be subject to hacking or vandalism, and there may be a decrease in demand for its services due to health concerns or a pandemic such as mad cow disease or avian flu.

    This section of the prospectus has come under close scrutiny in recent years as a result of the global financial crisis. The FCA in its Technical Note UKLA/TN/621.2 Risk factors (available on the FCA's website) reminds companies that these factors should be directly relevant to the company, its industry and the shares being offered, and it noted recent tendencies towards more generic and standardised risk factors which went beyond this. The FCA will challenge the use of certain risk factors in appropriate circumstances. There is further information on the interaction between the risk factors and the need for a working capital statement in the prospectus in the FCA's Technical Note UKLA/TN/321.1 Working Capital Statements and risk factors (available on the FCA's website).

5.   *Information about the issuer.* The document must refer to the company's history and development, including information such as its date of incorporation, the address of its registered office and important events in the development of the company's business. The document must also contain a description of the company's principal investments, existing and future.

6. *Business overview.* The company's principal activities and markets must be described.

7. *Organisational structure.* The document must detail if the issuer is part of a group, a brief description of the group and the company's position within that group. It must also identify the company's significant subsidiaries.

8. *Property, plant and equipment.* The company's existing and planned material tangible fixed assets, such as leased properties, and any encumbrances to which they are subject, must be listed. The document must also highlight any environmental issues which may affect the company's ability to use such assets.

9. *Operating and financial review.* The document must include a description of the company's financial condition and other information which has materially affected, or could materially affect, the issuer's operations. In each case information is required for each of the years covered by the audited financial statements.

10. *Capital resources.* The document must detail the company's capital resources, including cash flow, borrowing requirements, any restrictions on the use of capital resources and information regarding the anticipated sources of funds for any future investments.

11. *Research and development, patents and licences.* Information must be provided about the company's research and development policy.

12. *Trend information.* Information is required about the most significant trends in production, sales and inventory, costs and selling prices, and any known trends or uncertainties which are reasonably likely to have a material effect on the company's prospects for the current financial year.

13. *Profit forecasts or estimates.* If an issuer chooses to include a profit forecast in the prospectus then it must also provide the information set out in para 13 of Annex I, including a statement setting out the assumptions on which the forecast is based and a report by the company's auditors or independent accountants that the forecast has been properly compiled.

14. *Administrative, management and supervisory bodies and senior management.* The document must provide information about the company's management, particularly the directors, but also potentially any founders (if the company is less than five years' old) and senior managers who are relevant to establishing that the company has appropriate expertise and experience for the management of the company's business. Some of this information could be seen as rather 'personal', such as details of any unspent convictions in relation to fraudulent offences, details of any insolvency events and details of any public criticisms of any director by any statutory or regulatory bodies. Ideally there will be no skeletons hiding in the directors' (or, if relevant, founders' or senior managers') closets which need to be aired in the prospectus (and if there are not, an appropriate 'negative statement' must be made in the document). However, if there are, then the due diligence process should ensure that they come to light sooner rather than later, so that the financial PR consultants have time to consider how they can manage the issues in a way that will not stop potential investors from investing in the company. Details of any conflict of interest between any of the people covered by para 14 must also be disclosed (and if there are none, an appropriate negative statement must be made).

15. *Remuneration and benefits.* Details of the remuneration (for the last full financial year) and benefits of the directors (and, if relevant, founders and senior managers) must be provided.

16. *Board practices.* Certain information about the running of the board, including periods of service, service contract information and corporate governance compliance (see **Chapter 8**), must be included.

17. *Employees.* The document must include information relating to employees, including the number of employees, information regarding their share or share option ownership,

and a description of any arrangements for involving the employees in the company's capital.

18. *Major shareholders.* The document must identify any major shareholder of the company (that is, anyone other than a director who has an interest in the company's capital or voting rights which is notifiable under national law (3% in the UK – see **Chapter 15**), and provide other information as to such shareholders, such as whether or not they have different voting rights.

19. *Related party transactions.* Details of any related party transactions (see **19.5**) must be provided, together with the amount to which such transactions form part of the company's turnover.

20. *Financial information concerning the issuer's assets and liabilities, financial position and profits and losses.* The prospectus must contain a significant amount of financial information, prepared with the help of the reporting accounts. Paragraph **4.2.5** above refers to some of this information. In particular, the short form report, containing information relating to the profits and losses, assets and liabilities, financial record and position of the group for the period of three years before the IPO, must form part of the document. The document must also include a statement as to whether or not there has been any significant change in the financial or trading position of the group since the date to which the last accounts or interim statements were made up. This paragraph also refers to the inclusion of the 'building block' pro forma financial information required by Annex II.

Information is also required, by para 20.8, about any litigation or arbitration (including any pending or threatened) which might have, or has had, a significant effect on the group's financial position. This can be a very sensitive area for the company, which would not usually consider publicising litigation, or the threat of it. However, the Prospectus Rules are very clear that it must do so, subject to the 'significant effect' qualification. If the company does not consider it has anything to disclose in this regard, it must include a 'negative statement' to that effect.

Information about the company's dividend policy must also be included.

21. *Additional information.* The document must include information about the company's share capital, such as the authorised and issued share capital, and certain details of the history of the company's share capital. In addition, various information about the company's memorandum and articles of association must be provided, including a description of the company's objects, a description of the rights attaching to each class of existing shares and a description of certain issues in the articles, such as any change of control clause or any conditions governing changes in capital which are more stringent than those required by law.

22. *Material contracts.* The document should summarise the principal contents of certain contracts referred to as 'material contracts', namely those contracts which have been entered into other than in the ordinary course of business by the company or any member of the company's group:

    (i)   in the two-year period preceding the publication of the document (if the contract is material); or

    (ii) at any time (if the contract provides the company or any member of the company's group with any entitlement or obligation which is still material to the company or the group as at the date the prospectus is published).

The lawyers will help the company to identify which documents fall within the definition and draft the summaries of those contracts for inclusion in the document.

23. *Third party information and statement by experts and declarations of any interest.* If the document includes a statement or report attributed to a person as an expert, it must provide information about the expert. If the document contains any information sourced from a third party, the source of that information must be identified, and confirmation must be

provided that the information has been reproduced accurately and that, as far as the issuer is aware, no facts have been omitted which would render the information inaccurate or misleading.

24. *Documents on display.* The document should include a statement that, for the life of the registration document, certain documents (set out in para 24) are available at a named location for inspection. These documents include the company's memorandum and articles of association and historical financial information. The lawyers will assist the company in creating and indexing the files of display documents.

25. *Information on holdings.* Information must be provided about any undertakings in which the company holds shares which are likely to have a significant effect on the assessment of the company's finances.

The securities note

The securities note must contain information about the securities (for our purposes, shares) to be offered or admitted. Prospectus Rule 2.3.1EU provides that the securities note should contain the information set out in Annex III of the PD Regulation (set out at Appendix 3 of the Prospectus Rules). The main content requirements of Annex III are summarised below. Again this is intended to provide only a flavour of the content of the prospectus, and for a comprehensive list of the content requirements, you should refer to the Prospectus Rules themselves. The numerical paragraph references below correspond to the paragraph numbers of Annex III.

1. *Persons responsible.* As with the registration document, a responsibility statement must be included; this time by all those responsible for the information given in the prospectus.

2. *Risk factors.* Again, there is a requirement similar to that which exists for the registration document, that the securities note must include prominent disclosure, under the section headed 'risk factors', of risk factors that are material to the shares being offered and/or admitted. This is to enable investors to assess the market risk associated with the shares.

3. *Essential information.* The document must include what is referred to as the 'working capital statement', namely a statement that, in the company's opinion, the working capital is sufficient for the issuer's present requirements or, if not, how it proposes to provide the additional working capital it requires. Of course, this ensures the directors address their minds to the ability of the company to thrive, or at least survive, after flotation, and address the likelihood of insolvency problems after the IPO. (The working capital statement is, in effect, a statement that the company is not going to 'go belly up' (ie become insolvent) straight after the IPO.) The document must also include a capitalisation and indebtedness statement. In addition, information must be provided in relation to anyone with any particular interest in the issue/offer of shares (including any conflicting interest), and in relation to the reasons for the offer and how it is intended any proceeds will be used.

4. *Information concerning the securities to be offered/admitted to trading.* Information must be provided about the shares which are to be offered or admitted, including a description of the type and class of shares, the legislation under which the securities were created (until 1 October 2009, the CA 1985; thereafter, the CA 2006), the rights which attach to the shares (such as voting rights, rights to share in capital, dividend rights and pre-emption rights: see **Chapters 13** and **14**). In the case of new issues, the resolutions, authorisations and approvals by virtue of which the shares have been created and/or issued must also be stated (see **Chapter 14**).

5. *Terms and conditions of the offer.* The document must set out detailed terms and conditions of the offer, including the total amount of the offer, the period for which the offer will be open and the circumstances under which the offer can be revoked, and an indication of

the offer price. Details of any underwriters and when the underwriting agreement was or will be reached are also required.

6. *Admission to trading and dealing arrangements.* As a prospectus is required for all public offers (unless an exemption applies), there is a requirement to include a statement as to whether the shares offered will be admitted to trading with a view to their distribution on a regulated market. For our purposes, in the context of an IPO the shares will be admitted to trading on the Main Market, a regulated market.

7. *Selling securities holders.* If the IPO involves an offer for sale of shares (see **4.4.1.1**) then specific details must be provided, including the name and address of the selling shareholders and the number and class of shares being sold by each shareholder.

8. *Expense of the issue/offer.* The securities note must detail the total net proceeds and an estimate of the total expenses of the issue/offer.

9. *Dilution.* The amount and percentage of immediate dilution (see **14.6.2**) resulting from the offer must be included in the document.

10. *Additional information.* There is a requirement, to mirror the requirement in para 23 of Annex I relating to the registration document, that if the securities note includes a statement or report attributed to a person as an expert, then it must provide information about the expert. If it contains any information sourced from a third party, the source of that information must be identified, and confirmation must be provided that the information has been reproduced accurately and that, as far as the issuer is aware, no facts have been omitted which would render the information inaccurate or misleading. Other additional information which must be included is a statement of the capacity in which any advisers, referred to in the securities note, have acted, and to identify and reproduce, or summarise, audited information referred to in the document.

6.5.2.2 Incorporation by reference

Information can be incorporated by reference into the registration document or the securities note, in certain circumstances, without, therefore, having to be restated in full. To be incorporated, the information must:

(a) have been approved by, filed with, or notified to the FCA (PR 2.4.1R);

(b) be the latest available to the company (PR 2.4.3R);

(c) be accessible using a cross-referenced list in the prospectus (PR 2.4.5R); and

(d) not endanger investor protection (PR 2.4.6EU, para 5).

Prospectus Rules 2.4.2G and 2.4.6EU, para 1 set out examples of information which can be incorporated by reference, such as information in the audited report and accounts of the company, or the company's memorandum and articles of association. As explained at **5.3.6.2** above, the company must submit to the FCA a copy of any document incorporated into the prospectus by reference (annotated to indicate to which item of the schedules and building blocks in the PD Regulation it relates). To date reference to information incorporated by reference seems to have been made in the rubric on the cover page of the prospectus.

Unlike the registration document and the securities note, the summary cannot incorporate information by reference (PR 2.4.4R).

6.5.2.3 Omission of information

Prospectus Rule 2.5.2UK and s 87B of the FSMA 2000 provide that the FCA has the discretion to authorise the omission of any information required by the Prospectus Rules or s 87A of the FSMA 2000 if:

(a) disclosure of the information would be contrary to the public interest; or

(b)   disclosure of the information would be seriously detrimental to the company and the omission of the information is not likely to mislead investors in their assessment of the investment; or

(c)   the information to be omitted is of minor importance for a specific offer or admission and is unlikely to influence the investors' ability to make an informed choice as to whether to invest.

As mentioned at **5.3.6.2** above, any request to omit information under PR 2.5.2R must comply with the requirements of PR 2.5.3R.

The lawyers must make the directors aware of this discretion of the FCA, but they must manage the message carefully. As we have seen, the Prospectus Rules and the FSMA 2000 require significant disclosure in the prospectus. The directors may not want certain information to be included in the prospectus, and will ask the lawyers how they can avoid disclosure of that information. The general message is that if the Prospectus Rules, or the general disclosure requirement in s 87A of the FSMA 2000, require such disclosure then the prospectus must contain that information. The FCA will exercise its discretion to omit information only in exceptional circumstances. Indeed, the very fact that directors wish to omit certain information may suggest that they think that such information would deter investors from investing in the company. This means that the information is likely to be highly relevant to investors, and so would not fall within the FCA's discretion in any event. Lawyers need to be firm with directors who try to conceal facts, because ultimately the directors themselves may be personally liable to investors for inaccuracies in or omissions from the prospectus (see **6.7** below).

6.5.2.4   Checking content

Chapter 5 describes how the prospectus is submitted to the FCA for approval. To help the FCA check that the document complies with its content requirements, PR 3.1.4R requires that the draft document must be annotated in the margin to indicate which Prospectus Rule requirement the text complies with. So, for example, the margin opposite the list of directors' names and addresses would be annotated with 'I.14' to indicate that the list fulfils the content requirements of Annex 1, para 14. Subsequent drafts must comply with PR 3.1.5R. The FCA asks that deleted text should be retained (eg by using 'strike-through') to speed up the approval process.

6.6   RESPONSIBILITY

It is all very well requiring the production of a prospectus which will usually run to well in excess of 100 pages (Royal Mail plc's October 2013 IPO prospectus ran to 450 pages!), but what if any of the information included in the prospectus proves to be incorrect, or what if a relevant piece of information has been omitted? This may lead to investors losing money if they have invested as a result in a company which is in reality not what it appears to be from the prospectus. Can the investors be compensated in such circumstances? The answer is yes. The FSMA 2000 provides the authority to make certain people involved in the preparation of the prospectus take responsibility for the accuracy of its contents. It then makes those responsible liable for any mistakes or omissions which cause investors loss.

6.6.1   Who is responsible for the contents of the prospectus?

The answer lies in the Prospectus Rules as authorised by s 84(1)(d) of the FSMA 2000. Where, as in our case, the prospectus relates to equity securities (ordinary shares) for which the UK is the home Member State, PR 5.5.3R(2) provides that the following people will be responsible for the prospectus:

(a)   the issuer (ie the company) (PR 5.5.3R(2)(a));

(b)   the directors of the company (as at the date the document is published) (PR 5.5.3R(2)(b)(i));

(c)   anyone who has agreed to be named, and is named, in the prospectus as a director, or as having agreed to become a director, either immediately or in the future (after the IPO, for example) (PR 5.5.3R(2)(b)(ii));

(d)   anyone who accepts, and is stated in the prospectus as accepting, responsibility for the prospectus (PR 5.5.3R(2)(c));

(e)   anyone, other than the company, who is offering shares (and if this is another company, the directors of that company at the time the prospectus is published) (PR 5.5.3R(2)(d));

(f)   the person requesting admission to trading of the shares (if not the company) (and if this is another company, the directors of that company at the time the prospectus is published) (PR 5.5.3R(2)(e)); and

(g)   anyone else who authorises the contents of the prospectus (PR 5.5.3R(2)(f)).

Paragraph (e) above will be of particular concern to any selling shareholders if an offer for sale forms part of the IPO. They may well be individuals who would not be comfortable taking such responsibility. However, comfort is at hand. Prospectus Rule 5.5.7R provides that a person will not be responsible under PR 5.5.3R(2)(d) if the shareholder is making the offer in association with the issuer and it is primarily the issuer, or the issuing company's advisers, who draw up the prospectus. This will usually be the case with IPOs, so usually the lawyer will be able to reassure any selling shareholders on the issue of responsibility.

Paragraph (g) above will, for example, cover the accountants (because they have authorised financial information prepared specifically for the prospectus) (Annex I, para 23 and Annex III, para 10 – see **6.5.2.1** above). As a result, they must set out a statement in the prospectus that they are responsible for such content. However, they will not be required to give such a statement in respect of financial information incorporated by reference which was not prepared specifically for the prospectus.

It appears that the FCA does not consider the sponsor to have authorised the prospectus for the purposes of the responsibility regime, as current practice is for sponsors not to provide such a statement under PR 5.5.9R.

Lawyers similarly are covered by the exemption in PR 5.5.9R. They do not have responsibility by reason only of giving advice about the content of the prospectus in a professional capacity.

6.6.2   What does responsibility mean?

The persons with responsibility for the document must ensure that the document complies with the general disclosure obligation imposed by the FSMA 2000 (see **6.5.1** above), the specific content requirements set out in the Prospectus Rules (see **6.5.2** above) and the requirements of the Listing Rules in relation to the listing application to the FCA (see **Chapter 5**). In other words, they must ensure that all relevant information is included in the prospectus. The consequences of this are discussed at **6.7** below.

6.6.3   Practicalities

6.6.3.1   Responsibility statement

As mentioned at **6.5.2.1** above, a responsibility statement must be included in the prospectus pursuant to para 1.2 of both Annex I and Annex III of the Prospectus Rules.

6.7   LIABILITY

As stated in **6.6.2** above, those with responsibility for the prospectus must ensure that it meets the content requirements of the Prospectus Rules and the FSMA 2000, and the rules relating to the application for listing under the Listing Rules. The document must not omit any information or contain information which is incorrect or misleading. The consequence of this is that the persons responsible for the document may incur civil and/or criminal liability in relation to any inaccuracies or misstatements in, or omissions from, the document.

6.7.1 Civil liability

6.7.1.1 Section 90 of the FSMA 2000

This is the liability which a person responsible is most likely to face for problems arising out of the content of the prospectus.

The effect of s 90 of the FSMA 2000 is that those responsible for listing *particulars* must pay compensation to anyone who has acquired shares which are the subject of the listing particulars, and has suffered loss as a result of any inaccurate or misleading statement in the document, or any omission of information which should have been disclosed under s 87A. Section 90(11) (added by para 6 of Sch 1 to the Prospectus Regulations 2005) provides that this applies equally in relation to a *prospectus*. While it includes specific reference to the general disclosure requirement under s 87A of the FSMA 2000, in practice s 90 is construed to apply not only to a failure of the prospectus to meet this requirement, but also to any failure to meet the content requirements of the Prospectus Rules.

Note that s 90(12) provides that a person can be liable solely on the basis of the contents of the summary (see **6.5.2.1**) only if the summary is misleading, inaccurate or inconsistent, or does not include the required 'key information' (see **6.5.2.1** above) when read together with the rest of the prospectus.

It may help to consider the issue of liability by way of an example.

> **EXAMPLE**
>
> Imagine that an investor, Mr X, encouraged by the positive messages in the prospectus, invests in Company A. In fact, the prospectus failed to include information about a very real risk that a rival's new invention could significantly reduce Company A's sales. Imagine that, after the IPO, the rival's new invention goes terribly wrong. Company A continues to prosper and Mr X makes a good profit. Mr X has suffered no loss and the persons responsible for the inaccurate prospectus, through sheer luck, will incur no liability under s 90.
>
> Consider now what would happen if, in fact, the rival's new invention is a huge success, to the extent that Company A loses significant sales and ultimately goes belly up. Mr X loses his entire investment. He has suffered loss and wants compensation. Section 90 of the FSMA 2000 provides that he should obtain compensation from those persons responsible for the incorrect selling document (that is, mainly, the directors).

What is the scope of s 90? There are two particular phrases in the provision which have caused some debate:

(a) 'who has acquired' – s 90 concerns the loss suffered by a person 'who has acquired' securities. Is this restricted to the original investor, or does it include those who buy the shares from that original investor?

(b) 'as a result of' – for any investor to have a claim to compensation under s 90, he must prove that he suffered loss 'as a result of' the deficiencies in the document. Does this mean that the investor must have relied on the document? Must the investor have read the document?

These phrases leave open the possibility that any aggrieved original investor who had not even read the document, or any subsequent purchaser of the shares from the original investor, could try to run the argument that s 90 is wide enough to afford him a claim for compensation.

There are some exemptions from liability under s 90, which are set out in Sch 10 to the FSMA 2000. These exemptions include:

(a) if, at the time the prospectus was submitted to the FCA, the persons responsible (having made reasonable enquiries) believed the erroneous information was true and not misleading;

(b) where loss arises as a result of a statement by an expert;

(c) where a correction had been published before shares were acquired;

(d) where the erroneous information was reproduced from a public official document; and

(e) where the person seeking compensation acquired the shares knowing the information was deficient.

The first ever case relying on s 90 was commenced in the High Court in 2013. It relates to a prospectus prepared for a rights issue (see **17.7** below) rather than an IPO, but it is still instructive for us as s 90 relates to prospectuses used whatever the circumstances. Thousands of investors in Royal Bank of Scotland (RBS) (both institutional, such as the UK Mineworkers' Pension Fund, the Dutch bank ING and the teachers' retirement system of Illinois, USA and private individuals) started the action against RBS and four of its former directors (including the former CEO, Fred Goodwin, who became the public's principal hate figure over the financial crisis in the UK) for what they claim is the loss caused by misleading statements and omissions in RBS's prospectus arising out of its emergency £12 billion share offer in 2008. At the time RBS was desperately trying to raise money from its shareholders to stay afloat, having been caught up in the global financial crisis. The fundraising failed to save RBS, and four months later it announced the second biggest loss ever by a bank in UK. Eventually RBS ended up being taken over by the UK Government to prevent it from collapsing. The investors claim that if RBS had provided the correct information in the prospectus, they would not have taken up the shares offered at the time, and they are claiming the difference between the price paid (£2) and what they say the shares were really worth (in one initial statement by 21 claimants this was said to be just 28 pence).

At the time of writing the case is still at the early procedural stage and, in light of the massive number of claimants, will proceed slowly, but it will undoubtedly be one of the most important UK financial services cases ever heard should it reach trial.

6.7.1.2 Liability in tort

The persons responsible for the prospectus may also incur tortious liability under the following heads:

(a) *Negligent misstatement.* Those with responsibility for the prospectus owe a duty of care to those investing at the time of the IPO. The publication of a deficient document breaches this duty. If an investor relies on a deficient prospectus and suffers loss because of that reliance then, on the basis of *Hedley Byrne & Co Ltd v Heller & Partners Ltd* [1964] AC 465, those responsible for the prospectus will be liable to that investor. Note that, applying *Caparo Industries v Dickman* [1990] 1 All ER 568, the persons responsible for the document would not owe any duty to any subsequent purchasers of the shares. This, and the fact that the investor must have *relied* on the erroneous information or omission, can be contrasted with the position under s 90 of the FSMA 2000 (see **6.7.1.1**) and therefore makes this a less attractive claim for an aggrieved investor.

(b) *Deceit.* If an investor can prove that any misstatement in the prospectus was made fraudulently, he may have a claim in damages for deceit.

(c) *Misrepresentation Act 1967.* If an investor chooses to invest in the company on the basis of an incorrect or misleading prospectus, he may be able to rescind the contract for the purchase of shares and/or claim damages from the other party to the contract (see also

CA 2006, s 655). Note that the other party usually will be the issuer of the shares, ie the company (in the case of an offer for subscription) or the selling shareholder (in the case of an offer for sale), rather than the directors.

6.7.1.3 Liability in contract

The prospectus will form either the whole or part of any contract between an investor buying shares and either the company issuing shares to the investor, or any existing shareholder selling shares to the investor (the circumstances will vary depending on the IPO). If the prospectus is deficient, the investor may be able to rescind the contract, or sue the other party to the contract (the company or the selling shareholder) for damages.

6.7.1.4 Advertisements relating to a prospectus

Prospectus Rule 3.3 lays down a number of requirements relating to advertisements in connection with a prospectus. Advertisements are defined as relating to a specific offer to the public of securities (such as shares) or admission to trading and aiming specifically to promote the possible acquisition of securities. This covers a wide range of communications to investors and the media, including those made via printed matter, the Internet, email, television, text messages, road-shows, briefings, conference calls and presentations to promote the offer. Crucially, the information in each such advertisement must not be inaccurate or misleading. It must also be consistent with the information in an existing prospectus, or one which will be published in due course if the prospectus is not yet finalised. If the information is inaccurate, misleading or inconsistent then liability can also arise for breach of the Prospectus Rules, and the sanctions in **3.6** above may be applied by the FCA. Care must therefore be taken, particularly by management of a company undertaking a high-profile IPO, when discussing it on television (especially in a live interview) or with a journalist, or if a director feels the urge to tweet about it.

6.7.2 Criminal liability

The threat of paying compensation or damages may be bad enough for the persons responsible, but it could get worse. Reflecting the importance of protecting the investing public, there may even be the possibility of criminal liability. Mentioning this sanction does tend to help any director, who is tiring of the legal due diligence or verification process, to re-focus.

Criminal offences are usually prosecuted by the Crown Prosecution Service, but the FCA has special powers to bring criminal prosecutions, including for the offences set out in ss 401 and 402 of the FSMA 2000.

6.7.2.1 Sections 89 and 90 of the Financial Services Act 2012

A director risks criminal liability under the following provisions of the Financial Services Act 2012:

(a) *Section 89 (misleading statements)*. This provision makes it a criminal offence for any person to make a statement which he knows to be false or misleading in a material respect, to conceal dishonestly any material facts or recklessly make a statement which is misleading.

(b) *Section 90 (misleading impressions)*. This provision catches anything any person does to create a false or misleading impression as to the market in, or price or value of the shares, if he does so deliberately to induce investors to buy investments, sell them, underwrite them or refrain from so doing or, while knowing the impression to be false or misleading makes a gain or causes a loss.

Sections 89 and 90 of the Financial Services Act 2012 are considered in more detail at **9.5** below.

6.7.2.2   Theft Act 1968

Section 19 of the Theft Act 1968 imposes criminal penalties on any director who makes false or misleading statements with intent to deceive shareholders. Clearly this could apply to any director who is responsible for a deficient prospectus, if intent can be proved.

6.7.2.3   Section 85(3) of the FSMA 2000

It is a criminal offence for a person to offer shares to the public or request their admission to trading without providing an approved prospectus to the public.

6.7.2.4   Fraud Act 2006

It is a criminal offence under s 2 of the Fraud Act 2006 dishonestly to make a representation and in doing so intend to make a gain or cause a loss. Under s 3 it is a criminal offence for a person to fail to disclose information which he is legally obliged to do and in doing so make a gain or expose another to the risk of loss. Under s 12, if the offence is committed by a company then a director or other officer of the company is (in addition to the company) liable for that offence if he consents to or connives in that offence. The penalties for these offences under s 1 are a maximum of 10 years' imprisonment and an unlimited fine.

6.7.3   Fines

As seen at **3.6** above, s 91 of the FSMA 2000 provides that the FCA can fine the company for breach of Part 6 Rules, including the Prospectus Rules, and if it can prove that any director or former director was knowingly concerned in the breach, can also fine that director.

6.7.4   Censure

As seen at **3.6** above, s 91 of the FSMA 2000 provides that the FCA may choose privately or publicly to censure the company, or a director or former director knowingly concerned in the breach, as an alternative to a fine.

6.8   VERIFICATION

As the range of possible liability set out at **6.7** above makes clear, it is not a good idea for the directors to make incorrect statements in the prospectus, or to omit required material from it. During the IPO process, therefore, great care is taken to ensure that the prospectus meets the requirements of the Prospectus Rules and the FSMA 2000. As **6.6.1** above explains, directors are not the only people with responsibility for the document, but they do have responsibility, and their responsibility is for the entire document. Accordingly, a process has emerged which aims to ensure that the directors make all reasonable enquiries to satisfy themselves that:

(a)   each material statement of fact or opinion in the document is not only true, but also not misleading in the context in which it appears;

(b)   the document as a whole gives a true and fair impression of the history, business and prospects of the company; and

(c)   the document does not omit any information which makes it misleading or which contravenes the Prospectus Rules and/or s 87A of the FSMA 2000.

This process is called verification. It protects the directors by providing evidence that they have taken reasonable care to ensure the information required by s 87A of the FSMA 2000 has been included. It also helps to avoid breaching ss 89 and 90 of the Financial Services Act 2012 (see **9.5**) and the market abuse regime (see **Chapter 10**), and so provides comfort to the sponsor. The verification process is considered in more detail at **5.3.5** above.

6.9   TYPES OF PROSPECTUS

6.9.1   Full/final

So far, this chapter has considered the document which will ultimately be submitted to the FCA for approval as part of the company's application for admission to listing. This is known as the full or final prospectus. However, references to other forms of the prospectus may be made during the IPO process in adition to the abbreviated prospectus under the PD Regulation discussed at **6.5.2** above. These references are explained below.

6.9.2   Preliminary/price-range prospectus

This is virtually identical to the full prospectus. It too has to be approved by the FCA before it can be sent out to prospective investors. The key difference is that the price for the shares being offered will not be specified in the document as a fixed amount, instead there will usually be a price range. This type of prospectus is also commonly known as a 'price-range prospectus'. It is even possible to issue the preliminary prospectus without a price or the number of shares being offered being mentioned at all. Approval by the FCA means that this document can be sent out to any potential investor. A pricing statement will subsequently be issued setting out the final price before the offer closes under PR 2.3.2R. This statement does not require prior approval by the FCA (possibly with a supplementary prospectus (see **6.9.4** below) if, for example, there has been a material change to the information in the preliminary prospectus).

6.9.3   Pathfinder prospectus

This is a draft of the prospectus which is sent out to prospective investors to stimulate interest in the IPO. A full prospectus will be sent out once expressions of interest have been received. The crucial difference from the preliminary prospectus (see **6.9.2**) is that it is sent to prospective investors without prior FCA approval. This causes a potential problem in that it could result in a breach of s 21 of the FSMA 2000 (see **Chapter 12**). The impact of s 21 is that it is an offence for a company to send out a pathfinder to induce investors to buy shares. The company can avoid this problem by sending the pathfinder only to persons exempt from s 21 (mainly institutional investors) (see **12.9**). In addition, a pathfinder must comply with the rules relating to advertisements set out in PR 3.3 (see **5.3.6.6**), as clarified in the FCA's Technical Note UKLA/TN/604.1 PD Advertisement regime (available in the UKLA section of the FCA's website).

Note that under PR 3.2.3R, an approved prospectus (be it full or preliminary) must be made available to investors at least six working days before the close of the offer (see **5.4.2.1**).

6.9.4   Factors to take into account

There are a number of factors to weigh up before the company decides whether to issue a preliminary or pathfinder prospectus.

A pathfinder can be distributed only to limited categories of person (such as institutional investors) whereas a preliminary prospectus can be sent out to any investor, including a member of the public.

If a preliminary prospectus is used, a supplementary prospectus may have to be prepared which will need to be approved by the FCA before it is distributed (see **6.9.5**). This does not arise with a pathfinder, as no prior prospectus relating to the offer is in existence. The publication of a supplementary prospectus grants investors the right to withdraw their acceptance of the offer (FSMA 2000, s 87Q(4)).

Another potential disadvantage of the company choosing to use a preliminary prospectus (which does not arise with a pathfinder) is that investors have the right to withdraw their acceptances of the offer within two working days of the date the company provides the price of the offer to the FCA under s 87A(7) of the FSMA 2000 (FSMA 2000, s 87(Q)(1) and (2)). However, if the prospectus details the method and conditions for determining the price and amount (or, in relation to the price, states a maximum offer price) then this right to withdraw will not arise (FSMA 2000, s 87Q(3)).

Note that under PR 3.2.3R, an approved prospectus (be it full or preliminary) must be made available to investors at least six working days before the close of the offer (see **5.4.2.1**).

6.9.5 Supplementary

Section 87G of the FSMA 2000 and PR 3.4.1UK provide that if, in the period following the approval of the prospectus but before dealings in shares commence, there arises or is noted any significant new factor, material mistake or inaccuracy relating to the information included in the approved prospectus, the company must produce a supplementary prospectus. This document must contain details of the new factor, mistake or inaccuracy, and must be approved by the FCA. As mentioned at **6.9.4** above, investors have the right to withdraw their acceptances of the offer during the two working days following publication of the supplementary prospectus (FSMA 2000, s 87Q(4)), so this is a situation to be avoided if at all possible and demonstrates another reason for having the thorough due diligence process in the period leading up to the IPO.

6.10 VALIDITY

A prospectus is valid for 12 months after its approval, for any further offers or admissions to trading, provided that it is updated by a supplementary prospectus, approved by the FCA (see **6.9.5**) (PR 5.1.1R). As mentioned at **6.5.2.1** above, the registration document is valid for a period of up to 12 months after it has been filed and approved, but this is also subject to updating, using a new securities note, which again requires the approval of the FCA (PR 2.2.5R and PR 5.1.4R).

Given the requirements for FCA approval of any update to either the prospectus (by supplementary prospectus) or the registration note (by a new securities note), any advantage of this extended validity period may be limited, as explained at **6.5.2.1** above.

6.11 PASSPORTING

The Prospectus Directive has ensured that each Member State has the same rules regarding the drawing up of a prospectus. This reflects the principal aim of the European Commission's Financial Services Action Plan (FSAP), to create a single financial market across the EU. It also applies to non-EU EEA States, such as Norway and Iceland. This has enabled the introduction of a 'passporting' procedure, whereby a company will not need to produce a prospectus for an offer of shares to the public, or an admission of shares to trading, in one EEA Member State ('MS2') if another EEA Member State ('MS1') has already approved and published a prospectus in the previous 12 months. Subject to updating (see **6.10** above), the company simply must translate the summary (not, interestingly, any other part of the prospectus) into a language acceptable to MS2 and obtain a 'certificate of approval' from the competent authority in MS1 (in the UK, the FCA) that the prospectus has been drawn up and approved in accordance with the Prospectus Directive. Prospectus Rule 3.1.6G states that any request for such a certificate should be included with the company's application for approval of the initial prospectus. Prospectus Rule 5.3 and ss 87H and 87I of the FSMA 2000 set out the rules relating to the certificate of approval, and the UKLA Publications Factsheet No 4 (available from the UKLA section of the FCA's website) provides further information on the procedure to be followed. The competent authority in MS1 will have to notify the company or the person drawing up the prospectus that the certificate has been issued.

While the passporting procedure is easier to use than the previous mutual recognition procedure, a potentially lengthy due diligence exercise may still be required to ensure any previously issued prospectus is up to date. In addition, the eligibility criteria for listing are not covered by the Prospectus Directive and so remain diverse in each of the EEA Member States (remember that in the UK the conditions for listing are set out in Chapters 2 and 6 of the Listing Rules for a premium listing and Chapters 2 and 14 for a standard listing – see **4.3.1.2** and **4.3.1.3**). The company may have to meet further criteria in order to list shares in MS2 which it did not have to meet to list shares in MS1.

To date, a number of companies in the UK have taken advantage of the passporting procedure for an offer of shares in more than one EEA Member State. For example, the prospectus approved for the Royal Mail plc IPO in October 2013 was passported into Belgium, Cyprus, Germany, Gibraltar and Italy. Most EEA Member States have been requesting that the summary be translated into their national language, although certain EEA Member States (such as Austria, Luxembourg, The Netherlands and, in certain cases, Norway) accept the English language version. The Royal Bank of Scotland summary had to be translated into Dutch (for Belgium), French (for Belgium), German (for Germany), Greek (for Cyprus) and Italian (for Italy).

The FCA maintains a database (accessible through the UKLA section of its website) of companies which have passported prospectuses from non-UK EU jurisdictions.

PART II

BEING A LISTED COMPANY

CHAPTER 7

CONTINUING OBLIGATIONS

7.1 INTRODUCTION

Chapter 1 explained that once a company is listed, it becomes subject to continuing obligations. Both the FCA (in the DTRs, the Prospectus Rules and the Listing Rules) and the Stock Exchange (in the Admission and Disclosure Standards) impose continuing obligations on listed companies. As with the IPO process, however, the FCA and the Stock Exchange have worked together to dovetail their requirements. To what extent the company is subject to continuing obligations depends on whether it has a premium listing or a standard listing on the Main Market of the Stock Exchange.

7.2 WHY HAVE CONTINUING OBLIGATIONS?

The continuing obligations exist to protect both existing and potential investors. They seek to ensure that there is an orderly market for investments (stability being crucial to investors' confidence in the markets) and that all investors have access to information at the same time (in the interests of fairness).

Put into context, it makes sense that listed companies should bear these obligations. Remember that their shareholder base is diverse, and the vast majority of shareholders will not be involved in the management of the company and may know little about its day-to-day running (see **2.6** above). They therefore require increased protection to ensure that their investment in the company is safe.

At first glance, there may seem to be so many continuing obligations that you might wonder why any company would choose to float. However, the full array of obligations is imposed only on companies with a premium listing; standard listed companies are subject to far fewer obligations. Before embarking on the IPO process a company should of course consider, as part of its pre-IPO preparation, whether it is capable of meeting the continuing obligations that will be imposed on it after the IPO. If it cannot or does not want to meet the premium listed requirements then there is always the option of the less regulated standard listing or a quotation on AIM. However, the obligations are certainly not meant to deter companies from listing. In practice, once companies have put in place the administrative processes to enable them to deal with the obligations, most find that meeting the continuing obligations simply becomes part of the day-to-day running of the business.

That said, it does seem that, periodically, greater regulation imposed on listed companies trading on stock markets leads to a change in behaviour. Particularly tough restrictions imposed in the US, on stock exchanges such as the NYSE and NASDAQ, principally as a result of the Sarbanes-Oxley Act of 2002 (a name once guaranteed to get the pulse racing amongst bankers, lawyers, entrepreneurs and investors across the globe), led to an increase in (particularly non-UK) companies seeking to list in London rather than in the US. Some foreign companies (including UK ones such as lastminute.com) even 'delisted' from US stock markets to avoid the increased liability for directors and the greater cost of compliance with new accounting rules and other new continuing obligations brought in under the Sarbanes-Oxley Act. The Act was introduced in the US as a direct result of the financial scandals involving US listed companies, such as Enron and Worldcom, with the aim of increasing investor protection. Interestingly it did nothing to stop the practices of listed and unlisted US financial services companies which caused the global financial crisis in 2007/08.

More recently the UK has, together with all other EU Member States and the US, strengthened controls on listed companies in light of the failure of regulators to prevent the global financial crisis of 2007/08 and the tendency of listed companies, particularly banks, to put themselves in a position which imperilled their very existence. It remains to be seen how effective these more restrictive continuing obligations on listed companies will be, and the ultimate test will be whether the next financial crisis can be arrested before it develops into the global depression which the last one caused.

The recent deep recession in the UK resulted in a dramatic drop in the number of companies listing on the Stock Exchange. In an attempt to lure companies back to seek a listing, the Stock Exchange introduced a two-tier system of listings with a fully regulated premium listing and a minimum EU law regulated listing, known as the standard listing. The Stock Exchange's strategy therefore was that, while maintaining a gold-standard listing at the very highest standards of regulation, it was hoping to attract companies which might otherwise be put off from listing with a more appealing, less regulated option for listing. As at the end of 2013, approximately 200 companies had a standard listing of equity shares, with the majority being overseas companies which had already listed on the Main Market and chose to take advantage of the lesser regulation, such as Toyota, JP Morgan Chase and General Electric (all valued at over £100 billion).

Whichever option the company chooses, it will, of course require advice on the continuing obligations from its advisers from time to time. If the company was impressed by the work of its advisers on the IPO, it may well retain those advisers on a permanent basis after flotation. Due to the day-to-day nature of the continuing obligations, the in-house legal department of the listed company will often take responsibility for ensuring that the company meets those obligations. However, where a second opinion is required, or where the in-house solicitors are not available, the company will often call on its external lawyers, who will be expected to know what the continuing obligations are and how to meet them. As is explained below, due to the need to meet the obligations in a timely manner, the company will often require advice on an urgent basis.

7.3   WHERE TO FIND THE CONTINUING OBLIGATIONS

The continuing obligations imposed on listed companies can be found in the CA 2006, Chapters 9–20 of the Listing Rules, the DTRs (including the Corporate Governance Rules) and in the Stock Exchange's Admission and Disclosure Standards. Chapters 15–20 of the Listing Rules relate to special types of issuer or security and so fall outside the scope of this textbook. Chapters 10 and 11 of the Listing Rules, which deal with transactions, are discussed at **19.4** and **19.5** respectively. The remainder can be tackled more manageably if they are grouped together as follows:

(a)   obligations with continuing application (see **7.4**);

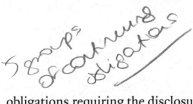

(b) obligations requiring the disclosure and notification of information about the company (see **7.5**);

(c) obligations relating to the shareholders of the company (see **7.6**);

(d) obligations relating to financial information about the company (see **7.7**); and

(e) obligations in the Admission and Disclosure Standards (see **7.10**).

Please note that what follows in this chapter applies only to a premium listed company unless expressly stated to apply to a standard listed company.

The Association of General Counsel and Company Secretaries of the FTSE 100 (GC100) produced a set of Guidelines (the GC100 Guidelines) in three parts, with the latest version published in May 2012. Part I seeks to assist its members (who are employed by the biggest listed companies) in establishing procedures, systems and controls to ensure that they comply fully with the Listing Rules and the DTRs. The Guidelines are neither legally binding nor part of the FCA's Handbook, although the FCA has agreed to include the following wording in the Guidelines: '... the FCA has seen this material in draft and recognises these Guidelines as a useful contribution to a difficult area'. In practice, therefore, the corporate lawyer needs to be aware of their existence.

7.4 OBLIGATIONS WITH CONTINUING APPLICATION

Listing Rule 9.2 sets out some of the requirements for a premium listing (see **Chapter 4**) which will continue to apply even after the IPO has taken place.

7.4.1 Admission to trading

You will recall that a condition for listing is that the shares are admitted to trading (LR 2.2.3R) (see **4.3.1.1**). Listing Rule 9.2.1R provides that it is a continuing obligation that the company's shares are admitted to trading at all times. This seeks to ensure that shares in a company are always freely marketable.

Listing Rule 14.3.1R requires the shares to be admitted to trading at all times for a standard listed company.

7.4.2 Compliance with the Disclosure, Transparency and Corporate Governance Rules

Under LR 9.2.5G and LR 9.2.6R, a premium listed company must comply with Chapter 2 of the DTRs (that is, the general obligation of disclosure and related matters discussed at **7.5** below).

Under LR 9.2.6AG and LR 9.2.6BR, a premium listed company must comply with the Transparency Rules (Chapters 4–6 of the DTRs) and the Corporate Governance Rules (Chapter 7 of the DTRs).

These continuing obligations explicitly reinforce compliance with the DTRs.

A company with a standard listing must comply with the Disclosure Rules and the Transparency Rules (LR 14.3.11G and LR 14.3.22R). The company must also comply with the Corporate Governance Rules (LR 14.3.24R and DTR 1B.1).

7.4.3 Compliance with the Model Code

Listing Rule 9.2.8 provides that a premium listed company must require persons discharging managerial responsibilities (PDMRs) to comply with a code governing how they deal in shares which they own in their listed company, called the Model Code, and to take all proper and reasonable steps to ensure their compliance. This is designed to ensure that the terms of the Model Code are complied with. It is annexed to Chapter 9 of the Listing Rules as Annex 1. The Model Code does not apply to standard listed companies.

Further detail on the Model Code is provided at **7.8** below.

7.4.4 Contact details

The company must provide to the FCA contact details of at least one person which it nominates to be the first point of contact with the FCA in relation to matters of the company's compliance with the Listing Rules and the DTRs (LR 9.2.11R and LR 9.2.12G). The chosen person must be knowledgeable about the company, the Listing Rules and the DTRs, and must be contactable on business days between 7 am and 7 pm. It is advisable for the company to appoint more than one person to perform this role, to ensure that there is always someone available.

This is also required for a company with a standard listing (LR 14.3.8R).

7.4.5 Shares in public hands

One of the conditions for listing is that at least 25% of the company's shares are in public hands (LR 6.1.19R) (see 4.3.1.1). Listing Rule 9.2.15R provides that the company must comply with this rule at all times. It must give written notice to the FCA without delay if the proportion of listed securities in public hands falls below 25% (LR 9.2.16R). This underpins a fundamental rule of listing on the Stock Exchange. It seeks to ensure a sufficient market is maintained in the shares of the listed company.

The standard listed company must continue to comply with LR 14.2.2R at all times (LR 14.3.2R). This is the mirror requirement to maintain at least 25% of the shares of the company in public hands.

7.4.6 Control over assets and independent business

Listing Rule 9.2.2AR states that a premium listed company must continue to comply with the requirements of LR 6.1.4R(2) and (3) once it has listed. These are that the company controls a majority of its assets and that it is an independent business.

7.5 DISCLOSURE AND NOTIFICATION OF INFORMATION ABOUT THE COMPANY

This encompasses one of the most important sets of continuing obligations imposed on listed companies. In order to ensure that shareholders and the market have all the information that they need to decide whether to buy, sell or continue to hold shares in a listed company, all manner of information about the company's activities, management and finances must be publicly disclosed. The rules seek both to protect investors and to maintain confidence in the financial markets. Disclosure of financial information is dealt with at 7.7.

Many of these disclosure and notification obligations arise under the DTRs. As explained at 3.5.3, the DTRs were introduced in the UK to give effect to the Market Abuse Directive (MAD), creating the Disclosure Rules, the Transparency Directive, introducing the Transparency Rules, and the Statutory Audit Directive and the Company Reporting Directive, introducing the Corporate Governance Rules. In addition, further obligations are set out in LR 9.6.

The most important requirement of all is the general obligation to disclose 'inside information' about the company under DTR 2.2.1R (considered at 7.5.1 to 7.5.3), and this obligation applies to both premium and standard listed companies.

7.5.1 The obligation to disclose 'inside information'

The general obligation to disclose inside information reflects Listing Principles 4 and 5, and ensures that the company gives information to the market as a whole (rather than just to a few select investors) and in a timely manner. Remember that there could be many hundreds or thousands of shareholders in the listed company, ranging from an institutional investor based in the City to a retired, civilly-partnered couple in Cleethorpes. The overwhelming majority of them will have no contact with the management who run the listed company on a day-to-day basis. They will therefore be reliant on information provided by the company to assess whether they should continue with their investment in the company. The provision of this information is not left to chance: the company is compelled continually to release important news regarding the company, be it good or bad, under this obligation. The release of this information to the market as quickly as possible will also help ensure that the share price accurately reflects the company's true value, thereby reducing the scope for people with inside knowledge of the company's affairs to profit secretly at the expense of others.

The obligation is set out at DTR 2.2.1R and requires that, subject to DTR 2.5.1R (see **7.5.2.8**), the company:

(a)   must notify an RIS;

(b)   as soon as possible;

(c)   of any inside information (see **7.5.2.1**) which directly concerns the company.

Where an issuer has a website, the company must also disclose the information on its website in accordance with DTR 2.3.

7.5.2   Satisfying the requirements of the obligation

To comply with the obligation an understanding of the following issues is required.

7.5.2.1   What is inside information?

Disclosure and Transparency Rules 2.2.3G to 2.2.8G contain guidance as to how to identify inside information. Disclosure Rule 2.2.3G refers to the definition of inside information in s 118C of the FSMA 2000. It is information:

(a)   of a *precise nature* (see **7.5.2.2**):

(b)   which is not *generally available* (see **7.5.2.3**) ;

(c)   which relates, directly or indirectly, to an issuer of a *financial instrument* (see **7.5.2.4**) or to the *financial instrument* itself; and

(d)   if generally available, would be likely to have a *significant effect* (see **7.5.2.5**) on the price of the *financial instrument* or the price of related investments.

The FCA believes that the company and its advisers are best placed to make an initial assessment of whether information is 'inside information' which therefore must be disclosed (DTR 2.2.7G). The board must continuously monitor any changes in the company's circumstances which may mean an announcement is required (DTR 2.2.8G). The criteria referred to in the above definition of 'inside information', which the board must understand in order to decide whether to disclose information, are set out at **7.5.2.2** to **7.5.2.5**.

7.5.2.2   What is information of a 'precise nature'?

Section 118C(5) of the FSMA 2000 provides that information is of a precise nature if it:

(a)   indicates circumstances that:

    (i)   exist; or

    (ii)   may reasonably be expected to come into existence; OR

(b)   indicates an event that:

    (i)   has occurred; or

    (ii)   may reasonably be expected to occur; AND

(c)   is specific enough to enable a conclusion to be drawn as to the possible effect, on the price of the financial instrument, of those circumstances or that event.

This, of course, is wider than the natural meaning of the words used. It underscores the very wide scope of this general disclosure obligation. In *Geltl v Daimler AG* (Case C-19/11), the ECJ, in considering the definition of inside information for the purposes of MAD, held that information about intermediate steps taken in connection with bringing about a future event may constitute precise information (in this case about the forthcoming departure of a CEO). It also decided that a reasonable expectation that an event will occur means there must be a realistic prospect that the event will occur, not merely a high probability.

7.5.2.3   When is information 'generally available'?

Information which can be obtained by research or analysis conducted by, or on behalf of, users of a market is regarded as being generally available (FSMA 2000, s 118C(8)).

7.5.2.4   What is a financial instrument?

The s 118C definition of inside information uses the term 'qualifying investments'. However, when considering the definition of 'inside information' for the purpose of the general obligation of disclosure under the Disclosure Rules, the term 'financial instrument' is substituted. This is defined in Section C of Annex I to MiFID. Most importantly for our purposes it includes shares (transferable securities), but it also includes other investments such as options to acquire shares, and interest rate, currency and equity swaps.

7.5.2.5   What is a 'significant effect' on a price?

The inside information test hinges on this criterion.

There is no specific figure (percentage or otherwise) which can be set which constitutes a 'significant effect' on the price (DTR 2.2.4G(2)). The aim is to prevent an over-rigid application of the rules. The test will be satisfied if a reasonable investor would be likely to use the information as part of the basis of his investment decision (DTR 2.2.4G(1)). This is referred to as the 'reasonable investor test'.

Further guidance on how to apply this test is set out at DTR 2.2.5G and DTR 2.2.6G. In particular, DTR 2.2.6G provides that information about the following matters is likely to fulfil the reasonable investor test (and therefore likely to have a 'significant effect' on price):

(a)   the company's assets and liabilities;

(b)   the performance, or the expectation of the performance, of the company's business;

(c)   the company's financial condition;

(d)   the course of the company's business;

(e)   major new developments in the company's business; or

(f)   information previously disclosed to the market.

This test has been interpreted by the Upper Tribunal (Tax and Chancery Chamber) in *David Massey v FSA* [2011] UKUT 49 (TCC) to mean any information which would inform the decision of a reasonable investor. There is therefore no need to show that the information is actually price sensitive.

Information which is therefore likely to amount to 'inside information' includes changes in management, acquisitions and disposals, group restructurings, litigation, loss of key customers/contracts, granting of intellectual property rights, development of new products, and receiving a takeover approach (see **22.3.1**). Examples of disclosure of this and other information can be searched for via the RNS section of the Stock Exchange's website.

7.5.2.6   What is a Regulatory Information Service (RIS)?

An RIS is a Primary Information Provider (PIP) service, which has been approved by the FCA and is on the list of Regulatory Information Services maintained by the FCA. Listed companies use an RIS to discharge their continuing obligations to make announcements to the public. The best known RIS (for historical reasons as it used to have a monopoly) is the Stock Exchange's own Regulatory News Service, known as RNS. As at the time of writing, there were seven other RISs, all of which are listed in Appendix 3 to the Listing Rules.

The PIP service criteria, published on the UKLA section of the FCA website, set out so-called 'headline categories' which the RIS must use when releasing information. For example, the release of information about the admission of shares to listing must be headed 'Official List Notice' and (with undisputed accuracy) information about an acquisition must be headed 'Acquisition'. Lawyers will need to learn to use their firms' databases to access copies of company announcements made through an RIS. Announcements made through RNS can be accessed by anyone from the Stock Exchange's website.

Transparency Rule 6.3.2R requires that all regulated information (which includes information disclosed under DTR 2.2.1R) must be disclosed in accordance with DTRs 6.3.3R to 6.3.8R which set out minimum standards. These are that the information must be:

(a) disseminated in a way ensuring it is capable of being disseminated as widely as possible;

(b) usually communicated in unedited full text;

(c) communicated in a way which ensures the security of the communication and provides certainty as to the source of the information; and

(d) communicated in a way which makes it clear it is regulated information and who the issuer is, and the date, time and subject matter of the communication.

As part of a review into the impact of the implementation of the Transparency Rules under the Transparency Directive at the start of 2007, the FCA's forerunner, the FSA, concluded that the pre-existing RIS system met the requirements of the Transparency Directive.

7.5.2.7 What does a Primary Information Provider (PIP) do?

A PIP is an organisation which ensures that information from listed companies (such as regulatory announcements and company news) is disseminated to secondary news sources (Secondary Information Providers, or SIPs), such as Reuters, Bloomberg or Hemscott online, at the same time. Due to the electronic nature of these communications, when the information is disseminated by the PIP it is often referred to as being 'sent down the wire'. Most importantly of all, the SIPs then pass on the information to the public at large.

7.5.2.8 What if dissemination of the information will have adverse consequences for the company?

Often this is precisely the reason for the requirement that the information is announced, and the FCA will not permit breaches of the disclosure obligation just because the obligation may result in a fall in the company's share price or result in the share price not representing the true value of the company.

It is not possible to offset good news against bad news in order to avoid making an announcement. Companies should disclose both types of information and let the market decide whether they cancel each other out. This principle was reaffirmed in a decision to fine Wolfson Microelectronics plc in January 2009 for a breach of DTR 2.2.1R and Listing Principle 4. Wolfson had received notification from a customer that it was going to reduce demand for one of Wolfson's products but that it expected to increase demand for another of its products. Wolfson initially failed to make an announcement of the bad news that demand was going to be reduced. Further, in FCA Technical Note UKLA/TN/521.1 Assessing and handling insider information, the FCA emphasises that generally it is not acceptable to 'choreograph' the disclosure of offsetting information which individually meets the test under DTR 2.2.1R.

However, there are two further points to note:

(a) *Delaying disclosure.* Disclosure and Transparency Rule 2.5.1R provides that the company can delay disclosure, in order to avoid prejudicing its legitimate interests, if:

(i) it would not mislead the public;

(ii)   anyone who does receive the information owes a duty of confidentiality to the company; and

(iii)   the company can ensure the confidentiality of that information.

If the company does choose to delay disclosure, it should continue to monitor the situation and be ready to disclose as soon as circumstances change which means that the proviso in DTR 2.5.1R no longer applies (DTR 2.5.2G(1)). This reinforces the guidance in DTR 2.2.8 that the board must carefully and continuously monitor any changes in the company's circumstances (see **7.5.2.1**).

The Disclosure Rules provide two specific examples of circumstances when the company is likely to be able to make use of the delay permitted by DTR 2.5.1R. The one in DTR 2.5.3G(1) in particular is likely to be very useful. It provides that disclosure of matters in the course of negotiation may be delayed where the outcome of negotiations would be affected by the disclosure.

The company can, however, disseminate such information to those who owe it a duty of confidentiality in the normal exercise of employment, profession or duties (including its lawyers and other advisers, and the people with whom it is negotiating (eg, the other contracting party)) pursuant to DTR 2.5.7G. This is an exception from the general rule, under DTR 2.5.6R, that inside information should not be given to anyone (including advisers) until it has been given to an RIS. It is only if there is a leak during these negotiations that the information must be given to the RIS (see **7.5.1**). The company can, therefore, talk to its lawyers about an impending deal without having to make the information public through an RIS.

The lawyers who receive such information should note two things. First, it would clearly not be very professional to be responsible for any leak of information which would force the company to make an announcement. This means that the lawyers need to make sure that they limit the number of people in their team who have access to such information, and that everyone in their team is aware of the confidential nature of the information. A piece of advice from the Second World War seems pertinent here: 'Loose lips sink ships'. Expecting lawyers to keep quiet presents obvious challenges, but the importance of maintaining confidentiality cannot be over-emphasised. Disclosure Rule 2.5.9G highlights the fact that the wider the group of people to whom information is provided, the greater the risk that there will be a leak, leading to the triggering of the full disclosure obligation. Secondly, the lawyers themselves (and other advisers who receive information pursuant to DTR 2.5.7G) cannot deal in the company's shares until the information has been made public.

In the FCA's Technical Note UKLA/TN/520.1 Dealing with leaks and rumours (available in the UKLA section of the FCA's website), the FCA emphasises the importance of responding where necessary to rumours about the company. Under DTR 2.7.3R there is no need to respond to press speculation or market rumours which are inaccurate. However, if a rumour is largely accurate and amounts to inside information then the company must issue an announcement as soon as possible (DTR 2.7.2G). This of course means that the speculation does not have to be entirely accurate. For example, rumours which are correct about a company seeking to raise money from its shareholders would probably have to be disclosed if it is only the amount of money which is erroneously reported.

(b)   *Dispensation.* The FCA has the discretion to grant a dispensation in relation to any of the Disclosure Rules, including the disclosure requirements under DTR 2.2.1R. Disclosure Rule 1.2 provides that the company must apply to the FCA in writing, usually at least five business days before the proposed modification or dispensation is required. The application must contain the information required by DTR 1.2.2R. However, the FCA is likely to grant this dispensation only in very limited circumstances (for example, when an announcement at a particular time might jeopardise the company's ability to continue to trade).

An example of what this disclosure obligation can mean in practice, and the accompanying effect on share price, is set out below.

SuperGroup issues warning after mix-up

By Andrea Felsted and Adam Jones

Shares in SuperGroup lost more than a third of their value on Friday after the clothing retailer issued its third profit warning in six months, partly because of a mix-up between a plus sign and a minus sign in its forecasting.

The owner of the Superdry brand said that partly as a result of "arithmetic errors" its pre-tax profit would be about £43m for the year to April 29 – a marked reduction from its guidance in a previous profit warning in February, when it had predicted a figure of about £50m.

SuperGroup shares fell 38 per cent to 351.80p, after the fourth profit warning since its float just over two years ago, valuing the group's equity at £283m. The shares now stand about 30 per cent below their 500p float price.

The company said it was "terribly embarrassing to have to come to the market and say we have made a mistake".

It had made an error in its forecast for its wholesale business, where a negative figure had accidentally been treated as a positive during the forecasting process, it said. The adding-up mistake accounted for £2.5m of the profit shortfall.

Julian Dunkerton, chief executive, said the company had been growing fast but recognised that there were weaknesses that it was addressing, citing recent executive appointments that would bring more "formality" to the business.

But John Stevenson, analyst at Peel Hunt said: "This is the latest in a fairly long list of communication errors and problems, and from our point of view it is one too many."

Mr Dunkerton, who owns 32 per cent of the company, said he had no intention of resigning after the latest profit warning.

"I feel that would be a little harsh," he said. "Nobody is more affected than myself if you look at the share register. You must understand that my devotion to this company is 100 per cent, and I have nothing but its progress and its success embedded in my psyche."

SuperGroup said there was a separate profit shortfall of £2m in its wholesale business resulting from demand for stock coming later than expected, although it said most of those sales would fall into its next financial year.

In addition, SuperGroup said its margins had been hit by a greater-than-expected proportion of its sales going through lower-margin channels such as eBay and outlet stores, while an increase in operating costs partly linked to new executive hiring had also been a factor.

Together, these two issues would have a further impact of about £2m on profit, it said. The company said all the problems would have a "minimal impact" on its projections for its next financial year.

SuperGroup is awaiting the arrival of a new chief financial officer, Shaun Wills, who is due to start work at the company on Monday.

Source: *Financial Times*, 20 April 2012

7.5.2.9   What does 'as soon as possible' mean?

The Disclosure Rules require general disclosure to be made 'as soon as possible'. The FCA has said that it does not consider that the Disclosure Rules allow a longer period of time to make disclosures than was allowed under the old listing regime. The following statement, released by the FSA, the forerunner to the FCA, in relation to the breach by Marconi plc of its general obligation of disclosure under the former listing rules, is still useful guidance, therefore, regarding the meaning of 'as soon as possible':

> On 2 July 2001 Marconi changed its expectation as to its performance for the half year ending 30 September 2001 and the full year ending 31 March 2002. That change, if made public, was likely to lead to a substantial movement in the price of its listed securities and gave rise to the obligation to notify the [RIS] without delay. The notification should have been made by, at the latest, the evening of 3 July 2001. By not making that notification until 18:41 on 4 July 2001 Marconi contravened Rule 9.2(c) of the Listing Rules …
>
> By reason of his absence overseas and the decision not to involve him between 26 June 2001 and 3 July 2001, the Deputy Chief Executive's concurrence was not required for the change in Marconi's expectation to take place. Fulfilment of this obligation involved reporting the matter to the Board without delay to enable the Board to make a formal decision to issue the necessary trading statement. It was not necessary to await the return of the Deputy Chief Executive before accelerating steps to do so …
>
> The period of time which it is reasonable for a listed company to take in making an announcement under the Listing Rules regarding a change in its expectations will depend upon all the circumstances relevant to the particular situation in which the change occurs. However, save in exceptional circumstances, a listed company must prioritise its disclosure obligations under the Listing Rules.

(FSA Final Notice: Marconi plc, 11 April 2003)

Obviously, there might be a temptation to delay disclosure of information which would allow the market to determine the true value of the company's shares when the news about the listed company is bad. However, a failure to follow the rules can be costly. Lamprell plc was fined over £2.4 million in 2013 for breaches of DTR 2.2.1R and other provisions as a result of failing to a issue a profit warning for 18 days when senior management had become aware of a deterioration in the financial performance of the company. The delay in the announcement created a false market in the shares, which was demonstrated by a 57% drop in the company's share price once the announcement was made. Another company, JJB Sports plc, was fined £455,000 in January 2011 for breaches of the same rules, for delaying disclosure by over nine months of inside information relating to the price of a company which it bought.

Both cases mentioned above emphasise the importance of the listed company contacting qualified advisers, including lawyers, in a timely manner whenever there is doubt about the need to disclose inside information.

Companies which envisage that they will not be able to comply with the 'as soon as possible' requirement should discuss with the FCA whether they can waive this obligation (DTR 2.2.9G(4)). Alternatively, it may be possible that the company is in a position to make an announcement 'as soon as possible', but it would prefer to include more detail than is strictly required, and collating this information would delay the announcement. In this case, the company should publish what is known as a 'holding announcement', which discharges its formal obligations under the Disclosure Rules, but which informs the market that further information will be announced in due course. Disclosure Rule 2.2.9G(2) sets out further information about the content of a holding announcement.

The ability of the company to delay an announcement is discussed at **7.5.2.8** above. Again, if the company is delaying a disclosure in accordance with the Disclosure Rules, it must prepare a holding announcement which can be released quickly in the event of a breach of confidentiality (DTR 2.6.3G).

7.5.2.10   Further guidance on handling inside information

There are two UKLA Technical Notes which offer guidance on various aspects of inside information: UKLA/TN/521.1 Assessing and handling inside information and UKLA/TN/520.1 Delaying disclosure/dealing with leaks and rumours. In addition there are further recommendations which were published by the forerunner to the FCA, the FSA, in its newsletter *Market Watch*, issues No 21, 27 and 37. They contain non-binding commentary and good practice guidelines with a view to increasing awareness of the ways to protect inside information and to limiting the potential misuse of inside information, including in the context of public company takeovers. For example, among the recommendations are that enquiries from the media should be handled by a dedicated media relations team and that any non-media relations personnel should be prohibited from responding to initial enquiries from the media. In addition, firms' employees should be regularly reminded of the prohibition on leaks.

7.5.2.11   National Storage Mechanism

As part of the UK's obligations under the Transparency Directive, all regulatory announcements made by listed companies are stored in the online National Storage Mechanism (NSM) which is run by Morningstar plc and which can be found at www. morningstar.co.uk/uk/NSM.

7.5.3   Consequences of breaching the general obligation of disclosure

7.5.3.1   Breach of the Disclosure Rules

Any breach of the general obligation of disclosure could lead to the FCA imposing any of the sanctions set out at **3.6** above. Real-life illustrations of sanctions imposed may be found at **7.5.2.9** and **7.11** below.

7.5.3.2 Criminal offences

Any breach of the general obligation of disclosure may also constitute a criminal offence under s 89 and 90 of the Financial Services Act 2012, which contain provisions relating to misleading statements and misleading impressions. This section is considered in more detail at **9.5**.

It may also give rise to an offence under Pt V of the Criminal Justice Act 1993 relating to insider dealing (see **Chapter 11**).

It is a criminal offence, under s 3 of the Fraud Act 2006, punishable by up to 10 years' imprisonment and/or a fine, fraudulently to fail to disclose information which a person is under a legal duty to disclose in certain circumstances. In extreme cases this could be relevant here.

7.5.3.3 Civil offences

Under s 90A of and Sch 10A to the FSMA 2000, a listed company will be liable to pay compensation to a person who has acquired shares, continues to hold shares or disposes of them and has suffered loss as a result of reliance on any untrue or misleading statement in, or omission from, any published information. This includes all information announced via an RIS, whether required to be so or not. It also covers information disclosed by any other means but whose availability is announced by an RIS. For example, a listed company's announcement via an RIS of the publication of its annual accounts means that liability under s 90A extends to all of the information contained in the accounts.

A company will be liable if a PDMR (see **7.8.2.1**) for the company knew that the statement was wrong or misleading, was reckless as to whether it was, or knew any omission was a dishonest concealment of a material fact.

It is also an offence dishonestly to delay the publication of information which is released through an RIS under s 90A of the FSMA 2000.

Only the company can be directly liable for these offences, but a director could still bear liability to his company for negligence, or could have sanctions imposed on him if he was knowingly concerned in the breach under s 91(2) of the FSMA 2000 (see **3.6** above).

Failure to comply with the general obligation of disclosure may well constitute the civil offence of market abuse under s 118 of the FSMA 2000 (see **Chapter 10**).

7.5.4 Information gathering and publication

In a related provision, DTR 1.3.1R provides that the company (premium or standard listed), PDMR (see **7.8.2.1**), or connected person must provide to the FCA as soon as possible following a request:

(a) any information which the FCA considers appropriate to protect investors or ensure the smooth operation of the market; and

(b) any other information or explanation that the FCA may reasonable require to verify whether the Disclosure Rules are being and have been complied with.

The FCA can require the company to publish information disclosed under DTR 1.3.1R (or, after giving the company an opportunity to make representations as to why it should not be published, the FCA itself may publish the information) (DTR 1.3.3R).

7.5.5 Misleading information

The company (premium or standard listed) must also take all reasonable care to ensure that the information it provides to an RIS (see **7.5.2.1**) is not misleading, false or deceptive and does not omit anything likely to affect the import of the information (DTR 1.3.4R). The company must not combine any marketing of its activities with an RIS announcement if this is likely to be misleading (DTR 1.3.5R).

7.5.6   Insider lists

Disclosure Rule 2.8.1R provides that both the premium and standard listed company must compile a list of those persons who work for it who have access (on a regular or occasional basis) to inside information relating directly or indirectly to the company.

'Persons who work for it' is not restricted to employees. The list should include the company's own employees who have access to inside information, but it should also include principal contacts at any other firm or company acting on its behalf, or on its account, with whom it has had direct contact and who have access to inside information about it (DTR 2.8.7G).

In addition, and of particular interest to the lawyer, the company must ensure that persons acting on its behalf, or for its account, such as advisers, compile such lists.

'Access to inside information' is not defined, and the FCA has provided little guidance in the Disclosure Rules as to the contents of the list (see DTR 2.8.3). However, it has provided informal guidance in a newsletter (see *Market Watch Newsletter*, issue 12, available on the FCA's website). It remains to be seen whether the FCA develops this idea by encouraging firms of advisers to restrict as far as possible those employees (including secretaries) who have access to inside information on a transaction.

Part II of the GC100 Guidelines (see **7.3**) contains guidance for the GC100 member companies on the requirement to maintain insider lists. The Committee of European Securities Regulators (CESR), the forerunner to the ESMA produced guidance on insider lists in Section 1 of its third set of guidance on MAD, dated 15 May 2009, available on the ESMA website at http://esma.europa.eu.

7.5.7   Notifications

In addition to the general obligation to disclose 'inside information' under the Disclosure Rules, the Listing Rules and DTRs set out various specific disclosures, or 'notifications', that a listed company must make.

Transparency Rule 6.3.2R requires that all regulated information (which includes information required to be disclosed under **7.5.7.1** to **7.5.7.12**) must be disclosed in accordance with DTRs 6.3.3R to 6.3.8R which sets out minimum standards of dissemination. The RIS system complies with these rules (see **7.5.2.6** and **7.5.2.7** above). This applies to companies with a premium or a standard listing.

7.5.7.1   Copies of documents

Listing Rules 9.6.1R to 9.6.3R provide that a premium listed company must file two copies of the following documents with the FCA:

(a)   all circulars, notices, reports (at the same time they are issued); and

(b)   resolutions, other than resolutions concerning ordinary business at an AGM (as soon as possible after the relevant meeting).

The company must also notify an RIS that it has filed such documents with the FCA, and set out where copies of the document can be obtained. Alternatively, the company can provide the full text of such documents to the RIS, but this is likely to be impractical with more weighty documents.

These provisions have now been superseded by the obligation on listed companies to file documents with the NSM (see **5.3.6** above). An amendment to the Listing Rules, although not yet forthcoming at the time of writing, is expected in the near future to amend this and similar provisions.

7.5.7.2 Notification relating to capital

Under LR 9.6.4R a listed company must notify an RIS as soon as possible of the following information in relation to its capital:

(a)   proposed changes to capital structure;

(b)   any redemption of listed shares ; and

(c)   the results of any new issue or offer of listed securities.

Under DTR 6.1.9R, the company must disclose to the public any change in the rights which attach to any class of listed securities.

Transparency Rule 5.5.1R requires the company to disclose the acquisition or disposal of its own shares, and DTR 5.6.1R requires the total number of voting rights and capital for each class of shares to be announced at the end of each month in which there has been an increase (eg, after a rights issue – see **17.7**) or decrease (eg, after a buyback). In addition, under DTR 5.6.1AR, this information must be disclosed at any time after there has been a transaction which produces a material change in the total number of voting rights. A material change is defined in DTR 5.6.1BG as an increase or decrease of 1% or more.

There is also a rule relating to notifications about underwriting.

All of these provisions apply to both premium and standard listed companies.

7.5.7.3 Notification of major interests in shares

Chapter 15 considers Chapter 5 of the DTRs, which requires every shareholder (of a premium and standard listed company) to notify the company if his, her or its shareholding:

(a)   has fallen from above 3% to below 3%;

(b)   has risen from below 3% to above 3%; or

(c)   is over 3% and rises or falls to a different percentage level.

The notification referred to at **7.5.7.2** under DTRs 5.6.1R and 5.6.1AR enables shareholders to check whether a change in capital has triggered this requirement.

It also sets out the right of the company, pursuant to s 793 of the CA 2006, to investigate who has an interest in its shares.

Transparency Rule 5.8.12R obliges the company to disclose to the public the information it receives under Chapter 5 of the DTRs or under s 793 of the CA 2006. The company must make this disclosure in the usual way, that is, by notifying the information to an RIS as soon as possible (DTR 3.1.4R). See further at **15.7.1**.

7.5.7.4 Notifications of board charges and directors' details

The company must notify an RIS when a new director is appointed, an existing director resigns, retires or is removed, or there is a change to any important function or executive responsibility of a director (LR 9.6.11R).

A search of the RNS archive (available on the Stock Exchange's website) under 'Bumi plc' reveals on 15 October 2012 a terse announcement outlining the dramatic resignation of Nat Rothschild, a non-executive director as a result of corporate governance concerns over the running of the company.

Listing Rule 9.6.13R provides that the company must notify an RIS of certain information about new directors, including details of certain current and past directorships, unspent convictions, bankruptcies and any public criticism by a regulatory or statutory body. Listing Rule 9.6.14R requires this information to be updated where necessary and to include details of a current director's new directorships in other publicly quoted companies. An example of this type of notification is set out below:

18 August 2008

Bradford & Bingley plc

Bradford & Bingley Announces Appointment of New Chief Executive

The Board of Bradford & Bingley plc is delighted to announce that Richard Pym has agreed to join the Board as Chief Executive with immediate effect.

Richard Pym retired as Group Chief Executive of Alliance & Leicester plc (A&L) in July 2007. He joined A&L in 1992 as Group Finance Director, and became Managing Director of Retail Banking in 2001 and Chief Executive in 2002. He was responsible for fundamental changes in A&L's product and channel strategies, including the substantial development of internet capabilities.

He is currently an independent non-executive director of Old Mutual plc, the international asset management group and non-executive Chairman of BrightHouse Group Ltd, an investment of private equity firm Vision Capital. He is also non-executive Chairman of Halfords Group plc, the UK car parts, car accessories and cycle retailer, and will be standing down from this role in due course. He is a qualified Chartered Accountant.

Chairman of Bradford & Bingley, Rod Kent, said: "It has been a key priority for the Board to find a new Chief Executive, and we believe that Richard Pym is ideal for the role."

Richard Pym commented: "Bradford & Bingley has developed strong customer franchises in savings and lending and I am delighted to have been invited to lead the business. I look forward to working with the Board and executive team in building a successful future."

Pursuant to Listing Rule 9.6.13 (1), details of directorships held by Mr Pym in Publicly quoted companies during the past five years are set out below:

Halfords Group plc (current)
Old Mutual plc (current)
Alliance & Leicester plc (ceased 2007)
Selfridges plc (ceased 2003)

Bradford & Bingley also confirms that there are no matters relating to Mr Pym that would require disclosure under Listing Rules 9.6.13 (2) to (6). Mr Pym does not currently have any beneficial interests in Bradford & Bingley shares.

7.5.7.5   Notification of lock-up arrangements

Listing Rules 9.6.16R and 9.6.17R provide that the premium listed company must notify an RIS of any lock-up arrangements that have not already been disclosed, or of any changes to any lock-up arrangements previously disclosed. A lock-up arrangement is also known as an irrevocable undertaking (see **21.10**).

7.5.7.6   Notification of shareholder resolutions

The premium listed company must notify an RIS as soon as possible after a general meeting of all resolutions passed (other than resolutions concerning ordinary business passed at an AGM) (LR 9.6.18R). Rather unhelpfully, there is no definition of 'ordinary business'. It is for listed companies to determine themselves what is ordinary. It usually includes, eg, the re-appointment of directors and the payment of dividends.

7.5.7.7   Change of name

If the premium listed company changes its name, LR 9.6.19R provides that it must, as soon as possible:

(a)   notify an RIS (stating the date on which the change has effect);

(b)   inform the FCA in writing; and

(c)   send the FCA a copy of the revised certificate of incorporation.

For example, on 23 September 2013 Lloyds TSB Bank plc announced it changed its name to Lloyds Bank plc as part of a restructuring.

7.5.7.8 Change of accounting date

The premium listed company must notify an RIS as soon as possible of any change in its accounting reference date. If the change extends the accounting period to more than 14 months, the company must produce a second interim report (LR 9.6.20R to LR 9.6.22G).

7.5.7.9 Amendments to constitution

If the company proposes to amend its articles or memorandum of association, it must (whether it has a premium or standard listing), under DTR 6.1.2R, communicate the draft amendment to both the FCA and the Stock Exchange without delay, but by no later than the date of calling the relevant shareholders meeting.

7.5.7.10 Transactions by persons discharging managerial responsibility

Disclosure and Transparency Rule 3.1.2R requires PDMRs (see **7.8.2.1**) and their connected persons (see **7.8.2.2**) to disclose certain transactions to their company (premium or standard listed), including their dealings in the company's shares. This is considered further in **15.7.1**. A listed company must pass on the information it receives to an RIS no later than the end of the next business day (DTR 3.1.4R).

7.5.7.11 Directors' interests in shares

Listing Rule 9.8.6R(1) requires a statement setting out the directors' holdings of shares in their premium listed company to be included in the annual report, together with any changes to this information over the past year. Disclosure and Transparency Rule 3.1.4R requires this information to be notified to an RIS no later than the end of the next business day.

7.5.7.12 Notification when the RIS is not open for business

It should now be clear that the method prescribed by the DTRs and the Listing Rules for making disclosures to the public is through the company's chosen RIS. What happens when the company suddenly discovers it needs to make an announcement, to comply with the 'as soon as possible' requirement, and the RIS is closed? The answer lies in DTR 1.3.6R and LR 1.3.4R, which provide that the company must ensure that it distributes the information to at least two national newspapers in the UK and to two newswire services operating in the UK. This is an exception from the general rule, under DTR 2.5.6R, that price-sensitive information should not be given to anyone before it has been notified to an RIS. The information should be notified to an RIS as soon as it re-opens. This is a useful paragraph to know about, as the client may well call its lawyers late at night (when its RIS has closed), needing to know very quickly how to effect the disclosure that same night.

7.6 OBLIGATIONS RELATING TO THE SHAREHOLDERS OF THE COMPANY

There a number of continuing obligations imposed on listed companies which relate specifically to the shareholders of the company.

7.6.1 Equality of treatment

Under Listing Principle 5 (LR 7.2.1R) and DTR 6.1.3R, a listed company (premium and standard listed) must ensure equal treatment of all holders of shares who are in the same position.

7.6.2 Prescribed information to shareholders

Under DTR 6.1.4R, a listed company must ensure that all facilities and information necessary to enable shareholders to exercise their rights are available. A company can convey information to shareholders electronically (DTR 6.1.8R) (see **7.9.5**).

Transparency Rule 6.1.12R requires a listed company to inform its shareholders about the time, place and agenda of shareholder meetings, the total number of shares and voting rights, and the rights of shareholders to participate in the meetings. Disclosure and Transparency Rule 6.1.13R requires a notice or circular to be sent to shareholders regarding the payment of dividends and the allotment of new shares.

All of these rules apply to both a premium and standard listed company.

7.6.3 Pre-emption rights

Listing Rule 9.3.11R provides that if a premium listed company issues equity shares for cash, the company must first offer those shares to the existing equity shareholders pro rata (that is, in proportion to their existing holdings). This right reflects the statutory rights of shareholders under s 561 of the CA 2006. However, the shareholders of a listed company can agree to dispense with their pre-emption rights, and LR 9.3.12R makes it clear that any general disapplication by the shareholders of their statutory pre-emption rights will also dispense with the pre-emption rights under LR 9.3.11R.

For further information on pre-emption rights, see **Chapter 14**.

7.6.4 Transactions

In order to ensure that the rights of shareholders in premium listed companies are fully protected, the Listing Rules set out obligations on the company in relation to certain key transactions. These require the disclosure of information and, in certain cases, also the prior approval of the company's shareholders by way of an ordinary resolution. This approval may be necessary even though the CA 2006 or the listed company's articles do not require it.

Listing Rule 9.4 requires employee share schemes and long-term management incentive schemes to be approved by ordinary resolution before they are implemented, or alternatively the disclosure of information on the schemes in the annual report, depending on the terms.

Listing Rule 9.5 sets out requirements for the issue of further shares after the company has been listed, and these are discussed in more detail in **Chapter 17**.

Chapter 19 deals with further transactions (principally acquisitions and disposals) and related party transactions (LR Chapters 10 and 11 respectively).

7.7   FINANCIAL INFORMATION ABOUT THE COMPANY

7.7.1 Transparency Rules

The Transparency Rules, introduced to implement the Transparency Directive, require more information to be disclosed on the finances of the listed company, more often than was previously the case. The aims of the new rules are to increase investor protection and to promote more efficient investment across the EU. They therefore apply to both premium and standard listed companies.

7.7.2 Annual financial reports

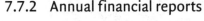

Chapter 4 of the DTRs requires an issuer whose transferable securities are admitted to trading on a regulated market and whose home Member State is the UK to publish an annual financial report (DTRs 4.1.1R and 4.1.3R) (often described as the Annual Report and Accounts). This includes UK companies whose ordinary shares are trading on the Main Market of the Stock Exchange, and so covers the companies dealt with by this book (both premium and standard listed). It is important to remember that these provisions are in addition to those set out in Part 15 of the CA 2006 dealing with company accounts and reports. Part 15 includes specific provisions for both public companies and quoted companies.

A listed company's annual financial report is required to be published no later than four months after the end of each financial year (DTR 4.1.3R). The forerunner to the FCA, the FSA, issued a warning to listed companies in June 2008 that it would take action in the future against companies that did not comply with this rule. Some listed companies had only been submitting preliminary results rather than a full report by this deadline.

The annual financial report must include:

(a) its audited financial statements (the accounts) prepared in accordance with the applicable accounting standards;

(b) a management report; and

(c) a responsibility statement (DTR 4.1.5) made by the 'persons responsible in the company' (DTR 4.1.12R).

The responsibility statement must certify that, to the best of the persons' knowledge, the financial statements, prepared in accordance with the applicable set of accounting standards, give a true and fair view of the assets, liabilities, financial position and profit and loss of the issuer. It must also certify that the management report includes a fair review of the development and performance of the business and the position of the issuer, together with a description of the principal risks and uncertainties they face (DTR 4.1.12R). The FCA has stated in Technical Note UKLA/TN/501.1 Half-yearly and annual reports (available in the UKLA section of its website) that it would usually be the directors who are the persons responsible.

There is a series of additional obligations relating to the annual accounts and reports placed on listed companies under LR 9.8. The Financial Reporting Council (FRC) has issued guidance (available on its website) on how this statement should be prepared.

7.7.3 Half-yearly reports

Chapter 4 of the DTRs requires an issuer whose shares are admitted to trading on a regulated market (ie the Main Market) and whose home Member State is the UK to publish a half-yearly financial report covering the first six months of the financial year (DTR 4.2.1R).

The half-yearly report must be made public as soon as possible but no later than two months after the end of the period to which the report relates (DTR 4.2.2R). *When the Directive amending the Transparency Directive is implemented in the UK (see **3.7.3** above), the two-month period will become three months.*

The half-yearly financial report must include:

(a) a condensed set of financial statements (ie accounts), which can be, but do not need to be, audited or reviewed by auditors;

(b) an interim management report; and

(c) responsibility statements (DTR 4.2.3R).

The interim management report must include an indication of important events that have occurred and their impact on the accounts, and a description of the main risks and uncertainties for the remaining six months (DTR 4.2.7R). It must also include a fair review of major related party transactions (DTR 4.2.8R) (see **Chapter 19**).

7.7.4 Interim management statements

The DTRs further require listed companies whose shares are admitted to trading on a regulated market (ie the Main Market) and whose home Member State is the UK to produce an interim management statement (IMS) (DTR 4.3.1R) during each half-year (DTR 4.3.2R).

An IMS must be made in the period between 10 weeks after the beginning and six weeks before the end of the relevant period (DTR 4.3.3R) and must contain information covering the period from the beginning of the relevant six-month period to the date the statement is published (DTR 4.3.4R).

An IMS must include an explanation of material events and transactions that have taken place during the relevant period, their impact on the financial position of the company and a general description of the financial position and performance of the company during the relevant period (DTR 4.3.5R).

This requirement does not apply to a listed company which already produces quarterly financial reports (DTR 4.3.6R). There is no responsibility statement requirement for an IMS.

Following the adoption of the Directive amending the Transparency Directive on 26 November 2013 (see **3.7.3** *above), the FCA is expected to use powers to abolish the need for an IMS by amending DTR 4 in the first half of 2014. Companies will continue to be able to publish them voluntarily if they wish. Under the Directive, Member States can continue to require companies to have an IMS provided this is proportionate, so these may be retained in Member States other than the UK. The change has been made principally to reduce the administrative burden on smaller listed companies.*

An extract from an IMS is set out below.

Company	British Airways PLC
TIDM	BAY
Headline	Improved performance from revenue and costs
Released	07:00 30-Jul-2010

INTERIM MANAGEMENT STATEMENT

Period April 1, 2010 - June 30, 2010 (Unaudited)

IMPROVED PERFORMANCE FROM REVENUE AND COSTS

British Airways today (July 30) presented its interim management statement for the three months ended June 30, 2010.

Period highlights:

- Operating loss of £72 million (2009: £94 million)
- Strong yield performance in both cargo and passenger business
- Loss before tax of £164 million (2009: £148 million)
- Cash balance of £1,749 million, up £35 million from year end
- Pensions agreements approved by the UK Pensions Regulator
- Regulatory approval received for transatlantic joint business and Iberia merger

British Airways' chief executive Willie Walsh, said:

"Despite both revenues and cost being hit by the closure of UK airspace following the Icelandic volcanic eruption and the impact of industrial action, our financial performance improved during the quarter from underlying revenue increases and further cost reductions.

"The trends in our passenger and cargo traffic continue to be positive with yields up and costs down. Together this led to a reduced operating loss for the period though pre tax losses increased as a result of additional finance costs and the impact of non cash foreign exchange movements.

"Our cost performance continues to follow last year's trend with total costs for the quarter down 3.3 per cent. Our focus must remain on cost control as we grow and continue our quest for permanent structural change across the business.

"Both the airline's cash and debt position remained strong in the quarter.

"The impact of all disruptions was in line with previous estimates, some £250 million in the quarter.

"We have achieved some major strategic milestones in the last couple of weeks. Our transatlantic joint business with American Airlines and Iberia has received regulatory approval from the US and EU authorities and will start this autumn. In addition, we've received the green light from regulators for our merger with Iberia.

"In June, we agreed with our pension trustees on a recovery plan to address our pension deficits that avoids closing the schemes and maintains our annual contributions at the current level of £330 million. The recovery plan was finalised following consultation with our trade unions who agreed on reductions in future benefits. It was submitted to the UK Pensions Regulator which has now completed its review of the funding agreements and recovery plans and has confirmed that the plans are acceptable. Iberia has until September 30, 2010 to review the recovery plan as part of our merger agreement.

"We continue to invest in our customers and have taken delivery of the first of six Boeing 777-300ER aircraft which have all new interiors including new First, our award winning new Club World cabin, new World Traveller and World Traveller Plus cabins and a new in-flight entertainment system. The state-of-the art aircraft is bigger, quieter and more fuel efficient than its predecessors and showcases the future face of British Airways.

"In June, we welcomed our 50 millionth customer through Terminal 5. Since T5 opened we have raised our flight punctuality to record levels and now have the best baggage performance of any major European hub based carrier. We're also achieving excellent operational performance at Gatwick where we are consistently the most punctual major airline. In the quarter, 89 per cent of Gatwick flights departed on time".

Financial review:

Total revenue in the period was down 2.3 per cent. Passenger revenue was down 3.4 per cent, on capacity down 11.2 per cent. Yields improved by 13.5 per cent, 12.7 per cent excluding exchange, driven by a change in mix especially within cabin. Without the disruption during the period, passenger revenue would have increased by some 11 per cent year on year.

Our cargo business has seen strong performance, with revenue increasing by 36.7 per cent. Cargo yields increased by 33.9 per cent, driven by demand, mix and fuel surcharges. Cargo volumes, measured in cargo tonne kilometres, increased by 2.1 per cent.

Operating costs were down 3.3 per cent. Fuel costs were down 0.7 per cent, and other non fuel costs reduced by 4.3 per cent.

Our cash position at the end of June 2010 was £1,749 million, up £35 million from the end of March 2010. Our net debt position reduced by £37 million to £2,251 million from £2,288 million at the end of March 2010.

The retranslation of foreign debt and the marked to market movement on fuel and currency hedges along with the loss for the period have reduced reserves by £214 million to £481 million.

Loss before tax for the period was £164 million.

The effective tax rate for the quarter was 26 per cent.

Business review:

Our four key business priorities remain unchanged.

Upgraded customer experience

Our new First cabin has been installed on seven aircraft and will be fitted across the longhaul fleet by the end of next year.

A new British Airways App gives customers access to real time flight information about their bookings, full integration with their Executive Club details, a dedicated travel news section, a Twitter news feed and a link to the ba.com mobile website. Executive Club iPhone users can use the new App to display mobile boarding passes on their phones, which can be scanned at check-in to speed up and enhance the boarding process.

BA CityFlyer now operates the youngest airline fleet in the UK after the final Avro RJ100 left the fleet this month. The RJs are being replaced by 11 brand new Embraer 170 and 190SR aircraft, the first of which was delivered 10 months ago with the final one being delivered this November.

Capacity and fleet

From November 2010, we will launch a new two-per-week service from Gatwick to Cancun and double daily flights from Heathrow to Gothenburg. Our subsidiary BA CityFlyer will launch double daily flights from London City to Copenhagen in September.

As already announced, we have decided to re-introduce one Boeing 747 into service this winter and will keep capacity under review as market conditions develop.

Competitive cost base

We continue to work closely with our staff and key suppliers to reduce costs, improve productivity and ensure that the improvements that we have made during the past 21 months remain in place as the business starts to grow.

Corporate responsibility

Our new global charity partnership with Comic Relief, "Flying Start", was launched with a pledge to raise up to £8 million by 2013 for vulnerable and disadvantaged children in the UK and around the world.

We are establishing, in partnership with the Solena Group, Europe's first sustainable jet-fuel plant and plan to use the low-carbon fuel to power part of our fleet from 2014. The new fuel will be derived from waste biomass and manufactured in a state-of-the-art facility that can convert a variety of waste materials, destined for landfill, into aviation fuel.

We have made further improvements to our carbon offset scheme as customers can now offset their carbon emissions based not only on the distance flown but also by the cabin they fly in. This means that customers travelling in premium cabins, who have more space on the aircraft, will pay more to offset their emissions. Likewise, those in economy will pay less.

We won the Wildlife Trust's Biodiversity Benchmark award for the Harmondsworth Moor parkland at our Heathrow head office - an award we have held since 2003.

Our Corporate Responsibility report was published during the period and is available online at www.britishairways.com/travel/csr-corporate-responsibility.

Trading Outlook

While some economic experts are flagging the risk of a "double dip" recession, the steady recovery continues and, on that basis, we continue to target to break even at a profit before tax level for the full year as we move forward on our strategic objectives and continue to build on our excellent customer service.

ends

July 30, 2010   074/LG/2010

Note to Editors:

There will be a webcast of an analyst conference call and slide presentation at 2pm (BST) available through our website www.bashares.com.

Appendix

Financial Position and Performance for the three months ended 30 June 2010

		Three months ended June 30		
		2010	2009	Change
Revenue	£m	1,937	1,983	(2.3)%
Operating (loss)	£m	(72)	(94)	23.4%
Loss before tax	£m	(164)	(148)	(10.8)%
Loss after tax	£m	(122)	(106)	(15.1)%
EBITDAR	£m	139	118	21
Net debt	£m	2,251	2,268	17
Cash & cash equivalents	£m	1,749	1,258	491
Basic earnings/(loss) per share	P	(10.9)	(9.6)	(13.5)%
Cash in/(out) from operating activities	£m	186	(29)	215
Passenger revenue per RPK	P	6.88	6.06	13.5%

7.7.5 Exemptions

The periodic financial reporting requirements set out at **7.7.2** to **7.7.4** above do not apply in certain circumstances (DTR 4.4). These are not relevant to this book.

7.7.6 Liability

Liability may arise under s 90A of the FSMA 2000 (see **7.5.3.3** above).

Under s 463 of the CA 2006, directors can be liable to their company for any untrue or misleading statement made in or omissions from the directors' report, the directors' remuneration report (see 8.4 below), and summary financial statements taken from them.

A director will be liable only if:

(a)   he knew the statement to be untrue or misleading, or was reckless as to whether it was untrue or misleading, or

(b)   he knew the omission to be dishonest concealment of a material fact.

If the company fails to publish the required financial information within the prescribed time limits, the FCA may impose any of the sanctions set out at **3.6** above.

7.8 THE MODEL CODE

As stated at **7.4.3**, the premium listed company must ensure that its PDMRs (see **7.8.2.1**) comply with the Model Code, which is set out at Annex 1 to Chapter 9 of the Listing Rules. The company can, however, impose more rigorous obligations than those required by the Model Code if it wishes (LR 9.2.9G). The Model Code restricts when and how PDMRs can deal in the company's shares. It is in addition to the other rules which apply to dealing by such persons, such as:

(a)   the market abuse provisions of the FSMA 2000 (see **Chapter 10**);

(b)   the insider dealing regime of the CJA 1993 (see **Chapter 11**);

(c)   the notification obligations under DTR 3.1.2R; and

(d)   the statutory duties of directors.

The task of making sure the directors comply with the Model Code is usually dealt with in-house, by the company secretary or an in-house lawyer, because the day-to-day nature of compliance means that it would be administratively difficult (and expensive) for external lawyers to police. For example, the Model Code contains detailed provisions relating to share schemes, trusts and options, which require a detailed knowledge of the company's affairs before they can be applied. To this end, Part III of the GC100 Guidelines offers assistance to the GC100 member companies on compliance with the Model Code. However, external lawyers will be expected to advise on aspects of the Model Code on occasion, for example if they want a second opinion. As always, recourse should be made to the detail of the Model Code itself. However, the following provides a flavour of those parts of the Model Code with which the external lawyer will need to be familiar.

7.8.1   Purpose of the Model Code

Why is so much attention paid to the dealings of PDMRs, over and above the dealings of any other shareholder? Well, PDMRs, including directors, manage the day-to-day business of the company. They are best placed to know when they can trade in shares to make a personal profit. For example, say the directors receive an approach from a bidder with a lucrative offer to take over the company. Imagine at this point that the company's shares are worth £1 each and the offer is that bidder will pay £2 for each share. The shareholders do not know it yet, but they are about to double their money. The PDMRs, however, will know it, so what is to stop them from using their advantage over the other shareholders by suddenly investing huge amounts in the company before the offer becomes public knowledge? Answer: the Model Code (or its equivalent). The integrity of the market and the protection of investors require that directors do not abuse their position in this way. The Model Code, therefore, restricts the ability of PDMRs to deal in the company's shares.

7.8.2   Applicability of the Model Code

The Model Code applies to PDMRs (see **7.8.2.1**).

In addition, the PDMRs must also comply with the following rules in relation to 'connected persons' (Model Code, paras 20 to 22):

(a)   take reasonable steps to prevent any dealings in the company's shares, by, or on behalf of, his connected persons, on considerations of a short-term nature (see **7.8.4.3**) (para 20); and

(b)   seek to prohibit dealings in the company's shares, by, or on behalf of his connected persons (or by an investment manager on the connected person's behalf) during a close period (see **7.8.4.3**) (para 21).

In order to fulfil the obligation set out in paras 20 and 21, the PDMR must comply with para 22 and advise the connected persons and investment managers of:

(a)   the listed company's name;

(b)   the close periods during which they cannot deal; and

(c)   the fact that they must advise the company immediately after they have dealt in the company's shares.

Note that the Model Code will not apply to PDMRs once they leave the company. They will, however, still be caught by the market abuse and insider dealing regimes (see **Chapter 10** and **Chapter 11**). The FCA can also impose a financial penalty on any former director who, while a director, was knowingly concerned in a breach of the Listing Rules (FSMA 2000, s 91(2)).

7.8.2.1 Persons discharging managerial responsibilities

A PDMR is defined in s 96B of the FSMA 2000 as:

(a)   a director; or

(b)   a senior executive of a company who:

    (i)   has regular access to inside information relating, directly or indirectly, to the company; and

    (ii)   has power to make managerial decisions affecting the future development and business prospects of the company.

Practically this will include directors and a few other managers of sufficient seniority to be classified as PDMRs. As regards a senior executive who is not a director, LR 9.2.8A(2) makes it clear that the nature, or even absence, of a contractual arrangement between him and the company will not prevent that person being a PDMR if he has regular access to the company's inside information and he can take managerial decisions affecting the company.

7.8.2.2 Connected person

This is defined in Sch 11B to the FSMA 2000 (FSMA 2000, s 96B(2)). Note that the wider definition in s 252 of the CA 2006 does not apply here. The definition includes:

(a)   the PDMR's family, that is his:

    (i)   spouse,

    (ii)   civil partner,

    (iii)   child or step-child under 18,

    (iv)   relative with whom, as at the date of the transaction, he has shared a house for at least 12 months;

(b)   a body corporate with which the PDMR is associated (that is, the PDMR or connected person is a director or senior executive with the power to make managerial decisions affecting the future development of the body coporate, or the PDMR and connected persons control, or can exercise, more than 20% of its voting power in general meeting, or are interested in at least 20% of its equity shares);

(c)   the trustee of certain trusts of which the beneficiary or potential beneficiary includes the PDMR, his spouse, civil partner, children or step-children under 18, relative sharing the house or an associated body corporate; and

(d)   any partner of the PDMR, or any connected person's partner.

7.8.3 Prohibited dealings

The key provision of the Model Code is para 3: a restricted person (that is, a PDMR) must not deal in any of the company's shares unless he obtains advance clearance to deal.

Dealing is defined by para 1(c) of the Model Code. At its simplest, it includes buying and selling shares, or agreeing to buy and sell shares. Paragraph 2 of the Model Code sets out dealings which are not subject to the Model Code.

— not important if already dealt

7.8.4 Clearance to deal

This is dealt with in paras 4 to 7 of the Model Code.

7.8.4.1 Who can give clearance to deal?

Person seeking clearance	Person able to give clearance
Director (other than Chairman or Chief Executive)	Chairman, or other director designated by the board (para 4(a))
Company Secretary	As above
Chairman	Chief Executive (para 4(b)), or the senior independent director, or a committee of the board or a nominated officer
Chief Executive	Chairman (para 4(c)), or the senior independent director, or a committee of the board or a nominated officer
If Chairman and Chief Executive are the same person	Board of Directors (para 4(d))
PDMR (other than a director)	Company secretary, or designated director (para 4(e)).

7.8.4.2 The clearance procedure

The company must:

(a) keep a written record of the requests for clearance it receives, and of any clearance given (para 6);

(b) respond within five business days of the request for clearance (para 5); and

(c) provide a copy of the response and any clearance to the restricted person concerned (para 6).

Once clearance has been given, the restricted person must deal as soon as possible, and in any event within two business days of clearance being received (para 7).

7.8.4.3 Refusal of clearance to deal

Clearance to deal must not be given during a prohibited period or on considerations of a short-term nature. Each is considered in turn below.

During a prohibited period (Model Code, para 8(a))

A prohibited period means:

(a) any close period (see below); and

(b) any period during which inside information exists in relation to the company.

Broadly, a 'close period' is the 60-day period prior to publication of the preliminary announcement of the company's annual results or the annual financial report (see **7.7.2**) and the period from the end of the relevant financial period up to the publication of the half-yearly report (see **7.7.3**). (If the company reports on a quarterly basis, the close period is the 30-day period before the announcement of the quarterly results. Note that this does not include the IMSs (see **7.7.4**).) See the definition at para 1(a) of the Model Code for further information.

'Inside information' is as defined by s 118C of the FSMA 2000 (see **7.5.2**, substituting 'qualifying investments' for 'financial instruments'). Remember that, usually, if inside information does exist about the company, it should be disclosed to an RIS under the general obligation of disclosure provided by DTR 2.2.1R (see **7.5.1** above), and so would no longer be inside information. The prohibition on giving clearance while such inside information exists assumes that an exception to the obligation to disclose must exist, for example because the matter is still under negotiation (DTR 2.5.3G(1) – see **7.5.2.8**). The fact that any request for clearance would have to be refused, however, may well flag up, to a restricted person otherwise unaware of it, that there is some inside information – perhaps an acquisition or disposal in the course of negotiation – in existence. (In addition, it is possible that the restricted person might then consult the company's insider list (see **7.5.6**) to see who might well have access to that information, and so who might be interesting to take to lunch to pump for gossip.) For this reason, the lawyer will advise the company to train its restricted persons in relation to the requirements of the Model Code and the DTRs, and the importance of avoiding any breach.

On considerations of a short-term nature (Model Code, para 8(b))

An investment of less than one year will usually be considered to be of a short-term nature.

Why will clearance to deal not be given in such circumstances? Most shareholders can buy and sell shares as quickly as they like. For example, if you or I invest £100 in Company X tomorrow, and the next day our investment has grown to £1,000, we might well choose to realise our investment that day and treat ourselves to a cheeky long weekend away. We have made what is known as a 'fast buck'. Persons discharging managerial responsibilities subject to the Model Code cannot do this. Why? Directors' shareholdings are seen as a barometer of the company's fortunes. If a director buys shares, it sends a certain message to the market (usually positive). Similarly, if a director sells shares, it can send a negative message to the market. If a director was buying or selling shares left, right and centre, the market might well lose confidence in the company and the share price might become unstable. The Model Code's aim is to protect investors and maintain the integrity of the market; hence it prohibits such short-term trading.

7.8.4.4 Exception for severe financial difficulty and other exceptional circumstances

Despite the rules set out at **7.8.4.3** above, paras 9, 10 and 11 provide that clearance to sell (but not buy) shares may be given during a prohibited period as restricted under para 8(a) (see **7.8.4.3**) where the restricted person:

(a)   is not in possession of inside information; and

(b)   either:

    (i)   is in severe financial difficulty (eg, she has a pressing financial commitment which cannot be satisfied otherwise than by selling the shares, but this would not include a liability to tax unless the person had no other means of satisfying the liability); or

    (ii)   is in other exceptional circumstances (eg, there is a court order, or other overriding legal requirement, for the sale).

Ultimately, the person with responsibility for giving clearance to deal must decide whether the exception applies, but FCA guidance can be (and, in the case of exceptional circumstances, should be) sought.

In practice it is likely to be very rare that circumstances will arise permitting the use of this exception.

If the 'exceptional circumstances' exception is used, the company must notify an RIS of the information under DTR 3.1.4R, including the nature of the exceptional circumstances (LR 9.2.10R).

7.8.4.5 Trading plans

The Model Code permits PDMRs to deal in their company's securities during 'prohibited periods' in certain circumstances without breaching the Model Code.

It would otherwise be difficult for PDMRs to adopt long-term trading strategies in relation to their company's shares without breaching the Model Code due to the significant number of times when there would be a 'prohibited period' during any given year due to the regular release of financial information and the unpredictability of when inside information would arise.

Further, some companies are listed in more than one country, some of which already permitted dealing by PDMRs in circumstances where there would be no suspicion of abusing inside information even during a 'prohibited period'. This meant that a PDMR would be able to deal in the company's shares in one country but breach the Model Code in the UK.

The dealing must occur in line with a pre-determined agreement, known as a trading plan, entered into with an independent third party. The terms of the plan must have been fixed outside of a 'prohibited period'. Due to the independence of the third party and the fact that the terms of dealing have been agreed in advance, there will not be the same concerns about PDMRs abusing inside information.

Entering a trading plan

A PDMR can at any time which is not a 'prohibited period' enter into a 'trading plan' (para 24). This is defined in the Glossary as a written plan between a PDMR and an independent third party setting out a strategy under which the third party will be given authority for the acquisition or disposal of specified securities in the PDMR's company and either it:

(a) specifies the amount, date and price of securities to be dealt; or

(b) gives discretion to the independent third party as to when, how many and at what price to deal in the securities; or

(c) includes a written formula setting this out.

Clearance is required to be given to enter a trading plan in accordance with para 4 of the Model Code. This cannot be given during a 'prohibited period' (para 24).

Dealing under a trading plan

A PDMR can deal in securities of his company during *both* 'prohibited' and non-prohibited periods. Dealing can take place during a 'prohibited period' only if (para 25):

(a) the trading plan was entered into before the 'prohibited period';

(b) clearance has been given to the plan in accordance with para 4 before the 'prohibited period'; and

(c) the trading plan does not allow the PDMR to exert any influence or discretion over the third party as to how, when, or whether to deal in the company's securities.

The PDMR must notify the company at the same time as making the required DTR 3.1.2 notification of the fact that the dealing was under the trading plan and the date the plan was entered into (para 26).

The company must notify an RIS of information provided to it by a PDMR in accordance with para 26 (DTR 3.1.4R(d)).

Amending a trading plan

A trading plan cannot be amended without clearance in accordance with para 4, and this cannot be given during a 'prohibited period' (para 24).

Cancelling a trading plan

A trading plan cannot be cancelled without clearance in accordance with para 4 (para 24).

A trading plan can only be cancelled during a 'prohibited period' in the exceptional circumstances set out in paras 9 and 10 of the Model Code (para 24) (see **7.8.4.4**).

7.8.5 Sanctions for breach of the Model Code

The Model Code forms part of the continuing obligations of the Listing Rules, and is enforceable against the company itself by virtue of LR 9.2.8R. If the company has not required PDMRs to comply with the Model Code and to take all proper and reasonable steps to ensure their compliance, the FCA may impose the sanctions on it for a breach of the Listing Rules referred to at **3.6** above. The FCA may also impose a financial penalty under s 91(2) of the FSMA 2000 on a PDMR, but only if the PDMR is a director or former director who was knowingly concerned in a breach of the Listing Rules by the company.

The first ever penalty for breach of LR 9.2.8R (as well as Listing Principles 1 and 2) was imposed in February 2013 on Nestor Healthcare Group Limited. The £175,000 fine was imposed because clearance had been given by the wrong person, dealing had taken place two months after clearance instead of within two days, and also because of serious deficiencies in record-keeping. The following month Lamprell plc was fined £2.4 million for breaches of the DTRs, Listing Principles and para 8 of the Model Code by allowing a PDMR to trade during a prohibited period. It is worth noting that the forerunner to the FCA, the FSA, decided that there had been a direct breach of para 8 and thereby Appendix 1 to the Listing Rules by the company without making reference to LR 9.2.8R.

If the company has complied with its obligations under LR 9.2.8R but a PDMR has still breached the Model Code (for instance by failing to seek clearance before dealing), the PDMR could potentially be liable for market abuse or insider dealing, and such action may also amount to a breach of his employment contract with the company.

7.9 COMMUNICATION WITH SHAREHOLDERS

As we have seen, the Listing Rules, Prospectus Rules and DTRs set out many different circumstances when the company must communicate information to its shareholders.

7.9.1 The circular

The usual way of communicating with shareholders is by way of a document known as a circular. The Listing Rules define a circular as:

> Any document issued to holders of listed securities including notices of meetings but excluding prospectuses, listing particulars, annual reports and accounts, interim reports, proxy cards and dividend or interest vouchers.

Chapter 13 of the Listing Rules, entitled 'Contents of Circulars', prescribes general content requirements for all circulars (LR 13.3) (see **7.9.3**) and specific content requirements for particular types of circular (see **7.9.2**). This Chapter applies only to premium listed companies.

7.9.2 When is a circular required?

The Listing Rules set out the circumstances when a circular is required. The following are the most commonly encountered by the lawyer. The Chapter 13 Listing Rule governing the specific content requirements of the required circular is provided in brackets.

- Class 1 transactions (LR 13.4, LR 13.5 and LR 13, Annex 1R) (see **19.6.1**)
- Related party transactions (LR 13.6) (see **19.6.2**)
- Circulars regarding the purchase of own securities ('buyback') (LR 13.7)
- Authority to allot shares (LR 13.8.1R) (see **14.5.6**)
- Disapplying pre-emption rights (LR 13.8.2R) (see **14.6.15**)
- Reduction of capital (LR 13.8.4R)

- Capitalisation or bonus issue (LR 13.8.5R)
- Scrip dividend alternative (LR 13.8.6R)
- Scrip dividend mandate schemes/dividend reinvestment plan (LR 13.8.7R)
- Notices of meetings (including business other than ordinary business at an AGM) (LR 13.8.8R)
- Amendments to the company's constitution (LR 13.8.10R)
- Employees' share scheme arrangements (LR 13.8.11R to LR 13.8.14R)
- Discounted option arrangements (LR 13.8.15R)
- Reminders of conversion rights (LR 13.8.16R)

7.9.3 General content requirements

The basic content requirements of all circulars are prescribed by LR 13.3. To provide a flavour of what is in a circular, a sample of the requirements include:

(a) a clear and adequate explanation of the subject matter;

(b) a statement why the shareholder is being asked to vote, or otherwise why the circular is being sent;

(c) if voting or other action is required:

    (i) all information necessary to allow the shareholder to make a properly informed decision; and

    (ii) a heading drawing attention to the importance of the document and advising the shareholder to consult an independent adviser if he is unsure what action to take;

(d) if voting is required, a recommendation from the board as to how shareholders should vote, indicating whether the proposal is, in its opinion, in the shareholders' best interests.

Under LR 13.1.7R, the FCA can authorise the omission of information which would otherwise be required to be included if it would be against the public interest or seriously detrimental to the listed company (provided it would not be likely to mislead the public).

7.9.4 FCA approval

Some circulars require prior approval by the FCA before the company can circulate them to shareholders, and others do not. The lawyer will need to be able to advise on whether a circular requires prior approval.

Once published, any circular, approved or otherwise, must be sent to the NSM for publication on its website (see **7.5.7.1**), and an approved circular must be sent to the company's shareholders as soon as practicable after approval.

7.9.4.1 Circulars which do not require approval

Listing Rule 13.2.2R provides that circulars which do not require prior approval are those which:

(a) are listed in LR 13.8 (or relate only to a proposed change of name, or are information-only circulars which do not relate to a shareholder vote);

(b) comply with LR 13.3 and any requirements of LR 13.8; and

(c) have no unusual features.

As can be seen from the list at **7.9.2** above, there are many circulars listed in LR 13.8. They include circulars relating to share capital changes, such as an increase in authorised share capital, the grant of an authority to allot and the disapplication of pre-emption rights.

7.9.4.2 Circulars which require approval

All other circulars require approval (LR 13.2.1R). By definition, these will be circulars which:

(a)   are not listed in LR 13.8R; and

(b)   have unusual features.

Examples include circulars produced in connection with Class 1 transactions (see **19.4**) and related party transactions (see **19.5**).

The approval process is detailed in LR 13.2.4R to 13.2.9G. The company must submit the draft circular to the FCA at least 10 clear business days before the intended publication date.

7.9.5   Electronic communication

The CA 2006 has introduced provisions in ss 308, 309, 333 and 1143 to 1148 which apply to all companies. They permit (but do not compel) documents or information to be sent from the company to the shareholder or *vice versa* electronically (including via e-mail and on a website), provided the conditions in Schs 4 and 5 are met.

These provisions are supplemented for listed companies by Chapter 6 of the DTRs. Transparency Rule 6.1.7G permits (but does not compel) listed companies to communicate with their shareholders by 'electronic means', provided certain conditions are met, the most important of these being (DTR 6.1.8R) the need for prior approval of the shareholders by ordinary resolution and for identification arrangements to be put in place.

'Electronic means' is defined in the DTRs as a 'means of electronic equipment for the processing (including digital compression), storage and transmission of data, employing wires, radio optical technologies, or any other electromagnetic means.' A pretty impenetrable definition for most lawyers (except that rarity the lawyer-geek, who will doubtless be salivating at the prospect of explaining the full extent of these terms to his or her colleagues) – it includes e-mail, websites and a fax.

The ICSA has produced a guidance note for electronic communication with shareholders under the CA 2006 and the DTRs (available on its website) setting out recommended best practice.

7.10   THE ADMISSION AND DISCLOSURE STANDARDS

As stated at **7.1** above, the Admission and Disclosure Standards contain continuing obligations which are additional to those set out in the Listing Rules. These obligations are set out at ADS 3 (see **Appendix 1**), and they include that the company must comply with the Part 6 Rules. The other continuing obligations are mercifully very brief, compared with the requirements of the Listing Rules. They include:

(a)   requirements relating to the timetable for what are referred to as 'corporate actions', that is, payment of dividends, open offers, rights issues and the like (ADS 3.5 to 3.9);

(b)   a requirement that proposed amendments to the company's constitution must be communicated to the FCA and Stock Exchange in draft form, at the latest on the date of calling the relevant GM (ADS 3.11);

(c)   that the Stock Exchange will suspend the admission to trading of any shares which are suspended from admission to listing (ADS 3.15) (this is a mirror image of LR 9.2.1R – see **7.4.1** above); and

(d)   that the company must pay an annual fee to the Stock Exchange (ADS 3.14).

7.11   SANCTIONS

7.11.1   Sanctions for breach of the Disclosure Rules, the Transparency Rules, the Corporate Governance Rules, the Prospectus Rules or the Listing Rules

Sanctions for breach of the Part 6 Rules are set out at **3.6** above. The article below gives an example.

FSA fines Prudential £30m and censures chief Tidjane Thiam over AIA deal

Alistair Osborne

The Financial Services Authority has fined Prudential up to £30m and censured its chief executive Tidjane Thiam.

The penalty, first revealed in The Daily Telegraph, relates to the insurer's failure to have followed the correct protocol in notifying the City regulator ahead of its abortive $35.5bn (£23.4bn) bid for Asian rival AIA in 2010.

The FSA said in a statement: "Prudential failed to deal with the FSA in an open and cooperative manner when it was seeking to acquire AIA in early 2010, because it did not inform the FSA of the proposed acquisition until after it had been leaked to the media on 27 February 2010."

The insurer is thought to have agreed the fine as a settlement after a lengthy stand-off with the regulator. Talks between the two sides are understood to have been going on for more than a year, with the FSA initially demanding a fine of as much as £80m and a further £400,000 penalty for Mr Thiam.

The size of the FSA fine is expected to raise eyebrows in the City. A penalty of £30m would be one of the biggest the regulator has levied - topping the £29.7m handed to UBS in November last year for failing to prevent "large-scale unauthorised trading" by rogue trader Kweku Adoboli.

The FSA said: "The failure to inform the FSA was significant because it resulted in the FSA having to consider highly complex issues within a compressed timescale before making a decision as to whether to suspend Prudential's shares.

"It narrowed the FSA's options in scrutinising the transaction, risked delaying the publication of Prudential's subsequent rights issue prospectus and hampered the FSA's ability to assist overseas regulators with their enquiries in relation to the transaction."

Prudential launched one of the most controversial bids the City has seen when it agreed to buy AIA, the Asian wing of insurer AIG, for $35.5bn in March 2010. The deal was partly funded by a £14.5bn rights issue but triggered a massive shareholder revolt among investors opposed to the ambitious transaction.

Prudential's deal would have transformed the insurer's financial position, the regulator said, and had the "potential to impact upon the stability and confidence of the financial system in the UK and abroad".

Tracey McDermott, FSA director of enforcement and financial crime, said: "The FSA expects to have an open and frank relationship with the firms it supervises and with listed companies. It is essential that firms give due consideration to their regulatory obligations at all times. In particular, timely and proactive communication with the FSA is of fundamental importance to the functioning of the regulatory system and the integrity of the market.

"Prudential, led by Thiam as chief executive, failed to give due considera-tion to its obligation to inform the FSA of this transaction, which would have had a huge impact on the group had it gone through. That was a serious error of judgement for which Prudential is paying the price. Firms should be in no doubt as to the importance of early communication with the regulator in respect of transformational transactions to avoid market and investor disruption.

"Thiam has also been censured in relation to his role in this matter. This case should send a clear message to all board members of their collective and individual responsibility for the decisions they make on behalf of their companies."

The FSA said the Prudential wrongly allowed its judgement to be overly influenced by its concern about the risk of leaks.

"This concern meant Prudential failed to give due weight to the importance of complying with its regulatory obligations, even when explicitly advised by its own advisers of the importance of keeping the regulator informed," she said.

The deal's failure left the Prudential nursing a £377m bill for advisor fees and other expenses, while the company was forced to rebuild many bridges with its investors.

Some shareholders took their anger out on former chairman Harvey McGrath, who stepped down in December 2011, though he is not criticised by the FSA.

Source: *Telegraph*, 27 March 2013

Of this £30 million, Prudential plc was fined £14 million for breaching Listing Principle 6 for failing to deal with the FCA in an open and co-operative manner. Another example is Lamprell plc which was fined £2.4 million in March 2013 for breaches of the DTRs 1.2.4R and 3.3.1R, Listing Principle 2 and para 8 of the Model Code (see **7.8.5** above). On 2 November 2007 the FSA cancelled the listing of shares in Simon Group plc because it was no longer satisfying its continuing obligations for listing as the percentage of shares in public hands had fallen below 25% in breach of LR 6.1.19R.

7.11.2 Sanctions for breach of the Admission and Disclosure Standards

The sanctions are set out in ADS 3.23. In the event of breach of any continuing obligation, the Stock Exchange may privately or publicly censure a company, fine it, order the company to make a payment to any person, or alternatively cancel the company's admission to trading.

7.12 FUTURE DEVELOPMENTS

7.12.1 Enhancing the listing regime

The FCA is at the time of writing consulting on:

a package of measures designed to strengthen minority shareholder rights and protections where they are at risk of being abused. It is particularly intended to deal with cases when a controlling shareholder does not maintain an appropriate relationship with a premium listed company. In designing this package, we have sought to be both effective and proportionate, while enabling all shareholders to play an active role in the governance of premium listed companies. Taken together, we view this package as an important and necessary step in promoting the integrity of the Listing Regime and ensuring an appropriate degree of investor protection. (FCA Consultation Paper CP 13/15)

These proposed changes form part of a package of measures to restore confidence in the Main Market following problems with controlling shareholders in two companies, Bumi plc and ENRC.

The main changes will:

- place requirements on the interaction between a premium listed company and a controlling shareholder, where one exists, via a mandatory relationship agreement;
- provide additional voting power for minority shareholders when electing independent directors where a controlling shareholder is present by requiring that they must be separately approved both by the shareholders as a whole and the independent shareholders as a separate class;
- enhance voting power for the minority shareholders where a company with a controlling shareholder wishes to cancel its premium listing.

This will necessitate changes to Listing Rules Chapters 6, 7, 9, 11, 13 and 14. Of particular relevance to this chapter is a series of proposed amendments to Listing Rules 9.2 and 9.8.

The consultation finishes in February 2014 and any changes to the Listing Rules are likely to come into force in mid-2014. The latest developments will be available on the FCA website.

7.12.2   Regulatory Information Services

The FCA is currently consulting on changing the regime governing RISs. This is likely to involve changes to the definition of an RIS and to the rules governing them, including to the approval process, the criteria for becoming an RIS and the continuing obligations on RISs. This would involve changes to DTR 6.3 and a new rule, DTR 8. The FCA is intending to introduce the changes in early 2014 once they have been finalised. You can find out the latest developments on the FCA website.

7.12.3   Inside information

The definition of 'inside information' in DTR 2.2.1R is expected to change once the new Market Abuse Regulation becomes law (see **3.7.2** above). This is unlikely to happen before 2016.

CHAPTER 8

CORPORATE GOVERNANCE

8.1 WHAT IS CORPORATE GOVERNANCE?

Corporate governance refers to how a company is run. This includes not only how a company is directed and controlled, but also how a company is performing, how that performance can be enhanced, and how a company should account to interested parties such as shareholders and employees.

Corporate governance is relevant to all companies, but once a company is listed, those who control the company (directors and controlling shareholders) are not the same as, and therefore may have conflicting interests to, those who own the company (shareholders). This means that corporate governance is a particularly important issue for listed companies.

Corporate governance is once again very much in the news. It jumped to the top of politicians' and regulators' agendas worldwide as a result of the global financial crisis in 2007/08 which triggered the deepest recession in over 70 years. Listed companies stood at the heart of the crisis, and poor corporate governance of banks and other financial companies has been identified as a major contributory factor. The consequences of these failings continue to reverberate, several years on, and some of the largest UK banks only exist today thanks to government intervention. Although financial services companies are the main focus of many of the recent changes to corporate governance rules, it is worth noting that in the UK the rules have been amended for listed companies beyond the financial services industry.

8.2 THE UK FRAMEWORK

Common law, the CA 2006, the Listing Rules (in particular, the continuing obligations, Model Code and Listing Principles), the Corporate Governance Rules, the UK Corporate Governance Code, the Stewardship Code, the Large and Medium-sized Companies and Groups (Accounts and Reports) Regulations 2008 (SI 2008/410), the FCA's Code of Market Conduct and various non-legal guidelines produced by institutional shareholders (such as the ABI, the NAPF and PIRC) and the accountancy profession all contain provisions which address corporate governance issues. The UK Corporate Governance Code, the Corporate Governance Rules and the 2008 Regulations are discussed further below.

The EU has increasing influence in this area. Generally the European Commission does not believe in the introduction of an EU-wide corporate governance code. However, it does support the introduction of a limited number of measures to harmonise national codes.

The European Commission introduced a new Action Plan on company law and corporate governance (A modern legal framework for more engaged shareholders and sustainable companies) in December 2012. The Action Plan contains six initiatives to address:

> a perceived lack of shareholder interest in holding management accountable for their decisions and actions, compounded by the fact that many shareholders appear to hold their shares for only a short period of time. There is also evidence of shortcomings in the application of the corporate governance codes when reporting on a 'comply or explain' basis.

It will seek to do this by:

(a) enhancing transparency – companies need to provide better information about their corporate governance to their investors and society at large;

(b) engaging shareholders – shareholders should be encouraged to engage more in corporate governance;

(c) supporting companies' growth and their competitiveness – there is a need to simplify cross-border operations of European businesses, particularly in the case of small and medium-sized companies.

8.3   THE UK CORPORATE GOVERNANCE CODE

8.3.1   Nature

The UK Corporate Governance Code ('UK CGC') is the most prominent part of the UK corporate governance framework. It is a codification of best practice in corporate governance. The UK CGC does not have the force of law. Rather, as **8.3.4** below explains in more detail, companies are required to comply with the UK CGC or, if they do not, to explain their non-compliance. The UK CGC is not included in the Listing Rules but instead is available on the FRC's website (www.frc.org.uk).

8.3.2   Background

The UK CGC replaces the previous set of rules known as the Combined Code on Corporate Governance ('Combined Code'). There were four editions of the Combined Code: the original of 1995 and revised versions published in 2003, 2006 and 2008.

8.3.2.1   Background to the original Combined Code of 1995

The provisions of the original Combined Code were based on the findings of three reports, namely the Cadbury, Greenbury and Hampel Reports, which were commissioned in the 1990s to consider corporate governance in detail. The Hampel Committee 'combined' the recommendations of all three reports to produce the original Combined Code. This Combined Code was annexed to the Listing Rules in 1995 and the Listing Rules were amended to refer to compliance with it. In 1999 a further report (the Turnbull Report) was commissioned, to provide guidance to listed companies regarding implementation of the requirements in the original Combined Code relating to internal control.

8.3.2.2   Background to the Combined Code of 2003

In 2002, massive financial scandals involving the US companies Enron and WorldCom put corporate governance in the spotlight again. In the UK, two further reports were commissioned immediately. The Financial Reporting Council commissioned the Smith Report (concerning audit issues) and the DTI commissioned the Higgs Report (concerning non-executive directors and remuneration). Those responsible for compiling these reports worked closely together to propose a consolidated revised code. Some of the proposals proved controversial, however, so the Financial Reporting Council set up a working group to revise the code further. The final text of this revised code was published in July 2003.

8.3.2.3 Background to the UK Corporate Governance Code

As part of the UK Government's response to the near collapse of the UK banking system in 2008, the Prime Minister appointed Sir David Walker in February 2009 to conduct a review of the corporate governance of UK banks (later extended to other financial companies) and to make recommendations (the 'Walker Review'). In his report of July 2009 published by HM Treasury, Sir David made 39 recommendations covering board size, composition and qualification; functioning of the board and evaluation of performance; the role of institutional shareholders; remuneration; and risk governance.

As a consequence of the Walker Review, the FRC undertook a further review of the impact and effectiveness of the Combined Code in March 2009, which applied to all listed companies, not just to those in the financial services industry. The FRC also took account of the European Commission's recommendations on the remuneration of executive directors of listed companies and the relevant recommendations of the House of Commons Treasury Committee's third report on the banking crisis.

As a result it replaced the 2008 version of the Combined Code with the UK CGC, which although based on the Combined Code, has been rewritten and contains a number of new provisions. The latest version, dated September 2012, applies to company reporting years beginning on or after 1 October 2012. At the same time certain provisions which were in the Combined Code were extracted and used to form the basis of another new code, the Stewardship Code, which sets out the responsibility of institutional investors with regard to their ownership of listed companies (see **8.5** below).

8.3.3 Application

The UK CGC only applies to companies with a premium listing on the Main Market of the Stock Exchange. These companies have an obligation to 'comply or explain' with the UK CGC under LR 9.8.6R (see **8.3.6** below). Standard listed companies do not have to comply with the UK CGC.

In recognition that smaller listed companies can find it difficult to achieve full compliance with all of the demands of the UK CGC, certain provisions do not apply to premium listed companies below the FTSE 350.

8.3.4 Structure

The UK CGC consists of three introductory sections ('Governance and the Code', a preface and 'Comply or Explain') and 18 main principles of good governance. In addition there are two schedules and an appendix.

Each principle is supplemented by a set of supporting principles and code provisions. The supporting principles were drafted with the intention of affording companies an element of flexibility regarding the implementation of the main principles.

The principles of the UK CGC are divided into five sections. Each section sets out the main principles relating to:

A. Leadership (four principles);
B. Effectiveness (seven principles);
C. Accountability (three principles);
D. Remuneration (two principles); and
E. Relations with shareholders (two principles).

8.3.5 Associated guidance

The following guidance on the UK CGC is also available from the FRC website.

8.3.5.1 Internal Control: Guidance to Directors

Formerly known as the Turnbull Guidance, this sets out best practice on the internal control of companies. Following a review by the FRC, the guidance was updated in October 2005.

8.3.5.2 The FRC's Guide on Board Effectiveness

This updated and replaced the Good Practice Suggestions from the Higgs Report. Companies are not obliged to follow this guide, which offer assistance on how to apply the principles of the UK CGC, but they may find it helpful. The guidance, published in March 2011, provides assistance on each of the sections of the UK CGC, but principally on sections A and B on the leadership and effectiveness of the board.

8.3.5.3 The FRC's Guidance on Audit Committees

The latest version of this guide to best practice in relation to audit committees (formerly known as the Smith Guidance) was published in September 2012. It includes guidance on how to establish a committee, the relationship of the committee with the board, the role and responsibilities of the committee, and how it should communicate with shareholders. As with the Guide on Board Effectiveness, companies are not obliged to follow this Guidance.

8.3.6 Compliance

8.3.6.1 The principles

While any company can choose to follow the provisions of the UK CGC, the Listing Rules provide that, strictly, it applies only to premium listed companies. Even these companies are not subject to any formal requirement to comply with the UK CGC. Instead, the requirement is that any such company must include in its annual financial report (ie the annual report and accounts) a statement, known as a 'disclosure statement', which details:

(a)   how it has applied the main *principles* set out in the UK CGC in a way which would enable shareholders to evaluate how the principles have been applied (LR 9.8.6R(5)); and

(b)   whether it has complied throughout the relevant accounting period with the code *provisions* set out in the UK CGC and, if it has not, which provisions it has not complied with, the period of non-compliance, and why it has not complied (LR 9.8.6R(6)).

The disclosure requirements are therefore referred to as the 'comply or explain' approach. This approach encourages compliance even though strictly it does not require it, because the requirement to disclose any failure to comply carries with it a risk of adverse publicity. The institutional investors have made it clear, however, that they do generally expect compliance and, in practice, companies which do not comply with the UK CGC without good reason are often subject to significant pressure from institutional investors such as the ABI, the NAPF and PIRC.

In the introductory section to the UK CGC headed 'Comply or Explain', the FRC makes it clear that an alternative approach to following a specific provision is permissible if good governance can be achieved by that other means. If this applies in a particular company's case then it must ensure that it explains clearly and carefully to its shareholders its reasons for choosing, so that it is and be able to illustrate how its actual practices achieve both the principle concerned and good governance. The UK CGC goes on to state that shareholders should not automatically treat a departure from the UK CGC as a breach, but should pay due regard to the company's explanation, individual circumstances, size, complexity, and the nature of the risks and challenges it faces. Both parties should also be prepared to discuss the matter before a decision is reached.

There is no prescribed form of disclosure statement, which, as with other aspects of the corporate governance regime, is intended to afford companies a degree of flexibility.

Listing Rule 9.8.10R(2) provides that, before it publishes its annual report, the company must ensure that its auditors review the disclosure statement in relation to nine provisions of the UK CGC which deal with audit and accountability, and which are objectively verifiable (namely C1.1, C2.1 and C3.1 to C3.7).

Listing Rule 9.8.7R sets out the obligations of any overseas company with a premium listing on the UK CGC, in relation to the matters referred to above. Such companies are required to meet the requirements of LR 9.8.6R(5) and (6) (ie 'comply or explain'), but do not need to satisfy LR 9.8.10R(2) (requiring the auditors to comment on the company's compliance with certain parts of the UK CGC).

8.3.6.2   Disclosure of corporate governance arrangements

In addition to the disclosure statement referred to at 8.3.6.1 above, several of the UK CGC provisions require further disclosure, including in the company's annual report, of other information relating to corporate governance. These provisions are highlighted in Schedule B to the UK CGC, together with disclosures required in the LRs and in DTR 7 (Corporate Governance Rules).

8.3.6.3   Corporate governance statement

The Corporate Governance Rules (see **3.5.3**) require a listed company (premium or standard) to include a corporate governance statement in its directors' report in the company's annual report (DTR 7.2.1R), or in a separate report or on the company's website (DTR 7.2.9R), containing the information set out in DTR 7. It should be noted that there is some overlap with the requirements of DTR 7 and the Listing Rules and the UK CGC. For example, DTR 7.2.4G explains that compliance with LR 9.8.6R(6) (see **8.3.6.1**) satisfies DTR 7.2.2R and 7.2.3R, which together require information about the corporate governance code followed by the company, how the company applies it in practice and an explanation of any non-compliance with the code. As the UK CGC requires this information to be included anyway, these provisions of the DTRs will usually be superfluous. However, where a listed company chooses to 'explain' rather than 'comply' with the UK CGC, it will have to show that it still meets the minimum requirements in DTR 7 (Schedule B to the UK CGC).

8.3.6.4   Directors' remuneration

Further, Listing Rule 9.8.8R sets out the information on directors' remuneration which must be included in a report to shareholders in a premium listed company's annual report.

*At the time of writing, the FCA is consulting on deleting most of LR 9.8.8R because listed companies now have to comply with rules flowing from the CA 2006 (see **8.4** below). It intends to retain provisions affecting certain overseas companies which fall outside the CA 2006 provisions.*

8.3.7   Key features

As explained at **8.3.4** above, the UK CGC provides guidance for good corporate governance in relation to leadership, effectiveness, accountability, remuneration and relations with shareholders. The key features of the provisions relating to each area are discussed below, to provide a flavour of the issues the UK CGC addresses.

The UK CGC does, of course, go into some detail in relation to each of these, and other, issues; therefore any in-depth analysis must involve recourse to the UK CGC itself.

Numerous practical guides are also available. The website of the Institute of Chartered Secretaries and Administrators (ICSA) features guidance notes on how to implement the requirements of the UK CGC, which are useful to lawyers seeking to draft corporate governance documentation. The Institute of Directors has also collated some useful corporate governance information on its website, which is updated regularly, and the

Institutional Voting Information Service website of ABI contains a useful monitoring checklist on the UK CGC.

8.3.7.1   Section A: Leadership

The following is a selection of the main provisions from Section A of the UK CGC.

The Preface encourages the chairman to report personally on the implementation of Section A of the UK CGC in his statement in the company's annual report.

The role of the board

The powerfully worded Preface to the UK CGC makes it clear that the challenge of achieving good corporate governance should not be underrated:

> To run a corporate board successfully is extremely demanding. Constraints on time and knowledge combine with the need to maintain mutual respect and openness between a cast of strong, able and busy directors dealing with each other across the different demands of executive and non-executive roles. To achieve good governance requires continuing and high quality effort.

The UK CGC highlights the important role of the board of directors in taking the company forward. The following is a selection of some of the main provisions in Section A regarding the role of the board:

(a)   All companies should be headed by an effective board, which has collective responsibility for the long-term success of the company (A.1).

(b)   The board should set the company's strategic aims, ensure the necessary financial and human resources are in place and review management performance. The board should also set the company's values and standards (Supporting Principle A.1).

(c)   The board should meet regularly to discharge its duties effectively, and there should be a formal schedule of matters reserved for its decision (A.1.1).

Division of responsibility

The chairman and the chief executive are both responsible for the leadership of the company, but in different ways. While the chief executive is responsible for running the business, the chairman must ensure that the board runs effectively.

(a)   The role of chairman and chief executive should be held by separate individuals, and the division of responsibility sbould be set out in writing (A.2.1).

(b)   No one individual should have unfettered powers of decision (A.2).

There has been much discussion over the importance of splitting these roles. It is, for example, less common for this to happen in US listed companies. The debate has, however, now largely been settled in the UK, but sometimes even the bluest of blue-chip listed companies is prepared to run the risk of incurring the wrath of its investors by going against this core principle of the UK CGC. Sir Stuart Rose, former Chairman and Chief Executive of M&S, survived a shareholder resolution at its 2009 AGM which was proposed for M&S's breach of this principle: 37.7% of shareholders voted against Sir Stuart Rose's dual role, while 62.3% voted in favour. Sir Stuart had previously noted that it had even resulted in him being described as the 'Robert Mugabe of retail'. This remains an exceptional step to take, and in M&S's case signified the depth of its worries at the time about its future trading performance in an increasingly tough economic climate.

Role of the chairman

The emphasis in Section A is on the role of the chairman as a leader of the board. Section E (see **8.3.7.5** below) explains that the chairman has a further important role as a channel of communication between the shareholders and the board (E.1.1). Additional responsibilities of the chairman can also be found in other sections of the UK CGC.

Guidance on the role of the chairman is set out in the FRC's Guide on Board Effectiveness (see **8.3.5.2**). The ICSA has also published a guidance note on the roles of the chairman and the chief executive:

(a)   The chairman is responsible for leadership of the board and ensuring its effectiveness on all aspects of its role (A.3).

(b)   The chairman's responsibilities (as proposed by the Higgs Report) are incorporated into the UK CGC as a Supporting Principle A.3. The chairman will draw up the agenda for board meetings and ensure that there is sufficient time to discuss the matters. He will also be responsible for ensuring contributions, particularly of non-executive directors, and that there are good relations between executive and non-executive directors.

(c)   When appointed, the chairman should be independent, measured against criteria set out at B.1.1 of the UK CGC (A.3.1).

(d)   The chief executive should not go on to become the chairman. This principle was introduced by the Higgs Report and was controversial, as many listed companies had a tradition of 'sending the chief executive upstairs' to be chairman. This provision can be waived in exceptional circumstances if the board consults with major shareholders first, and discloses the reasons behind the decision in the annual report and accounts (A.3.1).

Non-executive directors

Guidance on the role of the non-executive director (commonly referred to as a NED) is set out in the FRC's Guide on Board Effectiveness (see **8.3.5.2**).

Some of the main provisions in Section A of the UK CGC relating to NEDs are as follows:

(a)   The role of the NED is fully set out at Supporting Principle A.4. In essence it requires NEDs to scrutinise the performance of management, satisfy themselves that the financial and risk control mechanisms are robust, and determine appropriate levels of executive pay.

(b)   The board should appoint one of the NEDs to be the senior independent director (A.4.1).

(c)   The chairman should hold some meetings with the NEDs alone, where the executive directors are not present (A.4.2).

(d)   The NEDs must appraise the performance of the chairman at least annually (A.4.2).

The ICSA has produced guidance notes on the role of NEDs and the senior independent director.

The role of the NED is not a particularly easy one in today's climate. Companies need to take care to select a suitable NED who will take the role seriously and be able to meet the dramatically increased expectations of his performance and legal duties in light of the perceived failings of NEDs in preventing the poor decision-making which ultimately led to the global financial crisis. The website of the Institute of Chartered Accountants maintains a register of independent directors.

It is worth remembering that in company law a NED is treated no differently from an executive director and shares the same potential liability. In light of these risks the ICSA has produced guidance for prospective directors (both NED and executive), 'Guidance on joining the right board', available on the ICSA's website at www.icsa.org.uk, to help them to evaluate whether they are joining the board of a listed company which meets their skills and requirements.

8.3.7.2   Section B: Effectiveness

The Preface encourages the chairman to report personally on the implementation of Section B of the UK CGC in his statement in the company's annual report.

The BIS has published on its website a guide to best practice in recruitment and performance in the boardroom, entitled 'Building Better Boards', which although based on the 2003 version of the Combined Code, is still useful.

The following is a selection of the main provisions from Section B of the UK CGC.

Composition of the board

(a)   The board should have an appropriate mix of skills, experience, independence and knowledge (B.1).

(b)   The board should consist of a balance of executive and non-executive directors (in particular *independent* NEDs). At least half of the board should comprise independent NEDs, unless the company is below the FTSE 350, in which case there should be at least two independent NEDs (B.1.2).

(c)   To be effective, NEDs ideally should be 'independent'. The board should identify, in the annual report, each NED it considers to be independent. Guidance as to the meaning of 'independent' is provided in B.1.1.

Compliance with these requirements of the UK CGC is the reason that companies tend to announce new NED appointments prior to the IPO.

Appointments to the board

(a)   The procedure for appointment of directors should be formal, rigorous and transparent. A nomination committee, a majority of which are independent NEDs, should lead the appointment process (B.2, B.2.1).

(b)   Due regard should be had to diversity, including gender, when considering candidates for the board (Supporting Principle B.2). In addition, the UK CGC seeks to encourage listed companies to take more women on to their boards. Provisions B.2.4 and B.6 require a special section of the company's Annual Report to include a description of the board's policy on diversity, including gender, and require the board to consider factors including the gender balance in assessing the board's effectiveness. Although there is currently no suggested or compulsory quota for women on boards as in some other countries, these references represent an acknowledgement of how woefully underrepresented women are on the boards of UK listed companies (see further **8.7** below).

(c)   The chairman should ensure that new directors receive a full, formal and tailored induction into the company (B.4.1).

Commitment

(a)   The chairman's other significant commitments should be disclosed to the board before his appointment and be included in the company's annual report (B.3.1).

(b)   Non-executive directors should ensure that they have sufficient time to perform their role for the company (B.3.2).

Evaluation

(a)   Directors' performance, both as a board and individually, should be evaluated formally and rigorously every year (B.6).

(b)   The board of a FTSE 350 company should be subject to an external review every three years (B.6.2). This is a new development brought in with the UK CGC.

Re-election

All directors should be subject to annual re-election by the shareholders (B.7.1). The votes will take place at the company's AGM. This is a significant change from the Combined Code when a vote was expected every three years. The hope is that this requirement will encourage directors to engage more with their shareholders, particularly institutional investors.

Other provisions in Section B cover the directors' development and training, and ensuring that the board receives the necessary information and support to perform its role.

8.3.7.3 Section C: Accountability

As explained at **8.3.5.3** above, it is useful to consult the FRC's Guidance on Audit Committees when considering what the UK CGC has to say on this issue. Some of the key provisions in the UK CGC relating to accountability and audit are as follows:

(a)   The board should present a fair, balanced and understandable view of the company's position and prospects (C.1).

(b)   The board should explain the company's business model in the company's annual report (C.1.2).

(c)   The board is responsible for determining the significant risks which the company is prepared to take in order to achieve its strategic objectives, and should conduct a review of the risk management system and internal controls at least annually (C.2 and C.2.1).

   At the time of writing, the FRC is consulting on changes to C.2, C.2.1 and introducing a new C.2.2. See further **8.7.1** *below.*

(d)   There should be an audit committee with at least three members (unless the company is below the FTSE 350, in which case there should be at least two members) who are all independent NEDs. At least one member should have recent and relevant financial experience (C.3, C.3.1).

(e)   The main role and responsibilities of the audit committee should be set out in written terms of reference, which are available both on the company's website and on request, and a section in the company's annual report should describe the committee's work in discharging those responsibilities (C.3.2, C.3.3). The lawyer may be required to draft the terms of reference for the audit committee. The ICSA has published standard form terms of reference for audit committees.

(f)   The role of the audit committee is set out at C.3.2.

(g)   FTSE 350 companies should put the external audit contract out to tender at least every 10 years (C.3.7).

The implementation of the EC's Statutory Audit Directive in the UK through the Corporate Governance Rules introduced a statutory requirement for an Audit Committee for listed companies, including at least one independent member and one member with suitable accounting experience. A statement must be made publicly disclosing which body carries out these functions and how it is comprised. This may be included with the corporate governance statement (see **8.3.5.4**). There is of course an overlap with the provisions of the UK CGC, and the FCA states in DTR 7.1.7G that compliance with the UK CGC's provisions for audit committees will result in compliance with those in the Corporate Governance Rules. It is worth noting that the UK CGC places additional requirements on listed companies beyond those in the EU-inspired Corporate Governance Rules.

8.3.7.4 Section D: Remuneration

(a)   Remuneration should be sufficient to attract, retain and motivate directors of the quality required to run the company successfully, but the company should avoid paying more than is necessary for this purpose. A significant proportion of executive directors' remuneration should be linked to corporate and individual performance (D.1).

(b)   Policy on directors' remuneration should be formal and transparent. A remuneration committee, of at least three (two in the case of a company below the FTSE 350) independent NEDs, should determine the remuneration of directors (D.2, D.2.1).

(c)   In designing performance-related schemes the remuneration committee should take account of Schedule A to the UK CGC (D.1.1). Schedule A includes guidance on the approach to be taken, for example that share options should not be exercisable in less than three years after being awarded to the director and that only basic pay should be pensionable.

(d)   Notice periods under service contracts should not exceed one year. The remuneration committee should avoid rewarding poor performance in the event of an early termination of a director's service contract (D.1.4, D.1.5).

Remuneration, and indeed the remuneration committee, has been creating headlines well beyond the financial pages of the press for some years now. 'Good Practice Suggestions from the Higgs Report' (see **8.3.5.2**) sets out guidance on the role of the remuneration committee. The ICSA has produced specimen terms of reference for the remuneration committee.

The result of the remuneration committees' actions has been a phenomenal rise in the pay and benefits of listed company directors. Somewhat grotesquely, this trend continues apace, even in light of the current economic reality that for most workers average pay is rising less than inflation and living standards have dropped for the last five years, a public sector pay freeze is in place and, increasingly, part-time employment and so-called 'zero hours' employment contracts are replacing full-time employment. The average remuneration for FTSE 100 chief executives in 2013 is over 120 times greater than that of the average full-time worker in the UK, standing at over £4 million per year (including pay, bonus and awards under share-based performance schemes). In 1998 it was just 45 times greater.

For further information on directors' remuneration, see **8.4**.

8.3.7.5   Section E: Relations with shareholders

(a)   The chairman should ensure that the views of shareholders are communicated to the board (E.1.1).

(b)   The board should use the AGM to communicate with shareholders and to encourage their participation (E.2).

Ashley labels unhappy investors 'cry babies'

Marianne Barriaux

Mike Ashley, the Sports World billionaire, has accused unsupportive investors of being 'cry babies'.

The sports retailer, which owns Lillywhites and Dunlop, has faced accusations of a lack of transparency. Since the group's flotation five months ago, its share price has almost halved.

But Mr Ashley told the Sunday Times: 'I've got balls of steel. Some investors have been great and have been very supportive. But some of these City people act like a bunch of cry babies.'

He said some investors were too focused on the near-term share price, and not on the future prospects of the company.

Source: *Guardian*, 30 July 2007

8.4   DIRECTORS' REMUNERATION

8.4.1   Background

There are rules governing the remuneration of listed company directors in both the Listing Rules (see **8.3.6.4**) and the UK CGC (see **8.3.7.4**). Listed company directors must also comply with the rules set out in Chapters 6 and 9 of Pt 15 of the CA 2006.

In addition, the Large and Medium-sized Companies and Groups (Accounts and Reports) Regulations 2008 (SI 2008/410) supplement the regime regulating the remuneration of directors of listed companies. Finally, the IPCs regularly produce non-binding guidance for their members on directors' remuneration to assist them in deciding whether to vote in favour of or against shareholder resolutions on the matter.

The issue of excessive remuneration for directors of listed companies has once again risen to the top of the political agenda in the UK. Not least because this time institutional investors have joined in the criticism. In response to this, there have been changes to the law in the UK, which came into force on 1 October 2013, introducing a much more rigorous regime of transparency and shareholder control.

In the EU, recent efforts to control excessive remuneration have concentrated on the financial services industry, including a currently hotly disputed proposal to put a cap on bonuses paid to bankers.

8.4.2   Nature of the CA 2006 rules and the 2008 Regulations

The latest version of the CA 2006 rules and the 2008 Regulations apply in respect of financial years beginning on or after 1 October 2013.

The CA 2006 rules and the 2008 Regulations (that part which applies to remuneration) apply to 'quoted companies', which are defined by s 385(2) of the CA 2006 as including not only companies admitted to the Official List and the Main Market (referred to as 'listed companies' in this book, see **1.3** above), but also companies listed on a market in an EEA Member State and NYSE and NASDAQ in the USA. The scope of the CA 2006 rules and the 2008 Regulations is therefore wider than the scope of the Listing Rules and the UK CGC (see **8.3.5** above). The CA 2006 rules and the 2008 Regulations do not, however, apply to companies quoted on AIM.

8.4.3   Key features

The CA 2006 rules have three key requirements, set out below. Any director of a company which fails to comply with these requirements will be guilty of an offence under the CA 2006 and liable to a fine. A director can also be personally liable to the company for any loss it suffers under s 437 of the CA 2006 for any false or misleading statements in the report, or an omission from it, if he knew or was reckless as to whether the statement was false or misleading, or knew the omission to be a dishonest concealment of a material fact.

8.4.3.1   Directors' remuneration report

Under s 420 of the CA 2006, the company must produce an annual directors' remuneration report (DRR) which contains the information required by Sch 8 to the 2008 Regulations, made under s 421 and s 422A(4) of the CA 2006, in the form prescribed by the Regulations. The information which the report must disclose is considerable, and goes beyond the disclosure requirements of both the Listing Rules and the UK CGC. The DRR has two parts, an annual report on remuneration and a directors' remuneration policy.

Annual report on remuneration

This must set out the directors' actual remuneration for the financial year in a specified table form. It must include a single figure for total remuneration for each director together with a breakdown for salary, taxable benefits (eg expenses), annual bonus, long-term performance related awards (eg shares) and pension benefits. Each director's remuneration figures, including the total, are to be listed on a single line in the table for ease of comparison. The preceding year's figures must also be included. The company can use a separate table for the NEDs. Additional comparative graphs and tables must also be included (eg comparing the CEO's remuneration to company performance).

The annual report must also include a statement of how the directors' remuneration policy (see below) is being implemented for the coming year and details of the required shareholder votes (see **8.4.3.3** below) together with the board's response to a significant negative vote.

Directors' remuneration policy

This must be drawn up and included in the annual report when it is to be voted upon by the shareholders, which must be at least once every three years (see **8.4.3.3** below). Again there are rules as to the content and presentation of the information in the policy. For example, for each of the elements of remuneration mentioned in the table in the annual report, the policy must address how that element supports the company's short- and long-term objectives, and the policy must contain details of how termination payments for loss of office will be approached.

The report forms part of the annual report and accounts and must be filed at Companies House (CA 2006, s 439).

8.4.3.2   Audit of DRR

Under s 497 of the CA 2006, the company's auditors must, in addition to auditing the company's accounts and financial information, audit the DRR and state in its report to shareholders whether the information set out in Pt 3 of Sch 8 to the 2008 Regulations relating to the directors' single total remuneration figure, pension benefits, payments for loss of office and other specified matters in the report has been properly prepared in accordance with the CA 2006.

This is of course part of the control mechanism on listed companies to ensure that they reveal all the necessary information correctly.

8.4.3.3   Shareholder approval

Every listed company must send a copy of its annual accounts and reports (including, under CA 2006, s 471(3), the DRR) to every shareholder (CA 2006, s 423). The company must then table the DRR at a general meeting (CA 2006, s 437). Two separate shareholder votes need to be considered, one for each part of the DRR.

Annual report on remuneration

Once a year the company must obtain approval of the annual report on remuneration (by ordinary resolution) of the shareholders (CA 2006, s 439). Note that this requirement does not mean that any specific director's service contract is conditional upon shareholder approval (CA 2006, s 439). If shareholders do not approve the annual report on remuneration, the effect is advisory only. In other words, the board can ignore the vote. Although it does have other consequences, both practical and legal, as explained below.

Directors' remuneration policy

Under s 439A of the CA 2006, at least once every three years the shareholders must hold a binding vote by ordinary resolution on the directors' remuneration policy for the company, or sooner if it wishes to alter the policy.

Companies must have received approval for their remuneration policy by the end of their first financial year commencing on or after 1 October 2013. In other words, a company with its year end at 31 December 2013 will need to hold its first vote by 31 December 2014 at the latest (although in practice it is likely to hold it at the AGM in early 2014).

According to BIS, if the ordinary resolution is not passed, the company can either:

(a)   continue to use the previously approved policy;

(b)   continue with the previous policy and seek shareholder approval of specific remuneration; or

(c)   put a revised policy forward for a vote at a later GM (after the AGM).

Once the company has received approval for its new remuneration policy, any obligation to make a payment that would be in contravention of the policy will have no effect under s 226E(1) of the CA 2006. If, however, a payment has already been made, it is deemed to be held by the director on trust for the company, and any director who authorised the payment will be jointly and severally liable to indemnify the company for any loss resulting from the making of the payment under s 226E(2) of the CA 2006.

Note also that under s 439A(2) of the CA 2006, if the ordinary resolution on shareholders approval of the directors' remuneration report is not passed, it will need to put the directors' remuneration policy back to the shareholders the following year for re-approval in a binding vote.

It remains to be seen how shareholders and companies will react to these powers. Institutional investors have become much more active in this area in light of a public outcry at the bloated bonuses and remuneration packages of some directors of listed companies even when the companies' share price had dropped sharply.

8.4.3.4   Further measures

There are additional measures which apply to and are being considered for certain financial services companies including banks (some of which are listed on the Main Market). For example, the FCA Remuneration Code requires such companies to have in place remuneration policies that are consistent with effective risk management. This code of practice is designed to ensure that these companies' boards of directors focus more closely both on ensuring that the total amount distributed by a firm is consistent with good risk management and sustainability, and that individual compensation practices provide the right incentives. The code was introduced in an attempt to try and limit the remuneration policies which encourage excessive risk-taking and which are believed to have played a significant role in provoking the global financial crisis in 2007/08.

Boards wake up to a shareholder Spring

By Kate Burgess and Dan McCrum

A new mood of militancy is bowling through this year's season of public get-togethers between companies and their shareholders. And it is extraordinary for several reasons.

For decades annual meetings have been polite affairs. The big institutional insurance and pension fund managers, who own the bulk of shares, usually back management having thrashed out concerns privately long before they reach the ballot box.

Not this year. There has been a breakdown in discussions with several boards after institutions accused them of persistently rewarding executives with multimillion-pound bonuses despite anaemic performances. This comes against a backdrop of deepening anxieties about jobs, wages, and returns on savings. Shareholders have simply lost patience with persistently poor returns over five years.

This week investors in Aviva refused to back the UK insurer's pay plans for top executives. It is only the fourth FTSE 100 company to lose the vote in Britain's decade-long history of having a say on pay.

The backlash started against banks paying large chunks of profits to staff. Just over half of Citigroup's shareholders refused to back its remuneration scheme last month. Then swaths of UBS' shareholders this week voted against the management's performance and its pay plans.

In the UK, nearly a third of Barclays' investors refused to back its pay report, despite a last-minute dash to deflect shareholder anger by publicly promising to boost dividends and cut the bonus of its chief executive Bob Diamond.

One seasoned adviser to Barclays remarked: "After that, Barclays remuneration committee meetings will never be the same again".

And it is not hedge funds, activist arbitrageurs or corporate governance nuts that are leading the protests. "This is the City turning on the City. That is what is so remarkable about this so-called shareholder spring," says one UK-based proxy adviser.

Those rebelling are long-term corporate backers such as BlackRock, Invesco, Aviva's investment arm and Standard Life. Now they are taking the battle beyond the banks to other companies and other countries.

In Europe, the backlash over executive pay is still largely confined to the banks. But Susannah Haan, secretary-general of the Federation of European Issuers, says: "European companies understand it is coming".

So far the uprising has cost two UK chief executives their jobs. Two weeks ago David Brennan, chief executive of AstraZeneca, bowed to pressure from the pharmaceutical group's top shareholders and stepped down at the annual meeting. This week Sly Bailey quit as chief executive of media group Trinity Mirror days before the annual meeting and after the company failed to find a compromise over her £1.7m pay package.

Investors are not going into battle lightheartedly. "Bringing these things to a head is very destabilising – for companies, employees and our investment," says the chief investment officer of one group.

But the head of another leading shareholder group says: "We are fed up with companies coming back with poorly structured pay plans year after year." Another says: "We have reached a point where we are saying we have to change the mindset and if that requires sacrificing a head, so be it."

The no-votes do not simply reflect poor communication between boards and owners, says Robert Talbut, chief investment officer of Royal London Asset Management. Nor, he adds, should the no-votes be seen as a sudden knee jerk. Instead, they reflect calls for "fundamental reform" aligning pay to performance.

Keith Skeoch, chief executive of Standard Life Investments, says: "Boards have to get away from the idea of delivering large lumps of annual income [to executives]".

Pay is also the flashpoint for wider shareholder dissatisfaction. The no-votes signal concerns about a wider board malfunction, explains Sarah Wilson, chief executive at Manifest, a voting agency. "Remuneration is the window to the soul of the company. It objectively measures the links between incentives, behaviour, strategy and outcomes," she says.

The sudden burst of protest has in part been driven by the US where investors have had an advisory vote on pay for two years.

Last year 41 companies' pay plans were turned down within the Russell 3000 index. So far this year, eight have suffered the same fate, with the Citi vote setting a new high water mark.

"The Citi vote was electrifying. It shook us all up big time," says an EU-based investor. It shows that – contrary to the beliefs of some chief executives – US shareholders do care about pay if not aligned to performance.

Bank boards in the US, UK and Europe redoubled attempts to allay investor concerns over bonuses, says ISS, a proxy voting adviser. The say on pay in the US "has stiffened the sinews of shareholders and regulators and the contagion is spreading to other territories, such as Australia, South Africa and Europe," says Tom Gosling, pay consultant at PwC.

Even without the US impetus, many shareholders in Europe who have long had a vote on remuneration reports have been spoiling for a fight. Politics has been driving pay up the agenda amid criticism that investors failed to act like owners and did not curb the outsize executive incentives blamed for fuelling the financial crisis.

In 2010 the European Commission issued a green paper on the governance and pay at banks querying "the effectiveness of corporate governance rules based on the presumption of effective control by shareholders". Confidence in the model "has been severely shaken, to say the least," it said.

That year the UK came up with the Stewardship Code setting out a blueprint for enhancing shareholders' engagement with companies.

Mr Skeoch of Standard Life says the code has galvanised shareholders. "Investors are a lot more joined up about issues. They are much more prepared to vote to signal intentions – and they will do so internationally."

The code has not, however, staved off government intervention. UK politicians are proposing to make the vote on pay binding. Shareholders do not much like the idea but recognise the political will behind it, given the widening gap between ordinary workers' pay and bosses' bonuses.

As one investor comments: "Boards can't sack lots of people and then immediately come back with a pay rise for executives. Consciously or unconsciously it is distasteful."

But some shareholders resent being squeezed between what one described as "unembarrassable" boards and policy makers who expect investors to act as board consciences.

Ms Wilson from Manifest adds: "Shareholders don't want to micromanage or set pay. That is not their job. This is about stiffening the resolve of remuneration committees."

So will companies continue to suffer public beatings? We've seen these shareholder springs before. In 2009, 59 per cent of shareholders voted Shell's pay plans down. But the threatened wider revolt never materialised as corporate returns recovered.

"Is the trend here to stay?" asks Amra Balic, head of corporate governance for Europe Middle East and Africa at BlackRock. "It depends on whether companies learn anything from this year's experience."

Source: *Financial Times*, 4 May 2012

8.5 INSTITUTIONAL INVESTORS

As explained at **8.3.6.1** above, it is really the institutional investors (see **2.6.2**) who enforce the UK CGC by making life difficult for those companies who do not comply. Regulators are looking to these investors to assist listed companies in achieving better corporate governance.

8.5.1 UK Stewardship Code

As part of the review of corporate governance in the UK and the subsequent introduction of the UK CGC, the ISC's Code on the Responsibilities of Institutional Investors formed the basis of a new voluntary code published by the FRC, the UK Stewardship Code (see the FRC's website, www.frc.org.uk).

The purpose of the Stewardship Code is to improve corporate governance and long-term returns to shareholders through promoting better dialogue between shareholders and the boards of directors of listed companies. The Stewardship Code applies to firms who manage assets on behalf of institutional investors, but the FRC encourages all institutional investors to comply. As with the UK CGC, the Stewardship Code operates on a 'comply or explain' basis. Institutional investors should provide a statement on their website of how they have applied the Stewardship Code and, if not, why not.

The key principles cover public disclosure of policies on stewardship responsibilities, managing conflicts of interest, monitoring investee companies, guidelines on when to escalate activities as a shareholder, to act with other shareholders where appropriate, voting policies and to report periodically on stewardship and voting activities. The latest version is dated 28 September 2012.

The ICSA has published guidance on its website entitled Enhancing Stewardship Dialogue. It is intended to provide practical advice on creating a more meaningful dialogue between companies and institutional investors on strategy and long-term performance.

8.5.2 Investment Protection Committees

The global financial crisis has led to an increased awareness of the importance of good corporate governance. One side-effect has been an increase in shareholder activism, particularly by institutional investors, and greater turnout and voting at listed companies' AGMs. Certain IPCs, such as the ISC, NAPF and PIRC, publish their corporate governance expectations and circulate them to shareholders and listed companies. Recent examples include:

(a) 'The Responsibilities of Institutional Shareholders and Agents – Statement of Principles' and 'The Code on the Responsibilities of Institutional Investors', published by the Institutional Shareholders' Committee in June 2007 and November 2009 respectively and available from the Institutional Voting Information Service (IVIS) website.

The IVIS website also offers a subscription service, where reports including recommendations for voting at AGMs are provided. A decision is reached dependent on the listed company's compliance with the ABI Guidelines and the UK CGC.

(b) 'Corporate Governance Policy and Voting Guidelines', published in November 2013 by NAPF, the UK representative body for pension providers, on its website.

(c) 'Shareholder Voting Guidelines', 17th edn, published in February 2013 by PIRC.

(d) 'The ABI Principles of Remuneration', published in November 2013 by the ABI.

8.6 SHAREHOLDER RIGHTS DIRECTIVE

As we have seen, better corporate governance can be achieved by greater shareholder involvement in the running of listed companies. To further this aim the EU Shareholder Rights Directive (2007/36/EC) was adopted in June 2007. It was implemented in the UK on 3

August 2009 by the Companies (Shareholders' Rights) Regulations 2009 (SI 2009/1632), which amended Pt 13 of the CA 2006, and seeks to improve the way that companies trade on regulated markets in the EU by improving shareholder information and rights to participate in general meetings. The Directive applies to companies on the Main Market but not to those on AIM. The most important rights are set out below.

8.6.1 Notice period for general meetings

The CA 2006 allowed general meetings of listed companies (not being the AGM) to be held on not less than 14 clear days' notice. Under a new s 307A the notice period must be 21 clear days unless:

(a)   the company offers all shareholders the right to vote electronically (which can be met by the company enabling all shareholders to appoint a proxy via a website); and

(b)   shareholders pass a special resolution each year at the AGM resolving that only 14 clear days' notice is required for such meetings,

in which case the notice period can be 14 clear days.

Some IPCs have produced guidance on this provision. For example, the National Association of Pension Funds (NAPF) has issued guidance on when it will consider the use of a 14-day notice period for listed companies' general meetings to be acceptable, instead of the 21-day period.

Despite the fact that, until this change, general meetings to consider ordinary resolutions only required 14 days' notice, NAPF has adopted a restrictive position, stating that the 14-day period should only be used in limited circumstances and for time-sensitive matters where its use would be in the interests of shareholders as a whole. NAPF suggests that shareholders vote against any resolution proposed at a 14-day notice meeting if the use of this shorter notice period has not been adequately justified, or the shareholders need more time to consider their voting decision due to the complexity of the matters proposed. However, it should not prevent a meeting being called on 14 days' notice to approve a transaction with significant time pressures.

When companies propose the resolution to enable meetings to be held on 14 days' notice, NAPF also requires a statement in the AGM notice of 'the circumstances in which a short notice meeting may be called'. NAPF members should vote in favour of the enabling resolution as long as satisfactory language is included in the AGM circular.

PIRC, in its UK Shareholder Voting Guidelines, also states that it will not support meetings held on the shorter notice period if there is a lack of justification and the proposals are complex.

8.6.2 Contents of notice

The following additional information must now be included in the notice calling a meeting of a listed company (s 337(3) for (f)(ii) and (iii) below and s 311(2) for the remainder):

(a)   details of the website containing the information relating to the general meeting (see **8.6.3** below);

(b)   a statement that the right to vote is by reference to the Register of Members and the time when the right to vote will be determined;

(c)   details of how to attend and vote including deadlines;

(d)   details of forms for appointing proxies;

(e)   where the company allows voting in advance or electronic voting then the procedure for doing so; and

(f)   if the AGM notice is sent out more than six weeks before the meeting it must contain a statement about the shareholders' rights to:

  (i) ask questions at the meeting (see **8.6.4** below);

  (ii) give notice of a resolution at the meeting; and

  (iii) include a matter in the business of the meeting (see **8.6.5** below).

8.6.3 Publication of information on a website

Section 311A requires a listed company to publish certain specified information in advance of the meeting on a website on or before the date on which notice of a meeting is given including the matters set out in the notice itself and details of the company's share capital. The information must be kept on the website for at least two years.

After the meeting s 341(1A) requires additional information about poll votes to be posted on the website, such as the number of votes for and against and abstentions.

8.6.4 Right to ask questions

There is a new right, under s 319A, for shareholders to ask questions at a meeting which the company must cause to be answered unless an exception applies. The exceptions include if it would involve revealing confidential information and if it is undesirable in the interests of the company or good order of the meeting.

8.6.5 Right to requisition a resolution

In addition to the existing right of shareholders (holding either at least 5% of the voting rights of the company or being at least 100 in number owning shares with an average paid-up capital of at least £100 per shareholder) to requisition a resolution at an AGM, they have a new right in s 338A to require the company to include 'a matter' (not being a resolution) in the business of the AGM.

8.6.6 Appointment of proxies

The company must provide an electronic address for the return of proxies (s 333A). Section 327(A1) and s 330(A1) require the appointment and termination respectively of a proxy by a shareholder in a listed company to be in writing. This can be done by electronic means.

8.7 WOMEN ON BOARDS

In 2010, only 12.5% of FTSE 100 directors were female, and 21% of FTSE 100 companies had no women on their boards (producing rather predictable headlines in the UK press about there not being enough women on top). As part of the UK Government's strategy to increase the number of women in the boardrooms of listed companies, the UK Government commissioned Lord Davies (note the gender) to conduct a review. He produced a number of recommendations in his report with the target of improving the gender balance on the boards of FTSE 100 and FTSE 250 companies to 25% by 2015.

As at October 2013, the proportion had risen to 19% for FTSE 100 companies with just five all-male boards (including, not without irony, the London Stock Exchange Group plc). This improvement has been achieved through measures such as the leading executive search firms launching a voluntary code of conduct to meet the 25% goal. It is worth noting that, although the trend is very encouraging, the vast majority of new positions have been as part-time non-executive directors (NEDs).

Also, the UK CGC was amended to require a section in the listed company's annual report to describe its policy on board diversity together with other gender-related provisions.

The European Commission has taken a series of measures to try and increase the representation of women on the boards of listed companies voluntarily throughout the EU. Indeed it was in response to EU proposals that the UK instructed Lord Davies to conduct his review. However, frustration at the very slow pace of change led to the European Commission adopting a proposal for a Directive aimed at improving the gender balance on the boards of listed companies in November 2012. A minimum target of 40% of women (or 'members of the under-represented sex' as the Directive puts it in gender-neutral language) NEDs by 2018 for listed companies is proposed. However, it is not a binding 40% quota as such but an obligation on listed companies to put in place procedures to achieve the 40% level. A target for executive directors would, however, be entirely voluntary for the listed companies. Some in the European Parliament feel that the Directive does not go far enough, but in the Council a number of Member States are resistant to the idea of binding quotas even for NEDs, including, of course, the UK. Negotiations between the EU institutions are continuing at the time of writing.

8.8   FUTURE DEVELOPMENTS

Unsurprisingly there has been much soul-searching by governments and regulators as to why existing corporate governance rules were so ineffective in preventing the global financial crisis. Given the role of listed companies in contributing to the crisis, especially those in the financial services industry, and the size of these companies and their importance to the economy, a plethora of reviews has been and continues to be undertaken in the UK, by the EU and elsewhere, all with one aim in mind – never again. A summary of some of the reviews affecting UK listed companies follows. One consequence of these reviews is that amendments to existing rules and legislation and the creation of new rules are expected in the coming year and beyond. As lawyers, you will of course be called upon to advise listed companies of the changes. It is therefore imperative that you keep a beady eye on developments in this area.

8.8.1   UK CGC

The FRC announced in November 2013 that it will be consulting on aspects of the UK CGC and replacing its Internal Control: Guidance to Directors with new guidance entitled 'Integrated Code Guidance' (IGC). These changes would affect rules and guidance on going concerns, risk management and internal controls. A new version of the UK CGC is expected to come into force on 1 October 2014 together with the new IGC subject to the results of the consultation.

The FRC is also consulting on whether to change the UK CGC's provisions in light of the new regime for reporting directors' remuneration (see **8.4** above). Any changes would be incorporated into the updated version of the UK CGC expected on 1 October 2014. You will find details on the FRC's website, www.frc.org.uk.

8.8.2   EU corporate governance

The European Commission has published a Green Paper to strengthen corporate governance in financial institutions. It has since issued a feedback statement of the responses received, but so far has not produced any proposal.

8.8.3   UK Government review

BIS announced in October 2010 the first stage in a review of corporate governance in the UK in which views are sought on whether the boards of directors of listed companies and their shareholders have a sufficiently long-term view of their development. Improvements to governance of directors' remuneration are also considered. Following the consultation, BIS appointed Professor Kay in June 2011 to conduct a review on the effect of equity markets on the long-term competitive performance and governance of UK listed companies. His report was published in July 2012 and his proposed reforms include the following:

(a) Long-term performance incentives for directors should only be provided in the form of shares to be held at least until the director has retired.

(b) Amendments should be made to the UK Stewardship Code, focusing on strategic issues.

(c) An independent investors' forum should be established.

(d)   Directors should consult major long-term investors over significant board appointments.

In November 2013, the House of Commons BIS Committee published the Government's response to the BIS Committee's report following its inquiry into the Kay Review. The Government agrees with the BIS Committee's recommendation that the Government should play an active role in ensuring progress to deliver the Kay Review recommendations. The Government has not ruled out legislative or regulatory measures to bring about these changes but, in many areas, the Government believes that the development of best practice and cultural change is preferable to additional regulation.

The Government intends to publish a more detailed progress report in summer 2014.

CHAPTER 9

THE FINANCIAL SERVICES AND MARKETS ACT 2000 AND THE FINANCIAL SERVICES ACT 2012

9.1 BACKGROUND

The Financial Services and Markets Act 2000 (FSMA 2000) came into force on 1 December 2001. At this point the FSA became the single regulator for the financial services industry. On 1 April 2013 the majority of the Financial Services Act 2012 (FSA 2012) came into force. This resulted in a fundamental overhaul of the system of financial services regulation in the UK. The UK Government introduced the reforms following a thorough post-mortem into the causes of the global financial crisis in 2007/08 which, aside from the deepest recession since World War II, resulted in some of the UK's biggest banks (Lloyds TSB, HBOS (no longer in existence) and Royal Bank of Scotland) being taken into public ownership to prevent them from collapsing.

The single regulator, the FSA, was generally felt to have been 'asleep on its watch' in the years leading up to the crisis. It became known for its light touch regulatory approach. As one senior regulator put it, 'the whole culture of the system fell apart to "anything goes, as long as the compliance officer doesn't say no".' It has been replaced by three new regulators, the Financial Policy Committee (FPC), the Prudential Regulation Authority (PRA) and the Financial Conduct Authority (FCA). The FPC is a committee of the Bank of England and its role is to protect and enhance the stability of the financial system in the UK. The intention is that it spots and neutralises threats to the UK financial system (such as an asset bubble) before they become damaging. Operating at the macro-economic level, the FPC does not therefore regulate individual firms. You can find out more about the FPC at its website www.bankofengland.co.uk/financialstability.

The PRA regulates financial services institutions which are deemed to be systemically important to the UK economy. This covers banks, building societies, insurance companies and certain investment firms such as credit unions. The PRA is currently regulating approximately 1,400 such entities. You can find out more about the PRA at its website www.bankofengland.co.uk/pra.

The FCA has a multi-faceted role. It is responsible for:

(a) the conduct of business regulation of all regulated firms (including those authorised by the PRA);

(b) the regulation of all non-PRA authorised firms;

(c)   the regulation of the UK's financial markets including the Stock Exchange;

(d)   fighting financial crime;

(e)   the regulation of consumer credit (from 1 April 2014); and

(f)   a number of other roles as set out in the FSMA 2000.

The FCA is therefore of most interest to us for the purposes of this book in its role as markets regulator, since it oversees the Stock Exchange and the regulation of listed companies. In practice, a listed bank or insurance company will be regulated by both the FCA and the PRA and subject to the rules in both the FCA and PRA Handbooks. This dual regulation, widely known as 'twin peaks' regulation, aims to minimise the possibility of a financial crisis damaging the UK economy again. In light of their highly specialised nature, the roles and rules of the FPC and the PRA are beyond the remit of this book.

You can access the PRA's rules (the PRA Handbook) online at http://fshandbook.info/FS/html/PRA and the FCA's (the FCA Handbook) online at http://fshandbook.info/FS/html/FCA.

The FCA has also signalled a change in approach to regulation with a more 'hands on' style. As the head of the FCA, Michael Wheatley, put it in an interview to the *Financial Times* on 1 April 2013, 'I characterise it as a move away from looking in the rear-view mirror. The conversations will be much more geared towards… tell us about your growth plans; where do you see your business moving to over the next six months [and] where do you see the risks in those areas?'

9.2   THE FCA'S OBJECTIVES

Some of the provisions of the FSMA 2000 are complex. They are easier to understand if you consider them in the context of the objectives set out in the Act. The FCA's strategic objective is ensuring that the relevant markets as defined in s 1F of the FSMA 2000 (including the financial markets) function well (FSMA 2000, s 1B(2)). In addition, the FCA has three operational objectives (FSMA 2000, s 1B(3)):

(a)   the consumer protection objective: to secure an appropriate degree of protection for consumers (FSMA 2000, s 1C);

(b)   the integrity objective: to protect and enhance the integrity of the UK financial system (FSMA 2000, s 1D) (which includes the Stock Exchange); and

(c)   the competition objective: to promote effective competition in the interests of consumers in the markets for regulated financial services and services provided by the recognised investment exchanges (RIEs) (which includes the Stock Exchange) (FSMA 2000, s 1E).

9.3   RELEVANCE TO PRACTICE

No corporate finance lawyer can avoid the FSMA 2000. Together with the CA 2006, the 2000 Act will be the most thumbed statute on the lawyer's desk. It affects all professional firms which carry on regulated activities, and also affects how companies, particularly listed companies, conduct their day-to-day corporate and trading activities. The lawyer will have most involvement with the following provisions of the FSMA 2000:

(a)   the general prohibition on carrying on a regulated activity in the United Kingdom (s 19);

(b)   the financial promotion regulatory framework (s 21);

(c)   the rules relating to the official listing of securities (Pt VI and in particular ss 85, 86, 87A–87Q, 90, 90A and 91); and

(d)   the market abuse regime (s 118).

This chapter considers (a) above. **Chapter 12** considers financial promotion; **Chapter 6** explores the rules of the FSMA 2000 relating to the listing of securities; and **Chapter 10** considers market abuse.

9.4 THE GENERAL PROHIBITION ON CARRYING ON A REGULATED ACTIVITY

Lawyers must be aware of the general prohibition in s 19 of the FSMA 2000 not only so that they can advise their clients accordingly, but also so that they can ensure that neither they nor their law firm breach that section.

9.4.1 The general prohibition

Section 19 of the FSMA 2000 prohibits any person from carrying on a regulated activity in the United Kingdom unless he is:

(a) an authorised person; or

(b) an exempt person.

This is known as the 'general prohibition'. Contravention of the general prohibition is a criminal offence (s 23). Any agreement which results from a breach of s 19 will be unenforceable (s 26). A company which enters into an agreement in breach of s 19 can be wound up in the public interest by the FCA (*Digital Satellite Warranty Cover Ltd v FSA* [2011] EWCA Civ 1413).

9.4.2 Regulated activities

The general prohibition relates to the carrying on of a 'regulated activity'. What is a regulated activity? The actual definition is provided by s 22 of the FSMA 2000. It is:

> an activity of a specified kind which is carried on by way of business and:
>
> (a) relates to an investment of a specified kind; or
>
> (b) in the case of an activity of a kind which is also specified for the purposes of this paragraph, is carried on in relation to property of any kind.
>
> An activity is also a regulated activity if it is an activity of a specified kind which is carried on by way of business and relates to:
>
> (a) information about a person's financial standing, or
>
> (b) the setting of a specified benchmark.

This is not particularly helpful. Schedule 2 to the Act, together with a number of statutory instruments, including the Financial Services and Markets Act 2000 (Regulated Activities) Order 2001 (SI 2001/544) ('Regulated Activities Order 2001') (as amended over 15 times!), seeks to clarify the definition. Schedule 2 to the FSMA 2000 provides examples of regulated activities, and the Regulated Activities Order 2001 details the meaning of specified activities (Pt II) and specified investments (Pt III). In practice, recourse should be made to these sources. However, for our purposes it is more useful to consider a few of the more common examples of 'regulated activities' which a corporate finance lawyer might encounter, namely those relating to investments (such as shares). The regulated activities include:

(a) dealing in investments (Regulated Activities Order 2001, Chapters IV and V) – this includes dealing as principal or agent;

(b) arranging deals in investments (Regulated Activities Order 2001, Chapter VI) – this includes making arrangements with a view to another person buying or selling shares;

(c) managing investments (Regulated Activities Order 2001, Chapter VII) – this includes managing someone else's shares;

(d) advising on investments (Regulated Activities Order 2001, Chapter XII) – this includes giving advice to someone buying or selling shares. It will not include general advice in relation to an investment, or merely explaining the implications of exercising rights. So, for example, explaining the meaning of technical jargon, or advising how to complete an application form will not amount to advising on investments. (It could, however, still amount to arranging deals in investments – see (b) above.)

The definition of 'regulated activities' is very wide. The prohibition prevents any person carrying on a regulated activity, unless that person is an authorised person or an exempt person. So who are these persons?

9.4.3   Authorised person

Section 31(1) of the FSMA 2000 defines an 'authorised person'. The most common example of an authorised person is someone who has obtained permission from the FCA or PRA (depending on the type of business – see **9.1** above) to carry on regulated activities (under Pt IV of the Act), such as an investment bank seeking to act as a sponsor or broker (see **Chapter 4**). Part IV of the Act contains the detail of how such permission is obtained. From the lawyer's point of view, however, the important issue is that, unless a client is an authorised person or an exempt person, it will be prohibited from carrying out any regulated activity, and the lawyer must advise the client to instruct an authorised person (or, more rarely, an exempt person) to carry out the activity instead.

9.4.4   Exempt person

A person is exempt if he has been granted an exemption order under s 38(1) of the FSMA 2000, or is exempt as an 'appointed representative' under s 39(1) of the Act. In practice, exempt persons are encountered rarely. However, the most common 'exempt person' with which lawyers will be familiar is any RIE or recognised clearing house pursuant to s 285 of the FSMA 2000. For example, in certain circumstances (see s 285(2)) the Stock Exchange as an RIE will be exempt from the general prohibition.

9.5   THE FINANCIAL SERVICES ACT 2012

As stated at **9.1** above, the FSA 2012 implemented the substantial changes to the FSMA 2000. In addition, Pt 7 of the FSA 2012 repealed the former offences of misleading statements under s 397 of the FSMA 2000 and replaced them with new offences in ss 89–91 of the FSA 2012. These are very important as they are criminal offences punishable by imprisonment and directly cover the activities of listed companies and their directors. It is therefore essential that the corporate finance lawyer is able to advise in relation to them. In this book we will only be considering the first two offences of misleading statements (s 89) and misleading impressions (s 90). The third offence (s 91) sets out offences for misleading statements and impressions in relation to benchmarks, which currently only applies to LIBOR, a benchmark for interest rates. As such, it does not relate directly to the content of this book.

9.5.1   Misleading statements

9.5.1.1   The criminal offence

Section 89 of the FSA 2012 provides that it is a criminal offence for a person either to:

(a)   make a statement which he *knows* to be false or misleading in a material respect; or

(b)   make a statement which is false or misleading in a material respect, being reckless as to whether it is; or

(c)   dishonestly conceal any material facts whether in connection with a statement made by that person or otherwise (s 89(1))

if the person makes the statement or conceals the facts with the intention of inducing, or is reckless as to whether making it or concealing them may induce another person to:

(i)   enter into, or offer to enter into, or refrain from entering or offering to enter into a *relevant agreement*, or

(ii)   exercise, or refrain from exercising, any rights conferred by a *relevant investment* (s 89(2)).

Note that the person who is induced does not have to be the recipient of the statement.

9.5.1.2   'Relevant agreement'

A relevant agreement is defined by s 93(3) of the FSA 2012. The definition refers to 'specified kinds of activity', which are contained in art 2 of the Financial Services Act 2012 (Misleading Statements and Impressions) Order 2013 (SI 2013/637) ('Misleading Statements Order'). An example of a relevant agreement is an agreement to sell (or not sell) shares.

9.5.1.3   'Relevant investment'

A relevant investment is defined by s 93(5) of the FSA 2012. Reference is made to 'specified kinds of investment', which are contained in art 4 of the Misleading Statements Order. Shares and bonds are examples of relevant investments.

9.5.1.4   'Reckless'

'Reckless' includes not only someone not giving any thought to the accuracy of a statement, but also someone making a statement when he is aware that he should first make some enquiries as to the accuracy of the statement yet fails to make such enquiries (provided those enquires would have revealed that the statement was false or misleading).

9.5.1.5   The Disclosure and Transparency Rules

Failure to comply with the DTRs, and in particular the general obligation of disclosure set out at DTR 2.2.1R (see **7.5.1**), may constitute the dishonest concealment of material facts for the purpose of s 89 (see **9.5.1.1(b)**).

9.5.1.6   Example

The most common s 89 scenario which a corporate finance lawyer will encounter is where a client makes a misleading statement so that shareholders continue to buy, or do not sell, shares, when if the statement was actually truthful, those shareholders might be tempted not to buy, or to sell, their shares.

There have been no cases under the FSA 2012 yet. Under its predecessor, s 397 of the FSMA 2000, the former chief executive and former finance director of a software company called AIT were convicted for publicly issuing a statement on the company's turnover and profits knowing it to be untrue. The former chief executive was sentenced to three and a half years' imprisonment (reduced to 18 months on appeal). The former finance director was sentenced to two years' imprisonment (reduced to 9 months on appeal).

In another case in June 2011, Stuart Pearson, the CEO of an AIM-quoted company, who was found guilty of making misleading statements about the company's assets contrary to s 397, was sentenced to 12 months' imprisonment and disqualified as a director for five years.

9.5.2   Misleading impressions

9.5.2.1   The criminal offence

This is an offence under s 90 of the FSA 2012. Section 90(1) provides that it is a criminal offence to:

(a)   do any act, or engage in any course of conduct;

(b)   which creates a false or misleading impression;

(c)   as to the market in, or the price or value of, any relevant investment (see **9.5.1.3**);

(d)   if that person intends to:

(i)   create that impression, and

(ii)   by creating the impression, to induce another person to acquire, dispose of, subscribe for or underwrite the investments or to refrain from doing so; and/or

(iii)   is misleading or reckless as to whether it is, and the person intends to produce the results in s 90(4) or is aware that creating the impression is likely to produce any of the results in s 90(4).

The results in s 90(4) are the making of a gain for that person or another person, or the causing of loss to another person or the exposing of another person to the risk of loss.

9.5.2.2   Examples

One scenario in which this offence might arise is as follows. Bidder plc plans to make a takeover offer for Target plc. It therefore seeks to build up a stake in Target plc (see **Chapter 21**). Target plc suspects that Bidder plc is going to make a bid for it, and is not pleased. It arranges for its associate companies to buy shares in Target plc, so that the share price of Target plc rises, which makes Bidder plc's stakebuilding exercise more costly. Bidder plc will have to pay more for its stake. This contravenes s 90 of the FSA 2012, because Target plc has deliberately created a misleading impression in the shares of Target plc with the intention of making Bidder plc refrain from dealing in the shares of Target plc.

Two *Daily Mirror* journalists were found guilty of conspiracy to commit a similar offence under a forerunner to s 90 of the FSA 2012. The journalists bought shares in listed companies and then tipped them as a buy in their column in the *Daily Mirror*, 'City Slickers'. The share price rose post-publication and the two men then sold the shares, making a profit. They were aided by a third person (who pleaded guilty to the same charge), who used Internet message boards to stimulate interest in the same companies. As an indication of how serious the offence is, one of the journalists was sentenced to six months' imprisonment, having made approximately £40,000 profit. The second, who co-operated with the investigation, made £15,000 profit and was sentenced to community service. On the steps of the court after sentencing he remarked, 'That was a close one!' The third person was sentenced to three months' imprisonment, having made £17,000.

9.5.2.3   Defence

Section 90(9) provides a defence for a person charged under s 90(1) if he can show that he reasonably believed his conduct would not create a false or misleading impression.

9.5.3   Relationship between s 89 and s 90

The provisions are not mutually exclusive. One act can give rise to charges under both provisions.

9.5.4   Sanctions

Section 92(1) of the FSA 2012 provides that the offences of making a misleading statement or creating a misleading impression are punishable by imprisonment and/or a fine. On summary conviction, the maximum sentence is 12 months and/or a fine up to the statutory maximum, and on conviction on indictment the maximum sentence is seven years and/or an unlimited fine. As mentioned in **9.5.1.6** above, a CEO was sentenced to 12 months' imprisonment and disqualified as a director for five years in June 2011.

The risk of directors breaching s 89 and s 90 by making a misleading statement in a prospectus was examined at **6.7.2.1** above. As noted in that paragraph, the verification process is used to try to ensure that s 89 and s 90 are not breached during the marketing of an IPO, and the threat of a prison sentence is usually enough to focus the directors' attention on this process.

CHAPTER 10

MARKET ABUSE

10.1 INTRODUCTION

As discussed in **Chapter 9**, the market abuse regime is one of the key features of the FSMA 2000. Part VIII (ss 118 to 131A) of the Act sets out that regime. Market abuse is a civil offence which was created by the FSMA 2000. It supplements the criminal offences of:

(a) misleading statements and misleading impressions under the FSA 2012 (see **9.5** above); and

(b) insider dealing under the CJA 1993 (see **Chapter 11**),

which target the same kind of behaviour covered by the market abuse regime.

It is one of the FCA's statutory objectives, the integrity objective (ss 1B(3) and 1D of the FSMA 2000), to protect and enhance the integrity of the UK financial system. Section 1D(2)(c) defines 'integrity' to include 'its not being affected by behaviour that amounts to market abuse'.

The enforcement of market abuse has increased significantly in recent times. In the last few years we have seen some of the world's and the UK's biggest banks driven to failure, nationalisation or a rescue takeover in the space of days by a loss of confidence expressed in part through a collapsing share price. Rumours abounded as to which institution might be next to be in trouble, and this resulted in breathtaking falls and rises in share prices as panic spread and confidence ebbed and flowed depending on the latest developments.

This presents opportunities to make huge amounts of money, not just legitimately (however morally questionable this may be) but also for the unscrupulous at a potentially devastating cost to the companies, investors, employees and ultimately economies involved. Now that the financial crisis has passed, it remains important to maintain investor confidence and stability in the markets in light of the crucial role they play in the UK economy. Tackling market abuse helps achieve this, and the FCA is expected to continue the robust approach of its predecessor.

10.1.1 The civil offence

The civil offence of market abuse was introduced so that market manipulators, who might otherwise have escaped punishment for the criminal offences referred to at (a) and (b) above, would be caught. It has, at least in theory, the following advantages over the criminal regime:

(a) it is wider in scope;

(b)   it is easier to prove. The standard of proof in criminal cases is 'beyond all reasonable doubt'. This high standard means that it is very difficult to convict anyone of insider dealing, or of making misleading statements and/or manipulating the market. To date there have been very few convictions for these offences. Market abuse, however, as a civil offence, has a lower standard of proof, namely 'on the balance of probabilities';

(c)   it assesses behaviour according to its effect rather than the intention behind it (although there is an element of intention lurking in the detail of the regime);

(d)   it can be committed by anyone – an individual or a company (contrast insider dealing, which can only be committed by an individual, see **11.7** below);

(e)   a jury is not required to try the offence; and

(f)   it is possible to settle a case of market abuse, unlike with a criminal offence, and the FCA has powers to to offer leniency to wrongdoers, to encourage co-operation where more than one individual is involved.

10.1.2   The Code of Market Conduct

Section 119 of the FSMA 2000 requires the FCA to provide guidance to market users as to what behaviour amounts to market abuse. The FCA has obliged with the Code of Market Conduct (CoMC). The CoMC confirms that the scope of market abuse is wide, and the FCA has significant power to tackle market abusers. It is not binding but it does have evidential weight. The CoMC forms Chapter 1 of the FCA Market Conduct Sourcebook (known as 'MAR'), which is part of the FCA Handbook and can be viewed under 'Business Standards' in the FCA Handbook section of the FCA's website. To follow market practice, references below to 'MAR 1' are to paragraphs of the CoMC.

The FCA also provides information periodically on the market abuse regime through its *Market Watch* publications (available on the FCA's website).

10.1.3   The Market Abuse Directive

The Market Abuse Directive (MAD) came into force in the UK on 1 July 2005, as part of the EU's FSAP.

The MAD was implemented in the UK through:

(a)   the Disclosure Rules; and

(b)   amendments to Pt VIII of the FSMA 2000 (made by the MAD Regulations 2005); and

(c)   a new version of the CoMC.

*Note that the MAD will be replaced by a new EU regime once the relevant legislation is agreed and becomes law. See further **10.8** below.*

10.2   WHAT IS MARKET ABUSE?

Market abuse, in layman's terms, is certain behaviour (see **10.3.4** below), relating to certain investments which trade, or are seeking admission to trade, on certain markets, which is deemed improper. The offence punishes those who seek to manipulate the market for their own benefit.

10.3   THE MAIN OFFENCE

Sections 118(1) and 118A(1) of the FSMA 2000 sets out the test which must be satisfied for behaviour to constitute market abuse. The behaviour of the market abuser must:

(a)   occur in the UK; and

(b)   occur in relation to:

(i)   a *qualifying investment* admitted to trading on a *prescribed market*, or

  (ii) a *qualifying investment* in respect of which a request for admission to trading on a prescribed market has been made, or

  (iii) (in the case of 'insider dealing' or 'improper disclosure' offences – see **10.3.4** below) an investment *related* to such a qualifying investment; and

(c) fall within any one or more of the types of behaviour set out at **10.3.4**.

10.3.1 Qualifying investment

This term is defined by the Financial Services and Markets Act 2000 (Prescribed Markets and Qualifying Investments) Order 2001 (SI 2001/996) ('PMQI Order 2001'), which refers to the definition of 'financial instrument' under art 1(3) of the MAD. For our purposes, note that qualifying investments include shares and bonds.

10.3.2 Prescribed market

The PMQI Order 2001 specifies the prescribed markets for the purposes of the market abuse regime. For our purposes, note that both of the Stock Exchange's markets (ie, the Main Market and the AIM) are prescribed markets. Other markets in the UK, such as ISDX, are also included.

10.3.3 Related investments

This term is defined by s 130A(3) of the FSMA 2000 as an investment whose price or value depends on the price or value of the qualifying investment. This includes more complex investments, for example an equity swap on a share traded on the Main Market.

10.3.4 The seven types of behaviour

The Court of Appeal in *Winterflood Securities Ltd v FSA* [2010] EWCA Civ 423, on appeal from the Upper Tribunal (Tax and Chancery Chamber) (on appeal from fines imposed by the FSA, the forerunner to the FCA, in June 2008 on a market maker, Winterflood, and two of its traders), has held that it is not necessary for a person to have an intention to commit market abuse under s 118. This is in keeping with MAR 1.2.3G.

Section 118(2) to (8) provide that the following types of behaviour will constitute market abuse:

Type 1: Insider dealing (s 118(2))

This is behaviour where an insider (as defined by the FSMA 2000, s 118B) deals, or attempts to deal, in a qualifying investment (see **10.3.1**) or related investment (see **10.3.3**), on the basis of inside information (see the very detailed definition at **7.5.2.1**, substituting 'qualifying investment' for 'financial instrument') relating to that investment. Further guidance is provided in MAR 1.3.

This would cover, for example, the situation where a director of a company is aware of a takeover offer which has not yet been announced, and buys shares in the company with the expectation that the share price will rise on the announcement of the offer.

In January 2010, the Court of Justice of the EU ruled in *Spector Photo Group and Van Raemdonck v Commissie voor het Bank- Financie- und Assurantiewezen (CBFA)* (Case C-45/08) that where a person has dealt while in possession of inside information, the use of that information may be presumed. In other words, the FCA in the UK does not need to show that the decision to deal was influenced by the possession of inside information; it need only demonstrate possession of inside information by an insider and dealing whilst in possession of that information. It is a rebuttable presumption, but the burden falls on the defendant to show that he was dealing legitimately.

Remember this is a type of behaviour under the civil offence of market abuse and is quite separate from the criminal offence of insider dealing referred to in **Chapter 11**.

Type 2: Improper disclosure (s 118(3))

This is behaviour where an insider (as defined by the FSMA 2000, s 118B) discloses inside information (see **7.5.2.1**, substituting 'qualifying investment' for 'financial instrument') to another person other than in the proper course of his employment, profession or duties. Further guidance is provided in MAR 1.4.

This would include, for example, a director telling a friend in the gym that her company was going to sell off a major division of the company before it was publicly announced.

Type 3: Misuse of information (s 118(4))

This is behaviour based on information *not generally available* to those using the market, but which, if available to a regular user of the market, would be, or would be likely to be, regarded by him as *relevant* when deciding the terms on which transactions in investments of the kind in question should be effected. (This 'relevant information not generally available' is sometimes abbreviated to RINGA.) The behaviour must fail the regular user test (see **10.3.5** below). Further guidance is provided in MAR 1.5. This type of behaviour may also amount to the criminal offence of insider dealing (see **Chapter 11**).

Note that this provision is due to expire on 31 December 2014 (SI 2011/2928). It will be reviewed by HM Treasury in light of the progress of the new market abuse regime at an EU level.

Note also that behaviour falls within type 3 behaviour only if it does not fall within type 1 or type 2 behaviour (s 118(4)).

'Relevant information'

The CoMC (see **10.1.2**) sets out the factors to be taken into account to determine whether information is relevant. The information must relate to matters which regular users would reasonably expect to be disclosed to market users. The CoMC also gives examples of relevant information. Of particular interest to the corporate lawyer is the example of information concerning business affairs or prospects (such as entering into a significant contract with a supplier).

'Not generally available'

The CoMC states that information is generally available if it can be obtained by research or analysis conducted by, or on behalf of, users of the market. Information notified to an RIS, or sent to a public registry such as Companies House, would be classed as generally available information.

Type 4: Manipulating transactions (s 118(5))

This is behaviour which effects a transaction (other than for legitimate reasons, in conformity with accepted market practices – as defined by s 130A(3) and MAR 1, Annex 2G) which either:

(a)   gives, or is likely to give, a false or misleading impression as to the supply of, or demand for, or as to the price of, a qualifying investment (see **10.3.1**); or

(b)   secures the prices of such an investment at an abnormal or artificial level.

This offence is most likely to be committed by a market professional, such as a trader. Further guidance is provided in MAR 1.6. It includes two specific situations:

(a)   An *abusive squeeze*. This is perhaps less interesting than it sounds. It describes a situation where a person corners the market and uses that position to distort the market.

(b)   *Price positioning*. This consists of entering into a transaction, or series of transactions, to position the price at a distorted level (that is, materially different to that which reflects the operation of usual market forces).

Type 5: Manipulating devices (s 118(6))

This is behaviour which effects transactions which employ fictitious devices or any other form of deception or contrivance. Again, this is most likely to be committed by a market professional, such as a trader. Further guidance is provided in MAR 1.7. An example of this type of behaviour is a trader who buys shares, then spreads misleading positive information about the shares to increase their price, before selling the shares at a profit (known as a 'pump and dump').

Type 6: Dissemination (s 118(7))

This is behaviour which disseminates information which gives, or is likely to give, a false or misleading impression as to a qualifying investment (see **10.3.1**), by a person who knew, or could reasonably be expected to have known, that the information was false or misleading.

Posting false information on a website about a listed company's financial position would fall under this type of behaviour.

Type 7: Distortion (s 118(8))

This is behaviour which is:

(a)   likely to give a regular user of the market a false or misleading impression as to the supply of, or demand for, or price or value of, a qualifying investment (see **10.3.1**); or

(b)   would be, or would be likely to be, regarded by a regular user of the market as behaviour that would distort, or would be likely to distort, the market in such an investment.

The behaviour must fail the regular user test (see **10.3.5** below). Further guidance is given in MAR 1.9.

By way of example, Henry Cameron, the former CEO of Sibir Energy plc, was fined £350,000 in July 2010 for breaching ss 118(7) and (8) of the FSMA 2000, for causing Sibir to make misleading announcements to the market by significantly understating payments made by Sibir to one of its largest shareholders.

Note that s 118(8) is due to expire on 31 December 2014 (SI 2011/2928). It will be reviewed by HM Treasury in light of the progress of the new market abuse regime at an EU level.

Note also that behaviour falls within type 7 (distortion) behaviour only if it does not fall within type 4, 5 or 6 behaviour (s 118(4)).

10.3.5   The regular market user test

10.3.5.1   Application

The test applies only to type 3 (misuse of information) and type 7 (distortion) behaviour.

10.3.5.2   The test

The test is whether a regular user of the market would regard the behaviour of the person (let us call him X) as failing to observe the standard of behaviour reasonably expected of a person in X's position. If so, X has failed the regular market user test.

10.3.5.3   The regular market user

The regular market user is 'a reasonable person who regularly deals on that market in investments of the kind in question' (s 130A(3)). There are difficulties in applying this test. It is not easy to identify a hypothetical regular market user, or to identify the standards of behaviour which that user would expect of someone else. Guidance on the application of type 3 and type 7 is set out in the CoMC (see **10.3.4** above).

10.3.6 Summary

The main offence under s 118 of the FSMA 2000 is summarised in **Figure 10.1**.

10.4 THE SECONDARY OFFENCE

The main offence under Pt VIII of the FSMA 2000 is that of market abuse (under s 118), which is considered at **10.3** above. However, there is also a secondary offence under Pt VIII; that of 'requiring or encouraging market abuse'. Section 123(1)(b) of the FSMA 2000 provides that penalties can be imposed on a person (let us call him A) if, by taking or refraining from taking any action, he 'requires or encourages' another person, X, to engage in behaviour which, if engaged in by A, would amount to market abuse. This secondary offence is designed to catch those people who might otherwise circumvent the market abuse offence by asking someone else to carry out their instructions.

Further guidance is provided in MAR 1.2.22 and 1.2.23. Examples include a director, in possession of relevant and disclosable information which is not generally available, who instructs an employee to deal in qualifying investments in respect of which the information is relevant information. If the director did the dealing, it would constitute market abuse and would be an offence under s 118. Section 123 ensures that the director will still be caught, albeit under the s 123 offence of requiring or encouraging, rather than the s 118 offence of market abuse.

Figure 10.1: Section 118 flowchart

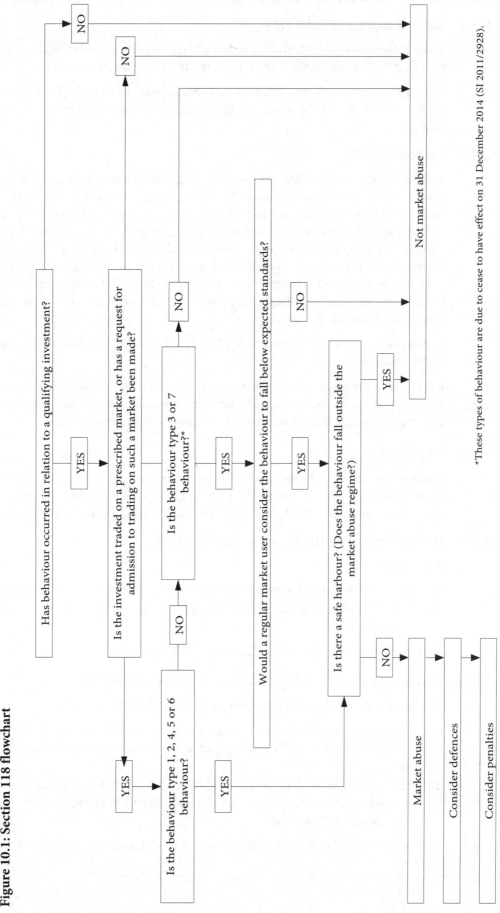

*These types of behaviour are due to cease to have effect on 31 December 2014 (SI 2011/2928).

10.5   BEHAVIOUR WHICH DOES NOT AMOUNT TO MARKET ABUSE

10.5.1   Safe harbours under the MAD

A safe harbour is a type of behaviour which will not constitute market abuse, even if it satisfies the test in s 118 of the FSMA 2000. It is therefore equivalent to an exception.

The MAD provides only two safe harbours, one relating to share buyback (s 118A(5)(b) and MAR 1.10.1G(1)) and the other relating to price stabilisation activities (s 118A(5)(b) and MAR 2).

10.5.2   Section 118A(5)

Section 118A(5) of the FSMA 2000 stipulates specific behaviour which will not amount to market abuse. It includes not only the two safe harbours referred to at **10.5.1**, but also behaviour which conforms to a rule which includes a provision to the effect that behaviour conforming with that rule does not amount to market abuse (s 118A(5)(a)). This includes the parts of the Listing Rules (LR 1.4.7R) and the Disclosure Rules (DTR 1.5.2R) which relate to a disclosure, announcement, communication or release of information. In addition, MAR 1.10.2G and MAR 1.10.3G specify that there are no FCA rules or rules in the Takeover Code (relating to takeovers, see **Chapter 21**) which permit or require a person to behave in a way which amounts to market abuse.

In practice, behaviour falling within s 118A(5) will also be referred to colloquially as falling within a 'safe harbour'.

Behaviour on the part of a person acting on behalf of a public authority in pursuit of monetary policies, policies in respect of exchange rates, the management of public debt or foreign exchange reserves will also not amount to market abuse (s 118A(5)(c)).

10.6   DEFENCES

If behaviour falls outside the market abuse regime (see **10.5** above) then it is not market abuse. However, even if behaviour falls within the regime, and is market abuse, the perpetrator may still be able to avoid any penalty, by raising a defence under s 123(2).

10.6.1   Defences to the s 118 offence of market abuse

If the market abuser, X:

(a)   believed, on reasonable grounds, that his behaviour did not amount to market abuse; or

(b)   had taken all reasonable precautions and exercised all due diligence to avoid engaging in market abuse,

then the FCA cannot impose a penalty on X (s 123(2)).

10.6.2   Defences to the s 123 offence of requiring or encouraging

If A, the person requiring or encouraging X to abuse the market:

(a)   believed on reasonable grounds that his behaviour did not require or encourage X to engage in behaviour which, if engaged in by A, would have amounted to market abuse; or

(b)   had taken all reasonable precautions and exercised all due diligence to avoid requiring or encouraging X to engage in behaviour which, if engaged in by A, would have amounted to market abuse,

then, under s 123(2) of the FSMA 2000, the FCA cannot impose a penalty on A.

10.7 SANCTIONS

If the FCA suspects that market abuse may have occurred, it can use its statutory powers to investigate the issue.

One of the biggest problems in proving market abuse is evidence. In an attempt to tackle this, the FCA requires the firms it regulates to record telephone conversations (on landlines and on company mobile phones) and other electronic communications (including e-mail, texts and instant messages) relating to client orders and the conclusion of transactions in the equity and other markets, and keep the records for six months. Although personal mobiles are exempt, authorised firms are expected to ensure that transactions are not made on personal phones.

Once market abuse has been proved, though, and no defence applies, the FCA can:

(a) choose not to act (FSMA 2000, s 123);

(b) impose an unlimited fine (s 123) (see also **3.7.4**);

(c) make a public statement that the person has engaged in market abuse (s 123). Clearly, the hope here is that 'naming and shaming' will serve as a deterrent;

(d) apply to the court for an injunction (s 381);

(e) require the person to pay back profits made, or losses avoided (s 383); or

(f) require the person to compensate any victims (s 384).

The largest fine of £17 million for market abuse and for breaches of the Listing Rules was imposed on Royal Dutch Shell in 2004. In 2013 the Upper Tribunal upheld a £8 million fine for market abuse on a Canadian company, Swift Trade Inc. The Tribunal said it was 'as serious a case as might be imagined, and there is nothing which could possibly be said by way of mitigation'. The company systematically and deliberately engaged in a form of manipulative trading activity known as 'layering' or 'spoofing' in relation to shares traded on the Stock Exchange. This is a method of trading whereby a person attempts to increase the price of shares in order to benefit from selling them at a high price and then attempts to decrease the price of the shares so that they can buy them again at a lower price. Details of current and recent investigations can be found on the FCA's website.

10.8 FUTURE DEVELOPMENTS

The European Commission has introduced changes to EU legislation in this area. In particular, it has identified gaps in the regulation of certain financial instruments and markets which it would like to see plugged. Furthermore, it considers enforcement of the current rules to be uneven across the EU and has proposed strengthening enforcement generally, introducing more harmonised standards and enhancing co-operation between national regulators. The European Commission's proposals (known as MAD II) are to replace MAD with a new Market Abuse Regulation (known as MAR) and a new Directive on Criminal Sanctions for insider dealing and market manipulation (known as CSMAD). The proposals will have to be agreed by both the European Parliament and the Council of the EU. At the time of writing, agreement had been reached on the text of MAR and negotiations had started on CSMAD. The text of MAR, however, cannot be finalised until the text of MiFID II (see **6.7.3** below) has been agreed as this will affect the scope of MAR. It therefore seems likely that the new rules will not come into force until 2016 at the earliest. The UK Government has already stated that it intends to opt out of CSMAD on the basis that it already has the offences covered in criminal law in the UK. In doing so, it is exercising a right it acquired under the Lisbon Treaty.

CHAPTER 11

INSIDER DEALING

11.1 INTRODUCTION

Part V of the Criminal Justice Act 1993 (CJA 1993) contains the insider dealing provisions. These provisions existed before the FSMA 2000 came into force. As explained at **10.1** above, the criminal offence of insider dealing overlaps considerably with the civil offence of market abuse. The market abuse regime, however, does not affect the insider dealing regime. It is therefore possible to commit both the offences of insider dealing under the CJA 1993 and market abuse under s 118 of the FSMA 2000.

Lord Lane explained the reason for the insider dealing regime very effectively in layman's terms as follows: '... the clear intention to prevent, so far as possible, what amounts to cheating when those with inside knowledge use that knowledge to make a profit in their dealing with others' (*Attorney-General's Reference (No 1 of 1988)* [1989] 2 WLR 729).

As part of its ongoing get-tough strategy for market misconduct, the FCA has been using its criminal powers of prosecution for insider dealing with vigour. There have been at least 25 convictions for insider dealing, leading to prison sentences of up to four years, and further arrests have been made (see **11.6**).

11.2 THE OFFENCE

Section 52 of the CJA 1993 provides that the offence of insider dealing can be committed in three ways, namely, if an *individual who has information as an insider*:

(a) *deals* in price-affected securities, when in possession of *inside information*;

(b) *encourages another* to deal in price-affected securities, when in possession of *inside information*, or

(c) *discloses inside information* other than in the proper performance of his employment, office or profession.

Whichever way the offence is committed, there are two common requirements, namely, an individual as an 'insider' and 'inside information'.

11.2.1 Insider

Section 57(1) of the CJA 1993 defines what it is for a person to have information as an insider. This is where a person:

(a) has information which is *inside information*;

(b)   has received that information *from an inside source*; and

(c)   he *knows* (a) and (b).

11.2.2   Inside information

Unlike the market abuse regime and the DTRs, which use the definition under s 118C of the FSMA 2000, the insider dealing regime uses the definition of 'inside information' under s 56 of the CJA 1993. This is information which:

(a)   relates to particular, rather than general, securities or companies;

(b)   is specific or precise;

(c)   has not been made public; and

(d)   is price-sensitive (that is, would be likely to have a significant effect on the price of securities, such as shares, if it were made public).

This definition has been criticised because there is not much guidance about the meaning of the terms used. Until these words are defined, or their meaning falls to be decided by the courts, they must be given their ordinary dictionary meaning. It is not clear, for example, whether a rumour which turns out to be false would be 'specific or precise' (although common sense would suggest it would not).

11.2.2.1   Particular not general

This includes information which may affect a company's prospects (which may be about the sector in which the company operates rather than about the company itself).

11.2.2.2   Specific or precise

As discussed at **11.2.2** above, there is no definition of these terms.

11.2.2.3   Not made public

If information has been made public it is not inside information. Think back to Lord Lane's comments at **11.1** above; how can someone cheat if he is using freely available information? Section 58 provides some guidance as to when information has been made public. Information which a company provides to an RIS has been made public and therefore will not be inside information. Further s 58 provides that information made available only to a section of the public can also be treated as having been made public. It is difficult to see the logic in this. Surely it is unfair if, in order to make a profit, you use information I am unable to access? There is no guidance as to what constitutes a 'section' of the public.

11.2.2.4   Price-sensitive

There is no guidance on what amounts to a 'significant effect' on price, and so this has to be considered on a case-by-case basis.

11.2.3   From an inside source

Section 57(2) provides that a person has information from an inside source if he:

(a)   is an inside source (that is, a director, employee or shareholder) of 'an issuer of securities' (for our purposes, a company (but not necessarily the company whose securities are the subject of insider dealing)); or

(b)   has access to the information because of his employment, office or profession; or

(c)   obtained the information from someone who obtained it by way of (a) or (b) above.

Persons falling within (a) and (b) are known as 'primary insiders'. Persons falling within (c) are known as 'secondary insiders', or 'tippees'. An example of a tippee is a director's relative, who overhears talk about an impending takeover bid and then invests in the target company.

11.3   THREE WAYS THE OFFENCE CAN BE COMMITTED

As explained at **11.2**, the offence can be committed in three different ways.

11.3.1   The dealing offence (s 52(1))

It is an offence to *deal* in price-affected *securities* on a *regulated market*, or by or through a *professional intermediary*.

11.3.1.1   Dealing

Section 55 of the CJA 1993 explains the meaning of 'dealing'. It includes:

(a)   the acquisition, or disposal, of securities;

(b)   any agreement to acquire securities (for example, entering into a share option agreement);

(c)   any agreement to create securities (for example, subscribing for shares), whether as principal or agent; and

(d)   procuring an acquisition or disposal of securities by any other person.

11.3.1.2   Securities

Securities are defined by s 54 of and Sch 2 to the CJA 1993. The definition is wide and includes shares, bonds, warrants and options.

11.3.1.3   Regulated market

Under powers granted by s 60 of the CJA 1993, this has been defined by the Insider Dealing (Securities and Regulated Markets) Order 1994 (SI 1994/187) as including both the Main Market and the AIM, as well as other, lesser-known UK markets, such as ISDX. Dealing on a regulated market is referred to as an 'on-market' transaction. If you or I decide to buy shares in Marks and Spencer Group plc through the Stock Exchange, that is an on-market transaction. The dealing offence is concerned with on-market transactions.

11.3.1.4   Professional intermediary

A professional intermediary is a person who carries on a business of acquiring or disposing of securities, or who otherwise acts as a professional intermediary between persons taking part in any dealing in securities (s 59). A stockbroker acting in the normal course of business will be a professional intermediary, but lawyers and accountants acting in their normal course of business will not.

> **EXAMPLE**
>
> Imagine that B plc is considering making a takeover bid for X plc, a listed company. B's investment bank acquires some shares in X plc on B's behalf, as a preliminary stake-building exercise. The shares are purchased privately, directly from a shareholder in X plc. This is known as an 'off-market' transaction. Although this acquisition has not taken place on a regulated market, B plc made the deal through a professional intermediary, the merchant bank, and therefore the deal has the potential to be within the scope of the dealing offence.

11.3.2   The offence of encouraging another to deal (s 52(2)(a))

It is not necessary for the person who is encouraged to deal either:

(a)   actually to deal; or

(b)   to realise the securities are price-affected.

A simple statement such as 'I cannot tell you why, but now is a good time to buy shares in X plc' could be caught by s 52(2)(a).

11.3.3 The disclosing offence (s 52(2)(b))

This prohibits any individual from disclosing inside information to another person other than in the proper performance of the functions of his employment, office or profession.

EXAMPLE

Imagine that X plc, a listed company, is a weapons manufacturer. X plc is about to sign a lucrative deal with the Ministry of Defence. D, a director of X plc, knows about the deal. L is the company's lawyer. B is L's brother. Over a family dinner at which much wine is consumed, L mentions to B that this deal is pending. B, D and L all buy shares in X plc on the Stock Exchange before details of the deal have been made public. Who is guilty of an offence (subject to any defences)?

(a)   D is guilty of insider dealing under s 52(1) (see **11.3.1**). He is an insider. He has inside information (he knows about the proposed takeover, which is specific information relating to X plc which has not been made public and is likely to have a significant effect on X plc's share price). D, presumably, knows that he is an insider with inside information. He received the information from an inside source (he has the information as a director of X plc). He has dealt in price-affected securities (the shares) on a regulated market (the Main Market).

(b)   L is also guilty of insider dealing under s 52(1). He is in a similar position to D, although L is an insider because he has information through having access to it by virtue of his profession.

L is also guilty of an offence under s 52(2)(b) (see **11.3.3**) as he has disclosed the information to his brother, which is not in the proper performance of his profession.

If L encouraged his brother to buy shares in X plc, L is also be guilty of an offence under s 52(2)(a) (see **11.3.2**).

L is also guilty of serious professional misconduct and liable to be punished by the Solicitors Regulatory Authority (SRA) for breaches of the SRA Code of Conduct 2011, such as breach of his duty of confidentiality.

(c)   B may also be guilty of the dealing offence under s 52(1) (see **11.3.1**). Is he an insider? He is a tippee (see **11.2.3**). The source of the information is a primary insider (his brother, a lawyer) and B knows this. B has inside information. Does B know this? If B does, he will be guilty of the dealing offence.

11.4 TERRITORIAL SCOPE

11.4.1 Dealing

Section 62(1) of the CJA 1993 provides that a person is not guilty of the dealing offence unless:

(a)   he was within the UK at the time of dealing;

(b)   the market is a UK regulated market (such as the Main Market, or AIM); or

(c)   the professional intermediary was within the UK at the time he is alleged to have committed the offence.

11.4.2 Encouraging or disclosing

Section 62(2) of the CJA 1993 provides that a person is not guilty of the encouraging or disclosing offence unless:

(a)   he was within the UK at the time of the encouragement or disclosure; or

(b)   the recipient of the encouragement or information was within the UK when he received that encouragement or information.

11.5   DEFENCES

11.5.1   General defences

Section 53 of the CJA 1993 provides defences to each of the three ways of committing the offence.

11.5.1.1   Dealing or encouraging

No offence will be committed if the defendant can prove that:

(a)   he did not expect to gain an advantage. This is a difficult defence to run. The prosecution will have proved already that he was an insider and knew he had insider information;

(b)   he believed the information had been (in the case of the dealing offence) or would be (in the case of the encouraging offence) disclosed widely enough to ensure no-one would be prejudiced; or

(c)   he would have traded anyway, even if he did not have inside information. This could be used, for example, if he had to meet urgent financial commitments.

11.5.1.2   Disclosing

No offence will be committed if the defendant can prove that:

(a)   he did not expect dealing to occur; or

(b)   he did not expect profit to result.

Again, the defence set out at (b) is a difficult defence to run once the prosecution has proved the defendant was an insider who knew he had inside information.

11.5.2   Special defences

Schedule 1 to the CJA 1993 includes some special defences relating to market-makers, market information and price stabilisation.

11.5.2.1   Market-makers

A market-maker (see **2.5.2**) has a special defence to the dealing and encouraging offences (but not the disclosing offence) if he acts in good faith in the course of his business as, or employment by, a market-maker.

11.5.2.2   Market information

There are special defences available to those who have inside information which qualifies as 'market information'. Market information is information consisting of any of the following facts:

(a)   that securities of a particular kind have been, or are to be, acquired or disposed of, or that their acquisition is under consideration or the subject of negotiation;

(b)   the number or price (or range of prices) of those securities;

(c)   the identity of those involved, or likely to be involved, in any capacity in an acquisition or disposal; or

(d)   the fact that securities of a particular kind have not been, or are not to be, acquired or disposed of.

There are two separate defences available. In each case, the defences are only available to an individual charged with dealing and/or encouraging. They are not available in relation to the disclosing offence. The defences are:

(a)   The information which the individual had as an insider was *market information* and it was *reasonable* for a person in his position to have acted as he did, despite having that information as an insider at the time. Paragraph 2(2) of Sch 1 sets out a non-exhaustive list of factors to be taken into account in determining reasonableness (the content of information, the circumstances and the capacity in which the individual first had the information and the capacity in which he now acts).

(b)   The individual acted in connection with an acquisition or a disposal which was under consideration or the subject of negotiation (or in the course of a series of such acquisitions or disposals), and with a view to *facilitating the accomplishment* of the relevant transaction(s). The individual must also show that the information he had was *market information* arising directly out of his involvement in the transaction(s) in question. This is referred to as the 'facilitation defence'. Note that there is no reasonableness element for this defence.

It may help to consider an example of the 'market information' defence.

EXAMPLE

Imagine that X plc is considering making a takeover bid for Y plc, a listed company. The directors of X plc decide that, as a preliminary to the bid, X plc should purchase shares in Y plc on the Stock Exchange. X plc's directors instruct the company's stockbrokers to buy shares in Y plc. Are the directors guilty of insider dealing?

At the time of dealing the directors are insiders. They have inside information (namely, that X plc is about to make a bid for Y plc). The directors have that information from an inside source (in their capacity as directors). They will know that they have inside information from an inside source. The directors are dealing in price-affected securities (remember that the definition of dealing includes the situation where a person procures an acquisition of securities by another, here X plc (see **11.3.1.1**)) on a regulated market (the Main Market). It would seem that they are guilty of insider dealing under s 52(1).

Nonetheless, in these circumstances, the directors may be able to rely on the market information defence if they can show they acted to facilitate the accomplishment of the takeover of Y plc, and the information they had was solely market information arising directly out of their involvement in the takeover, and not any other confidential price-sensitive information.

11.5.2.3   Price stabilisation

There is a special defence for individuals engaged in price stabilisation operations within any price stabilisation rules made under s 144(1) of the FSMA 2000. Price stabilisation is market activity undertaken to support the price of shares offered on an IPO (see **Chapter 4**) and some secondary issues (see **Chapter 17**), as there is often a disproportionately large amount of selling at these times. The defence is available as the practice is justified on policy grounds (that it encourages equity finance and shores up confidence in the market).

11.6   SANCTIONS

The offence of insider dealing is punishable in the same way as the criminal offence of making a misleading statement or manipulating the market (under the FSMA 2000 – see **9.4** above), namely by imprisonment and/or a fine. On summary conviction, the maximum sentence is six months, and on conviction on indictment the maximum sentence in seven years.

Note that s 63(2) provides that no contract shall be void or unenforceable solely because an offence has been committed under s 52.

Insider dealing may also amount to a breach of the Model Code (see **7.8** above).

The FCA has responsibility for enforcing the insider dealing provisions of the CJA 1993, and has the power to launch criminal prosecutions in its own right without the need for permission from the Secretary of State of BIS or the Director of Public Prosecutions. A challenge to this power in an action brought by three individuals who were prosecuted for insider dealing failed in the High Court in December 2008.

In the first-ever criminal prosecution for insider dealing brought by the forerunner to the FCA, the FSA, in *R v McQuoid and Melbourne* in relation to TTP Communications plc, the two defendants, one a solicitor, were sentenced to eight months' imprisonment (one suspended for 12 months) in March 2009. In June 2010, Anjam Ahmad was sentenced to 10 months' imprisonment suspended for two years, 300 hours' community service and a £50,000 fine. Mr Ahmad was the first person to take advantage of new powers granted to the FCA under the Serious Organised Crime and Police Act 2005 allowing it to offer lower sentences or immunity from prosecution for co-operating witnesses.

The article below explains one of the most egregious examples of insider dealing brought before the courts to date. In addition to the prison sentences mentioned, a confiscation order of £767,000 was subsequently made for each of Mr and Mrs Littlewood, failing payment of which an extra three years each would be added to their sentences. Mr Sa'aid was ordered to pay £640,000.

More recent prosecutions have led to the imprisonment of insider dealing 'rings' of several people working together and generally increased prison sentences. In March 2013 Richard Joseph, a former trader, was sentenced to four years imprisonment for insider dealing. He used inside information provided by the former print room manager, Ersin Mustafa, whom he paid out of the profits made from trading on this information. Mr Mustafa also provided inside information to six other men in a separate case which resulted in them receiving prison sentences of between 18 months and three-and-a-half years in July 2012. Mr Mustafa is thought to have fled to north Cyprus.

11.7   SCOPE OF THE OFFENCE

The offence of insider dealing is narrower in scope than the offence of market abuse (see **Chapter 10**). Unlike market abuse, only an individual can commit the offence of insider dealing; a company cannot (although an individual can commit the offence by requiring a company to deal). A company can, however, be convicted of aiding and abetting the offence. Anything done by an individual acting on behalf of a public sector body in pursuit of monetary policies, or policies with respect to exchange rates, the management of public debt or foreign reserves, cannot be the subject of an insider dealing offence.

As the offence is so narrow and subject to the criminal burden of proof and the vagaries of the jury system, it is difficult to convict anyone of it, and this explains the lack of prosecutions until 2008.

As one of the FSA's (the forerunner to the FCA) leading officials said in a speech on 22 May 2007 to leading financial institutions:

> Insider dealing cases are amongst the most difficult cases we are called upon to prove, they are time consuming and complex and we may not be able to establish all of the facts necessary to support an insider trading charge. Insider dealing may have been conducted by a number of defendants, involved multiple trades over a number of months and have been of a sophisticated nature. The trading may have been conducted through a number of accounts and attempts made to hide the distribution of proceeds. The investigation into such activities increasingly involves a number of foreign jurisdictions.
>
> It is rare to find a 'smoking gun' and often cases hinge on circumstantial evidence. It is quite common for insider traders to come up with alternative rationales for their trading strategies that can be difficult to disprove. In the consultative document preceding the legislation, the Government stated it would be inappropriate to impose criminal penalties if the individual did not realise that the information he had was inside information. This is something which can be very difficult to establish, for example in the face of a defendant who states that he was simply fortunate in the timing of his dealing.

For example in the Littlewoods case (see **11.6** above and the article opposite) the FSA amassed 1,700Gb of computerised material, 43,000 hard-copy pages, and 10 years' worth of banking and trading records across 150 bank accounts and 18 trading accounts.

This was one of the reasons, of course, for the introduction of the market abuse regime. However, the FCA's keenness to use the criminal provisions seems to be bearing fruit.

11.8 FUTURE DEVELOPMENTS

Trials and further charges and arrests are expected in the coming year.

Unremarkable couple who amassed a fortune from insider trading

Simon Goodley

On 31 March, 2009, a knock at the door of Christian Littlewood's North London home caused panic. The corporate financier knew immediately why police were stationed outside and exactly what their visit meant.

His secret life as an insider trader – which dated back at least eight years – was about to come to a swift halt, unless decisive action could be taken.

Wearing only a pair of boxer shorts, Littlewood bolted through the back door as police officers trailed behind, anxious to stop their suspect from destroying crucial evidence, as well as escaping.

It proved a futile dash. The half-naked banker was tackled by his pursuers, who soon discovered where he was heading: his garden shed was found to contain a floppy disc which recorded much of the crime in extraordinary detail.

That disc provided the Financial Services Authority's "Operation Duke" with important evidence in a case that resulted in Littlewood, his wife Angie and her friend, juice-bar owner Helmy Sa'aid, pleading guilty last week to an insider dealing conspiracy that netted profits of at least £590,000. Littlewood was sentenced to three years and four months in prison. Angie's 12-month sentence is suspended for two years and Sa'aid was jailed for two years.

Investigators say the crimes were merely the most egregious and clear-cut examples of the conspirators' trading. In total they identified 51 suspect trades which were believed to have generated gross profits of about £1m. The whole tale is expected to lead to calls for tougher sentencing for insider dealers and has been dubbed the biggest case of its type yet prosecuted in Britain.

The trio's downfall can be traced back to trades placed seven months before the raids, in the two weeks before a small publicly listed motor insurance company called Highway was acquired by larger rival Liverpool Victoria for £153m in August 2008. That deal was no surprise to the Littlewoods or Sa'aid, who had bought 684,701 shares in the insurer worth £338,000. A fortnight later those trades had netted the team a £160,000 profit.

That raised the FSA's suspicions. It was soon discovered that Sa'aid had enjoyed an extraordinary run of successful investments, trading at or just before 22 merger or acquisition announcements between 2000 and 2008. Of those, 15 were linked to investment bank Dresdner Kleinwort, though Dresdner had not been involved with Highway.

A link soon emerged, however. Sa'aid first bought Highway shares on 13 August, the same day that Littlewood had been classified as an "insider" on the transaction by his then employer Shore Capital. Littlewood, it was soon discovered, had previously worked for Dresdner, yet phone and banking records failed to establish a connection between the two men. What did exist were large cash transfers between a Siew-Yoon Lew and Littlewood and Sa'aid. Lew, it transpired, was Angie Littlewood's Singaporean maiden name.

The method of the scam was now clear, but why risk it? Littlewood's gross salaries, including huge bonuses, ranged from £200,000 to more than £400,000 over the period he abused his position and the court was told the couple did not lead a "champagne lifestyle".

That rather dull image is consistent with the portrait painted by ex-colleagues. "He was never a joyous character," says one. "He was never the charming mover and shaker ... he was the one chained to his desk doing the work. He never stood out and you would never have guessed [what he was up to]."

What did stand out was the private property empire the unremarkable couple had assembled. Despite the Littlewoods only being in their 30s, it is estimated they owned assets worth £3m. They had no mortgage on their flat in Rosslyn Court, Hampstead, which Land Registry records show they bought for £669,000 just before Christmas 2004. Nor was there any debt on seven rental properties located nearby. "They traded on around 50 lines of stock associated with Littlewood's employers," recalls one source close to the investigation. "But they were rolling over the money rather than taking much profit."

In fact, about £400,000 of profit remains in the trio's share trading accounts. So if the deals were not about making fast money and living lavishly, what was the motivation?

In his recent blogpost on the drivers of insider trading, US psychologist and Wall Street commentator Dr Doug Hirschhorn writes: "Commonly, the outside observer assumes that because trading involves money that it has to be about greed. Well, I don't believe it is. I believe it is about winning. About finding an advantage and beating your competitors. The money is just a way of keeping score."

The Littlewood's computer contained a mountain of electronic data for the FSA to study. The investigation unearthed 1,700 gigabytes of information – equivalent to a skyscraper-size pile of A4 paper – which perhaps means it is not surprising when aspects of insider trading cases are overlooked.

In fact, the latest statistics produced by the FSA suggest as much. In 2009, 30.6% of takeover announcements generated so-called abnormal pre-announcement price movements (though these statistics include people making good guesses and price rises after press speculation, as well as insider deals). Even within successful investigations such as the Littlewood case, important details get missed.

Three years before the Highway transaction, the FSA had suspicions about Angie Littlewood. A letter was sent to Siew-Yoon Lew – the name under which she then traded – that led her to stop using knowledge from her husband to buy shares. Instead, she passed information to Sa'aid and the trio split the profits. Angie Littlewood did not respond to the FSA's 2005 request for explanations and the regulator, which sends out many such letters, did not pursue her.

The judge said Angie had been under her husband's influence, was suffering from "moderate depression and possible alcoholism" and was a good mother to her children – aged three, five and eight – at least one of whom has a serious medical condition. These mitigating factors were taken into account when sentencing.

Sa'aid, who has spent almost a year in jail, will be deported to Singapore after serving his sentence. Christian Littlewood is due for release in 2014, but some suggest his case will have a longer-lasting legacy.

"The maximum sentence for insider dealing is seven years," says one lawyer. "This is supposedly the most "serious insider dealing case" yet. They have nicked £600,000 and yet they get just over three years. It would not surprise me to see the start of some kind of lobbying process to get insider-dealing sentences increased."

Source: *Guardian*, 5 February 2011

CHAPTER 12

FINANCIAL PROMOTION

12.1 INTRODUCTION

As **Chapter 9** stated, the regulation of financial promotion is one of the key features of the FSMA 2000. The main restriction on financial promotion is in s 21 of the Act, but there are two other important sources which provide further detail about the financial promotion regime.

The first is the Financial Services and Markets Act 2000 (Financial Promotion) Order 2005 (SI 2005/1529) ('FPO 2005'), as amended.

The second is Chapter 8 of a regulatory guide, the Perimeter Guidance Manual ('PERG'), available in the FCA Handbook section of the FCA's website. The guidance is not legally binding, but may be persuasive.

The FCA's Conduct of Business Sourcebook ('COBS'), in particular Chapter 4, is also relevant, as it contains the rules for authorised persons on financial promotion.

The financial promotion regime is not confined to listed companies. The majority of the provisions referred to in this chapter are equally applicable to unlisted companies, other than the exemptions referred to in **12.9.2**, some of which apply to listed companies only.

12.2 SECTION 21 OF THE FSMA 2000

Section 21(1) provides that a person must not, in the course of business, communicate an invitation or inducement to engage in investment activity. This is referred to as the 's 21 restriction'; the criteria are explored in more detail at **12.7** below. Section 21(2) provides that s 21(1) does not apply if:

(a)   the person making the communication is an authorised person; or

(b)   the content of the communication has been approved by an authorised person.

Section 21(1) will also not apply if the communication is covered by an *exemption* (see **12.9**).

12.3 CONSEQUENCES OF BREACH

The consequences of a breach of s 21 of the FSMA 2000 are as follows:

(a)   it is a criminal offence punishable by a fine and/or imprisonment (a maximum of six months on summary conviction; two years on conviction on indictment) (s 25);

(b)   any agreement which results from a communication made in breach of s 21 may be unenforceable (s 30);

(c)   any third party to the unenforceable agreement can sue for any loss incurred (s 30);

(d)   there may be an order for an injunction or for restitution (ss 380, 382); and

(e)   there may be an action for damages (s 150).

Standard Life Assurance Ltd was fined a record £2.45 million for failures resulting in the production of misleading marketing material for one of its investment funds.

The FCA can also take lesser action, such as requiring the amendment or withdrawal of a promotion with immediate effect, or censuring the wrongdoer.

12.4   WHAT IS A FINANCIAL PROMOTION?

Before we proceed, it would be helpful to identify what a financial promotion actually is. The term 'financial promotion' can be confusing. It is the name of an entire regime, yet the term is not actually referred to in the FSMA 2000, other than in the heading and side note to s 21. There is certainly no definition of the term. It does not mean much to the layman, or indeed to the lawyer who has not encountered it before. So what is a 'financial promotion'? Well, consider it as a generic term to refer to a communication covered by s 21. In very basic layman's terms, it is a communication that contains information which might entice someone to invest in a company, or do certain other activities in relation to investments in that company.

The key point to note at this stage is that what amounts to a financial promotion may not be immediately obvious. Of course, some financial promotions should set off alarm bells immediately. Take, for example, the company secretary who calls to inform you that the company is about to place a newspaper advertisement, 'Need extra cash? Invest in us – we are doing really well'. Hopefully, even the most inexperienced lawyer would consider that this might fall foul of s 21. However, consider a company which is planning to run a television advertising campaign to raise its profile. You happen to know that the company is preparing an IPO within the next month. The TV advertising campaign does not mention this at all. Would s 21 spring to mind? Would the company even consider bringing the existence of the campaign to the notice of its lawyers? Perhaps not, but it should, as in the context of the impending IPO, the advertisements might well fall within s 21.

Even advertising on the carrier bags used by sandwich shops for a spread-betting company has been held to be a financial promotion.

Its importance is reflected by the fact that every year in the UK hundreds of millions of pounds are spent by financial services companies across all media.

12.5   RELEVANCE IN PRACTICE

In practice, the rules relating to financial promotion mean that, if a client company is proposing to make a communication, the lawyer must check whether that communication will fall within s 21 of the FSMA 2000. If it does then this is not good, for the reasons set out at **12.3** above. The lawyer must advise the client that it needs to ensure that the communication falls outside s 21. The easiest way to do this is to instruct an authorised person (see **9.4.3**) to approve the communication before it is made (see **12.2** above). Sometimes it is not possible for an authorised person to approve the communication (see **12.9.1.1** below), and in such circumstances the lawyer must advise the client not to make the communication at all, or to change it to a form which can be approved. This approach is summarised by the flowchart in **Figure 12.1** below.

To put this into context, it is important for a lawyer advising a listed company to be alert to the types of communication that company might make, and to analyse whether these communications might fall within s 21. For example, if a company is raising funds, as considered in **Chapter 17**, then the company will publish a prospectus, perhaps a preliminary prospectus or a pathfinder document (see **6.9.3**), and a press announcement. If the company is effecting a takeover, as considered in **Chapters 20, 21** and **22**, then the company may seek irrevocable undertakings and will make a r 2.5 announcement, circulate an offer document and announce levels of acceptance. The lawyers must advise as to whether these communications fall within the s 21 restriction or not, and the consequences of this. This advice will depend on the individual circumstances of the communication (which may affect, for example, whether an exemption applies).

Figure 12.1: Financial promotion flowchart

12.5.1 Example

Below is an extract from Foxton Group's announcement of its IPO.

Company	Foxtons Group PLC
TIDM	
Headline	Intention to Float
Released	07:00 27-Aug-2013
Number	4547M07

NOT FOR RELEASE, DISTRIBUTION OR PUBLICATION, IN WHOLE OR IN PART, DIRECTLY OR INDIRECTLY, IN OR INTO THE UNITED STATES OF AMERICA (THE "UNITED STATES") (INCLUDING ITS TERRITORIES AND POSSESSIONS, ANY STATE OF THE UNITED STATES AND THE DISTRICT OF COLUMBIA), AUSTRALIA, CANADA, JAPAN OR SOUTH AFRICA OR ANY OTHER JURISDICTION WHERE IT IS UNLAWFUL TO DISTRIBUTE THIS ANNOUNCEMENT.

This announcement is not an offer of securities for sale in the United States or any other jurisdiction. This announcement is an advertisement and not a prospectus. Investors should not subscribe for or purchase any transferable securities referred to in this announcement except on the basis of information in the prospectus (the "Prospectus") intended to be published by Foxtons Group plc (the "Company" and, together with its subsidiaries, the "Group") in due course in connection with the proposed admission of its ordinary shares to the premium listing segment of the Official List of the Financial Conduct Authority and to trading on the main market for listed securities of the London Stock Exchange plc (the "London Stock Exchange"). Copies of the Prospectus will, following publication, be available for inspection from the Company's registered office: Building One, Chiswick Park, 566 Chiswick High Road, London W4 5BE.

For immediate release

27 August 2013

Foxtons Group plc

Announcement of intention to float on the London Stock Exchange

Foxtons Group plc today announces its intention to launch an initial public offering (the "Offer" or "IPO"). The Company intends to apply for admission of its ordinary shares (the "Shares") to the premium listing segment of the Official List of the Financial Conduct Authority and to trading on the main market for listed securities of the London Stock Exchange (together "Admission"). The Offer will comprise an offer of Shares to institutional investors.

Important Notice

The contents of this announcement, which has been prepared by and is the sole responsibility of the Company, have been approved by Credit Suisse and Numis solely for the purposes of section 21 of the Financial Services and Markets Act 2000 (as amended).

12.6   PURPOSE

The s 21 restriction on making financial promotions, like so many other statutory provisions in the field of corporate finance, is to protect investors. A financial promotion is basically a business communication which could encourage the recipient to take some action in relation to an investment. Section 21 controls how those communications are made and what they say, so that advantage is not taken of investors and potential investors.

12.7   THE DETAIL OF s 21

The following paragraphs consider some of the detail of the s 21 restriction and the exemptions from it. The FCA has provided a lot of guidance on the interpretation of the restriction and the main exemptions in PERG. This does not bind the courts, but it may be persuasive.

12.7.1   Person

'Person' includes a corporate entity such as a company.

12.7.2   Course of business

Section 21(4) of the FSMA 2000 gives HM Treasury the power to define this term, but to date it has not done so. This requirement excludes from the ambit of s 21 communications of a personal nature. So, if tonight in the pub I mention that I am going to buy a few shares in company X, and suggest that my friends do the same, my suggestion will not be caught by the s 21 restriction; the communication would not have a commercial nature. Further guidance is provided by PERG 8.5.

12.7.3   Communication

'Communication' means all communication, through whatever medium, so it includes oral and written communication as well as electronic communication (for example, a website announcement). 'Communicate' includes causing a communication to be made (FSMA 2000, s 21(13)). This means that if a company makes an announcement through, for example, financial PRs, and the announcement is in breach of s 21, then, subject to any exemptions which apply, not only the company but also the financial PRs would be responsible for the communication, and therefore caught by the s 21 restriction. PERG 8.6.3 sets out categories of persons whom the FCA does not consider will communicate or cause a communication to be made.

12.7.4   Invitation or inducement

Neither term is defined by the FSMA 2000. 'Invitation' will catch direct invitations to engage in investment activity, such as an invitation to buy shares. It can range from a polite request to an encouragement. A prospectus, together with an application form (see **Chapter 6**) would constitute an invitation to buy shares. 'Inducement' is thought to be wider. The Treasury stated that the term is intended to catch any communication which contains a degree of incitement to engage in an investment activity and that a communication of purely factual information would not amount to an inducement. It is unclear how wide this could be: what if a company embarks on a marketing campaign to raise its profile? It is possible that this could amount to an inducement if it contains any incitement to invest in that company. If the campaign involves putting the company's name onto a few umbrellas, then it would probably not amount to an inducement. PERG 8.4 provides further guidance.

12.7.5   Engaging in investment activity

Section 21(8) and (9) of the FSMA 2000, together with art 4 of and Sch 1 to the FPO 2005, define 'engaging in investment activity' as:

(a)   entering into an agreement which constitutes a 'controlled activity' (such as buying, selling and underwriting shares; see Pt I of Sch 1 to the FPO 2005); and

(b)   exercising any rights conferred by a 'controlled investment' (such as shares and bonds; see Pt II of Sch 1 to the FPO 2005) to buy, sell, underwrite or convert that investment.

This definition could affect how a company chooses to structure transactions. For example, while share sales constitute 'investment activity', asset sales do not.

12.8   TERRITORIAL SCOPE

The s 21 restriction will apply to any communication which is:

(a)   made from the UK; or

(b)   made from overseas, but is capable of having an effect in the UK (s 21(3)).

(However there are exemptions, under art 12 of the FPO 2005, for certain communications which are made to a recipient who receives the communication outside the UK, or which is directed only at persons outside the UK.)

Additional guidance is to be found in COBS 4.

12.9   EXEMPTIONS

As the s 21 restriction is so wide, to counterbalance this, the FPO 2005 contains over 65 exemptions from the restriction. Remember that while approval by an authorised person brings the communication outside the scope of s 21, it is not an exemption. If an exemption applies, there is no requirement for the communication to be approved by an authorised person.

The exemptions do contain some new terminology, however. The application of certain exemptions depends on the nature of the communication, in particular whether it is 'real time' or 'non real time' and, if real time, whether it is 'solicited' or 'unsolicited'. The meaning of these terms is explained at **12.9.1** below.

The s 21 restriction applies to both listed and unlisted companies. Nevertheless, there are some very useful exemptions which apply to listed companies only. The exemptions are detailed in, and in practice recourse must be made to, the relevant article of the FPO 2005 and PERG. However, the exemptions of particular use to listed companies are summarised at **12.9.2** below.

12.9.1   Terminology

In **12.9.1.1** and **12.9.1.2** below, references to 'art' are references to articles of the FPO 2005.

12.9.1.1   Real time and non-real time communications (art 7)

A real time communication is any communication made in the course of a personal visit, telephone conversation or other interactive dialogue. A non-real time communication is any communication which is not a real time communication. Examples include letters, e-mails and newspaper announcements. Article 7(5) contains a list of indicators that the communication is 'non-real time'.

The reason that the exemptions distinguish real time communications from non-real time communications is that the FCA considers that investors require more protection from real time communications (because people can get carried away in interactive dialogue and there is less opportunity for a cooling-off period). The exemptions which apply to real time communications therefore are narrower in scope than those exemptions which apply to non-real time communications. In fact, it is not possible for even an authorised person to approve real time communications, so care must be taken to ensure that any real time communication does fall within the scope of an exemption.

Further guidance on this issue is provided by PERG 8.10.

12.9.1.2   Solicited and unsolicited real time communications (art 8)

A solicited real time communication is a real time communication which has been initiated by the recipient, or which has been made in response to a request from the recipient. An unsolicited real time communication is a real time communication which is not a solicited communication.

12.9.2   Exemptions useful to listed companies

In **12.9.2.1** to **12.9.2.9** below, references to 'art' are references to articles of the FPO 2005.

12.9.2.1   Communications to shareholders and creditors (art 43)

The s 21 restriction does not apply to non-real time or solicited real time communications made by, or on behalf of, a company to, or directed at, its shareholders, provided that the communication does not relate to an investment (for example, shares) issued, or to be issued, outside the company's group. (However, any individual who sends such a communication, for example the chairman, may be at risk of breaching s 19 of the FSMA 2000; see **9.4**.)

12.9.2.2   Group companies (art 45)

The s 21 restriction will not apply to any communication between a company and any of its group companies.

12.9.2.3   Annual report and accounts (art 59)

The s 21 restriction will not apply to the distribution by a company of its annual report and accounts, provided it meets certain criteria, such as not including any invitation or advice to persons to buy, sell, underwrite or subscribe for any investments.

12.9.2.4   Employee share schemes (art 60)

The s 21 restriction will not apply to any communications by the company, or its group companies or trustees, which are for the purpose of any employee share scheme (see **13.9**).

12.9.2.5   Sale of body corporate (art 62)

This is subject to certain conditions. The intention of this exemption seems to be to enable controlling shareholders of small companies to buy and sell those companies without being caught by the s 21 restriction. However, as drafted, the scope of this exemption is not clear. If read literally, this exemption would apply to takeovers of public companies, which many consider cannot have been intended. The Treasury recognised this issue and, during 2004, drafted proposals to narrow the exemption. It was expected that the exemption would be amended when the FPO 2005 replaced the previous Financial Promotion Order. However, surprisingly, no changes were made, and the Treasury has not clarified why it has not implemented its proposals.

12.9.2.6   Other communications by listed companies (art 69)

The s 21 restriction will not apply to some communications made by listed companies, provided that certain criteria are met.

12.9.2.7   Promotions included in listing particulars, etc (art 70)

The s 21 restriction will not apply to any non-real time communication in a prospectus or supplementary prospectus which has been approved in accordance with the Prospectus Rules, or to any other document required or permitted to be published by the Listing Rules or the Prospectus Rules (except an advertisement within the meaning of the Prospectus Directive). This is because it is presumed that the FCA will provide sufficient protection to investors in these rules, so protection under the financial promotion regime is unnecessary.

The FCA considers that 'permitted' means something which is expressly permitted rather than simply not expressly prohibited (PERG 8.21.14G).

12.9.2.8   Material relating to prospectus for public offer of unlisted securities (art 71)

The s 21 restriction will not apply to any non-real time communication relating to a prospectus or supplementary prospectus, in the circumstances set out in art 71.

12.9.2.9   Investment professionals (art 19), certified high net worth individuals (art 48), high net worth companies (art 49) and certified and self-certified sophisticated investors (arts 50 and 50A)

Section 21 will not apply to communications made to the above-mentioned recipients. This can be useful to a company seeking to raise funds; by targeting these recipients only, the communication will be exempt from the s 21 restriction. There is the problem, of course, of how a company would know that the high net worth individuals and sophisticated investors it targets are certified.

Note that arts 48 and 50A apply only to communications relating to investments in *unlisted* companies.

12.10   CONCLUSION

Section 21 of the FSMA 2000 is very wide in its application. It covers most of the communications a listed company would make in its day-to-day corporate and trading activities. The exemptions, and the ability of authorised persons to approve non-real time communications, narrow the scope of the s 21 restriction. The exemptions are drafted with the rationale of s 21 in mind (see **12.6** above), namely investor protection. The more inexperienced the recipient, the more likely it is that the exemptions will not apply, and that s 21 will either prohibit the communication, or ensure that the communication is approved by an authorised person, in order to protect that recipient.

At the start of 2010, the forerunner to the FCA, the FSA, completed a three-year review of firms' compliance with its financial promotions regime in the press and on the Internet. It found that there was generally a high level of compliance with the rules and no significant concerns were identified.

EQUITY FINANCE

SHARES

13.1 INTRODUCTION

Shares are not unique to listed companies, or even to public companies. Most companies have limited liability. Most companies with limited liability have a share capital, and are limited by shares rather than by guarantee. So why dedicate a whole chapter of this book to shares? Well, any corporate finance lawyer needs to have a sound understanding of the basic law relating to share capital. **Chapter 1** established that the principal reason most companies choose to float is to take advantage of the opportunities afforded by the market to raise funds, both on an IPO (considered in **Chapters 4, 5** and **6**) and once listed (considered in **Chapter 17**). **Chapter 1** also set out the requirements that a company's share capital has to meet before the company can re-register as a public company. **Chapter 4** explained that the company's share capital has to meet further requirements before the company can seek an IPO. **Part IV** of this book also explains that listed companies often use their share capital as consideration when entering into various transactions, such as acquisitions or takeovers of other companies.

So listed companies are always making changes to their share capital. It is the lawyer's job to make sure they do so in a way permitted by law. **Chapters 13** to **16** explore the law relating to the share capital of a company, with particular focus on the law relating to listed companies.

13.2 WHAT IS A SHARE?

A share represents ownership of a company. A person who owns a share owns a bundle of rights in the company, such as the right to receive a dividend and, maybe, the right to vote. This person is referred to as a 'member', or 'shareholder', of that company. This book uses the term 'shareholder', but 'member' means exactly the same thing. The term 'investor' may be used to describe someone who has invested cash in return for shares in a company, but it could also be used to describe someone who has provided a loan to the company. In the former scenario, the investor will be a shareholder; in the latter, she will not.

13.3 SOME TERMS RELATING TO SHARE CAPITAL

13.3.1 Nominal value (also known as par value)

Shares must have a fixed nominal value (CA 2006, s 542). A company can have shares with a nominal value of 1p ('1p shares'), 10p ('10p shares') £1 ('£1 shares') – in fact, shares of any nominal value, although the nominal value should not be too high, as, under s 580 of the CA 2006, a company cannot issue a share at a discount to (that is, for any less than) its nominal value. This means, for example, that a company could not issue a £1 share for 80p. If it wanted to issue the share for 80p, the nominal value of that share would have to be equal to or less than 80p.

Note that the nominal value will usually bear no correlation to the current market value of the share (see **13.3.5**). Most shares will be sold at a premium (see **13.3.2**). A share with a nominal value of £1 (a £1 share) could be worth, say, £5 when sold on the market.

13.3.2   Premium

A premium is the difference between the nominal value of the share and the price paid for that share. For example, if I pay £5 for a share which has a nominal value of £1, I have paid £1 nominal value and a premium of £4.

13.3.3   Restrictions on share capital

Under the CA 2006 a company may restrict the number of shares that it can issue by including a provision in the company's articles of association.

Companies formed before 1 October 2009, before the relevant provisions of the CA 2006 came into force, had restrictions on the number of shares they could issue in their pre-CA 2006 memorandum of association (the authorised share capital). Under s 28 of the CA 2006 these provisions are automatically treated as restrictions in the articles with effect from 1 October 2009. The restrictions can be removed by passing an ordinary resolution or by adopting new articles by special resolution with no limit on the issue of shares or authorising the directors to issue shares in excess of the current limit.

Remember that there is a minimum authorised share capital requirement for a public company of at least £50,000 or its euro equivalent (see **1.9.2** and **1.9.3.2** above).

13.3.4   Issued share capital

This is the total nominal value of the shares a company has in issue, ie owned by shareholders.

Remember that there is a minimum issued share capital requirement of £50,000 for a public company which is trading (see **1.9.2.2** and **1.9.3.2** above).

13.3.5   Market value

The market value is the price that investors are willing to pay for a share on the market. It usually bears no correlation to the nominal value of the share (see **13.3.1**). By way of example, the ordinary shares in J Sainsbury plc, the supermarket chain, have a nominal value of 28.57p. On 22 November 2013, the closing market value on the Main Market was 404.60p. Market-makers (see **2.5.2**) will set a price at which they are willing to buy shares and a price at which they are willing to sell shares. The market value of shares which are quoted in the newspaper is, in fact, a middle price between these two prices.

13.3.6   Market capitalisation

Market capitalisation is one method of valuing a company. It represents the market value of the company's issued share capital. It is calculated as follows:

number of issued shares × current market value of each share

J Sainsbury plc had a market capitalisation of (ie was worth) £7.692 billion (1,901,348,215 issued shares × 404.60p) at the close of trading on 22 November 2013.

13.3.7   Fully, nil or part paid

A share is 'fully paid' when the shareholder has paid the company the nominal value of the share together with any premium payable on it. If the shareholder has paid nothing in this regard, the share is 'nil paid'. If the shareholder has made a payment towards this, but has not paid the full amount, the share is 'part paid'.

Remember that there are specific requirements as to the amount which must be paid up on any share if the company is a public company. Each share (other than a share allotted pursuant to an employee share scheme – see **13.9**) must be paid up at least as to one-quarter of its nominal value together with the whole of any premium paid on it (see **1.9.2.2** and **1.9.3.2** above).

13.4 WHAT BENEFITS DOES A SHARE HAVE?

The share has a number of benefits.

13.4.1 Limited liability

Any shareholder is liable to pay the company the amount due on the share. Once the share is fully paid, the shareholder (together with any person to whom the shareholder transfers that share) will have no further liability to the company. Even if the share is nil paid or part paid (see **13.3.7** above), the shareholder will have liability only up to the balance due on the share.

Why is this relevant? Well, imagine that Marks & Spencer Group plc goes bust tomorrow. I have 100 shares of 25p (nominal value) in the company, for which I paid £270. I am a humble lecturer (from the corporate lawyer's viewpoint) living on the breadline. Should I be worried? Might I have to stand behind the company's debt and help to satisfy all those unpaid suppliers of ladies underwear? No, because my shares limit my liability to the company and to any liquidator of the company. In paying the amount due on the shares, I discharged my liability in full. The only issues that may concern me are that I might have lost some or all of the £270 I paid for my shares (see **13.5.2.3**) and I have lost the potential for further capital growth.

13.4.2 Rights

A share will convey various rights on the shareholder. The rights may be set out in the company's memorandum of association (but this is rare), or in a special resolution, but usually they are set out in the company's articles of association, under the following headings (or similar):

(a) *Income rights.* This is the right to share in the profits of the company, through the right to a dividend.

(b) *The right to receive notice of, attend and vote at meetings.* The right which gives the shareholder the most power is the right to vote.

(c) *Capital rights.* This is the right to share in the capital of a company, on a winding up, after payment of the company's debts. This may be a right to be repaid the capital paid up on the shares (that is, the nominal value and any premium paid for the shares), or an additional right to share in any surplus assets once the amount paid up on all classes of shares has been repaid.

13.4.3 Capital growth

Many investors are attracted to shares because of the opportunity they afford for capital growth. A shareholder will buy shares on the Main Market at a certain price. The price of those shares is likely to change throughout the period the shareholder owns the shares. The shareholder's original investment will rise or fall in value. The shareholder therefore takes the risk of capital gains or losses. Investors hope, of course, that they will be able to weather any storms and sell when their investment has increased in value. The reality, of course, can be very different. Some will remember (and the author's wallet can testify to this) the dotcom 'boom and bust' in the late 1990s, when shareholders who bought shares in dotcom businesses early enough became millionaires overnight. Some of these shareholders had the good sense (or luck?) to sell some shares and bank the profit, but others lost considerable amounts when the dotcom bubble burst in 2000.

In the summer of 2007, dramatic uncertainty returned to the world's stock markets. Wild surges in share prices were caused by the global financial crisis brought on by the collapse in the housing market in the US. Since then, there has been a dramatic recovery in stock markets, with the FTSE 100 Index of the Stock Exchange's leading companies having risen almost 50% from its low in March 2009 of 3,500 points.

13.5 CLASSES OF SHARE

Often the company will want to create different types of share, with different rights attaching to each type. The company may, for example, be pre-IPO, and want to attract a venture capital company to invest, in return for shares. Usually, the venture capital company will be in a position to demand enhanced rights over the other ordinary shareholders. Alternatively, perhaps the company wants to reward its loyal employees for their commitment, or the original owners who built up the company, with some shares, but does not want to give them the power to vote, which ordinary shares would convey. The company will create a separate class of shares to issue to the venture capital company, or to its employees. Again, the company's articles will detail the rights attached to each class of share, using the headings set out at **13.4.2** above. The lawyer may well have to draft these rights, and they can be quite complex.

The common classes of shares are discussed below. Note, however, that it is impossible to list all the classes you are ever likely to encounter. That is another advantage of the share; there is an infinite number of permutations. Take care, however, not to presume anything from the name of the class of share; always check the articles for the specific rights, and any restrictions, which attach to a share.

13.5.1 Ordinary shares

Ordinary shares are the most common class of share. Usually listed companies will list their ordinary shares. They may, however, choose not to list other classes of share. Remember that if a company chooses to list a class of shares, it must list all the shares in that class (see **4.3.1.1** above). It is Marks & Spencer Group plc's ordinary shares of 25p that you or I are able to buy on the Main Market.

Typical rights attaching to ordinary shares are examined at **13.5.1.1** to **13.5.1.3** below.

13.5.1.1 Income rights

The holders of other classes of shares might be entitled to a preferential dividend payment before the ordinary shareholders (see **13.5.2.1** below), but usually any profits to be paid out over and above that preferential dividend will be paid entirely to the ordinary shareholders. Shares which carry this unlimited right to income are referred to as equity shares (to draw an analogy with a law firm, equity shareholders are like equity partners; they have an unlimited, but proportionate, right to share in profits). Note, however, that the company is not obliged to declare a dividend. It may not declare one if it has not had a profitable year and there are insufficient profits available for distribution (see **18.2.1**).

13.5.1.2 The right to receive notice of, attend and vote at meetings

The ordinary shareholders are usually entitled to receive notice of, attend and vote at company meetings. Occasionally, however, non-voting ordinary shares are created, for example to raise capital without diluting control of the company. Usually, other classes of share will not afford the right to vote save in very limited circumstances.

13.5.1.3 Capital rights

On a winding up of the company, the company's assets are used, first, in paying off the company's liabilities, then in repaying the capital (that is, the amount paid up) on all the classes of shares other than ordinary shares. Only then will the ordinary shareholders be repaid the amount paid up on their shares. However, if there are any surplus assets once all these payments have been made, they will usually be distributed between the ordinary shareholders.

13.5.2 Preference shares

A preference share is any share which has preferential rights over other classes of share, particular ordinary shares. A company may have more than one class of preference shares, for example it may have 'A' preference shares, with one set of rights, and 'B' preference shares, with another set of rights. Again, the company's articles will list the rights which attach to the shares.

Often, as stated in **13.5** above, preference shares are tailor-made for a particular scenario and with particular preference shareholders in mind. The bargaining position of these shareholders might dictate the rights which attach to the shares. If preference shares are being created as a 'freebie' reward, the company will have a free hand in drafting the rights. However, if the company is keen to bring on board a venture capital company, that venture capital company might well be demanding as to the share rights it obtains in return for its cash injection into the company.

Typical rights which may attach to preference shares are examined at **13.5.2.1** to **13.5.2.3** below.

13.5.2.1 Income rights

Preferential dividend

The holders of preference shares might be entitled to a fixed preferential dividend payment from distributable profits before the ordinary shareholders are entitled to their dividend (see **3.5.1.1** above). This is often expressed as a percentage of the nominal value of the share. For example, a '5% preference share' will entitle a preference shareholder, on the declaration of a dividend, to a fixed payment of 5% of the nominal value of his shareholding before any dividend is paid to ordinary shareholders. To continue the analogy with a law firm from **13.5.1.1** above, preference shareholders are like salaried partners; they have a limited right to share in profits.

If the company does not declare a dividend then, subject to any cumulative rights (see below), the shareholders are not entitled to a dividend payment.

Cumulative right to a dividend

Unless the articles expressly state to the contrary, all preference shares will be 'cumulative'. Usually the articles state expressly that preference shares are cumulative. This means that if the company does not declare a dividend, or if it declares a dividend so small that the preference shareholders do not receive their full dividend, then the dividend (or the shortfall, as the case may be) will be carried forward to the next year automatically; and if there is no dividend that year, it will be carried forward to the following year, and so on.

EXAMPLE

Imagine that X plc has an issued share capital of £100m, divided into 90 million ordinary shares of £1 each and 10 million cumulative 5% preference shares of £1 each. This means that in any year in which a dividend is declared, the first £500,000 (5% of £10 million, the nominal value of the shares) is payable to the preference shareholders. Any excess is payable to the ordinary shareholders. The table below shows the dividend payments over a five-year period.

Year	Total dividend	Preference dividend	Ordinary dividend	Preference entitlement carried forward to following year
1	£900,000	£500,000	£400,000	Nil
2	£400,000	£400,000	Nil	£100,000
3	£550,000	£550,000	Nil	£50,000
4	Nil	Nil	Nil	£550,000
5	£1,200,000	£1,050,000	£150,000	Nil

In year 3, although a total dividend of £550,000 is declared, the ordinary shareholders do not receive £50,000. Instead, that is also paid to the preference shareholders, to make up some (but not all) of the £100,000 arrears carried forward from year 2. The rest of the shortfall (£50,000) is not paid to the preference shareholders in year 4; no dividend at all was declared then. Instead, it, together with the arrears of £500,000 from year 4, is made up in year 5, and there is even some left for the ordinary shareholders this year.

Dividend on a winding up

When preference shares are cumulative, the articles should make clear whether any arrears of the preference dividend are payable to the preference shareholders on a winding up of the company. For example, in the example used above, if X plc was wound up in year 4, the articles should clarify whether the £550,000 arrears would be payable to the preference shareholders.

Participating preference shares

Participating preference shares have further rights to a dividend, not just a preferential right to a fixed amount before the ordinary shareholders. Participating preference shares can be cumulative, but they do not have to be. Take again the example above. You can see that once the preference shareholders have taken their 5% dividend, the remainder goes to the ordinary shareholders in their entirety. Take year 5. The remaining £150,000 is paid to the ordinary shareholders. If the preference shares had been participating preference shares, the preference shareholders would have had some right to part of this amount. In other words, they get a second bite at the dividend cherry. The articles will provide what that right is, but it could be, for example, that the ordinary shareholders also take a fixed percentage, then the balance is divided equally between the preference shareholders and the ordinary shareholders. Participating preference shares may also have further rights to capital (see **13.5.2.3** below).

13.5.2.2 The right to receive notice of, attend and vote at meetings

Usually, preference shares will give preference shareholders the right to receive notice of general meetings and to attend meetings. However, they will seldom give preference shareholders the right to vote, other than in relation to certain limited matters, such as on a resolution to wind up the company, or to vary the rights which attach to the preference shares.

13.5.2.3 Capital rights

Just because a preference shareholder has a preferential right to a dividend does not necessarily mean that he will have a preferential right on a return of capital, and vice versa. Often in practice, however, preference shareholders do have preferential rights as to capital. It may be that once the company has repaid its debts, the preference shareholders are repaid their capital before the ordinary shareholders. If there are any surplus assets remaining after even the ordinary shareholders have been repaid, then the preference shareholders may have some rights over the surplus, for example to divide it between themselves and the ordinary shareholders. In this case the preference shares would be participating preference shares. Unless there is an express provision to the contrary, however, this surplus will belong to the ordinary shareholders alone.

13.5.3 Redeemable shares

13.5.3.1 Creation

Under s 684 of the CA 2006, a company can issue shares which will, or may, be redeemed at the option of the company or the shareholder, if the company has in issue other shares which are not redeemable.

For a public company only, the company must be authorised to do this by its articles of association. A private company may include a provision in its articles excluding or restricting its ability to issue redeemable shares.

A company may find it useful to issue redeemable shares if, for example, a venture capital company wishes to invest in the company for a fixed period of time. Any lawyer drafting redeemable share rights should pay particular attention to s 685 of the CA 2006, which provides some guidelines as to the terms and manner of redemption which must be dealt with on creation of the shares.

13.5.3.2 Redemption

The general rule under s 687(2) of the CA 2006 is that redeemable shares can be redeemed only out of either:

(a)   distributable profits of the company; or

(b)   the proceeds of a fresh issue of shares made for the purpose of the redemption.

Any premium payable to redeemable shareholders on redemption must be paid out of distributable profits rather than capital (but see s 687(4) of the CA 2006, which provides that any premium payable in relation to redeemable shares which were issued at a premium may be made out of the proceeds of a fresh issue of shares, up to a certain amount). There is, however, an exception for private companies, which can redeem out of capital, subject to any restrictions in the articles of association and provided the company adopts the procedure in Chapter 5 of the CA 2006 to effect the redemption (s 687(1)). *Business Law and Practice* considers further the law relating to the redemption of redeemable shares.

13.5.3.3 The effect of redemption

Pursuant to s 688 of the CA 2006, the effect of redemption is that the shares are treated as cancelled. This means that the issued share capital of the company will be reduced by the nominal value of the shares redeemed.

13.5.4 Convertible shares

A company may issue convertible shares, which, as their name suggests, can be converted into ordinary shares. The conversion may be at a specified time, or may be triggered by the happening of some event (eg, an IPO). The attractions to a convertible shareholder of converting to ordinary shares may be the acquisition of voting rights, or the fact that the market value of the ordinary shares has risen above the conversion price of the convertible shares.

13.5.5   Bonus shares (also known as 'scrip' or 'scrip issues')

If its articles permit, a company can transfer profits to a fund called its 'capital redemption reserve' and use it to issue 'bonus' shares to the shareholders in proportion to their existing shareholdings. Since the issue may reduce the amount of money available for paying dividends, the term 'bonus' is not really appropriate. The correct term is 'capitalisation of reserves' (or 'capitalisation issue'), but the terms 'scrip', or 'scrip issues' are also used to describe such shares.

13.5.6   Subscriber shares

The memorandum will show the names of the people who agreed to own shares when the company was first registered. These people are called the subscribers, and the shares which were allotted to them on the company's registration are referred to as subscriber shares (see CA 2006, s 8(1)). Section 584 of the CA 2006 provides that in a public company the subscriber shares must be paid up in cash.

13.5.7   Summary

You will now appreciate that, usually, ordinary shares bear the greatest financial risk, because, unlike preference shares, typically they do not afford any prior right to a dividend or return of capital. It is because ordinary shareholders bear this risk that, generally, they also are afforded full voting rights. However, ordinary shares also carry the greatest potential for financial gain, because the rights they do afford in relation to income and capital tend to be unlimited, unlike preference shares, which often afford fixed rights to income and capital.

13.6   SHARES OR DEBT?

This book is concerned with equity finance. There is another book in the series which deals with debt finance (see **Banking and Capital Markets**). **Chapter 18** of this book provides an overview of the difference between equity and debt finance.

Some classes of share, which are equity finance, can easily be confused with debt finance. Take, for example, a 5% cumulative redeemable preference share. It will yield a return (the 5% fixed dividend), like interest on a loan, and it is redeemable, so repayable, like a loan. However, a closer inspection reveals that preference shares are in fact equity finance, not debt finance, for the following reasons:

(a)   The 5% return is a dividend, not interest. It will therefore have different tax consequences. It will not be a deductible expense in the calculation of the taxable profits of the company.

(b)   There is no guaranteed right to a dividend. The company will pay a dividend only to the extent that distributable profits are available for that purpose. The cumulative nature of preference shares does not alter this fact, as it is a benefit only if there are distributable profits in the future which are sufficient to cover the arrears of the preference dividend (or if the preference shareholder is afforded a right to arrears on a winding up). Conversely, an investor would expect the company to guarantee interest payments on a loan.

(c)   The fact that the shares are redeemable is not a guarantee that the shareholder will be repaid. The company can redeem the shares only out of distributable profits or a fresh issue of shares (unless it is a private company; see **13.5.3.2** above). If it cannot redeem the shares this way, the shareholder will not be repaid.

13.7 VARYING CLASS RIGHTS

13.7.1 Introduction

Section 630 of the CA 2006 provides that rights attaching to a class of shares, 'class rights', can be varied. This is good news for a company, as it provides a degree of flexibility, for example to reduce the amount of a preference dividend, or to create a new class of preference shares which rank ahead of an existing class of preference shares.

In both of these examples, however, there will be a class of shareholders who are worse off as a result of the variation of the rights of the existing preference shares, namely, the existing preference shareholders. As you might expect, the CA 2006 provides some protection for these shareholders in the procedures it prescribes for the variation of class rights. The Act provides different procedures, and the procedure the company must follow is dictated by whether the articles of association provide a variation procedure or not.

13.7.2 Class rights-defined in the articles of association

If the articles do not contain a procedure for variation, s 630(4) provides that class rights can be varied if:

(a) the holders of 75% in nominal value of the issued shares of the class of shares to be varied consent in writing to the variation; or

(b) a special resolution, passed at a separate general meeting of the class in question (known as a 'class meeting'), sanctions the variation (this means that 75% of those who attend the class meeting and vote in person or by proxy must vote in favour of the resolution).

While this affords protection to the holders of the shares whose rights are to be varied, in that a majority of them must agree to the variation, it does mean that the rights attached to the 25% minority of shares can be changed without their owners' consent.

Section 633 of the CA 2006 addresses this. It provides a procedure by which those shareholders who hold, in aggregate, not less than 15% of the issued shares of the class can (provided they did not consent to, or vote for, the variation) apply to the court within 21 days of the consent to, or vote for, the variation to have it cancelled. The court can then choose either to disallow (if satisfied the variation would unfairly prejudice the shareholders), or to confirm the variation. If a s 633 application is made, the variation has no effect until the court confirms it.

13.7.3 Class rights defined in the articles of association

If the articles contain a procedure for varying class rights, s 630(2) states that it is this procedure which should be followed, not the statutory procedure under s 630. The rationale behind this is that the class of shareholders need no extra statutory protection; they had notice of the articles when they became shareholders, and also have power to change the articles.

The articles can specify a procedure for varying class rights which sets a higher or, importantly, a lower standard than the statutory procedure.

The same right to apply to court to have the variation cancelled under s 633 (see **13.7.2**) applies to variations made in accordance with the articles' procedure.

13.8 REGISTRATION OF SHARE RIGHTS

A company must send details of share rights it has created or varied to the Registrar of Companies (that is, to Companies House). This obligation arises under ss 636–640 of the CA 2006.

13.9 EMPLOYEE SHARE SCHEMES

It was explained at **1.7.6** above that one of the benefits of listing is that companies can issue shares with an identifiable value to their employees to incentivise and reward them. Companies do this through schemes known as employee share schemes, which, if structured correctly, have the following tax benefits:

(a)   for the company – the cost to the company is a deductible expense for corporation tax purposes;

(b)   for the employee – the benefit is not normally subject to income tax or national insurance contributions (if all the criteria of the individual plan are met). The shares do have some tax consequences, however; capital gains tax will be charged when the employee disposes of the shares.

Note that share schemes do not usually create a separate class of share; in fact, this is specifically avoided, as it can mean that the scheme does not attract the beneficial tax treatment outlined above.

The law relating to share schemes is particularly specialised, and firms will often have a discrete team dedicated to advising solely in relation to such schemes. The corporate lawyer will, however, need to know about the existence of any share schemes, because they will be referred to in documents he drafts, such as a prospectus (see **Chapter 6**) or an offer document (see **22.4.1**). A noddy guide to the four share schemes which are currently approved by the Revenue is provided at **13.9.1** to **13.9.4** below. It covers the basics but not much more.

The corporate lawyer should also appreciate the following points about employee share schemes:

(i)   they are exempt from the application of s 551 of the CA 2006 (see **14.5.2**);

(ii)   they do not trigger pre-emption rights under s 561 of the CA 2006, although they do entitle their holders to pre-emption rights (see **14.6.8.2**);

(iii)   there is an exception for employee share scheme shares from the prohibition on financial assistance (see **16.5.3**);

(iv)   shares allotted in pursuance of an employee share scheme are also excluded from the requirement, under s 586 of the CA 2006, that shares must be paid up to at least one quarter of their nominal value, together with the whole of any premium (see **13.3.7**); and

(v)   generally a prospectus is not required where shares are offered by a listed company to existing or former directors or employees. Instead, a short document giving details of the company, the offer and the shares will suffice (see **6.4.1.5(h)** and **6.4.2.4(e)**).

13.9.1 Approved savings-related share option scheme or save as you earn (SAYE)

This scheme must be open to all employees. The company grants options to purchase shares in the company. At the time the option is granted, the price of the shares is fixed and the employees start to make regular monthly contributions to savings accounts. When an employee's account matures, the employee can use the proceeds to fund the exercise of the option.

13.9.2 Share incentive plan (SIP)

This scheme must also be open to all employees. There is a number of possible features. The company may:

(a)   issue up to £3,000 worth of shares each year to an individual employee;

(b)   allow an individual to purchase shares each year up to a value of the lower of £1,500, or 10% of salary; or

(c)   issue up to two shares for each share purchased by an individual employee.

13.9.3   Approved company share option plan (CSOP)

This scheme can be made available to selected employees, and so is often used to reward senior executives. The company grants options to purchase shares in the company. As with the approved savings-related share option scheme (see **13.9.1** above), at the time of the option is created, the price for the shares is fixed. However, with this scheme there is no associated savings account; the employee must provide his own funds to exercise the option.

13.9.4   Enterprise management incentives (EMI)

This scheme can also be made available to selected employees, and, like the approved company share option plan (see **13.9.3** above), it is often used to reward key employees. The company grants options to purchase shares in the company. Again, at the time the option is created, the price for the shares is fixed. There is no associated savings account. A number of significant conditions attach to this scheme (for example, the scheme is only available to companies with gross assets not exceeding £30m and fewer than 250 employees).

CHAPTER 14

ISSUING SHARES

14.1 INTRODUCTION

Chapter 13 explored the concept of the share and the classes of share which may comprise a company's share capital. Once a listed company has created a class of share, it will want to use those shares to raise capital. This will involve issuing shares to shareholders, in return for consideration.

The legislation relating to the issue of shares is relatively easy to apply when the issuing company is a private company. However, the application of those rules to the issue of shares by a public company can be more complex, not because the legislation is fundamentally different (it is not), but because usually public companies have more complex share structures, so it is necessary to delve a little further into the detail of the legislation. In the case of the issue of shares by listed companies, there are other considerations in addition to the legislation to take into account, namely guidelines issued by the IIC and the ABI, the Statement of Principles issued by the Pre-Emption Group and the requirements of the Listing Rules. This chapter considers share issues by a listed company.

In this Chapter we shall be examining only those rules which apply to public companies.

14.2 TERMINOLOGY

Some terminology, which has the potential to be confusing, is explained below.

14.2.1 Issuing shares or transferring shares?

'Issuing' relates to the issue of a share from the company to a shareholder. It is different to 'transferring' or 'selling' a share, which is when a shareholder transfers a share to another person. On a share issue, the company is party to the transaction and receives money for the share. On a share transfer, the parties will be the shareholder selling the share and the shareholder buying the share, not the company, and so the selling shareholder receives the proceeds and not the company. This chapter considers only the issue of shares. **Chapter 19** considers the transfer of shares.

14.2.2 Allotted shares or issued shares?

When considering the subject of issuing shares, the terms 'allotted' and 'issued' arise frequently. Let us be clear from the outset what they mean and the distinction between them. In practice the terms are used interchangeably and, usually, it is entirely appropriate to do this. However, it is essential for the corporate finance lawyer to be aware of the specific meaning of terminology he uses when advising a client.

14.2.2.1 Allotted

Pursuant to s 558 of the CA 2006, shares are allotted when a person acquires the *unconditional right to be included* in the company's register of members in respect of those shares.

14.2.2.2 Issued

Although there is no statutory definition of the meaning of 'issued', case law suggests that shares are issued when the allottee's name is *registered* in the company's register of members in respect of those shares (*Ambrose Lake Tin and Copper Co, Re (Clarke's Case)* (1878) 8 Ch D 635, CA and *National Westminster Bank plc and Another v IRC and Barclays Bank plc* [1994] 2 BCLC 30, CA).

14.2.2.3 The distinction

The above explanations reveal the minute difference between the two terms. The distinction lies in whether the shareholder's name has been included in the register of members, with allotment preceding issue. Of course, the majority of companies ensure that the register of members is kept up to date. This will remove any distinction between the two terms, as one will equate to the other; as soon as a person has an unconditional right to be entered into the register of members in respect of certain shares, his name will be entered into the register of members in respect of those shares. At that stage, the shares will be both allotted and issued.

14.3   ISSUING SHARES: THREE VITAL QUESTIONS

Now that the terminology is clear, let us turn to the topic of issuing shares. There are three important questions which the lawyer must consider in relation to any issue of shares, namely (and in this order):

(a)   Limit on the number of shares – does the company have a limit in its articles of association on the number of shares that it can issue?

(b)   Authority to allot – do the directors have sufficient authority to allot the shares under s 551 of the CA 2006?

(c)   Pre-emption rights – do the pre-emption rights under s 561 of the CA 2006 apply to the issue and, if so, does the company need to disapply them?

The detail of, and the potential action required by, these questions is considered at **14.4** to **14.6** below.

14.4   LIMIT ON NUMBER OF SHARES

The first question the lawyer must consider, then, on a share issue, is whether there is a provision in the company's articles of association which limits the number of shares the company can issue.

Companies formed after 1 October 2009 under the CA 2006 can place a limit in their articles on the number of shares which can be issued.

Companies formed before 1 October 2009, before the relevant provisions of the CA 2006 came into force, were required to have restrictions on the number of shares they could issue in their pre-CA 2006 memorandum of association (known as the 'authorised share capital'). Under s 28 of the CA 2006 these provisions are automatically treated as restrictions in the articles with effect from 1 October 2009.

If there is a limit in the articles and the proposed issue of shares will result in that limit being exceeded then that provision must either be removed or altered to permit the issue.

14.4.1   Checking articles and issued share capital

14.4.1.1   Locating the filings at Companies House

The lawyer should first locate and check the articles to see if there are any restrictions on the issue of shares. In a company formed before 1 October 2009 the lawyer should also check the memorandum of association (as the authorised share capital clause became a limit under the articles on that date).

The lawyer must check back through the records the company has filed at Companies House, to identify the current articles. If these contain a limit on the number of shares then the lawyer must also check the existing issued share capital to see if the new issue of shares will exceed this limit. The easiest way to find the existing issued share capital is to take the figures provided in the latest filed annual return, then to check all the filings made since that annual return to see if any of them alter either the authorised share capital, or the issued share capital. Note that with effect from 1 October 2009 the annual return is known as Form AR01. However, if the company has not kept up to date with its filings, the last annual return you find on file for a company may well be a Form 363 (which was required under the CA 1985). You can see a copy of both forms on the Companies House website. Subsequent changes to the company's share capital will be recorded in a statement of capital, which will be included on the relevant form which must be filed at Companies House. For example, after the allotment of new shares, the company must file a return of allotment Form SH01 within one month, which form will include a statement of capital. The lawyer should then check that the figure on record at Companies House corresponds with the company secretary's records (see **14.4.1.2** below).

Once the lawyer has identified the current figures, and knows how many shares the company is proposing to issue, it should be easy to calculate whether the company needs to remove the limit.

EXAMPLES

X plc wants to issue 50,000 shares in return for cash consideration. It has a restriction in its articles limiting its issued share capital to £1m divided into 1 million ordinary shares of £1 each. Let us take a couple of scenarios and analyse whether X plc needs to remove the restriction.

(a)   *Issued share capital is £1m*

It is easy to see that in this case, X plc must remove or increase the limit by £50,000 to £1.05 million.

(b)   *Issued share capital is £500,000*

In this case, X plc can issue a further 500,000 shares; it does not need to remove the limit.

(c)   *Issued share capital is £975,000*

X plc needs to remove the limit or increase it, but only by £25,000 to £1.025 million; as it is currently below the £1 million limit by 25,000 shares.

14.4.1.2   Ensuring filings are up to date

The lawyer should always check that the issued share capital figures on record at Companies House correspond with the company secretary's records. This is to make sure the company is up to date with its filings. If it is not, it will need to make late filings, otherwise this may lead to problems later on in the share issue.

14.4.2   Checking the guidelines

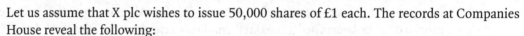

If the company is a listed company, the guidelines issued by the ABI and the Statement of Principles issued by the Pre-Emption Group have a bearing on the extent to which the company can issue new shares. It is preferable to check these guidelines and principles at this stage, to identify from the outset whether they will affect the proposed share issue. If they will, the company may decide not to proceed with the issue, and any preliminary steps, such as removing the limit in the articles on issued share capital. The provisions of the guidelines and principles are considered at **14.5.7** and **14.6.16** below.

14.4.3   Removing the limit on issued share capital

Let us assume that X plc wishes to issue 50,000 shares of £1 each. The records at Companies House reveal the following:

(a)   Issued share capital is £1m, divided into 1 million shares of £1 each.

(b)   The articles contain a restriction preventing the company from issuing shares which would take the issued share capital over £1 million, being one million shares of £1 each.

The company secretary has confirmed that the records at Companies House accord with his records and are up to date. The lawyer has checked, and the issue will be within the guidelines issued by the ABI and the Pre-emption Group (see **14.5.7** and **14.6.16** below).

X plc instructs its lawyer to draft the documentation to remove the limit on its issued share capital in its articles to enable the 50,000 shares of £1 each to be issued. How can this be done?

14.4.3.1   Special resolution

Section 21 of the CA 2006 provides that the company can change its articles by special resolution of the shareholders.

The lawyer must now draft the special resolution. The shareholders must pass this resolution by way of a special resolution in general meeting. The written resolution procedure under s 288 of the CA 2006 is not available to a public company.

If the company is formed before 1 October 2009 and there is an existing limit (see **14.4**) then it can be removed in one of three ways:

(a)   by passing an ordinary resolution to remove the limit; or

(b)   by passing a special resolution to adopt new articles without a limit; or

(c)   by passing a special resolution amending the articles authorising the directors to allot shares in excess of the limit.

Of course if there is no limit in the articles of association in the company concerned then this step can be dispensed with altogether.

14.4.3.2   Notifying Companies House

Under ss 29 and 30 of the CA 2006, a copy of the resolution and the amended articles must be sent to Companies House within 15 days of the date of the resolution (s 30(1)). Failure to comply with s 30 renders the company, and every officer who is in default, liable to a fine (s 30(2) and (3)).

14.4.4   The Listing Rules

The lawyer must also ensure that if the issuing company is a listed company it complies with the continuing obligations of the FCA in relation to communicating with its shareholders about the increase in issued share capital. These requirements are explained at 7.9 above. In particular, a premium listed company must publish a circular giving information on the change of articles (if relevant) and on the issue of new securities, including the arrangements for the allotment. The circular does not require the approval of the FCA (LR 13.2.2R). Listing Rule 13.8.10R provides that it must include the following information relating to the new articles (if relevant):

(a) an explanation of the effect of the proposed amendments; and

(b) either the full terms of the proposed amendments or a statement that they will be available for inspection:

    (i) from the date of the sending of the circular until the close of the relevant GM at a place in or near the City of London or such other place as the FCA may determine; and

    (ii) at the place of the GM for at least 15 minutes before and during the meeting.

In addition, the circular must contain certain information relating to the directors' authority to allot the new securities (see **14.5.6** below) and the disapplication of pre-emption rights (see **14.6.15** below).

The company must file a copy of the resolution and circular with the NSM, and notify an RIS that it has done so (LR 9.6.2R, LR 9.6.1R and LR 9.6.3R as amended by the introduction of the NSM) (see **7.5.7.1**). Any proposed alteration of a premium or standard listed company's capital structure must be notified to an RIS as soon as possible (LR 9.6.4R(1) and LR 14.3.17R(1)).

The aim of the additional rules is, of course, to maximise the protection for shareholders in the listed company and to ensure the markets have all the information on the company as quickly as possible.

14.5 AUTHORITY TO ALLOT

Once the company has removed any limit (if this is required) on the issue of shares in the articles, the second question the lawyer must consider is whether the directors have authority to allot the shares.

14.5.1 Section 551 of the CA 2006

Section 551 of the CA 2006 applies to public companies (and private companies with more than one class of share). It prohibits directors from allotting 'relevant securities' unless they are authorised to do so by:

(a) the company's articles of association; or

(b) ordinary resolution of the shareholders.

14.5.2 Shares

Section 551 applies to:

(a) the allotment of any type of share (ordinary and preference) (s 551(1)(a)) *other than–*
    (i) the subscriber shares (s 559), and
    (ii) shares allotted under an employee share scheme (see 13.9) (s 549(2)(a)); and

(b) the grant of any right to subscribe for, or convert to, any type of share (s 551(1)(b)) *other than* under an employee share scheme (s 549(2)(b)).

The exceptions are clear; no s 551 authority is needed to issue the initial subscriber shares in a company (see 13.5.6), or to issue employee share scheme shares.

Clearly, most shares fall outside the exceptions referred to at (a)(i) and (ii) above and so are caught by s 551(1)(a); s 551 authority is therefore needed before those shares can be allotted.

What is not so obvious, however, is the effect of s 551(1)(b). Basically, this brings more than just shares within the ambit of s 551. A few typical examples, which often are the source of some confusion as to *when* s 551 authority is required in respect of them, are considered below.

14.5.2.1 Convertible loan stock

Convertible loan stock is a class of debt security which carries the right to convert into shares.

Is it within s 551?

Yes, provided the stock does not convert to employee share scheme shares.

When is s 551 authority needed?

There are three possibilities. Is it:

(a)   when the debt securities are allotted; or

(b)   when the debt securities are converted into shares; or

(c)   both (a) and (b)?

The answer is (a) – s 549(3). This is important; *at the time the debt securities are allotted* there must be sufficient s 551 authority to cover the ordinary shares into which the debt securities will convert.

14.5.2.2 Options

Is an option within s 551?

The grant of an option to subscribe for shares (other than employee share scheme shares) will fall within s 551.

When is s 551 authority needed?

Section 551 authority is required *at the time of the grant*, not at the time of the exercise, of the option.

14.5.2.3 Convertible preference shares

A convertible preference share is a share which carries the right to convert into ordinary shares.

Is it within s 551?

Yes. In fact, both parts of s 551 (see above) catch these shares. Section 551(1)(a) catches the initial allotment of preference shares. However, the preference shares also carry a right to convert into ordinary shares, and this right is caught by s 551(1)(b) (see **14.5.2.1** above).

When is s 551 authority needed?

Again, the question is whether s 551 authority is required:

(a)   when the convertible preference shares are allotted; or

(b)   when the shares are converted into ordinary shares; or

(c)   both (a) and (b)?

The answer is (a). Note, however, that, on the basis of the analysis set out above, the s 551 authority will need to cover *both* of the shares comprised in this type of shares, namely, the convertible preference shares and the ordinary shares they will convert into. For example, if the company is issuing 50 preference shares, which carry the right to convert into 50 ordinary shares, *at the time the convertible preference shares are allotted* the directors require authority to allot both share 1 and share 2, so two separate s 551 authorities are required.

A flowchart summarising the application of s 551 is set out at **Figure 14.1** below.

Figure 14.1: Section 551 flowchart

14.5.3   Checking the existing s 551 authority

We now know that it is necessary to examine carefully the nature of the securities to be issued, to determine whether s 551 authority is required. However, our example of X plc wishing to issue 50,000 ordinary shares (see **14.4.3** above) is relatively straightforward. The shares fall within s 551(1)(a). Section 551 authority is required. So now what? First the lawyer will need to check the existing s 551 authority, to see whether the directors already have authority to allot the 50,000 shares or whether a new s 551 authority is required.

As explained at **14.5.1**, any s 551 authority will be either in the articles of association, or in an ordinary resolution. The lawyer must check the articles and the records at Companies House to identify the most recent s 551 authority. The lawyer must then check this authority to identify two key features, namely:

(a)   the date on which it expires; and

(b)   the maximum amount of relevant securities which can be allotted under it.

If the expiry date has passed then the answer is obvious; a new s 551 authority is required for the new issue in its entirety.

If the expiry date has not passed, so the s 551 authority is still current, then the lawyer must identify how many shares have been issued pursuant to that authority. If the maximum amount of shares has been issued, or if the proposed issue would exceed that amount, then a new s 551 authority is required. If not, then the existing s 551 authority will suffice.

Note that an authority given under s 80 or 80A of the CA 1985 (the forerunners to s 551) that is in force immediately before 1 October 2009 has effect on and after 1 October 2009 as if given under s 551 of the 2006 Act. This means that for companies formed before 1 October 2009 you will need to check to see whether such an authorisation exists, as it may still be valid. This is because authorisations under the CA 1985 had a maximum potential validity of five years.

14.5.4   Obtaining a new s 551 authority

Section 551(8) provides that whether the original authority was given in the articles of association, or by ordinary resolution, it can be renewed by ordinary resolution. This is clearly a departure from the usual rule that changes to the articles require a special resolution. The lawyer will need to draft this resolution.

14.5.5   The resolution

Under s 551(2) of the CA 2006, the authority can be restricted to a specific allotment, or it can be drafted as a general power to allot. It may be made subject to conditions, or it can be unconditional. An example of a resolution granting a general, unconditional s 551 authority is set out in resolution 1 of the ABI Guidelines on directors' powers to allot share capital and disapply shareholders' pre-emption right (see **Appendix 2**).

As **14.5.3** explained, s 551(3) provides that the authority must include two key pieces of information:

(a)   the date on which it expires; and

(b)   the maximum amount of shares which can be allotted under it.

The lawyer must bear this in mind, not only when checking any existing s 551 authority, but also when drafting a new s 551 authority. The two key pieces of information are considered at **14.5.5.1** and **14.5.5.2** below.

14.5.5.1   The expiry date

Under s 551(3)(b) of the CA 2006, the expiry date must not be more than five years from either:

(a)   the date on which the company was incorporated (if the authority is contained in the articles of association); or

(b)   the date of the resolution giving the authority.

Clearly (a) is relevant only in relation to drafting the original s 551 authority, and therefore it is (b) which applies in relation to drafting the majority of s 551 authorities. The authority can be for up to a fixed period of five years. In an abundance of caution, this is usually expressed in the resolution as being the fifth anniversary of the resolution less one day.

Note that in practice, listed companies usually grant the directors a new s 551 authority each year, at the AGM, as a safeguard against inadvertently allowing an authority to expire. Another safeguard in relation to the expiry date which can be drafted into a s 551 authority is to allow the directors to allot shares, even if the s 551 authority has expired, if they do so pursuant to an offer or agreement made by the company before the authority expired (see resolution 1 of the ABI Guidelines in **Appendix 2**).

14.5.5.2 Maximum amount of relevant securities

The s 551 authority must state the maximum amount of shares which can be allotted under it. The amount is usually stated in terms of the maximum nominal amount (for example, £50,000), rather than the number of shares (for example, 50,000 shares of £1 each), so that if the company consolidates or subdivides its shares (for example, into shares of £2 or 10p), it will not need to amend the s 551 authority.

In relation to s 551(1)(b) (see 14.5.2 above), the maximum amount relates to the shares which will be issued on exercise of the right. If the issue were of 10 debt securities, for example, which will be converted to a maximum of 100 ordinary shares of £1 each, then the maximum amount would be £100.

When determining this maximum amount, if the company is a listed company, regard must be had to the ABI guidelines, which impose a limit on the amount. The provisions of the guidelines are considered at **14.5.7** below.

14.5.5.3 Notifying Companies House

Under s 555 of the CA 2006 the company must file with Companies House within one month a return of the allotment together with a statement of capital. These are contained in one Companies House form, Form SH01. Under s 554, directors must register an allotment as soon as practicable, but no later than two months after the allotment, otherwise an offence will have been committed.

The lawyer must also ensure that the s 551 ordinary resolution is filed at Companies House within 15 days of it being passed.

14.5.6 The Listing Rules

Again, if the company issuing the shares is a listed company then it must comply with the continuing obligations of the Listing Rules regarding communications with shareholders (see **7.9** above). In particular, LR 13.8.1R provides that when a premium listed company sends out the s 551 resolution to its shareholders, the explanatory circular (which does not require approval by the FCA (LR 13.2.2R)) must include the following information:

(a) a statement of:
   (i) the maximum amount of relevant securities which the directors will have authority to allot, and
   (ii) the percentage which that amount represents of the total issued ordinary share capital as at the latest practicable date before publication of the circular;
(b) a statement by the directors as to whether they have any present intention of exercising the authority, and if so for what purpose; and
(c) a statement as to whether the authority will lapse.

The circular must also include information relating to any treasury shares held by the company.

The company must file a copy of the resolution and circular with the NSM, and notify an RIS that it has done so (LR 9.6.1R, LR 9.6.2R and LR 9.6.3R as amended by the introduction of the NSM) (see **7.5.7.1**).

14.5.7 The ABI Guidelines

The ABI has issued guidelines (see **Appendix 2**) which restrict the amount of share capital which can be included in a s 551, CA 2006 authority given by listed companies. The ABI Guidelines provide that the maximum amount of relevant securities for which authority can be given is one-third of the issued ordinary share capital.

The ABI will accept an authority to allow the allotment of a further one-third of the issued share capital, provided that the additional authority is only used for fully pre-emptive rights issues and both the general and additional authorities expire at the next AGM (rather than up to five years for a general authority). Further, the entire board of directors must put itself up for re-election at the next AGM if more than one-third of the issued share capital is actually allotted in one year; in other words, if recourse is had to the additional authority.

The permission for this additional one-third authority was introduced by the ABI in 2008 in response to the frequency with which some listed companies, principally banks, were having to exceed the original one-third limit to raise sufficient funds from its shareholders to stave off possible insolvency.

EXAMPLES

Let us use X plc as an example. X plc is now a listed company and has an authorised share capital of £1.05m and an issued share capital of £1m.

(a) X plc wants to issue 50,000 shares of £1 each (not by way of rights issue).

    (i) The authorised but unissued ordinary share capital is £50,000.

    (ii) The sum equal to one-third of the issued ordinary share capital is £333,333.

    (iii) £50,000 is the lesser figure, so it is fine to give the directors the s 551 authority for issuing the £50,000 shares.

(b) Imagine instead that X plc wants to issue 500,000 rather than 50,000 shares (not by way of rights issue). X plc has already increased its authorised share capital to £1.5m. The issued share capital is still £1m.

    (i) The authorised but unissued ordinary share capital is £500,000.

    (ii) The sum equal to one-third of the issued ordinary share capital is £333,333.

    (iii) £333,333 is the lesser figure, so the ABI Guidelines would prevent X plc giving s 551 authority over the entire amount of shares X plc wants to issue, namely £500,000. It could issue only 333,333 shares.

(c) Imagine instead that X plc wants to issue 500,000 rather than 50,000 shares but this time fully pre-emptively by way of rights issue. X plc has already increased its authorised share capital to £1.5m. The issued share capital is still £1m.

    (i) The authorised but unissued ordinary share capital is £500,000.

    (ii) The sum equal to two-thirds of the issued share capital is £666,666.

    (iii) £500,000 is the lesser figure so the ABI Guidelines would permit X plc to give s 551 authority to issue the number of shares it wants. This is only because the issue will be by way of fully pre-emptive rights issue. The further conditions mentioned above must also be satisfied.

This is why, as stated in **14.4.2** above, it is important to analyse the ABI guidelines upfront.

The ABI Guidelines are non-statutory and designed to prevent the dilution of (principally institutional investors') shareholdings without the shareholders' prior approval. If the company considers that it has good reason to exceed the limit set out in the Guidelines, it can discuss this with the ABI in advance of any allotment.

14.5.8   Sanctions for breach of s 551

Breach of s 551 does not actually invalidate the share allotment (CA 2006, s 549(6)). However, s 549(4) and (5) provide that any director who knowingly and wilfully contravenes, or permits or authorises a contravention of, s 551 is liable to a fine.

14.5.9   Sanctions for breach of the Listing Rules

The sanctions for breach of the Listing Rules are as set out at **3.6** above.

14.6 PRE-EMPTION RIGHTS ON ALLOTMENT

Now that X plc has removed any limit in the articles on issuing the 50,000 shares, and the directors have authority to allot the 50,000 shares, what is preventing the company from allotting the shares? Well, there is one final question to consider: do the pre-emption rights under s 561 of the CA 2006 apply to the allotment and, if so, does the company need to disapply them?

(Remember not to confuse pre-emption rights on allotment of new shares with pre-emption rights on the transfer of existing shares. This chapter is considering the issue of new shares, not the transfer of existing shares, and therefore is concerned only with pre-emption rights on allotment.) Any pre-emption rights on transfer will be drafted into the company's articles of association or, if the company has issued any convertible securities, or warrants and options etc, the deeds or agreements setting out the terms of issue may also contain specific pre-emption rights on transfer.)

14.6.1 What is a pre-emption right on allotment?

A pre-emption right on allotment is a right of first refusal for existing shareholders on an issue of shares by a company. This means that when a company wants to issue shares, it must first offer those shares to the existing shareholders in proportion to their existing shareholdings.

14.6.2 Rationale

The right of pre-emption protects the shareholders against the dilution of their shareholdings. If each shareholder takes up the shares offered to him under the right of pre-emption, although the number of shares held by him will increase, his percentage shareholding will be preserved. Of course, the right helps the existing shareholder to preserve his percentage shareholding only if he can afford to buy the shares offered to him.

14.6.3 Where are pre-emption rights on allotment?

The main provisions relating to pre-emption on allotment are in the CA 2006 and the Listing Rules. A company's articles of association may also contain specific provisions relating to pre-emption on allotment. If a listed company has issued any convertible securities, or warrants and options etc, the deeds or agreements setting out the terms of issue may also contain specific pre-emption provisions on allotment.

14.6.4 Obstruction

We are about to consider the complex provisions relating to pre-emption rights. Bear in mind, while you are reading, that from the company's perspective (acting through its directors) pre-emption rights can be a pain. They may prevent, at least initially, the company from issuing shares to those to whom it would prefer to issue and compel the company to offer those shares to existing shareholders. We shall come back to this at **14.6.13** below.

14.6.5 Section 561 of the CA 2006

Section 561 of the CA 2006 provides statutory pre-emption rights on allotment. A company proposing to issue *equity securities* in return for *cash* must first offer the shares to holders of *ordinary shares* in proportion to the nominal value of their existing shareholdings.

Let us be very clear: this means that there are two types of securities we need to analyse:

(a)   equity securities – that is, the shares the company is proposing to issue which might *trigger* pre-emption rights, so that those equity securities must be offered first to those people who have pre-emption rights; and

(b)   ordinary shares – that is, the shares which *entitle* their owners to pre-emption rights, so that their owners are offered first refusal over an issue of equity securities.

These two types of securities are considered further at **14.6.6** and **14.6.8** below.

14.6.6   Equity securities

This term relates to the shares the company is proposing to issue. If the company is proposing to issue an equity security, it will trigger pre-emption rights under s 561. Section 560(1) of the CA 2006 defines 'equity securities'. It does so by reference to the term 'ordinary shares'.

Basically, equity securities are:

(a)   any 'ordinary shares' in the company (see **14.6.8** below) *other than*:
  (i)   a subscriber share (s 577) (see **13.5.6**),
  (ii)   a bonus share (s 564),
  (iii)   shares held under an employees' share scheme (s 566), and
  (iv)   shares allotted *pursuant to* a right to subscribe (s 549(3)); and

(b)   any *right to subscribe* for, or convert securities into, ordinary shares.

14.6.7   For cash

Section 565 provides that the pre-emption rights under s 561(1) will apply only if the issue of shares is *wholly* in return for cash. If the consideration for the issue is partly or wholly anything other than cash (for example, shares or land), the s 561 pre-emption rights on allotment will not apply. Section 583 of the CA 2006 defines a payment of cash to include cash or cheque.

14.6.8   Ordinary shares

This term relates to the shares that entitle their owners to benefit from pre-emption rights in the event that the company issues equity securities. Section 560(1) defines 'ordinary shares' as any shares *other than* a share which, in relation to both dividends and capital, carries a right to participate only up to a specified amount (the definition therefore includes shares such as an ordinary share and a participating preference share, and excludes, for example, non-participating preference shares – see **13.5.2.1**).

If you compare the definition of 'equity securities' (see **14.6.6**) with the definition of 'ordinary shares', you will notice several important distinctions between the two.

14.6.8.1   The right to subscribe for, or convert into, ordinary shares

This falls within the definition of equity securities but outside the definition of 'ordinary shares'. This means that while the issue of a right to subscribe for, or convert securities into, ordinary shares will *trigger* the pre-emption rights (see (a) and (b) below for more detail), those rights to subscribe or convert will not *entitle* their owners to pre-emption rights. Let us delve a little further into this by exploring the position regarding two different types of convertible security and whether they *trigger* pre-emption rights:

(a)   *Convertible loan stock.* The loan stock will fall within para (b) of the definition of 'equity securities' at **14.6.6** above and the issue of convertible loan stock for cash will *trigger* s 561 pre-emption rights.

By 'triggering pre-emption rights' we are saying that the company must first offer the loan stock to existing shareholders *pro rata*. Why? the loan stock is convertible into shares, and if this conversion takes place it will dilute the existing shareholders' ownership if converted shares are held by outsiders.

(b)   *Convertible preference shares.* The issue here is whether the convertible preference shares are participating or non-participating shares. If they are participating, they will be caught by the definition of 'equity securities' (para (a) at **14.6.6** above: they are 'ordinary shares' for these purposes) and will *trigger* s 561 pre-emption rights, assuming they are issued for cash. If they are non-participating, they will fall outside para (a) at **14.6.6** above (they are not 'ordinary shares'); however, they will be caught by para (b) at **14.6.6**. The issue of those shares will *trigger* the pre-emption rights, assuming they are issued wholly for cash.

14.6.8.2 Employee share scheme shares

Section 566 states that s 561 pre-emption rights do not apply to shares held under an employees' share scheme (see **14.6.5** above). This means that employee share scheme shares will not trigger the s 561 pre-emption provisions when they are issued, but, once issued, they will *entitle* their owners to pre-emption rights in the event that the company issues equity securities.

Employee share schemes are explored in more detail at **13.9**.

14.6.8.3 Bonus/subscriber shares

Sections 564 and 577 state that the allotment of bonus/subscriber shares will not trigger pre-emption rights, but holders of bonus and subscriber shares will be *entitled* to pre-emption rights provided they are ordinary shares and are not excluded because they carry only a limited right to participate in income and share capital.

14.6.9 How to consider pre-emption rights

When analysing whether s 561 will apply to a share issue, you need to separate your analysis of the securities the company is proposing to issue, which might *trigger* pre-emption rights, from your analysis of the securities which might *entitle* their holders to a pre-emption right on an issue of equity securities.

Now, two pieces of good news. The first is that the summary at **14.6.10** below, and the examples at **14.6.11** below, should simplify the application of s 561. The second is that, if the company decides to disapply the pre-emption rights, you will not need to apply s 561 at all (see **14.6.15** below) (although unfortunately you do need to be capable of applying s 561 to find out whether you need to disapply it in the first place).

14.6.10 Summary of statutory pre-emption rights on allotment

(a) Equity securities which *can trigger* pre-emption rights when they are issued (that is they must be offered pro rata to the existing shareholders):

  (i) ordinary shares;

  (ii) participating preference shares; and

  (iii) rights to subscribe for, or convert into, ordinary or participating preference shares.

(b) Securities which are not equity securities and *cannot trigger* pre-emption rights when they are issued:

  (i) non-participating preference shares;

  (ii) employee share scheme shares;

  (iii) any share issued for non-cash consideration;

  (iv) bonus shares; and

  (v) subscriber shares.

(c) 'Ordinary shares' which *entitle* their owners to pre-emption rights on an issue of equity securities (in other words, these shareholders will expect a pro rata offer of the equity securities being offered):

  (i) ordinary shares;

  (ii) participating preference shares;

  (iii) employee share scheme shares (if they are (i) or (ii) above);

  (iv) bonus shares (if they are (i) or (ii) above); and

  (v) subscriber shares (if they are (i) or (ii) above).

(d)   Shares which *do not entitle* their owners to pre-emption rights on an issue of equity securities (in other words, these shareholders cannot expect a pro rata offer of the equity securities being offered):

(i)   non-participating preference shares;

(ii)   rights to subscribe for, or to convert into, ordinary or participating preference shares.

14.6.11   Examples

The following examples assume that there is not already in place a disapplication of the statutory pre-emption rights on allotment and that, unless otherwise stated, the consideration for the proposed issue is wholly cash.

EXAMPLE 1

A plc is proposing to issue ordinary shares. The company's existing share capital comprises ordinary and participating preference shares. The shares to be issued are equity securities and the proposed issue is for cash consideration. Therefore, unless a disapplication of s 561 is obtained, the directors must offer the shares first to the holders of the ordinary and the preference shares (both are 'ordinary shares') pro rata to their respective holdings.

EXAMPLE 2

B plc is seeking to acquire the entire issued share capital of Z plc and is offering Z's shareholders two B plc shares for each of their Z shares. Section 561 does not apply to the issue of B shares because the consideration for them is not cash. The consideration comprises the shares in Z.

EXAMPLE 3

C plc intends to issue ordinary shares. The existing capital structure comprises ordinary shares and convertible loan stock. This is an issue of equity securities but the new shares will be offered only to the holders of the ordinary shares. Convertible loan stock does not fall within the definition of 'ordinary shares' and so does not entitle its owners to pre-emption rights.

EXAMPLE 4

D plc intends to issue convertible loan stock. The existing capital structure comprises ordinary shares and non-participating preference shares. The issue of convertible loan stock does amount to an issue of equity securities. On this assumption, s 561 applies. Unless the section is disapplied the directors must offer the convertible loan stock first to the ordinary shareholders. The holders of the non-participating preference shares do not have statutory pre-emption rights as they are not the holders of 'ordinary shares'.

14.6.12   Pre-emption rights on allotment under the Listing Rules

As explained at **7.6.3** above, premium listed companies only must, in addition to the statutory pre-emption rights, comply with pre-emption rights on allotment (LR 9.3.11R). The statutory rights under the CA 2006 apply to all companies registered in the UK, whether public or private, including standard listed companies. The Listing Rules rights apply just to premium listed companies. These will usually be UK-registered, but they may also be registered overseas and so not subject to the CA 2006. On an issue of *equity shares for cash*, there is a continuing obligation on a premium listed company to offer those shares first to the *existing equity shareholders* (of shares of that class, or of another class who are entitled to be offered them) in proportion to their existing holdings.

An issue by a premium listed company pursuant to the pre-emption rights set out in LR 9.3.11R is known as a 'rights issue' or an 'open offer'. **Chapter 17** considers these in more detail.

These rights of pre-emption on allotment under the Listing Rules reflect the statutory rights of shareholders of any company, listed or not, under ss 561 to 577 of the CA 2006, but the pre-emption rights on allotment under the Listing Rules are not identical. For example:

(a) The definition of 'equity shares' in the Listing Rules is different from 'equity securities' in the CA 2006. Under the Listing Rules, equity shares are just:

   (i)   ordinary shares; and

   (ii) participating preference shares.

(b) Listing Rule 9.3.12R(2) provides that a company does not need to comply with the pre-emption rights in LR 9.3.11R in relation to equity shares which:

   (i)   represent fractional entitlements; or

   (ii) the directors think it is necessary or expedient to exclude from any offer due to legal problems under the laws of any territory or due to any regulatory body,

   where there is a disapplication in a rights issue or an open offer, used solely in respect of the shares covered by (b)(i) and (ii) above, rather than generally for *all* shares.

   In addition, LR 9.3.12R(3) and LR 9.3.12R(4) provide that the pre-emption rights under the Listing Rules will not apply if the company is selling treasury shares for cash to an employee share scheme, or if the company is an overseas company with a primary listing.

   Section 561 makes no provision for fractional entitlements so, in practice, entitlements are rounded down. Further, in order to comply with s 561 without making an offer in jurisdictions outside the EEA with onerous requirements, companies must follow the procedure under s 562(3) of the CA 2006, known as the '*Gazette* route'.

These differences are easier to understand in the context of a rights issue. Their practical effect is considered at **17.7.6** below. Pre-emption rights under the CA 2006 can cause problems on a rights issue in a way that the pre-emption rights under the Listing Rules do not.

Note that there are no pre-emption rights on *transfer* in the Listing Rules. (Indeed, this would be contrary to the requirement that the shares of listed companies should be freely transferable – see **4.3.1.1**.)

14.6.13   What is the problem with pre-emption rights?

By now (perhaps with the help of a cold towel) you should be able to work out whether the proposed issue will trigger pre-emption rights either under the CA 2006, or under the Listing Rules. Let us consider the example of X plc again. X plc is proposing to issue 50,000 ordinary shares. These fall within limb 1 of the 'equity securities' test. The shares are to be issued wholly for cash. They will therefore *trigger* statutory pre-emption rights; they must first be offered to holders of relevant shares and relevant employee shares who are entitled to pre-emption rights.

Does this suit the company's purposes? Well usually no, not really. If pre-emption rights apply, the company must follow the detailed procedure set out in s 562 of the CA 2006, regarding the form the offer must take and the length of time for which it must remain open (14 days from the date the offer is made). Only once this period has expired, or the company has received a reply from each shareholder who benefits from the pre-emption rights, can it allot any shares which have not been taken up through pre-emption.

This usually inconveniences the company, so it will normally disapply the statutory pre-emption rights.

14.6.14 Disapplication of pre-emption rights under the CA 2006

The CA 2006 provides a number of ways in which a company can disapply s 561 when allotting equity securities for cash. Those under ss 567 and 569 are available only to private companies. We are not concerned with private companies, and so do not consider these methods any further.

Public companies can disapply pre-emption rights under ss 570 and 571 of the CA 2006. These sections provide that the company can disapply the s 561 pre-emption rights:

(a)   specifically (see **14.6.14.1**); or

(b)   generally (see **14.6.14.2**).

14.6.14.1 Specific disapplication (s 571)

A disapplication of pre-emption rights in relation to a specific allotment must be effected by a special resolution. However, this is not a popular method because of the requirements of s 571(5)–(7). This provides that before the resolution is proposed, the directors must recommend that the resolution be passed and circulate a written statement setting out:

(a)   their reasons for making the recommendation;

(b)   the amount of consideration for the shares; and

(c)   the justification of that amount.

The statement must be circulated to the members before the general meeting to pass the special resolution. The directors risk up to 12 months' imprisonment or a fine if the statement contains anything which is materially misleading, false or deceptive (s 572).

14.6.14.2 General disapplication (s 570)

This is the most common method of disapplying pre-emption rights, and can be used where there is in place a general authorisation for the purposes of s 551 of the CA 2006. The disapplication can be effected either by special resolution, which is most common, or by a provision in the articles. Unlike under s 571, the directors are not required to make any recommendation in relation to the resolution (see **14.6.14.1**).

14.6.14.3 Duration

Whether the disapplication is specific or general, it will be effective only until the s 551 authority to which it relates expires (s 570(3)). This means that the disapplication cannot last more than five years. Whenever a new s 551 authority is obtained, a new s 570 or 571 disapplication should also be obtained.

14.6.14.4 Example

An example of a general s 570 disapplication, which shows how it relates to the s 551 authority, is set out in resolution 2 of the ABI Guidelines on directors' powers to allot share capital and disapply shareholders' pre-emption right (see **Appendix 2**).

14.6.14.5 Notifying Companies House

The company must file a copy of the s 570 (or 571) resolution at Companies House within 15 days of its being passed (s 29(1)(a) and s 30).

14.6.15 Disapplication of pre-emption rights under the Listing Rules

As explained at **7.6.3** above, the shareholders of a premium listed company can also agree to dispense with their pre-emption rights under the Listing Rules. Listing Rule 9.3.12R(1) makes clear that a general disapplication by the shareholders of their statutory pre-emption rights in accordance with s 570 of the CA 2006 will also dispense with the pre-emption rights under LR 9.3.11R. In practice, most public companies effect a general disapplication of the statutory pre-emption rights at each AGM, at the same time that they take any s 551 authority. Although in theory this also dispenses with the pre-emption rights under the Listing Rules in their entirety, listed companies prefer to state in the resolution that they will nevertheless comply with the pre-emption rights under the Listing Rules. The s 570 disapplication, set out in resolution 2 of the ABI Guidelines on directors' powers to allot share capital and disapply shareholders' pre-emption right (see **Appendix 2**), is a typical example. This allows directors to make small, non pre-emptive issues and rights issues or open offers that follow the pre-emption provisions in the Listing Rules. The rationale for the provision that rights issues and open offers should follow the pre-emption rights under the Listing Rules but not the pre-emption rights under the CA 2006, is explained at **14.6.12** and **17.7.6**.

Again, if the company has a premium listing, it will need to observe the continuing obligations of the Listing Rules relating to communications with shareholders. These obligations are considered at 7.9 above. Listing Rule 13.8.2R provides that a circular should accompany the s 570 or s 571 disapplication containing the following information (the circular does not require approval by the FCA – LR 13.2.2R):

(a) a statement of the maximum amount of equity securities that the disapplication will cover; and

(b) (in the case of a general disapplication in respect of equity securities for cash made otherwise than to existing shareholders in proportion to their existing shareholdings) the percentage which the amount generally disapplied represents of the total ordinary share capital in issue as at the latest practicable date before publication of the circular.

The company must file a copy of the resolution and circular with the NSM, and notify an RIS that it has done so (LR 9.6.2R, LR 9.6.1R and LR 9.6.3R as amended by the introduction of the NSM) (see **7.5.7.1**).

14.6.16 The Pre-Emption Group's Statement of Principles

The institutional investors do not generally support issues of new shares by listed companies other than by way of a rights issue, because otherwise the issue will dilute a shareholder's shareholding, resulting in a smaller share of the company's profit (dividend) and a smaller percentage of voting rights. The original Pre-Emption Group was established in 1987 under the auspices of the Stock Exchange and consisted of representatives of listed companies, institutional investors and corporate finance practitioners. The Group issued Pre-Emption Guidelines advising shareholders not to vote in favour of any annual disapplication of pre-emption rights unless certain conditions were met.

Following concerns that the Guidelines were out of date, and after a Government-sponsored report by Paul Myners in 2005, a new Pre-Emption Group was established in 2005. The Group's members represent listed companies, investors and intermediaries. In May 2006, the Group produced a 'Statement of Principles' to provide guidance to shareholders and companies on the disapplication of pre-emption rights, and which were updated in July 2008. The Principles, supported by the ABI, the NAPF and the IMA, replaced the Pre-Emption Guidelines. They are set out in full at **Appendix 3**. They can also be viewed at the Pre-Emption Group's website (www.pre-emptiongroup.org.uk).

The Principles do not have the force of law but are stated to be a basis for discussion between companies and their investors. In practice, they reflect the position that the powerful institutional shareholders will take in relation to any s 570 or 571 disapplication. Paragraph 5 of the Statement makes clear that the Principles apply to equity issues for cash, other than on a pre-emptive basis, by UK companies which are listed on the Main Market. AIM companies are encouraged to comply too, although it is recognised that they may require a greater degree of flexibility. Paragraph 5 also makes clear that the Principles do not apply to issues of equity securities for cash if the issue is on a pre-emptive basis.

The Pre-Emption Group has stated that it will monitor the application of the Principles.

Note that, at the time of writing, reference was still being made in the Principles to the CA 1985 which was replaced by the CA 2006 on 1 October 2009.

14.6.16.1 Routine disapplications

The Statement recognises that shareholders will consider some requests to disapply pre-emption rights as non-controversial, or 'routine'. While the company needs to explain why the disapplication is required, and notify shareholders of the need for it in good time, shareholders are likely to agree in principle with such requests and will require less in-depth discussion about them. Typically, a routine disapplication can be made by way of an appropriate resolution at an AGM (para 18).

The Statement sets out the following guidance as to what constitutes a 'routine disapplication':

(a) A request is more likely to be 'routine' when the company is seeking authority to issue non-pre-emptively 5% or less of ordinary share capital in any one year (regardless of how the issue is structured) (paras 8 and 9);

(b) a company should not issue more than 7.5% of its ordinary share capital for cash, other than to existing shareholders, in any rolling three year period, unless:

(i) it has consulted suitably in advance; or

(ii) the matter was specifically highlighted when the disapplication request was made (para 10); and

(c) the price at which the shares are proposed to be issued is relevant; a discount of greater than 5% is not likely to be regarded as routine (paras 11, 20 and 21).

14.6.16.2 Non-routine disapplications

As recommended by the Myners Report, the Principles recognise that some requests to disapply pre-emption rights might be non-routine but nevertheless in the interests of the company and its shareholders. The Principles emphasise that the limits set out above are intended to ease the granting of authority to routine requests to disapply pre-emption rights, not prohibit the granting of non-routine disapplications. Rather, any request for a non-routine disapplication should be considered by shareholders on a case by case basis.

The Principles set out examples of issues which are likely to be critical to shareholders in terms of voting on any non-routine disapplication, such as the size and stage of development of the company in the sector in which it operates and the extent to which the issue would dilute the value and voting control of existing shareholdings (para 16). Any non-routine disapplication should be made at a specially convened GM, unless the company is in a position to provide all the necessary information to shareholders at its AGM, in which case the request can be made at the AGM (para 18). A disapplication should not be granted for more than 15 months or until the next AGM, whichever is the shorter (para 19).

14.6.16.3 The disapplication procedure

For both routine and non-routine disapplications, the company must communicate with shareholders as soon as possible (para 4). Following the granting of any disapplication, the company should publish in its annual report certain information about the non-pre-emptive issue, such as the level of discount, the amount raised and how it was used (para 22).

EXAMPLE

Let us apply the Statement of Principles to our example of X plc. The issued ordinary share capital at the date of the last published accounts was £1m. 5% of £1m is £50,000, so the disapplication required relating to the issue of 50,000 shares of £1 is 'routine', provided X plc has not made any other issues in the last three years which would exceed the 7.5% cumulative total referred to at **14.6.16.1(b)**. The lawyer needs to check that the consideration complies within the requirement set out at **14.6.16.1(c)**, then, finally, X plc will be in a position to issue shares.

14.6.17 Sanctions for breach of s 561

A breach of s 561 will not invalidate or cancel an allotment. However, s 563 of the CA 2006 provides that the company and any director who knowingly permitted the breach are jointly and severally liable to compensate any person to whom the shares should have been offered under the pre-emption rights.

14.6.18 Sanctions for breach of the Listing Rules

The sanctions for breach of the Listing Rules are as set out at **3.6** above.

14.7 ISSUING THE SHARES

Once the three questions listed at **14.3** above have been considered and the appropriate action taken, the company is in a position to issue the shares. However, the lawyer must check that the circumstances of the issue do not trigger any other legal problems. The areas to check are as follows.

14.7.1 Directors' duties

The directors must issue the shares in accordance with their statutory obligations under the CA 2006 and the remaining common law and fiduciary obligations. In particular, they must:

(a) act in a way they consider, in good faith, would be most likely to promote the success of the company for the benefit of the company as a whole (CA 2006, s 172); and

(b) act in accordance with the company's constitution and only exercise their powers for their proper purpose (CA 2006, s 171).

14.7.2 Financial assistance

There is a general prohibition on a public company providing financial help to anyone acquiring its shares. This can cause problems on a share issue, and the lawyer must analyse the terms of the issue carefully to identify any potential problems relating to financial assistance. **Chapter 16** considers this topic in detail.

14.7.3 Consideration

'Consideration' means the price paid for the shares. Generally, this does not have to be cash; a subscriber may pay cash, but may also pay in money's worth, such as with other shares (if the subscriber is a company) or other assets. However, where the issuer of shares is a public company, s 585(1) of the CA 2006 provides that it cannot accept consideration in the form of an undertaking:

(a) to do work; or

(b) to perform services.

In addition, a public company cannot allot shares as fully or partly paid up otherwise than in cash, if the consideration is or includes an undertaking which will, or may, be performed more than five years after the date of the allotment (s 587(1)). This is referred to as a 'long-term undertaking'.

14.7.4 Issuing shares at a discount

As explained at **13.3.1** above, s 580 of the CA 2006 provides that no company, public or private, listed or unlisted, can issue a share at a discount to its nominal value. The company can, of course, issue a share which is partly paid, but, as discussed at **13.3.7** above, in the case of a public company, each share (other than a share allotted pursuant to an employee share scheme – see **13.9**) must be paid up at least as to one-quarter of its nominal value together with the whole of any premium paid on it.

Finally, as **14.6.16** above explained, the Pre-emption Group's Principles provide that a listed company should not issue any share under a s 570 or s 571 disapplication (on a non pre-emptive basis) at a discount of more than 5% of its market value. This restriction does not apply, however, if the pre-emption requirements of the Listing Rules are followed.

14.7.5 Valuation of non-cash consideration

Section 593(1) of the CA 2006 provides that if the consideration for the allotment is not cash ('non-cash consideration'), the consideration must be independently valued, and a report of the valuation must be given to the company and the subscriber. There are some exceptions to this rule, however, and one important exception relates to a 'share-for-share exchange', that is, when the consideration for the issue of shares by one company is shares in another company. In this case no valuation is required (s 594).

14.7.6 Class rights

The procedure required to vary rights which attach to a certain class of shares was examined at **13.7** above. The lawyer must examine the rights attaching to the shares the company proposes to issue, to check that the issue will not, in fact, vary any existing class rights (for example, if the shares to be issued are a new class which will rank above an existing class in terms of dividend rights). If they will vary class rights, the procedures detailed in **13.7** above will need to be followed.

14.7.7 The Prospectus Rules

The lawyer must analyse the terms of the share issue to check whether a prospectus is required. **Chapter 17** considers this in relation to listed companies which are seeking to issue further shares.

14.7.8 Filing details of the issue

The company must notify the Registrar of any allotment of shares within one month of the allotment, by completing and delivering Form SH01 to Companies House. Note that the form must include a brief description of the consideration for which the shares were allotted. If the consideration was other than for cash, a simple description of the asset which comprises the consideration will suffice, such as '100 ordinary shares of £1 in Z Limited' if the consideration for the issue is shares. A statement of capital (contained in the form) must also be completed.

14.8 CONCLUSION

This chapter has shown that, while it is common for a company to issue shares, it can cause a few headaches for the lawyer. However, a methodical approach will ensure that all the required checks are made, and appropriate action taken. Do not forget, either, that while the lawyer should consider the three vital questions outlined at **14.3** above in relation to all issues of shares, not all issues will require action to be taken in relation to all three questions. For example, it may be that the company does not have a restriction in its articles on the number of shares it can issue, the directors already have authority to allot those shares, and the pre-emption rights have already been disapplied.

Also, the introduction to this chapter stated that it is not that the legislation which applies to listed companies is any more onerous than that applying to private companies, it is simply that the share capital of listed companies tends to be more complex. We have considered some of the more complex classes of securities that a listed company may have, such as convertible debt securities and convertible preference shares, in the context of whether an issue of such securities would require a s 551 authority, or trigger, or entitle recipients to, s 561 pre-emption rights on allotment. However, often listed companies will be issuing ordinary shares, like our example of X plc, where the process is much more straightforward because it is easier to determine whether the shares fall within the definitions in the CA 2006.

CHAPTER 15

DISCLOSURE OF INTERESTS IN SHARES

15.1 INTRODUCTION

People become shareholders of a company, public or private, in one of two ways. They either subscribe for shares which the company issues (see **Chapter 14**), or they buy shares from existing shareholders (see **Chapter 19**). In both cases, the new shareholder will identify himself (or itself) to the company, so that the company can record the shareholder's details in its register of members and send out a share certificate.

This chapter considers the rules which require certain shareholders of public companies to disclose their interests in shares to the company, and why, despite the seemingly adequate process outlined above, a public company requires this extra protection.

15.2 NOMINEE SHAREHOLDERS

A 'nominee' shareholder is the registered owner of a share, but he holds that share on trust for the benefit of another person, the 'beneficial owner'. The nominee will hold the legal title to the share but will have no beneficial interest in that share. Usually the beneficial owner will require the nominee to execute a declaration of trust in respect of the share, in which the nominee will give various undertakings to the beneficial owner, such as:

(a) to account to the beneficial owner for dividends and other income received in respect of the share;

(b) to exercise rights attaching to the share, such as voting rights, as the beneficial owner directs; and

(c) to transfer the share as the beneficial owner directs.

For example, stockbrokers use companies to act as nominee shareholders, to manage the accounts of their clients more efficiently. We have also seen an example with the CREST system of holding shares in listed companies in electronic form (see **2.5.3.1**).

15.3 THE REGISTER OF MEMBERS

All companies must maintain a register of members, pursuant to s 113 of the CA 2006. However, s 126 of the CA 2006 prohibits a company from recording notice of any trust in the register of members. This means that the register will record details of the holder of the legal title only. It will not record any details of the holder of the beneficial title. In some cases, of course, this is one and the same person. If I buy a share in Marks and Spencer Group plc tomorrow, I will own both legal and beneficial title to it. However, anyone who buys shares through a nominee will remain off the register; it is the nominee's details which the register will record.

15.3.1   Advantages of s 126

The purpose of s 126 is to make the company's administration easier, because the company does not have to concern itself with matters of beneficial entitlement to shares. The company has no obligation to identify the beneficial owner, or to involve itself in the detail of what a nominee shareholder can or cannot do in relation to the shares. As far as the company is concerned, no one has an interest in the share other than the person entered in the register of members. This is so helpful to a company that it will often reiterate this provision in its articles of association.

15.3.2   Disadvantages of s 126

Section 126 does have its disadvantages. It means that the company is not aware of who has beneficial ownership of its shares. Why is this a problem? For private companies it does not tend to be problematic. Often in private companies the shareholders are a relatively small group of people who know each other.

However, with public companies whose shares are traded on the Stock Exchange this is not the case. There are many shareholders. Nominee shareholders can be useful to market abusers or insider dealers seeking to hide their true identities (see **Chapter 10** and **11**). The value of those companies whose shares are traded on the Stock Exchange means that they are often targets for a takeover offer (see **Chapters 20** to **23**). If the company is not aware of the beneficial ownership of its shares, what is to stop a potential bidder secretly building up a large shareholding in the target company by buying shares through a nominee? These shares would come in very useful when it comes to securing acceptance of the offer from target company shareholders.

For these reasons, there are rules which require the disclosure to the company of certain interests in shares. Some of them should be familiar, as we encountered them briefly in **Chapter 7** when we examined the continuing obligations of listed companies.

15.4   RULES REQUIRING THE DISCLOSURE OF SHARE INTERESTS

In implementing the Transparency Directive in the UK (see **3.1** and **3.5.3** above), Chapter 5 of the DTRs was introduced, requiring major shareholdings to be disclosed to the company. Chapter 5 is considered at **15.5** below.

Part 22 of the CA 2006 concerns a public company's right to investigate who has a beneficial interest in its shares. This is examined at **15.6** below.

There are certain other provisions under the DTRs and the Takeover Code which also require the disclosure of the beneficial ownership of a public company shares in particular circumstances. These requirements are discussed at **15.7**.

15.5   NOTIFICATION OF THE ACQUISITION OR DISPOSAL OF MAJOR SHAREHOLDINGS

The Transparency Directive requires rules to be in place in every EU Member State relating to the notification of the acquisition or disposal of major shareholdings in certain companies. The relevant provisions were introduced by Pt 43 of the CA 2006, which enacted new provisions in Pt VI of the FSMA 2000. Pursuant to these provisions the Transparency Rules were drawn up by the FCA. Chapter 5 contains the particular rules relating to the notification of major shareholdings. Chapter 5 applies to companies whose shares are admitted to trading on a *regulated* market (such as the Main Market). The rules therefore apply to the companies considered by this book. In addition, Chapter 5 of the DTRs applies to companies whose shares are admitted to trading on a *prescribed* market. This includes AIM. Chapter 5 is therefore the only part of the DTRs which extends beyond Main Market companies to include AIM-quoted companies. Chapter 5 requires a shareholder of such companies to disclose his shareholding to the company in certain circumstances. Paragraph **15.3.2** above explains why this protection extends only to certain public companies.

In looking at these rules for this book we shall only consider the position of a UK plc which has its shares admitted to the Official List and admitted to trading on the Main Market. The notification obligations apply equally to premium listed and standard listed companies. We shall not be considering either AIM-quoted companies or non-UK companies. There is detailed guidance provided by the FCA on the application of the rules for all types of company in the UKLA's Technical Notes.

15.5.1 Purpose

The purpose of Chapter 5 of the DTRs is to ensure that companies whose shares are traded on the Stock Exchange are made aware of the identity of the beneficial owners of their shares, and therefore who controls voting rights in the company. As explained in **15.3.2** above, this is particularly helpful in terms of assisting the company to expose insider dealing or market abuse and to defend against a possible unwanted takeover bid.

15.5.2 When the obligation arises

The obligation to disclose interests in shares is triggered when the percentage of voting rights a person holds either as a shareholder, or directly or indirectly through his holding of financial instruments, crosses certain thresholds, the lowest of which is 3% (DTR 5.1.2R). Although 3% may not seem like a major shareholding, it is worth remembering that companies whose shares are trading on the Stock Exchange are the biggest in the country. A 3% stake in Royal Dutch Shell plc, one of the Stock Exchange's largest companies, is worth approximately £4 *billion* at the time of writing. So a shareholder with such a stake in the company has influence well beyond the apparently unimportant percentage, as so few shareholders will be able to reach this level.

15.5.3 The thresholds triggering disclosure

The applicable thresholds depend on two factors:

(a)   whether the company is a UK company or a non-UK company; and

(b)   the type of person holding voting rights in a company.

15.5.3.1 UK company

A person must notify a UK company if the percentage of voting rights he holds reaches, exceeds or falls below 3% and every whole percentage above 3% up to 100% (DTR 5.1.2R(1)).

It is important to note that a decrease as well as an increase in voting rights may be caught by the obligation to notify. Also, DTR 5.1.2R requires further changes, up or down, in the whole percentage figure of voting rights held by the person after an initial notification to be notified.

EXAMPLE

Miss C buys 2% of listed UK company Z plc in January 2015. No obligation to notify arises (she has not reached 3%). In March 2015 she buys a further 1%. She must make a notification under DTR 5.2.1R as she now owns 3% of Z plc. Miss C buys a further 2% in June 2015. She must make a further notification under DTR 5.1.2R as she now owns 5% and her voting rights have changed by a whole percentage figure from 3% to 5%. In July 2015 Miss C sells 1% of her shares in Z plc. Again, as her voting rights have changed by a whole percentage figure (from 5% to 4%), she must make another notification.

15.5.3.2   Specialist holders of voting rights

Certain institutional investors (such as an asset manager) need make a notification only at 5% and 10% and every whole percentage above 10% for certain types of share (DTR 5.1.5R).

15.5.3.3   Change in voting rights

Under DTR 5.6.1R, a listed company is obliged, at the end of each month during which there has been an increase or decrease in the number of its issued voting shares, to publish a statement of the new total number of voting rights in the company through an RIS. In addition, under DTR 5.6.1AR, a listed company must publish the same information after a transaction which produces a material change in its voting rights. This is defined in DTR 5.6.1BG as an increase or decrease of 1% or more. An increase can occur, for example, after a rights issue or an issue of shares under an employee share scheme. A decrease can occur, for example, after a buyback of shares by the company. The importance of this is that the percentage voting rights of a person who owns, say, 10 shares in a company with 100 issued shares (10%) changes if the number of issued shares in that company increases to 1,000 shares (now 1%) or decreases to 50 shares (now 20%) and that person does not buy or sell any shares.

Transparency Rule 5.1.2R(2) therefore obliges a person whose voting rights reach or cross one of the required thresholds by virtue of a change in the company's issued share capital, to make the necessary notification. This is a logical extension of the basic rule, for even though the person has not bought or sold any shares, his relative voting power (as shown in the example above) has now changed, and 3% is still 3% of the voting rights in the company even if it arose without any shares being bought or sold by the holder.

An example of an announcement made under DTR 5.6.1R is set out below.

Company	Rentokil Initial PLC
TIDM	RTO
Headline	Total Voting Rights
Released	17:30 21-Nov-2013
Number	6808T17

21 November 2013

Rentokil Initial plc
("the Company")
Total Voting Rights

In conformity with provision 5.6.1R of the Financial Conduct Authority ("FCA's") Disclosure and Transparency Rules the Company notified the market of the following:

As at 1 November 2013 the Company's issued share capital consisted of 1,817,498,329 ordinary shares of 1 pence each. The voting rights of these shares are identical with each share carrying the right to one vote per share. No shares are held in Treasury.

This total number of voting rights in the Company is 1,817,498,329 and this figure may be used by shareholders in the Company as the denominator for the calculations by which they will determine if they are required to notify their interest in, or a change to their interest in, the share capital of the Company under the Disclosure and Transparency Rules.

15.5.3.4   Percentage level

For the purposes of calculating whether any of the percentage thresholds in **15.5.3.1** and **15.5.3.2** has been reached, exceeded or fallen below, the percentage figure shall be rounded down to the next whole number (DTR 5.1.1R(6)): 3.5% therefore becomes 3% for the purposes of Chapter 5 of the DTRs; 14.99% becomes 14%; 6.07% becomes 6%, and so on. What this means is practice is that the notification obligation kicks in only when a whole percentage number changes. A person who buys more shares in a company, resulting in a change in voting rights from 3.2% to 3.9%, does not need to make a notification. Both figures are rounded down to the whole number 3% (that person will of course have made a notification on first crossing the 3% threshold). However, a person who sells shares, resulting in a drop in voting rights from 8.1% to 7.9%, must make a notification. The 8.1% is rounded down to 8% and 7.9% is rounded down to 7%. So although the sale represents a drop of only 0.2% in actual voting rights in the company, for the purposes of Chapter 5 it is a drop of whole percentage, thereby triggering a notification under DTR 5.1.2R.

15.5.3.5 Indirect holdings of voting rights

Under DTR 5.1.2R, for the purposes of calculating whether any of the percentage thresholds in **15.5.3.1** and **15.5.3.2** has been reached, exceeded or fallen below, a person must include any indirect holdings of voting rights (by virtue of the definition of 'shareholder' in the Glossary to the FCA Handbook). Direct holdings, which we have considered up to now, are those in shares fully owned in the name of the person concerned. Indirect holdings are specified in DTR 5.2.1R. They cover scenarios where a third party has ownership of the shares but another person is entitled to acquire, exercise or dispose of the voting rights in certain circumstances. Three examples are set out below.

Controlled companies

Disclosure and Transparency Rule 5.2.1R(e) includes voting rights held by a company which another person controls. So, for example, if Mr T owned 2.5 % of the voting shares in A plc in his own name, no notification obligation would arise as he owns below 3% of the voting rights. If, though, a company, ACME Limited, owned 100% by Mr T, subsequently bought 1% of the shares in A plc then this indirect holding would be aggregated with Mr T's direct holding and take him to 3.5%, and therefore require him to make a notification under DTR 5.1.2R.

Proxies

Where the chairman of a company is given proxy votes to exercise at his discretion at a general meeting then this too will amount to an indirect shareholding; and if totalling 3% or more of the voting rights, will also have to be notified (DTR 5.2.1R(h)).

Concert parties

Disclosure and Transparency Rule 5.2.1R(a) covers people who have an agreement to adopt a lasting common policy towards the directors of the company by the exercise of their joint voting rights. If such people hold 3% or more of the shares in a company then they must make a notification. This would catch people otherwise seeking to avoid the disclosure thresholds by clubbing together to acquire voting rights in a company, but with each holding of voting rights falling below the relevant threshold. For example, if G, H and J each own 2.5% of V plc's shares individually they have no notification obligation. However, if they had an agreement in accordance with DTR 5.2.1R(a) then the obligation would arise. This is particularly useful for a company in defending it against a surprise takeover bid. The rule seeks to ensure that the company is aware not only of a potential bidder's stake in the company (if it breaches 3%), but also of the group companies and the financial advisers of the bidder who may also be buying up shares.

15.5.3.6 Holdings of qualifying financial instruments

Under DTR 5.1.2R and DTR 5.3.1R, for the purposes of calculating whether any of the percentage thresholds in **15.5.3.1** and **15.5.3.2** has been reached, exceeded or fallen below, a person must consider not only direct holdings of voting rights and indirect holdings of voting rights (**15.5.3.5**), but also direct or indirect holdings in qualifying financial instruments which give the right to acquire shares with voting rights in the company. Transparency Rule 5.3.2R gives examples of such instruments, which could include convertible loan stock, options, etc.

15.5.4   Procedure for the making the notification

We now know what the disclosure obligation is and when it must be made. The question now arises as to how the holder of voting rights fulfils his obligation.

15.5.4.1   Who is notified and how?

The person must notify the company in which he holds the voting rights (DTR 5.1.2R and DTR 5.8.2(2)R). Furthermore, a copy of the notification must also be sent to the FCA (DTR 5.9.1 and 5.8.2(2) and the FCA's Technical Note UKLA/TN/543.1 Shareholder obligations).

In accordance with DTR 5.8.10R and DTR 5.9.1R, the notification must be made on Form TR1 (available on the FCA's website) and the copy sent to the FCA must be submitted electronically. The content of the Form TR1 can be seen in the example at **15.5.4.3** below.

15.5.4.2   Deadline for making the notification

The notification must be made by the relevant person to the company and the FCA within two trading days after the day when the person became aware, or should have become aware, of the acquisition or a disposal, or possibility of exercising voting rights (DTR 5.8.3R). This deadline is also triggered by the publication of a statement of a change in voting rights made under DTR 5.6.1R. The deadline for disclosure triggered by DTR 5.6.1AR is by the end of the next trading day after the material transaction. The FCA provides a link to a calendar of trading days through its website (DTR 5.8.9G). Basically, weekends and public holidays are excluded.

15.5.4.3   Content of the notification

The notification must include the information in DTR 5.8.1R for a notification of a direct or indirect holding of voting rights in shares, and DTR 5.8.2R sets out the required contents for a notification of voting rights in qualifying financial instruments. As explained at **15.5.4.1** above, a Form TR1 should be used. An example of a Form TR1 is set out below. Note that in the copy sent to the FCA only there must be an additional Annex containing contact details (DTR 5.9.1R).

Company	French Connection Group PLC
TIDM	FCCN
Headline	Holding(s) in Company
Released	11:23 21-Nov-2013
Number	6278T11

TR-1: NOTIFICATION OF MAJOR INTEREST IN SHARES[i]		
1. Identity of the issuer or the underlying issuer of existing shares to which voting rights are attached:[ii]	French Connection Group	
2 Reason for the notification (please tick the appropriate box or boxes):		
An acquisition or disposal of voting rights		X
An acquisition or disposal of qualifying financial instruments which may result in the acquisition of shares already issued to which voting rights are attached		
An acquisition or disposal of instruments with similar economic effect to qualifying financial instruments		.
An event changing the breakdown of voting rights		
Other (please specify):		
3. Full name of person(s) subject to the notification obligation:[iii]	Schroders plc	
4. Full name of shareholder(s) (if different from 3.):[iv]		
5. Date of the transaction and date on which the threshold is crossed or reached:[v]	30.10.13	

6. Date on which issuer notified:	30.10.13
7. Threshold(s) that is/are crossed or reached:[vi, vii]	14% - 13%

8. Notified details:

A: Voting rights attached to shares[viii, ix]

Class/type of shares	Situation previous to the triggering transaction		Resulting situation after the triggering transaction				
if possible using the ISIN CODE	Number of Shares	Number of Voting Rights	Number of shares	Number of voting rights		% of voting rights[x]	
			Direct	Direct[xi]	Indirect[xii]	Direct	Indirect
Ordinary GB0033764746	14,368,105	14,368,105	13,418,779	N/A	13,418,779	N/A	13.993%

B: Qualifying Financial Instruments

Resulting situation after the triggering transaction

Type of financial instrument	Expiration date[xiii]	Exercise/Conversion Period[xiv]	Number of voting rights that may be acquired if the instrument is exercised/converted	% of voting rights

C: Financial Instruments with similar economic effect to Qualifying Financial Instruments[xv, xvi]

Resulting situation after the triggering transaction

Type of financial instrument	Exercise price	Expiration date[xvii]	Exercise/ Conversion period[xviii]	Number of voting rights instrument refers to	% of voting rights[xix, xx]	
					Nominal	Delta

Total (A+B+C)

Number of voting rights	Percentage of voting rights
13,418,779	13.993%

9. Chain of controlled undertakings through which the voting rights and/or the financial instruments are effectively held, if applicable:[xxi]

Schroder Investment Management Limited	13,418,779 13.993%

Proxy Voting:

10. Name of the proxy holder:	
11. Number of voting rights proxy holder will cease to hold:	
12. Date on which proxy holder will cease to hold voting rights:	
13. Additional information:	The shares referred to in section 9 are held in portfolios managed by those firms on a discretionary basis for clients under investment management agreements. This disclosure has been calculated based on issue share capital amount 95,899,754
14. Contact name:	[removed]
15. Contact telephone number:	[removed]

15.5.5   The company's response to the notification

The notification made to the company concerned must be made public through an RIS by the end of the next trading day following receipt, in accordance with DTR 5.8.12R. The FCA provides a link to a calendar of trading days through its website (DTR 5.8.9G). The company must comply with DTR 6.3 when releasing the information. There is no set format for such an announcement, but if the Form TR1 is published the Annex must be removed (FCA's Technical Note UKLA/TN/543.1 Shareholder obligations).

15.5.6 Sanctions for breach

The FCA can impose the following sanctions for breaches of Chapter 5 of the DTRs:

(a)   private or public censure;

(b)   an unlimited fine;

(c)   require the relevant information to be disclosed to it (FSMA 2000, s 89H); and

(d)   may suspend or prohibit trading in the shares (FSMA 2000, s 89L).

For example, in August 2011 the FSA, the forerunner to the FCA, fined Sir Ken Morrison, the former Chairman of Wm Morrison Supermarkets Plc, £210,000 for breaching DTR 5.8.3R for failure to notify the company of a drop in his voting rights below 6, 5, 4 and 3%.

15.6   THE COMPANY'S POWER TO INVESTIGATE BENEFICIAL OWNERSHIP

We have already established that direct and indirect major owners of shares (and certain financial instruments) in companies whose shares are trading on the Stock Exchange must disclose certain levels of voting rights to the company. Part 22 of the CA 2006 supplements Chapter 5 of the DTRs by allowing public companies (whether listed or not) to be proactive and investigate the beneficial ownership of its shares in certain circumstances either:

(a)   on its own initiative, pursuant to s 793 of the CA 2006; or

(b)   because a shareholder has compelled it to do so, under s 803 of the CA 2006.

This power reflects just how important it is considered to be that a public company, particularly one trading on the Stock Exchange, is able to identify the ultimate ownership of its shares. The aim is to enable the company to identify any shareholder who may have predatory intentions toward the company and may be considering or seeking to launch a takeover bid. This power has become all the more important due to the increasing use of nominee shareholder accounts in CREST (the dematerialised system for owning shares in listed companies – see **2.5.3.1**).

15.6.1 Section 793 notice

If a public company knows, or has reasonable cause to believe, that a person:

(a)   is interested; or

(b)   has been interested, at any time within the last three years,

in the company's shares, the company can serve a s 793 notice on that person, requesting him to confirm whether or not he does have such an interest, details of those interests and certain other relevant information. The notice may be served in writing or electronically. Section 793 details the specific information which the company can request, but it also includes, for example, details of any concert party arrangements (see **15.5.3.5** above). In fact, the company can request information which is not covered by the disclosure obligation; for example, even if the recipient of the notice has interests which are less than 3%, the recipient can still be requested to disclose his interests.

The s 793 notice must specify a reasonable time within which the recipient must respond. This is not defined. In practice, this seems to be interpreted as two days in an emergency situation (such as when the company suspects it is the target of an impending takeover bid), and five days in all other circumstances.

Of course, s 793 is particularly welcome when a company suspects it is about to be the target of an unwanted takeover bid. Imagine that the share price of X plc has been falling dramatically and that the press has speculated that now would be a good time for one of X plc's competitors to launch a takeover bid. The company secretary of X plc will send out s 793 notices in order to expose any prospective bidder. In the event that the bidder then makes the bid, the company secretary will continue to send out s 793 notices, to monitor the level of acceptances. Of course, the bidder should also comply with the disclosure obligations under Chapter 5 of the DTRs and notify the company whenever its shareholding increases by a percentage level.

In practice, while the company secretary will often draft the notice (as it is the company secretary who will have daily contact with the company's registrars), he will often consult the company's lawyers about the interpretation of aspects of the legislation, for example what the current practice is as to the minimum 'reasonable time' within which the company can demand a reply.

The CA 2006 does not specify a format for a s 793 notice, but in light of the minimal changes to the position under the CA 1985, there is a specimen notice available on the BIS website, under s 212 of the 1985 Act, which is still instructive. At the time of writing, BIS had yet to update this specimen.

15.6.2   Shareholders' s 803 requisition

Section 803 of the CA 2006 provides that shareholders who hold at least one-tenth of the company's paid-up voting share capital can requisition the company to use its powers under s 793. The requisition must:

(a)   be in hard copy or electronic form;

(b)   state that the company is requested to exercise its powers under s 793;

(c)   give reasonable grounds for requiring the company to exercise its powers in that way;

(d)   be authenticated; and

(d)   be served in accordance with Pt 37 of the CA 2006.

Section 805 provides that the company must respond by carrying out the requested investigation and compiling a report of its findings, which it must make available at the company's registered office or at a place specified under regulations to be made in accordance with s 1136 of the CA 2006.

The company must act on the request within certain time limits set out in s 805. If it fails to do so, sanctions may be imposed (see **15.6.3.2**).

15.6.3   Sanctions

15.6.3.1   Criminal penalties

It is a criminal offence under s 795(2) of the CA 2006 to fail to comply with a s 793 notice, or knowingly or recklessly to make a false statement in reply. The offence is punishable with up to two years' imprisonment and/or a fine.

Fines can be imposed under s 798 of the CA 2006 for attempts to evade the restrictions placed under a s 794 order (see **15.6.3.2** below).

Fines can also be imposed for a failure to comply with a s 803 shareholder requisition, and for failing to meet various requirements relating to the obligation to provide a report under s 805 and allow access to it.

15.6.3.2   Imposing restrictions on shares

Section 794 of the CA 2006 allows the company to apply to court to have restrictions placed on shares covered by a s 793 notice where the recipient of the notice has failed to respond in time. Section 797 of the 2006 Act sets out the consequences of such an order if it is made:

(a)   any transfer of the shares is void;

(b)   no voting rights are exercisable in respect of the shares;

(c) the shareholder cannot benefit from any rights given by his shares to receive new shares in the company (such as a bonus or rights issue); and

(d) except on liquidation, no payment can be made of any sums due from the company on the shares, such as a dividend.

These restrictions are onerous, and are intended to prevent the person in breach of the s 793 notice from taking advantage of the breach, such as by launching a surprise takeover bid (the shares acquired could not be used to vote in favour of the bid) or by profiting from insider dealing or market abuse (the transfer is void). The company or any aggrieved person can apply to court for the removal of the restrictions under s 800 of the CA 2006. The court shall remove the restrictions only if it is satisfied that the relevant facts about the shares have been disclosed to the company and that no unfair advantage has accrued to anyone as a result of the breach of the disclosure obligation, or the shares are sold and the court approves the transfer.

15.6.4 The register of share interests

Section 808 of the CA 2006 provides that the company must keep a separate register which records interests disclosed to it pursuant to a s 793 notice. The company must keep the register, and the public have the right to inspect this register under s 811 of the CA 2006.

Section 817 of the CA 2006 provides protection for anyone who has been entered into the register who does not consider they should be in that register. It can arise in the process of complying with the s 793 notice that a shareholder identifies another person as being interested in shares. Section 817 provides a process whereby that person can insist on being removed from the register, provided the information which has been supplied is incorrect.

15.7 OTHER REQUIREMENTS

There are further disclosure requirements under the DTRs and the Listing Rules. Both sets of rules apply only to listed companies.

15.7.1 Transactions by PDMRs and their connected persons

As mentioned at **7.5.7.10** above, DTR 3.1.2R requires PDMRs and their connected persons to disclose to the company all transactions conducted on their own account in the shares of the company (or derivatives or any other financial instruments relating to those shares). This must be done within four business days of the day on which the transaction occurred. The PDMR must include in the disclosure the information required by DTR 3.1.3R.

A listed company must then notify an RIS of the information it receives under DTR 3.1.2R (DTR 3.1.4R(1)(a)). The company must include the information required by DTR 3.1.3R (DTR 3.1.5R), and provide the information to the RIS as soon as possible, and in any event no later than the end of the business day following the receipt of the information (DTR 3.1.4R(2)).

An example of such a notification is set out below. They can be found on the RNS section of the Stock Exchange's website under the heading 'Director/PDMR shareholding'.

Company	Prudential PLC
TIDM	PRU
Headline	Director/PDMR Shareholding
Released	12:15 21-Nov-2013
Number	6310T12

NOTIFICATION OF TRANSACTIONS OF DIRECTORS/PERSONS DISCHARGING MANAGERIAL RESPONSIBILITY AND CONNECTED PERSONS

This announcement is made in accordance with the requirements of DTR 3.1.4R(1)(a).

Prudential plc was notified on 20 November 2013 that the following transactions in the Company's shares took place on 20 November 2013 in London:

Purchase of shares

PDMR	Shares Purchased	Share Price	% of beneficial interest issued Share Capital acquired	Beneficial interest in shares held and % of issued share capital held beneficially
Philip Remnant	2,609 ordinary shares of 5p each	£12.5785	Less than 0.0002%	4,709 ordinary shares of 5p each, less than 0.0002%

Disposal of shares

PDMR	Shares Disposed	Share Price	% of beneficial interest issued Share Capital disposed	Beneficial interest in shares held and % of issued share capital held beneficially
Pierre-Olivier Bouee	5,000 ordinary shares of 5p each	£12.61	Less than 0.0002%	43,381 ordinary shares of 5p each, less than 0.002%

15.7.2 Directors' interests in shares

As mentioned at **7.5.7.11** above, LR 9.8.6R(1) requires a statement, setting out the directors' holdings of shares in their premium listed company, to be included in the annual report, together with any changes to this information over the past year. Disclosure Rule 3.1.4R requires this information to be notified to an RIS no later than the end of the next business day.

15.7.3 The Model Code

As explained at **7.8** above, PDMRs and their connected persons are required to seek clearance before dealing in shares they own in their listed company.

15.7.4 Takeovers

15.7.4.1 Application of the Takeover Code

Chapter 20 explores this in more detail, but, broadly speaking, the Takeover Code applies during the offer period for a takeover of, for example, a UK plc listed on the Stock Exchange (see **22.3.4**). If the Takeover Code does apply, it applies to everyone participating in the takeover, such as the offeror (the bidder) and the offeree (the target company), and their directors and any advisers.

15.7.4.2 Nature of the Takeover Code

The Takeover Code has the force of law under the Takeover Directive which has now been implemented in the UK. It exists to ensure that all takeovers are conducted fairly and in an orderly manner (see **Chapter 20**).

15.7.4.3 The obligations

Disclosure of issued shares (r 2.10)

The two main disclosure obligations are under r 8 of the Takeover Code (see below) and relate to the shareholdings at the announcement of the offer and subsequent dealings in shares during the offer period. However, as a precursor to those disclosure obligations, those companies whose securities will be subject to the disclosure obligations must notify the market, via an RIS, of the exact number of relevant securities which are in issue during the offer period.

Rule 2.10 of the Takeover Code provides that:

(a)   as soon as possible after the commencement of the offer period (and in any event by 9.00 am on the next business day) the target company; and

(b)   by 9.00 am on the business day after any announcement of a firm intention to make an offer (unless it has already stated that its offer will be, or is likely to be, solely in cash)

the bidder, or a publicly identified potential bidder, must each announce details, through an RIS, of all classes of relevant securities it has in issue, together with the numbers of such securities in issue.

Relevant securities are defined as:

(a)   voting shares in the target company;

(b)   any other shares in the target company which are the subject of the offer;

(c)   equity share capital in the target company and the bidder;

(d)   securities of the bidder which carry substantially the same rights as any to be issued as consideration for the offer; and

(e)   any securities in the target company and the bidder which are convertible into, or carry subscription rights over, any of the shares referred to at (a) to (c) above.

Disclosure of opening positions (r 8)

Rule 8 of the Takeover Code provides that an 'Opening Position Disclosure' must be made by:

(a)   the offeror;

(b)   the offeree company; and

(c)   holders of 1% or more of the offeror's or offeree's shares.

This disclosure is an announcement containing details of (inter alia) interests in or rights to subscribe for relevant securities (see above). It must be made both to an RIS and electronically to the Takeover Panel no later than 12 noon, 10 business days following the start of the offer period or, for the offeror only, from the earlier of the announcement which first identifies the offeror and the time of the announcement of the offer.

The offeror and offeree must include the holdings of any concert parties (see below) in their disclosure.

This provision ensures that all parties to a takeover, the Takeover Panel and, ultimately, members of the public are aware of who could be an important player in deciding the outcome of the takeover. It will also highlight any shareholders who have a stake in both the offeror and the offeree.

Disclosure of subsequent dealings by the offeror or offeree (r 8)

Rule 8 of the Takeover Code provides in addition that, once the offer period has commenced:

(a)   the offeror;

(b)   the offeree company; and

(c)   anyone 'acting in concert' with the offeror or offeree company,

must make a 'Dealing Disclosure', disclosing any dealings (as defined by the Takeover Code) in relevant securities (see above) to an RIS and the Takeover Panel no later than 12 noon on the business day following the date of the transaction.

People 'acting in concert' (also known as a 'concert party') are defined in the Takeover Code as persons who co-operate to obtain or consolidate control of a company or to frustrate its successful outcome. The term is intended to cover those who have an interest in the outcome of the offer. The Code gives the following examples of persons who typically will be concert parties:

(a) the offeree group companies or the offeror group companies (and their associated companies, being companies in which they have a shareholding of 20% or more);

(b) the offeree or offeror with any of its directors (and their close family and related trusts);

(c) the offeree or offeror group of companies and its pension funds;

(d) a fund manager of any investment company, unit trust or other person whose investments are managed by the fund manager on a discretionary basis;

(e) connected advisers of the offeree company and the offeror (and any members of the connected adviser's groups);

(f) directors of a company which is subject to an offer or where the directors have a bona fide belief that an offer is imminent.

Disclosure of subsequent dealings by 1%+ shareholders (r 8.3)

Rule 8.3 of the Takeover Code provides that if a person is interested or, as the result of any transaction, will be interested (directly or indirectly) in 1% or more of any class of relevant securities of an offeror or offeree, then he must make a Dealing Disclosure, disclosing his dealings in any relevant securities of that company, as well as the dealings of any other person through whom he derives his interest. The disclosure must be made by 3.30 pm on the business day following the date of the transaction (Note 2).

If disclosure is required under r 8.1 (offeror) or r 8.2 (offeree) or r 8.4 (concert party), then the same information does not also need to be disclosed under r 8.3.

The aim is therefore to ensure maximum transparency in share dealings by parties involved in a takeover. It is very important that the offeree company is aware of how big a stake the offeror has in it and when it changes.

Although r 8 applies only during the offer period, in Takeover Panel Statement 2011/3 (see **20.5.6.2** below), the Takeover Panel in one case extended the need for r 8 disclosures beyond the end of the offer period due to the special circumstances of that takeover.

15.7.4.4 Content of the notification

The 'Disclosure Forms' section of the Takeover Panel's website contains specimen Opening Position Disclosure and Dealing Disclosure forms which set out the format these r 8 notifications should take. Further information on the content can be found in Note 8 to r 8. A real-life example of a r 8.1 Opening Position Disclosure is set out below.

Company	News Corporation
TIDM	NCRA
Headline	Form 8 (OPD) NewsCorp/BSkyB
Released	11:56 29-June-2010
Number	4207O11

FORM 8 (OPD)

PUBLIC OPENING POSITION DISCLOSURE BY A PARTY TO AN OFFER

Rules 8.1 and 8.2 of the Takeover Code (the "Code")

1. **KEY INFORMATION**

(a)	Identity of the party to the offer making the disclosure:	News Corporation
(b)	Owner or controller of interests and short positions disclosed, if different from 1(a): *The naming of nominee or vehicle companies is insufficient*	

(c)	Name of offeror/offeree in relation to whose relevant securities this form relates: *Use a separate form for each party to the offer*	British Sky Broadcasting Group Plc
(d)	Is the party to the offer making the disclosure the offeror or the offeree?	OFFEROR
(e)	Date position held:	28 June 2010
(f)	Has the party previously disclosed, or is it today disclosing, under the Code in respect of any other party to this offer?	NO

2.   POSITIONS OF THE PARTY TO THE OFFER MAKING THE DISCLOSURE

(a)   Interests and short positions in the relevant securities of the offeror or offeree to which the disclosure relates

Class of relevant security:	50p ordinary			
	Interests		Short positions	
	Number	%	Number	%
(1) Relevant securities owned and/or controlled:	686,021,700	39.1%		
(2) Derivatives (other than options):				
(3) Options and agreements to purchase/ sell:				
TOTAL:	686,021,700	39.1%		

All interests and all short positions should be disclosed.

Details of any open derivative or option positions, or agreements to purchase or sell relevant securities, should be given on a Supplemental Form 8 (Open Positions).

Details of any securities borrowing and lending positions or financial collateral arrangements should be disclosed on a Supplemental Form 8 (SBL).

(b)   Rights to subscribe for new securities

Class of relevant security in relation to which subscription right exists:	
Details, including nature of the rights concerned and relevant percentages:	

If there are positions or rights to subscribe to disclose in more than one class of relevant securities of the offeror or offeree named in 1(c), copy table 2(a) or (b) (as appropriate) for each additional class of relevant security.

(c)   Irrevocable commitments and letters of intent

Details of any irrevocable commitments or letters of intent procured by the party to the offer making the disclosure or any person acting in concert with it (see Note 3 on Rule 2.11 of the Code):

3.   POSITIONS OF PERSONS ACTING IN CONCERT WITH THE PARTY TO THE OFFER MAKING THE DISCLOSURE

Details of any interests, short positions and rights to subscribe of any person acting in concert with the party to the offer making the disclosure
J.P. Morgan Securities Ltd. has a non-exempt short position of 106,407 in British Sky Broadcasting Group Plc representing 0.006% of the 50p ordinary shares issued by British Sky Broadcasting Group Plc

If there are positions or rights to subscribe to disclose in more than one class of relevant securities of the offeror or offeree named in 1(c), copy table 3 for each additional class of relevant security.

Details of any open derivative or option positions, or agreements to purchase or sell relevant securities, should be given on a Supplemental Form 8 (Open Positions).

Details of any securities borrowing and lending positions or financial collateral arrangements should be disclosed on a Supplemental Form 8 (SBL).

4. **OTHER INFORMATION**

(a) **Indemnity and other dealing arrangements**

Details of any indemnity or option arrangement, or any agreement or understanding, formal or informal, relating to relevant securities which may be an inducement to deal or refrain from dealing entered into by the party to the offer making the disclosure or any person acting in concert with it: *If there are no such agreements, arrangements or understandings, state "none"*

(b) **Agreements, arrangements or understandings relating to options or derivatives**

Details of any agreement, arrangement or understanding, formal or informal, between the party to the offer making the disclosure, or any person acting in concert with it, and any other person relating to: (i) **the voting rights of any relevant securities under any option; or**   (ii) **the voting rights or future acquisition or disposal of any relevant securities to which any derivative is referenced:**   *If there are no such agreements, arrangements or understandings, state "none"*

(c) **Attachments**

Are any Supplemental Forms attached?

Supplemental Form 8 (Open Positions)	NO
Supplemental Form 8 (SBL)	NO

Date of disclosure:	**29 June 2010**

15.8 SUMMARY

The table below summarises the key notification obligations, relating to the disclosure of interests in shares, covered by this chapter. The table is intended to be an overview only, and recourse should be made to the text for the specific detail of the rules.

Rule	Notifier	Notifiee	Interest	Deadline
DTR 5.1.2R	Shareholder of public company	Company	Acquires 3% (or further increase beyond whole percentage point), or falls by a whole percentage point or below 3% (see **15.5.3** for detail)	2 trading days after they become aware of interest
DTR 5.8.12R	Listed company	RIS	Information received under DTR 5.1.2R	By end of trading day following the day the company receives the information
DTR 3.1.2R	PDMRs of listed company (and their connected persons)	Company	All transactions conducted on their own account in the company's shares (or derivatives or any other financial instruments relating to those shares)	4 business days of day on which transaction occurred
DTR 3.1.4R (1)(a)	Listed company	RIS	Information received under DTR 3.1.2R	By end of the business day following the day the company receives the information
Takeover Code Rule 2.10	Offeror and offeree company	RIS	Number of relevant securities in issue	By 9 am on the next business day after the start of the offer period (offeree) By 9 am on business day after announcement of firm intention to make offer (offeror)
Takeover Code Rule 8	Offeror, offeree company and those holding interests of 1%+	RIS and Takeover Panel	Opening Position Disclosure (interests in and rights to subscribe to relevant securities)	12 noon 10 business days after offer period starts (offeree/1+%) 12 noon 10 business days after earlier of date offeror first publicly identified or firm offer announcement (offeror)
Takeover Code Rule 8	Offeror, offeree company and concert parties	RIS and Takeover Panel	Dealing Disclosure (dealings in relevant securities)	12 noon on business day following date of transaction

FINANCIAL ASSISTANCE

16.1 INTRODUCTION

So far, **Part III** of this book has considered the concept of shares: what they are; the different classes of share; the law relating to share issues; and how a company can find out who owns its shares. This chapter considers a potential problem which can arise on the *acquisition* of shares; the problem that, subject to certain exceptions, a public company cannot give 'financial assistance' for the purchase of its shares.

In its simplest form this means that if I want to buy shares in X plc, X plc cannot give me any financial help to buy those shares.

The rule itself is straightforward enough. So why is it described as a problem? In practice, financial assistance can arise in ways which are not easy to spot. In addition, the lawyer is often removed from the detail of the funding arrangements and is concentrating, instead, on the negotiation of the transaction. These two factors can conspire to make financial assistance an area that can inject an element of last-minute panic into a share acquisition that is otherwise running quite smoothly.

16.2 RATIONALE

To achieve a good understanding of the financial assistance rules, it can help to consider the rationale behind those rules. Why is financial assistance prohibited?

Let us consider a practical example of financial assistance. I am a financier and I want to buy a company. I lack significant funds. I find a company, X plc, which has substantial cash reserves and easily realisable assets (that is, they can be sold for cash readily). I agree to buy X plc for cash consideration. I am the buyer, and the shareholders of X plc are the sellers. I structure the transaction so that X plc uses its cash reserves, and cash realised from selling some of its assets, to advance me the cash I need to pay consideration to the shareholders of X plc. I then buy the company, but in effect X plc has funded the transaction.

The question is, who has lost out in this transaction? X plc's creditors. Their security is that X plc is cash-rich. This cash is now lining the pockets of the shareholders who sold shares in the company. It is no longer in X plc. X plc has misused its assets.

The prohibition on financial assistance would not permit the transaction described above. The reason? To protect creditors.

16.3   THE FINANCIAL ASSISTANCE PROHIBITION

Sections 678 and 679 of the CA 2006 contain the prohibitions on financial assistance. Section 678 prohibits the giving of financial assistance for the acquisition of shares in a public company. Section 679 prohibits the giving of financial assistance by a public company subsidiary for the acquisition of shares in its private holding company. Each section contains two prohibitions. The difference between them is:

(a)   s 678(1) and s 679(1) apply to financial assistance given *before or at the same time as* the acquisition of shares; and

(b)   s 678(3) and s 679(3) apply to financial assistance given *after* the acquisition of shares.

16.3.1   Financial assistance given before or at the same time as the acquisition of shares

We shall start by looking at s 678(1), which provides that:

(a)   where a person is acquiring or *proposing to acquire* shares in a *public* company;

(b)   it is not lawful for the company;

(c)   or any of the company's *subsidiaries*;

(d)   to give financial assistance;

(e)   directly or indirectly;

(f)   *for the purpose* of that acquisition;

(g)   before or at the time the acquisition takes place.

The following points are of interest here:

(i)   Section 678(1) only applies to the acquisition of shares in a *public* company (whether listed or not).

(ii)   'Proposing to acquire' means that there does not actually have to be an acquisition of shares for s 678(1) to apply; it is the fact that the person *intends* to acquire shares which is important.

(iii)   The person giving the financial assistance (Assistor) does not necessarily have to be the company whose shares are being acquired (Target); if the Assistor is a subsidiary of Target, s 678(1) will apply even if it is a private company.

(iv)   'For the purpose' (see (f) above) means that this is a purpose-based, not a results-based, test. It is not sufficient simply that financial assistance results in the acquisition, or is somehow connected with the acquisition. The Assistor must have *intended* to facilitate the transaction by giving the assistance. It is vital, therefore, to identify why the Assistor has provided the assistance.

For the s 679(1) prohibition, the test is broadly the same as in (a)–(g) above, but in (a) substitute 'private' for 'public', and (b) and (c) will read 'it is not lawful for a public company that is a subsidiary of that company'.

16.3.2   Financial assistance given after the acquisition of shares

Once again we shall start by considering s 678(3), which provides that:

(a)   where a person has acquired shares in a *public* company;

(b)   and a *liability has been incurred* (by that, or *any other*, person) for the purpose of that acquisition;

(c)   it is not lawful for the company;

(d)   or any of the company's *subsidiaries*;

(e)   to give financial assistance;

(f)   directly or indirectly;

(g)   *for the purpose of reducing or discharging the liability incurred*.

Again, note the following points:

(i)   Section 683(2) provides that 'incurring a liability' includes a change in financial position (there is no indication that this change must be for the worse). The obvious example of this is someone borrowing money to fund an acquisition.

(ii) The liability does not have to have been incurred by the person acquiring the shares.

(iii) As with s 678(1), the Assistor does not have to be Target; if the Assistor is a subsidiary of Target, s 678(3) will apply even if it is a private company.

(iv) As with s 678(1), the words 'for the purpose' feature in s 678(3) too. This means that the financial assistance does not actually have to reduce or discharge the liability incurred, as long as it was *intended* to reduce or discharge that liability. As with s 678, it is vital to identify why the Assistor has provided the assistance.

(v)   Section 683(2) provides that 'reducing or discharging the liability incurred' includes wholly or partly restoring a person's financial position to what it was before the acquisition.

For the s 679(3) prohibition, the test is broadly the same as in (a) to (g) above, but in (a) substitute 'private' for 'public', and (b) and (c) will read 'it is not lawful for a public company that is a subsidiary of that company'.

16.4   WHAT IS FINANCIAL ASSISTANCE?

Section 677 of the CA 2006 defines 'financial assistance' as:

(a)   financial assistance given by way of gift (that is, where the Assistor transfers an asset of value for nil consideration);

(b)   financial assistance given by way of:
      (i)   guarantee, security, indemnity (subject to a limited exception); or
      (ii)   release or waiver; or

(c)   financial assistance given by way of loan (or certain other types of agreement such as credit); or

(d)   any other financial assistance given by a company:
      (i)   the net assets (defined by s 677(2) as the actual value of assets less liabilities) of which are thereby reduced to a material extent (this is not defined, but appears to be a de-minimis level), or
      (ii)   which has no net assets.

You will note that the 'definition' of financial assistance actually uses the words 'financial assistance'. Section 677(1) therefore does not really define what financial assistance is, rather it gives examples of financial assistance.

Nethertheless, this definition makes clear that financial assistance is not limited to the more obvious situations, such as where the Assistor makes a gift or loan to the buyer to fund the acquisition of shares. Assistance of an indirect nature, such as when a bank gives a loan to the buyer to fund the acquisition, but the Assistor guarantees that loan or gives any type of security for it, will also constitute financial assistance. As mentioned in the introduction to this chapter at **16.1** above, these less obvious examples of financial assistance can cause problems for the corporate lawyer.

EXAMPLE

Imagine a typical day in practice. The chief executive of X plc calls you, its lawyer, to instruct you in relation to a share disposal. X plc is selling the entire issued share capital of its wholly-owned subsidiary, Target plc, to Buyer plc. The acquisition must be completed urgently. X plc needs the cash consideration from the sale by the end of the month (three days' time) or it will go bust.

You download your firm's precedent agreement and launch yourself into a series of meetings, first with your client, X plc, to find out the detail of the transaction, then with Buyer plc and its lawyers, to thrash out a deal.

Can you imagine how easy it is, in that first meeting with your client, for the client to say to you, 'We are selling all the shares in our subsidiary, Target plc. The buyer, Buyer plc, is paying a good price; it has secured a loan on really good terms from the bank', for you to make a note of this, then move on to more pressing areas of detail, such as the structure of the deal and the warranties X plc is prepared to give?

Forty-eight hours later you have an agreement ready to sign. At that point, you receive a call from a colleague in your firm's banking department, who says she has just received a call from the assistant company secretary of Target plc, asking her to review the form of guarantee Target plc is giving to Buyer plc's bank.

Suddenly you have a problem. Target plc cannot give Buyer's bank a guarantee, as this would be financial assistance and prohibited under s 677(1). The bank will not provide the loan to Buyer plc unless it receives the guarantee from Target plc it was promised. Without the bank loan, Buyer plc cannot purchase the shares in Target plc. Without the consideration, X plc will go bust. You have to explain this problem to X plc.

How could this situation have been avoided? Well if, at that first meeting, you had probed a little more into the funding arrangements with Buyer plc's bank, you might have prompted the client to mention the bank guarantee. This is clear with hindsight, but can be very easy to miss in the rush to make a start on the acquisition agreement within the time constraints imposed.

16.5   WHAT IS NOT FINANCIAL ASSISTANCE?

The CA 2006 provides three categories of exceptions to the financial assistance prohibition. These exceptions are considered below.

16.5.1   The purpose exceptions

It was explained at **16.3.1** and **16.3.2** above that purpose and intention are important when considering the prohibition on financial assistance. It should come as no surprise, then, to find that one of the exceptions to the financial assistance prohibition is concerned with purpose.

Section 678(2) and s 679(2) provide that s 678(1) and s 679(1) respectively (that is, pre-acquisition financial assistance) do not prohibit the Assistor from giving financial assistance if:

(a)   either:
    (i)   the Assistor's *principal purpose* is not to give the financial assistance for the purpose of the acquisition (principal purpose exception), *or*
    (ii)   the giving of the financial assistance for the purpose of the acquisition was only an incidental part of some *larger purpose* of the Assistor (larger purpose exception); *and*

(b)   the Assistor gives the financial assistance in good faith in the interests of the Assistor.

Section 678(4) and s 679(4) provide principal purpose and larger purpose exceptions for financial assistance under s 678(3) and s 679(3) respectively too (that is, post-acquisition financial assistance), but the words 'the acquisition' (see (a)(i) and (ii) above) are replaced with 'reducing or discharging the liability which has been incurred'.

The 'principal purpose' and 'larger purpose' exceptions are somewhat vague, and it is difficult for the lawyer to be able to state definitively that they will apply. The decision in *Brady v Brady* [1989] AC 755 has made the application of the purpose exceptions even less clear.

16.5.1.1 *Brady v Brady*

In this case, an arrangement was made in good faith to divide a family company's assets into two new companies, so that the two brothers who ran the family company could go their separate ways. The arrangement involved the family company giving financial assistance, as Assistor. At first instance, it was held that while the arrangement was prohibited by the forerunner to s 678(1), it was saved by the larger purpose exception; the Assistor's giving of the assistance for the purpose of the acquisition was only an incidental part of the Assistor's *larger purpose*. The House of Lords, however, did not agree that the exception applied.

16.5.1.2 The principal purpose exception

In *Brady v Brady*, Lord Oliver explained that, for this exception to apply, there must be a principal and a secondary purpose behind the giving of the financial assistance. For example, if the principal purpose of the Assistor is to obtain an asset that it really wants, but the secondary purpose is to put the person who is willing to sell the asset in a position to acquire shares in the company, then, as long as the Assistor genuinely enters into the transaction in the belief that it is in the Assistor's best interests, the transaction will fall within the exception. There may be difficulties, however, in proving that the secondary purpose was not, in fact, the primary purpose.

16.5.1.3 The larger purpose exception

This exception covers transactions where the financial assistance is intended but it is incidental to the Assistor's 'larger purpose'. As outlined at **16.5.1.1** above, the House of Lords has interpreted this exception very narrowly and, as such, it is not relied upon in practice.

16.5.2 Section 681: unconditional exceptions

Section 681(2) permits the following (which all involve removing value from the company) on the basis that they are not anything against which creditors require protection:

(a)   (i)   a dividend lawfully made – this would allow, for example, the Assistor to pay a pre-sale dividend to its shareholders before its shares are sold (this may have tax benefits, as it allows shareholders to take some of the value of the company as income not capital);

    (ii)   a distribution in a winding up;

(b)   the allotment of bonus shares;

(c)   a reduction of capital under Chapter 10 of Pt 17 of the CA 2006;

(d)   a lawful redemption or purchase of own shares;

(e)   schemes of arrangement made pursuant to a CA 2006, s 899 court order;

(f)   anything done pursuant to an arrangement under s 110 of the Insolvency Act 1986 (this will cover a liquidator accepting shares as consideration for property sold in a winding up); and

(g)   anything done pursuant to a voluntary arrangement made between the company and its creditors.

16.5.3 Section 682: conditional exceptions

Section 682(2) provides the following exceptions:

(a)   the lending of money by money lending companies in the ordinary course of their business;

(b)   where the financial assistance is given in good faith to fund an employee share scheme; and

(c)   loans to bona fide employees (not directors) to allow them to buy shares in the company, or its holding company (no share scheme is required for the exception to apply).

The s 682(1) proviso

Section 682(1) adds an important proviso to the application of the s 682(2) exemptions where the Assistor is a public company. If the Assistor is a public company, it can rely on the s 682(2) exemptions only if the company has *net assets*:

(a)   which are not thereby reduced; or

(b)   to the extent those assets are thereby reduced, the assistance is provided out of distributable profits.

Note that net assets are defined as the *book value* of assets less liabilities (that is, their value for accounting purposes). This is different to the definition of net assets for the purposes of s 677(1) (see **16.4** above), where the definition is the *actual value* of net assets less liabilities. (Liabilities are defined by s 682(4)(b) and distributable profits by s 683(1).)

16.6   AVOIDING THE RESTRICTIONS

There is always the option of re-registering a public company as a private company, under s 97 of the CA 2006, so that the company is a private company at the time the financial assistance is given, and that financial assistance can then be given. This is, of course, a little extreme, and certainly would not be appropriate in the case of a listed company.

16.7   SANCTIONS

16.7.1   Criminal sanctions

Section 680 provides that breach of the prohibition on financial assistance is a criminal offence. The company is liable to a fine, and any officer in default is liable to a fine and/or imprisonment.

16.7.2   Consequences for the share acquisition

The acquisition will be void and unenforceable (*Brady v Brady*) unless the offending term can be severed from any acquisition agreement (*Carney v Herbert* [1985] AC 301).

If the provision of financial assistance breaches the directors' duty to act in good faith in the way most likely to promote the success of the company (CA 2006, s 172) and the breach has not been ratified by a shareholder resolution, the directors may have to compensate their company for any loss it has incurred.

Any third party who received the financial assistance may be required to account for any cash or assets received in breach of s 678 or s 679 (*Belmont Finance Corp Ltd v Williams Furniture Ltd (No 2)* [1980] 1 All ER 393).

16.8   CONCLUSION

The prohibition on financial assistance has the potential to cause serious problems with share acquisitions involving public companies.

The key is to consider the issue of financial assistance as soon as possible in any share acquisition transaction. This will involve asking questions about how the transaction is funded and, if necessary, making changes to the structure of the deal.

CHAPTER 17

EQUITY FINANCE

17.1 BACKGROUND

Part I of this book considered the IPO process, that is (for the purposes of this book) how a company can admit its shares to listing on the Official List and to trading on the Main Market.

As was seen at **4.4** above, a company seeking to float can do so in a number of different ways:

(a) a public offer (encompassing an offer for subscription and/or sale);

(b) a placing;

(c) an introduction; or

(d) an intermediaries offer.

These methods were considered in some detail in **Chapter 4**.

Chapter 1 explained that one of the advantages of an IPO is that, after it has taken place, a listed company can raise further finance through issuing new shares ('equity finance') in a way that an unlisted company cannot. This chapter explores the various methods by which a listed company can seek a listing for further share capital, in order to raise equity finance.

17.2 WHAT IS EQUITY FINANCE?

Equity finance involves a company using its equity, namely securities (and more specifically for our purposes, shares), in order to raise finance. An example of a company raising equity finance is when it issues new shares in return for cash, or in exchange for an asset.

As you will realise on reading this chapter, equity finance involves both:

(a) the issue of shares; and

(b) the admission of those shares to listing and to trading on the Main Market of the Stock Exchange.

It is the dual admissions of those shares which gives them their value. The issue and admissions of shares in a listed company in this way is often referred to as a 'secondary issue'. The 'primary issue' is when the company floats and its issued shares are listed for the first time. Subsequent issues of new shares, and the listing of those shares, are therefore 'secondary issues'. (Be aware that this terminology can be confusing, as sometimes the term 'primary issue' is used to describe any issue of shares by the company, and the term 'secondary issue' is used to refer to a sale (transfer) by a shareholder of existing shares. However, for the purposes of this book, the terminology is given the meanings outlined above: a 'primary issue' is an issue of shares by the company on an IPO; and a 'secondary issue' is any subsequent issue of shares by the company.)

When a company raises equity finance, then, the lawyer must be aware of, and be able to apply, not only the law which relates specifically to the raising of equity finance, but also the wider set of rules and regulations which apply to listed companies:

(a)   generally;

(b)   on the issue of shares; and

(c)   on the admission of those shares to listing and trading.

This chapter looks at the law which relates specifically to the raising of equity finance. However, at **17.4** below there is a brief reminder of the other rules and regulations which relate to (a), (b) and (c) above, and an indication of where you can read about them in this book.

Note that for the period 1 January to 31 October 2013, companies listed on the Main Market raised over £11.7 billion through secondary issues. Reflecting a steady improvement in UK and global economic conditions, this was dramatically up on the previous year's figure of £3.3 billion.

17.3   WHY A COMPANY NEEDS EQUITY FINANCE

There are numerous reasons why a company might want to raise equity finance. Just like us, it needs money. It may want to pay off debt, buy something, or just make its bank balance look a little healthier. It may be concerned about gearing (its ratio of debt to equity). By increasing the amount of share capital in issue, the company will improve its gearing ratio without having to repay any debt. This may enhance the company's ability to borrow in the future. The company will also have the option to use the cash proceeds from the rights issue to pay off debt, which will improve the company's gearing even more. **Chapter 18** considers the concept of gearing. It also considers briefly the concept of debt finance, and examines the issues a company will take into account in deciding whether to raise equity or debt finance.

Since the outbreak of the global financial crisis in 2007/08, many billions of pounds have been raised on the Stock Exchange by listed companies, initially by banks as they desperately scrambled to access whatever money they could to fend off their collapse as a result of the powerful shockwaves emanating from the global financial crisis. This included rights issues by the Royal Bank of Scotland Group plc and HSBC Holdings plc, which raised £12 billion in June 2008 and £12.5 billion in March 2009 respectively, to ensure they had sufficient capital. This was followed by the UK's largest ever rights issue by Lloyds Banking Group plc, which raised £13.5 billion in November 2009. The money was raised to prevent the company from having to sell more of its shares to the UK Government in return for further State insurance for its toxic debt. In 2009 and 2010, over £100 billion was raised on the Main Market through secondary issues. More recently, the continued lack of availability of debt finance led companies in other business sectors to turn to rights issues to raise money, and in the past couple of years the demand for equity finance continues to be strong, reflecting companies' and shareholders' improving sentiment about the UK and global economy.

17.4   LISTED COMPANY RULES AND REGULATIONS

17.4.1   General rules

The general rules relating to listed companies are set out in **Part II** of this book. The general obligation of disclosure under the Disclosure Rules (see **7.5.1**) and the continuing obligations of the Listing Rules, relating to the disclosure of new issues (see **7.5.7** above) and communicating with shareholders in relation to new issues (see **7.9** above), are particularly relevant to any company seeking to raise equity finance. The lawyer must also be alert to any suggestion that the issue might fall foul of the rules relating to corporate governance (see **Chapter 8**), misleading statements and market manipulation (see **Chapter 9**), market abuse (see **Chapter 10**) or insider dealing (see **Chapter 11**). Finally, the lawyer must ensure that the issue is not marketed in a way which would breach the financial promotion rules of the FSMA 2000 (see **Chapter 12**). Account must also be taken of the differing levels of regulation for premium and standard listed companies.

17.4.2 Issuing shares

Part III of this book considers the rules of the CA 2006, the Prospectus Rules, the Listing Rules, the Takeover Code, and the ABI Guidelines and the Pre-Emption Statement of Principles which relate to the issue of shares. The following are particularly important, from the company's perspective, when raising equity finance.

17.4.2.1 The Companies Act 2006

Chapters 2 to 4 of Pt 17 of the CA 2006 are all relevant to the issue of shares (see **Chapter 14**). The 2006 Act also sets out the procedure which companies must follow if a share issue will vary the class rights of any existing shares. Again, this may be relevant in an equity finance transaction (see **13.7** above). Finally, the issue must be structured in a way which does not cause the company to fall foul of the prohibition on financial assistance (see **Chapter 16**).

17.4.2.2 The Listing Rules

Listing Rules 9.3.11R and 9.3.12R set out the pre-emption rights provisions which are relevant on an issue of shares for premium listed companies only (see **14.6.12** above).

17.4.2.3 Guidelines and Principles

Institutional investors such as the ABI impose their own requirements relating to the issue of shares. These requirements do not have the force of law, but they are significant because listed companies do not want to get on the wrong side of their largest shareholders. **Chapter 14** considers the ABI Guidelines (see **14.5.7**) and the Statement of Principles of the Pre-Emption Group (see **14.6.16**) which are relevant on an issue of shares. In addition, in May 2011 the IIC published its Best Practice Guidance for Issuers when Raising Equity Capital. The IIC is a group of trade bodies representing institutional investors comprising the ABI, IMA and NAPF. The IIC Guidance includes steps to be taken by listed companies well before equity finance is raised as well as during and after the process, and is available on the IIC's website at www.iicomm.org.

17.4.3 Admitting new shares to listing and trading

Part I of this book considered the admission of shares on an IPO. Many of the issues addressed by **Part I** are also relevant to the admission of shares on a secondary issue.

It was explained at **4.3.1.1** above that a company cannot choose to list only part of a class of shares. It must list all of the shares in a class. So, if a listed company proposes to issue more shares *of a class which is already listed*, it must seek admission to listing on the Official List and admission to trading on the Main Market in respect of those shares. As mentioned above, this is not only a requirement of the Listing Rules, it also makes the issues commercially attractive, as a listing gives the shares value.

In relation to the listing aspects of a secondary issue, the lawyer must be aware of the following rules and regulations:

(a)   *The FSMA 2000.* Part VI of the FSMA 2000 sets out the rules relating to the listing of shares. Sections 87A (general duty of disclosure) and 90 (compensation for loss) are particularly important. See **Chapter 6**.

(b)   *The Prospectus Rules.* The requirement for a prospectus under the Prospectus Rules (and s 85 of the FSMA 2000) is discussed at **17.5.1** below. The requirement for a prospectus on an IPO was considered in **Chapter 6**. The prospectus and accompanying documents must be submitted to the FCA as required by the Prospectus Rules (see **5.3.6.1** and **5.3.6.2** above; but note that the submission date for a secondary issue is 10 working days before the prospectus is due to be published (impact day), rather than the 20 working days required for an IPO).

It is worth remembering that approval of the prospectus is not a foregone conclusion. Prudential plc embarrassingly had to delay publication of its prospectus for what would have been a record £14.5 billion rights issue in May 2010 because the forerunner to the FCA, the FSA, needed clarification that Prudential's finances could withstand the takeover of the company (AIA) for which it was going to use the proceeds of the rights issue. Ultimately the rights issue was cancelled due to shareholder opposition.

(c)   *The Listing Rules.* A formal application for admission of the shares to the Official List must be made to the FCA under the Listing Rules. This involves a process very similar to that set out at **5.3.6.3** to **5.3.6.5** above, in the context of an IPO, namely the submission of:

(i)   '48 hour' documents;

(ii)   'on the day' documents (note the documents differ on a secondary issue to those required for an IPO; a Pricing Statement, rather than a Shareholder Statement signed by the sponsor, is required – see LR 3.3.3R); and

(iii)   certain information following admission.

Where the requirements are the same as those for an IPO, see **5.3.6** for further detail. Any raising of equity finance will be made conditional upon admission to listing on the Official List. Admission will be effective when the FCA makes its Official List announcement (see **5.4.3.1**).

(d)   *The Admission and Disclosure Standards.* A formal application for admission of the shares to the Main Market must be made to the Stock Exchange under the Admission and Disclosure Standards. Again, the process involved practically mirrors that required for the application for admission to trading set out in **5.3.7** in relation to an IPO, namely (under ADS 2) the submission of:

(i)   an application for admission to trading – Form 1 (note that for a secondary issue this is submitted with the other two-day documents, rather than 10 days in advance, as on an IPO);

(ii)   various two-day documents in electronic form;

(iii)   written confirmation of the number of securities to be allotted;

(iv)   a copy of the RIS announcement relating to the admission; and

(v)   certain information following admission.

Where the requirements are the same as those for an IPO, see **5.3.7** for further detail. Any raising of equity finance will be made conditional upon admission to trading on the Main Market. Again, admission will be effective when the Stock Exchange makes an announcement on its website (see **5.4.3.2**).

Note that, in the context of a rights issue, once the shares have been admitted to listing and trading nil paid, no further application is required to admit the shares fully paid (see **17.7.3.2** below).

17.5   EQUITY FINANCE DOCUMENTATION

The lawyer spends much of his time drafting, and therefore any lawyer will need to know what documentation is required on a secondary issue. Specific documentation required for each method of raising equity finance considered by this chapter is detailed at **17.7** to **17.11** below. However, the reason these documents are required is explained below.

17.5.1 Prospectus

As referred to at **6.4**, the effect of PR 1.2.1UK and s 85 of the FSMA 2000 is that if the company wishes to do either or both of the following:

(a) *offer* transferable securities *to the public in the* UK (s 85(1)); or

(b) request *admission* of transferable securities *to trading* on a regulated market situated or operating *in the* UK (even if there is no offer to the public) (s 85(2)),

an FCA-approved prospectus is required. These rules apply equally to a secondary issue as they do to an IPO (see **6.4** above).

Section 85(5) of the FSMA 2000 (which in turn refers to Sch 11A to the FSMA and PR 1.2.2R) and s 86 of the FSMA 2000 set out various circumstances when an *offer to the public* will not require a prospectus. Section 85(6) (which in turn refers to Sch 11A to the FSMA and PR 1.2.3R) sets out the circumstances when an *admission to trading* will not require a prospectus.

17.5.1.1 Full prospectus

Once the need for a prospectus has been established, there are two possibilities regarding the content of the prospectus. The first includes the full content as required in an IPO, as set out at **6.5.2** above, where the content requirements are prescribed by the articles and Annexes of the PD Regulation (which are set out at PR 2.3.1EU and PR Appendix 3). For a secondary issue of ordinary shares the appropriate schedules will be the share schedules (Annexes I and III) and the pro forma financial information building block (Annex II), so the level of disclosure required in any prospectus relating to a secondary issue of ordinary shares in this case is exactly the same as for a prospectus relating to an IPO of ordinary shares. The prospectus for Prudential plc's potentially record-breaking £14.5 billion rights issue (which was aborted for financial reasons and management incompetence in May 2010) ran to a record 940 pages, and if copies for each of its 71,700 shareholders were stacked up, the pile would have reached 3.5 miles high!

17.5.1.2 Proportionate disclosure prospectus

The second possibility arises if the secondary issue falls within the Prospectus Directive's proportionate disclosure regime. This applies in two situations:

(a) for certain smaller companies; and

(b) for certain types of secondary issue.

Smaller companies

These are small and medium-sized entreprises (SMEs) and companies 'with reduced market capitalisation' (RMCs).

An SME is a company which, on the basis of its last accounts, met two of the following three criteria:

(a) an average of fewer than 250 employees during the year;

(b) a balance sheet not exceeding €40 million;

(c) an annual net turnover not exceeding €50 million.

An RMC is a company with an average market capitalisation of less than €100 million on the basis of year-end quotes at the end of the last three calendar years.

In this case, the company is able to produce an abbreviated prospectus containing less information, in accordance with Annexes XXV–XXVIII of the PD Regulation (as set out at PR Appendix 3) instead of Annexes I–III, for either an offer of shares to the public or an admission of shares to trading. This rule was introduced to encourage offers by smaller companies by reducing the preparation time and cost of preparing a prospectus.

Secondary issues

These are:

(a)   rights issues where statutory pre-emption rights are followed; and

(b)   secondary issues where statutory pre-emption rights have been disapplied and replaced with 'near identical rights'. In practice, this would include certain rights issues and compensatory open offers (see **17.8.3** below).

Again, in this case the company is able to produce an abbreviated prospectus containing less information, but this time in accordance with Annex XXIII and Annex XXIV of the PD Regulation (as set out at PR Appendix 3) instead of Annexes I–III. This rule was introduced to recognise the reality that issues in accordance with, or nearly identical to, statutory pre-emption rights are offers to existing shareholders of the company, who will usually already be aware of its financial situation and the risks of investing in it and so need less information.

Both the smaller companies and the secondary issues covered by the proportionate disclosure regime may still elect to produce a full prospectus instead. They may have to do this, for example, for regulatory approval of the prospectus overseas, eg an offer involving the US.

17.5.1.3 Supplementary prospectus

An approved supplementary prospectus (see **6.9.4**) will also be required if, for example, during a rights issue, there arises or is noted any significant new factor, material mistake or inaccuracy relating to the information included in the approved prospectus. This supplementary prospectus will trigger statutory withdrawal rights under s 87Q of the FSMA 2000 (see **6.9.4**). The FCA's Technical Note UKLA/TN/605.2 Supplementary prospectuses confirms that the right to withdraw will cease when shareholders pay up their subscription in full.

17.5.1.4 Exemptions

The only difference is that exemptions, which may not apply in the context of an IPO (see **6.4**), may apply on a secondary issue, depending on its circumstances, with the effect that a prospectus is not required. Clearly, if the lawyer can structure a secondary issue so that no prospectus is required, this will save the company considerable time and expense. **Table 17.1** below analyses whether the exemptions are likely to apply to the key methods of raising money via a secondary issue (see **17.6**): a rights issue, open offer, placing, acquisition issue or vendor consideration placing. As you can see, it is likely that only a placing, acquisition issue or vendor consideration placing can be structured in a way which avoids the need to prepare a prospectus.

Table 17.1

Method of equity finance	Public offer under s 85(1)?	Admission to trading under s 85(2)?	Prospectus required?
Rights issue	Yes. Unlikely to benefit from any exemption. (As a pre-emptive offer made to all shareholders, is unlikely to benefit from the '150 persons' or 'qualified investors' exemptions.)	Yes, however small rights issues may be structured so that '10%' exemption applies.	Yes.
Open offer	As for rights issue.	As for rights issue.	As for rights issue.

Method of equity finance	Public offer under s 85(1)?	Admission to trading under s 85(2)?	Prospectus required?
Placing	Yes ; however, likely to benefit from 'qualified investor' or '150 persons' exemption.	Yes, however small placings may be structured so that '10%' exemption applies.	Yes, unless structured so that is exempt from the requirement for a prospectus.
Acquisition issue	May benefit from 'qualified investor' or '150 persons' exemption, depending on target shareholder profile.	Yes, however small rights issues may be structured so that '10%' exemption applies.	Yes, unless structured so that is exempt from the requirement for a prospectus. (Where shares are issued in the context of a takeover, the publication of a document the FCA deems to be 'equivalent to' a prospectus will suffice – see **22.4.4.2**.)
Vendor consideration placing	As for acquisition issue.	As for acquisition issue.	As for acquisition issue.

17.5.2 Circular

The Listing Rules require a premium listed company to communicate to its shareholders by way of circular on a new issue (see **7.6.2** above). This may take the form of a notice of GM, and incorporate by reference information in any prospectus. The circular must conform with the requirements of LR 13.3 (see **7.9.3**).

In practice, often the requirement for the circular is met by the prospectus, which will contain all the information required to be in the circular. However, the prospectus also contains an offer of securities, which can cause problems with regard to very strict securities law in certain overseas jurisdictions. One solution is not to send the prospectus to such jurisdictions but a circular. If there are overseas shareholders therefore, the company may prepare both a prospectus and a separate circular. Also, if time is of the essence, the company may (with the permission of the FCA) send out a brief circular outlining the main reasons for the issue, together with a notice of GM, and then send out the prospectus once the document has been completed (as happened, for example, with Bradford and Bingley's £400 million rights issue in the summer of 2008).

17.5.3 RIS notification/press announcement

Any new issue of listed securities must be notified to an RIS under the specific disclosure requirements of the Listing Rules (see **7.5.7.2** above). This will usually take the form of a press announcement to announce the issue to the market. It will contain all material information about the issue, and any related acquisition. Further announcements will be required as the rights issue progresses.

17.5.4   Sale and purchase agreement

If the company is issuing shares as consideration for the acquisition of a non-cash asset, such as shares in another company, then a sale and purchase agreement (also referred to as an acquisition agreement, an S&P or an SPA) will be required for the transfer of that asset.

17.5.5   Underwriting agreement

The concept of underwriting in the context of an IPO was introduced at **4.2.7** above. It is also relevant on a secondary issue. In return for a fee, the underwriters will agree to take up any shares which are not subscribed for. The underwriting agreement will record the agreement between the company and the underwriter.

17.5.6   Placing agreement

If the chosen method of raising equity finance involves a placing of shares, a placing agreement will also be necessary (see **4.4.1.2** above).

17.6   METHODS OF RAISING EQUITY FINANCE

As **17.1** above explained, a company can float in a number of different ways. However, once listed, a company can bring securities to listing using a wider variety of methods.

The main methods by which a company can raise equity finance once it is listed are:

(a)   a rights issue;

(b)   an open offer;

(c)   a placing;

(d)   an acquisition issue; and

(e)   a vendor consideration placing (LR 9.5.9R).

These methods are considered in detail at **17.7** to **17.11** below, and we examine why a company might choose one method rather than another. As with an IPO, however, more than one method may be combined, depending on the circumstances (such as the combined placing and open offer by Thomas Cook Group Plc in May 2013 which raised £400 million). Specific documentation required for each method is also set out.

Note that some of the less common methods of raising equity finance are not discussed in detail in this chapter. Two of these, an offer (for subscription and/or sale) and an intermediaries offer, are considered in **Chapters 4** and **6**, albeit in the context of an IPO rather than a secondary issue.

Chapter 9 of the Listing Rules contains the rules relating to the methods by which secondary issues can be listed. The vast majority of these rules apply only to premium listed companies. Where they do apply to standard listed companies, a note is made by the relevant provision in the following commentary.

17.7   RIGHTS ISSUE

17.7.1   What is a rights issue?

A rights issue was referred to at **14.6.12** above, when considering pre-emption rights. Appendix 1.1 of the Listing Rules defines a rights issue. Basically, it is:

(a)   an offer to issue new shares or transfer existing shares (or other securities);

(b)   to existing shareholders (or security holders) in proportion to their existing holdings;

(c)   made by way of the issue of a renounceable letter;

(d)   which may be traded 'nil paid' for a period before payment for the shares (or other securities) is due.

The aim is to raise money for the company by issuing new shares. For example, a company could offer to issue two shares to each shareholder for every one share that shareholder already holds (known as a '2-for-1' offer). There is no magic to this figure. The key calculation is how much money the company wishes to raise. It considers how many shares are in issue and then makes the offer accordingly, because of course all shareholders must be offered the right to buy the new shares. In March 2013 William Hill plc had a '2-for-9' rights issue; shareholders were entitled to buy 2 new shares for every 9 existing shares held.

In the period 1 January to 31 October 2013, £7.39 billion was raised by companies on the Main Market through rights issues, making it the most popular form of secondary issue. This compares with only £658 million in the same period in 2012. In 2012 the market was still suffering from the effects of the sovereign debt crisis in Europe and renewed concerns about a possible break-up of the eurozone and ongoing economic weakness in the UK, which uncertainty meant that a general fundraising from the company's shareholders was less popular than other secondary issues. However, a return to stronger economic growth in the UK, coupled with greater hopes for the global economy, has led to a dramatic pick up in rights issues, reflecting increased shareholder confidence.

17.7.2   Price

The shares are usually allotted for cash, at a discount to the market price of the existing shares. Why is that? Well, if the company is going to raise finance, it requires shareholders to take up their rights under the rights issue and pay the cash consideration for the shares to the company. This means that the price for the shares must be better (that is, cheaper) than the price of buying shares on the open market. If it is not, the shareholders might choose to buy shares on the market instead, in which case they will pay the selling shareholder, not the company, for the shares.

Current market practice is for a company to make what is known as a 'deep-discount rights issue', when it issues shares at a substantial discount to market value. Originally this was done so that the company did not have to pay for the issue to be underwritten (because no shareholder is likely to refuse to take up the rights) (see **17.7.5**), or because the company had an urgent need for the new money, although it is now the norm for even deeply discounted rights issues to be underwritten (eg William Hill plc £375 million rights issue in March 2013) and this reflects the market turmoil post the global financial crisis. Issuing shares at a deep discount will make the issue more attractive to shareholders, so it can increase the chances of success of the rights issue, particularly in a weak market (which, in turn, can help to reduce any underwriting costs, as the company may be able to negotiate lower fees with the underwriter to reflect the reduced risk that shareholders will not take up the shares).

Note that as long as the price exceeds the nominal value of the share (CA 2006, s 580), there is no legal limit to the discount at which the company can sell the shares. As explained at **14.6.16**, the Pre-Emption Group's Statement of Principles does not apply if the company observes the pre-emption requirements of the Listing Rules. Before the financial crisis in 2007/08, the rule of thumb was that companies can usually discount by up to 50%, a typical discount being 15–20%, and a deep discount being 40–50%. More recently, a typical discount is 40% with a deep discount exceeding 50%. However, in these financially uncertain times, some companies are so desperate for money that they have even exceeded the 50% threshold. Talvivaara Mining Company, a Finnish Company listed on the Main Market, announced in February 2013 a deep discount rights issue of 84.5% to the market price of its shares. As with humans, so with companies – desperation is often eye-catching but never pretty.

One disadvantage of the discount applied to shares is that it tends to cause a drop in the market value of the shares for a period following the rights issue.

17.7.3   Structure

17.7.3.1   The PAL

The offer to shareholders of the right to buy new shares in the company is made by way of a renounceable letter, known as a provisional allotment letter (PAL). This does exactly what its name suggests: it provisionally allots to the shareholder her pro rata entitlement of shares. At this stage no money has changed hands. The company has given the shareholder a document which sets out her *right* to buy the new shares. The PAL will provide details of the rights issue, including the number of shares to which the shareholder is entitled and the price of those shares. The PAL is a temporary document of title, and as such it must comply with the requirements of LR 9.5.15R for a premium listed company and with the requirements of LR 14.3.9R for a standard listed company. (It is not a permanent document of title such as a share certificate, because so far the shareholder has not paid for the shares offered to her.)

On receiving the PAL, the shareholder then has a number of options. She can:

(a)   take up the rights, by subscribing for the shares (see **17.7.3.2** below);

(b)   renounce the rights and sell them on to a third party, nil paid (see **17.7.3.3** below);

(c)   combine (a) and (b), by taking up some rights and renouncing the rest (**17.7.3.4** below); or

(d)   do nothing (**17.7.3.5** below).

17.7.3.2   Taking up the rights to subscribe

Before the end of the offer period (as **17.7.4** below explains, the offer must be open for at least 14 days) the shareholder who holds the rights to subscribe, and who wishes to exercise them, must submit the consideration and the PAL to the company's receiving agents. (At the end of the offer period, this right will lapse.) This means that the shareholder will have bought the new shares and ensure her existing percentage shareholding is not diluted.

17.7.3.3   Renouncing the rights to subscribe

Rationale

As we have seen in **17.7.3.2** above, if the shareholder takes up the rights, she ensures that her existing percentage shareholding is not diluted. However, if the shareholder renounces the rights, her shareholding will be diluted, meaning a smaller share of the company's profits and a lower percentage share of the voting rights. So why would a shareholder renounce the right to subscribe for shares? As ever with listed companies, usually the motivation is financial.

> **EXAMPLE**
>
> Imagine that shares in X plc have a current market value of £2 each. X plc gives its shareholders the right to subscribe for more shares, in proportion to their existing shareholdings, for £1.60 per share (that is, at a discount of 20%). The right to subscribe has a value, therefore, of 40p per share. However, the fact that the market value in the shares is likely to drop (see **17.7.2** above) must be taken into account. Imagine that the market value drops to £1.95. If the shareholder renounces her rights and sells them for 35p each, she will have made a profit of 35p per share (less any dealing costs). If the shareholder has, say, 1,000 shares, she can make £350 with no capital outlay. She might consider that this makes diluting her shareholding worthwhile.
>
> (Note, however, that the shareholder may incur an immediate capital gains tax charge if she sells her rights. If she exercised the rights, however, capital gains tax would arise only on a subsequent disposal of the shares.)

The shareholder wishing to renounce and sell rights should not find it too difficult to find a buyer for those rights, as the buyer will be able to buy shares from the shareholder at the market value, here £1.95. The buyer will pay £1.60 per share to the company under the rights issue, plus 35p per share to the shareholder for the right to subscribe. Of course, the risk to the buyer is that the market price drops further.

> **EXAMPLE**
>
> Imagine the market price of shares in X plc drops not to £1.95 but to £1.50. The buyer has already paid 35p per share to the selling shareholder for the right to subscribe and must pay an additional £1.60 to the company for shares he can buy in the market for £1.50. In this case, the buyer will probably cut his losses; while he cannot claim back the price he has paid to the selling shareholder for the right to subscribe, he can avoid paying the remaining £1.60 to the company simply by not exercising the right and letting it lapse.

Nil paid dealings

So how does the shareholder renounce and trade her rights to subscribe? The PAL is negotiable, which means that it can be transferred by delivery (ie it can be bought and sold). As **17.7.4** below explains, the offer must be open for at least 14 days. 'Nil paid dealings' can take place during this 14-day period. This means that a shareholder can trade the rights to subscribe simply by signing the PAL and passing it on to someone else. These dealings are referred to as 'nil paid dealings' because trading takes place before any subscription monies have been paid for the shares represented by the PAL. The third party can then exercise the right to subscribe in the manner described at **17.7.3.2** above and will become the owner of the new shares mentioned in the PAL. It is on the admission of the shares to trading in nil paid form that the FCA will grant admission of the shares to the Official List (LR 9.5.3G). (Once the shares are paid up, and the allotment becomes unconditional, there is no need for a further listing application.)

17.7.3.4 Taking up some rights and renouncing the rest

Alternatively, the shareholder may choose to take up some rights (using the procedure outlined at **17.7.3.2**) and renounce the remainder (using the process outlined at **17.7.3.3**). This may be used where the shareholder has insufficient funds to buy the whole allocation or does not wish to take up all her rights. The proceeds received from trading some of the rights may help to finance the purchase of the balance of these rights (known as 'tail swallowing').

17.7.3.5 Doing nothing

Shareholders who do nothing are known as 'lazy shareholders'. Even lazy shareholders can benefit from a rights issue, because arrangements are made for the sale of any shares not taken up. Even if a shareholder does not take up the shares and does not trade the PAL, she may still receive a cash payment to the extent that the shares which were provisionally allotted to her are sold in the market for more than their subscription price. For premium listed companies only, the proceeds must exceed £5 (LR 9.5.4R). (As explained in **17.7.3.3**, the nil paid rights have a value.)

17.7.4 Timing

The FCA does not allow shares in listed companies to be allotted provisionally on a conditional basis (LR 2.1.5G). This means that if any shareholder approvals are required in relation to the issue (such as to give the directors authority to allot – see **Chapter 14**), the PALs can be posted only after all necessary shareholder approvals have been obtained at the GM.

Premium listed company

Once the PALs are posted, LR 9.5.6R provides that the offer must remain open for at least 10 business days. Section 562(5) states that the offer must be open for 14 days. This section will only be relevant if s 561 is not disapplied. If s 561 does apply then the premium listed company must still also comply with the 10 business days requirement under LR 9.5.6R. This matters because this could be slightly longer than the 14-day period under s 562(5) (due to the definition of business day in the Listing Rules which excludes public holidays).

When calculating the 10 business days under LR 9.5.6R, the first business day will be the first day the rights issue offer is open for acceptance. This will be the day of the posting of the PAL. When calculating the 14 days under s 562(5), the first day is counted from the day of making the offer. This therefore starts from the day of posting the PAL.

Standard listed company

A standard listed company is only subject to the requirements of the CA 2006, including s 562(5) above.

Conclusion

The combination of the time required for the GM notice (14 clear days for a special resolution at a GM (and not an AGM) under the CA 2006 provisions assuming the conditions in s 307A of the CA 2006 – see **8.6.1** – are met), added to the subsequent minimum offer period of 14 days under the CA 2006/10 business days (under the Listing Rules for premium listed companies) or 14 days (under the CA 2006 for standard listed companies where s 561 has not been disapplied), means that the rights issue will often take weeks to complete.

17.7.5 Underwriting

The role of underwriters on an IPO was explored at **4.2.7** above. The process of underwriting is equally relevant to a secondary issue. The underwriters (usually an investment bank or a broker) basically guarantee that the company will receive the equity finance it seeks, by agreeing to take up, at no less than the subscription price under the rights issue, any shares which are not taken up by shareholders and which cannot be sold in the market (including fractional entitlements if s 561 has been disapplied – see **17.7.6.1**). These shares are referred to as 'the rump'. As explained at **17.7.3.5**, any premium received over the subscription price must be given to the person to whom the shares were provisionally allotted.

The underwriters must buy any of the rump which is left (that is, which they have been unable to sell). These leftover shares are referred to as 'the stick'. The stick represents the underwriter's risk, and the underwriter will try to predict what the stick, and therefore the risk, will be, in calculating his commission (see **17.7.5.1** at (a) below). As with an IPO, it is common for a secondary issue to be sub-underwritten either in part, or in its entirety (see **4.2.7**).

Events in the second half of 2008 demonstrated in stark terms both the need for underwriting arrangements and the risks involved for underwriters. The article below shows the effect of HBOS's disastrous rights issue which left the underwriters and sub-underwriters having to pay almost £2.5 billion to buy the stick. Of course such failures are extremely rare and reflect the turmoil caused by the problems in the financial markets and the collapse of the share price of banks listed on the Stock Exchange.

HBOS rights issue flops

**Julia Kollewe and
Jill Treanor**

Underwriters to HBOS's £4bn rights issue have been left with almost £3.8bn of shares after investors shunned its cash call in one of the biggest fund-raising flops in UK history.

Shares in HBOS dropped 6% to 265p in early trading, below the offer price of 275p.

Investors took up just 8.3% of shares at 275p, even fewer than expected. The level of support is one of the lowest ever registered for a rights issue and deals a blow to HBOS's management.

When HBOS announced the rights issue on April 29, it was priced at a near-50% discount to its then market price of just under 500p.

Shareholders subscribed to buy 124m shares in the rights issue, leaving underwriters Morgan Stanley and Dresdner Kleinwort with 1.375bn shares. The banks have until 4.30pm tomorrow to offer them to new and existing shareholders. If the shares are not placed in the market, the underwriters pass them on to other financial institutions which have agreed to "sub-underwrite" the issue.

The two investment banks keep the leftovers and it is thought they could end up with a maximum of £1bn worth each as a quarter of the bank's shareholder base is made up of retail investors who do not tend to support corporate cash calls.

The rights issue has cost HBOS £160m, including paperwork and underwriting fees.

HBOS's shares fell below 275p in the days before the offer deadline and plunged to 225p at one point. They ended the week at 282p - above the rights issue price but the rally came too late to entice shareholders to the cash call.

Barclays didn't fare much better in its cash call on Friday - with shareholders taking up only 19% of shares offered in a £4.5bn fundraising, forcing "anchor" investors including the Qatar Investment Authority to come to its rescue.

Royal Bank of Scotland and Bradford & Bingley have also tried to raise fresh funds to shore up their balance sheets in the face of the credit crunch. It took B&B three attempts to get through a £400m fundraising, which was finally approved at a special shareholders' meeting last week.

Source: *Guardian*, 21 July 2008

17.7.5.1   The underwriting agreement

The underwriting arrangements will be recorded in an underwriting agreement, which typically includes the following:

(a)   *Details about the commission payable.* Underwriting costs increase with the length of time for which the underwriter is 'on risk' to take up shares, because the longer the period, the less certain the underwriter can be about how the market in those shares will move. The higher the risk for the underwriter, the more the underwriter will charge for his services. With a rights issue, the underwriter is 'on risk' for a considerable period of time (see **17.7.4** above); therefore the underwriting costs can be high. Traditionally, a typical underwriting agreement might provide, for example, that the underwriter's fees will be 2% of the amount underwritten for the first 30 days of the rights issue, and a further commission of 0.125% of the aggregate amount raised in respect of any further period (although the amount and formula will vary depending on factors such as the amount of the rights issue and the amount of discount). However, in light of the financial crisis, underwriting fees soared to an average of 3.5%, which resulted in a Rights Issue Underwriting Fee Report by the IIC and prompted an inquiry by the OFT (see **17.7.5.2** below). More recently, fees seem to have settled into the 2–3.25% range.

(b)   *Conditions.* These will include the passing of any necessary resolutions at a GM and the admission of the shares to the Official List and the Main Market, nil paid (known as the 'admission condition'). In other words, the agreement is a conditional contract. If these conditions are not met, the underwriter can walk away from the agreement.

(c)   *Representations and warranties from the company.* Breach of these may give rise to the right to terminate the agreement, in addition to damages.

(d)   *Material adverse change (MAC) clause and force majeure clause.* These clauses will allow the underwriter to terminate the agreement in very limited circumstances. There has been greater attention paid to these clauses in light of the financial crisis. Underwriters are increasingly drafting termination rights more precisely rather than relying on generally-worded MAC clauses. It is also worth noting that a recent case, *Tandrin Aviation Holdings Ltd v Aero Toy Store* [2010] EWHC 40 (Comm), reiterated the accepted principle that extraordinary economic or financial difficulties do not fall within a generally-worded force majeure clause, and that explicit reference to such events must be made to discharge the parties from contractual liability.

As stated at **17.7.4**, the FCA does not allow shares in listed companies to be allotted provisionally on a conditional basis. This means that underwriters should not have any right to terminate their underwriting obligation once the nil paid rights have been admitted, because once this point is reached shareholders will begin trading in the rights. Companies must therefore ensure that their underwriting arrangements do not allow the underwriters to invoke withdrawal rights (see **6.9.4** and **17.5.1**) under any circumstances.

17.7.5.2   Underwriting fees

The OFT in August 2010 held an inquiry into underwriting fees charged for different types of secondary issue, including rights issues and placings. It was held in the light of increasing dissatisfaction from companies and investors caused by increased fees, particularly at a time of perceived lower risk due to larger than usual discounts in the offer price.

The inquiry was limited to secondary issues (not IPOs) and to the largest 350 firms on the Main Market (FTSE 350). The inquiry took the form of a market study which reported back in January 2011 that fees and discounts had risen significantly, even when risks had reduced. Rather than take further action, the OFT decided that it was more efficient to allow the market itself to resolve the problem. At the same time the IIC, made up of representative bodies of institutional investors, conducted its own investigations which have resulted in its 'Best Practice Guidance for Issuers when Raising Equity Finance' of May 2011, available on its website at www.iicomm.org. The guidance it provides to listed companies includes advice on how to raise equity finance as cost-effectively as possible through controlling the underwriting fees payable.

17.7.6   Pre-emption rights

A rights issue is a pre-emptive offer, that is, it is in accordance with the statutory pre-emption rights on allotment under s 561 of the CA 2006; the company is issuing *equity securities* (for our purposes, ordinary shares) to holders of *ordinary shares* in proportion to the nominal value of their existing shareholdings, in return for cash consideration (see **14.6.5**). This therefore accords with the rationale behind pre-emption rights, namely to allow existing voting shareholders to protect their proportionate share of the votes at the company's GM and of the profits paid by way of dividend.

As the issue is in accordance with s 561, there is no requirement to disapply s 561; however, the company must also comply with s 562 of the CA 2006, which sets out how to make the offer. In particular, the offer:

(a)   must be in hard copy or electronic form (s 562(2));

(b)   must state a period of not less than 14 days during which it can be accepted (s 562(5)) (see **17.7.4**); and

(c)   such period begins:

    (i)   for an offer made in hard copy, with the date on which the offer was sent or supplied; or

    (ii)   for an offer made electronically, with the date on which the offer was sent.

However, having said that there is no *legal requirement* to disapply s 561 for a rights issue, *in practice* s 561 is often disapplied, for the reasons set out at **17.7.6.1** to **17.7.6.3** below. As explained at **14.6.15**, for this reason typically listed companies effect a general disapplication of the statutory pre-emption rights (that is, s 561) at each AGM, in a way which allows directors to make small rights issues provided they follow the pre-emption rights in the Listing Rules (see **17.7.6.5**). Remember, however, that any existing s 561 disapplication will relate to an existing s 551 authority (see **14.6.14.3**). If the rights issue requires a new s 551 authority (because the existing s 551 authority has expired in terms of time or number of shares) then the existing s 561 disapplication will be of no use. If this is the case, the company will need to pass a new s 561 disapplication specifically for the issue if the statutory procedure is not to be followed.

The differences outlined below should be familiar to you from **14.6.12**.

17.7.6.1 Fractional entitlements

If the company offered shareholders their exact proportional entitlements under a rights issue, the calculation may entitle some shareholders to fractions of shares. The CA 2006 is unclear as to how a company should deal with fractional entitlements, so, in practice, the company rounds down each shareholder's entitlement to the nearest whole share. The fractional entitlements which have not been offered have the potential to raise further finance, if the company can aggregate them and sell the aggregate. Unfortunately, the CA 2006 is not clear as to whether fractional entitlements are covered by s 561. Selling the aggregate might infringe the existing shareholders' pre-emption rights. However, if those pre-emption rights are disapplied, the company can sell the aggregate fractional entitlements. The company can take both the subscription price and any premium over the subscription price which it receives.

> **EXAMPLE**
>
> The company has 500,000 shareholders. One of them, X, holds 302 shares. The company announces a '1 for 3' rights issue, that is 1 new share is offered for every 3 shares held. Strictly X is entitled to 100 shares plus two-thirds of a share (302 divided by 3).
>
> However, as the CA 2006 is unclear as to whether fractional entitlements can be allocated, the company rounds down X's entitlement to 100 shares. This leaves two-thirds of a share unissued. A similar situation has arisen for most of the other 499,999 shareholders, so that, together with X's two-thirds of a share, there is an aggregate of, say, 200,000 shares unissued.
>
> If s 561 applies to the issue, it is thought that selling these 200,000 shares to a third party may infringe the pre-emptive right of X (to his two-thirds of a share) and of each of the other existing shareholders (to their respective fractional entitlements), so the company cannot do anything with these shares.
>
> However, if s 561 is disapplied, these shares can be sold to one or more third parties, raising further finance for the company. The company will take the subscription price for the 200,000 shares and can take any premium received.

17.7.6.2 Overseas shareholders

Certain jurisdictions, such as Japan, Canada and the USA, have very strict laws concerning the offering of securities. These laws mean that it can be so expensive and time-consuming to make an offer of securities in those jurisdictions that many companies prefer not to make an offer there. If the pre-emption rights have not been disapplied and the company has shareholders in those jurisdictions, the company has a problem. Section 561 of the CA 2006 does provide for this situation; it allows companies to make an offer to those overseas shareholders by way of a notice in the *Gazette* (known as the '*Gazette* route'). However, companies often prefer instead to disapply the pre-emption rights, and arrange for the entitlements of those shareholders to be aggregated and sold in the market, nil-paid. Any premium the company receives over the subscription price will then usually be given to those overseas shareholders. For premium listed companies this will be done in accordance with LR 9.5.4R (subject to the company's right to retain amounts under £5 per shareholder if it wishes). Standard listed companies are not subject to LR 9.5.4R but would typically pay the premium anyway to keep their overseas shareholders happy.

Note that the FCA will not usually permit the exclusion of shareholders in another EU Member State from a rights issue on the grounds of local securities laws. In such cases it encourages companies to take advantage of the procedure for the 'passporting' of prospectuses (see **6.11**).

17.7.6.3 Convertible securities

If a company has issued securities and the terms of those securities state that they will entitle the holder to pre-emption rights, but under the CA 2006 the holder is not entitled to pre-emption rights (because the securities do not fall within the definition of 'ordinary shares': see **14.6.8** above), the company must disapply s 561. This will ensure that the company will be able to make the rights issue to those holders, in accordance with the terms of the securities.

> **EXAMPLE**
>
> The company has in issue convertible loan stock. The terms of the loan stock state that the holders of the stock are entitled to pre-emption rights on any rights issue. However, under s 561, convertible loan stock does not fall within the definition of ordinary shares (it is not a share), and so, under s 561 the loan stock does not entitle its holders to pre-emption rights. There is a conflict. It would be very difficult to change the terms of the stock, so instead s 561 is disapplied to resolve the conflict; and the rights issue is offered to the holders of the convertible loan stock.

17.7.6.4 Pre-emption rights under the Listing Rules for premium listed companies

As **14.6.12** explained, the pre-emption rights under the Listing Rules for premium listed companies are slightly more flexible than the pre-emption rights under the CA 2006, and they do not raise the problems listed at **17.7.6.1** and **17.7.6.2** above (although they do raise similar problems relating to convertible securities). When the company disapplies s 561, although this also disapplies the pre-emption rights under the Listing Rules (see LR 9.3.12R and **14.6.15**), the company will nevertheless still offer the rights pre-emptively (except to overseas shareholders and fractional entitlements) as envisaged by the Listing Rules. This removes the practical problems of the statutory pre-emption rights in relation to fractional entitlements and overseas shareholders, but keeps the IPCs happy.

17.7.6.5 The IPCs

If the statutory pre-emption rights are disapplied, does this mean that the Pre-emption Group will no longer support the issue? No. As explained at **14.6.16** above, para 5 of the Pre-Emption Group's Statement of Principles makes clear that the Principles do not apply to issues of equity securities on a pre-emptive basis. Paragraph 16 of the Pre-Emption Group's Statement of Principles (see **14.6.16**) evidences the IPC's preference for pre-emptive issues. It states that the choice of financing options (that is, the method of raising equity finance) is one of the critical considerations relating to a request for a non-routine disapplication (see **14.6.16.2**). The Group notes that a wide variety of financing options are now available to companies, and if a non-pre-emptive issue of shares is the most appropriate means of raising capital, companies should explain why that is, and why other financing methods have been rejected.

17.7.7 Timetable

Table 17.2 below is an example of a basic rights issue timetable, assuming that a GM is required. Please note that in practice most documents are submitted to the FCA and to the Stock Exchange in draft form well before the required deadline. Similarly, applications may be made in advance of the date required by the regulatory rules. Remember also that the timetable will be dependent on the particular circumstances of the listed company involved (for example, the time period in the company's articles for receipt of documents sent in the post may vary from company to company). The timings may therefore vary from rights issue to rights issue.

Table 17.2 GM REQUIRED

Date	Event
1.5 to 3 months (deadline is 10 working days) before impact day.	Submit draft prospectus and related draft documentation to FCA for approval under the Prospectus Rules.
Day before impact day	Board meeting to approve rights issue. Underwriting agreement signed and held in escrow.
Impact day	Press announcement released. Underwriting agreement released from escrow. Prospectus published, containing notice of GM. (PALs cannot be sent out until after GM.)
2 business days before D day (LR 3.3.2R)	Apply for admission of shares, nil paid, to the Official List and Main Market (by submitting '48 hour' documents to FCA under the Listing Rules, and 'two- day' documents to the Stock Exchange under the Admission and Disclosure Standards).
14 clear days after impact day (assuming a GM (and not an AGM) held) (s 307A and s 360, CA 2006)	GM to pass shareholder resolutions (eg grant directors authority to allot, disapply s 561, create a new class of shares, alter articles of association, and/ or approve any related acquisition). PALS sent out immediately after GM.
One business day after GM ('**D day**')	Submit 'on the day' documents to the FCA under the Listing Rules (LR 3.3.3R). Shares admitted to Official List and Main Market, nil paid. Statement made by FCA to an RIS and statement published by the Stock Exchange on its website. 'Admission condition' in underwriting agreement is satisfied. Nil paid dealings in shares begin. Sale of overseas shareholders' shares and fractional entitlements (if s 561 pre-emption rights disapplied).
10 business days (LR 9.5.6R) from posting of PALs if s 561 disapplied (premium listing); or 14 days (CA 2006, s 562(5)) and 10 business days (LR 9.5.6R) if s 561 not disapplied (premium listing); or 14 days (CA 2006, s 562(5)) if s 561 not disapplied (standard listing) ('Close of offer')	End of nil paid dealing period. Deadline for acceptance and payment in full.

Date	Event
1 business day after close of offer	Dealings in shares commence, fully paid. Notify underwriters of acceptances. Underwriters try to sell rump.
2 business days after close of offer	Identify stick. Final confirmation of acceptances announced. Announce result of rights issue to RIS (for premium listed companies) see **17.7.11** below.
Week after close of offer	Underwriters pay company consideration for the stick, if any. Company receives net proceeds of the issue and dispatches share certificates to shareholders/credits CREST accounts.

17.7.8   Advantages of a rights issue

A rights issue has the following advantages:

(a)   *Price.* If the issue is in accordance with the pre-emption requirements of the Listing Rules, there is no limit on the level of discount at which the company can issue the shares (save that the shares must not be issued at a discount to their nominal value in breach of s 580 of the CA 2006).

(b)   *The IPCs.* The IPCs are more likely to support this pre-emptive method of raising equity finance (see **17.7.6.6**).

17.7.9   Disadvantages of a rights issue

A rights issue has the following disadvantages:

(a)   *Cost.* The costs of underwriting can be high.

(b)   *Market value.* The shares issued under a rights issue are usually issued at a discount. This can cause the market value of the shares to fall.

(c)   *Timing.* The offer period is 10 business days under LR 9.5.6R for premium listed companies, or 14 days under CA 2006, s 562(5) for standard listed companies (assuming s 561 not disapplied), which cannot run concurrently with the GM notice.

(d)   *Pre-emption.* Even though the offer is on a pre-emptive basis, a s 561 disapplication is often required (see **17.7.6** above).

17.7.10   Is a rights issue appropriate?

When considering whether a rights issue is the most appropriate method to raise equity finance, the following questions will be useful:

(a)   Is the company concerned about underwriting costs? If so, a rights issue may not be the best method.

(b)   Does the company need to raise finance quickly? If so, a rights issue may not be the best method.

(c)   Does the company need flexibility in the amount by which it can discount shares? If so, a rights issue has some advantage over the other methods of equity finance in this regard.

17.7.11   Documentation

The following documentation may be required for a rights issue:

(a)   press announcement of rights issue on impact day and of the results of the issue, issued via an RIS and satisfying the need for an RIS notification (LR 9.5.5R and LR 9.6.6.R for premium listed companies);

(b)   underwriting agreement;

(c)   PAL;

(d)   notice of GM;

(e)   prospectus;

(f)   perhaps, a separate circular (see **17.5.2**);

(g)   documents required for admitting shares to listing and to trading (see **17.4.3**);

(h)   if the rights issue involves CREST shareholders, additional documents to enable dealing in the rights; and

(i)   *Gazette* notice (for overseas shareholders).

Barclays issues £5.8bn new shares as it reveals £12.8bn shortfall

Nick Goodway

Banking giant Barclays today revealed plans to plug up a £12.8bn shortfall identified by the City watchdog through an issue of £5.8bn-worth of new shares.

Barclays also took another £2 billion hit for mis-selling payment protection insurance and interest rate swaps, taking the total set aside for mis-selling to £5.5 billion.

However, in a sweetener to investors, the bank said that once it had closed the capital gap identified by the Prudential Regulation Authority (PRA), it would be able to increase its dividend payouts by more than expected from 2014.

Chief executive Antony Jenkins, who took over after Bob Diamond quit in the wake of the Libor-rigging scandal last year, said: "After careful consideration of the options, the board and I have determined that Barclays should respond quickly and decisively to meet this new target.

"We have developed a bold but bal-

anced plan to do so."

Barclays' first-half profits fell 17 per cent to £3.59 billion, which was slightly lower than City estimates and included a £640 million charge for Jenkins' restructuring plan, which aims to save £1.5 billion in annual costs and will see a total of 3,700 jobs go by 2015.

Under the rights issue, existing shareholders will be offered one new share for every four they own at 185p a share, which is a 40 per cent discount to last night's closing price. Today Barclays shares dropped more than 6 per cent to 287.80p by mid-afternoon but are still up more than 12 per cent this year.

The PRA and Bank of England said they welcomed Barclays' move, calling it "a credible plan to meet a leverage ratio of 3 per cent, after adjustments, by June 2014 without cutting back on lending to the real economy".

Barclays will sell up to an additional

£80 billion of assets, raise another £2 billion through the issue of "CoCos", loss-absorbing securities, and retain more of its earnings in order to meet the PRA's £12.8 billion target.

Jenkins said: "The board and I are aware of the implications of a rights issue for shareholders. We hope to balance this with reduced uncertainty in the outlook for Barclays and with enhancement of our dividend payout from 2014."

He added that once the new capital is in place, Barclays could increase the amount of earnings it pays in dividends to shareholders from his original target of 30 per cent to somewhere between 40 per cent and 50 per cent.

Barclays is paying some £150 million in fees for the rights issue, much of which will go to the lead underwriters and bookrunners: Credit Suisse, Deutsche Bank, Bank of America Merrill Lynch and Citi.

Source: *Independent*, 30 July 2013

17.8   OPEN OFFER

17.8.1   What is an open offer?

Appendix 1.1 of the Listing Rules defines an open offer. Like a rights issue (see **17.7** above), an open offer is:

(a)   an offer to issue new shares, or transfer existing shares (or other securities);

(b)   to existing shareholders (or security holders) in proportion to their existing holdings.

Again, the offer is usually for cash. However, unlike a rights issue, the offer is not made by means of a PAL (see **17.7.3.1** above), but by an application form. The structure of the offer is considered at **17.8.3** below.

17.8.2   Price

The shares are offered at a discount, but the discount tends to be less than that for a rights issue (see **17.7.2** above). The default position is that an open offer for a premium listed company cannot be priced at a discount of more than 10% of market value (LR 9.5.10R(1)). Listing Rule 9.5.10R(3) provides that this rule does not apply if:

(a)   the company's shareholders have specifically approved the terms of the open offer at a discount of more than 10%; or

(b)   the shares are being issued for cash consideration under a pre-existing general authority to disapply s 561 of the CA 2006.

Note that any shares issued under the exception at (b) above will render the disapplication 'non-routine' under the Pre-Emption Group's Statement of Principles, which advocate limiting any discount to 5%, unless the issue is in accordance with the pre-emption requirements of the Listing Rules (see **14.6.16**).

17.8.3   Structure

The company sends a personal application form to each shareholder. Unlike the PAL used in a rights issue, this form simply offers shares; it does not provisionally allot them. The shareholder can either take up the offer, or do nothing. No shareholder can assign or sell the benefit of the offer. There is no trading in rights. In addition, no arrangements are made for the sale of shares which shareholders do not take up. This is bad news for the 'lazy shareholder'; in contrast to a rights issue (see **17.7.3.5** above), if a shareholder does nothing in relation to the offer, he will receive nothing under the offer.

The traditional structure of an open offer gives shareholders less flexibility than on a rights issue (the shareholder cannot trade the rights nil paid, and the lazy shareholder receives nothing) and open offers tend to be cheaper for companies than rights issues. The IPCs have stated, informally and not through formal guidance, that if an issue represents more than 15–18% of a company's issued share capital, or if the discount is greater than 7.5%, this may cause them concern (if the issue does not otherwise protect shareholders adequately). In such circumstances, the IPCs prefer a rights issue to an open offer. In any event, in the period 1 January to 31 October 2013 there was just one open offer combined with a placing (see **7.9** below) at a discount of 6.3%. In order to mitigate some of this criticism, it is possible to have so-called 'compensatory' open offers (eg Lloyds Banking Group plc open offer in May 2009) which are structured so that shareholders who do not take up their entitlement are compensated as on a rights issue by receiving any premium above the offer price when the rump is sold in the market by the underwriters.

17.8.4   Timing

Listing Rule 9.5.7R provides that the timetable for an open offer for a premium listed company must be approved by the RIE on which the shares are traded. For our purposes this is the London Stock Exchange. Listing Rule 9.5.7AR states that the offer period must be a minimum period of 10 business days from the date of posting the application forms. This mirrors the Stock Exchange's requirement in Admission and Disclosure Standards, ADS 3.9 – see **Appendix 1**. The offer period is therefore the same for a rights issue. Admission and Disclosure Standard 3.9 applies equally to a standard listed company undertaking an open offer.

In addition, and of more significance to timing, is the fact that, unlike with a rights issue, the application forms do not provisionally allot shares. This means that the problem with provisionally allotting shares on a conditional basis does not arise. Therefore, if a GM is required in order to obtain the consent of the shareholders in connection with the share issue (to increase the company's share capital and such like – see **Chapter 14**), the offer period can run concurrently with the GM notice. This means that, compared to a rights issue, the underwriting commission is less and the company will receive its cash sooner.

17.8.5   Advantages of an open offer

An open offer has the following advantages for the company:

(a)   *Timing.* The offer period can run concurrently with the GM notice.

(b)   *Cost.* For a premium listed company the default position is that shares cannot be offered at a discount of more than 10%. Unless the offer is structured to fall within one of the exceptions to this, the open offer will be cheaper for the company (but see **17.8.6**(b) below).

17.8.6 Disadvantages of an open offer

An open offer has the following disadvantages for the company:

(a) *Pre-emption.* Even though the offer is on a pre-emptive basis, a s 561 disapplication is usually required, because the statutory pre-emption rights have the potential to cause problems (as they do on a rights issue; see **17.7.6**).

(b) *Flexibility.* For a premium listed company the default position is that shares cannot be offered at a discount of more than 10%. Unless the offer is structured to fall within one of the exceptions to this, an open offer might be less attractive to shareholders than a rights issue.

(c) *The IPCs.* The IPCs prefer rights issues to open offers in certain circumstances (see **17.8.3**).

17.8.7 Documentation

The following documentation may be required for an open offer:

(a) press announcement/RIS notification;

(b) underwriting agreement;

(c) notice of GM;

(d) prospectus;

(e) perhaps, a separate circular (see **17.5.2**); and

(f) other documents required for admitting shares to listing and to trading (see **17.4.3**).

17.9 PLACING

A placing is one of the methods by which a company can float (see **4.4.2** above). It is also a method which can be used for a secondary issue.

In the period 1 January to 31 October 2013, approximately £3.25 billion was raised by companies on the Main Market through full or partial placings, making this the second most popular form of secondary issue.

17.9.1 What is a placing?

The formal definition of a placing is in Appendix 1.1 of the Listing Rules. Basically, a placing is:

(a) an offer by the company to issue new shares and/or an offer by existing shareholders to transfer existing unlisted shares (or other securities);

(b) to specified persons or clients of any financial adviser assisting in the placing;

(c) which does not involve an offer to the public or to existing holders of the company's securities.

Again, a placing is usually for cash. The key distinguishing feature is therefore that a placing involves a much smaller number of people than a rights issue or an open offer, and they are usually institutional investors.

17.9.2 Price

Paragraph 11 of the Pre-Emption Group's Statement of Principles (set out at **Appendix 3**) provides that a request for a discount of more than 5% of market value is not likely to be regarded as 'routine' (see **14.6.16**).

Listing Rule 9.5.10R also provides that for a premium listed company, a placing, as with an open offer, cannot be priced at a discount of more than 10% of market value unless it is structured to fall within either of the exceptions set out at LR 9.5.10R(3)(a) or (b) (see **17.8.2**).

17.9.3   Advantages of a placing

The advantage of a placing is its cost. The limitations on the discount that can be applied (see **17.9.2**) mean that a placing can be cheaper for the company than a rights issue. As soundings will be taken from the market as to likely demand and an acceptable price, underwriting fees, if any, are likely to be lower than on a rights issue.

17.9.4   Disadvantages of a placing

A placing is not a pre-emptive offer, so:

(a)   a s 561 disapplication is required; and

(b)   the Pre-Emption Group's Statement of Principles will restrict the number of shares which can be issued (see **14.6.16** above) (and the discount which can be applied – see **17.9.2**).

17.9.5   Documentation

The following documentation may be required for a placing:

(a)   press announcement/RIS notification;

(b)   placing agreement;

(c)   underwriting agreement;

(d)   prospectus, unless the placing is exempt (see **17.5.1**);

(e)   if the placing is exempt, or possibly if overseas shareholders, a separate circular (see **17.5.2**); and

(f)   other documents required for admitting shares to listing and to trading (see **17.4.3**).

17.9.6   Example

G4S plc completed a placing in August 2013 which raised £348 million to invest in its business to support further organic growth, particularly in its developing markets businesses, to resource both business and product development and to make acquisitions.

17.10   ACQUISITION ISSUE

17.10.1   What is an acquisition issue?

An acquisition issue is also known as a 'share-for-share exchange', or a 'securities exchange offer'. It is:

(a)   an issue of new shares by the company;

(b)   to the seller(s) of an asset or assets (which includes shares);

(c)   in consideration for the acquisition by the company of that asset or assets.

17.10.2   Structure

An acquisition issue does not involve marketing shares, as in the case of a rights issue, an open offer or a placing. Instead, it consists of the offer of shares as consideration for an acquisition.

EXAMPLE

Imagine that X plc wants to buy the entire issued share capital of another company, Y Ltd. The buyer is X plc. The sellers are all the shareholders of Y Ltd. The sellers will transfer the shares they hold in Y Ltd to X plc. X plc will then issue shares in itself to the shareholders of Y Ltd, as consideration. See **Figure 17.1** below.

Figure 17.1: Acquisition issue

Before the acquisition

The acquisition

1. Shareholders in Y Ltd *transfer* all the shares in Y Ltd to X plc, so X plc becomes the sole shareholder of Y Ltd.

2. X plc *issues* shares in itself to the shareholders of Y Ltd, as consideration for the transfer, so the former shareholders of Y become additional shareholders of X plc.

After the acquisition

17.10.3 Advantages of an acquisition issue

An acquisition issue has the following advantages:

(a) *Timing*. There are no significant timetabling issues.

(b) *Cost*. An acquisition issue is inexpensive.

(c) *Pre-emption*. The issue is not for cash, so s 561 pre-emption rights are not triggered.

17.10.4 Disadvantages of an acquisition issue

An acquisition issue has the disadvantage that a valuation may be required under s 593 of the CA 2006 (see **14.7.5** above), if the asset to be acquired is anything other than shares.

17.10.5 Documentation

The following documentation may be required for an acquisition issue:

(a)   press announcement/RIS notification;

(b)   sale and purchase agreement;

(c)   prospectus, unless the acquisition issue is exempt;

(d)   circular; and

(e)   other documents required for admitting shares to listing and to trading (see **17.4.3**).

17.11   VENDOR PLACING

17.11.1   What is a vendor placing?

A vendor placing (also known as a 'vendor consideration placing') is used in the context of an acquisition only. It is useful when:

(a)   the company wants to make an acquisition; but

(b)   the company does not have sufficient cash to buy the company or business; and

(c)   the seller is not willing to accept non-cash consideration (so that an acquisition issue (see **17.10** above) is not appropriate).

Instead, the vendor placing is structured so that:

(a)   there is an acquisition issue; then

(b)   the company arranges for its investment bank to place the shares it has issued to the seller as consideration; then

(c)   the company's investment bank gives the proceeds of the placing, in cash, to the seller.

So the listed company acquires the company or business it wants. The seller gets the cash it wants.

17.11.2   Price

Listing Rule 9.5.10R provides that, as with an open offer and a placing, a vendor placing for a premium listed company cannot be priced at a discount of more than 10% of market value unless it is structured to fall within either of the exceptions set out at LR 9.5.10R(3)(a) and (b) (see **17.8.2**). The vendor placing is not an issue of shares for cash, so it will not fall within the exception at LR 9.5.10R(3)(b).

17.11.3   Advantages of a vendor placing

(a)   *Cost.* The limitation on the discount that can be applied for a premium listed company (see **17.11.2**) means that a vendor placing can have cost advantages for the company.

(b)   *Pre-emption.* A vendor placing is not an issue for cash. The company issues the shares for non-cash consideration (it exchanges them for shares). The pre-emption rules do not apply, therefore, so no s 561 disapplication is required. However, the ABI has issued guidelines which provide that vendor placings:

(i)   of over 10% of the company's issued equity share capital; or

(ii)   at more than 5% discount,

must be placed on a basis which gives existing shareholders the right to 'claw back' their pro rata share of the issue. The claw-back is usually offered by way of an open offer (vendor placing with open offer), but it can also be made by way of rights issue (vendor consideration rights issue).

17.11.4   Disadvantages of a vendor placing

A valuation may be required under s 593 of the CA 2006 (see **14.7.5** above), if the asset to be acquired is anything other than shares.

17.11.5 Documentation

The following documentation may be required for a vendor placing:

(a)   press announcement/RIS notification;

(b)   sale and purchase agreement;

(c)   placing agreement;

(d)   underwriting agreement;

(e)   prospectus, unless the vendor placing is exempt;

(f)   circular; and

(g)   other documents required for admitting shares to listing and to trading (see **17.4.3**).

CHAPTER 18

EQUITY FINANCE OR DEBT FINANCE?

18.1 INTRODUCTION

Chapter 17 considers that when a company needs finance to provide working capital, reduce borrowings, fund a specific acquisition, or, indeed, for any other reason, it may decide to raise equity finance. This involves the company issuing shares in return for cash or assets. Another book in the series, **Banking and Capital Markets**, discusses another way in which a company may raise finance – debt finance. This involves the company using debt to obtain the cash or assets it requires.

The remainder of this chapter provides a brief overview as to why a company might choose to raise equity finance rather than debt finance, and vice versa. It then examines why most companies, regardless of their size, are financed by a combination of both debt and equity, and considers the key to the right combination.

18.2 INCOME

18.2.1 Equity finance

A company does not have to declare a dividend. If it does not, the shareholders will not receive any income from their investment. The company does not have to pay any interest to the shareholders. The shareholders do not have a *right* to income.

However, in the real world, any listed company will be aware that if it does not declare a dividend, it risks both losing the support of its shareholders and damaging its reputation as a good investment. It is not a good idea, therefore, for a company to perceive a dividend as something which it can withhold without good reason.

To the extent a company does declare a dividend, the shareholders will share in the profits of the company. For equity shareholders, this right is infinite (see **13.5.1.1**).

18.2.2 Debt finance

Lenders will negotiate a rate of interest with the company. The cost of debt to the company depends on the interest rate which a lender charges. The company will have to pay interest regardless of profits (unlike a dividend). Interest provides lenders with income from their investment (unlike a dividend, this income is finite).

The term 'leverage' is often used in this regard. Leverage is the opportunity to create profit by financing a business through debt which is entitled to a finite return. Imagine that you and nine of your friends own a company; you are its shareholders. You have no more cash to invest. If you finance the business solely through equity, you need to bring on board other shareholders who are willing and able to inject cash into the company in return for shares. All the profits of the company will now be shared not just between you and your nine friends, but between all the other shareholders too. Now imagine that you decided to finance the company solely through debt. Any profits which are surplus, once the interest on the debt has been paid, will be shared just between you and your nine friends.

18.3   CAPITAL

18.3.1   Equity finance

On a winding up of the company, the company repays its debts first, then it pays to the shareholders the nominal value of their shares, together with any premium they paid on those shares. The shareholders do not have a *right* to capital. This risk, that shareholders will lose their capital, is balanced by the opportunity, described at **18.2.1** above, to share in the profits of the company without limit, and the potential, described at **18.4** below, for capital growth.

18.3.2   Debt finance

Ultimately, the company must repay the capital to the lender. The holders of debt securities will be paid in priority to shareholders on a winding up.

18.4   CAPITAL GROWTH

18.4.1   Equity finance

There is scope for capital growth. The share value will reflect the success of the company. This can help a successful company to market shares.

18.4.2   Debt finance

There is no scope for capital growth. The lender has a right to be repaid only the capital sum, plus interest, no matter how well the company is performing.

18.5   TAXATION

18.5.1   Equity finance

Dividends are not a deductible expense in calculating the company's corporation taxation liability.

18.5.2   Debt finance

Interest payable on a loan is tax deductible.

18.6   RIGHTS

18.6.1   Equity finance

When a company issues shares, unless it issues such shares in proportion to the existing shareholders' shareholdings, the issue will dilute those shareholdings.

If the issue is of voting shares, the balance of power within the company could change. This may be a high price to pay for raising finance.

18.6.2 Debt finance

Debt finance will not affect the power structure of the company, nor afford the lender any right to vote in the company.

18.7 INVESTORS

The differences between debt and equity considered above mean that investors have different priorities, depending on how they intend to invest in a company.

The extent to which a potential investor will investigate a company before choosing to invest will differ, depending on whether the investor is seeking to invest by way of equity or debt.

18.7.1 Equity investors

Substantial equity investors include pension funds and other similar financial institutions. Potential equity investors will analyse not only the company's current financial position, but also how the company is placed in the long term, by considering the business sector in which the company operates, the company's expenditure on research and development for new products (R&D), and the company's future earning potential. This reflects the fact that once equity investors invest in a company, they pass the point of no return. They have no right to recover their cash, unless they can sell the shares. They risk losing all their capital.

18.7.2 Debt investors

Substantial debt investors include banks and finance houses. Potential lenders tend to confine their analysis to whether the company can service a loan (and any other loans taken out by the company which would rank ahead of, or equal with, the investor's loan) from current earnings.

This reflects the fact that lenders are entitled to be repaid their capital, and also that it is common for the lender to negotiate the right to monitor the financial position of the company through a series of tests known as 'financial covenants' (which relate to issues such as the net worth, cash flow and gearing (see **18.9.1** below) of the company).

18.8 THE PROBLEM

It should now be clear that equity finance and debt finance both bring advantages and disadvantages for a company.

With equity finance, there comes the significant risk for shareholders that they will lose capital. This risk usually means that it is impossible for a company to find enough shareholders with sufficient funds to enable it to finance itself solely through equity. Even if it could, a company would still be likely to use debt finance in order to achieve some leverage.

Why not finance the company entirely through debt, to achieve complete leverage, as in the example at **18.2.2** above? The company must repay debt on a regular basis, regardless of the profits the company has made. Imagine what happens if there is a downturn in business. Perhaps the company's major customer goes bust and cannot repay its debts to the company, or perhaps interest rates rise dramatically, or there is a world event which adversely impacts on trading (consider, for example, the impact on the travel industry of the ash cloud from the volcano in Iceland in 2010). If a business is financed through too much debt, any of these events might mean that the company cannot generate enough cash to enable it to pay its debts as they fall due. (With equity, of course, the company would not have to declare a dividend.)

18.9 THE SOLUTION

The solution is for a company to achieve a proper balance between debt and equity finance. What is a 'proper balance'? The company needs:

(a)   sufficient equity to provide a cushion against any unexpected problems with the business and/or cash flow; and

(b)   sufficient debt to achieve appropriate leverage and an appropriate return to the equity shareholders.

18.9.1   Gearing

The ratio of a company's debt to equity is referred to as 'gearing'. The higher the proportion of debt, the higher the gearing will be.

Prospective investors in the company will be interested in the company's gearing. In particular, lenders will consider the company's gearing before they negotiate the terms of a loan. If the gearing is high, then, as considered above, there is a greater risk that unexpected problems with the business and/or cash flow will render the company unable to service its debt. This means that there is a higher risk of the company going bust. A lender will demand a higher interest rate, therefore, for a loan to a company which is highly geared.

18.9.2   Articles of association

A company seeking to raise equity finance must involve its shareholders in the decision at some point in the process (for example, to authorise the directors to allot shares). However, the decision whether a company should enter into a loan is usually reserved to the board.

A company's articles of association can protect shareholders in this regard. The articles can provide that while the ratio of debt to equity is at a certain level, the company can borrow without having to seek permission from the shareholders; but that once gearing reaches a certain level, the company will require the authorisation of the shareholders in order to borrow.

18.10   CONCLUSION

A public company must think carefully about whether it should use debt or equity to raise the finance it needs. The company needs to monitor its gearing carefully. Not only might a highly-geared company bear a greater risk of going bust, but prospective investors will also scrutinise a company's gearing before deciding whether to invest in the company. It is important, therefore, that the company gets it right.

There are, very rarely, periods of time when it is difficult for a listed company to raise money, by way either of debt or equity. The summer of 2007 was one such rare occasion. The so-called 'credit crunch' in the financial markets, brought on by the housing crisis in the US caused by excessive mortgage lending to the highest credit risk (so-called 'sub-prime' mortgages) and the subsequent problems of borrowers defaulting on repayments, led to banks across the world dramatically cutting back on their lending to one another. This in turn led to the supply of money for lending (including to companies) temporarily drying up. The ability of companies to raise money through equity finance was also affected by the uncertainty of the impact of the losses incurred by financial institutions.

At the time of writing, there are still difficulties for many companies in accessing debt finance, although secondary issues in the equity market have now recovered (see **Chapter 17**).

PART IV

LISTED COMPANY TRANSACTIONS

CHAPTER 19

ACQUISITIONS AND DISPOSALS

19.1 INTRODUCTION

Chapters 10 and 11 of the Listing Rules regulate 'transactions' by premium listed companies. They do not apply to companies with a standard listing. The term 'transaction' is defined in LR 10.1.3R (see 19.4.1). The definition refers principally to acquisitions and disposals by the listed company. **Chapters 20** to **23** discuss the specific rules relating to takeovers and mergers. This chapter considers the main issues which arise when a listed company enters into an acquisition or a disposal.

19.2 BASIC CONSIDERATIONS

The basic issues which a listed company must consider when it is proposing to enter into a transaction are no different to those an unlisted company would consider. They are:

(a) Structure – purchasing/selling assets or shares?

(b) Consideration – cash or non-cash?

(c) Finance – existing cash, equity or debt?

(d) Due diligence – how much?

(e) Contractual protection – warranties and indemnities?

The Legal Practice Guide, *Acquisitions* explores these basic issues.

However, if a listed company is involved in the transaction, the approach of the company to these issues may differ in the following ways:

(a) *Consideration.* As **Chapter 17** explained, if the buyer is a listed company, it has the option of using its shares as consideration.

(b) *Finance.* Even if the seller does not want shares in the buyer as consideration, if the buyer is a listed company it can choose from a variety of methods (not available to an unlisted company) to raise equity finance (see **Chapter 17**).

(c) *Due diligence.* If the target company is a listed company, there will be information about it in the public domain, which will assist the due diligence process.

(d) *Contractual protection.* If the target company is a listed company and its shares are widely held by members of the public or institutions, they, as sellers, will not provide much (if any) contractual protection to any buyer. (Would you be willing to vouch for anything Vodafone Group plc might warrant about its business in a sale and purchase agreement, just because you own a few ordinary shares?)

As well as having a different approach to the basic issues of a transaction, a listed company will also have some additional considerations. These are examined at **19.3** below.

19.3 LISTED COMPANY CONSIDERATIONS

Most of the additional considerations for listed companies should be familiar to you already, as they have been explained in the preceding chapters of this book. A summary of the main issues follows.

19.3.1 Consideration

If the company is:

(a)   issuing shares as consideration; or

(b)   using equity finance to raise cash to use as consideration

for the acquisition, then the rules and regulations considered in **Chapter 17** will be relevant.

19.3.2 The continuing obligation of disclosure

The general obligation of a listed company, under DTR 2.2.1R, to disclose major new developments in its sphere of activity if the information is not already public knowledge and may lead to substantial movement in its share price, is discussed in **Chapter 7**. This obligation will require companies to disclose significant acquisitions and disposals. An exception to this rule – that a company does not need to disclose information about matters in the course of negotiation, unless there is a breach of confidence during those negotiations – is examined at **7.5.2.8** above. These rules are relevant during an acquisition or disposal, to make sure the company discloses the transaction, through an RIS, in a timely manner as soon as the DTRs require.

19.3.3 The disclosure of interests in shares

Chapter 15 considers the obligation of a listed company:

(a)   under DTR 5.8.12R, to disclose to the public the information it acquires under Chapter 5 of the DTRs (see **15.5.5**);

(b)   under DTR 3.1.4R, to disclose to the public certain transactions by PDMRs and their connected persons (see **15.7.1**);

(c)   under DTR 3.1.4R, to disclose to the public a statement on directors' holdings in their listed company (see **15.7.2**); and

(d)   under the Takeover Code, to disclose its interest in shares to the public once its shareholdings exceed a certain level (see **15.7.4**).

These requirements can be particularly relevant in the context of acquisitions or disposals of shares.

19.3.4 Misleading statements, misleading impressions, market abuse and insider dealing

Chapters 9, **10** and **11** consider the civil offence of market abuse and the criminal offences of misleading statements, misleading impressions and insider dealing. These offences can be relevant on an acquisition or a disposal. The acquisition or disposal of shares by a listed company has the potential to increase that company's value. There is scope for the company's directors, and others, to abuse their inside knowledge that the transaction will take place, by investing in shares which will increase in value once the transaction becomes public knowledge.

19.3.5 Financial regulation

As **Chapter 9** explains, anyone who carries out regulated activities in the process of the transaction must be either authorised, or (less likely) exempt.

19.3.6 Financial promotion

Any communication which persuades someone to do something in relation to an investment must comply with the rules of the FSMA 2000 relating to financial promotion. This is discussed in more detail in **Chapter 12**.

19.3.7 Financial assistance

Chapter 16 explains that the lawyer must always check the structure of any share acquisition, to make sure that it does not give rise to financial assistance problems. There may be further scope for such problems if the consideration also involves shares (that is, the consideration is the issue of shares, or the consideration has been raised through equity finance).

19.3.8 The Model Code

Chapter 7 considers the Model Code. As explained at **7.8.4.3**, directors will not obtain clearance to deal in a premium listed company's shares if an acquisition or a disposal has not been made public and the announcement of the transaction would be likely to lead to a significant movement in the company's share price, unless the trading takes place under a 'trading plan'.

19.3.9 The classification of transactions

The remainder of this chapter examines:

(a)   how acquisitions and disposals by premium listed companies are classified under the Listing Rules; and

(b)   the consequences for the premium listed company of that classification.

19.4 THE CLASSIFICATION OF TRANSACTIONS

19.4.1 What is a 'transaction' under the Listing Rules?

Listing Rule 10.1.3R defines 'transaction'. It includes all agreements entered into by a listed company or any of its subsidiaries, other than:

(a)   a transaction in the ordinary course of business (eg, a foreign exchange company buying more currency, or a travel agency selling a holiday);

(b)   an issue of shares, or a transaction to raise finance, which does not involve the acquisition or disposal of any fixed asset of the listed company or subsidiary (eg, a rights issue or open offer);

(c)   a transaction between a listed company and its wholly-owned subsidiary, or between its wholly-owned subsidiaries (that is, certain intra-group transactions).

It also includes the grant of certain options.

Listing Rule 10.1.4G provides general guidance as to the FCA's intention regarding the Chapter 10 regime. It states that it is intended to cover transactions that are outside the ordinary course of a company's business and may change a shareholder's (or other security holder's) economic interest in the company's assets or liabilities (whether or not any change is registered in the balance sheet). This clarifies that the regime is focused on the potential impact of the transaction on the company

Broadly, 'transaction' means acquisitions and disposals of assets or shares. This would therefore cover a listed company buying or selling another company or a business. It also includes a listed company entering into a joint venture.

19.4.2 The classification regime

Chapters 5, 10 and 11 of the Listing Rules contain rules relating to the classification of transactions. The rules in Chapters 5 and 10 divide transactions into three different classes, according to the size of the transaction compared with the size of the listed company. This comparison is made using four calculations referred to as the 'class tests', set out at LR 10, Annex 1 (see **19.4.3**). Each calculation results in a figure which is expressed as a percentage and referred to as a 'percentage ratio'. The percentage ratios determine how the transaction is classified (see **19.4.5.1**, **19.4.6.1** and **19.4.7.1**).

Why is this classification necessary? As ever, it is to protect shareholders. The purpose of classifying a transaction is so that the Listing Rules can determine the extent to which the transaction needs to be regulated, in order to protect the interests of shareholders. Chapter 10 regulates transactions on the basis of size. If a transaction is of a significant size, it is classified in a way which means that the company must follow strict procedural requirements before it can complete the transaction (for example, the company must seek shareholder approval of the transaction). On the other hand, if a transaction is not so significant, it is classified in a way which means that the company does not have to follow such strict procedural requirements. This reflects the practical reality that the bigger the transaction (say, the acquisition of a new company), the greater the risk to the purchasing listed company and its shareholders.

19.4.3   The class tests

If the thought of taking figures and applying percentage ratio tests to them brings unwelcome flashbacks of school and makes you break out in a cold sweat, do not worry. The company's financial advisers and its reporting accountants will actually apply the tests to the relevant figures. However, the lawyer must be aware of and understand the need for, and the principles behind, the class tests. In particular, the lawyer must make sure that the company considers these class tests at an early stage in the transaction in light of the implications for timing, certainty and cost which the results of these class tests may bring.

So, the first stage is to apply all of the relevant class tests. The class tests, set out in LR 10, Annex 1, are as follows:

(a)   Gross assets test (para 2R)

$$\frac{\text{Gross assets which are the subject of the transaction}}{\text{Gross assets of the listed company}} \times 100\%$$

(b)   Profits test (para 4R)

$$\frac{\text{Profits attributable to the assets which are the subject of the transaction}}{\text{Profits of the listed company}} \times 100\%$$

(c)   Consideration test (para 5R)

$$\frac{\text{Consideration for the transaction}}{\text{Aggregate market value of the listed company's ordinary shares}} \times 100\%$$

(d)   Gross capital test* (para 7R)

$$\frac{\text{Gross capital of the company or business being acquired}}{\text{Gross capital of the listed company}} \times 100\%$$

*This test is to be performed only for the acquisition of a company or business and not for a disposal (para 7R(2)).

Annex 1 to the Listing Rules, Chapter 10 provides further guidance on the application of the class tests.

The 'listed company' referred to in the class tests is the premium listed company that is party to the transaction and which you are advising. If both parties to the transaction, that is, buyer and seller, are listed companies, then the transaction will need to be classified twice, once from the buyer's perspective, where the buyer's details will be the 'listed company' referred to above (which will establish the formalities the buyer needs to comply with to make the acquisition), and once from the seller's perspective, where the seller will be the 'listed company' referred to above (this will establish the formalities the seller needs to comply with to make the disposal).

It is possible that one transaction can fall within two different classes, depending on from whose perspective the transaction is classified. For example, a disposal by small listed company A of a third of its assets is likely to be a really significant transaction for company A, probably Class 1. However, for the buyer, huge listed company B, the acquisition is less significant, say Class 2.

Note that in share sales the sellers are the shareholders rather than the company itself, so, even if the target is a listed company, the transaction will need to be classified from one perspective (the listed company buyer's) only.

[handwritten margin note: remember this if share sale]

A joint venture entered into by a listed company must be classified twice – once for the disposal into the new joint venture company and again for the acquisition of an interest in the joint venture company (see the FCA's Technical Note UKLA/TN/302.1 Classification Tests, available in the UKLA section of the FCA's website, for further information).

Listing Rule 10, Annex 1, para 10G provides that the FCA can modify the class tests, to substitute other relevant indicators of size, in the event that they produce an anomalous result, or if the calculation is inappropriate to the activities of the listed company.

Listing Rule 10.2.10R provides that, for the purposes of the calculations, the transaction must be aggregated with certain other transactions (broadly those involving the same parties, the acquisition or disposal of shares in the same company, or which, taken together, result in a substantial involvement in a new business activity) which took place in the preceding 12 months. The aim is to ensure that a series of transactions over a relatively short space of time, which cumulatively may have the same risks for the listed company and its shareholders as one big transaction, are subjected to the same regulatory protection. The FCA also has discretion to aggregate in other circumstances (LR 10.2.11G). The FCA has provided further information on how it aggregates transactions in its Technical Note UKLA/TN/307.1 Aggregating transactions, available on the UKLA section of the FCA's website.

In practice, typically the consideration test proves to be the key test.

19.4.4   The classification of transactions

Ordinarily three class tests will be applied for a disposal, and all four on an acquisition (see **19.4.3**). This will produce either three or four separate percentage ratios. These figures determine the class of the transaction, but what classes are there? There are three classes of transaction, the first two under Chapter 10 of the Listing Rules and the third under Chapter 5, namely:

(a)   Class 1 transaction;

(b)   Class 2 transaction; and

(c)   reverse takeovers.

As mentioned at **19.4.2** above, the purpose of classifying a transaction is to determine the level of procedural safeguards which the Listing Rules will impose to protect the shareholders. Let us now consider:

(a)   the percentage ratios required for the class to apply;

(b)   the requirements of Chapters 5 and 10 of the Listing Rules in relation to transactions of that class.

19.4.5 Class 2

19.4.5.1 Percentage ratios

If *any* of the percentage ratios is 5% or more, but *each* percentage ratio is less than 25%, the transaction will be classified as a Class 2 transaction (LR 10.2.2R(2)).

A recent example is Tate & Lyle plc, the chemicals conglomerate, which made a Class 2 announcement via the RNS on 1 July 2010 that it had disposed of its sugar business to American Sugar Refining.

19.4.5.2 Chapter 10 requirements

Listing Rule 10.4.1R(1) provides that the company must notify an RIS as soon as possible after the terms of any Class 2 transaction are agreed. The announcement (referred to as a 'Class 2 announcement') must contain the information prescribed by LR 10.4.1R(2).

If the company later becomes aware that:

(a)   there has been a significant change which affects any matter in the Class 2 announcement; or

(b)   a significant new matter has arisen which the company would have been required to mention in the Class 2 announcement if it had arisen at the time it was preparing that announcement,

the company must make a supplementary announcement through an RIS without delay (LR 10.4.2R(1)).

19.4.6 Class 1

19.4.6.1 Percentage ratios

If *any* of the percentage ratios is 25% or more, the transaction will be classified as a Class 1 transaction (LR 10.2.2R(3)). For example, imagine that X plc, a listed company, is acquiring Y Ltd. The profits of X plc are £100m. The profits of Y Ltd are £30m. The percentage ratio resulting from the profits class test is 30% (30/100 × 100%). The transaction is a Class 1 transaction.

19.4.6.2 Chapter 10 requirements

Listing Rule 10.5.1R provides that the company must:

(a)   comply with the Class 2 requirements, that is, make an announcement through an RIS which complies with LR 10.4.1R(1) (note that, in practice, this is still referred to as a Class 2 announcement, even when it relates to a Class 1 transaction), and make a supplementary announcement, if required;

(b)   send an explanatory circular, approved by the FCA, to shareholders in the form prescribed by LR 13 (Class 1 circular: see **19.6.1** below);

(c)   obtain the shareholders' approval of the transaction (by ordinary resolution in general meeting) before completing the transaction (the notice of GM will be sent out with the circular referred to at (b) above); and

(d)   ensure that, if the agreement is to be entered into before shareholder approval is obtained, completion of the transaction is conditional on shareholder approval being obtained.

These are significant additional procedural steps imposed on the listed company. They will require the calling and holding of a GM if the AGM is not conveniently timed. The requirement for shareholder approval, however, is the best form of protection, as it gives the shareholder a veto over what is, in relation to the listed company, a large transaction and therefore a bigger risk for their investment.

The following (very brief) extract from the required RIS announcement released by Xchanging plc demonstrates this in practice.

Company	Xchanging PLC
TIDM	XCH
Headline	Acquisition
Released	07:00 06-Oct-08
Number	1123F07

XCHANGING PLC ("XCHANGING")

PROPOSED ACQUISITION OF CAMBRIDGE SOLUTIONS LIMITED ("CAMBRIDGE SOLUTIONS")

KEY HIGHLIGHTS

- Xchanging announces that it has today agreed to acquire 75% of the fully diluted share capital of Cambridge Solutions from a group of Cambridge Solutions' major shareholders (the "Acquisition"). Cambridge Solutions, with approximately 4,500 employees, is an international BPO and IT services provider with a global presence through offices in eight countries across four continents. Cambridge Solutions provides its services to a blue-chip customer base and is listed on the Bombay, National, Madras and Ahmedabad stock exchanges in India.

- The consideration for the Acquisition will be approximately £83 million, comprising Rs 3,712 million in cash (equivalent to approximately £45 million at current rates) and the issue of 15,249,998 New Xchanging Shares. The New Xchanging Shares amount to 7% of the Company's current issued ordinary share capital.

  ...

- The Acquisition is conditional on receiving the approval of Xchanging Shareholders. Details of a meeting convened to seek this approval will be set out in a circular which will be sent to Xchanging Shareholders in due course.

  ...

1. INTRODUCTION

...

In view of its size, the Acquisition constitutes a Class 1 transaction for Xchanging for the purposes of the Listing Rules and accordingly Completion of the Acquisition is subject to, amongst other things, Xchanging Shareholder approval which will be sought at a general meeting of Xchanging shareholders to be convened in due course.

Under LR 10.5.2R, if there is a material change in the terms of the transaction after shareholder approval has been given but before completion of the transaction, the company must repeat the requirements set out in LR 10.5.1R. For example, this would cover an increase of 10% or more in the consideration payable (LR 10.5.3G).

If a material new matter arises or there is a material change before the GM but after the circular has been sent out, a supplementary circular will need to be sent out to the shareholders and the FCA notified in accordance with LR 10.5.4R.

19.4.6.3 Waiver of the requirements to prepare a circular and obtain shareholder approval

If the company is making a Class 1 disposal (not acquisition) because it is in severe financial difficulty, then LR 10.8.1G provides that the FCA may waive the requirement for a circular and shareholder approval referred to at **19.4.6.2(b)** and **(c)** above. If the company wants to make use of this waiver, it must demonstrate to the FCA that it is in severe financial difficulty and must satisfy the conditions in LR 10.8.2G to LR 10.8.6G. The conditions are onerous, and include:

(a)   the company demonstrating to the FCA that it could not reasonably have entered into negotiations earlier (thereby allowing time to seek shareholder approval);

(b)   the sponsor confirming that the company is in severe financial difficulty and will not be in a position to meet its obligations as they fall due unless the disposal takes place according to the proposed timetable;

(c)   the company's finance providers confirming that further finance or facilities will not be made available and, unless the disposal is effected immediately, current facilities will be withdrawn; and

(d)   the company making a full announcement to an RIS, no later than the terms of the disposal are agreed, containing the information set out in LR 10.8.4G and LR 10.8.5G.

A very rare example of this waiver being granted is set out in the article below relating to the disposal of a business by a listed company, JJB Sports. It also demonstrates how in practice a listed company often needs advice from lawyers of differing legal expertise at the same time. This matter will involve employment law (eg the dismissal), property law (eg the leases), debt finance (eg standstill agreement) and insolvency law (eg possible CVA) as well as company law. Ultimately, JJB Sports lost its battle for survival and was put into administration in September 2012.

JJB sells gyms and fires chief executive

Jonathan Russell and Rowena Mason

Retailer JJB Sports has sold its chain of fitness clubs to Wigan Athletic chairman Dave Whelan and confirmed it has sacked its chief executive Christopher Ronnie for gross misconduct.

In a widespread shake-up of the struggling sports retailer, finance director David Madeley has also resigned, while the company is to seek an agreement with its landlords over changing the terms of leases on its outlets.

In a statement on Wednesday night, the company said it had agreed to sell the 55-strong fitness club chain to Mr Whelan, the founder of JJB Sports, for £83.4m.

Proceeds from the sale will initially be used to prop up the indebted company. Although Mr Whelan announced the purchase of the chain of gyms on Wigan Athletic's website in the after-

noon, it wasn't until six hours later that it was confirmed by JJB Sports.

The company had to seek a waiver from the UK Listing Authority, available to companies in "severe financial difficulty", to conduct the sale without seeking shareholder approval.

A standstill agreement between JJB Sports and its banks expired on Tuesday, before the sale had been completed, to help the struggling retailer pay down some of its debt.

JJB Sports is believed to owe its lenders – Lloyds and Barclays – around £50m.

Following on from the disposal of the fitness club chain, the company has agreed new short and medium-term debt facilities with its banks.

Sir David Jones, JJB executive chairman, said: "In announcing our se-

ries of measures today, we have taken the first step in securing JJB's long-term future after months of speculation."

As part of the restructuring, JJB is also seeking a company voluntary arrangement to settle claims of landlords against 140 closed retail stores and to vary the terms of leases on the company's remaining 250 trading stores.

It is understood Mr Ronnie was sacked for failure to disclose details of loans relating to the ownership of his shares.

In January the company warned of losses of up to £10m when it publishes its full-year results in April.

Its shoe businesses, Qube and the Original Shoe Company, have already fallen into administration with the loss of 400 jobs.

Source: *Telegraph*, 26 March 2009

19.4.6.4   The sponsor's role

It is a requirement that a listed company must obtain guidance from a sponsor as to the application of Chapter 10 if the transaction could be a Class 1 transaction (or a reverse takeover) (LR 8.2.2R).

19.4.6.5   Specific transactions

In addition to the acquisition and disposal of a company or a business, the rules can also result in the following specific types of transactions being classified as Class 1 transactions:

(a)   *Joint ventures.* On entering a joint venture, a company should consider the exit provisions of the venture, to determine whether they result in the transaction being classified as a Class 1 transaction (see LR 10.8.9G).

(b)   *Reverse takeovers.* Listing Rule 5.6.3R provides that a reverse takeover (see **19.4.8** below) must comply with the requirements of a Class 1 transaction if it meets the conditions set out in LR 5.6.

(c) *Indemnities.* It is common, in a sale and purchase agreement, for a buyer to seek an indemnity from the seller, to cover specific areas of risk. An indemnity is an undertaking by the seller to meet a specific potential legal liability of the buyer. The indemnity will entitle the buyer to a payment from the seller if the event giving rise to the indemnity takes place. Unlike a claim for breach of warranty, there is no need for the buyer to establish that he has suffered loss.

Listing Rule 10.2.4R provides that certain exceptional indemnities, where the maximum liability is unlimited, or equal to or more than 25% of the average of the company's profits for the last three financial years, will be treated as Class 1 transactions. (The FCA has discretion to substitute other indicators of the size of the indemnity, in the event that this calculation gives an anomalous result.) Listing Rule 10.2.5G sets out the types of indemnity which are not exceptional (including indemnities customarily given in connection with sale and purchase agreements).

(d) *Break fees.* A break fee is an arrangement the purpose of which is that a compensatory sum will become payable by a listed company to another party (or parties) to a proposed transaction if the proposed transaction fails or is materially impeded and there is no independent substantive commercial rationale for the arrangement. It therefore acts as a financial incentive to get the deal done.

Listing Rule 10.2.7R provides that any break fee payable in respect of a transaction will itself be treated as a Class 1 transaction if the total value of break fees in aggregate exceeds 1% of the value of the company, calculated by reference to the offer price (where the company is being acquired) or 1% of the company's market capitalisation (in all other circumstances).

(e) *Issues by major subsidiary undertakings.* Listing Rule 10.2.8R provides that if a major *unlisted* subsidiary of a listed company issues shares:

(i) for cash;

(ii) in exchange for other securities, or

(iii) to reduce indebtedness,

which will cause a dilution with an economic effect equivalent to the sale of 25% or more of the group, then the share issue will be classified as a Class 1 transaction.

19.4.7 Reverse takeover

19.4.7.1 Percentage ratios

If:

(a) a listed company, one of its subsidiaries or a new holding company of it acquires:

(i) a business,

(ii) an unlisted company, or

(iii) assets; *and*

(b) either:

(i) *any* percentage ratio is 100% or more, *or*

(ii) the transaction will result in:

– a fundamental change in the business, or

– a change in the board, or in voting control of the listed company,

then the transaction will be a reverse takeover (LR 5.6.4R(4)). What this means, in layman's terms, is that the listed company is acquiring a company which is either bigger than it is (on the basis of the class tests), or will, in any event, cause fundamental changes to the listed company's business, or, the balance of power at either board or shareholder level. In other words, it is a really significant transaction.

In practice, reverse takeovers can be a useful way for an unlisted company to list shares when it might otherwise not meet the criteria of the Listing Rules considered in **Chapters 4**, **5** and **6**. In effect, the unlisted company 'reverses into' a listed company.

> **EXAMPLE**
>
> Imagine that X plc, our listed company, has fallen on hard times. A large private company, Z Ltd, is doing very well. The shareholders of Z Ltd negotiate a deal, whereby they will sell Z Ltd to X plc in return for an issue of shares in X plc. The shareholders in Z Ltd will become shareholders in X plc, a listed company. The original shareholders of X plc hope that the acquisition by X plc of the successful company, Z Ltd, might help X plc back on its feet.

Figure 19.1 below shows the reverse takeover process in simplified form, using the details in the example above.

Figure 19.1: Reverse takeover

Before the reverse

The reverse

1.   Shareholders in Z Ltd *transfer* shares in Z Ltd to X plc
2.   X plc *issues* shares in itself to the shareholders of Z Ltd, as consideration for the transfer.

Conclusion

19.4.7.2   Chapter 10 requirements

Listing Rule 5.6.3R provides that the company must comply with the Class 1 requirements. In addition, LR 5.6.19G provides that generally the FCA will cancel the listing of the company's shares. The company must then reapply for the listing of those shares and satisfy the relevant conditions for listing (other than one requirement relating to the company's accounts).

This reflects the reality that a listed company is, in effect, being used as a 'Trojan horse' by the unlisted company's shareholders to gain a listing. As we saw in **Chapter 4**, the directors and the company are normally scrutinised intensely before a company can float on the Stock Exchange. To prevent this process being circumvented by a reverse takeover, the company under new ownership must reapply for listing of the company's shares.

Under LR 5.6.8G, generally the FCA will suspend the listing on its announcement, but it is not compulsory.

19.4.7.3   The sponsor's role

A listed company must obtain guidance from a sponsor as to the application of Chapter 10 if the transaction *could* be a reverse takeover (LR 8.2.2R).

19.5   RELATED PARTY TRANSACTIONS

While Chapter 10 of the Listing Rules sets out the rules relating to the classification of transactions on the basis of the *size* of the transaction compared to the size of the listed company, Chapter 11 is dedicated to related party transactions. Related party transactions are classified by the *nature* of the relationship between the parties to the transaction, one of which will be the premium listed company or one of its subsidiaries.

The rationale behind the related party classification is the same as that behind the Chapter 10 classifications: the protection of investors. Related party transactions are subject to certain safeguards which are designed to prevent those who have considerable power over a listed company from taking advantage of their position.

19.5.1   What is a related party transaction?

A related party transaction is defined by LR 11.1.5R as:

(a)   a transaction (other than a transaction in the ordinary course of business) between a listed company (or any of its subsidiary undertakings) and a related party;

(b)   any arrangements (other than an arrangement in the ordinary course of business) pursuant to which a listed company (or any of its subsidiary undertakings) and a related party each invests in, or provides finance to, another undertaking or asset; or

(c)   a transaction (other than a transaction in the ordinary course of business) between a listed company (or any of its subsidiary undertakings) and any person, the purpose and effect of which is to benefit a related party.

If the transaction falls within any of the above definitions, it will be a related party transaction, regardless of the size of the transaction. However, the transaction does still need to be classified by size, using the Chapter 10 classification system. This is because one of the consequences of a transaction being a related party transaction is that the company must publish a circular to its shareholders, and some of the content requirements of that circular depend on whether the related party transaction is the size of a Class 1 transaction or not (see **19.6.2** below). The size of the related party transaction can also affect whether the transaction is exempt from, or subject to more relaxed requirements than, the usual rules (see **19.5.4** below).

19.5.2   Who is a related party?

A 'related party' means a substantial shareholder, director or shadow director, a person exercising significant influence and any of their associates (LR 11.1.4R).

19.5.2.1   Substantial shareholder

This is defined in LR 11.4.1AR and refers to anyone who is entitled to exercise, or control the exercise of, 10% or more of the votes able to be cast on all or substantially all matters at a general meeting of either the listed company, *or any other company in the listed company's group* (but see **19.5.4.1** below in relation to insignificant subsidiaries). This does not apply to shareholders who hold 10% or more for only five days or less, do not attempt to influence the management of the company and do not exercise the votes, for instance investment banks conducting trades on behalf of a group of clients.

19.5.2.2   Director or shadow director

This refers to anyone who is (or, at any time in the 12 months before the transaction, was) a director or shadow director of the listed company, or of *any other company in the listed company's group* (but see **19.5.4.1** below in relation to insignificant subsidiaries). The Listing Rules define 'shadow director' as anyone who falls within the definition of a director in s 417(1)(b) of the FSMA 2000. This covers anyone in accordance with whose directions or instructions the directors of the company are accustomed to act. There is, however, some protection for the likes of lawyers; a person will not be a shadow director just because the directors act in accordance with advice he provides in a professional capacity.

19.5.2.3   Person exercising significant influence

This is a person who exercises significant influence over the company.

19.5.2.4   Associate

This means anyone who, at the time of the transaction, was an associate of the substantial shareholder, director, shadow director, or person exercising significant influence, referred to at **19.5.2.1** to **19.5.2.3** above. 'Associate' is defined in LR Appendix 1.1 as follows:

- In relation to a director, substantial shareholder, or person exercising significant influence, who is an individual:
  (1)   that individual's spouse, civil partner or child (together 'the individual's family');
  (2)   the trustees (acting as such) of any trust of which the individual or any of the individual's family is a beneficiary or discretionary object (other than a trust which is either an occupational pension scheme or an employees' share scheme which does not, in either case, have the effect of conferring benefits on persons all or most of whom are related parties);
  (3)   any company in whose equity securities the individual or any member or members (taken together) of the individual's family or the individual and any such member or members (taken together) are directly or indirectly interested (or have a conditional or contingent entitlement to become interested) so that they are (or would on the fulfilment of the condition or the occurrence of the contingency be) able:
     (a)   to exercise or control the exercise of 30% or more of the votes able to be cast at general meetings on all, or substantially all, matters; or
     (b)   to appoint or remove directors holding a majority of voting rights at board meetings on all, or substantially all, matters;
  (4)   any limited partnership or limited liability partnership in which the individual or any member or members (taken together) of the individual's family are directly or indirectly interested (or have a conditional or contingent entitlement to become

interested) so that they hold or control or would on the fulfilment of the condition or the occurrence of the contingency be able to hold or control:

(a)   a voting interest greater than 30% in the partnership; or

(b)   at least 30% of the partnership.

For the purpose of paragraph (3), if more than one director of the listed company, its parent undertaking or any of its subsidiary undertakings is interested in the equity securities of another company, then the interests of those directors and their associates will be aggregated when determining whether that company is an associate of the director.

- In relation to a substantial shareholder, or person exercising significant influence, which is a company:

(1)   any other company which is its subsidiary undertaking or parent undertaking or fellow subsidiary undertaking of the parent undertaking;

(2)   any company whose directors are accustomed to act in accordance with the substantial shareholder's, or person exercising significant influence's directions or instructions;

(3)   any company in the capital of which the substantial shareholder, or person exercising significant influence and any other company under (1) or (2) taken together, is (or would on the fulfillment of a condition or the occurrence of a contingency be) interested in the manner described in (3) above.

As you can see, the definition is not particularly user-friendly. It may help to consider an example of who is an associate:

EXAMPLE

Mr A is a non-executive director (NED) of X plc, a fashion retailer. He also owns 30% of Y Ltd, a marketing company. X plc decides to acquire the business (ie all of the assets) of Y Ltd, to provide an in-house marketing facility for its business.

Y Ltd is an associate of Mr A. This is because Mr A is a director of X plc, and an individual. Y Ltd is caught by para (3) of the appropriate part of the definition; it is a company in whose equity securities Mr A is directly interested and in which he can exercise 30% of the votes.

As a result of Y Ltd's being an associate of a director of X plc, Y Ltd is also a related party of X plc. The acquisition by X plc of the business of Y Ltd is not a revenue transaction in the ordinary course of business (retailers do not buy marketing businesses on a day-to-day basis). The acquisition therefore is a related party transaction. There is a risk that Mr A could abuse his position as a director of X plc, for example in negotiating the price, and so the shareholders of X plc will be afforded extra protection under Chapter 11 of the Listing Rules.

19.5.3   Chapter 11 requirements

Subject to the exceptions referred to at **19.5.4** below, the following 'related party rules' apply. The listed company must:

(a)   make a Class 2 announcement (see **19.4.5.2** above), which must also contain the name of the related party and details of the nature and extent of the related party's interest, and make a supplementary announcement, if required (again, do not be confused by the fact that the announcement is still referred to as a Class 2 announcement even though it is being made in relation to a related parties transaction) (LR 11.1.7R(1));

(b)   send an explanatory circular, approved by the FCA, and containing the information prescribed by LR 13.3 and LR 13.6, to shareholders (see **19.6.2** below) (LR 11.1.7R(2));

(c)   obtain the shareholders' approval of the transaction (by ordinary resolution in general meeting before completing the transaction – the notice of the GM will be sent out with the circular referred to at (b) above) (LR 11.1.7R(3)(a));

(d)   if the agreement is to be entered into before shareholder approval is obtained, ensure that completion of the transaction is conditional on shareholder approval being obtained (LR 11.1.7R(3)(b)); and

(e)   ensure that the related party does not (and takes all reasonable steps to ensure that its associates do not) vote on any resolution to approve the transaction (LR 11.1.7R(4)). For example, in August 2011 Sports Direct plc bought property from its director and CEO, Mike Ashley. He owned 70% of the shares in the company but was not allowed to vote on the resolution which was decided by the remaining 30% of votes.

Under LR 11.1.7AR, if there is a material change in the terms of the transaction after shareholder approval has been given but before completion of the transaction, the company must repeat the requirements set out in LR 11.1.7R. For example, this would cover an increase of 10% or more in the consideration payable (LR 11.1.7BG).

If a material new matter arises or there is a material change before the GM but after the circular has been sent out, a supplementary circular will need to be sent out to the shareholders and the FCA notified in accordance with LR 11.1.7CR.

19.5.4   Exceptions

There are two categories where the related party rules referred to at **19.5.3** above will not apply. The first is a full exception, where none of the related party rules will apply. The second is a limited exception, where the rules which apply are substantially more relaxed than the full related party rules.

19.5.4.1   When the related party rules will not apply

Listing Rule 11.1.6R provides that the related party rules will not apply if the transaction or arrangement is:

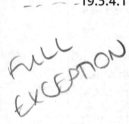

(a)   a small transaction (defined by LR 11, Annex 1R, para 1 as any transaction where each of the Chapter 10 class tests (see **19.4.3** above) results in percentage ratios which are equal to or less than 0.25%); or

(b)   a transaction of a kind referred to in LR 11, Annex 1R, paras 2 to 10, provided it does not have any unusual features.

This includes the following transactions:

New issues (LR 11, Annex 1R, para 2)

The rules will not apply to any issue of new securities to a related party:

(a)   pursuant to a pre-emptive offering; or

(b)   pursuant to the exercise of conversion or subscription rights attaching to listed securities.

The rationale behind this exception is that the shareholders have been protected by other means.

Employees' share schemes (LR 11, Annex 1R, para 3)

The rules will not apply to various awards made pursuant to an employees' share scheme.

Directors' indemnities (LR 11, Annex 1R, para 5)

The rules will not apply to the grant of an indemnity to a director of a listed company or any of its subsidiaries, if the terms of the indemnity are in accordance with those specifically permitted under the CA 2006.

Underwriting (LR 11, Annex 1R, para 6)

The rules will not apply to the underwriting by a related party of certain share issues by the listed company or any of its subsidiaries, provided the consideration to be paid to the underwriter:

(a)   is no more than the usual commercial underwriting consideration; and

(b)   is the same as will be paid to any other underwriters.

Insignificant subsidiaries (LR 11, Annex 1R, para 9)

The rules will not apply if the related party is a related party only through being a substantial shareholder, director or shadow director of an insignificant subsidiary of the listed company (or the associate of any such person). An insignificant subsidiary is a subsidiary which has:

(a)   contributed less than 10% of the profits, and

(b)   represented less than 10% of the assets of,

the listed company for each of the three financial years preceding the date of the transaction for which accounts have been published (or for each financial year for which accounts have been published, if the insignificant subsidiary has been part of the group for less than three years).

Note that this exception will not apply in certain circumstances, such as if the insignificant subsidiary has been part of the group for less than one year, or if the insignificant subsidiary itself is party to the transaction and the ratio of consideration to market capitalisation is more than 10%.

19.5.4.2   When the related party rules will be relaxed

CLIMITED EXCEPTION

The rules will be relaxed, rather than not apply at all, in relation to any transaction where each of the Chapter 10 class tests (see **19.4.3** above) results in percentage ratios which are less than 5%, but where one or more exceeds 0.25%. In other words, the related party transaction is small, but not small enough to benefit from the full exception referred to at **19.5.4.1** above. How are the rules relaxed? The following rules apply instead of the rules referred to at **19.5.3** above (LR 11.1.10R). The company must:

(a)   inform the FCA in writing of the details of the proposed transaction;

(b)   provide the FCA with written confirmation, from an independent adviser acceptable to the FCA, that the terms of the proposed related party transaction are fair and reasonable so far as the shareholders of the company are concerned; and

(c)   undertake in writing to the FCA to include details of the transaction in the company's next published annual accounts.

Compared to the time and effort required to comply with the usual related party rules by making a Class 2 announcement, publishing a Class 1 circular, and seeking shareholder approval, these rules are much less demanding of the company.

19.5.5   The sponsor's role

A listed company must obtain guidance from a sponsor as to the application of Chapter 11 if the transaction *could be* a related party transaction (LR 8.2.3R).

19.5.6   Sanctions

In April 2012, the FSA, the forerunner to the FCA, imposed the first ever fine for a breach of the Listing Rules relating to related party transactions. It fined Exillon Energy plc £292,950 for failing to identify certain payments made to its Chairman as related party transactions, and breaching the requirements of LR 11.1.10R(2) and LR 11.1.11(3) as a result.

19.5.7 The Companies Act 2006

The Listing Rules operate alongside the statutory provisions of the CA 2006. In the event of a related party transaction, the following sections of the CA 2006 may also be relevant.

19.5.7.1 Sections 177 and 182 of the CA 2006

These sections require directors to declare their interests in a transaction.

19.5.7.2 Section 190 of the CA 2006

This section requires shareholder approval of substantial property transactions between directors (but not substantial shareholders) and the company.

19.5.8 The memorandum and articles

The company's memorandum and articles may also contain provisions regulating transactions between the company and its directors.

19.6 THE CIRCULAR

As explained in **Chapter 7**, the circular is a means by which a company communicates with its shareholders, particularly where the company requires the shareholders to approve a transaction. The circular should provide enough information to shareholders to allow them to make an informed decision whether to vote for or against the transaction. The circular will also contain the notice of GM, convening the meeting at which the shareholders will vote on the transaction.

Chapter 13 of the Listing Rules prescribes the content of a circular. Listing Rule 13.3 sets out the content requirements for circulars generally (see **7.9.3**); specific content requirements for specific types of circular are then prescribed by other chapter 13 Listing Rules. For example, LR 13.4, LR 13.5 and LR 13, Annex 1R set out the specific requirements, over and above the general LR 3.3 requirements, for a Class 1 circular, and LR 13.6 sets out the specific content requirements for a related party circular.

Just as the Prospectus Rules allow information to be incorporated by reference into a prospectus (see **6.5.2.2** above), so LR 13.1.3R allows information in a prospectus, or other published document filed with the FCA, to be incorporated into a circular.

It was explained at **7.9.4** above that the FCA categorises circulars either as requiring approval prior to being sent out to the listed company's shareholders, or as not requiring prior approval. The Class 1 circular and related party circular both require FCA approval.

Once a circular has been finalised and approved, the company must file a copy of the circular with the NSM, and notify an RIS that it has done so (LR 9.6.1R and LR 9.6.3R as amended by the introduction of the NSM) (see **7.5.7.1**).

Note that the preparation of the circular can be very time-consuming and costly in light of the information required to be included, and may also delay the timing of the transaction to which it relates (see **19.7** below).

19.6.1 The Class 1 circular

19.6.1.1 Content

As explained at **19.6**, LR 13.3 sets out the general requirements, and LR 13.4, LR 13.5 and LR 13, Annex 1R the specific requirements for a Class 1 circular. Listing Rule 13, Annex 1R cross-refers to Annex 1 and Annex 3 of the PD Regulation (replicated at Appendix III of the Prospectus Rules). This aligns the content requirements of a circular with some of the content requirement for a prospectus (see **6.5.2**). Some of the information in LR 13, Annex 1R must be provided not only for the listed company buyer or seller, but also for the company the subject of the transaction. The requirements of the rules referred to above include the following:

(a) *General disclosure (LR 13.3.1R(3))*. All information necessary for shareholders to be able to make a properly informed decision on the proposal.

(b) *Recommendation (LR 13.3.1R(5))*. A recommendation to shareholders from the directors as to how they should exercise their votes for each resolution, and a statement from the directors as to whether they consider the proposal to be in the shareholders' best interests.

(c) *The directors' responsibility statement (LR 13.4.1R(4))*. A statement by the directors, in the form set out at LR 13.4.1R(4), that they take personal responsibility for the circular.

(d) *Major interests in shares (LR 13, Annex 1R)*. The names of the shareholders holding 3% or more of the company's shares (or an appropriate negative statement if there are none).

(e) *Material contracts (LR 13, Annex 1R)*. See **6.5.2.1** above.

(f) *Litigation (LR 13, Annex 1R)*. See **6.5.2.1** above.

(g) *Significant changes (LR 13, Annex 1R)*. A statement about any significant change since the last published accounts, in respect of the listed company, any other company in the listed company's group and the target company.

19.6.1.2 The sponsor's role

As explained at **19.4.6.4** above, the company must obtain the guidance of a sponsor before it enters into a Class 1 transaction. The sponsor has various obligations under the Listing Rules relating to a 'sponsor service', the definition of which includes a company preparing a Class 1 circular. The obligations include the following:

(a) The sponsor owes a general duty of skill and care and taking reasonable steps to ensure that the company understands its obligations under the Listing Rules and the Disclosure Rules (LR 8.3.3R and LR 8.3.4R).

(b) Listing Rule 8.4.12R provides that, before the sponsor submits the Class 1 circular to the FCA for approval, it must be of the opinion, having made due and careful enquiry, that:

    (i) the company has satisfied all requirements of the Listing Rules relevant to the production of a Class 1 circular;

    (ii) the transaction will not have an adverse impact on the company's ability to comply with the Listing Rules or the DTRs; and

    (iii) the directors have a reasonable basis on which to make the working capital statement required by LR 13.4.1R.

The requirement at (ii) above is particularly onerous from the sponsor's point of view.

(c) Listing Rule 8.4.13R sets out further tasks for the sponsor, including:

    (i) submitting to the FCA a Sponsor's Declaration for the Production of a Circular (on the day the circular is to be approved, but before such approval has been given); and

    (ii) ensuring that all matters known to it, which, in its reasonable opinion, should be taken into account by the FCA in considering the transaction, have been disclosed with sufficient prominence in the documentation or otherwise in writing to the FCA.

The proforma Sponsor's Declaration for the Production of a Circular is available from the UKLA section of the FCA's website.

19.6.2 The related party circular

Listing Rule 13.3 lists the general content requirements, and LR 13.6 the specific content requirements, of a related party circular. These requirements include:

(a)   *Full particulars (LR 13.6.1R(3))*. Full particulars of the transaction, including the name of the related party and the nature and extent of that party's interest in the transaction.

(b)   *The fair and reasonable statement (LR 13.6.1R(5))*. A statement by the board that the transaction is fair and reasonable so far as the shareholders of the company are concerned, and that they have been so advised by an independent adviser acceptable to the FCA.

If the acquisition or disposal is of an asset for which appropriate financial information is not available, an independent valuation of that asset is also required (LR 13.6.1R(4)).

On receipt of the circular, the shareholders will have all the information to hand to enable them to make an informed decision as to whether or not to approve the transaction by ordinary resolution at the general meeting to be held (**19.5.3** above).

19.6.3 Verification

The verification process in the context of an IPO is explained at **5.3.5** and **6.8** above. Verification is also required in relation to other documents published by listed companies, such as circulars, to protect directors against claims from shareholders on the basis set out at **6.7** above.

19.7 THE TRANSACTION TIMETABLE

The requirements of Chapter 10 and Chapter 11 of the Listing Rules can have a significant effect on the transaction timetable. The detail of an acquisition or disposal timetable for any company, listed or unlisted, is considered in another book in the series (see LPC Guide, **Acquisitions**).

The skeleton timetable below should provide a basic understanding of how the requirements for listed companies impact on an acquisition timetable. The listed company requirements are italicised. Remember, however, that not every listed company will need to follow these requirements; whether it does depends on the classification of the transaction.

(a)   Sign heads of agreement.

This document will include legally binding provisions. It will contain important provisions about confidentiality and exclusivity.

(b)   Sign the (*conditional*) agreement.

If the transaction is a Class 1, reverse takeover or related party transaction, the agreement must be conditional upon shareholder approval.

(c)   *Make a Class 2 announcement.*

If the transaction is a Class 2, Class 1, reverse takeover or related party transaction, the company must make a Class 2 announcement through an RIS.

(d)   *Post the circular and the GM notice.*

If the transaction is a Class 1, reverse takeover or related party transaction, a circular is required.

(e)   *Hold a GM.*

If the transaction is a Class 1, reverse takeover or related party transaction, shareholder approval is required.

(f)   Completion.

Company/business finally bought/sold.

Note that there are several steps in between steps (b) and (f) for a listed company. Usually an unlisted company can sign and complete a sale and purchase agreement simultaneously.

19.8 CONCLUSION

The Listing Rules regulate the process by which a premium listed company can make acquisitions and disposals. Depending on the size of the transaction and the relationship between the parties to the transaction, the Listing Rules can require a company to notify an RIS of the transaction and, for more significant transactions, circulate an explanatory circular and obtain shareholder approval of the transaction. These requirements can impact significantly on the timing and cost of the transaction, but reflect the pervasive aim of the regulation of listed companies: to protect investors.

19.9 FUTURE DEVELOPMENTS

The FCA is, at the time of writing, consulting on changes to the Listing Rules, including to LR Chapters 11 and 13. For example, the proposals seek to change the formalities for a smaller related party transaction (see **19.5.4.2** above) and include 'controlling shareholders' within the definition of 'associate' (see **4.6** above). You can find details of the consultation CP13/15 on the FCA's website. The final version of the changes is expected to be available on the FCA's website in the second half of 2014.

CHAPTER 20

TAKEOVERS: REGULATION

20.1 INTRODUCTION

Chapters 21 and **22** consider the detail of a takeover offer (also known as a 'takeover bid'). The purpose of this chapter is to introduce the regulation which will be relevant to any lawyer who advises on such an offer.

20.2 THE PANEL

The Panel on Takeovers and Mergers (the 'Panel') was established in 1968 as a non-statutory body with the support of the Bank of England. Since then it has supervised the regulatory aspects of takeovers. On 20 May 2006 it was designated as the statutory supervisory authority to carry out certain regulatory functions in relation to takeovers pursuant to the Takeovers Directive (see **20.3**), and on 20 April 2007 it gained statutory powers to regulate takeovers beyond the Takeovers Directive under Chapter 1 of Pt 28 of the CA 2006.

20.2.1 What does the Panel do?

The Panel is an independent body with two roles:

(a) *Rule-making.* The Panel issues and administers the Takeover Code, the rulebook relating to takeovers (see **20.5** below).

(a) *Judicial.* The Panel supervises and regulates takeovers and other matters dealt with in the Takeover Code.

20.2.2 Who is on the Panel?

The Panel comprises a maximum of 34 members. It self-appoints a Chairman, up to two Deputy Chairmen and a maximum of 20 other members. Certain financial institutions and professional bodies such as the ABI, the CBI and the NAPF appoint the remaining members.

20.2.3 The Panel Executive

The full Panel itself meets rarely. Instead the Panel Executive carries out the day-to-day work of the Panel, monitoring takeovers and interpreting, consulting on and giving rulings on the Takeover Code. The Panel Executive is headed by the Director General, typically an investment banker seconded to the Panel, and is staffed not only by employees, but also by secondees, including accountants, brokers, investment bankers and, significantly, corporate lawyers. In practice, the term 'Panel Executive' is rarely used; if a lawyer is consulting the Panel Executive, he will invariably refer to this as 'consulting the Panel'. Further information about the Panel Executive is contained in para 5 of the Introduction to the Takeover Code and is available on the Panel's website.

20.2.4   The Panel Committees

The Panel operates principally through the following committees.

20.2.4.1   The Code Committee

The Code Committee, comprising up to 12 members appointed by the Panel, carries out the rule-making role of the Panel (see **20.5**). This Committee is responsible for reviewing and amending the Takeover Code. Typically, the Committee will announce a period of public consultation before amending the Code. The Public Consultation Papers ('PCPs') are published on the Panel's website. Paragraph 4(b) of the Introduction to the Takeover Code provides further detail on the Code Committee.

20.2.4.2   The Hearings Committee

The Hearings Committee carries out the judicial role of the Panel (see **20.2.1**). The Committee reviews the Panel Executive's rulings, and also hears any disciplinary proceedings (which the Panel Executive instigates – see **20.5.7.4**), relating to breaches of the Takeover Code. Usually the secretary to the Hearings Committee is a senior lawyer (such as a partner in a law firm). Paragraphs 4(c) and 7 of the Introduction to the Takeover Code provide further detail on the Hearings Committee.

There is a right to appeal to the Takeover Appeal Board in relation to a decision of the Hearings Committee (Introduction to the Takeover Code, para 8). The Takeover Appeal Board is a separate organisation from the Panel. Further information can be found at www.thetakeoverappealboard.org.uk.

Paragraph 4(d) of the Introduction to the Takeover Code ensures that membership of the Committees are kept separate: a member of the Code Committee (see **20.2.4.1**) cannot be or become a member of the Hearings Committee or the Takeover Appeal Board.

20.2.4.3   The Nomination Committee

The Nomination Committee monitors the size, composition and balance of the Panel. It will therefore doubtless be aware of the fact that (at the time of writing) there are only two women on the full Panel of 31, and that the Panel Executive is led by a man and three male deputies. Only in the Support Group do women predominate, and even here the Office Manager is a man.

20.2.5   The nature of the Panel

Originally, the Panel was a wholly non-statutory body. In cases such as *R v Panel on Takeovers and Mergers, ex p Datafin plc and Another (Norton Opax plc and Another intervening)* [1987] 1 All ER 564 and *R v Panel on Takeovers and Mergers, ex p Guinness plc* [1989] 1 All ER 509, the courts marvelled at the unique nature of the Panel, which in practice had enormous power as a regulator of some of the largest, most expensive transactions in the financial industry, despite its lack of actual statutory powers. For example, when Guinness breached r 11 of the Takeover Code during its offer for Distillers, the Panel had the power to force Guinness to pay a considerable sum to the former Distillers shareholders, despite its non-statutory footing at the time (see the article in **Chapter 21**).

However, on 20 May 2006, the implementation of the Takeovers Directive in the UK (see **20.4**) placed the exercise of the Panel's powers on a statutory footing in relation to takeover offers to which the Takeovers Directive applies (see **20.3**). This was extended on 20 April 2007 to include other takeovers covered by the Takeover Code but outside the Takeovers Directive.

20.3   THE TAKEOVERS DIRECTIVE

The Directive on Takeover Bids (Directive 2004/25/EC) (the 'Takeovers Directive') came into force on 20 May 2004 after 20 years of trying to reach agreement in the EU. It aims to impose minimum adequate takeover regulation across the Member States. Each Member State had to implement the Directive into its own law by 20 May 2006.

20.3.1 Application

The Directive applies to takeover *offers* of companies whose shares are admitted to a *regulated market*.

20.3.1.1 Offers

Article 2.1(a) of the Directive states that the Directive applies only to public offers to acquire control of a company. Therefore the Directive does not apply to takeovers effected by way of scheme of arrangement (see **21.12**) (although the Takeover Code does – see **20.4.2**).

20.3.1.2 Regulated market

The reference to a regulated market is to a market within the meaning of art 4.1(14) of MiFID (see **6.4.2.3** above). A list of regulated markets can be found on the websites of the FCA and the European Commission. For the purposes of this book it is important to note that the Main Market is a regulated market, but AIM is not.

To summarise, the Directive applies to takeovers of companies listed on the Main Market (the focus of this book), but not to takeovers of unlisted public companies or companies quoted on AIM (which are not regulated markets), or takeovers made by way of a scheme of arrangement (which does not involve an offer).

20.3.2 Implementation

In the UK, the original intention was to implement the Takeovers Directive through Pt 28 of the CA 2006. However, the 2006 Act progressed through Parliament more slowly than originally anticipated and was not enacted in time to meet the Directive's implementation date of 20 May 2006. As an interim measure, therefore, the Takeovers Directive (Interim Implementation) Regulations 2006 (SI 2006/1183) were drawn up specifically to implement the Takeovers Directive in the UK on a temporary basis, to remain in force until Pt 28 of the CA 2006 was brought into force. This happened on 6 April 2007, and the Regulations were repealed at the same time.

20.4 PART 28 OF THE COMPANIES ACT 2006

This is now the legal basis for the Panel exercising certain statutory powers in relation to public company takeovers in the UK. Section 942 of the CA 2006 grants the Panel the power to do anything it thinks is necessary or expedient to carry out its functions.

Section 943 of the CA 2006 gives the Takeover Code a statutory basis (formerly it operated without statutory backing, as an informal set of rules which in practice all listed companies observed). The Panel must make rules governing certain matters required by the Takeovers Directive (which are now in the Takeover Code) and it has also been given the power to make rules for takeovers other than those covered by the Takeovers Directive. As discussed in **20.5.1**, the Takeover Code extends well beyond such takeovers and these rules now have statutory effect.

The CA 2006 has also given the Panel statutory powers of investigation and the right to impose sanctions for breaches of the Takeover Code (see **20.5.7**).

20.5 THE TAKEOVER CODE

The main source of regulation of takeovers is called the Takeover Code on Takeovers and Mergers. This is often referred to as the 'Takeover Code', or the 'City Code'. This book refers to it as the Takeover Code. It may be viewed in full on the Panel's website. (It is also known, in practice, as the 'Blue Book', not for any particularly titillating content but with unquestionable accuracy in describing the colour of the book containing the Takeover Code.)

20.5.1   When does the Takeover Code apply?

The application of the Takeover Code is set out in para 3 of the Introduction to the Takeover Code. It applies to offers (see **20.5.1.2**) for certain companies (see **20.5.1.1**).

20.5.1.1   Companies within the Takeover Code

The Takeover Code will apply if the offeree company falls into any of the following categories:

1. Intro section 3(a)(i)

- a public company, or Societas Europaea
- with its registered office in the UK, the Channel Islands or the Isle of Man
- whose securities are admitted to trading:
  - (i)   on a regulated market in the UK (such as the Main Market, which is the focus of this book); or
  - (ii)   on a multilateral trading facility (such as AIM); or
  - (iii) on any stock exchange in the Channel Islands or the Isle of Man.

2. Intro section 3(a)(ii)

- any other public company, or Societas Europaea (including unlisted public companies), or, in limited circumstances, a private company (namely a private company which during the last 10 years has:
  - (i)   had its securities admitted to trading on a regulated market or MTF in the UK or on any stock exchange in the Channel Islands or the Isle of Man; or
  - (ii)   advertised dealings for a six-month continuous period; or
  - (iii) has filed a prospectus; or
  - (iv)   had securities subject to a CA 2006, s 693(3) marketing arrangement)
- which:
  - (i)   has its registered office in the UK, the Channel Islands or the Isle of Man, and
  - (ii)   in the Panel's opinion, has its place of central management and control in the UK, the Channel Islands or the Isle of Man.

3. Intro section 3(a)(iii)

- a company which has its registered office in the UK but whose securities are traded on an EEA regulated market outside the UK
- a company which has its registered office in the EEA but outside the UK and whose securities are traded solely on a regulated market in the UK
- certain companies which have their registered office in the EEA but outside the UK and whose securities are traded both on a regulated market in the UK and in another EEA country but not the country in which the registered office is located.

The Takeover Code uses the word 'offeree company' to describe the target company (or potential target company) whose shares are the subject of the offer (or potential offer). In practice, the offeree company is frequently referred to as the 'target'.

In summary, then, for UK companies it is the offeree company's status as a *public* company (or former public company) which is important for the purposes of the Takeover Code, regardless of whether the offeree company happens to be listed or unlisted. The Takeover Code therefore generally excludes offers for private companies. These are subject to contract law and certain statutory provisions.

For companies falling under 3. above there is provision for shared jurisdiction with takeover regulators in other EEA Member States.

20.5.1.2 Offers within the Takeover Code

The Takeover Code applies to 'offers' for those companies mentioned at **20.5.1.1** above. 'Offer' is defined to include those transactions set out in para 3(b) of the Introduction to the Takeover Code. These are principally 'takeover bids and merger transactions however effected, including by means of statutory merger or scheme of arrangement'. (The Takeover Code does extend to less common and more technical transactions as well, but these are beyond the scope of this book.) Usually such a transaction will involve the offeror seeking control of the offeree company. Section 943(7) of the CA 2006 defines takeover bids by reference to Art 2.1(a) of the Takeovers Directive. This refers to an offer to acquire control of the offeree company as defined in national rules, which in the UK is the Takeover Code. 'Control' is defined in the Takeover Code as 30% or more of the voting rights in the offeree company. This book concentrates on the most common situation in practice, of an offeror seeking to gain 100% control of the offeree company.

It is worth noting that sometimes it can be difficult to pin down whether a transaction is a 'takeover' or a 'merger'. A merger denotes a union of equals, but frequently the term is used in practice when a takeover (one company taking ownership of another) is occurring. This use of 'merger' is usually done for PR reasons to give the impression that the offeree company is not being swallowed up by the offeror. Ultimately this has no impact on the application of the Takeover Code as it covers both situations.

The Takeover Code even applies to transactions which are in contemplation but not yet announced. For example, there are strict rules governing secrecy in r 2 of the Takeover Code (see **21.3**) and dealing in shares (r 4, see **21.8.10.1**) which apply even if a takeover offer has not yet been firmly decided upon.

Note also that the Takeover Code will apply regardless of how the takeover is carried out. For example, it applies to a takeover effected by way of a general offer or by way of a scheme of arrangement – see **21.12**. Again, the Takeover Code is broader than the Takeovers Directive, which, for example, does not apply to schemes of arrangement (see **20.3.1**).

20.5.1.3 The offeror/bidder

There are no rules in the Takeover Code regarding the status or nature of the offeror making the offer. The offeror may be any company, listed or unlisted, public or private, UK or foreign registered. It could be a partnership or limited liability partnership, UK or foreign registered. It could even be an individual or group of individuals. As mentioned in **20.5.1.1** above, it is the status of the *offeree company* which is important. In practice, the offeror may also be referred to as the 'bidder'.

20.5.2 To whom does the Takeover Code apply?

Paragraph 3(f) of the Introduction to the Takeover Code confirms that the Code applies to everyone who is involved in a transaction to which it applies. This includes not only the offeror and the offeree company, but also the directors of the offeror and the offeree company, and their respective professional advisers. The lawyers advising on the transaction, therefore, will be subject to the Takeover Code.

20.5.3 The purpose of the Takeover Code

The Introduction to the Takeover Code explains, in para 2, that its purpose is to:

(a)   ensure fair and equal treatment of all shareholders in an offeree company in relation to takeovers;

(b)   provide an orderly framework within which takeovers are conducted; and (c)　promote the integrity of the financial markets.

Importantly, the Takeover Code is *not* concerned with the commercial advantages or disadvantages of a takeover. For example, whether the offer price fairly reflects the offeree company's true value. These are matters for the directors and shareholders of the offeree company to decide upon. The Takeover Code's purpose is not to facilitate or impede takeovers, and also is not concerned with other regulatory issues, such as competition policy, which are subject to their own sets of rules and regulatory bodies (see **20.7**).

20.5.4　The nature of the Takeover Code

As discussed at **20.4** above, s 943 of the CA 2006 gives statutory effect to the previously non-statutory Takeover Code.

The Takeover Code comprises six general principles (see **20.5.5**), 38 rules which are based on, and develop, these principles, and seven Appendices. The rules must be read in conjunction not only with the general principles but also with the accompanying notes, which give practical guidance on the applicability of the rules.

The six general principles are taken directly from the Takeovers Directive and are essentially statements of standards of commercial behaviour.

The Takeover Code is an interesting creature from the common law lawyer's perspective, as, under para 2(b) of the Introduction, it is the *spirit*, and not just the letter, of both the general principles and the rules which is to be applied. This means that the Panel Executive may be willing to modify or relax the wording of the rules, on a case-by-case basis, if this is consistent with the underlying purpose of the rules. This, of course, is a significant departure from normal practice and clearly affects how the lawyer must advise in relation to the Takeover Code (see **20.5.6** below).

20.5.5　The general principles

The general principles are the key to understanding the spirit of the Takeover Code. They are the cornerstone of the Code, and they may apply in situations which the rules of the Takeover Code do not cover expressly. The six general principles are set out below, together with (the author's) summaries to help reinforce the essence of each principle:

1.　All holders of the securities of an offeree company of the same class must be afforded equivalent treatment; moreover, if a person acquires control of a company, the other holders of securities must be protected.
　Summary: shareholders should be treated equally and fairly.

2.　The holders of the securities of an offeree company must have sufficient time and information to enable them to reach a properly informed decision on the bid; where it advises the holders of securities, the board of the offeree company must give its views on the effects of implementation of the bid on employment, conditions of employment and the locations of the company's places of business.
　Summary: sufficient information should be made available to shareholders in a timely fashion, to enable them to decide whether to accept or reject the offer.

3.　The board of an offeree company must act in the interests of the company as a whole and must not deny the holders of securities the opportunity to decide on the merits of the bid.
　Summary: Directors have duties of fairness in relation to takeovers.

4.　False markets must not be created in the securities of the offeree company, of the offeror company or of any other company concerned by the bid in such a way that the rise or fall of the prices of the securities becomes artificial and the normal functioning of the markets is distorted.
　Summary: Parties should not commit market abuse, etc.

5. An offeror must announce a bid only after ensuring that he/she can fulfil in full any cash consideration, if such is offered, and after taking all reasonable measures to secure the implementation of any other type of consideration.

    Summary: The bidder must be in a position to pay for the offeree company's shares.

6. An offeree company must not be hindered in the conduct of its affairs for longer than is reasonable by a bid for its securities.

    Summary: The offer timetable should not drag on.

The practical effect of these general principles is considered in **Chapters 21** and **22**.

20.5.6 The Takeover Code in practice

If there is any doubt as to how the Takeover Code might apply in a certain situation, the parties and their advisers should consult the Panel Executive, who will provide a ruling on the issue. In fact, para 6(b) of the Introduction to the Takeover Code states expressly that legal advice is not an appropriate alternative to obtaining a ruling from the Panel Executive. Does this mean that the lawyer does not need to know anything about the Takeover Code? Far from it. In fact, the lawyer plays a pivotal part in the interpretation of the Code.

First, the lawyer will be involved in trying to identify a 'third way', in circumstances where the company will struggle to comply with the letter of the Takeover Code, but there is a possibility of an alternative approach which would not compromise the spirit of the Takeover Code. The Panel Executive is likely to be much more receptive to a company which approaches it in the hope of modifying the interpretation of a rule if the company has a well thought-out suggestion for such modification. Obviously the lawyer's knowledge and experience, of previous occasions when the Panel Executive has been willing to modify the interpretation of rules of the Takeover Code, will assist in this role.

The second role of the lawyer in relation to the Takeover Code is that, together with certain of the company's other advisers, he will have regular contact with the Panel Executive during the takeover process.

20.5.6.1 Practice Statements

The Panel Executive publishes Practice Statements, which it posts, in date order, on its website. These statements provide informal guidance on how the Panel Executive interprets and applies the Takeover Code in certain circumstances. The Practice Statements do not form part of the Takeover Code, and so are not binding and no substitute for consulting the Panel Executive.

20.5.6.2 Panel Statements

The Panel also publishes Panel Statements on its website in date order. These statements record decisions taken by the Panel in relation to real-life takeovers, including enforcement decisions.

20.5.7 Enforcement of the Takeover Code

The Takeover Code has the force of law in relation to all takeovers to which it applies.

20.5.7.1 Monitoring powers

The Panel has powers to monitor the progress of a takeover. Those dealing with the Panel must do so in an open and cooperative way, and disclose all relevant information (subject to legal professional privilege) (Introduction to the Takeover Code, para 9(a)). The Panel also has the power to require documents and information from persons dealing with the Panel (CA 2006, s 947 and Introduction to the Takeover Code, para 9(b)).

20.5.7.2   Enforcement powers of the Panel

Anyone reporting a breach to the Panel must do so promptly, otherwise the Panel may exercise its discretion to disregard the complaint (Introduction to the Takeover Code, para 10(a)).

Once it is certain that the Code has been breached, the Panel has several powers of enforcement, set out below.

Compliance rulings

The Panel has the power to make a compliance ruling, either to prevent a breach of the Code (if there is a reasonable likelihood of a breach of the Takeover Code or a Panel ruling) or, if the breach has already occurred, to ensure the breach is remedied (Introduction to the Takeover Code, para 10(b)).

Compensation rulings

The Panel has a limited power to make a compensation ruling to order a party to compensate any offeree company shareholders who have suffered financially as a result of a breach of the Code (Introduction to the Takeover Code, para 10(c)). The Panel can exercise this power only in relation to breaches of those rules which deal with the offer consideration (namely rr 6, 9, 11, 14, 15, 16.1 and 35.3). The effect of a compensation ruling is to put the shareholders into the position they would have been had the breach not occurred. The Panel can also order that simple or compound interest be paid to the shareholders.

Enforcement by the courts

The Panel can ask the courts to enforce the Takeover Code (CA 2006, s 955 and Introduction to the Takeover Code, para 10(d)). The Panel has stated that it will exercise this power only as a last resort, or in urgent cases.

Bid documentation rules

For offers to which the Takeovers Directive applies only (see **20.3.1**), there is a criminal offence under s 953 of the CA 2006 for non-compliance with the 'bid documentation rules'. These are defined in the Introduction to the Takeover Code, para 10(e), and set out in Appendix 6.

The bid documentation rules relate to the content requirements of the main takeover document, known as the offer document (see **22.4.1**) (the 'offer document rules'), and any defence documents (see **22.4.2**) (the 'response document rules'). In the event that the documents do not comply with the rules, a criminal offence is committed (in the case of a breach of the offer document rules) not only by the offeror but also by any director, officer or member of the offeror who caused the document to be published, and (in the case of a breach of the response document rules) by any director or officer of the offeree company if they knew, or were reckless as to whether, the document did not comply with the Takeover Code, and failed to take all reasonable steps to ensure compliance. The offence is punishable by a fine. The offence applies only to those takeover offers which are subject to the Takeovers Directive (see **20.3.1**), namely those covered by this book, ie takeovers of companies listed on the Official List and trading on the Main Market (so not to schemes of arrangement or to offers for unlisted companies, or companies listed on AIM).

In certain circumstances, disciplinary action may be taken (see **20.5.7.4**).

20.5.7.3   Enforcement powers of the FCA

Under the Introduction to the Takeover Code, para 11, the Panel can request the FCA to take enforcement action against any person authorised by the FSMA 2000 who contravenes the Takeover Code or a ruling of the Panel. The definition of 'authorised person' is considered at

9.4.3. In practice, this will cover the stockbroker (see **21.5.3**) and the financial adviser (see **21.5.1**) acting for the company in relation to the takeover. The stockbroker and financial adviser will not continue to act unless the takeover complies with the Takeover Code, as otherwise they risk the sanctions listed below. Note that the FCA can also take enforcement action against an 'approved person', for example a director of an authorised firm.

The FCA can take the following enforcement action in the event of a breach of the Takeover Code:

(a) public censure;

(b) fine;

(c) the removal of authorisation under the FSMA 2000;

(d) injunction; and

(e) order for restitution.

Note also the requirement, referred to at **20.5.7.4(e)** below, that the rules of the FCA prohibit a person authorised by the FSMA 2000 from acting for any offender.

20.5.7.4 Disciplinary powers

Paragraph 11 of the Introduction to the Code allows the Panel Executive to deal with a matter on its own where the offender agrees to the facts and the action to be taken. It also outlines the power of the Panel Executive to institute disciplinary proceedings before the Hearings Committee (see **20.2.4.2**). If the Committee finds that there has been a breach of the Takeover Code, it can impose the following sanctions:

(a) private reprimand;

(b) public statement of censure;

(c) suspension or withdrawal of, or the imposition of conditions on, any exemption, approval or other special status the Panel has granted;

(d) reporting the offender's conduct to another regulatory body such as BIS, the Stock Exchange or the FCA; or

(e) publishing a Panel Statement indicating that the offender is unlikely to comply with the Takeover Code. This can trigger other requirements of the FCA and certain professional bodies which oblige their members, in certain circumstances, not to act for the offender in a transaction to which the Takeover Code applies. This in effect means the party is 'cold shouldered' by financial institutions and is unable to be involved in takeover activity in the UK.

There is an example of (b) in Panel Statement 2010/14, available on the Panel's website. The Panel publicly criticises the US food company Kraft for a breach of r 19.1 of the Takeover Code (see **22.4.5.1** below). Kraft made pledges during an £11.7 billion bid for Cadbury that it would keep open a particular factory if it won control of Cadbury. It did take over Cadbury and promptly announced the closure of the factory. It demonstrated a shocking disregard for the spirit of the rules, as well as a brutal change in fortunes for employees of a company whose original Quaker owners went to great lengths to improve the living and working conditions of its workers. The impact of Kraft's decision has been dramatic, with a review of certain provisions of the Takeover Code instituted by the Panel which resulted in a new version of the Takeover Code being issued. It has also resonated well beyond the City. As a direct result of Kraft's actions, the UK Government is conducting a review of the law governing takeovers in the UK (see **21.14** below).

An extremely rare example of (e) was imposed on Brian Myerson, an investor and AIM company director, in 2010 when he was banned from takeover activity for three years for serious breaches of the Takeover Code.

The Panel Executive has set out, in the 'compliance' section of its website, the issues it will take into account when considering whether to take disciplinary action.

20.6   OTHER RULES AND REGULATIONS

Chapter 17, which considers the methods of raising equity finance, and **Chapter 19**, which considers listed company acquisitions and disposals, explain that the specific subject matter of those chapters cannot be considered in a vacuum; most of the rules and regulations examined in this book are relevant to the specific areas of law those chapters consider. The same can be said of takeovers. In addition to the Takeover Code, takeovers are subject to other rules and regulations, all of which are considered in this book. They are summarised below.

20.6.1   Consideration

If the company is:

(a)   issuing shares as consideration, or

(b)   using equity finance to raise cash to use as consideration,

for the acquisition, then the rules and regulations considered in **17.4** above will be relevant.

20.6.2   Acquiring shares

A takeover is, after all, just an acquisition of shares. This means that all the rules and regulations summarised at **19.3** above are relevant, including rules under the CA 2006, the Listing Rules, the DTRs, FSMA 2000 and the Model Code.

20.6.3   Merger control

The takeover of a UK company can give rise to merger control issues in the UK under the EA 2002, or in the EU under the EC Merger Regulation. **Chapter 23** considers this issue further.

20.6.4   Sector-specific regulatory controls

Certain sectors have their own specific regulatory provisions. Examples include the defence, travel and broadcasting industries. The lawyer may need to take advice from his client as to the sector-specific regulations which may apply to any takeover transaction.

20.6.5   Compulsory acquisition of minority shareholdings

The provisions of ss 974 to 991 of the CA 2006, which are important in the context of a takeover, are discussed at **22.7** below.

20.7   REGULATORY BODIES

The rules and regulations which may apply to a takeover, and which are considered in this chapter, mean that the following regulatory bodies may become involved in a takeover bid:

(a)   The Panel, which administers the Takeover Code (see **20.2** above).

(b)   The FCA, which has powers of enforcement in relation to the Takeover Code (see **20.5.7.3** above).

(c)   The FCA (acting in its capacity as UKLA). If the offeror is listed and is issuing new shares as consideration, or to raise cash consideration, those shares must be admitted to listing on the Official List by the FCA. Also, if the acquisition is a Class 1 transaction, the FCA will need to approve the Class 1 circular (see **19.6** above).

(d)   The Stock Exchange. If the offeror is listed and is issuing new shares as consideration, or to raise cash consideration, those shares must be admitted to trading on the Main Market by the Stock Exchange.

(e)   The OFT, the Competition Commission and the European Commission. If the takeover raises competition issues, these bodies may become involved (see **Chapter 23**). *Note that* on 1 April 2014 the OFT and the Competition Commission will be replaced by the Competition and Markets Authority (CMA).

(f)   Sector-specific regulatory bodies. This will depend on the sector in which the parties to the takeover specialise. For example, the Civil Aviation Authority is likely to be involved in the takeover of an airline company, to check the company holds an ATOL licence.

CHAPTER 21

TAKEOVERS: PREPARATION

21.1 INTRODUCTION

Chapter 20 introduces the concept of a takeover and considers the rules and regulations which the lawyer will need to apply in relation to a takeover. In particular, it explains that the Takeover Code contains the key rules relating to takeovers, and that the unique nature of the Code means that the lawyer will need to consult the Panel Executive (referred to in this chapter as 'the Panel') to determine how the Takeover Code might apply in the circumstances of a particular takeover.

It is very exciting to be instructed in relation to a takeover. Of all the listed company issues considered in this book, it is the takeover which arrests the attention not only of your client, but also, once announced, of shareholders, your colleagues, the press and the general public.

Chapter 22 considers the takeover process once the bid has been announced. However, the lawyer's work begins long before that. This chapter considers the work which the lawyer undertakes prior to the announcement of a takeover bid.

Note that, as explained in **Chapter 20**, in practice the terms 'offer' and 'bid' are used interchangeably, as are the terms 'offeror' and 'bidder', and 'offeree' and 'target'. The Takeover Code uses the terms 'offer', 'offeror' and 'offeree'.

21.2 RECOMMENDED OR HOSTILE?

Rule 1 of the Takeover Code provides that the offeror must make the offer first to the directors (or advisers) of the offeree company. The most significant factor which will determine the nature of the offeror's preparation is whether the takeover is intended to be recommended or hostile. They could not be more different.

21.2.1 The recommended offer

If the directors of the offeree company consider that the offer is in the best interests of the company's shareholders, employees and (if the company's solvency is in issue) creditors, they must recommend the offeree's shareholders to accept the offer. The offer is described as 'recommended'. Remember, it is the shareholders of the offeree company who own it and who ultimately will determine the success of the offer, in other words, whether to sell their shares to the offeror or not.

Bear in mind that a takeover often results in a change in management. The directors of the offeree company risk losing their jobs, or being relocated, if the takeover goes ahead. The culture of the business may change. However, the directors of the offeree company must not allow personal considerations to influence the exercise of their duties to the company when considering whether to recommend the offer.

With a recommended offer, both the offeror and the offeree company have a common aim in ensuring the takeover goes ahead. A recommended offer to acquire all the securities in a company is the most straightforward form of takeover. The boards of directors of both companies will act consensually to try to achieve that takeover. It has the best chance of success, and it can be completed in the shortest period of time.

21.2.2   The hostile offer

If, having been approached under r 1 by the offeror, the board of the offeree company advises its shareholders not to accept the offer, it is described as a 'hostile' offer. The offeror and the offeree company have diametrically opposed aims. The offeror wants the takeover to be successful, while the offeree company will do everything in its power to ensure the offer fails so that it maintains its independence. For both sides there is much at stake. For the offeror, the takeover could be central to the company's strategy of expansion. The shareholders of the offeree company, who ultimately decide whether to accept the offer, need to balance the fact that their board is advising them to reject the offer against the claims of the offeror about how attractive the offer is, in terms of the consideration they will receive in exchange for their shares in the offeree company. The stakes are raised still further by the offer being played out in the public arena, with hard-won reputations on the line.

Of the 58 offers completed under the Takeover Code in the year to 31 March 2013, 9 were originally hostile and 45 were recommended. The remaining 4 were r 9 mandatory bids (see **21.8.10.3** below).

21.2.3   The effect on preparation

If the offeror has an existing relationship with the offeree company, it may know in advance whether the offeree company will recommend the offer or not. If so, the offeror can prepare accordingly. However, if the offeror does not have an existing relationship with the offeree company, it has a choice: it can either approach the offeree company with a view to negotiating a recommended offer (and consider whether it is prepared to 'go hostile' in the event the offeree company decides not to recommend an offer), or it can launch a surprise hostile offer for the offeree company without discussing this first with the offeree company.

Whether the offer is intended to be recommended or hostile, the offeror must also plan for the possibility that another offeror may make a rival offer for the offeree company.

21.3   THE NEED FOR SECRECY

Rule 2.1 of the Takeover Code provides that all persons with confidential information on an offer, particularly price-sensitive information, must treat that information as secret until the offer is announced to the public under r 2.4 or r 2.7 (see **22.3**). In practice, this means that the lawyer must advise his client company, together with all advisers who are instructed to work on the transaction, of the importance of secrecy and security (Note 1 on r 2.1). The number of people to whom confidential information is given should be kept to a minimum. Anyone who receives confidential information can pass it on only if it is necessary to do so, and they must ensure that they inform the recipient of any information of the need for secrecy in relation to that information. For the lawyer, this translates into ensuring that:

(a)   the team working on the transaction is no larger than it needs to be;

(b)   each member of the team is aware of the secrecy obligation;

(c)   due diligence (see **21.6**) is carried out discreetly;

(d)   documents relating to the takeover are kept confidential (for example, not left lying around on the printer); and

(e)   the transaction and each of the parties to the transaction are referred to by way of code name rather than their actual names. The code names should not be too obvious. The client may already have code names which it used while carrying out its initial research into the offeree company as a potential target. To take a facile example (although in real life the code names do tend to be facile), imagine a takeover of a company which has an American chairman. The transaction might be code-named 'Project Baseball', the offeror code-named 'Bat' and the offeree company code-named 'Ball'. This means that, in all conversations, meetings, telephone calls, documentation and such like, the code names will be used rather than the real names. The documentation will then be amended, to replace the code names with the real names, just before it is published. All very MI5!

To the layman (and, indeed, to a trainee who has not come across the concept before) this can all seem a little dramatic. It can also result in rather awkward situations for the lawyers. There will be a distinct buzz of activity around the offices of the team of lawyers who are working on a takeover. This can draw inquisitive comments from colleagues, regarding what the team is working on. The effect of r 2.1 is that those colleagues must be rebuffed in as polite a manner as you can manage. This can be particularly difficult for any trainee working on the takeover, who will not be able to discuss the transaction even with more senior lawyers who enquire what the trainee is doing. These measures, however, are vital. A leak can have disastrous consequences for the bid (see **22.3.3.2** and **22.3.3.3** below). While the secrecy obligation can be frustrating for the lawyer, consider just how much more embarrassing it would be if a leak was traced back to him.

The Panel reiterated the importance of r 2.1 in Practice Statement 2008/20, and expresses its support for the FCA's attempts to tackle the problem of misuse of inside information in takeovers.

21.4   AN EXAMPLE

Obviously, the work involved for a lawyer advising on a takeover depends on whether he is advising the offeror or the offeree company. This book examines the takeover principally from the point of view of the offeror. To make sense of what **Chapter 20** and **Chapter 21** have covered so far, let us consider an example.

21.4.1   The facts

Imagine that we advise X plc, a company whose shares are admitted to listing on the Official List and to trading on the Main Market, which is seeking to make an offer for the entire issued ordinary share capital of Y plc, also a company whose shares are admitted to listing on the Official List and to trading on the Main Market. The share price of X plc is looking healthy. Y plc, however, has had some bad press lately. It has been underperforming compared to its main rivals (which include X plc) and its share price is at an all-time low. The press have been speculating about whether Y plc is ripe for a takeover.

21.4.2   The analysis

The transaction is a takeover which is subject to the provisions of the Takeover Code. X plc is seeking to acquire 100% of the shares in a UK company whose securities are admitted to trading on a regulated market (ie the Main Market) (see **20.5.1.1** above), Y plc. X plc is the offeror. Y plc is the offeree company.

Note that the fact that X plc, the offeror, is a listed company is, in fact, irrelevant in terms of the application of the Takeover Code, where it is the identity of the offeree company which is important. It is, however, relevant in terms of applying the class tests and other continuing obligations imposed on listed companies, and in terms of the ability of X plc to offer shares as consideration, or raise cash consideration through the issue of shares.

For the purposes of the application of the Takeover Code, it is worth remembering (see **20.5.1.1**) that Y plc need not be listed. The takeover of *any* public company will fall under the Takeover Code.

21.4.3 Code names

The company secretary of X plc has decided that the code name for the transaction is Project Gotham. The code name of X plc is Batman. The code name of Y plc is Robin.

21.4.4 The parties

The main parties involved in Project Gotham will be as follows:

(a)   The offeror, Batman.

(b)   The offeree company, Robin.

(c)   The board of Batman.

(d)   The board of Robin.

(e)   The shareholders of Batman. The shareholders of Batman may need to be involved for two reasons:

    (i)   if the transaction is a Class 1 acquisition or a reverse takeover, Batman will require shareholder approval before it can complete the acquisition (see **Chapter 19**); and

    (ii)   if Batman decides to issue Batman shares to Robin's shareholders as consideration, the shareholders may need to increase Batman's authorised share capital and/or give the directors authority to allot the consideration shares under s 551 of the CA 2006. Batman shareholders would not need to disapply s 561 of the CA 2006 in these circumstances, as the shares are to be issued for non-cash consideration (see **14.6.7**, which sets out the position under the CA 2006).

(f)   The shareholders of the offeree, Robin. The shareholders of Robin own the shares which Batman wants to acquire. The fate of the takeover rests on whether they decide to accept the offer or not. Ultimately, they are the most important people in the takeover.

(g)   The advisers to both Batman and Robin. See **21.5** below.

21.5 APPOINTING A TEAM OF ADVISERS

As with an IPO, a takeover involves not only lawyers, but a wider team of advisers, who must all work together seamlessly to advise either the offeror or the offeree on all aspects of the transaction.

21.5.1 Financial advisers

Rule 3 of the Takeover Code provides that the offeree must have an independent financial adviser. In practice, the offeror will also have an independent financial adviser. An investment bank will usually adopt the role of financial adviser. In relation to advising the offeror, it will use its experience of other transactions, and its knowledge of the regulatory environment and the Takeover Code, to:

(a)   plan and coordinate the takeover (although increasingly the lawyers are leading coordination of the documentation);

(b)   advise the board in relation to tactics, such as:

    (i)   when to make the offer,

(ii) the level of consideration to be offered (including when to raise the level in the event that the offer is not well received),

(iii) the type of consideration to be offered (if equity finance is required to raise cash consideration, the financial advisers will advise on the method of equity finance to be used);

(c) be the offeror's principal point of contact with the Panel, to discuss any provisions of the Takeover Code which are causing concern;

(d) issue and approve the offer documentation under s 21 of the FSMA 2000 (unless an exemption applies);

(e) underwrite any cash offer or cash alternative;

(f) report on profit forecasts and quantified benefits statements (r 28.1(a), note 9); and

(g) advise in relation to any information released during the offer (r 19.1, note 1) (see **22.4.5.1**).

21.5.2 Lawyers

The offeror will require lawyers as, of course, will the offeree. However, the financial adviser of the offeror may also be advised, separately from the offeror, by a further team of lawyers.

The lawyers will advise in relation to the rules and regulations considered in **Chapter 20**. They will also be involved in speaking to the Panel in relation to the interpretation of the Takeover Code, and in drafting and, increasingly, coordinating the documentation for the takeover.

21.5.3 Stockbrokers

The investment bank acting as financial adviser will often take on the role of stockbroker. The stockbrokers play an important part in deciding tactics. They are able to do this because of the unique relationship they have with shareholders. Stockbrokers have day-to-day contact with key representatives of institutional shareholders. Remember that institutional shareholders have large stakes in public companies. Usually, therefore, the stockbrokers will have the 'inside track' on the appetite of the offeree company shareholders, and the market, for the offer. This is particularly important in a hostile bid, where the offeror will have to convince offeree company shareholders to accept the offer even though the offeree company board has advised them not to.

The stockbrokers will use this knowledge to:

(a) monitor market purchases and rumour;

(b) advise the offeror on the likely reaction of:

(i) its shareholders (see **21.4.4**) to the proposed acquisition, and

(ii) the offeree company's shareholders to the nature and amount of consideration to be offered; and

(c) arrange meetings with the offeree company's principal shareholders, before the offer is announced, to explain the basic terms of the offer and to see if those shareholders will commit irrevocably to accept the offer once it is made (see **21.10** below).

21.5.4 Accountants

The accountants will gather the financial information which must be included in the takeover documentation. They will also give comfort to the board in relation to financial information in the takeover documentation, and report on any profit forecast or merger benefits statement (or working capital or indebtedness statement in any prospectus or equivalent document).

21.5.5 Financial public relations consultants

The role of the public relations adviser is to liaise with the press to secure good coverage of the offer, and to ensure that the key messages in connection with the bid are published accurately.

The highly regarded 'Lex' column of the *Financial Times* (unfortunately subscription only) will comment on high-profile takeovers, as will the business editors of other national daily newspapers, websites and TV channels. The offeror, particularly on a hostile takeover, will hope that the media comment favourably on the offer, so that they might persuade offeree company shareholders to accept the offer.

21.5.6 Registrars or receiving bankers

The registrars or receiving bankers (often the same institution) will receive the forms of acceptance from the shareholders of the offeree company who want to accept the takeover offer. They will monitor the level of acceptances to determine whether the critical level necessary to allow the offer to be declared unconditional as to acceptances has been reached (see **22.4.7.1** below). If a meeting of the shareholders of the offeror is required (see **21.4.4** above), the registrars or receiving bankers will also receive and monitor the return of proxies for that meeting. Appendix 4 of the Takeover Code sets out a code of practice for receiving agents.

21.5.7 Printers

The role of the printers on a takeover is not unlike that on an IPO (see **4.2.11**). The takeover documentation will be created by word processor at the outset of the transaction, but ultimately the final version will be professionally printed. Once each document is substantially in final draft form, therefore, it will be taken to print, and thereafter each draft will be printed (referred to as 'proof printing'). The printers need to process the documentation quickly, accurately and securely.

21.6 DUE DILIGENCE

21.6.1 The requirement for due diligence

The effect of General Principle 5 (see **20.5.5** above) and r 2.7(a) of the Takeover Code is that an offeror should announce a takeover offer only after the most careful and responsible consideration, when it has every reason to believe that it can and will implement the offer. This means that the offeror must undertake some careful planning and investigation before it announces an offer.

21.6.2 What is 'due diligence'?

The concept of due diligence in the context of an IPO was explained at **5.3.4** above. The concept is not so different on a takeover. While due diligence on an IPO involves investigating the company seeking to float, and collating comprehensive information about the company which can then be used in the prospectus, due diligence on a takeover seeks to investigate the offeree company (and, in certain circumstances, such as if shares in the offeror are to be issued as consideration, the offeror) so that this information can be used in the offer document (**22.4.1**). However, the effect of the secrecy obligation outlined at **21.3** above, means that the due diligence exercise is more limited on a takeover than on an IPO.

21.6.3 The purpose of due diligence

Due diligence is used to discharge the offeror's obligations under General Principle 5 and r 2.7(a) of the Takeover Code (see **22.3.3.1**). For example, the Panel will not look too kindly on an offeror who announces an offer, only to discover that it does not have enough cash to fund it.

The information the offeror will require includes the following:

(a)   Is the offeree company really an attractive acquisition?

    (i)   How has it been performing lately?

    (ii)   What are its main assets and liabilities?

  (iii) Where is it located?

  (iv) What do its latest report and accounts reveal?

(b) Can the offeror successfully integrate the offeree company into its business? What costs savings could be made after the takeover?

(c) How should the offer be structured?

  (i) Might the offeree company be willing to recommend the offer?

  (ii) If not, is the offeror willing to proceed on a hostile basis?

  (iii) Should the offeror offer cash or shares as consideration?

  (iv) If offering shares, does the offeror have sufficient unissued authorised share capital, and do the directors have sufficient authority to allot those shares?

  (v) If not, will the offeror's shareholders be willing to pass the necessary resolution(s)?

  (vi) Will the offer constitute a Class 1 acquisition, or a reverse takeover? If so, will the offeror's shareholders be willing to approve it?

  (vii) Are there any issues which might affect the timing of the offer; for example, should the offeror company wait until the offeree company's next annual report or accounts are published?

(d) What are the chances of success?

  (i) Who are the main shareholders of the offeree company, whom the offeror would need to persuade to accept the offer?

  (ii) How many offeree company shareholders might be willing to provide irrevocable undertakings? (See **21.10** below.)

  (iii) How many shares does the offeror hold which it can vote in favour of the bid? (See **21.8** below.)

  (iv) Is anyone else interested in the offeree company: might there be a more attractive competing bid?

  (v) Are there any competition or regulatory issues which could jeopardise the bid? (See **Chapter 23.**)

21.6.4 The due diligence process

21.6.4.1 If the offer is recommended

The offeror will undertake some initial due diligence itself, using publicly available information, before it approaches the offeree company. If the offeree company is receptive to the offer, it will then assist the offeror with its due diligence exercise and provide the information the offeror requires. However, the offeree company must be careful. Rule 20.2 requires any information provided to an offeror, whether publicly identified or not, to be provided to a competing offeror (should one arise). While the original offeror might have been welcomed by the offeree, the competing offeror may be unwanted, and sensitive information on the offeree, given to the original offeror, will have to be revealed to this new, unwelcome suitor.

21.6.4.2 If the offer is hostile

If the offer is hostile, the offeror will not receive the help from the offeree company which is outlined above. However, as noted at **21.6.4.1**, if the offeree company has provided information to any competing offeror, then r 20.2 of the Takeover Code provides that the offeree company must provide the same information on request to all other offerors or potential offerors. In practice, however, it is probable that a hostile offeror will want to launch a 'surprise' offer on the offeree company, so it will not avail itself of its rights under r 20.2 until its hostile offer has been announced, by which time it should already have completed its due diligence exercise, in order to comply with General Principle 5 and r 2.7(a) of the Takeover Code (see **22.4.5.4**).

21.6.5   Publicly available information

The following information about the offeree company should already be in the public domain:

(a)   articles of association (Companies House);

(b)   details of directors (Companies House, annual report and accounts, RIS disclosures, the offeree's register of directors);

(c)   details of shareholders and share capital (Companies House, annual report and accounts, RIS disclosures, the offeree's register of members and register of directors' interests);

(d)   financial information (annual report and accounts). Section 415 of the CA 2006 provides that a company must prepare a directors' report as part of its annual report and accounts, which contains the information required by Chapter 5 of Part 15 of the CA 2006. The report must contain a business review (CA 2006, s 417), which must contain a fair review of the company's business and a description of the principal risks and uncertainties facing the company. The review should be a balanced and comprehensive review of the development and performance of the business of the company during the financial year and the position of the company's business at the end of that year;

(e)   the directors' remuneration report (see **8.4.3.1**);

(f)   any published prospectus (the NSM (see **7.5.7.1** above)); and

(g)   any analyst research (available from investment banks).

Plenty of other information will be available on the company's website, in trade magazines, and possibly in the newspapers.

Section 992 of the CA 2006 requires additional information to be disclosed in the directors' report for companies whose voting shares are admitted to trading on a regulated market (ie the Main Market but not AIM). This implements provisions of the Takeovers Directive. Although the requirements are not limited to companies which are the subject of a takeover offer, the effect of the additional disclosure is to ensure that more information on the share structure of the company, including any share transfer or voting restrictions which might be triggered on a takeover, becomes public information.

21.7   FINANCING THE OFFER

The offeror must know, before announcing a takeover offer, how it will finance that offer. This is not only a practical consideration; it is a requirement of General Principle 5 and r 2.7(a) of the Takeover Code.

The choices available to the offeror are as follows.

21.7.1   Cash consideration

21.7.1.1   Debt finance

The offeror could obtain a loan to fund the takeover. However, as **Chapter 18** explained, this will affect the company's gearing and so may not be desirable. It will also depend on the prevailing bank interest rates and the prevailing economic climate. Currently, of course, debt finance is very difficult to come by.

21.7.1.2   Equity finance

The offeror could obtain the funds from its existing shareholders, using one of the methods described at **17.7** to **17.9** above. This depends on the existing shareholders being willing to subscribe to a fresh issue of shares.

21.7.2   Paper consideration

21.7.2.1   Debt finance

The company could offer loan notes to the shareholders of the offeree company rather than cash.

21.7.2.2   Equity finance

The company can offer shares (often referred to as 'paper') as consideration rather than cash. This is discussed at **17.10** above.

21.7.3   The option to take cash or shares

It is relatively common for an offeror to offer the offeree company's shareholders the option to take either cash or shares in the offeror in return for their shares in the offeree company. This sounds complicated, but in fact the method by which a company does this should be familiar to you already. This is achieved through a vendor placing, described at **17.11** above. The offeror will actually issue only shares as consideration, but the issue will be on the basis that, for those shareholders in the offeree company who want to take up the cash alternative, the offeror will have those shares placed, and the shareholders will receive the cash proceeds of that placing.

The idea behind this is to make the offer as appealing as possible to the offeree shareholders who decide the success of the offer. Some shareholders may be more likely to accept the offer if they receive cold, hard cash rather than shares in the offeror. Other shareholders may prefer to receive shares rather than cash, for tax reasons.

In some offers, the offeror may offer the offeree shareholders *both* cash and shares. This may be accompanied by a 'mix and match' election, where the shareholders can choose to vary the split of cash and shares being offered. Say that X plc offered offeree shareholders three shares in X plc and £1 in cash for every one share in the offeree. The offeror may allow the offeree shareholders to take four shares in X plc and 50p in cash, or any other combination, so long as the total value paid for each offeree share remains the same.

21.8   STAKEBUILDING

21.8.1   What is stakebuilding?

Stakebuilding is the strategic purchase of shares in the offeree company by the offeror, in the period before the announcement of an offer, and during the offer period (see **22.3.4**).

21.8.2   The purpose of stakebuilding

The key to the success of the offer depends on reaching a minimum threshold of just over 50% of the voting rights in the offeree company. Once that level is reached, the offeror controls the offeree company. Of course the offeror often wants 100% control, but just over 50% is the minimum required (Takeover Code, r 10). If the offeror buys shares in the offeree it reduces the number of shares required to reach the level necessary to complete the offer and successfully take over the offeree company.

21.8.3   Advantages of stakebuilding

The advantages of stakebuilding are as follows:

(a)   Rule 10 of the Takeover Code provides that the offer can be declared unconditional as to acceptances (see **22.4.7.1**) once the offeror holds over 50% of the voting rights in the offeree company. In other words, the offeror has won control of the offeree. Imagine, then, that an offeror already has a stake of 25% in the offeree company. The offeror would only need to persuade the owners of just over 25% of the offeree company shares to accept the offer in order to be able to declare the offer unconditional as to acceptances.

(b)   The offeror can acquire shares at the market price before the offer is announced. Once the offer is announced the price of the shares in the offeree will rise, often substantially, to reflect the fact that the offeror wants to buy all the shares and they have therefore become more valuable.

(c)   The offeror does not need to alert the offeree to the acquisition if it acquires the shares before it announces the offer and it acquires fewer than 3% of the shares (remember that the disclosure of interest obligations under Chapter 5 of the DTRs would require disclosure of the offeror's interest once that interest reached 3% (see **Chapter 15**)) – but see **21.8.4(e)** below.

(d)   If the offeror has a substantial shareholding by the time it announces the offer, other shareholders may be more inclined to accept the offer.

21.8.4   Disadvantages of stakebuilding

The disadvantages of stakebuilding are as follows:

(a)   The offeror will own the shares even if the offer fails. The offeror will usually want all or nothing – total control of the offeree company, not just to be a minority shareholder.

(b)   If anyone finds out about the strategic purchase (and this is likely given the requirement for the company to pass on to an RIS information it receives under Chapter 5 of the DTRs – see **Chapter 15**), market rumour about a possible takeover may raise the market price of the offeree company's shares. As the consideration for a takeover offer is usually at a premium to the market price, this may make the offeror's intended offer price less attractive.

(c)   The increase in price and/or rumour referred to at (b) above may trigger an announcement under r 2.2 (see **22.3**), thereby removing any element of surprise.

(d)   Purchases prior to the publication of the offer document do not count towards the 90% compulsory acquisition threshold (see **22.7.2** below).

(e)   The purchase may dictate the level or nature of the consideration the offeror must pay pursuant to the offer, under r 6 and r 11 (see **21.8.10.4**), or trigger a mandatory offer under r 9 (see **21.8.10.3**).

21.8.5   Rules and regulations relating to stakebuilding

Some of the rules relating to stakebuilding are considered at **21.8.6** to **21.8.11** below. **Table 21.1**, at **21.9** below, summarises the various stakebuilding thresholds.

The lawyer must be familiar with these rules in order to advise an offeror client whether there are any reasons why it cannot build a stake in the offeree company, or whether it is restricted in building its stake in any particular way. (Note also that the provisions of any standstill letter (see **21.13.4**) will also affect the offeror's ability to build a stake in the offeree company.)

21.8.6   Insider dealing

The fact that the offeror is buying shares in the offeree company at a time when the takeover bid is not public knowledge might suggest that the directors of the offeror are guilty of insider dealing (by requiring the offeror to buy shares; remember that the offeror, as a company, cannot commit the offence – see **11.7**). However, as **11.5.2.2** above explains, in fact the directors may be able to make use of the 'market information' defence.

21.8.7   Market abuse

Again, you could be forgiven for thinking that the offeror's stakebuilding exercise might fall foul of the market abuse regime under the FSMA 2000 (see **Chapter 10**). However, the Code of Market Conduct provides protection which is similar to the defence that exists for insider dealing. MAR 1.3.17C provides that an offeror should not be prevented by the market abuse regime from acquiring shares in a potential target with a view to pursuing a takeover offer, simply because the offeror knew that it would be making an offer.

21.8.8 The Listing Rules

If the offeror seeks to acquire a large stake, consideration must be given to how the acquisition of the stake would be classified under the Listing Rules, and to related requirements of the Listing Rules (see **Chapter 19**).

21.8.9 Disclosure requirements

Stakebuilding can trigger the disclosure requirements under Chapter 5 of the DTRs and (during the offer period – see **22.3.4**) the Takeover Code, as set out in **Chapter 15**.

21.8.10 The Takeover Code

The following rules of the Takeover Code may affect any attempt to acquire a stake in an offeree company.

21.8.10.1 Rule 4.1: prohibited dealings

Rule 4.1(a) prevents anyone other than the offeror from building a stake in the offeree where they have confidential price-sensitive information about an intended offer, until the offer, or approach, is announced. Note 1 on r 4 also prohibits the offeror, and 'other persons', from dealing before an announcement if the offeree company has given the offeror confidential price-sensitive information in the course of offer negotiations.

To prevent a would-be stake builder avoiding this rule simply by asking someone else to buy the stake on his behalf, r 4.1(b) prohibits anyone who has confidential price-sensitive information about an intended offer from recommending to another person to buy offeree company shares.

21.8.10.2 Rule 5.1: acquiring 30% or more

Subject to exceptions, this rule prevents the offeror (or anyone acting in concert with it – see **22.6.1.2**) acquiring any interest in offeree company shares (see **21.8.10.5**), which, when aggregated with the offeree company shares in which he is already interested, would carry 30% or more of the voting rights in the offeree company. Paragraph 5 of the definition of 'interests in securities' and the preamble to r 5 confirm that irrevocable undertakings count towards the 30% threshold for the purpose of r 5.1 (see **21.10**).

The Takeover Code considers that a 30% shareholding represents 'control' of a company (see 'Definitions' section of the Takeover Code). The aim of r 5.1 is to prevent a person gaining control of an offeree company without making a full takeover bid for that company, governed by the Takeover Code with all its protection for offeree company shareholders.

Rule 5.2 sets out the exceptions to r 5.1 referred to above. This rule provides that r 5.1 does not apply to an acquisition of an interest in shares:

(a) from a single shareholder, when it is the only acquisition within a 7-day period (r 5.2(a)). (Note that the offeror cannot then make any further acquisitions, other than pursuant to the exceptions below (r 5.3), and details of the acquisition must be disclosed (r 5.4));

(b) immediately before (and conditional upon) the r 2.7 announcement (see **22.3.3.1**) of a firm intention to make a *recommended* offer (r 5.2(b));

(c) after a r 2.7 announcement (see **22.3.3.1**) of a firm intention to make a bid (not subject to a pre-condition), and:

    (i) the offeree company board has agreed to the acquisition,

    (ii) the offeree company board has recommended the offer, or a competing offer,

      (iii)   the first closing date of the offer, or a competing offer, has passed (at least 21 days after publishing the offer document; see **22.5.2**) and the offer, or competing offer, has been cleared on competition grounds (see **Chapter 23**), or

      (iv)   the offer is unconditional in all respects (see **22.4.7**) (r 5.2(c));

(d)   by way of acceptance of the bid (r 5.2(d)); or

(e)   which is permitted by Note 11 on r 9.1 or Note 5 on the Dispensations from r 9 (r 5.2(e)).

In the context of a *hostile* offer (see **21.2.2**) these exceptions tend to prevent the offeror from building a stake of more than 29.9% until after the first closing date (see **22.5.2**).

21.8.10.3   Rule 9: mandatory offer

Rule 5.1 of the Takeover Code provides that a person can acquire an interest in shares carrying between 30% and 50% of the voting rights in the offeree company only if the acquisition falls within an exception to that rule. What happens if one of the exceptions to r 5.1 applies and the potential offeror does acquire such an interest? The answer is that r 9 will apply, and for the offeror the consequences of this can be serious.

Rule 9 provides that if:

(a)   a person acquires an interest in shares (see **21.8.10.5**) in a company which results in that person holding 30% or more of the voting rights of that company; or

(b)   a person already interested in shares carrying between 30% and 50% of the voting rights in a company for someone in concert with that person acquires an interest in any other voting shares of that company;

that person must make an offer to acquire all the equity share capital and all other transferable voting capital of that company on the terms set out in r 9.

If r 9 applies, therefore, not only is the potential offeror forced to make a takeover offer, but he cannot even choose the terms of that offer. The terms imposed by r 9 are not favourable to the offeror. Consideration must be cash, or there must be at least a cash alternative. The consideration must be at a level which is equal to the highest price paid by the offeror (or any person acting in concert with the offeror – see **22.6.1.2**) for any interest in shares of that class in the 12 months preceding the announcement of the offer (r 9.5(a)). If the offeror acquires shares above the offer price during the course of the r 9 offer, then it must increase its offer to the highest price it has paid for the shares (r 9.5(b)). The only conditions which can be attached to the offer are that over 50% of the offeree company shareholders must vote in favour of the offer, and that the offer will lapse if referred on competition grounds. It is explained at **22.4.7** why relying on just these conditions is not ideal. However, as set out in the extract from the regulatory announcement below, sometimes an offeror is happy to follow this route.

The reason for r 9 is that same as that for r 5; if r 9 is triggered, the offeror has acquired 'control', that is 30%, of the offeree company, and so must make a full takeover offer for the company, governed by the Takeover Code.

Note that, in contrast to r 5; irrevocable undertakings do not count towards the 30% threshold for the purposes of r 9 (see **21.10** below).

Company	St James Holdings Limited
Headline	Offer for Newcastle United
Released	14:12 23-May-07
Number	1114X

For immediate release

NOT FOR RELEASE, PUBLICATION OR DISTRIBUTION IN, INTO OR FROM AUSTRALIA, CANADA, JAPAN OR THE UNITED STATES

Cash Offer
by
St James Holdings Limited
for
Newcastle United PLC

Summary

- St James Holdings Limited (SJHL) (a company formed at the direction of Mike Ashley) announces that it has today acquired 55,342,223 Newcastle United Shares, representing approximately 41.6 per cent. of the issued share capital of Newcastle United, from Wynyard (Guernsey) Limited, Cameron Hall Developments Limited and Cameron Hall Developments Limited Executive Pension Scheme (the ultimate beneficial owners of each of which are all members of Sir John Hall's family) at a price of 100 pence for each Newcastle United Share.

- SJHL is a UK private limited company which is wholly-owned by Mike Ashley and which has been incorporated for the specific purpose of acquiring Newcastle United Shares and making the Offer.

- In accordance with the provisions of Rule 9 of the City Code, SJHL also announces the terms of a cash offer to be made for all of the issued and to be issued share capital of Newcastle United which is not already owned by SJHL. SJHL intends to seek a recommendation of the Offer from the board of Newcastle United.

- The Offer will, when formally made, be conditional only upon the receipt of acceptances in respect of Newcastle United Shares which, together with the Newcastle United Shares acquired or agreed to be acquired before or during the Offer, will result in SJHL holding Newcastle United Shares carrying more than 50 per cent. of the voting rights in Newcastle United.

- The Offer will be **100 pence in cash for each Newcastle United Share**, valuing the entire issued share capital of Newcastle United at £133.1 million

- The Offer represents:
  — a premium of approximately 19 per cent. to the Closing Price of 84 pence for each Newcastle United Share on 22 May 2007; and
  — a premium of approximately 50 per cent. to the average Closing Price of 66.9 pence for each Newcastle United Share in the three month period up to and including 22 May 2007,
  22 May 2007 being the last business day prior to the announcement of the acquisition.

21.8.10.4   Rule 11 and rule 6: consideration

The offeror cannot consider stakebuilding in isolation from the takeover offer itself. The acquisition of a stake may dictate the level (in the case of r 6), or the nature (in the case of r 11) of the consideration the offeror must pay for shares in the offeree company pursuant to the takeover offer. The rationale for these rules is General Principle 1, which provides that shareholders should be treated similarly.

EXAMPLE

Imagine that A plc, seeking to make a takeover bid for Y plc, acquires a stake in Y plc from Shareholder 1 on Monday at £2.00 per share. A plc then announces a takeover offer on Tuesday for the entire issued ordinary share capital of Y plc at a price of £1.95 per share. Shareholder 1 has clearly been given an advantage over the other shareholders. What if A plc had announced a takeover offer on Tuesday for the entire issued ordinary share capital of Y plc where the consideration was shares in A plc? Again, Shareholder 1 has received special treatment. The effect of r 6 and r 11 is to prevent an offeror breaching General Principle 1.

Rule 11

Rule 11.1: cash consideration

The consideration the offeror might offer to the offeree's shareholders is examined at **21.7** above. However, r 11.1 provides that in certain circumstances the offeror *must* offer cash consideration (or a cash alternative).

If:

(a)   the offeror (or any concert party) purchased interests in shares in the offeree company, of a class which is now under offer, during the offer period or within 12 months prior to the start of the offer period, and:

   (i)   the purchase was *for cash*, and

   (ii)   the shares carry 10% or more of the voting rights currently exercisable at a meeting of that class; or

(b)   the offeror (or any concert party) purchased interests in voting or non-voting shares in the offeree company, of a class which is now under offer, during the offer period, and the purchase was *for cash*; or

(c)   the Panel considers that cash consideration is required in order to give effect to General Principle 1,

then, unless the Panel otherwise agrees, the offer for that class of shares must be in cash, or accompanied by a cash alternative (see **21.7.3**), at not less than the highest price paid by the offeror (or any concert party) for those shares.

Note that the words 'for cash' are very widely defined. Note 5 on r 11 provides that they actually include the situation where the offeror acquired interests in shares in exchange for *securities*, provided the seller of the offeree shares (or the other party to the transaction giving rise to the interest, if the interest is not the sale of the share itself) is not subject to selling restrictions, such as being required to hold the securities received in exchange for the interest in the offeree shares until the offer has lapsed, or the offer consideration has been published to accepting shareholders. If the offer falls within this meaning of 'for cash' then, unless the offeror or its concert parties arranged the immediate placing of those shares, it must also comply with the provisions of r 11.2 (see below).

EXAMPLE

Imagine that A plc intends to make an offer for the entire issued ordinary share capital of Y plc, offering two A plc shares as consideration for each Y plc share. A plc's lawyers will advise that A plc needs to consider whether it has purchased Y plc shares in the past. A plc provides information about its previous purchases of Y plc shares. It acquired a 4% stake at £3 per share 11 months ago, and a 6% stake at £4 per share 8 months ago. The lawyer must advise A plc that the consideration under the offer cannot be two A plc shares as consideration for each Y plc share, as A plc intended. It must be £4.00 per share, in cash, or at least include a cash alternative.

Rule 11.2: *paper consideration*

Rule 11.2 provides that if:

(a)   the offeror (or any concert party) purchased interests in shares in the offeree company, of a class which is now under offer, during the offer period or within three months prior to the start of the offer period; and

(b)   the purchase was *in exchange for securities*; and

(c)   the shares carry 10% or more of the voting rights currently exercisable at a meeting of that class,

then those securities must be offered to all other holders of shares of that class. As detailed above, an obligation will also arise, under r 11.1, to make an offer in cash, or to provide a cash alternative, unless the exchange falls outside the wide definition of 'for cash' in Note 5 on r 11.1 (because there are some selling restrictions on the seller of the offeree company shares, or, in the case of an interest in offeree company shares, the other party to the transaction giving rise to the interest).

Rule 6: minimum consideration

Rule 6.1

Rule 6.1 provides that, unless the Panel otherwise consents, if:

(a) an offeror (or a person acting in concert with the offeror) (see **22.6.1.2** for the meaning of 'in concert');

(b) has acquired an interest in the offeree company shares (see **21.8.10.5**);

(c) within three months before the beginning of an offer period (see **22.3.4** for the meaning of 'offer period');

(d) or during the period (if any) between the commencement of the offer period and a r 2.7 announcement (see **22.3.4** below);

then the offer to shareholders of the same class must be on the same, or better, terms.

Let us consider the example of A plc bidding for Y plc, referred to above. The effect of r 6 is that A plc will not be able to fix the offer price at £1.95 per share. Instead, A plc must offer the Y plc shareholders at least £2.00 per share under the takeover offer.

Note that the Panel has discretion to extend the three-month period if it considers it is necessary to give effect to General Principle 1 (r 6.1(c)).

Rule 6.2

While r 6.1 covers acquisitions the offeror makes *before* the offer period, r 6.2 covers acquisitions the offeror makes *during* the offer period. Rule 6.2 provides that, if:

(a) an offeror (or a person acting in concert with the offeror);

(b) has acquired an interest in the offeree company shares (see **21.8.10.5**) above the offer price;

(c) after a r 2.7 announcement (see **22.3.3.1**) has been made but before the offer closes for acceptance,

then the offeror must increase its offer to equal the highest price it has paid for the interest in those shares, and, immediately after the purchase, it must announce that the revised offer will be made.

Note that while the example below involves cash consideration, neither r 6.1 nor r 6.2 requires the offer to be in cash. However, any paper consideration offered must, as at the date the offer is announced, have a value equal to the highest price the offeror has paid for the relevant prior purchase of offeree shares. (Note, however, that if r 9 or r 11 also apply, the offer does have to be in cash (or accompanied by a cash alternative); see **21.8.10.3** and below.)

> **EXAMPLE**
>
> Imagine that A plc, having been advised that the offer price must be £2.00, pursuant to r 6.1, announces an offer for Y plc at a price of £2.00 per share on Tuesday. On Wednesday, A acquires some Y shares from Shareholder 2 at a price of £2.00 per share. On Thursday, A acquires some Y shares from Shareholder 3 at £2.05 per share. In breach of General Principle 1, Shareholder 2 has been treated differently from Shareholder 3. A plc must make an announcement, immediately after it acquires the shares from Shareholder 3, that a revised offer will be made in accordance with r 6.2. Shareholder 2 will get an unexpected bonus. She will receive the higher, revised price of £2.05 per share, not just £2.00 which she had originally expected.

Overlap between rules 11 and 6

Note that there is clearly the potential for overlap between r 6 and r 11, as both may apply where the offeror has purchased offeree shares *for cash*. Rules 6.1 and 6.2 provide that, in such a case, usually compliance with r 11 will be regarded as sufficient to satisfy the requirements of r 6.

21.8.10.5 Derivatives and options

In relation to disclosure and stakebuilding, the Takeover Code applies to dealings in derivatives referenced to shares and options over shares, as well as actual shares themselves. These terms are explained below. The effect of this is that the acquisition of 'interests in shares', and not just actual shares, are taken into account for the purposes of rr 5, 6, 9 and 11. In relation to r 4, the definition of 'dealing' includes the taking, granting, acquisition and disposal of an option over securities and a derivative referenced to securities, so if the rule applies, no interests in shares can be acquired.

Derivative

This term is defined in the Takeover Code. Broadly, it is a financial product whose value depends on the performance of an underlying security. An example of a derivative is a contract for differences ('CFD') under which the holder of the CFD benefits from a change in the price of a company's securities from the reference price agreed at the time the CFD is entered into.

Option

An option is the right to buy or sell a share at a fixed price within a particular time-frame.

Interests in shares

This term is defined in the Takeover Code (under 'interests in securities'). It includes:

(a) ownership of shares (para 1, definition of 'interests in securities');

(b) the right to exercise or direct, or having general control of, the voting rights attached to shares (para 2, definition of 'interests in securities');

(c) the right, option, or obligation to acquire shares (para 3, definition of 'interests in securities');

(d) being party to certain derivatives in relation to shares (para 4, definition of 'interests in securities'); and

(e) for the purposes of r 5 only (see **21.8.10.2**), irrevocable commitments (see **21.10**) in relation to shares (para 5, definition of 'interests in securities').

21.9 STAKEBUILDING THRESHOLDS

As the rules relating to stakebuilding are complex, **Table 21.1** below sets out a summary of the significant thresholds, and the consequences for the stakebuilder of acquiring certain stakes.

Table 21.1: Stakebuilding thresholds and consequences

Voting rights in target	Consequences for the stakebuilder
Any amount	Must disclose if issued with a notice under s 793 of CA 2006 (see **15.6**).
	If within three months prior to, or during, the offer period, any offer must not be on less favourable terms (r 6) (see **21.8.10.4**).
	If in exchange for cash, during the offer period, and these shares are now under offer, offer must be in cash, or accompanied by a cash alternative (r 11.1) (see **21.8.10.4**).
	Disclose dealings during an offer period (r 8.1) (see **15.7.4.3**).
1%	Must make Opening Position Disclosure and disclose dealings during an offer period (Dealing Disclosure) (r 8) (see **15.7.4.3**).

Voting rights in target	Consequences for the stakebuilder
3%	Disclose interests to the offeree company (DTR 5 – see **15.5**) and disclose subsequent movements through another percentage point level, or if the interest falls below 3%.
10% or more in exchange for cash in the 12 months prior to an offer period and during the offer period	If shares are voting shares, offer must be in cash, or accompanied by a cash alternative (r 11.1) (see **21.8.10.4**).
10% or more, in exchange for securities, in the 3 months prior to an offer period and during the offer period	Must offer those securities (r 11.2). May also need to make a cash offer, or provide a cash alternative under r 11.1 (see **21.8.10.4**).
25% + 1	Power to block special resolutions.
30%	May be prohibited from dealing (r 5) (see **21.8.10.7**). May have to make mandatory bid for the offeree (r 9) (see **21.8.10.3**).
50%	Power to block ordinary resolutions.
More than 50%	Power to pass ordinary resolutions. Offer capable of becoming unconditional as to acceptances (r 10) (see **22.4.7.1**). Takeover Code generally no longer applicable. A subsidiary as defined in CA 2006, s 1159.
75%	Power to pass special resolutions.
90% (applies to each class separately)	May be forced to buy the shares of offeree minority shareholders under s 983 of CA 2006 (see **22.7.3**).
90% of shares subject to the offer (applies to each class separately)	Power to purchase minority shareholdings under s 979 of CA 2006 (see **22.7.2**)

21.10 IRREVOCABLE UNDERTAKINGS

How a potential offeror can acquire interests in shares in order to secure some votes in favour of the takeover offer is considered at **21.8** above. As you will appreciate, the restrictions set out at **21.8.6** to **21.8.10** above mean that it is not easy for the potential offeror to do this. In practice, stakebuilding is usually restricted to an acquisition from a single shareholder, or made immediately before the announcement of a recommended offer (see **21.8.10.2**), so that it falls within the exceptions in the Takeover Code.

A more widely used technique, which also enables the potential offeror to improve the chances of success of the takeover offer, is the irrevocable undertaking (also known as an 'irrevocable commitment' or 'lock-up'). This is where the potential offeror obtains undertakings from certain offeree company shareholders (often major shareholders and directors who hold shares), in advance of the announcement of the offer and with the consent of the Panel (r 4.3), that they will accept the offer if it is made (and, sometimes also that they will vote in favour of any resolution that the offeree company may require to progress the offer).

While with stakebuilding the potential offeror knows that certain shares will vote in favour of the offer (because he owns interests in those shares), with irrevocable undertakings the potential offeror knows that certain shares will vote in favour of the offer because he has irrevocable undertakings from the shareholders which confirm that they will vote in favour.

Irrevocable undertakings fall into two categories:

(a)   Hard irrevocables, which remain binding even if a higher offer is made for the offeree.

(b)   Soft irrevocables, which will fall away to allow the shareholder to accept a higher offer which is made (typically one which is at least 10% higher than of the value of the offer to which the irrevocable relates).

The consideration for providing an irrevocable is the promise of the potential offeror to make the offer. As a safeguard against the irrevocable being held void for lack of consideration, the lawyer should ensure that any irrevocable is entered into by way of deed (see **21.10.4**).

If the offeror (or any associate of the offeror – as defined by the Takeover Code) obtains an irrevocable undertaking during an offer period (see **22.3.4**), it must disclose this through an RIS. The details it must disclose are set out in Note 5 on r 8 of the Takeover Code.

The effect of irrevocables on certain other public company issues is considered below.

21.10.1   Stakebuilding

Paragraph 5 of the definition of 'interests in securities' (which also covers 'interests in shares') and the preamble to r 5 confirm that, while irrevocable undertakings will not count towards the 30% shareholding threshold for the purposes of r 9 (see **21.8.10.3** above), they will count towards the 30% threshold for r 5 (see **21.8.10.2** above). Rule 5, therefore, acts as a cap on the level of undertakings the offeror can obtain. If one of the exceptions to r 5 applies, an offeror can obtain irrevocable undertakings over 30% or more of the offeree shares without triggering the r 9 mandatory bid provisions.

Is an irrevocable undertaking an 'interest in shares' for the purposes of rr 5, 6, 9 and 11? The effect of para 9(b) of Note 9 on the definition of 'interests in securities' is that the receipt of an undertaking falls outside the para 3 'right to acquire' category of interests (see **21.8.10.5(c)**). However, if the undertaking allows the offeror general control of the voting rights attached to the shares, the offeror will be treated as interested in those shares under para 2 of the definition of 'interests in securities' (see **21.8.10.5(b)**).

21.10.2   Financial promotion

Seeking an irrevocable undertaking may be capable of comprising an inducement or invitation to enter into investment activity. This means that any communication the company makes in order to persuade someone to provide such an undertaking will constitute a financial promotion under s 21 of the FSMA 2000 (see **Chapter 12**). Therefore the company must ensure that the communication either falls within an exemption (for example, because it is made to a professional investor under art 19 of the FPO 2005, or is a communication in relation to the sale of a body corporate under art 62 of the FPO 2005 – if takeovers do fall within this exemption), or that the communication is made by or authorised by an authorised person.

21.10.3   Insider dealing and market abuse

Giving an irrevocable undertaking may also amount to insider dealing (see **Chapter 11**); however, usually the market information defence (see **11.5.2.2**) will apply, unless the person providing the undertaking has confidential price-sensitive information other than simply knowledge that a takeover is proposed. Similarly, the provision of an irrevocable undertaking can amount to market abuse, but is likely to fall outside the regime under MAR 1.3.17C.

21.10.4 Squeeze-out provisions

Shares which are the subject of irrevocable undertakings are not considered to be shares already held by the bidder. Therefore they are 'shares to which the offer relates' and count towards the 90% threshold (see **22.7**) provided that they are entered into by way of deed, or for no consideration, for consideration of negligible value or for no consideration other than the promise of the potential offeror to make the offer (CA 2006, s 975(2)).

21.10.5 Acting in concert

A person who provides an irrevocable undertaking usually is not treated as acting in concert with the offeror or offeree company (Note 9 on the definition of 'acting in concert'). However, if the undertaking allows the offeror or the offeree company to exercise voting rights, or allows the person providing the undertaking to acquire shares, then the Panel should be consulted before the undertaking is given. In its Practice Statement 2008/22, the Panel has advised that where an undertaking on how to vote is given with an irrevocable commitment, it will not normally be acting in concert, provided it is limited to the duration of the offer at the latest and is limited to matters which relate to ensuring that the offer is successful.

21.11 NON-BINDING INDICATIONS OF INTENTION TO ACCEPT

Some shareholders, as a matter of policy, will not provide irrevocable undertakings. Sometimes, however, those shareholders will provide non-binding indications of their intention to accept the offer (also known as 'letters of intent'). While these indications are not legally binding, they can provide further reassurance to the potential offeror that the offer will be successful.

If the offeror (or any associate of the offeror – as defined by the Takeover Code) obtains a letter of intent during the offer period (see **22.3.4**) then, as with an irrevocable undertaking (see **21.10**), it must disclose this through an RIS under r 8.4(a) of the Takeover Code.

21.12 GENERAL OFFER OR SCHEME OF ARRANGEMENT?

The bidder must decide how to structure the takeover. A takeover can be effected by:

(a)   a general offer; or

(b)   a scheme of arrangement under Pt 26 of the CA 2006.

21.12.1 General offer

This involves the offeror (or the investment bank, on behalf of the offeror) making an offer to acquire shares in the offeree for consideration. As set out at **21.7**, the consideration can take several forms, such as cash, loan notes, shares or other securities. Sometimes the offer gives the offeree shareholders a choice of consideration, such as cash or shares (and under r 9 and, in certain circumstances, r 11.1, the offeror must provide a cash alternative – see **21.8.10** above). The shareholder accepts the offer by returning a form of acceptance (see **22.4.2**).

This structure is suitable for use with both recommended and hostile offers. This book, and in particular **Chapter 22**, focuses on this structure. The Thai company, PTT Exploration and Production Public Company Limited's £1.2 billion recommended takeover of Cove Energy plc in the summer of 2012 was conducted by way of an offer.

21.12.2 Scheme of arrangement

An alternative way of structuring a recommended takeover is by a scheme of arrangement pursuant to Pt 26 of the CA 2006. They are currently very much in favour as an alternative to a recommended takeover by way of general offer. Some of the largest recommended takeovers in the last few years were proposed as schemes of arrangement.

The £31.9 billion takeover of Xstrata plc by Glencore International plc in May 2013 was effected by a scheme of arrangement.

21.12.2.1   What is a scheme of arrangement?

A scheme of arrangement is a court-sanctioned arrangement between a company and its shareholders or creditors. It is a statutory procedure governed by Pt 26 (ss 896 to 901) of the CA 2006. Section 895 of the CA 2006 does not limit the subject matter of the arrangement (although the court's approval must be obtained). There is, therefore, considerable scope for using a scheme (for example, to effect a reorganisation or return or capital). While the section was not drafted with the takeover in mind, it has also come to be used as a way of effecting a takeover.

There are two forms of scheme, namely a reduction scheme and a transfer scheme. A reduction scheme involves the cancellation of the existing offeree shares and the issue of new offeree shares to the offeror in exchange for the payment of consideration by the offeror to the offeree shareholders. A transfer scheme involves the transfer of the existing offeree shares to the offeror, in exchange for the payment of consideration by the offeror to the offeree shareholders.

In theory, the consideration offered by the offeror to the offeree shareholders under a scheme can take any form, as with a general offer. However, given the longer overall timetable of a scheme, underwritten cash offers can prove too expensive.

As the scheme is arranged by, and so requires the cooperation of, the offeree, a scheme is suitable only for a recommended takeover.

Sections 896 to 899 of the CA 2006 set out the following main requirements for a scheme:

(a)   *Members' meeting (s 896(1))*. The court will (after an application to the Companies Court by the company) convene a meeting of the offeree shareholders (or the offeree company shareholders of the relevant class, as appropriate). At this meeting, the scheme must be approved by (s 899(1)):

   (i)   a majority in number;

   (ii)   representing 75% in value of the offeree company shareholders, or class of offeree company shareholders, voting at the meeting (in person or by proxy).

The resolution to approve the scheme must be by way of a poll in order to calculate whether the test referred to at (ii) above has been satisfied. Neither the offeror, nor any shareholder connected with the offeror, can vote. This means the offeror cannot increase its chances of success by stakebuilding and/or obtaining irrevocable undertakings.

(b)   *Explanatory statement (s 897(1) and (2))*. The offeree company must send an explanatory statement to its shareholders together with the notice of meeting. The statement should explain the effect of the scheme, and set out any material interests of directors and the effect of the scheme on those interests. The statement must be fair and, as far as possible, give all information reasonably necessary to enable the offeree shareholders to make an informed decision how to vote.

(c)   *Court approval (s 899)*. The scheme must obtain not only the approval of the offeree company shareholders, referred to at (a) above, but also the approval of the court. A copy of the court order must be filed at Companies House. The scheme takes effect on delivery of the order to Companies House or, if the court orders, on its registration by Companies House. The scheme will then bind the offeree company, its shareholders and the offeror (who will have agreed to be bound by it).

21.12.2.2   The Takeover Code

Paragraph 3(b) of the Introduction to the Takeover Code confirms that the Takeover Code governs a scheme of arrangement. Typically certain modifications to the Code will be required for a scheme (for example, as the scheme requires the involvement of the court, it may not be possible to adhere strictly to the timetable requirements set out in the Takeover

Code). Appendix 7 to the Takeover Code sets out the modifications to the Takeover Code which apply as a result of the takeover being effected by way of a scheme. It also lists those provisions of the Takeover Code which do not apply to a scheme.

21.12.2.3 Advantages of a scheme

A scheme has the following advantages over a general offer:

(a) A scheme requires a smaller percentage of offeree shareholder support (see **21.12.2.1(a)**), in order to obtain 100% control of the offeree company, than a general offer (where the offeror must acquire not less than 90% in value of the shares to which the offer relates – see **22.7.2.1**).

(b) Once the requisite majority of shareholders has approved the scheme, all shareholders are bound by it (with a general offer the offeror must compulsorily acquire the remaining 10% under s 979 of the CA 2006.

(c) Usually a scheme is quicker than a general offer in reaching the stage where all offeree company shareholders are bound. In the case of a general offer, the compulsory acquisition procedure can increase the timetable considerably. (However, overall, a scheme tends to take longer to effect – see **21.12.2.4(c)**.)

(d) A scheme is not deemed to be an offer to the public for the purposes of s 85(1) of the FSMA 2000 (but nevertheless a prospectus will be required if the offeror shares will be admitted to trading and none of the exemptions to s 85(2) apply).

(e) A reduction scheme can offer stamp duty savings (but see **21.12.2.4(g)**).

21.12.2.4 Disadvantages of a scheme

(a) A scheme cannot be used with a hostile offer (the application to court is made by the offeree company).

(b) It is more difficult to revise a scheme than a general offer, given the requirement for court approval.

(c) The requirement for court approval, filed at Companies House, means it can takes longer to effect the takeover than with a general offer (but see **21.12.2.3(c)**).

(d) There is more time for a competing bidder to intervene (unlike a general offer, a scheme cannot be declared unconditional on Day 21 – see **22.5.2**).

(e) Stakebuilding and irrevocable undertakings will not increase the offeror's chances of success (see **21.12.2.1(a)**).

(f) The offeree company controls the timing and implementation of the scheme (this may be a disadvantage from the offeror's perspective).

(g) A scheme involves greater costs (but see **21.2.2.3(e)**).

21.13 DEAL PROTECTION

If the offer is recommended, then the lawyer will be involved in drafting various documents to try to ensure that the takeover completes, and to protect their client's interest in the event that it does not. The documents are as follows:

(a) heads of agreement;

(b) exclusivity agreement;

(c) confidentiality agreement;

(d) standstill agreement; and

(e) (in rare cases) break fee letter.

The exclusivity, confidentiality and standstill agreements are often incorporated into one agreement. Brief details of the documents are set out at **21.13.1** to **21.13.5** below.

21.13.1   Heads of agreement

This agreement is also referred to as heads of terms, a letter of intent or a memorandum of understanding. It is not legally binding, but aims to record the parties' agreement in relation to certain fundamental issues at an early stage in negotiations. Key issues which it addresses include:

(a)   the parties;

(b)   the shares which are to be acquired;

(c)   consideration;

(d)   the extent of the due diligence exercise;

(e)   major terms and conditions;

(f)   timing; and

(g)   choice of law and jurisdiction.

21.13.2   Exclusivity agreement

This agreement is also referred to as a lock-out agreement. Its aim is to prevent a party negotiating with a third party for a certain period. In *Walford v Miles* [1992] 2 WLR 174, it was held that while this type of agreement is enforceable, an agreement which seeks to force a party to negotiate (a 'lock-in' agreement) would not be enforceable. This means the effect of an exclusivity is persuasive only; it will encourage (but not compel) a party to persevere with negotiations rather than start negotiations with another third party who may appear offering a better deal (as the agreement will prevent such negotiations within a certain time).

21.13.3   Confidentiality agreement

This agreement will set out the terms to govern the passing of confidential information from one party to another. It will provide what happens to the information if the deal falls through (usually that the information and any copies must be returned, but sometimes that it must be destroyed), and what will happen in the event of a breach of the agreement.

21.13.4   Standstill letter

A standstill agreement aims to prevent a recommended offeror from being able to launch a hostile offer. It will provide that the potential offeror will not buy any shares in the offeree for a specified period without the offeree's consent.

21.13.5   Break fee letter

The exclusivity, confidentiality and standstill arrangements referred to above are often recorded in a single agreement. Also known as an inducement fee, a break fee is a sum paid by one party to another on the occurrence of a specified event leading to the deal falling through, such as the directors of the offeree company failing to recommend the offer, or the offeree company shareholders failing to pass any necessary resolutions. An example of this is shown in the September 2008 £12.5 billion takeover of British Energy Group plc, listed on the Stock Exchange, by EDF. Each party agreed to pay a break fee of £50 million to the other. British Energy's fee was payable in two instalments. The first instalment of £20 million was payable if the directors did not unanimously recommend acceptance of EDF's offer, or withdrew their recommendations or recommended a competing offer. The second instalment of £30 million would have been payable if a competing offer was successful. Although no fee needed to be paid in the British Energy/EDF takeover, one example where it did was a failed takeover (not under the Takeover Code) by Prudential (listed on the Main Market) for AIG in Asia. Prudential's withdrawal of its bid resulted in its having to pay £153 million under its break fee.

The lawyer must be aware of the law relating to directors' statutory, common law and equitable duties, the financial assistance provisions of s 678 of the CA 2006 (see **Chapter 16**), r 21.2 of the Takeover Code and LR 10.2.7R (see **19.4.6.5(d)**) when drafting a break fee arrangement. Guidance on the application of r 21.2 to break fees can be found both in the notes on r 21.2 and in Practice Statement 2008/23. Details of any break fee must also be provided in the r 2.5 announcement of the offer (see **22.3.3.1(g)**).

Break fees used to be an integral part of a recommended takeover. However, following the review of the Takeover Code in light of the Cadbury takeover (see **20.5.7.4** above), they were generally prohibited with effect from 19 September 2011. There were concerns that break fees were acting as a disincentive to boards of offeree companies to recommend possible competing offers, this being contrary to the spirit of GP 3 and r 21. It was thought that break fees could have been causing a competing offeror to have been put off from making an offer by the cost of the break fee payable by the offeree company.

Rule 21.2(a) of The Takeover Code prohibits 'offer-related arrangements' between the offeree (and persons acting in concert) and the offeror during the offer period or when an offer is reasonably in contemplation. The prohibited arrangements are defined in r 21.2(b) and include arrangements having a similar effect to break fees. Rule 21.2(b) also excludes certain arrangements from the prohibition, including those relating to confidentiality and the non-solicitation of employees, customers or suppliers. In a couple of cases, though, a break fee can still be used despite the general prohibition. The most relevant for our purposes is in the context of a hostile offer when subsequently a preferred competing offeror also makes an offer which the offeree board then accepts (such an offeror is known as a 'white knight'). A break fee can be entered into by the white knight and the offeree, provided it does not exceed 1% of the value of the offer and other conditions are met (Note 1 to r 21.2). It is important to note that the offeree board's decisions to enter into a break fee (if permitted) and also which competing offer to recommend, if any, are still subject to their overriding duties as directors under the CA 2006 and other legal controls such as those on financial assistance.

21.14 FUTURE DEVELOPMENTS

In July 2010 the UK Government published a Command Paper produced in response to a BIS Committee Report addressing issues arising out of the Cadbury takeover. The Paper sets out the Government's position on the regulation of takeovers in the UK and states that, although happy with its powers to intervene where necessary to protect the UK's interests (particularly from overseas bidders), it is to review the regulatory framework now that the Takeover Panel has amended the Takeover Code in light of its own review. In particular, the BIS Secretary, Vince Cable, has indicated that he intends to discourage what he calls 'excessive' takeover activity in the UK.

The Government has most recently indicated in 2013 that it is seeking guidance on a possible policy to distinguish the treatment of long term owners and short term traders in a takeover. This has arisen out of reports made in connection with the Kay Review (see **8.8.3** above), which also made recommendations in relation to takeovers.

CHAPTER 22

THE TAKEOVER PROCESS

22.1 INTRODUCTION

Chapter 20 considered the rules and regulations which can apply to a takeover. **Chapter 21** explained that a substantial part of the lawyer's work on a takeover is undertaken before the offer is announced, to ensure that, once announced, the offer will run smoothly. This chapter looks at what happens after that.

22.2 TIMETABLE

Table 22.1 below sets out a typical timetable for a takeover offer. Note that the events which typically relate to hostile bids only are italicised. This chapter explains in more detail what happens at each stage, but it is useful to consider the timetable at the outset, as it provides an overview of the process.

The Takeover Code sets out the timetable of the offer by reference to the date on which the offeror publishes the offer document. There are three situations which might alter this timetable, namely:

(a) a rival offer is launched (Note 4 on r 31.6 provides that, usually, the timetable of the original offer will default to that of the later offer);

(b) no competition authority decision has been reached by Day 39 (the Panel will usually grant permission to freeze the timetable until the decision is announced); and/or

(c) if the Panel exercises any discretion given to it under the Takeover Code to extend any time periods.

Note also that if the offer is referred to the Competition Commission, or if the European Commission initiates Phase II proceedings, r 12.2 of the Takeover Code provides that the offer period will end (see **23.2.1**). *Note that the Competition Commission will be replaced by the Competition and Markets Authority (CMA) on 1 April 2014.*

22.3 ANNOUNCING THE OFFER

The lawyers will have worked extremely hard to plan the bid. The culmination of this work is when the offer is ready to announce. This is an exciting time, but again the lawyers need to make sure that the announcement is made pursuant to the provisions of the Takeover Code.

22.3.1 Timing

Chapter 21 explained that a considerable amount of the work required to plan a takeover happens behind closed doors. How does an offeror know when to open those doors and announce the bid?

Table 22.1: Timetable for a takeover offer

Date	Event	Rule
Before the announcement	Due diligence by offeror Approach offeree board Draft documents Obtain any irrevocable undertakings Build stake in offeree company Possibly make r 2.4 announcement (if so, the offer period will begin)	1 and 2.2 to 2.8
D – 28	Announce the offer under r 2.7 (earliest date) (if no prior r 2.4 announcement, the offer period will begin)	2.2 to 2.8
DAY 0	**Offeror publishes, displays, sends and announces offer document (and forms of acceptance) (normally within 28 days of r 2.7 announcement)** Market purchases now count towards CA 2006, s 979	24.1 and 30
D + 14	*Offeree dispatches, displays and announces first defence document if offer is hostile (latest date)*	25.1
D + 21	First closing date (earliest date)	31.1
By 8.00 am, the business day after first closing date	Announce acceptance levels Announce any extension of the offer	17.1
D + 39 (or 2nd day after any competition decision is announced, if later)	*Latest date for offeree to release any material new information*	31.9
D + 42 (assuming first closing date is D + 21)*	*Accepting shareholders can withdraw acceptances if offer not yet declared unconditional as to acceptances (earliest date)*	34
D + 46	*Latest date for offeror to improve offer*	32.1(c)
By midnight, D + 60	Latest date for offeror to fulfil acceptance condition and declare the offer 'unconditional as to acceptances' (ie wins control)	31.6(a)
D + 74 (assuming offer declared unconditional on D + 60)	Earliest date offer can close	31.4
D + 81 (assuming offer declared unconditional on D + 60)	Latest date for offeror to fulfil other conditions	31.7
14 days after offer becomes unconditional in all respects	Latest date to post consideration to offeree shareholders	31.8

*This rule also applies to recommended offers but in practice is rarely an issue.

Rule 1(a) provides that, when the offeror is ready to announce the bid, it must first put forward the offer to the offeree board or its advisers. Rule 2.2 then provides that where a serious source has notified the board of the offeree company of a firm intention to make an offer, this triggers the requirement for an announcement. The announcement must be made to an RIS (r 2.9). Note that a 'firm intention' excludes mere expressions of interest by a possible offeror. The obligation to announce arises only when, in accordance with r 2.7, the offeror has every reason to believe it can proceed with the offer. Financing must therefore be in place before this can be achieved. Subject to DTR 2.5.1R (see **7.5.2.8**), an announcement will also be required pursuant to the general obligation under DTR 2.2.1R (see **7.5.1**). In practice, the announcement required by r 2.2 will satisfy both obligations.

If everything goes to plan, the offeror will notify the offeree company board and then the offer will be announced under r 2.7 once it has been put together. In these circumstances, it is the offeree company's obligation to make the announcement (r 2.3(c)). In a hostile bid (see **21.2.2**), typically the offeror will seek to keep the amount of time, between putting the offer to the board and releasing the press announcement, to a bare minimum, and will telephone the offeree company's chairman just minutes before releasing the r 2.7 press announcement. This ensures that the offeree company is as ill-prepared as possible to deal with the takeover offer (and the offeree company's lawyers will have to get up to speed with the details of the offer from a standing start).

The obligation to announce the offer under r 2.2 can also arise in other circumstances, namely:

(a) there is an acquisition which gives rise to a r 9 mandatory bid (see **21.8.10.3** above);

(b) if the offeror has approached the board (but has not notified the offeree company board of a firm intention to make the offer) and the offeree company is then the subject of rumour and speculation, or there is an 'untoward' movement in its share price (the Panel will interpret 'untoward') (this is dealt with further in r 2.4 – see **22.3.3.2**);

(c) if the offeror has not even approached the board, but the offeree company is the subject of rumour and speculation, or there is an untoward movement in its share price, and there are reasonable grounds for concluding that it is the potential offeror's actions which have led to the situation (this is dealt with further in r 2.4 – see **22.3.3.2**);

(d) negotiations are about to be extended beyond the parties and their immediate advisers (see **21.3** above); or

(e) the offeree company is seeking a buyer for an interest or interests in 30% or more of its voting shares and there is either rumour and speculation, or an 'untoward' movement (as determined by the Panel) in the share price, or the number of potential purchasers approached is about to exceed a very restricted number.

You will note that rumour and speculation can lead to the need for the offer to be announced. This explains why secrecy is paramount in the preparation of any bid (see **21.3**), as the offeror will want to avoid having to announce its intentions before it is ready.

Note 1 on r 2.2 provides that parties should consult the Panel if they are in doubt as to whether an announcement is required. It is common for the Panel to be consulted in relation to (d) above in particular, as parties may wish to seek irrevocable undertakings (see **21.10**) or non-binding indications of intention to accept (see **21.11**) without triggering an obligation to announce the offer.

The Panel has reprimanded publicly financial advisers who have decided that no announcement is necessary without first consulting the Panel (see, for example, Panel Statement 2004/9, criticising Nabarro Wells & Co, financial adviser to Transcomm plc, which became the subject of a bid by British Telecommunications plc). However, if it is obvious that an announcement is required, the parties should not use consultation as a delaying tactic (see Panel Statement 2008/20).

22.3.2 Responsibility

Who is responsible for making the announcement in the circumstances listed at (a) to (e) above? Rule 2.3 of the Takeover Code provides that if the announcement is required before the offeror has approached the offeree company (which most likely will arise under r 2.2(c) due to rumour and speculation), or a r 9 obligation has arisen (see (a) above), responsibility for making the announcement lies with the offeror. If the announcement is required after the offeror has approached the offeree company, then responsibility lies with the offeree company. However, Panel Statement 2008/20 provides that if the offeror's approach has been rejected before the announcement is required, usually responsibility for making the announcement will revert back to the offeror.

22.3.3 Method

Rule 2.2 requires that an announcement should be made. To what type of announcement does this refer? There are two options:

(a)   the announcement of a firm intention to make an offer (r 2.7); and

(b)   the announcement of a possible offer (r 2.4).

22.3.3.1 The announcement of a firm intention to make an offer

The ideal scenario is that the announcement triggered by r 2.2 will be of a firm intention to make an offer. This is often referred to as the 'Rule 2.7 announcement', or the 'press announcement'. The potential offeror can make this announcement only after the most careful and responsible consideration, and only if it has every reason to believe that it can, and will continue to be able to, implement the offer (r 2.7(a)). It must also be certain that it can fulfil any cash consideration, and has taken all reasonable measures to secure the implementation of any other type of consideration (General Principle 5); in other words, it must have decided what consideration it will offer, and its financing arrangements must be in place. If it has any doubts, it must make a r 2.4 announcement rather than a r 2.7 announcement (see **22.3.3.2** below).

The r 2.7 announcement is a key document. Typically, it is the first public document to contain details of the offer. It is vital, therefore, that it contains the right message. As well as complying with r 2.7, there are certain conventions as to the matters which the announcement will address.

Content

Rule 2.7 sets out the content requirements of the announcement. The main requirements include:

(a)   the terms of the offer;

(b)   the identity of the offeror;

(c)   the conditions or pre-conditions of the offer (including details of any circumstances where the offeror cannot invoke the conditions or pre-conditions);

(d)   details of any dealing arrangements involving the offeror or concert parties for relevant securities (as defined by the Takeover Code; see **15.7.4.3**);

(e)   a summary of r 8 and confirmation that the offeror has made the necessary disclosures under r 8.1(a) (see **15.7.4.3**);

(f)   details of any offer-related arrangements under r 21.2 (see **21.13.5** above);

(g)   a list of documents which must be published on a website under r 26.1 and the website address, and the website on which the r 2.7 announcement will be published; and

(h)   if the offer is for cash, or includes an element of cash, confirmation by the offeror's financial adviser that the offeror's resources are sufficient to make the offer (known as the 'cash confirmation').

Publication

Rule 2.9 governs the publication of any r 2.7 announcement. The announcement must be typed and faxed or e-mailed to an RIS. If the announcement is submitted outside normal business hours, it must also be distributed to at least two national newspapers and two newswire services in the UK.

Rule 2.12 sets out what must be done following the publication under r 2.9. The offeree company must send a copy of the announcement (or a circular summarising the terms and conditions of the offer, together with a r 8 summary – see **15.7.4.3**) promptly to its shareholders, persons with information rights under s 146 of the CA 2006 and the Panel (r 2.12(b)(i) and (c)). In practice, the offeree company tends to send the announcement itself rather than a circular, so will arrange for a glossy version of it to be published for this purpose.

The offeror and offeree company must also make the announcement (or circular) available to their respective employee representatives (or, if there are none, to their employees) and to the trustees of its pension scheme (r 2.12(b)(ii)). If the company has chosen to distribute a circular rather than the announcement itself, nevertheless the announcement must be made readily and promptly available to them (and the circular must include a website address on which the announcement will be posted, such as the offeror or offeree company's website) (Note 1 on r 2.12).

Where necessary, the offeror or offeree company, as the case may be, should explain the implications of the announcement and, for an offeree company, the fact that contact information may be provided to the offeror (to enable it to send information) (r 2.12(c)).

If there has been no r 2.4 announcement then the publication of the r 2.7 announcement will start the offer period and the offeree company must make the disclosure required by r 2.10 (details of all classes of relevant securities issued by the offeree company). The offeror must also do this unless the offer is wholly for cash (see **15.7.4.3**).

Effect

Once the offeror has made a r 2.7 announcement, r 2.7(b) provides that it must proceed with the offer (unless the offer is stated to be subject to a pre-condition which has not been met, or is subject to a condition which could be invoked if the offer were made). In other words, once the r 2.7 announcement is made, usually there is no going back. The only way an offer can be withdrawn is with the consent of the Panel, which will be given only in exceptional circumstances. Panel Statements 2007/25, 2007/23 and 2007/13 give an example of how strictly this rule is applied in practice. An offeror's attempt to withdraw its offer for Freeport plc was rejected by the Panel, which ordered an offer to be made. However, in October 2007, the Panel did allow the offeror for Telent plc the right to withdraw its offer. This was due to exceptional intervention by the Government in the offeree to protect Telent plc's pension fund. Ultimately, the offeror proceeded with the offer.

22.3.3.2 The announcement of a possible offer

If the potential offeror must issue an announcement under r 2.2 but is not in a position to issue a r 2.7 announcement then, as a temporary measure, it, or the offeree company, may issue what is known as a 'possible offer announcement' or a 'holding announcement' under r 2.4.

Content

An extract from a holding announcement is set out below. As you can see, the announcement will contain limited information, such as a potential offeree company announcing that talks are in progress with a potential offeror, or a potential offeror announcing that it is considering making an offer for a potential offeree company. Crucially any announcement of a possible offer by the offeree company must usually include the identity of the potential offeror under r 2.4(a). This is important, because usually it will trigger a deadline by which the offeror must announce a r 2.7 firm announcement (see 'Effect' below). A r 2.4 announcement by the potential offeror does not need to identify the offeree company. This requirement to identify the offeror is part of the protections brought in with the new version of the Takeover Code on 19 September 2011 to strengthen offeree companies against hostile bids in particular. Previously it was not necesary to identify the potential offeror. The announcement should also include the deadline required by r 2.6(a) (see 'Effect' below) and a summary of the provisions of r 8 (see **15.7.4.3**).

Company	HBOS PLC
TIDM	HBOS
Headline	HBOS in Talks with LLoyds TSB
Released	13:25 17-Sep-08
Number	6588D13

In the light of market speculation, the Board of HBOS plc confirms that it is in advanced talks with Lloyds TSB Group plc which may or may not lead to an offer being made for HBOS.

A further announcement will be made when appropriate.

Publication

A r 2.4 announcement must be published under r 2.9 in exactly the same way as a r 2.7 announcement (see **22.3.3.1**).

As the r 2.4 announcement will start the offer period (see **22.3.4**), the offeree company must also:

(a)   send the announcement to its shareholders, persons with information rights under s 146 of the CA 2006 and the Panel under r 2.12(a); and

(b)   make the disclosure required by r 2.10 (see **15.7.4.3**). (The offeror must also do this unless the offer is wholly for cash.)

Effect

A typical example of when a holding announcement is required is if there has been a leak which breaches the secrecy requirement under r 2.1, and which starts rumours that trigger the requirement for an announcement under r 2.2.

Even though the leak may have occurred at a very early stage in planning the offer, once the potential offeror or offeree has made a r 2.4 announcement, in which the potential offeror is identified as required, then subject to an extension being granted by the Panel, the potential offeror has 28 days to 'put up or shut up'. This means that the potential offeror has 28 days from the announcement within which it must make either a r 2.7 announcement (ie that it definitely will proceed with an offer for the offeree company), or a statement under r 2.8 that it does not intend to make an offer (r 2.6(a)). This can leave an under-prepared offeror with little choice but to make a r 2.8 statement. This again can help to protect an offeree company from unwanted hostile offers as the potential offeror may not be ready or able to launch a takeover (including arranging the finance) within the 28 days. An example of a 'put up or shut up' notice is set out below.

Company	Sportingbet PLC
TIDM	SBT
Headline	Statement re approach by William Hill and GVC
Released	11:17 01-Oct-2012
Number	5849N11

Statement by the Board of Sportingbet regarding the approach by William Hill plc ('William Hill') and GVC Holdings plc ('GVC')

Sportingbet notes the recent press speculation regarding the approach by William Hill and GVC. The Board of Sportingbet confirms that it has received an indicative offer from William Hill and GVC of

52.5 pence comprising of 45 pence in cash from William Hill and 7.5 pence in shares in GVC. The Board of Sportingbet has responded that this indicative offer significantly undervalues the business and its future prospects.

This announcement is made without the consent of the potential offerors. There can be no certainty that an offer will be made nor as to the terms on which any offer might be made.

A further announcement will be made in due course.

In accordance with Rule 2.6(a) of the City Code on Takeovers and Mergers (the 'Code'), William Hill and GVC are required, by not later than 5.00 p.m. on 16 October 2012, to either announce a firm intention to make an offer for Sportingbet in accordance with Rule 2.7 of the Code or announce that they do not intend to make an offer, in which case the announcement will be treated as a statement to which Rule 2.8 of the Code applies. This deadline can be extended with the consent of the Panel in accordance with Rule 2.6(c) of the Code.

A copy of this announcement will be available at www.sportingbetplc.com. The content of the website referred to in this announcement is not incorporated into and does not form part of this announcement.

The offeree board can approach the Panel to ask it to extend this 28-day period, and will normally grant this in accordance with r 2.6(c). The usual reason for requesting an extension in these circumstances will be when the offeree board needs more time to negotiate a possible recommended offer with the potential offeror.

22.3.3.3   Statement of intention not to make an offer

The effect of a r 2.8 statement is that the potential offeror (or any concert party) must 'down tools'. It will not be able to:

(a)   make another offer for the offeree company;

(b)   acquire any interest in shares in the offeree company which would trigger a r 9 mandatory bid (see **21.8.10.3** above);

(c)   acquire any interest in, or procure an irrevocable undertaking (see **21.10**) in respect of, shares in the offeree company which, when aggregated with the shares of other concert parties, would carry 30% or more of the voting rights in the offeree company;

(d)   make any statement which raises or confirms the possibility that an offer might be made for the offeree company; or

(e)   take any steps to prepare a possible offer for the offeree company where knowledge of the possible offer might extend beyond the offeror and its immediate advisers,

for six months from the date of the r 2.8 statement, unless:

(i)   it has the consent of the Panel;

(ii)   the board of the offeree company agrees to the statement being set aside; or

(iii)   another offeror makes an r 2.7 announcement for the offeree; or

(iv)   the offeree announces a 'whitewash' under Note 1 on Dispensations from Rule 9 or a reverse takeover; or

(v)   there is a material change of circumstances; or

(vi)   an event has occurred which the potential offeror specified in the r 2.8 statement as an event which would enable the statement to be set aside.

These requirements are onerous (in fact, they mirror those which apply under r 35.1 to a failed bid (see **22.6.1.1**), albeit for a shorter period).

Much can happen to the fortunes of a potential offeror and offeree company during this six-month period, and of course the potential offeror can no longer launch a surprise offer, so a r 2.8 statement can mean the end of any takeover offer plans. Now it may be clearer why so much care is taken to ensure that the r 2.1 secrecy obligation (see **21.3**) is not breached.

Rule 2.8 will apply to any statement to the effect that the company does not intend to make an offer. The lawyer should advise the board not to make such a statement, simply with a view to keeping its intentions secret, if in fact it does intend to make an offer (and, in particular, warn about the severe implications of r 2.8 before the board members give interviews to the media).

An extract of a r 2.8 statement follows.

Company	Coms PLC
TIDM	COMS
Headline	Statement re Possible Offer
Released	14:18 03-Sep-2013
Number	1342N14

COMS PLC
("Coms" or the "Company")
Statement Regarding a Possible Offer

3 September 2013

The Board of Coms plc (the "Board") notes the recent share price movement in the shares of Pinnacle Technology Group plc ("Pinnacle") and confirms that it is considering a possible corporate transaction with Pinnacle that could result in an offer by Coms for the entire issued and to be issued ordinary share capital of Pinnacle being made. In the event that an indicative offer is made, it is the current expectation of the Board that any such indicative offer would be at or around 21p per Pinnacle share.

This is an announcement falling under Rule 2.4 of the City Code on Takeovers and Mergers (the "Code"). It does not represent a firm intention to make an offer under Rule 2.7 of the Code. Discussions are at a very preliminary stage and accordingly, there can be no certainty that any transaction or offer for Pinnacle will ultimately be forthcoming.

In accordance with Rule 2.6(a) of the Code, Coms must, by not later than 5.00pm on 30 September 2013, either announce a firm intention to make an offer for the Company in accordance with Rule 2.7 of the Code or announce that it does not intend to make an offer, in which case the announcement will be treated as a statement to which Rule 2.8 of the Code applies. This deadline will only be extended with the consent of the Takeover Panel in accordance with Rule 2.6(c) of the Code.

A further announcement will be made when appropriate.

22.3.4 The offer period

The offer period will begin:

(a)   when the offeror makes either a r 2.7 announcement of a firm intention to make an offer (see **22.3.3.1**), or a r 2.4 announcement of a possible offer (see **22.3.3.2**); or

(b)   when a company announces that shares carrying 30% or more of the voting rights in the company are for sale, or that the board is seeking potential offerors.

When an offer begins, the offeree company and, unless the offer is wholly for cash, the offeror, must make the disclosure required by r 2.10 (see **15.7.4.3**).

The offer period will end:

(a)   on the first closing date (a minimum of 21 days from the date the offeror publishes the offer document – see **22.5.2**); or

(b)   if later, the date the offer becomes or is declared unconditional as to acceptances (see **22.5.3**); or

(c)   all announced offers have been withdrawn or lapsed (see **22.4.7** and **22.5.7**) or all potential offerors have made r 2.8 statements (see **22.3.3.3**).

The Disclosure Table on the Panel's website lists all the companies which are currently in an offer period and offerors and potential offerors.

22.4 THE OFFER

22.4.1 The offer document

The offer document is the principal document that the lawyer must draft in relation to a takeover offer.

22.4.1.1 Nature

The offer document is addressed to the offeree shareholders. It makes the formal contractual offer to acquire their shares in the offeree. It will constitute a financial promotion under s 21 of the FSMA 2000 (see **Chapter 12**) and will therefore have to be approved by a financial adviser who is an authorised person (see **12.2**).

22.4.1.2 Timing

While the offer period can begin with either a r 2.4 or a r 2.7 announcement, the offer timetable will start to run with effect from the r 2.7 announcement. Rule 24.1(a) provides that the offeror normally has 28 days from the date of the r 2.7 announcement in which to send the offer document to shareholders and persons with information rights under s 146 of the CA 2006. In practice, however, it is unlikely that the offeror will want to leave 28 days between making the announcement and sending the offer document. This is because the offeror will want the offeree company shareholders to be reading its offer document, not that of any other offeror who announces a rival offer and sends an offer document during this 28-day period.

As the timetable at **Table 22.1** shows, the day the offer document is sent is referred to as 'D day', and other dates in the offer timetable are calculated from this day.

22.4.1.3 Publication

Before it is published the document must be sent in hard copy and electronic form to the Panel (r 30.3). In Response Statement 2005/5 the Code Committee confirmed that it will continue to be acceptable where, under the direction of a financial adviser, the document is sent to the Panel at the same time it is sent to the offeree shareholders.

The offer document is then published. The Takeover Code requires the offeror to:

(a) send the offer document to the offeree company shareholders and persons with information rights under s 146 of the CA 2006 (r 24.1(a));

(b) publish the offer document on a website, in accordance with r 30.4, on the date it sends the document to offeree company shareholders (r 24.1(b)(i));

(c) announce to an RIS, in accordance with r 2.9, that it has displayed the document, and where (r 24.1(b)(ii));

(d) make the document readily available to its employee representatives, and if there are none, to its employees (the offeree company must also do this) and to the trustees of the offeree's pension scheme (r 24.1(a)); and

(e) send the document in hard copy and electronic form to the advisers of the other parties to the offer (r 30.3(a)).

Note that under r 30.1 a document, announcement or other information (including the offer document) is deemed sent to a person under the Takeover Code if it is sent in hard copy or electronic form to him or it is published on a website provided a notification of website publication is sent to that person. This applies to both the offeror and the offeree. There are a number of exceptions to this:

(a) The Note on r 30.1 states that only hard copy versions are acceptable for acceptance forms (see **22.4.3**), withdrawal forms (see **22.5.5.1**), proxy forms and other forms required in the offer.

(b)   Rule 30.2(a) allows persons sent documents electronically or by website publication to request that the documents be sent to them in hard copy.

(c)   Certain rules, such as r 30.3(a), expressly state the method of communication, in that case hard copy and electronic. Website publication alone would therefore not be sufficient.

However, when an offeror or offeree sends the document, announcement or information, it must put a copy on its website under r 30.4(a) by midday of the next business day (subject to certain exemptions in Note 5). The document must be in a 'read-only' format to prevent alterations being made (Note 2).

Note 3 on r 30.4 extends the obligation to sending documents to shareholders outside the EEA unless there is an objectively good reason not to.

22.4.1.4   Content

Rule 24 (and, for a recommended offer, r 25) sets out the detailed content requirements of the offer document. Typically, it will include the following:

(a)   a section (sometimes in the form of a letter from the Chairman of the offeror), which explains the rationale of the offer and urges the offeree shareholders to accept it;

(b)   a letter from the Chairman of the offeree company (under r 25.2 of the Takeover Code), which recommends the offer to the offeree shareholders (if the offer is recommended: if not, see **22.4.2** below);

(c)   a formal letter from the offeror making the offer and setting out the principal terms and other important information. Following the implementation of the Takeovers Directive in the UK and the criminal offence under s 953 of the CA 2006 for a breach of the bid documentation rules (see **20.5.7.2**) by the person making the bid (amongst others), it is no longer common for the financial advisers to make the offer on the offeror's behalf;

(d)   a detailed appendix setting out the full terms and conditions of the offer;

(e)   a detailed appendix setting out the information relating to the offeror which is required by r 24 of the Takeover Code and, if the offer is recommended, the information relating to the offeree company which is required by r 25 of the Takeover Code; and

(f)   information about how the offeree company shareholders can accept the offer.

An example of the front page of an offer document is set out below.

THIS DOCUMENT IS IMPORTANT AND REQUIRES YOUR IMMEDIATE ATTENTION. If you are in any doubt as to the action you should take, you are recommended to seek your own personal financial advice immediately from your stockbroker, bank manager, solicitor, accountant or other independent professional adviser duly authorised under the Financial Services and Markets Act 2000 if you are resident in the UK or, if not, from another appropriately authorised independent financial adviser.

If you have sold or otherwise transferred all of your Amstrad Shares, please forward this document, together with the Form of Acceptance, at once to the purchaser or transferee or to the stockbroker, bank or other agent through whom the sale or transfer was effected, for onward transmission to the purchaser or transferee. However, these documents should not be forwarded or transmitted in or into any jurisdiction in which such act would constitute a violation of the relevant laws of such jurisdiction. If you have sold or otherwise transferred only part of your holding of Amstrad Shares, you should retain these documents and consult the stockbroker, bank or other agent through whom the sale or transfer was effected.

The distribution of this document into jurisdictions other than the United Kingdom may be restricted by the laws of those jurisdictions and therefore any person into whose possession this document comes should inform themselves about, and observe, any such restrictions. Failure to comply with any such restrictions may constitute a violation of the securities law of any such jurisdiction.

Recommended Cash Offer
by Sky Digital Supplies Limited
a wholly-owned subsidiary of
British Sky Broadcasting Group plc
for Amstrad plc

Your attention is drawn to the letter of recommendation from the Chairman of Amstrad, set out on pages 3 to 7 of this document, which explains why the Amstrad Directors are unanimously recommending acceptance of the Offer.

The procedure for acceptance of the Offer is set out on pages 15 to 18 of this document and in the Form of Acceptance. If you hold Amstrad Shares in certificated form, to accept the Offer, the Form of Acceptance should be completed, signed and returned in accordance with the instructions printed on it as soon as possible and, in any event, so as to be received by Capita Registrars no later than 3:00 p.m. on 21 August 2007. If you hold Amstrad Shares in uncertificated form, to accept the Offer, you should comply with the procedure for acceptances set out on pages 16 to 18 of this document and ensure that an electronic acceptance is made which settles no later than 3:00 p.m. on 21 August 2007. If you are a CREST sponsored member, you must refer to your CREST sponsor as only your CREST sponsor will be able to send the necessary TTE instruction to CRESTCo.

Merrill Lynch is acting exclusively as financial adviser to Sky and Sky Digital Supplies and no one else in connection with the Offer and the matters referred to in this document. Merrill Lynch will not be responsible to any person other than Sky and Sky Digital Supplies for providing the protections afforded to customers of Merrill Lynch, nor for providing advice in relation to the Offer or any other matters referred to in this document.

Rothschild is acting exclusively for Amstrad and no one else in connection with the Offer and the matters referred to in this document. Rothschild will not be responsible to any person other than Amstrad for providing the protections afforded to customers of Rothschild, nor for providing advice in relation to the Offer or any other matters referred to in this document.

The Loan Notes will not be listed on any stock exchange and have not been, and will not be, registered under the United States Securities Act of 1933, as amended, or under any relevant securities laws of any state of the United States and the relevant clearances have not been, and will not be, obtained from the regulatory authority of any province or territory of Canada. In addition, no prospectus in relation to the Loan Notes has been, or will be, lodged with or registered by the Australian Securities and Investments Commission and no steps have been, nor will be, taken to enable the Loan Notes to be offered in compliance with the applicable securities laws of Japan, New Zealand or any other country or jurisdiction outside the United Kingdom. The Loan Notes will not be offered, sold, resold, delivered or distributed, directly or indirectly, in or into the United States, Canada, Australia, New Zealand or Japan or any other jurisdiction if to do so would constitute a violation of the relevant laws in such jurisdiction.

Reproduced by kind permission of BSkyB plc.

22.4.2   The defence document

22.4.2.1   Nature

If the offer is recommended, the views of the board of the offeree company will usually be included in the offer document. However, if the offer is hostile, the offer document will have been prepared by the offeror only. Rule 25.1(a) requires the board of the offeree company to communicate with its shareholders and persons with information rights under s 146 of the CA 2006 by way of circular, which is often referred to as a 'defence document'.

Once the defence document has been sent, the offeror will usually send a further document, to respond to the arguments raised in the defence document and draw the attention of the offeree company shareholders once more to the merits of the offer. The offeree may then send a further defence document to the offeree shareholders in response to the offeror's latest claims, and so on.

22.4.2.2   Timing

Rule 25.1(a) provides that the offeree company board must publish a circular containing its opinion on the offer as soon as practicable following publication of the offer document and normally within 14 days. For lawyers advising a company which is the subject of a surprise hostile offer, this will involve some swift drafting and several late nights.

22.4.2.3   Publication

The defence document is also a public document. The Takeover Code requires the offeree company to:

(a)   send the defence document to its shareholders (and persons with information rights under s 146 of the CA 2006 (r 25.1(a));

(b)   put the defence document on display, in accordance with r 26, and publish it on a website in accordance with r 30.4, on the date it sends the document to offeree company shareholders (r 25.1(b)(i));

(c)   announce to an RIS, in accordance with r 2.9, that it has displayed the document, and where (r 30.2(a));

(d)   make the document readily available to its employee representatives, and if there are none, to its employees and to the trustees of its pension scheme (r 25.1(a)); and

(e)   send the document to the Panel and to the advisers to all other parties to the offer electronically and in hard copy (r 30.3(b)).

As mentioned at **22.4.1.3** above, Note 3 on r 30.4 extends the obligation in relation to sending documents to shareholders outside the EEA.

22.4.2.4   Content

The content of the defence document is prescribed by r 25.2 to r 25.9. The information the offeree company must set out includes:

(a)   the substance of the advice it has received from its r 3 advisers (see **21.5.1**);

(b)   the board's reasons for forming its opinions and its views on:

(i)   the effects of the offer on the offeree company's interests (including, specifically, employment); and

(ii)   the offeror's strategic plans for the offeree company and their likely repercussions on employment and the locations of the offeree company's place of business; and

(c)   an opinion from its employee representatives and a separate opinion from the trustees of its pension scheme on the effects of the offer on employment on the pension scheme respectively (provided the representatives and pension trustees provide the opinion in good time) (r 25.9).

The defence document will seek to make clear to the offeree company shareholders that the offeror's offer is poor (for example, it undervalues the offeree company, or the premium offered is too low) and will advise the offeree company shareholders to reject the offeror's offer. As acceptance of the offer involves offeree company shareholders relinquishing their offeree company shares to the offeror, the defence document tends to focus on the benefits to the shareholder of keeping their shares. However, it must be careful not to make a profit forecast unless it is willing to report on that forecast (see **22.4.5.1**). If the consideration for the offer is shares in the offeror (a securities exchange offer), the defence document may also attack the worth of the offeror, further fanning the flames of the hostile bid.

22.4.3   The forms of acceptance

The offeree company shareholder must complete a form of acceptance and return it to the offeror's registrars in order to accept the offer. These forms are of crucial importance, and the lawyer will make sure that they are as clear and straightforward as possible. They must be sent in hard copy (Note to r 30.1).

22.4.4 Other documentation

As you will now be aware, the lawyer cannot consider the takeover in isolation from the other rules relating to listed companies. While the main documents relating to the takeover itself are the r 2.7 announcement and the documents considered at **22.4.1** to **22.4.3** above, the following circumstances will also call for further documentation.

22.4.4.1 Class 1 transaction

The takeover is an acquisition of shares, and if the offeror is a premium listed company then the acquisition must be classified under the Listing Rules and the offeror must comply with the requirements which attach to that classification (see **Chapter 19**). It is likely that a large takeover will constitute a Class 1 transaction. This means that the offeror must make a Class 2 announcement, send a circular to its own shareholders (that is, the offeror shareholders) and obtain the prior consent of those shareholders to the takeover by ordinary resolution.

22.4.4.2 Securities exchange offer

If the offeror is offering shares as consideration then, if that class of shares is listed (which is likely, as a listing gives shares an identifiable value), the consideration shares will also need to be listed. This means that the offeror must prepare a marketing document.

The rule is that a prospectus will be required for a takeover unless the exemption in connection with takeovers applies. This exemption, referred to at **6.4.1.5(f)** and **6.4.2.4(c)** above, is that a prospectus is not required if the takeover involves a share-for-share exchange (that is, the consideration for the takeover is shares) and a document is available containing information regarded by the FCA as being 'equivalent to' a prospectus. The FCA's Technical Note UKLA/TN/602.1 Exemptions from the requirement to produce a prospectus provides further information about this exemption. In order to decide whether a document is 'equivalent to' a prospectus, the FCA will fully vet the document, which must be submitted at least 10 days before approval is required (PR 3.1.14R and PR 3.1.15R).

There is a disadvantage to using an equivalent document; it will not benefit from the passporting rights referred to at **6.11** above. However, if an equivalent document is used, then there is no obligation to produce a supplementary prospectus, so it has the advantage that it will not raise the potential problem of withdrawal rights outlined at **22.5.5**.

The prospectus (or equivalent document) will be published as a separate document, but sent out to shareholders at the same time as the offer document. Much of the information which would normally be included in the offer document will be contained in the prospectus (or equivalent document). WPP Group plc used an equivalent document in its £1 billion offer for Taylor Nelson Sofres plc in July 2008.

Finally, it is possible that the offeror will need the consent of its own shareholders to authorise the directors to allot shares under s 551 of the CA 2006. Remember that no disapplication of s 561 is required if the issue is for non-cash consideration. (See **Chapter 14**.)

22.4.4.3 Resulting extra documentation

As a result of either of the circumstances discussed at **22.4.4.1** and **22.4.4.2** above, the offeror might need to produce:

(a) a circular (which contains the Class 1 information, if appropriate, information relating to any required increase in share capital and/or the s 551 authority, and the notice of the GM which convenes the meeting where the shareholders of the offeror can vote on these issues); and

(b) a prospectus, or 'equivalent document'.

There will also be various r 17.1 press announcements (for example, of the level of acceptances (see **22.5.3**), or notifying an extension to the bid) during the course of the offer.

22.4.5   Standard of information

The Takeover Code sets high standards for any information provided to shareholders and persons with information rights under s 146 of the CA 2006 during an offer. As noted at **22.4.1.4**, the specific requirements regarding this information are contained in rr 24 and 25. However, the Takeover Code also sets out the following general rules about the nature and quality of that information.

22.4.5.1   Rule 19.1: accuracy of information

Rule 19.1 provides that:

(a)   any document or advertisement issued, or statement made, during the course of an offer must be prepared with the highest standard of care and accuracy; and

(b)   the information given must be adequately and fairly presented.

Again, the lawyers will use the verification process to help to protect the board in this regard.

The notes on r 19.1 provide valuable drafting guidance to the lawyer. They advocate the use of unambiguous language, citing sources for any material facts stated (typically this is done in a 'sources and bases' section in the document), and warn against using quotations out of context.

Note 1 on r 19.1 highlights certain areas of particular sensitivity, including profit forecasts, on which comment should be avoided. A profit forecast is any statement which puts a floor under, or a ceiling on, the expected profits for a certain period (for example, 'don't accept the bid as we are going to be much more profitable next year in any event'). As is the case with an IPO (see **6.5.2.1**), any profit forecast made during the course of a takeover must be reported on (r 28). Typically, a forecast will not be made unless it has already been decided that the benefit of making a forecast outweighs the work necessary to report on that forecast. This may be the case, for example, if the offer falls late in the financial year, and the most recent published accounts appear a little dated. Even then, as recognised by Note 1, it should not be the subject of media comment.

The Panel considers that the financial adviser is responsible for ensuring that its client complies with this rule (see **21.5.1(g)**). This can lead to something of a strain in relationships between the financial adviser, who needs to advise caution in making media statements, and the financial public relations consultants (see **21.5.5**), who want to deliver powerful messages to the media.

Note 3 on r 19.1 explains that where the offeror makes a statement of intention of action it intends to take or not in any document, announcement or other information then it is committed to that course of action for 12 months unless there is a material change. This clarification was introduced as direct result of the Kraft/Cadbury takeover (see **20.5.7.4**).

22.4.5.2   Rule 19.2: the responsibility statement

Rule 19.2 makes clear that it is the directors who must ensure that these standards are met. Each document issued to shareholders and persons with information rights under s 146 of the CA 2006, or advertisement published in connection with an offer, must contain what is referred to as a 'responsibility statement' from the directors of the offeror and/or, where appropriate, the offeree. The information that must be included in the statement is provided by r 19.2. Typically, the statement is drafted as follows:

> The directors of [the company], whose names appear on page [   ], accept responsibility for the information contained in this [document/advertisement]. To the best of the knowledge and belief of the directors (who have taken all reasonable care to ensure that such is the case) the information contained in this document is in accordance with the facts and does not omit anything likely to affect the import of such information.

In a recommended bid, the offer document will include a responsibility statement from the directors of the offeror in relation to the information provided about the offer and about the offeror. However, it will also include a responsibility statement from the directors of the offeree company in respect of the information it includes about the offeree.

In a hostile offer, the directors of the offeree company will not usually have provided the offeror with any of the information which is included in the offer document. The offer document will include a responsibility statement from the directors of the offeror only. However, any defence documents circulated by the offeree company must include a responsibility statement from the directors of the offeree company (see **22.4.2** above).

The wording of the responsibility statement should be familiar. As explained at **6.5.2.1** above, Appendix 3 of the Prospectus Rules requires a similar responsibility statement in a prospectus. You will remember that the purpose of the IPO verification process is to make sure that the directors are in a position to make this statement. The position on a takeover is no different. The junior lawyer will be involved in the process of ensuring that each statement in the offer document is properly verified, and will produce a verification note. The verification process is discussed in more detail at **5.3.5** above.

22.4.5.3 Rule 19.3: unacceptable statements

Rule 19.3 provides that the parties to the offer and their advisers must take care not to issue statements which, while not factually incorrect, may mislead shareholders and the market, or which may create uncertainty. In particular, the offeror should not make a statement which hints that it may improve the offer or that it may make a change to the structure, conditionality or the non-financial terms of its offer, without committing itself to doing so and specifying the improvement. To see an example of a breach of r 19.3 (by Universe Bidco Limited), see Panel Statement 2010/17.

22.4.5.4 Rule 20: equality of information

Rule 20.1

Rule 20.1 develops General Principle 1 (see **20.5.5**). It provides that information about companies involved in an offer must be made equally available to all offeree company shareholders as nearly as possible at the same time and in the same manner.

Note 3 on r 20.1 provides guidance in relation to meetings the board may have with shareholders, analysts, brokers or other investment professionals prior to the announcement of the offer, and during the offer itself. It provides that the directors must not disclose, in the case of a meeting prior to the announcement of the offer, any material new information or significant new opinions that will not be in the r 2.7 announcement and, in the case of a meeting during the offer period, any material new information or significant new opinions at all. Again, a profit forecast is capable of falling within r 20.1.

Of course, the board is very keen to enthuse the audience at such meetings with just the type of statements that r 20.1 seeks to prevent. The financial adviser or corporate broker of the party convening any such meeting must be present at the meeting and has the happy task of providing written confirmation to the Panel, by midday the following day, that the restrictions were complied with. The lawyers tend not to attend these meetings: the risk of soaring blood pressure is too high.

If any material information or significant new opinion is released at the meeting, a circular must be sent to shareholders and persons with information rights under s 146 of the CA 2006 (in the final stages of an offer, an advertisement in a newspaper may be required). If the information or opinion cannot be substantiated, this must be made clear and it must be withdrawn formally. This, of course, would be a public relations nightmare.

Rule 20.2

Rule 20.2 seeks to level the playing field for any competing offeror. It provides that the offeree, on request, must provide the same information to each offeror or genuine potential offeror, no matter how unwelcome that offeror's offer is.

The problem which r 20.2 can cause to an offeree company is illustrated well by the takeover of Midland Bank plc in 1992. Midland had provided information to its preferred offeror, HSBC Holdings Ltd (HSBC) (a subsidiary of the Hong Kong and Shanghai Banking Corporation). Lloyds Bank plc, a high street rival, then stated that it was also 'considering' making an offer for Midland. A pre-condition of Lloyds' offer was the receipt by Lloyds of all the information that Midland had provided to HSBC. Midland objected, on the grounds that it was not fair to oblige it to give commercially sensitive information to one of its arch rivals. Lloyds argued that, without the information, it would not be able to progress its offer and so the shareholders of Midland would lose out on an offer from Lloyds. The Panel upheld Lloyds' request. It saw no reason to modify or relax r 20.2. Lloyds was a genuine potential offeror, and it was in the best interests of Midland shareholders that Midland provide the information to Lloyds. It follows that an offeree company should exercise caution when revealing information, even to a preferred offeror.

Two practical points are worthy of note here. First, the potential offeror must specify the information it requires from the offeree company; it cannot simply ask the offeree company to provide everything which it gave to the preferred offeror. Secondly, r 20.2 is usually of use only once the rival bid is public. As many hostile bids are launched as surprise attacks, and all the preparation and due diligence is undertaken in secret, the usefulness of r 20.2 is limited.

Note also that r 20.2 extends to site visits and meetings with the offeree's management. So, if one bidder has met the offeree's directors, the competing offeror should, if it requests this, be given equivalent access.

22.4.5.5 Rule 23: sufficiency of information

Rule 23 relates to the documents which the offeror and the offeree company prepare during an offer. The rule embodies General Principle 2 of the Takeover Code (see **20.5.5** above) and provides that the offeree shareholders must be given sufficient information and advice, in a timely manner, to enable them to reach a properly informed decision as to the merits or demerits of the offer, and that no relevant information should be withheld from those shareholders.

Rule 27.1 sets out specific matters which must be updated, including irrevocable undertakings and letters of intent, interests and dealings in shares and changes to directors' service contracts.

22.4.5.6 Bid documentation rules

As detailed at **20.5.7.2**, the failure to comply with the bid documentation rules in Appendix 6 to the Takeover Code is a criminal offence punishable by a fine.

22.4.6 Consideration

In certain circumstances the Takeover Code will dictate the level and type of consideration which must be offered (see **21.8.10.4** above).

22.4.7 Conditions of the offer

The offeror will make the offer subject to certain conditions. The r 2.7 announcement and the offer document will set out the detailed terms of these conditions. If the conditions are not fulfilled, the offer will lapse, unless the offeror can waive the conditions.

There will always be a condition as to the number of offeree company shares which the offeror must acquire in order for the offer to succeed (the 'acceptance condition'; see **22.4.7.1** below), but usually there will be other conditions too. The Takeover Code regulates the conditions which the offeror can impose. Rule 13 provides that the offer must not normally be subject to conditions which depend solely on subjective judgements by the directors of the offeror, or the fulfilment of which is in their hands.

The most common conditions which may be attached to an offer are set out at **22.4.7.1** to **22.4.7.7** below. Note, however, that if the offeror seeks to rely on the non-fulfilment of a condition as justification for lapsing the offer, and invoke that condition, it must consult the Panel (Panel Statement 1999/14). In particular, it must satisfy the Panel that the issue in question could not have been discovered through the due diligence exercise carried out before the offer was announced (if the offer was recommended) and that the issue is genuinely material to the offeror. The exception to this rule is if the offer will lapse because any of the conditions referred to at **22.4.7.1**, **22.4.7.4** or, in practice, **22.4.7.2** below are not fulfilled.

Usually, the offeror will reserve the right to waive conditions (other than those set out at **22.4.7.2** and **22.4.7.3** below, which, in practice, must be fulfilled), and the acceptance condition cannot be waived in its entirety; see **22.4.7.1**). This means that the offeror can choose to declare an offer unconditional despite certain conditions not being fulfilled, if it so chooses.

22.4.7.1 Acceptance

This is a key condition which must reflect r 10 of the Takeover Code. Rule 10 provides that the offeror must have acquired, or agreed to acquire, shares carrying over 50% of the voting rights in the offeree company. Once the offeror has acquired such shares it can declare the offer 'unconditional as to acceptances'. In other words, it has won legal control of the offeree company.

However, in practice, the offer condition is usually drafted so that it will be fulfilled only if the offeror acquires 90% of the shares to which the offer relates. This is to enable the offeror to acquire the remaining 10% of shares by invoking s 979 of the CA 2006 (see **22.7** below). Typically the offeror will not want to be left with troublesome minority shareholders whom it is not entitled to buy out.

Usually the condition will specify that the offeror can waive the condition at a level of acceptances below 90% (but not 50% or below as this would breach the minimum acceptance requirement of r 10).

As explained at **22.5.5.1**, until the offer is declared unconditional as to acceptances, shareholders who have already accepted the offer can withdraw their acceptances (typically from Day 42 of the offer). However, once the offer is declared unconditional as to acceptances, such shareholders are bound by their acceptances, subject to the fulfilment of any other conditions to which the offer is subject.

22.4.7.2 Admission of consideration shares to listing and trading

If the offeror is issuing shares of a class which is already listed as consideration then, as explained at **17.4.3** above, in order to:

(a)   comply with the requirements of the Listing Rules; and

(b)   give value to the shares,

these shares must be admitted to listing on the Official List and to trading on the Main Market.

In this case a condition will be included which states that the offer will become wholly unconditional only once the consideration shares are effectively admitted to listing and to trading. In April 2011, the City of London Law Society agreed standard wording for this condition with the UKLA. It may be found on the Society's website at www.citysolicitors.org.

A similar condition is also required if the offeror is issuing shares in order to raise cash consideration for the offer (see r 13.4).

22.4.7.3   Offeror shareholder approval

If the takeover is a Class 1 transaction then the Listing Rules require the transaction to be approved by the offeror shareholders (see **Chapter 19**). In addition, the offeror shareholders may need to authorise the increase of share capital and the issue of shares (if the offeror is offering its shares as consideration). Again, if the offeror is issuing shares to raise cash consideration, then it will need to include a condition regarding any required shareholder approval, relating to issues such as increasing the share capital, issuing the shares and/or disapplying pre-emption rights (r 13.4).

It is usual for the offer to be conditional upon the passing at a GM of the offeror of all resolutions that are necessary to implement the offer.

22.4.7.4   Merger control clearance

Rule 12.1(c) of the Takeover Code allows an offeror to make the offer conditional on a decision being made that there will be no reference to the Competition Commission (see **23.4.3**), or, in the case of a takeover which falls within the scope of the EC Merger Regulation, that the European Commission will clear the offer within Phase I (see **23.3**). (Rule 12.1 of the Takeover Code also provides that it must be a *term* of the offer that it will lapse if the Competition Commission or the European Commission take certain action in relation to the offer – see **23.2.1**.) While the offeror can waive any condition relating to merger control, and proceed without clearance from the relevant UK or EU competition authority, it cannot waive the term imposed by r 12.1.

Note that the Competition Commission will be replaced by the Competition and Markets Authority (CMA) on 1 April 2014.

22.4.7.5   Authorisations

This condition states that all authorisations for carrying on the business of the offeree company and other offeree group companies are in full force and effect.

22.4.7.6   Material litigation

This condition provides that no material litigation or arbitration proceedings have been instituted or threatened against the offeree group.

22.4.7.7   Material adverse change

This condition (the 'MAC condition') states that there are no material adverse changes in the offeree company's financial or trading position, other than those which the offeree has already disclosed. In 2001, the Panel refused to allow an offeror, WPP, to invoke its MAC condition on the basis that a material adverse change had taken place in the prospects of the offeree company, Tempus, after the announcement of WPP's offer on 10 September 2001 and, in particular, following the terrorist attacks in the US on 11 September 2001. The Panel stated that a change in economic, industrial or political circumstances will not normally justify the withdrawal of an announced offer.

22.4.8   Frustrating action

This is relevant only in connection with a hostile bid. If an offeree company receives an unwelcome takeover offer, the directors may be tempted to frustrate the offer by taking some action which will make the offeree company more difficult to acquire, or less attractive to the offeror. Rule 21 expands General Principle 3 of the Takeover Code (see **20.5.5** above) by providing that directors of an offeree company cannot undertake frustrating action without the approval of the offeree company shareholders. Remember that an offer which may be unwelcome from the offeree company board's point of view may be very welcome from the offeree company shareholders' perspective. Account must also be taken of the offeree company's directors' statutory duties.

A non-exhaustive list of frustrating actions is set out in r 21.1(b). It includes:

(a)   the issue of, or granting of options over, unissued shares;

(b)   the sale, disposal or acquisition of assets; and

(c)   the entering into of contracts other than in the ordinary course of business (such as amending a director's service contract to improve his terms without justification).

22.4.9   Poison pills

A poison pill is a general term used to describe defensive measures a company may take even before a bid is imminent (when the Takeover Code rules on frustrating action described at **22.4.8** do not apply). An example of a poison pill is drafting change of control clauses into key agreements (for example, Marks & Spencer Group plc inserting a clause into its contracts with suppliers of all socks and underwear that such contracts would terminate if anyone made a takeover offer for Marks & Spencer Group plc, thus leaving an offeror potentially with a much less valuable offeree company). These are common in the UK, but in practice do not tend to pose too much of a deterrent to a hostile offeror (who may have its own contacts with whom to contract, or indeed have good relations with the party subject to the change of control clause in any event).

When considering whether to adopt a poison pill, the board must take care not to breach its fiduciary duty to the company. *Criterion Properties plc v Stratford Properties UK plc and Others* [2004] UKHL 28 provides some guidance on this issue. In that case, Criterion Properties plc ('Criterion') had entered into a joint venture agreement with Stratford Properties UK plc ('Oaktree') under which Oaktree had a put option, namely the option to require Criterion to purchase Oaktree's shares, in the event that there was a change of control of Criterion, or if two named directors left the Criterion board. The purchase price was so high that it guaranteed Oaktree a minimum return of 25% pa on the investment. Obviously, the effect of the change of control clause was to deter any potential offeror from making an offer for Criterion. Criterion applied to the court to set aside the agreement.

The House of Lords found that the case turned on whether the Criterion directors had authority to enter into the contract. If the directors had actual or apparent authority, the agreement would be valid. If they did not, the court discussed whether the directors had ostensible authority. The court noted that this issue raised a question of considerable public importance, namely whether the directors of a public company have the power to authorise the signing of a poison pill agreement intended to deter third parties from making offers to purchase the company's shares and, in particular, whether they had authority to do so when the deterrent consisted of divesting of some of the company's assets.

Unfortunately, the court of first instance and the Court of Appeal had not considered the issue of authority, and so the House of Lords could not resolve the issue further; however, the case contains some useful commentary on poison pills.

22.4.9.1   Breakthrough provisions

Article 11 of the Takeovers Directive (see **20.3**) sets out what it refers to as 'breakthrough provisions'. These provisions provide that, on a takeover, the offeror can override some poison pills in certain circumstances. Article 11 specifies the types of poison pill which can be overridden. It includes restrictions on transferring shares which are contained in the company's articles or contracts, and restrictions on voting rights.

However, the breakthrough provisions proved so controversial that art 12 of the Directive permits Member States to opt out of art 11. In the event that a Member State does opt out, however, the Directive provides that companies must be able to opt back into (and, if required subsequently, back out of) the breakthrough provisions if they so choose.

In the UK, the Government has opted out of art 11. It prefers to leave to shareholders the decision on whether to have enforceable poison pills. Under s 966 of the CA 2006 a UK company must opt into (and, if required, then opt to back out of) the breakthrough procedures.

In order to opt in, the company must, under s 966(1) of the CA 2006, pass a special resolution, and fulfil the following conditions:

(a) the company must have voting shares admitted to trading on a regulated market (see **20.3.1**) (that is, it must be a potential offeree company in a takeover to which the Directive applies (see **20.3**)) (s 966(2));

(b) the company's articles of association must not contain (s 966(3)):

   (i) any of the restrictions on share transfer or voting rights which are listed in art 11 (or if they do, they must fall away in the same circumstances as they would under the breakthrough provisions); or

   (ii) any other provisions that would be incompatible with art 11 of the Directive; and

(c) no shares conferring special rights in the company can be held by a Government minister, his nominees or any company he directly or indirectly owns or controls (s 966(4)).

Under s 970(1) and (2) of the CA 2006 the company must notify the Panel of any special resolution passed to opt in to (or subsequently opt out of) the breakthrough provisions, within 15 days after the passing of that resolution. Section 968 sets out the consequences of opting in, and in particular which poison pills will be invalid.

22.5 ACCEPTING THE OFFER

Once the offer documents and any defence documents have been published, the fate of the offer will be determined by whether the offeree shareholders choose to accept it.

22.5.1 Method of acceptance

The offeree company shareholders accept the offer by completing the forms of acceptance (referred to at **22.4.3**) and returning them to the company's registrars, who will then count the votes (as explained at **21.5.6**).

22.5.2 First closing date

Most forms of acceptance will urge shareholders to vote by a specified time and date, known as the 'first closing date'. Rule 31.1 provides that the offer must be open for a minimum of 21 days from the date the offeror publishes the offer document. The offeror will be keen to complete the takeover as soon as possible, and therefore the first closing date is usually the 21st day following the publishing of the offer document, but it can be a longer period. Most offers are extended beyond the first closing date, but the offeror could use the acceptance condition to lapse the offer at this date if it no longer wished to proceed.

Institutional shareholders may delay casting their votes, to see if anything happens to change their decision to vote for or against the offer (such as a rival offeror announcing a better offer, or a dramatic change in market conditions).

22.5.3 Announcing the level of acceptances

Rule 17.1 provides that the offeror must announce the level of acceptances by 8.00 am on the business day after the first closing date.

If the bid is recommended, the offeror will expect to be able to declare the offer unconditional as to acceptances on the first closing date. However, if the offer is hostile, the offeror is unlikely to have received the required level of acceptances (see **22.4.7.1** above), as shareholders may wait to see if the offeror will improve the offer, or whether another rival offer will be made.

The level of acceptances must also be announced, under r 17.1, after any further closing date and after any extension or revision of the offer (see **22.5.4**).

22.5.4 Extending and revising the offer

If the conditions of the offer, including the condition as to acceptances, have not been met by the first closing date, the offeror can withdraw the offer. Rule 31.3 provides that the offeror is not obliged to extend the offer. However, usually the offeror will extend the offer in the hope that it will eventually receive a sufficient level of acceptances. The offeror may also improve the terms of the offer. Typically the offeror will announce the extension or revision of the offer at the same time that it announces the level of acceptances.

If the offeror does decide to revise its offer, it must do as it did with the original offer (see **22.4.1.3**), namely:

(a) send a revised offer document to the offeree company shareholders and persons with information rights under s 146 of the CA 2006. This must comply with the content requirements of r 24, and also with r 27, which provides that any documents sent to shareholders after the offer document must contain details of any material changes to the documents published previously during the offer period (or state that there are no such changes) (r 32.1(a));

(b) publish the revised offer document on a website, in accordance with r 30.4, on the date it publishes the document to offeree company shareholders (r 32.1(a));

(c) announce to an RIS, in accordance with r 2.9, that it has published the document on the website (r 32.1(a));

(d) make the document available to its employee representatives, and if there are none, to its employees and to the trustees of its pension scheme (the offeree company must also do this) (r 32.1(b)); and

(e) send the document to the Panel and to the advisers to all other parties to the offer electronically and in hard copy (r 30.3(b)).

As mentioned at **22.4.1.3** above, Note 3 on r 30.4 extends the obligation in relation to sending documents to shareholders outside the EEA unless there is an objectively good reason not to.

Rule 32.1(c) provides that the revised offer must be open for at least 14 days following the publishing of the revised document. The effect of this requirement, together with the final day rule, referred to at **22.5.7** below, is that the offer cannot be revised after the 46th day following the publishing of the announcement of the original offer document. Usually this is relevant only on a hostile takeover.

Rule 32.3 provides that any shareholder who accepted the original offer is entitled to receive the revised consideration.

In the event of a revised offer in a hostile offer, the offeree company must do as it did with the defence document (see **22.4.2.3**), namely:

(a) send a circular to its shareholders and persons with information rights under s 146 of the CA 2006 setting out its views on the revised offer, as required by r 25.1(a), drawn up in accordance with rr 25 and 27 (see **22.5.4(a)**) (r 32.6(a)). The offeree company must append to the circular an opinion from its employee representatives on the effects of the offer on employment (provided the representatives provide the opinion in good time) (r 32.6(b));

(b)   publish the circular on a website, in accordance with r 30.4, on the date it sends the document to offeree company shareholders (r 32.6(a));

(c)   announce to an RIS, in accordance with r 2.9, that it has published the circular on the website (r 32.6(a));

(d)   make the circular available to its employee representatives, and if there are none, to its employees and to the trustees of its pension scheme (r 32.6(b)); and

(e)   send the document to the Panel and to the advisers to all other parties to the offer electronically and in hard copy (r 30.3(b)).

Again, Note 3 on r 30.4 extends the obligation in relation to sending documents to shareholders outside the EEA unless there is an objectively good reason not to.

22.5.5   The right of withdrawal

22.5.5.1   Withdrawal rights under the Takeover Code

Any shareholder who has accepted the offer can change his mind and withdraw that acceptance at any time after the date which is 21 days after the first closing date (so, usually, any time after the 42nd day following the announcement of the offer) until the date the offer has become, or is declared, unconditional as to acceptances.

This is why so much importance is attached to the offer becoming or being declared unconditional; once this has happened, shareholders who have accepted the offer are bound by this acceptance, and cannot withdraw.

In a hostile offer, the offeree company will send withdrawal forms to its shareholders to encourage them to take advantage of these rights.

22.5.5.2   Withdrawal rights under the FSMA 2000

We have just noted that, under the Takeover Code, usually withdrawal rights cease to be available after an offer has become or has been declared unconditional. As explained at **6.9.4** above, however, s 87Q of the FSMA 2000 provides that investors have the right to withdraw their acceptances during the two days following publication of any supplementary prospectus (referred to as a 'statutory withdrawal period'). So what happens if a takeover is made by way of share-for-share exchange, and a supplementary prospectus is required? Can withdrawal rights arise under the FSMA 2000 after the offer has become or has been declared unconditional, meaning that the offeror's acceptance level could drop below 50%? Neither the FSMA 2000 nor the Takeover Code is clear on this point. The Panel has addressed this issue in Panel Statement 2005/29. It states that it has received legal advice that the new FSMA 2000 provisions can be interpreted as meaning:

(a)   that the period for withdrawal by an acceptor of an offer ends once the offer has become or has been declared wholly unconditional and the relevant securities have been unconditionally allotted (that is, wholly unconditional bids, where the unconditional allotments of securities have been made, could not be reopened through the exercise of withdrawal rights); and

(b)   that the withdrawal rights under the FSMA 2000 will not arise if a share-for-share offer is made by way of an 'equivalent document' (see **22.4.4.2**) rather than a prospectus.

The FCA confirmed, in its Technical Note UKLA/TN/605.1 Supplementary prospectuses, that it agrees with this view. Until the courts ultimately decide this matter, practically it is prudent for the offeror to make use of the Panel Statement and either:

(i) make the offer by way of an equivalent document rather than a prospectus (but see **22.4.4.2** for the disadvantages in this approach); or

(ii) take steps to avoid becoming or being declared unconditional as to acceptances when a statutory withdrawal period is running, or when there is a possibility that a supplementary prospectus may be required (possibly by organising matters so that the offer becomes wholly unconditional at the same time the offer becomes or is declared unconditional as to acceptances, which is already common practice); and/or

(iii) include an extra condition to the offer which it can invoke should the exercise of withdrawal rights under the FSMA 2000 result in acceptance levels dropping below 50% after the offer has become or been declared unconditional as to acceptances.

22.5.6 Day 39

Rule 31.9 provides that the offeree company should not, without the consent of the Panel, announce any material new information after the 39th day following the publication of the initial offer document. If any relevant competition authority has not given its decision by this time, the Panel will usually grant permission to extend the deadline until the second day after the decision is announced.

22.5.7 Day 60: the final day rule

For reasons of the offeree's stability (and the advisers' sanity), the takeover process is not allowed to continue indefinitely. Rule 31.6 provides that, except with the consent of the Panel, the offer will lapse if the offeror cannot declare the offer unconditional as to acceptances by midnight on the 60th day after the initial offer document was published. The circumstances when the Panel will grant consent to an extension of this period are set out in r 31.6(a)(i) to (v). For example, if a competing offeror launches a bid for the offeree company, the timetables for both offers will be co-ordinated and run from the publication of the competing offeror's offer document, which will inevitably lead to an extension of Day 60 for the original offer.

22.5.8 Day 74: earliest date the offer can close

Rule 31.4 provides that, after the offer has become or been declared unconditional as to acceptances, it must still remain open for further acceptances for at least 14 days after the current closing date. As explained at **22.5.7**, the latest closing date will tend to be Day 60, and so, if this is the case, the earliest date the offer can close will be Day 74.

Rule 31.2 provides that if the offer remains open for acceptances beyond Day 70, the offeror must give at least 14 days' written notice to all offeree company shareholders who have not accepted the offer.

In practice, typically the offeror keeps the offer open until further notice, and then runs the offer in parallel to the compulsory acquisition procedure (see **22.7**).

22.5.9 Day 81: last date to fulfil other conditions

Rule 31.7 provides that, except with the consent of the Panel, the other conditions of the offer must be fulfilled or waived within 21 days of either the first closing date, or the date on which the offer becomes unconditional as to acceptances (whichever is the later), otherwise the offer will lapse.

The Panel's consent to the extension of this period will be granted only if the outstanding condition involves a material official authorisation or regulatory clearance relating to the offer, and it has been impossible to obtain an extension under r 31.6.

The effect of r 31.6 and r 31.7 is that the latest date on which the other conditions may be satisfied is the 81st day after the publication of the initial offer document. However, in practice most offers are declared wholly unconditional at the same time they are declared unconditional as to acceptances.

22.6   SUCCESS OR FAILURE?

22.6.1   The failed offer

22.6.1.1   The 12-month restriction

If the offeror withdraws the offer, or the offer lapses, r 35.1 of the Takeover Code provides that, without the consent of the Panel, neither the offeror nor any concert parties (see **22.6.1.2**) can:

(a)   make another offer for the offeree company;

(b)   acquire any interest in shares in the offeree which would trigger a r 9 mandatory bid (see **21.8.10.3** above);

(c)   acquire any interest in, or procure an irrevocable undertaking (see **21.10**) in respect of, shares in the offeree company which, when aggregated with the shares of other concert parties, would carry 30% or more of the voting rights in the offeree company;

(d)   make any statement which raises or confirms the possibility that an offer might be made for the offeree company; or

(e)   take any steps to prepare a possible offer for the offeree company where knowledge of the possible offer might extend beyond the offeror and its immediate advisers,

for at least 12 months from the date the offer is withdrawn or lapses. The rationale for this rule is to promote certainty in the market and avoid companies becoming embroiled in an endless takeover battle (as reflected in General Principle 6). Note that the requirements to 'down tools' mirror those that apply following a r 2.8 statement (see **22.3.3.3**), albeit for a longer period.

The note to r 35.1 of the Takeover Code sets out the usual circumstances when the Panel will waive the 12-month restriction imposed by r 35.1 These include:

(a)   if the offeror wants to announce a new offer which is recommended;

(b)   if the offeror wants to announce a new offer to compete with another offer;

(c)   if the original offer lapsed in accordance with r 12.2 (see **23.2.1**) and the offeror wants to announce a new offer following competition clearance; or

(d)   if there has been a material change of circumstances.

22.6.1.2   Acting in concert

The Takeover Code defines 'persons acting in concert' as persons:

> who, pursuant to an agreement or understanding (whether formal or informal), co-operate to obtain or consolidate control of a company or to frustrate the successful outcome of an offer for a company.

Affiliated persons (such as a majority shareholder; see Note 2 to the definition) are deemed to be acting in concert with each other.

Certain persons, such as directors and other companies in the same group, are presumed to be acting in concert unless the contrary is established.

22.6.1.3   Restrictions on dealings

If an offer has lapsed which was one of two or more competing offers, then, until the other competing offer(s) have also lapsed, or become wholly unconditional, r 35.4 prevents the failed offeror from acquiring any interest in shares of the offeree company on terms more favourable than under its lapsed offer.

22.6.2   The successful bid

Once the offer is declared wholly unconditional, the offeror can breathe a sigh of relief: the takeover has been successful. However, r 31.4 of the Takeover Code provides that the offer must still remain open for acceptance for not less than 14 days. This affords offeree company shareholders, who did not accept the offer before the offer was declared unconditional as to acceptances, an opportunity to accept the offer once the offeror has acquired control of the offeree.

Ideally, an offeror will want to acquire 100% of the offeree company's shares, to avoid being left to cope with unfriendly minority shareholders (see **22.7.1**). If the offeror has received acceptances in respect of at least 90% of the shares to which the offer relates, it can compel the other offeree company shareholders to sell their shares to the offeror using the compulsory acquisition procedure under s 979 of the CA 2006 (see **22.7** below). However, if the offeror cannot invoke the compulsory acquisition procedure, it must abide with the minority shareholders who rejected the offer. After six months following the closure of the original offer, however, the offeror may be able to buy the shares of this minority by offering them more favourable terms than those of the original offer.

22.7 BUYING OUT MINORITY SHAREHOLDERS

22.7.1 The problem with minority shareholders

The typical offeror will not want to become the majority shareholder of the offeree company alongside minority shareholders who did not accept the offer. Minority shareholders can be problematic for various reasons, including their ability to disrupt GMs and create bad publicity for the company. The presence of a minority can also prevent the company from carrying out its day to day business effectively (for example, the minority may be able to block special resolutions if they hold more than 25% of the company's shares, or prevent a GM from being held on short notice if they hold more than 5%).

The minority shareholders, too, may be less than happy to find themselves holding a minority stake in a company which is controlled by the offeror. In particular, if the offeror decides to take the company private after the takeover, the minority may struggle to find a market for their shares in order to exit from the company.

For the reasons outlined above, once the majority of shareholders have accepted the offer, ss 979 and 983 of the CA 2006 give a statutory right respectively:

(a)   to the offeror, to buy out the minority shareholders, and so acquire 100% of the offeree company (referred to as a 'squeeze-out' right); and

(b)   to each minority shareholder who has refused the takeover offer, to require the offeror to purchase his shares (referred to as a 'sell-out' right).

22.7.2 The right of the offeror to buy out minority shareholders ('squeeze-out')

22.7.2.1 The conditions

Two conditions must be satisfied before the offeror can invoke the compulsory acquisition provisions:

(a)   the takeover offer condition; and

(b)   the 90% squeeze-out threshold condition.

The takeover offer condition

There must be a 'takeover offer', which is defined by s 974 of the CA 2006 as:

(a)   an offer to acquire all the shares in the offeree company (or, where there is more than one class of shares, all the shares of one or more classes) other than the offeree company shares already held by the offeror, or contracted to be acquired by it; and

(b)   where the terms of the offer are the same in relation to all the shares to which the offer relates.

Note that, in relation to overseas shareholders, under s 978 of the CA 2006 the offer can constitute a 'takeover offer' for the purposes of the CA 2006 even if the offer is not communicated to an overseas shareholder, provided:

(a)   the shareholder does not have a registered UK address;

(b)   the offer is not made to the shareholder in order to avoid contravening the law of an overseas territory; and

(c)   the offer is either:

(i)   published in the *Gazette*; or

(ii)   available for inspection at, or can be obtained from, a place in an EEA State, or a website, and notice of this is published in the *Gazette*.

The 90% squeeze-out threshold condition

The rules differ according to whether the offer falls within the Takeovers Directive or not. Only the position under the Takeovers Directive has been considered (see **20.3**).

Under s 979 of the CA 2006 the offeror must have acquired or unconditionally contracted to acquire, by virtue of acceptances of the offer, not less than 90% in value of all the shares *to which the offer relates* and, where the shares to which the offer relates are voting shares, not less than 90% of the voting rights carried by those shares (or, if the offer is for more than one class of share, not less than 90% in value and, where voting shares, not less than 90% of voting rights, for any of the classes to which the offer relates). Note that under s 974(2) of the CA 2006 any shares acquired by the offeror or its concert parties *before* the offer document was published do not count towards the 90% threshold, but any shares acquired *after* the document was published will count towards the threshold (CA 2006, s 979(8)–(10)).

For example, if the offeror already owned 25% of the offeree company's shares before the offer document was published, the offer relates to only 75% of the offeree company's share capital. The offeror must, therefore, secure acceptances in respect of 90% (in both value and voting rights) of this 75%.

Under s 975(2) of the CA 2006, shares which are the subject of irrevocable undertakings (see **21.10**) as at the date of the offer (which is the date the offer document is published) do count towards the 90% threshold. Shares which the offeror's concert parties hold or have contracted to acquire as at the date of the offer (CA 2006, s 975(4)) do not count towards the 90% threshold.

Section 986(9) of the CA 2006 provides that the offeror can apply to the court for an order which allows it to serve a squeeze-out notice (see **22.7.2.2**) even though it has not acquired the 90% threshold, if it can prove that:

(a)   after reasonable enquiry the offeror has been unable to trace one or more of the persons holding shares to which the offer relates;

(b)   if account were taken of the shares of these missing persons, the 90% threshold would be reached; and

(c)   the consideration offered is fair and reasonable.

However, the court will make such an order only if it considers it just and equitable to do so, having regard to the number of shareholders who have been traced but who have rejected the offer.

22.7.2.2   The squeeze-out notice

Provided the offeror has acquired or unconditionally contracted to acquire 90% of the shares to which the offer relates and 90% of the voting rights before the expiry of three months after the last day on which the offer can be accepted, the offeror can give notice to those offeree company shareholders who did not accept the offer that it wishes to acquire their shares by the deadline just mentioned.

The squeeze-out notice under s 981 of the CA 2006 entitles, and also obliges, the offeror to acquire the offeree company shareholder's shares on the same terms as those of the takeover offer. For example, if the offer gave shareholders a choice of paper or cash consideration, the same choice must be given to shareholders who did not accept the offer. However, there are some exceptions, for example for certain overseas shareholders. Also, where a cash alternative was due to be provided by a third party who can no longer provide it (eg, through a vendor placing), the offeror must pay a cash equivalent to the offeree shareholder.

The notice must make clear:

(a) that the shareholder must make his choice of consideration known to the offeror, in writing, within six weeks of the notice; and

(b) the default consideration that the shareholder will receive if he does not make his choice known to the offeror.

The offeror must copy the first notice (they are usually distributed in the order they appear on the register of members) to the board of offeree company, together with a statutory declaration that the conditions referred to at **22.7.2.1** above have been satisfied.

22.7.2.3 The acquisition

Six weeks after serving the notice (CA 2006, s 981(6) and (7)) the offeror must send to the offeree:

(a) a copy of all the squeeze-out notices;

(b) a stock transfer form executed by a person the offeror nominates on behalf of the shareholder; and

(c) the consideration for the shares.

The offeree will then:

(a) register the offeror as the holder of the shares to which the s 979 notice relates (s 981(7)); and

(b) hold the consideration on trust for the relevant shareholders (s 981(9)).

Section 982(4) and (5) provide what should happen on the rare occurrence that a shareholder cannot be traced.

22.7.2.4 Preventing the acquisition

Section 986(1) of the CA 2006 provides that any shareholder who receives a s 979 notice can apply to the court, within six weeks of the date on which the notice was given, for an order preventing the acquisition or allowing the acquisition on such terms as the court thinks fit (ie on different terms). However, the courts are unlikely to be willing to investigate the merits of an offer which has already been endorsed by at least 90% of shareholders, unless there is a compelling reason to do so.

22.7.3 The right of minority shareholders to be bought out ('sell-out')

Section 983 of the CA 2006 provides a mechanism whereby an offeree company shareholder who has refused the takeover offer may be able to 'sell out', that is, force the offeror to purchase his shares.

22.7.3.1 The conditions

Two conditions must be satisfied before an offeree company shareholder can require the offeror to take his shares:

(a)   the takeover offer condition; and

(b)   the 90% sell-out threshold condition.

The takeover offer condition

This condition is the same as for squeeze out (see **22.7.2.1**).

The 90% sell-out threshold condition

A shareholder can compel the offeror to buy his shares only when the offeror has obtained an interest in 90% in value carrying 90% of the voting rights of *all the shares in the offeree company* (or the class of shares to which the shares of the minority shareholder belong). Note that the 90% sell-out threshold is different to the 90% squeeze-out threshold (see **22.7.2.1**). For squeeze-out purposes, only shares *to which the offer relates* are included. For sell-out, *all shares* in the offeree are included. Shares held by the offeror before the offer document was published will count, therefore, towards the 90% sell-out threshold but not towards the 90% squeeze-out threshold (as they would not be shares to which the offer relates). Irrevocable undertakings and shares held by any associate of the offeror also count towards the sell-out threshold.

The effect of this difference is that the offeror may meet the 90% sell-out threshold before it meets the 90% squeeze-out threshold.

> **EXAMPLE**
>
> Imagine that the offeror acquired a 25% stake in the offeree before it published the offer document. For squeeze-out, the offeror must acquire 90% of the remaining 75%, which will be triggered once the offeror has acquired an aggregate of 92.5% (90% x 75% + the existing 25%). For sell-out, the offeror must acquire only 90%, and the 25% already acquired will count towards this.

22.7.3.2   The sell-out notice

The average shareholder of an offeree company is unlikely to be aware of his sell-out rights. Therefore, within one month of reaching the 90% threshold, the offeror must notify those shareholders who have not accepted the offer of their sell-out rights (under CA 2006, s 984(3)). If the sell-out notice is served before the end of the offer period, it must state that the offer is still open for acceptance.

The offeror must specify the period within which the shareholder can take up his sell-out rights. Under the CA 2006 procedure, they must be exercised within three months from the last date on which the offer could be accepted or, if later, the date on which the offeror serves the sell-out notice.

Of course, if (as is usual) the offeror has already served a squeeze-out notice to acquire the minority shareholders' shares, the offeror does not need to notify the shareholders of their sell-out rights. For this reason, sell-out notices are not common.

If the minority shareholder exercises his sell-out rights, the offeror must acquire those shares on terms which are the same as the terms of the takeover offer, or on such other terms as may be agreed. If the offer included a choice of consideration, the position is similar to that under squeeze-out: if the chosen consideration is not available, the shareholder will receive the cash equivalent. The court has an overriding jurisdiction, on the application of either the shareholder or the offeror, to determine the terms on which the shares will be acquired.

22.7.3.3   The notice from the shareholder

The shareholder must give the offeror written notice of his desire to sell out. If there is a choice of consideration under the offer, the shareholder must state his choice of consideration.

22.8 FUTURE DEVELOPMENTS

The UK Government is undertaking a review of the regulation of takeovers in the UK which may result in changes to how takeovers are conducted (see **21.14** above).

CHAPTER 23

TAKEOVERS: MERGER CONTROL

23.1 INTRODUCTION

It is difficult to define exactly what constitutes a merger, and from a legal perspective the distinction between a takeover and a merger is not particularly important. It follows that the law relating to *merger* control can, in fact, apply to a *takeover*.

Why would the competition authorities be concerned with a takeover? Imagine that a supermarket chain, with a 40% market share, decides to make an offer for the entire issued share capital of one of its rivals, which also has a 40% market share. If the takeover is successful, the result will be a supermarket chain with a substantial share of the market. It will have considerable bargaining power and is likely to be able to source produce on very competitive terms. It is possible that other, smaller supermarket chains might be squeezed out of the market, and that others who wanted to break into the market would not be able to do so. The probable result of all of this is that consumers on their weekly shop will have less choice and may have to pay more. This is why the competition authorities will keep a close eye on any takeover offer.

Practically, the corporate lawyer will enlist the help of his colleagues who specialise in competition law, who will then advise in relation to any merger control issues relevant to the takeover. However, this means that the corporate lawyer must be aware of the merger control rules to know when he should consult such colleagues; and, as always, the corporate lawyer will need to know enough about the process to follow discussions at meetings and to understand the impact it may have on the takeover offer. This chapter aims to introduce the corporate lawyer to the basics of merger control.

23.2 MERGER CONTROL PROVISIONS IN THE TAKEOVER CODE

23.2.1 Rule 12

23.2.1.1 Rule 12.1

Rule 12.1 of the Takeover Code provides that it must be a term of the takeover offer that the offer will lapse if, before the first closing date, or the date the offer becomes or is declared unconditional as to acceptances (see **Chapter 22**), whichever is later:

(a) the offer is referred to the Competition Commission for investigation under the Enterprise Act 2002 (EA 2002) (see **23.4**); or

(b) the offer gives rise to a concentration with a Community dimension within the scope of the EU Merger Regulation (see **23.3**), and the European Commission either:

    (i) commences Phase II proceedings under art 6(1)(c) of the EU Merger Regulation (see **23.3.6**), or

(ii)   refers the matter back to the UK under art 9 of the EU Merger Regulation and there is then a reference to the Competition Commission (see **23.3.7**).

23.2.1.2   Rule 12.2

If the offer, or possible offer, is referred to the Competition Commission, or if the European Commission initiates Phase II proceedings, the offer period will usually end. A new offer period will begin when the 'competition reference period' ends. The competition reference period is defined in the Takeover Code. It covers the period between the date a reference is made, or Phase II proceedings are initiated, and the date the authorities reach a decision on the matter. The rationale for this is due to the fact that the investigation by the relevant competition authorities will usually take a substantial period of time. It would be unreasonable to leave the offeree company subject to the uncertainty of a bid, possibly for many months, which may or may not be permitted once the authorities reach a decision.

Note that the Competition Commission will be replaced by the Competition and Markets Authority (CMA) on 1 April 2014.

23.3   EU MERGER CONTROL

On 1 May 2004 the Regulation on the control of concentrations between undertakings (EU Council Regulation 139/2004) (the 'EU Merger Regulation') came into force.

The EU Merger Regulation will apply if the takeover constitutes a *concentration* with a *Community dimension*. If the takeover fulfils these criteria then, subject to limited exceptions (see **23.3.7** below), the Regulation will apply to the exclusion of any national competition law rules and the takeover will fall within the exclusive jurisdiction of the European Commission. This is intended to relieve the burden on the parties to the takeover, by reducing the number of regulatory authorities to which they are subject. For this reason the Regulation is often referred to as 'the one-stop shop'.

If the takeover does not fulfil these criteria, then it falls outside the scope of the EU Merger Regulation, but it may still be caught by domestic merger control rules (see **23.4**).

23.3.1   Concentration

Article 3 of the EU Merger Regulation provides that a concentration can arise on:

(a)   the merger of two or more independent undertakings;

(b)   the acquisition of direct or indirect control of the whole or part of an undertaking or undertakings; or

(c)   some joint ventures.

This definition reflects the fact that the EU Merger Regulation is drafted to catch more than simply takeovers. It is category (b) which may bring a takeover within the EU Merger Regulation. Note, however, that (b) can also can also catch acquisitions which do not constitute a takeover, for example the acquisition of assets.

'Control' in the context of the EU Merger Regulation is wider than the definition of 'control' in the Takeover Code. In this context, 'control' means more than just voting control. It includes, for example, where one party can exercise 'decisive influence' (art 3). An 18% shareholding was considered insufficient to confer control (EDF/AEM/Edison Case COMP/M.3729), whereas in Aker Maritime/Kvaerner Case COMP/M.2117 a 26.7% share constituted control for the purposes of the EU Merger Regulation.

23.3.2   Community dimension

Article 1 provides that a concentration will have a Community dimension if, subject to the two-thirds rule (see **23.3.3** below), it fulfils certain turnover criteria. There are two alternative sets of criteria, namely:

(a)   the aggregate *worldwide* turnover of *all* parties exceeds €5,000m (approx £4,250m); and

(b)   the aggregate *Community-wide* turnover of *at least two* of the parties exceeds €250m (approx £215m);

or

(a)   the aggregate *worldwide* turnover of *all* parties exceeds €2,500m (approx £2,125m);

(b)   the aggregate *Community-wide* turnover of *at least two* of the parties exceeds €100m (approx £85m); and

(c)   in at least three Member States:

   (i)   the aggregate *national* turnover of *all* the parties exceeds €100m (approx £85m), and

   (ii)   the aggregate *national* turnover of *at least two* of the parties exceeds €25m (approx £21m).

Even if the takeover does not have a Community dimension, art 4, para 5 of the EU Merger Regulation provides that, if the takeover is capable of being reviewed under the national competition laws of at least three Member States, the parties can request the European Commission to take jurisdiction over the offer instead of the national authorities.

23.3.3   The two-thirds rule

A concentration will not have a Community dimension if each of the parties achieves more than two-thirds of its Community-wide turnover within the same Member State. This means, practically, that if the main impact of the takeover is within one Member State, it will not have a Community dimension. It could, of course, still be caught by the national competition rules of that Member State.

Practically, when calculating whether a takeover falls within the jurisdiction of the Commission, it is helpful to check whether the two-thirds rule applies *before* applying the 'Community dimension' test referred to at **23.3.2** above. If the two-thirds rule applies then there is no need to apply the 'Community dimension' test; the Commission will not have jurisdiction.

23.3.4   Notification

If the takeover constitutes a concentration with a Community dimension then the EU Merger Regulation provides that the parties must notify the European Commission before completion. The takeover cannot complete until the European Commission clears it. The notification should answer the Commission's questionnaire, Form CO, which requires considerable information about the parties and the transaction. Form CO is annexed to Regulation 802/2004/EC, which implemented the EU Merger Regulation.

23.3.5   Phase I

Article 10 provides that the Commission has 25 working days from the date of notification to decide that it:

(a)   does not have jurisdiction because the offer does not fall within the scope of the EU Merger Regulation;

(b)   will clear the offer (because it does not create or strengthen a dominant position in any relevant Community market);

(c)   will allow the offer to proceed, subject to conditions (for example, the parties agreeing to dispose of part of the business);

(d)   will investigate the offer further (because it has serious doubts whether it creates or strengthen a dominant position in any relevant Community market); or

(e)   will refer the offer back to a Member State under art 9 (because the offer threatens to affect significantly competition in a distinct market within that Member State; see **23.3.7**).

This period of 25 days is referred to as Phase I. Phase I can be extended to 35 working days in certain circumstances, such as where remedies are offered, or where a Member State makes a request for an art 9 reference (see **23.3.7** below).

If the Commission decides (d) above, and commences a Phase II investigation, or decides (e) above, and refers the offer back to the OFT and there is then a subsequent reference to the Competition Commission, the takeover offer will lapse under r 12.1 of the Takeover Code (see **23.2.1.1(b)**).

Note that the Competition Commission will be replaced by the Competition and Markets Authority (CMA) on 1 April 2014.

23.3.6   Phase II

If, at the end of Phase I, the Commission decides to investigate the offer further (option (d) above), that period of investigation is referred to as Phase II. As explained at **23.2.1**, if the European Commission initiates Phase II proceedings, the offer period will end. Phase II can last up to 90 working days. It can be extended by 20 working days at the request of the parties or the Commission (if the parties so consent). Phase II will automatically be extended by 15 working days where the parties offer remedies after the 54th day of the Phase II investigation.

At the end of Phase II, the Commission can:

(a)   clear the takeover; or

(b)   allow the takeover to proceed subject to certain conditions; or

(c)   block the takeover.

23.3.7   Exceptions

As **23.3** explains, the EU Merger Regulation is intended to be a 'one-stop shop' and applies to the exclusion of any national competition laws. However, a Member State can intervene to request repatriation of a case if it can demonstrate to the Commission that a reference back to the national authorities is necessary:

(a)   to protect legitimate interests (such as national security) (art 21); or

(b)   because the takeover threatens to affect significantly competition in a distinct market within that Member State (art 9).

For an example of (a), Spain imposed conditions on E.ON's and Enel and Acciona's bids for Endesa, the Spanish energy company, even though the European Commission had cleared both bids, arguing that it was necessary to protect Spain's national interests. The ECJ ruled that Spain had broken EU law by not withdrawing conditions on E.ON's bid (*Commission v Spain* (E.ON/Endesa) Case C-196/07). Separately, Poland launched infringement proceedings against the European Commission claiming that it had failed to take account of its interests in clearing the Unicredito/HVB merger (Case COMP/M.3894).

For an example of (b), in 1996, under the original EU Merger Regulation, the European Commission granted the UK's request for an art 9 reference with regard to the offer by a German pharmaceuticals company for Lloyds Chemists.

23.4   UK MERGER CONTROL

The EA 2002 governs merger control in the UK. The merger control provisions of the EA 2002 will apply to a takeover if:

(a)   it is a *relevant merger situation*; and

(b)   it results, or may be expected to result, in a *substantial lessening of competition*.

23.4.1   Relevant merger situation

A takeover will constitute a 'relevant merger situation' if:

(a)   it is not caught by the EU Merger Regulation (see **23.3** above);

(b)   two or more enterprises cease to be distinct;

(c)   the time limit for a reference to the Competition Commission has not yet expired; and

(d)   either:

   (i)   the turnover test, or

   (ii)   the share of supply test,

   is fulfilled.

Note that the Competition Commission will be replaced by the Competition and Markets Authority (CMA) on 1 April 2014.

Let us now consider each criterion in turn.

23.4.1.1   Not caught by the EU Merger Regulation

As stated at **23.3** above, if the takeover constitutes a *concentration* with a *Community dimension* then, subject to limited exceptions (see **23.3.7** above), the Regulation will apply to the exclusion of any national competition law rules. It is only if the takeover falls outside the EU Merger Regulation that the provisions of the EA 2002 may apply.

23.4.1.2   Two or more enterprises cease to be distinct

Enterprise

Section 129(1) of the EA 2002 provides that an 'enterprise' is the activities, or part of the activities, of a business. 'Business' in this context includes an undertaking carried on for gain or reward, or in the course of which goods or services are supplied otherwise than free of charge.

At least one of the enterprises must be carried on in the UK (or by, or under the control of, a body corporate which is incorporated in the UK).

Ceasing to be distinct

Enterprises cease to be distinct under s 26 of the EA 2002 if they are brought under common ownership or control. An offeror will acquire 'control' for these purposes if:

(a)   it can materially influence the policy of the offeree ('influential control');

(b)   it can control the policy of the offeree ('de facto control'); or

(c)   it has a controlling interest (that is, more than 50% of the voting rights) in the offeree ('legal control').

The OFT has produced guidelines to assist in the determination of (a) and (b). BSkyB Group plc's 17.8% acquisition in ITV plc in 2006 was held to amount to 'influential control' by the Competition Commission. This was because, in practice, it would enable BSkyB to block special resolutions (due to average ITV shareholder turnout), BSkyB was the only significant industry shareholder and it could get board representation due to its shareholding. It was ordered in 2008 to cut its shareholding to 7.5%. BSkyB's appeals against the decision to the Competition Appeal Tribunal and to the Court of Appeal failed.

23.4.1.3   The time limit for a reference has not expired

Section 24 of the EA 2002 provides that the takeover must either:

(a)   not have completed; or

(b)   have completed less than four months ago (unless the takeover completed without a public announcement, and the OFT was not notified, in which case the four-month period will start from the time the takeover comes to the attention of the OFT).

23.4.1.4   The turnover test and the share of supply test

To qualify for investigation the takeover must satisfy at least one of the following tests:

Turnover test

This test (EA 2002, s 28(1)) will be fulfilled if the value of the UK turnover of the *offeree* exceeds £70m.

Share of supply test

This test (EA 2002, s 23) will be fulfilled if:

(a)   after the takeover, the offeror will supply, or be supplied with, at least 25% of a defined class of goods or services which are supplied in the UK (or a substantial part of it (see below)); or

(b)   if this was already the case before the takeover, then after the takeover the offeror acquires an even greater share of the market.

EXAMPLE

If X plc, which controls 20% of the market for the supply of cars, makes a bid for Y plc, another car manufacturer with a market share of 10%, this would fulfil the market share test, because after the takeover X plc would own at least 25% of the UK car market. Even if X plc owned 25% of the car market before the takeover, the takeover of Y plc would still qualify for a reference as it would increase further X plc's market share.

Note that the example above assumes that the car market is a distinct market. In practice it can be difficult for lawyers to predict what is a distinct market. Ultimately, the OFT has the discretion to determine what the criteria are for determining the market. For example, it may consider the number of units sold, the value of goods sold, or the number of employees engaged in the manufacture or supply of the goods.

In a case (decided under the Fair Trading Act 1973, the predecessor of the EA 2002) involving bus companies in the north of England, the House of Lords held that South Yorkshire, which amounts to 1.65% of the area of the UK and which contained 3.2% of the population, was a substantial part of the UK for the purposes of the EA 2002 (*South Yorkshire Transport Ltd and Another v Monopolies and Mergers Commission and Another* [1993] 1 All ER 289).

23.4.2   A substantial lessening of competition

The EA 2002 does not define this term, which is referred to in practice as an 'SLC'. However, the explanatory notes to the EA 2002 state the following:

> Similar language is used in the legislation controlling mergers in a number of other major jurisdictions including the US, Canada, Australia and New Zealand. The concept is an economic one, best understood by reference to the question of whether a merger will increase or facilitate the exercise of market power (whether unilateral or through co-ordinated behaviour), leading to reduced output, higher prices, less innovation or lower quality of choice. A number of matters may be potentially relevant to the assessment of whether a merger will result in a substantial lessening of competition. These matters include, but are not limited to:
>
> • market shares and concentration
>
> • extent of effective competition before and after the merger
>
> • efficiency and financial performance of firms in the market
>
> • barriers to entry and expansion in the relevant market
>
> • availability of substitute products and the scope for supply – or demand – substitution

- extent of change and innovation in a market
- whether in the absence of the merger one of the firms would fail and, if so, whether its failure would cause the assets of that firm to exit the market, and
- the conduct of customers or of suppliers to those in the market.

In fact, the OFT ('Mergers: Substantive Assessment' (OFT 516), May 2003) and the Competition Commission ('Merger References – Competition Commission Guidelines') produce their own guidance for determining whether or not there has been an SLC.

23.4.3 The competition authorities

The EA 2002 is administered by the following authorities:

23.4.3.1 The Office of Fair Trading ('OFT')

The OFT is the government department which conducts the initial merger control investigation. If the OFT decides that:

(a) the takeover constitutes a relevant merger situation (see **23.4.1** above); and

(b) the takeover has resulted, or may be expected to result, in an SLC within any UK market(s) for goods or services (see **23.4.2** above),

then s 33(1) of the EA 2002 provides that it must refer the case to the Competition Commission (see **23.4.3.2** below). In *OFT v IBA Health Limited* [2004] EWCA Civ 142, concerning the takeover by iSoft plc of Torex plc, the Court of Appeal clarified the meaning of 'or may be expected to result'.

The Court ruled that the relevant test is whether the OFT itself believes that a takeover may be expected to result in an SLC. The OFT does not have to predict what the Competition Commission might decide. The OFT's belief must be more than a mere suspicion, and must be reasonable and objectively justified. If the OFT believes the probability of the takeover resulting in an SLC is over 50%, it should refer. If it believes the probability is less than 50%, but more than fanciful, the OFT has discretion as to whether to refer.

As stated at **23.2.1** above, if the OFT does refer to the Competition Commission a takeover which is subject to the Takeover Code, the takeover must lapse.

Note that the Competition Commission will be replaced by the Competition and Markets Authority (CMA) on 1 April 2014.

23.4.3.2 The Competition Commission

The Competition Commission is a statutory body which is independent of the Government. It must investigate takeovers which the OFT refers to it. In doing so, under ss 35 and 36 of the EA 2002 it must decide:

(a) whether the takeover has resulted, or will result, in an anti-competitive outcome. Note that this involves deciding whether it is more likely than not that the takeover has resulted, or will result, in a substantial lessening of competition. The OFT, in contrast, only had to reasonably believe that there had been, or might be, an SLC; and

(b) (if there is, or will be, an anti-competitive outcome) what remedies are appropriate.

The Competition Commission has the power to require attendance of witnesses and production of documents. It must take into account any representations made to it by those with a substantial interest in the subject matter of the reference.

Within 24 weeks from the date of the reference, the Competition Commission must consider the reference and make its decisions. In exceptional circumstances the 24-week period can be extended by up to a further eight weeks. It will then publish a report on its assessment of the takeover, the remedies it recommends and the reasons for its decisions. The report will be made available on the Competition Commission's website.

A guidance note, 'Merger References – Competition Commission Guidelines', which sets out how the Competition Commission will assess cases, is also available on its website.

Note that the Competition Commission will be replaced by the Competition and Markets Authority (CMA) on 1 April 2014.

23.4.3.3   The Secretary of State for Business, Innovation and Skills

The Secretary of State's power to intervene in merger control decisions is limited to mergers involving particular public interest issues. In such cases, the Secretary of State, rather than the OFT, can decide, first, whether to refer the merger to the Competition Commission and, secondly, whether to follow the Competition Commission's decision.

In the first use of this power under the EA 2002, the Secretary of State intervened in relation to BSkyB Group plc's acquisition of 17.9% of the shares of ITV plc. The Competition Commission subsequently held the purchase to be anti-competitive and ordered the sale of just over 10% of the shareholding. This decision was subsequently upheld by the Court of Appeal.

23.4.4   Notification

23.4.4.1   Clearance

Unlike the EU merger control process, outlined at **23.3.4** above, under the EA 2002 there is no obligation on the parties to notify a merger or proposed merger to the OFT. However, most parties to a takeover choose to notify the OFT in advance in order to seek formal confirmation that it will not be referred to the Competition Commission. This is referred to as a 'clearance'. The takeover process is expensive in terms of both time and money, and the parties will want to be certain that they are not going to make such an investment only for the Competition Commission to block the takeover at a later stage in the process.

There are two methods by which the parties to a takeover can seek clearance:

(a) *Informal submission*. The offeror (possibly jointly with the offeree) submits a memorandum, together with supporting documentation, to the OFT, explaining why a Competition Commission reference is not required and why clearance should be given.

(b) *Pre-notification by statutory merger notice*. This method is for pre-notification only, ie, it can only be used for a takeover which has been announced but not yet completed. The parties file a merger notice which answers questions about the takeover and which markets it may affect.

23.4.4.2   Informal advice

In its guidance, 'Mergers – jurisdictional and procedural guidance' of June 2009, the OFT, as an alternative to the offeror seeking clearance, will consider applications for informal advice on competition and jurisdictional issues arising out of a prospective merger situation that has not yet been made public. This procedure is only available to confidential transactions where there is a good faith intention to proceed, and where the OFT's duty to refer to the Competition Commission is a genuine issue. Details of this guidance are available from the OFT website.

23.4.5   Undertakings

If the OFT concludes that, having considered the two issues referred to at **23.4.3.1** above, it is under an obligation to make a reference to the Competition Commission, the parties may be able to provide certain undertakings with the effect that the takeover will not result in an SLC and so no reference is necessary. A good example of the use of undertakings was in the bid in 2003 by the supermarket chain Morrison for Safeway, which was cleared when Morrison provided an undertaking (referred to as a 'divestment undertaking') that it would sell 53 Safeway stores.

Note that the provision of undertakings can have an impact on the takeover timetable (see **Table 22.1** above), so any party seeking to provide such undertakings must keep the Panel informed and seek any necessary extensions to the timetable.

Note that the OFT and the Competition Commission will be replaced by the Competition and Markets Authority (CMA) on 1 April 2014.

23.4.6 The lawyer's role

The competition lawyer's role will include the following:

(a) giving preliminary advice on the likelihood of the takeover being referred to the Competition Commission;

(b) co-ordinating other advisers who may be needed to formulate arguments in favour of the offeror, such as economists and, perhaps, political consultants;

(c) preparing submissions on behalf of the offeror, and representing the offeror at hearings before the Competition Commission; and

(d) negotiating undertakings to ensure the takeover falls outside the scope of the EA 2002.

23.4.7 EU v UK merger regimes

The relationship between the two merger control regimes is illustrated in the case of the takeover of Midland by HSBC (see **22.4.5.4**). After HSBC made its initial offer for Midland, Lloyds announced that it would make a rival offer subject to certain pre-conditions. One of the pre-conditions was that the merger authorities would treat the rival bids alike.

The HSBC offer amounted to a concentration with a Community dimension, and so fell within the scope of the EU Merger Regulation's one-stop shop. However, the European Commission cleared the takeover, as HSBC and Midland competed in only a few sectors and, even after the takeover, intense competition in those sectors would remain.

The proposed Lloyds offer, however, did not fall within the scope of the EU Merger Regulation. Instead, it became apparent that it would be referred under the UK merger control regime. Lloyds therefore withdrew its offer, and the takeover by HSBC was successful.

23.5 FUTURE DEVELOPMENTS

As part of the review of Government organisations, BIS announced in October 2010 that it planned to merge the OFT with the Competition Commission to form a single competition and markets regulatory authority. The aim is to simplify procedures while at the same time saving money and reducing the burden on businesses. The new Competition and Markets Authority (CMA) will take up its powers on 1 April 2014. You can find more information from the CMA's website https://www.gov.uk/government/organisations/competition-and-markets-authority.

AIM

AIM

24.1 BACKGROUND TO THIS CHAPTER

The focus of Parts I to IV of this book is the company which has its shares admitted to listing on the Official List and admitted to trading on the Main Market. However, in recent years much of the IPO activity in the UK has been on the Alternative Investment Market (AIM). As a result, it would be impossible to practise corporate law in today's climate without at least a basic understanding of AIM, how it compares to the Main Market, and the perceived advantages and disadvantages of an admission to AIM. This chapter seeks to help provide that basic understanding.

24.2 AN INTRODUCTION TO AIM

In 1995 the Stock Exchange established the AIM as its international market for smaller and growing companies. The Stock Exchange states that its objective 'was to offer smaller and companies – from any country and any industry sector – the chance to raise capital on a market with a pragmatic and appropriate approach to regulation. With this in mind, AIM was designed to be a highly flexible public market offering many unique attributes both for companies and investors'.

AIM has proved a great success. In fact, until recently it was the most successful growth market in the world. Since its launch in 1995, over 3,430 companies have joined the market, raising more than £82 billion between them. As at October 2013, approximately 1,090 companies were trading on AIM, with a total market capitalisation in excess of £60 billion. The market's appeal is not limited to the UK. The popularity of AIM with overseas companies rose sharply before the onset of the global financial crisis. In 2001, 16 overseas companies joined AIM; this rose to 124 in 2006, but fewer international companies are now joining, with only 20 new admissions in the year 2013 up to October, reflecting on-going economic uncertainty in certain parts of the world; although there were still some 232 overseas companies trading on AIM as at October 2013. That said, AIM is certainly under pressure. In the first 10 months of 2013, around 80 companies de-listed or left the market. Some went insolvent, a couple transferred to the Main Market, but for the majority it seems that the costs of being on AIM (Stock Exchange and professional advisers' fees) and the tighter regulatory controls outweighed the benefits of being on AIM. Since the financial crisis started in 2007, AIM now hosts one-third fewer companies. How long this trend will continue remains to be seen. Typically it is the smaller UK companies who list on AIM, particularly natural resources, technology and fast-growing companies. Some AIM companies are household names, such as Mulberry, Glasgow Rangers FC, Prezzo and Majestic Wine.

AIM is regulated by the Stock Exchange. The Listing Rules do not apply to AIM companies (see **3.5.2**). Instead, AIM companies are governed by a set of rules helpfully titled the 'AIM Rules', and they apply equally to companies incorporated in the UK and overseas. The AIM Rules are drafted with smaller companies in mind; they do not contain much legal or technical jargon, and this allows them to be applied flexibly and comprehensively. The AIM Rules are available from the AIM section of the Stock Exchange website.

24.3 WHY AIM?

The advantages of listing, set out at **1.7** above, apply equally to AIM as they do to the Main Market. As, typically, it is the smaller, emerging companies who join AIM, the accessible market, easy access to capital and acquisition opportunities and employee incentives AIM offers are a particular draw.

So why join AIM rather than the Main Market? This decision has become much more difficult for companies since the introduction of the two-tier system of premium and standard listings. The premium segment of the Main Market remains a significantly more regulated market than AIM, but the standard segment, which is subject just to the minimum EU regulation, is in some areas less regulated than AIM.

In addition to the benefits referred to above, the following aspects of AIM can render it more attractive than a premium listing on the Main Market, particularly for smaller companies:

(a)   AIM is easier to access:

    (i)   it has reduced eligibility requirements (see **24.4**); and

    (ii)   the role of the 'Nomad' (see **24.4.1**) means the admission process is more straightforward.

    However, a standard listing on the Main Market is also subject to much reduced eligibility requirements and, as an advantage over AIM, no Nomad is required.

(b)   AIM has a more relaxed regulatory regime. In particular:

    (i)   there are reduced disclosure requirements;

    (ii)   shareholder approval is required only for a reverse takeover (see **24.6.2.3**) and a disposal resulting in a fundamental change of business (see **24.6.2.4**). (However the company may still require shareholder approval for ancillary matters relating to other transactions, such as a disapplication of s 561 pre-emption rights);

    (iii)   the brevity of the AIM Rules means that the day-to-day regulatory work required for an AIM company costs less than that for a premium listed Main Market company; and

    (iv)   the requirement for a prospectus is confined to circumstances where there is a public offer; s 85(2) of the FSMA 2000 does not apply to AIM companies (see **24.5.1**).

    For a standard listing, although the full disclosure requirements apply, there is no need for the non-statutory shareholder approvals at (ii). It shares the advantage of (iii), but a prospectus is also required for admission under s 85(2) as the standard listing is on the Main Market, a regulated market.

(c)   AIM offers tax advantages for investors which the Main Market does not.

    This advantage is applicable equally over standard listings.

It seems that companies are choosing to list on AIM rather than on the standard segment of the Main Market.

24.4 ELIGIBILITY CRITERIA

The minimum requirements for admission to AIM are different from those of the Main Market (set out at **4.3.1.2** and **4.3.1.3** above). For example, unlike a premium listing on the Main

Market, there are no requirements in respect of market capitalisation, the number of shares in public hands, or a three-year trading record.

In order to seek admission to AIM, a company must comply with the following minimum requirements:

(a) *Incorporation.* The company must be legally established under the laws of its place of incorporation and be able to offer shares to the public. (For UK companies this means being a public company – CA 2006, s 755.)

(b) *Transferability.* Shares admitted to AIM must be freely transferable (AIM Rules, r 32).

(c) *Whole class to be listed.* All issued shares of the same class must be admitted (AIM Rules, r 33).

(d) *Electronic settlement.* All shares admitted must be eligible for electronic settlement (AIM Rules, r 36).

(e) *Accounts.* The company (if it is incorporated in an EEA country) must have published accounts which conform with International Accounting Standards ('IAS') (AIM Rules, r 19).

(f) *Nominated adviser.* A nominated adviser (known as a 'Nomad') (AIM Rules, r 1) and broker must be appointed and retained at all times (AIM Rules, r 35) (see **24.4.1**).

In the event that the company's main activity is a business that has been generating revenue and/or been independent for less than two years prior to its admission to AIM, it is subject to a condition that all directors (and their families) and employees who hold an interest in the company and certain substantial shareholders must agree not to dispose of their interests for at least one year following admission to AIM (AIM Rules, r 7).

24.4.1 The Nomad

One of the most significant differences between the Main Market and AIM is the role of the nominated adviser (or 'Nomad'). The Stock Exchange attributes the success of AIM largely to the role of the Nomad, which is to guide a company first through the admission process and then through its life as a publicly quoted company. Rule 1 of the AIM Rules requires every AIM company to retain a Nomad at all times. The Stock Exchange will suspend trading in the securities of any AIM company which ceases to have a Nomad, and cancel their admission if a replacement Nomad is not appointed within one month.

24.4.1.1 Duties and responsibilities

Under r 39 of the AIM Rules the Nomad must comply with a separate set of rules, the AIM Rules for Nominated Advisers (the 'Nomad Rules', available in the AIM section of the Stock Exchange website). These separate rules for Nomads were introduced on 20 February 2007 and strengthen the regulatory regime for AIM-quoted companies.

The Nomad owes its responsibilities solely to the Stock Exchange.

The Nomad must:

(a) ensure that the company is suitable for admission to AIM; and

(b) advise and guide the company through the admission process and, once quoted on AIM, on its on-going responsibilities; and

(c) most importantly, confirm to the Stock Exchange that any admission document or prospectus (see **24.5**) complies with the requirements of Sch 2 to the AIM Rules.

Schedule 3 to the AIM Rules for the Nominated Adviser sets out more detailed responsibilities which the Nomad must perform. These are split into three categories: Admission Responsibilities; Ongoing Responsibilities; and Engagement Responsibilities. Only the first two are relevant to a Nomad acting for a new applicant to AIM. A list of Nomads is available on the AIM section of the Stock Exchange website.

These various Responsibilities are presented as a group of overriding principles accompanied by supporting 'actions'. The Nomad must comply with the principles in all cases. The 'actions' provide examples of how the principles translate into practice.

For example, principle AR1 requires the Nomad to gain a sound understanding of the company and its business before admission to AIM. One of the listed actions states that usually this requires the Nomad to visit the material places of operation of the company and to meet the directors. This ensures a business trip to Qatar, Kazakhstan, China or Wigan, depending on the company concerned.

There are two points to note about these actions. First, they are not an exhaustive list of actions the Nomad should take and, secondly, although the Stock Exchange usually will expect all the actions listed to be taken, a Nomad can take alternative action if it feels it is better suited to achieving the principle. The Stock Exchange's AIM Regulation team has started to produce a periodic publication, somewhat uninspiringly called 'Inside AIM' (available on the Stock Exchange's website), to offer guidance on the AIM Rules and the market, particularly to Nomads.

24.4.1.2 Admission Responsibilities

In preparation for admission of the new applicant company to AIM the Nomad is obliged, in addition to AR1 mentioned at **24.4.1.1** above, to assess the suitability of the board of directors (individually and collectively), oversee the due diligence procedure leading up to flotation, satisfy itself that the admission document complies with Sch 2 to the AIM Rules, and ensure that procedures are in place for the new company and its directors to comply with the AIM Rules.

24.4.1.3 Ongoing Responsibilities

Once the company has been admitted to AIM, the Nomad must consult regularly with the company, review announcements before they are released to the market, monitor trading in the company's shares, particularly when there is unpublished, price-sensitive information in existence, and advise on any changes to the board of directors to the company and their impact.

On 17 November 2009, the Stock Exchange publicly censured and fined Regal Petroleum plc a record £600,000 for breaches of the AIM Rules and Nomad Rules for issuing misleading announcements and failing to release price-sensitive information.

24.4.2 The broker

An AIM company must retain a broker at all times (AIM Rules, r 35). If there is no registered market maker (see **2.5.2**), the broker must use its best endeavours to find a matching business. Any member firm of the Stock Exchange can act as broker, subject to any required authorisation by any other regulator. A list of member firms is available on the AIM section of the Stock Exchange website, together with a separate list of brokers which AIM companies have appointed.

24.5 THE MARKETING DOCUMENT

When a company applies for admission to AIM, or is raising further equity finance on AIM then, subject to exemptions (see **24.5.1.1**), the company must produce a prospectus or admission document.

24.5.1 Prospectus or admission document?

Chapter 6 sets out in detail when a company is required to publish a prospectus pursuant to the Prospectus Rules and s 85 of the FSMA 2000. As stated at **3.5.1** above, the Prospectus

Rules apply to AIM companies as well as to Main Market companies. A prospectus is required when a company either:

(a)   offers transferable securities to the public in the UK (s 85(1)); or

(b)   requests admission of transferable securities to trading on a regulated market situated or operating in the UK (s 85(2)).

The AIM is a Stock Exchange regulated market. This is not the same as a 'regulated market' for the purposes of s 85(2), so s 85(2) does not apply to an AIM company or a company seeking admission to AIM. Nevertheless, if an AIM company, or a company seeking admission to AIM, is offering transferable securities to the public in the UK then, subject to any applicable exemptions, a prospectus is required under s 85(1).

As a company seeks admission to AIM because of its more flexible and pragmatic regulation, typically AIM companies will seek to structure any public offer to fall within one of the exemptions set out in s 85(5) and s 86 of the FSMA 2000.

If a prospectus is not required, the company must instead produce an admission document, which must comply with a more relaxed version of the Prospectus Rules (see **24.5.3**). An admission document does not require approval by the FCA.

24.5.1.1   Exemptions to the requirement to produce a prospectus

The exemptions to s 85(1) are set out at **6.4.1.5** above. The most common exemptions relied upon by AIM companies are those set out at **6.4.1.5(a)** (offers to qualified investors), **6.4.1.5(b)** (offers to fewer than 150 persons in each EEA State who are not qualified investors), **6.4.1.5(c)** (offers involving significant investment by each investor), **6.4.1.5(d)** (small offers) and **6.4.1.5(f)** (offers in conjunction with takeovers by way of share for share exchange).

If any of the FSMA 2000 exemptions to s 85(1) apply, a prospectus will not be required (remember that s 85(2) is not relevant in relation to AIM). In practice, any sizeable rights issue or open offer to raise further finance will tend to be to more than 150 persons per EEA State (as is the case with the Main Market), and therefore in these circumstances it will be necessary to draft a prospectus and have it approved by the FCA.

24.5.2   Responsibility

The directors take overall responsibility for a prospectus or admission document (although a third party may take responsibility for a specific part of the document). The directors are responsible for ensuring compliance with the AIM Rules.

24.5.3   Content requirements

24.5.3.1   Prospectus

The content requirements of a prospectus are as set out in the Prospectus Directive (see **6.5**).

24.5.3.2   Admission document

The Stock Exchange has carved out certain requirements of the Prospectus Rules in relation to the content requirements of an admission document. The carve-outs reflect the nature of AIM and the companies admitted to it.

The content requirements for what lawyers refer to as 'an AIM-PD: compliant admission document' are set out in Sch 2 to the AIM Rules (which includes Annexes I–III to the Prospectus Rules, as amended by the AIM Rules).

24.6 CONTINUING OBLIGATIONS

24.6.1 The general obligation of disclosure

As stated at **3.5.3**, the Disclosure Rules do not apply to AIM companies. The AIM Rules set out continuing obligations of AIM companies. The primary obligation is a general duty of disclosure, set out in r 11. This provides that every AIM company must announce, without delay, any new developments which:

(a)   are not public knowledge; and

(b)   concern a change in its financial condition, its sphere of activity, performance of its business, or its expectation of its performance; and

(c)   if made public, would be likely to cause a substantial movement in the price of its securities.

The company must make the announcement through an RIS. Rule 10 of the AIM Rules requires that the company must take reasonable care to ensure that any information it notifies is not misleading, false or deceptive, and does not omit anything likely to affect the import of such information.

24.6.2 Specific disclosure obligations

In addition to the general obligation to disclose price-sensitive information, there are specific obligations of disclosure in relation to the following:

(a)   substantial transactions (AIM Rules, r 12 – see **24.6.2.1** below);

(b)   related party transactions (AIM Rules, r 13 – see **24.6.2.2** below);

(c)   reverse takeovers (AIM Rules, r 14 – see **24.6.2.3** below);

(d)   any disposal resulting in a fundamental change of business (AIM Rules, r 15 – see **24.6.2.4** below);

(e)   changes to significant shareholders (DTR 5 and AIM Rules, r 17 – see **24.6.2.5** below);

(f)   dealings by directors (AIM Rules, r 17);

(g)   changes in directors, directors' details, Nomad or broker (AIM Rules, r 17);

(h)   any material change in the company's actual trading performance or financial condition and between any profit forecast or estimate included in the company's admission document, or which is otherwise in the public domain (AIM Rules, r 17);

(i)   other matters set out in r 17 of the AIM Rules, including any change to the accounting reference date, registered office address or legal name;

(j)   details of the directors' remuneration in the audited annual report (AIM Rules, r 19); and

(k)   an AIM company must also disclose certain key information on its website, including its current constitutional documents and the number of AIM securities in issue (AIM Rules, r 26).

24.6.2.1 Substantial transactions

An AIM company must disclose details of any substantial transactions. A transaction is substantial if it exceeds 10% of any class test contained in Sch 3 to the AIM Rules (which are similar to the class tests set out in Chapters 10 and 11 of the Listing Rules; see **19.4**).

Schedule 3 sets out a comparison between the size of the transaction and the company itself in respect of the following:

(a)   gross assets;

(b)   profits;

(c)   turnover;

(d)   consideration to market capitalisation; and

(e)   gross capital (in acquisitions of a company or business).

If a transaction is revenue in nature and occurring in the ordinary course of the business of the company, or if it has undertaken to raise finance that does not involve a change in the fixed assets of the company, it will not constitute a substantial transaction.

If the transaction exceeds 10% of any of the Sch 3 class tests, and so constitutes a substantial transaction, an announcement must be made pursuant to Sch 3, which must include the prescribed information set out in Sch 4. However, there is no requirement for shareholder approval, or for a circular (unless required under another AIM rule). Directors of AIM companies often cite this as a reason for choosing AIM over the Main Market.

24.6.2.2   Related party transaction

If the transaction is with a related party (as defined by the AIM Rules) and exceeds 5% in any of the Sch 3 class tests referred to at **24.6.2.1** above, an announcement containing prescribed information as set out in Sch 4 to the AIM Rules is required. The announcement must include a statement that the directors (excluding any director involved directly in the transaction) having consulted with the company's Nomad, consider that the terms of the transaction are fair and reasonable.

Where the class test exceeds 0.25%, the company must include details of any related party transaction in the company's annual audited accounts (see **24.6.3**).

24.6.2.3   Reverse takeover

A transaction (or transactions) over a 12-month period which either:

(a)   exceeds 100% of any of the class tests sets out in Sch 3 to the AIM Rules (see **24.6.2.1**); or

(b)   results in a fundamental change to the AIM company's business, board or voting control (or, in the case of an investing company (as defined by the AIM Rules), departs substantially from the investing strategy set out in its prospectus or admission document),

constitutes a reverse takeover under r 14 of the AIM Rules.

The company must:

(a)   obtain shareholder approval (by ordinary resolution) for any reverse takeover (and any agreement relating to a reverse takeover must be conditional upon such approval);

(b)   prepare a prospectus or admission document, which must describe the circumstances and details of the transaction and convene the shareholders' general meeting to approve the transaction; and

(c)   make an announcement of the reverse takeover via an RIS without delay, disclosing the information specified by Sch 4 to the AIM Rules.

Trading in the company's securities will be cancelled. The enlarged entity must seek admission in the same manner as any other AIM company which is seeking admission for the first time.

24.6.2.4   Disposal resulting in a fundamental change of business

Any disposal which, when aggregated with any other disposal or disposals over the previous 12 months, exceeds 75% in any of the class tests set out in Sch 3 to the AIM Rules (see **24.6.2.1** above), is a disposal which results in a fundamental change of business ('DFCB') (AIM Rules, r 15).

A DFCB must be conditional on shareholder approval (by ordinary resolution). A circular containing the information specified in Sch 4 to the AIM Rules (and r 13 insofar as the disposal is to a related party) and a notice of GM will also be required. Where the proposed disposal will divest the company of all, or substantially all, of its trading business activities, the circular must state the company's investing strategy going forward.

The Company must notify an RIS of the DFCB without delay, disclosing the information specified by Sch 4 to the AIM Rules. If the transaction involves a related party, the information required by r 13 of the AIM Rules must also be disclosed.

The company must make the acquisition (or acquisitions) constituting a reverse takeover under r 14 of the AIM Rules within 12 months of receiving the consent of its shareholders.

24.6.2.5 Changes to significant shareholders

Under r 17 of the AIM Rules, any changes of 1% or more in the holdings of 'significant shareholders' must be notified to an RIS as soon as possible. A significant shareholder is one who holds at least 3% of the AIM company's issued share capital.

In addition, DTR 5 applies to AIM companies incorporated under the Companies Act or who have their principal place of business in the UK (see **15.6**).

Generally compliance with DTR 5 will satisfy r 17 of the AIM Rules, but the Stock Exchange has pointed out that whereas DTR 5 requires the disclosure to be made as soon as possible on receipt of a notification and by no later than the end of the third trading day following notification (DTR 5.8.12R), under r 17 it must be made without delay, which is a stricter standard.

24.6.3 Financial information

The AIM Rules supplement the financial obligations in the CA 2006 with more specific obligations.

The AIM Rules require companies incorporated in an EEA country to publish annual accounts in accordance with International Accounting Standards ('IAS'). The company must send the accounts to shareholders within six months of the end of the financial year to which they relate (AIM Rules, r 19). The accounts must disclose any transaction with a related party (see **24.6.2.2**), whether or not previously disclosed under the AIM Rules, where any of the class tests in Sch 3 to the AIM Rules exceed 0.25%, and specify the identity of the related party and the consideration for the transaction.

The AIM Rules also require listed companies to prepare interim reports in respect of the first six months of the company's financial period. The company must publish the interim reports within three months of the end of this half-year period and must notify an RIS that they have been published (AIM Rules, r 18).

In addition, although not mandatory, it is best practice for an AIM company to include a statement in its annual report which discloses the extent to which it has complied with the principles set out in the UK CGC (see **24.7**).

24.6.4 Share dealing code

Rule 21 of the AIM Rules prohibits dealings by directors and other key employees in the company's securities in certain circumstances, such as when they are in possession of unpublished price sensitive information, or during specified periods. Generally, companies admitted to AIM will adopt a share dealing code which complies with this Rule.

24.7 CORPORATE GOVERNANCE

The UK CGC does not apply to AIM companies, although they are encouraged to comply with it. In May 2013, the Quoted Company Alliance ('QCA') published a Corporate Governance Code for Small and Mid-sized Quoted companies which applies to AIM companies. The guidelines are available to order from the QCA website.

APPENDICES

The Admission and Disclosure Standards

Admission and Disclosure Standards

Admission

Conditions

1.1 An **application** for **admission to trading** of any **class** of **securities** must:

    (a) relate to all **securities** of that **class**, issued or proposed to be issued; or

    (b) if **securities** of that **class** are already **admitted to trading** on the **Exchange's** markets, relate to all further **securities** of that **class**, issued or proposed to be issued.

    Guidance to Rule:

    *For UK incorporated **issuers** that are subject to the **Listing Rules**, an **application** for **admission to trading** of any **class** of **securities** must relate only to **securities** which are **listed** or proposed to be **listed** or equivalent.*

1.2 An **issuer** must be in compliance with the requirements of:

    (a) any **securities regulator** by which it is regulated; and /or

    (b) any stock exchange on which it has **securities** admitted to trading.

1.3 In the case of **transferable securities**, all such **securities** must be **freely negotiable**.

1.4 **Securities** that are **admitted to trading** on any **regulated market** operated by the **Exchange** must be capable of being traded in a fair, orderly and efficient manner.

1.5 The **Exchange** may refuse an **application** for the **admission to trading** of **securities** if it considers that:

    (a) the **applicant's** situation is such that **admission** of the **securities** may be detrimental to the orderly operation of the **Exchange's** markets or to the integrity of such markets; or

    (b) the **applicant** does not or will not comply with the **Standards** or with any special condition imposed upon the **applicant** by the **Exchange**

1.6 **Issuers** must confirm that they meet the criteria and requirements of the market to which they are applying.

Guidance to Rule:

Issuers *are required to tick the relevant box on* **Form 1** *to indicate the market to which they are seeking* **admission**.

In addition to 1.5, as per our obligations under **MiFID** *Article 40(1), the* **Exchange** *has the right to refuse an* **application** *for the* **admission to trading** *of* **securities** *to a* <u>certain market or segment</u> *if it considers that the* **securities** *are better suited to another of the* **Exchange's** *markets or segments.*

Settlement

1.7   To be **admitted to trading**, **securities** must be eligible for electronic **settlement**. The **issuer** must inform the **Exchange** at the time of **application** of the chosen **settlement** mechanism and if **settlement** restrictions will apply to any **securities** to be considered for **admission**.

Guidance to Rule:

The **Exchange** *requires that an appropriate* **settlement** *solution is in place, dependent upon the trading platform on which the* **securities** *are to be traded. Accepted* **central security depositaries** *include Euroclear UK & Ireland, Euroclear Bank, Depository Trust Clearing Corporation (DTCC) or Monte Titoli S.p.A.. Other* **central securities depositaries** *will be considered on a case-by-case basis.*

Issuers *should note that certain of the* **Exchange's** *trading platforms have trades cleared by* **central counterparties**. *In these cases, the* **securities** *have to be eligible for the* **central counterparty** *as well as the central* **securities** *depositary. In addition, the* **central counterparties** *may restrict where* **settlement** *can occur.*

Communication

1.8   An **issuer** must identify a contact within their organisation who will be responsible for communications between the **Exchange** and the **issuer**, and the **Exchange** must be notified in writing of any changes thereafter. An **issuer** may also wish to use a **nominated representative**.

Guidance to Rule:

The contact should be fully conversant with the **issuer's** *responsibilities under these* **Standards** *and will be either a director or senior employee of the* **issuer** *in a position to act as the* **Exchange's** *point of contact. At the* **issuer's** *discretion, a* **nominated representative** *from another organisation may also be selected to act as the primary day-to-day contact point with the* **Exchange** *on regulatory matters. Details of the* **issuer's** *contact and any* **nominated representative** *must be provided to the* **Exchange** *at the time of* *the **application** for **admission to trading** and the **Exchange** must be notified in writing of any changes thereafter.*

1.9   An **issuer** must ensure that all information provided in connection with the **application** for **admission to trading** is in all respects accurate, complete and not misleading. An **issuer** must be open, honest and co-operative in all dealings with the **Exchange**.

Admission process

1.10   An **issuer** proposing to admit **securities** that will be the subject of an **application** for **admission to trading** must agree the timetable for the **admission to trading** of those **securities** <u>in advance</u> with **Market Operations**.

1.11   The **issuer** must contact the **Exchange** no later than ten **business days** before the **application** is to be considered.

Application

Provisional application

2.1 To ensure the **Exchange** can properly consider any **application** for **admission to trading** the **issuer** must:

- For new **issuers**, submit the **Form 1** and a draft copy of the **prospectus** to the **Market Operations** team by no later than 12:00 at least ten **business days** prior to the day on which the **issuer** is requesting that the **Exchange** consider the **application** for **admission to trading**.

- The submission of **Form 1** shall be provisional. Formal **application** will only be deemed to be made when a **prospectus** relating to the **securities** to be **admitted to trading** has been approved.

- The final **application** form and supporting documentation must be submitted in accordance with 2.4.

Guidance to Rule:

__Admission__ of __securities__ becomes effective only when the decision of the __Exchange__ to admit the __securities__ to trading has been announced by the __Exchange__ via an __RNS__ announcement. (Should __RNS__ suffer an outage; a notice will be made available at the __Exchange's__ ground floor reception).

Except where otherwise agreed by the __Exchange, applications__ for __admission to trading__ are considered on __business days__ between the hours of 09:00 and 17:30.

The __Exchange__ will not, except in exceptional circumstances, admit __securities__ to trading until each of the documents and items listed in 2.4 have been lodged with the __Exchange__ (marked for the attention of __Market Operations__) in so far as they are relevant. All documents submitted to the __Exchange__ must be written in English and submitted electronically.

An invoice for the __admission__ fee will be raised on __admission__. The __admission__ fee is calculated in accordance with the __Exchange's__ scale of fees (see 3.14). Payment of the __admission__ fee must be received no later than 30 days after the date of this invoice.

2.2 When further issues of **securities** are allotted of the same **class** as **securities** already **admitted to trading** on our markets, **issuers** must assess whether a **prospectus** or **listing particulars** is required. If applicable, these must be submitted to the relevant **EEA competent authority** for review and approval in accordance with its rules. **Application** for **admission** of such further **securities** by the submission of a **Form 1** must also be made, either at the same time as the **application** for **listing** where applicable, and in any event not later than 48 hours before the **application** is to be considered.

2.3   If a request for **when issued dealing** is to be considered:

- A provisional "**when issued dealing application** form" (which can be found at the **Exchange's** website: www.londonstockexchange.com/mainmarket/usefuldocuments) must be received with the provisional **Form 1**.

- The final "**when issued dealing application** form" must be submitted (with a draft **stabilisation** notice if appropriate) at least two **business days** prior to the day on which the **issuer** is requesting that the **Exchange** consider the **application** for **when issued dealing**.

    Guidance to Rule:

    *The **Exchange** reserves the right to refuse **when issued dealing**.*

    *Where applicable, we reserve the right to only allow unconditional dealing when confirmation has been received that **admission to trading** on a **regulated market** and/or **listing** is effective.*

Documents

Before admission

2.4   Except as set out in paragraphs 2.1, 2.2, 2.3 or 2.7, or as otherwise agreed by the **Exchange**, the following documents must be submitted to the **Market Operations** team by no later than 12:00 at least two **business days** prior to the day on which the **issuer** is requesting that the **Exchange** consider the **application** for **admission to trading**:

2.4.1   **Issuers** not covered by 2.4.2 or 2.4.3 below:

- an **application** for **admission to trading** on the finalised **Form 1** issued by the **Exchange** signed by a duly authorised officer of the **issuer**; and

- an electronic copy of any **prospectus**, **listing particulars**, **passport**, circular, announcement or other document relating to the issue, together with copies of any notice of meeting referred to in such documents; and

- written confirmation of the number of **securities** to be allotted or issued pursuant to the board resolution should be provided and must be received by the **Exchange** no later than 16:30 on the day before **admission** is expected to become effective. By prior arrangement this may be extended 07:00 on the day of **admission**. The **applicant** should keep a copy of the resolution on its records for six years; and

- a copy of the **Regulated Information Service** announcement relating to the **admission.**

Guidance to Rule:

*For **issuers** for whom the **EEA competent authority** is the **FCA:***

*If the **FCA** has considered an application for **listing** and the **securities** the subject of the **application** are not all allotted and **admitted** following the initial allotment of the **securities** (for example, under an **offer for subscription**), further allotments of **securities** may be **admitted** if, before 4pm on the day before **admission** is sought, the **Market Operations** team has been informed and the **FCA** has been provided with the information required under **Listing Rule** 3.3.4 A R.*

2.4.2   **Issuers** of **covered warrants** and **Listed Structured Products**:

- a finalised **Form 1**, a pricing supplement, indicative price and a completed trading form (depending on the number of products being launched simultaneously) and any additional forms, as appropriate. If products are to be launched under a new **prospectus** then it must also be provided. The relevant form(s) are available at: www.londonstockexchange.com/mainmarket/usefuldocuments

2.4.3   **Issuers** of **ETFs** or **ETCs** or similar products:

- a finalised **Form 1**, a static data form and Pricing Supplement. If products are to be launched under a new **prospectus**, then it must also be provided. For **ETFs**, written confirmation must be provided that the **ETF** is **listed** by an **EEA competent authority**. The relevant form(s) are available at: www.londonstockexchange.com/mainmarket/usefuldocuments

After admission

2.5   Where relevant, a statement of the number of **securities** which were, in fact, issued and, where different from the number which were the subject of the **application**, the aggregate number of **securities** of that **class** in issue must be lodged with the **Exchange** (marked for the attention of **Market Operations**) as soon as it becomes available.

techMARK™ and techMARK mediscience™

2.6   An **issuer** may also seek **admission** to **techMARK™** or **techMARK mediscience™**. The process and criteria for such **applications** are set out in the relevant **Eligibility Criteria**, which is updated from time to time and is available from our website (www.londonstockexchange.com/techMARK)

Block admission

2.7 Where an **issuer** admits **securities** that will not be allotted prior to **admission** and that do not require a **prospectus** or **listing particulars**, the **issuer** may make an **application** for a **block admission**. These **admissions** may be pursuant to employee share schemes or the exercise of options.

Guidance to Rule:

*Where an **issuer** wishes to admit **securities** on a regular basis, they may make an **application** for a **block admission**. **Block admissions** will usually be for the reasons stated in rule 2.7 but the Exchange will consider requests for other reasons. The Exchange will monitor the correct usage of this facility and the number of **block admission applications** per **issuer**.*

Issuance programmes

2.8 Where **specialist securities** or **certificates representing shares** are issued under an issuance programme, an **applicant** must submit a subsequent **application** for **admission to trading** in the case of an increase in the maximum number of **securities** which may be in issue and **listed** at any one time under an issuance programme.

If the **Exchange** approves the **application**, it will **admit to trading** all **securities** which may be issued under the programme within 12 months after the publication of the **prospectus** or **listing particulars**, subject to the **Exchange** receiving:

(a) advice of the final terms of each issue;

(b) electronic copies of any supplementary **prospectus** or **listing particulars**; and

(c) confirmation that the **securities** in question have been issued.

2.9 The final terms of each issue which is intended to be **admitted to trading** must be submitted in writing to the **Exchange** as soon as possible after they have been agreed and in any event no later than 14:00 on the day before **admission** is required to become effective. The final terms may be submitted by the **issuer** or its **nominated representative**.

Continuing obligations

General

3.1   In order for its **securities** to be **admitted to trading** and to remain on the **Exchange's markets**, **issuers** must be in compliance with:

    (a) the requirements of any **securities regulator** by which it is regulated; and/or

    (b) the requirements of any stock exchange on which it has **securities** admitted to trading, and

    (c) the provisions set out in the **Standards**, including any modification to the application of the **Standards** which has been notified via our website.

3.2   **Issuers** must notify the **Exchange** without delay of any change of status of the information provided under 2.1-2.2, in respect of the **listing** or **admission to trading** (or cancellation from trading) of the **issuer's securities** on any other exchange or trading platform, where such **admission** or cancellation is at the application or agreement of the **issuer.**

3.2A   An **issuer** admitted to trading on the **Main Market** that wishes to transfer between listing categories pursuant to **FCA Listing Rule 5.4A** must notify **Market Operations** of its intention to transfer listing category. Such notification must be made as early as possible and no later than 3 **business days** before the transfer is due to take place. The notification should include: details of the **issuer**, the relevant **security** and the change in listing category sought; an explanation of why the **issuer** is seeking to transfer; the date on which the **issuer** wishes the transfer to take effect and contact details of the person the **Exchange** should liaise with in relation to the transfer.

3.3   The **Exchange** may make additions to, dispense with or modify the application of the **Standards** (either unconditionally or subject to conditions) in such cases and by reference to such circumstances as it considers appropriate.

3.4   **Issuers** and their **nominated representatives** must provide to the **Exchange** any information or explanation that the **Exchange** may reasonably require for the purpose of verifying whether the **Standards** are being or have been complied with or which relates to the integrity or orderly operation of the **Exchange's** markets.

Guidance to Rule:

Where an issuer has a website where it regularly publishes company information, they should inform the Stock Situation Analysis Team of the website address.

Timetable for corporate actions

3.5   An **issuer** must contact the **Stock Situation Analysis Team** in advance of any announcement of the timetable for any proposed action affecting the rights of existing holders of its **securities** traded on our markets. Except in the case of a dividend timetable notification (which are subject to rule 3.8), the reference to 'in advance' means that the **Exchange** should receive the proposed timetable by no later than 09:00 on the day before the proposed announcement.

3.5 - 3.9 do not apply to **issuers** of **depositary receipts** or **specialist securities**. **Issuers** of **depositary receipts** must observe their obligations under 3.10.

3.6   The Exchange may require amendments to the timetable, as and when considered necessary. The **Stock Situation Analysis Team** will liaise with the **issuer** and its advisors as appropriate.

A timetable which has not been cleared in advance with the **Stock Situation Analysis Team** but which has been announced to the market, may be subject to change if required by the **Stock Situation Analysis Team**. If this situation occurs a further correcting announcement must be made to the market.

3.7   Any proposed amendments to a timetable, including amendment to the publication details of any announcement, must be immediately notified to the **Stock Situation Analysis Team**.

Guidance to Rules:

Rules 3.5 – 3.7 relate to proposed timetables for all corporate actions for ***securities admitted to trading*** *on the* ***Exchange's*** *markets, for example:*

- *Corporate actions where an **ex date** is required (dividends, **scrip dividends**, **DRIPs**, **DRISs**, dividend **currency elections**, **open offers**, **rights issues**, **bonus issues**, **capitalisation issues**, **return of capital/cash**, **demergers**, **enfranchisements**).*

- *Other events for which clearance of timetables is required are:*
  - ***tender/repurchase offers**,*
  - ***consolidations**, **subdivision**,*
  - ***capital reorganisations**,*
  - ***schemes of arrangement/ schemes of reconstruction**,*
  - *some types of **conversions/redemptions**, or*
  - *any other corporate event which could affect the rights of existing holders of **securities admitted to trading on our markets**.*

3.8   Where applicable, dividend payments must follow the procedures set out in the guidance below:

Guidance to Rule:

*A dividend timetable which follows the guidelines set by the Dividend Procedure Timetable, published on the **Exchange's** website at www.londonstockexchange.com/mainmarket/usefuldocuments, need not be notified to the **Exchange** in advance, provided the announcement of the dividend includes:*

- *the amount of the dividend (should state whether the dividend is net or gross); and*
- *the record and payment dates; and*
- *the availability of any **scrip dividend, DRIP** or **dividend currency option;** and*
- *publish the election date.*

*Dividends outside of the guidelines detailed in the Dividend Procedure Timetable must be agreed by the **Stock Situation Analysis Team** in advance of the announcement of the dividend. The **Scrip Dividend** and **DRIP** documentation must also be lodged with the **Stock Situation Analysis Team**.*

*The term 'dividend' includes all interest payments for **debt securities** (excluding **specialist securities**). An announcement is not required for interest payments, but the **Exchange** must receive notification of any payment no later than seven **business days** prior to the **record date**. This notification must include:*

- *the appropriate net or gross amount; and*
- *the record and payment dates; and*
- *any conversion period details.*

*Where fixed payment details are available, the **issuer** may use one timetable to inform the **Exchange** of all future payments, providing any subsequent amendments are notified to the **Exchange** immediately.*

*When an issuer publishes details of future interest payments, they must notify the **Stock Situation Analysis team**.*

Timetable for open offer

3.9   The timetable for an **open offer** must ensure that valid claims through the market can be promptly satisfied and must comply with the following:

- the open offer must remain open for acceptance for at least 10 **business days**. For the purposes of calculating the period of 10 **business days**, the first **business day** is the date on which the offer is first open for acceptance. The **business days** must also exclude the **'ex' date**;

- where possible, the **open offer record date** should be the **business day** before the expected **'ex' date**. A **record date** preceding the **'ex' date** by more than three **business days** will only be approved in exceptional circumstances; and

- the announcement by an **issuer** of an **open offer** should take place by 07:15 on the proposed **'ex' date**.

As per 3.5 and 3.6, an **issuer** must contact the **Stock Situation Analysis Team** in advance of any announcement of the timetable for any **open offer**. The reference to 'in advance' means that the **Exchange** should receive the proposed timetable by no later than 09:00 on the day before the proposed announcement. The **Exchange** may require amendments to the timetable, as and when considered necessary. The **Stock Situation Analysis Team** will liaise with the **issuer** and its advisors as appropriate.

A timetable which has not been cleared in advance with the **Stock Situation Analysis Team** but which has been announced to the market, may be subject to change if required by the **Stock Situation Analysis Team**. If this situation occurs a further correcting announcement must be made to the market.

Continuing obligations for depositary receipt issuers

Timetable for corporate actions for Depositary Receipts

3.10   An **issuer** or its **depositary bank** should contact the **Stock Situation Analysis Team** in advance of any announcement of a timetable for any proposed action affecting the rights of existing holders of its **securities** traded on our markets. The reference to "in advance" means that the **Exchange** should receive the proposed announcement by no later than 9:00 on the day before the proposed announcement.

The **Exchange** may require amendments to the timetable, as and when considered necessary. The **Stock Situation Analysis Team** will liaise with the **issuer** or **depositary bank** as appropriate.

Any proposed amendments to an agreed timetable, including amendment to the published details of any announcement, should immediately be notified to the **Stock Situation Analysis Team**.

3.10 and related guidance must be adhered to by an **issuer** or its **depositary bank** unless otherwise specifically agreed with, and confirmed by, the **Exchange**.

Guidance to Rule:

*3.10 relates to proposed timetables for all corporate actions for **securities admitted to trading** on the **Exchange's** markets, for example: corporate actions where an **'ex date'** is required (**bonus issues**, stock distributions,* *rights issues, demergers /spin offs).*

Issuers will have regard to their domestic regulatory requirements and should discuss possible conflicts between those and the Standards with Stock Situation Analysis Team in advance, as issuers deem necessary.

Wherever possible the record date should be announced in advance and the 'ex' date for any of the above corporate actions will be determined by the Exchange, dependent on the information received and the type of the corporate action proposed.

Other events for which clearance of timetables is required are:

- *stock splits,*
- *tender/repurchase offers,*
- *capital reorganisations,*
- *or any other corporate action which could affect the rights of existing holders of securities admitted to trading on our markets.*

Dividends

Dividends for depositary receipts should be notified to the Stock Situation Analysis Team by 09:00 at least three business days prior to the dividend record date, to allow the depositary receipt to be marked Ex Dividend in the normal way, two business days prior to the record date.

In most circumstances the dividend record date for the depositary receipt will be in line with that of the underlying security. In the event of late notification of the record date for the underlying security, or where notice is not received three days prior to the record date, the depositary bank will be required to set a separate record date for the depositary receipt to allow the security to be marked Ex Dividend in line with the above timetable.

Dividend notifications for depositary receipts should include the following details, where available:

- *name of company declaring dividend*
- *ISIN or CUSIP number*
- *whether dividend is an approximate or final rate*
- *amount of the dividend (should state whether the dividend is net or gross and include both rates (if available)*
- *record date*
- *payment dates*
- *any relevant fees or tax charges*
- *name of depositary bank announcing dividend (including contact details).*

Amendments to constitution

3.11   If an **issuer** of **transferable securities** that have been **admitted to trading** on a **regulated market** (or are the subject of an **application** for **admission to trading** on a **regulated market**) proposes to amend its constitution it must communicate the draft amendment to: (a) the **FCA**; and (b) the **regulated market** on which its **securities** have been **admitted to trading**[2].

In order to fulfil part (b) of this obligation, **issuers** should email details of the amendments to our **Market Operations** team: admissions@londonstockexchange.com

The communication must be effected without delay but at the latest on the date of calling the general meeting which is to vote on, or be informed of, the amendment.

Guidance to Rule:

*The document should be sent to us when the **issuer** is satisfied it is ready to do so and this should form a part of its communications plan.*

***Issuers** may also choose to make an announcement to the market, via a **Regulated Information Service**, including any draft amendment.*

ETFs

3.12   **Issuers** of **ETFs** for whom the **UKLA** is not the **listing** authority:

(i) must comply with the **listing** rules of the **EEA** state in which they are **listed**;

(ii) must notify a **Regulated Information Service** as soon as possible of all circulars, notices, reports (as required by the **listing** rules of the **EEA** state in which they are **listed**), at the same time as any such documents are issued;

Unless the full text of the document is provided to the **Regulated Information Service**, the notification must set out where copies of the relevant document can be obtained.

(iii) must appoint a registrar in the UK if: (a) there are 200 or more holders resident in the UK; or (b) 10% of more of the equity securities are held by persons resident in the UK.

---

[2] **DTR** 6.1.2

(iv) must notify a **Regulated Information Service** on a daily basis of the number of outstanding shares and the Net Asset Value per share.

*In relation to sub-paragraph (iii) above, an **issuer** should also consider the requirements of any settlement venue for a UK registrar.*

Guidance to Rule for issuers of ETFs for whom the UKLA is not the listing authority:

*An issuer must consider its obligations under the **Disclosure and Transparency Rules**. For example, the **Market Abuse Directive** will apply to **ETF**s traded on a **regulated market** and **FCA DTR** 1 and **DTR** 2 will apply to **ETF**s **admitted to trading** on a **regulated market** in the UK, even if **UKLA** is not the **listing** authority.*

*An **issuer** must also obtain fund recognition from the **FCA** and adhere to the continuing obligations contained within the UCITS Directives[3].*

Settlement

3.13   The **Exchange** requires that the **securities** continue to be eligible for electronic **settlement**, as set out in the Guidance to Rule 1.7.

Fees

3.14   An **issuer** with **securities admitted to trading** shall pay to the **Exchange** all applicable charges set out in the document "Fees for issuers". This publication, as updated from time to time, can be found on our website: www.londonstockexchange.com/mainmarket/usefuldocuments

Suspension

3.15   The **Exchange** will suspend the **admission** to and trading of any **securities** on its markets if a **listing** of such **securities** is suspended.

3.16   The **Exchange** may suspend trading of such **securities** with effect from such time as it may determine, and in such circumstances as it thinks fit where the ability of the **Exchange** to ensure the orderly operation of its markets is, or may be, jeopardised, even if only temporarily.

---

[3] [1] Council Directives 85/611/EEC and 85/611/EEC, as amended.

3.17 Any request by an **issuer** to suspend trading of its **securities** must be confirmed to the **Exchange** in writing by the **issuer** or its **nominated representative**.

3.18 Where trading has been suspended, the **Exchange** may impose such conditions as it considers appropriate prior to resumption of trading.

3.19 An **issuer** must continue to comply with the **Standards**, even when **admission** of its **securities** to trading is suspended, unless the **Exchange** otherwise agrees.

Cancellation

3.20 An **issuer** that wishes the **Exchange** to cancel the right of any of its **securities** to be traded must advise the **Exchange** in writing, not later than 20 **business days** before the date it intends trading in its **securities** to be discontinued. An **issuer** is also required to announce the intended cancellation of any of its **securities** through a **Regulated Information Service**. If agreed, the **Exchange** will announce the intention to cancel individual **securities** through the **Datasync Email Service** and the intention to cancel issuers through a **Regulated Information Service**.

3.21 Cancellation will only be effective subject to the **issuer** complying with any legal or regulatory obligation and providing the **Exchange** with appropriate confirmation. Cancellation will only be effective once all outstanding subscriptions, charges, fees or other sums due to the **Exchange** have been paid in full.

Compliance and Appeals

3.22 Where the **Exchange** considers that an **issuer** has contravened the **Standards** and considers it appropriate to impose any sanction as set out in paragraph 3.23, it will follow the procedure set out in the **Compliance Procedures**.

3.23 If an **issuer** has contravened the **Standards**, one or more of the following actions may result:

   a) censure of the **issuer** and, in addition, publication of such censure;

   b) a fine;

   c) an order that the **issuer** make restitution to any **person** (when the **issuer** has profited from a breach of the **Exchange**'s rules at that **person**'s expense);

   d) cancellation of the right of the **issuer** to have its **securities,** or any **class** of its **securities**, traded on the **Exchange's** markets.

3.24 An **issuer** may appeal against a decision of the **Exchange** in relation to the application and interpretation of the **Standards**. The procedures for such appeals are set out in the Compliance Procedures.

APPENDIX 2

The ABI Guidelines for Directors' Powers to Allot Share Capital and Disapply Shareholders' Pre-emption Rights

The requirement on companies to obtain shareholder authorisation of powers both for the general allotment of new shares and any disapplication of pre-emption rights is embodied in law. This guidance sets out the expectations of institutional investors in this regard. Model resolutions, updated to reflect changes consequent on implementation of the Companies Act 2006, are included in Annex 1.

This guidance, which replaces that previously issued by the ABI, addresses the particular recommendation of the 'Rights Issue Review Group' that the overall allotment headroom that shareholders should normally be invited to approve be increased from one-third to two-thirds of an issuer's issued share capital. The ABI Investment Committee recognises, in particular, the case for ensuring that the routine S.551 headroom should allow for capital raising when made by way of a fully pre-emptive rights issue within an overall value headroom of one third by reference to the company's prevailing market value rather than the quantity of shares issued.

The guidance will be reviewed after three years of operation. In the meantime the ABI will monitor the use by companies of the additional headroom.

S.551 General Power to Allot

ABI Members will regard as routine a request for authorisation to allot new shares in an amount of up to one third of the existing issued share capital[1].

In addition they will regard as routine requests to authorise the allotment of a further one third. Such additional headroom shall be applied to fully pre-emptive rights issues only and the authorisation shall be valid for one year only.

Where an additional authority of this kind is taken and where

- the aggregate actual usage of the authority exceeds one third as regards nominal amount and also,
- in the case of issuance being in whole or part by way of a fully pre-emptive rights issue, monetary proceeds exceed one third (or such lesser relevant proportion) of the pre-issue market capitalisation,

ABI Members will expect that all members of the Board wishing to remain in office will stand for re-election at the next Annual General Meeting of the company following the decision to make the issue in question.

S.570 General Power to Disapply Pre-emption Rights

The terms of the resolution to disapply pre-emption rights are designed to accord with the provisions of the Pre-Emption Group's Statement of Principles with regard to routine disapplications. It will assist shareholders if, when seeking such authorisations, companies take the opportunity to confirm their intention to adhere to the provisions in the Principles regarding cumulative usage of authorities within a rolling 3-year period where the Principles

---

1. It is emphasised that this recommended level is not an absolute limit on the amount of share capital the directors may allot: it will merely require the board to return to shareholders if the company proposes significantly to increase the amount of issued share capital.

provide that usage in excess of 7.5% should not take place without prior consultation with shareholders.

ANNEX 1

The attached example resolutions are intended to assist companies and their advisers in understanding the limitations which ABI Members have indicated they would expect to see placed on the directors' authority to allot share capital under S.551 of the Companies Act 2006 and the general authority to disapply shareholders' pre-emption rights under S.570.

Resolution 1 (S.551 General Power to Allot)

The figure inserted at 'A' in each of (i) and (ii) should be an amount not exceeding one-third of the issued Ordinary share capital[2].

To the one-third figure can be added amounts for which the company requires further additional powers under Section 551. For example, further powers may be required to allot shares in respect of deferred consideration.

If the resolution contains a figure greater than one-third of the issued Ordinary share capital (by reference to the total issued Ordinary share capital as disclosed in accordance with the Listing Rules) it is important to explain clearly in the supporting documents the basis on which the figure is calculated, including the nature of any amounts which have been specifically added to the basic one-third figure.

Resolution 2 (Section 570 General Power to Disapply Pre-emption Rights)

The figure inserted at 'B' should not be more than 5% of the issued Ordinary share capital of the company. If the resolution contains a figure greater than five per cent of the issued Ordinary share capital (by reference to the total issued Ordinary share capital as disclosed in accordance with the Listing Rules), it is important to explain clearly in the supporting documents the basis on which the figure is calculated.

Ordinary Resolution

1(i)   THAT the board be and it is hereby generally and unconditionally authorised pursuant to section 551 of the Companies Act 2006 to allot shares in the company and to grant rights to subscribe for or to convert any security into shares in the company up to an aggregate nominal amount of £...A... provided that this authority shall expire on ....*.... save that the company may before such expiry make an offer or agreement which would or might require shares to be allotted or rights to subscribe for or convert securities into shares to be granted after such expiry and the board may allot shares or grant rights to subscribe for or convert securities into shares in pursuance of such an offer or agreement as if the authority conferred hereby had not expired,
and further,

(ii)   THAT the board be and it is hereby generally and unconditionally authorised to exercise all powers of the company to allot equity securities (within the meaning of Section 560 of the said Act) in connection with a rights issue in favour of Ordinary shareholders where the equity securities respectively attributable to the interests of all Ordinary shareholders are proportionate (as nearly as may be) to the respective numbers of Ordinary shares held by them up to an aggregate nominal amount of £...A... provided that this authority shall expire on the date of the next annual general meeting of the company after the passing of this resolution save that the company may before such expiry make an offer or agreement which would or might require equity securities to be

---

2.   However, to the extent that the S.551 authority sought for general purposes is less than one third, the S.551 authority reserved for rights issues only may be increased commensurately to provide a rights issue headroom of up to two thirds by reference to the nominal value of the share capital being issued compared to that outstanding.

allotted after such expiry and the board may allot equity securities in pursuance of such an offer or agreement as if the authority conferred hereby had not expired.

* Where an authority is sought in respect of both (i) and (ii) the date of expiry specified should be the date of the next annual general meeting. Where an authority is sought in respect of (i) only, a period up to 5 years is acceptable

Special Resolution

2   THAT subject to the passing of the previous resolution the board be and it is hereby empowered pursuant to Section 570 of the Companies Act 2006 to allot equity securities (within the meaning of Section 560 of the said Act) for cash pursuant to the authority conferred by the previous resolution as if sub-section (1) of Section 561 of the said Act did not apply to any such allotment provided that this power shall be limited

(i)   to the allotment of equity securities in connection with a rights issue in favour of Ordinary shareholders where the equity securities respectively attributable to the interests of all Ordinary shareholders are proportionate (as nearly as may be) to the respective numbers of Ordinary shares held by them and,

(ii)   to the allotment (otherwise than pursuant to sub-paragraph (i) above) of equity securities up to an aggregate nominal value of £...B...

and shall expire {on the date of the next annual general meeting of the company after the passing of this resolution } save that the company may before such expiry make an offer or agreement which would or might require equity securities to be allotted after such expiry and the board may allot equity securities in pursuance of such an offer or agreement as if the power conferred hereby had not expired.

31 December 2008
(amended 30 November 2009)

APPENDIX 3

Pre-emption Group: Disapplying Pre-emption Rights: A Statement of Principles

OVERARCHING PRINCIPLES

1. Pre-emption rights are a cornerstone of UK company law and provide shareholders with protection against inappropriate dilution of their investments. They are enshrined in law by the 2nd Company Law Directive and the Companies Act 1985, which provides that they may be disapplied only by a special resolution of shareholders at a general meeting of the company.

2. Whilst not undermining the importance of pre-emption rights, a degree of flexibility is appropriate in circumstances where new equity issuance on a non-pre-emptive basis would be in the interests of companies and their owners.

3. The principles set out in this paper aim to provide clarity on the circumstances in which flexibility might be appropriate and the factors to be taken into account when considering the case for disapplying pre-emption rights and making use of an agreed authority for a non-pre-emptive share issue.

4. Companies, institutional investors and voting advisory services all have an important role to play in ensuring the effective and flexible application of this guidance:

    •   Companies have a responsibility to signal an intention to seek a non-pre-emptive issue at the earliest opportunity and to establish a dialogue with the company's shareholders. They should keep shareholders informed of issues related to an application to disapply their pre-emption rights.

    •   Shareholders have a responsibility to engage with companies to help them understand the specific factors that might inform their view on a non-pre-emptive issue by the company. They should review the case made by companies on its merits and decide on each case individually using the usual investment criteria. Where a shareholder does intend to vote against a resolution to disapply preemption rights, the Institutional Shareholders' Committee Statement of Principles[1] on the responsibilities of shareholders makes clear that it is best practice to explain in advance the reasons for the decision.

    •   While companies should in any case consult their main shareholders, advisory services should be prepared to receive representations from companies. In such circumstances the advisory services should explain any recommendations made in light of the reasons provided. This should involve setting out the pros and cons of the proposal so that the ultimate decision maker can take an informed view.

APPLICATION OF THE PRINCIPLES

5. The principles set out here relate to issues of equity securities for cash other than on a pre-emptive basis pro rata to existing shareholders by all UK companies which are primary listed on the Main Market of the London Stock Exchange. Companies quoted on AIM are encouraged to apply these guidelines but investors recognise that greater flexibility is likely to be justified in the case of such companies.

6. These principles are supported by the ABI, NAPF and IMA as representatives of owners and investment managers. These associations hope that the guidance they contain will

---

1. 'The Responsibilities of Institutional Shareholders and Agents – Statement of Principles'; Institutional Shareholders' Committee, June 2007 [available at: http://www.institutionalshareholderscommittee.org.uk/library.html]

be helpful to companies in approaching requests for disapplication and in gauging the likely reaction of shareholders to proposals they may wish to make.

ROUTINE DISAPPLICATIONS

7. In a significant number of situations a request for disapplication is likely to be considered non-controversial by shareholders. While this does not reduce the importance of effective dialogue and timely notification, routine requests are less likely to need in-depth discussion and shareholders will be more inclined in principle to support them.

8. Requests are more likely to be routine in nature when the company is seeking authority to issue non-pre-emptively no more than 5% of ordinary share capital in any one year.

9. This principle applies whatever the structure of the proposed issue. For example, an issue of shares which contains both a pre-emptive and non-pre-emptive element ('combination issues') would normally be considered routine provided that the non-preemptive element met the criteria specified for routine applications within these guidelines. This would include issues that comprised a placing of shares with a partial clawback by existing shareholders.

10. In the absence of (a) suitable advance consultation and explanation or (b) the matter having been specifically highlighted at the time at which the request for disapplication was made, companies should not issue more than 7.5% of the company's ordinary share capital for cash other than to existing shareholders in any rolling three year period.

11. Where a request is made for the disapplication of pre-emption rights in respect of a specific issue of shares, the price at which the shares are proposed to be issued will also be relevant. Shareholders' approach to the pricing of non-pre-emptive issues is set out in paragraphs 18 and 19 below. Companies should note that a discount of greater than 5% is not likely to be regarded as routine.

12. Treasury shares issued for cash will be counted within the guideline levels set out in paragraph 8, but not those in paragraph 10.

13. Convertible instruments will be counted within the guideline levels set out in paragraphs 8 and 10, and should be counted at the point when authority to issue the instruments is sought, not the point at which they are converted to ordinary shares.

14. **These principles are intended to ease the granting of authority below those figures, not to rule out approvals above them. Requests which, if granted, would exceed these levels should be considered by shareholders on a case by case basis.** In these instances it is particularly important that there is early and effective dialogue, and that the company is able to communicate to shareholders the information they need in order to reach an informed decision. The considerations set out in the following section are critical to making a decision.

CRITICAL CONSIDERATIONS RELATING TO NON-ROUTINE REQUESTS FOR DISAPPLICATION

15. It is neither possible nor desirable to define all the circumstances in which shareholders might be willing to agree to disapply pre-emption rights above the level set out in paragraphs 8 and 10 above. Nevertheless, there are some general considerations that are likely to be relevant in the majority of cases; these are set out below. Companies should ensure they are in a position to communicate such information to shareholders to help them make an informed decision.

16. The critical considerations are likely to include:

    - **the strength of the business case:** In order to make a reasoned assessment shareholders need to receive a clear explanation of the purpose to which the capital raised will be put and the benefits to be gained - for example in terms of product development or the opportunity cost of not raising new finance to exploit new commercial opportunities -and how the financing or proposed future financing fits in with the life-cycle and financial needs of the company.

- **the size and stage of development of the company and the sector within which it operates**. Different companies have different financing needs. For example, shareholders might be expected to be more sympathetic to a request from a small company with high growth potential than one from a larger, more established company.

- **the stewardship and governance of the company**. If the company has a track record of generating shareholder value, clear planning and good communications, this may give shareholders additional confidence in its judgement.

- **financing options.** A wide variety of financing options are now available to companies. Companies should explain why a non-pre-emptive issue of shares is the most appropriate means of raising capital, and why other financing methods have been rejected.

- **the level of dilution of value and control for existing shareholders.** If there would be no resulting dilution, for example if an investment trust sought authority to issue shares at a premium to the underlying net asset value per share, this would not normally raise any concerns;

- **the proposed process following approval:** Companies should make clear the process they would follow if approval for a non-pre-emptive issue were to be granted, for example how dialogue with shareholders would be carried out in the period leading up to the announcement of an issue.

- **contingency plans:** Company managers should explain what contingency plans they have in place in case the request is not granted, and the implications of such a decision.

TIMING OF REQUESTS FOR DISAPPLICATION

17. Companies should signal the possibility of their intention to seek a non-pre-emptive issue at the earliest opportunity. For example if, at the time of the initial public offering, a company is aware that it is likely to have a need relatively quickly for additional cash, it should alert potential investors to this in the prospectus. In other cases it might be appropriate for the company to signal a potential request in its annual report. In some cases it may be appropriate for companies to consult a small number of major shareholders before making any announcement. Companies and shareholders should be mindful of the possible legal and regulatory issues in doing this.

18. Authority to disapply pre-emption rights following a 'routine' request would normally be granted by shareholders' approval of an appropriate resolution at an AGM. As discussed above, shareholders will not generally agree to a non-routine disapplication request without a sufficiently strong business case for this course of action. Thus, non-routine requests would be made at an AGM only when the company is in a position to justify this approach by providing relevant information such as that set out in paragraph 16; otherwise a specially convened EGM would be needed.

19. Authorities should be granted for no more than 15 months or until the next AGM, whichever is the shorter period.

OTHER CONSIDERATIONS RELATING TO NON PRE-EMPTIVE ISSUES

20. Companies should aim to ensure that they are raising capital on the best possible terms, particularly where the proposed issue is in the context of a transaction likely to enhance the share price. Any discount at which equity is issued for cash other than to existing shareholders will be of major concern. Companies should, in any event, seek to restrict the discount to a maximum of 5% of the middle of the best bid and offer prices for the

company's shares immediately prior to the announcement of an issue or proposed issue.

21. Where an issue is priced on a date after the announcement date, the level of discount should be assessed at the time of pricing rather than the time of announcement. Companies should also have regard to any adverse impact on the share price of the earlier announcement, which may create the potential for a significant loss or transfer of value, in deciding whether to proceed with an issue in such circumstances.

22. The principles and critical considerations set out above apply to requests for the disapplication of pre-emption rights. Once a request to disapply pre-emption rights has been approved, shareholders expect companies to discharge and account for this authority appropriately. It is recommended that the subsequent annual report should include relevant information such as the actual level of discount achieved, the amount raised and how it was used and the percentage amount of shares issued on a non-pre-emptive basis over the last year and three years.

ROLE OF THE PRE-EMPTION GROUP

23. The Pre-Emption Group will monitor the development of practice in relation to disapplying pre-emption rights. It expects that this Statement of Principles will inform the way in which all interested parties participate in this process. It will monitor and report annually on the application of these principles. The Pre-Emption Group will not express a view on or otherwise intervene in specific cases.

APPENDIX

DEFINITIONS

Clawback

Clawback as it is referred to in paragraph 9 is the right of existing shareholders to subscribe for a share of an issue at the pre-agreed price. This differs from a full rights entitlement since it is non-renounceable and therefore does not permit the shareholder to sell this entitlement to another investor.

Discounts

In general terms, the 'discount' (paragraphs 20 and 21) is defined as the aggregate of (a) the amount by which the offering price differs from the market price, and (b) expenses directly relevant to the making of the issue. In the case of issues of a new class of deferred equity in the form of convertibles, warrants or other deferred equity, the amount of the opening market price above the issue price and any difference at point of pricing of the instrument to underlying fair value will be regarded as part of the discount.

Market Movements

Where the pricing takes place at a time later than that of the announcement of the proposed issue (paragraph 21), it is recognised that the achievable price of the placing may vary in accordance with general market conditions. For the purposes of these guidelines the measurement of discount therefore relates to the time and date of the pricing rather than the time and date of the announcement of the issue.

AIM Rules for Companies

Part 1 of the AIM Rules for Companies dated 17 February 2010 is reproduced below. Please check the Stock Exchange website for any updates.

Part One – AIM Rules

Retention and role of a nominated adviser

1. In order to be eligible for **AIM**, an **applicant** must appoint a **nominated adviser** and an **AIM company** must retain a **nominated adviser** at all times.

   The **nominated adviser** is responsible to the **Exchange** for assessing the appropriateness of an **applicant** for **AIM**, or an existing **AIM company** when appointed as its **nominated adviser,** and for advising and guiding an **AIM company** on its responsibilities under these rules.

   The responsibilities of **nominated advisers** are set out in the **AIM Rules for Nominated Advisers.**

   If an **AIM company** ceases to have a **nominated adviser** the **Exchange** will suspend trading in its **AIM securities**. If within one month of that suspension the **AIM company** has failed to appoint a replacement **nominated adviser**, the **admission** of its **AIM securities** will be **cancelled**.

Applicants for AIM

Pre-admission announcement

2. An **applicant** must provide the **Exchange**, at least ten **business days** before the expected date of **admission** to **AIM**, with the information specified by Schedule One.

   A **quoted applicant** must provide the **Exchange**, at least twenty **business days** before the expected date of **admission** to **AIM**, with the information specified in Schedule One and its supplement.

   If there are any changes to such information prior to **admission**, the **applicant** must advise the **Exchange** immediately by supplying details of such changes. Where, in the opinion of the **Exchange**, such changes result in the information being significantly different from that originally provided, the **Exchange** may delay the expected date of **admission** for a further ten **business days** (or twenty **business days** in the case of a **quoted applicant**).

   The **Exchange** will **notify RNS** of information it receives under this rule.

Admission document

3. An **applicant** must produce an **admission document** disclosing the information specified by Schedule Two.

   A **quoted applicant** is not required to produce an **admission document** unless otherwise required by the **Prospectus Rules**.

Omissions from admission documents

4. The **Exchange** may authorise the omission of information from an **admission document** (other than a **Prospectus**) of an **applicant** where its **nominated adviser** confirms that:

♦   the information is of minor importance only and not likely to influence assessment of the **applicant's** assets and liabilities, financial position, profits and losses and prospects; or

♦   disclosure of that information would be seriously detrimental to the **applicant** and its omission would not be likely to mislead investors with regard to facts and circumstances necessary to form an informed assessment of the **applicant's** securities.

Application documents

5.   At least three **business days** before the expected date of **admission**, an **applicant** must submit to the **Exchange** a completed **application form** and an electronic version of its **admission document**. These must be accompanied by the **nominated adviser's declaration** required by the **AIM Rules for Nominated Advisers**.

At least three **business days** before the expected date of **admission**, a **quoted applicant** must submit to the **Exchange** an electronic version of its latest report and accounts and a completed **application form**. These must be accompanied by the **nominated adviser's declaration** required by the **AIM Rules for Nominated Advisers**.

The **AIM fee** will be invoiced to the **applicant** and should be paid pursuant to rule 37.

Admission to AIM

6.   **Admission** becomes effective only when the **Exchange** issues a **dealing notice** to that effect.

Special conditions for certain applicants

Lock-ins for new businesses

7.   Where an **applicant's** main activity is a business which has not been independent and earning revenue for at least two years, it must ensure that all **related parties** and **applicable employees** as at the date of **admission** agree not to dispose of any interest in its securities for one year from the **admission** of its securities.

This rule will not apply in the event of an intervening court order, the death of a party who has been subject to this rule or in respect of an acceptance of a takeover offer for the **AIM company** which is open to all **shareholders**.

Investing companies

8.   Where the **applicant** is an **investing company**, a condition of its **admission** is that it raises a minimum of £3 million in cash via an equity fundraising on, or immediately before, **admission**.

An **investing company** must state and follow an **investing policy**.

An **investing company** must seek the prior consent of its **shareholders** in a general meeting for any material change to its **investing policy**.

Where an **investing company** has not substantially implemented its **investing policy** within eighteen months of **admission**, it should seek the consent of its **shareholders** for its **investing policy** at its next annual general meeting and on an annual basis thereafter, until such time that its **investing policy** has been substantially implemented.

Other conditions

9.   The **Exchange** may make the **admission** of an **applicant** subject to a special condition.

Where matters are brought to the attention of the **Exchange** which could affect an **applicant's** appropriateness for **AIM**, it may delay an **admission**. The **Exchange** will inform the **applicant's nominated adviser** and may **notify RNS** that it has asked the **applicant** and its **nominated adviser** to undertake further due diligence.

The **Exchange** may refuse an **admission** to **AIM** if it considers that:

- the **applicant's** does not or will not comply with any special condition which the **Exchange** considers appropriate and of which the **Exchange** has informed the **applicant's nominated adviser**; or

- the **applicant's** situation is such that **admission** may be detrimental to the orderly operation or reputation of **AIM**

Principles of disclosure

10.   The information which is required by these rules must be **notified** by the **AIM company** no later than it is published elsewhere. An **AIM company** must retain a **Regulatory Information Service** provider to ensure that information can be **notified** as and when required.

An **AIM company** must take reasonable care to ensure that any information it **notifies** is not misleading, false or deceptive and does not omit anything likely to affect the import of such information.

It will be presumed that information **notified** to a **Regulatory Information Service** is required by these rules or other legal or regulatory requirement, unless otherwise designated.

General disclosure of price sensitive information

11.   An **AIM company** must issue **notification** without delay of any new developments which are not public knowledge concerning a change in:

- its financial condition;

- its sphere of activity;

- the performance of its business; or

- its expectation of its performance,

which, if made public, would be likely to lead to a substantial movement in the price of its **AIM securities**.

Disclosure of corporate transactions

Substantial transactions

12.   A substantial transaction is one which exceeds 10% in any of the **class tests**. It includes any transaction by a subsidiary of the **AIM company** but excludes any transactions of a revenue nature in the ordinary course of business and transactions to raise finance which

do not involve a change in the fixed assets of the **AIM company** or its subsidiaries.

An **AIM company** must issue **notification** without delay as soon as the terms of any substantial transaction are agreed, disclosing the information specified by Schedule Four.

Related party transactions

13.   This rule applies to any transaction whatsoever with a **related party** which exceeds 5% in any of the **class tests**.

An **AIM company** must issue **notification** without delay as soon as the terms of a transaction with a **related party** are agreed disclosing:

♦   the information specified by Schedule Four;

♦   the name of the **related party** concerned and the nature and extent of their interest in the transaction; and

♦   a statement that with the exception of any **director** who is involved in the transaction as a **related party**, its **directors** consider, having consulted with its **nominated adviser**, that the terms of the transaction are fair and reasonable insofar as its **shareholders** are concerned.

Reverse takeovers

14.   A reverse takeover is any acquisition or acquisitions in a twelve month period which for an **AIM company** would:

♦   exceed 100% in any of the **class tests**; or

♦   result in a fundamental change in its business, board or voting control; or

♦   in the case of an **investing company**, depart materially from its **investing policy** (as stated in its **admission document** or approved by **shareholders** in accordance with these rules).

Any agreement which would effect a reverse takeover must be:

♦   conditional on the consent of its **shareholders** being given in general meeting;

♦   **notified** without delay disclosing the information specified by Schedule Four and insofar as it is with a **related party**, the additional information required by rule 13; and

♦   accompanied by the publication of an **admission document** in respect of the proposed enlarged entity and convening the general meeting.

Where **shareholder** approval is given for the reverse takeover, trading in the **AIM securities** of the **AIM company** will be **cancelled**. If the enlarged entity seeks **admission**, it must make an application in the same manner as any other **applicant** applying for **admission** of its securities for the first time.

Fundamental changes of business

15.   Any disposal by an **AIM company** which, when aggregated with any other disposal(s) over the previous twelve months, exceeds 75% in any of the **class tests,** is deemed to be a disposal resulting in a fundamental change of business and must be:

♦   conditional on the consent of its **shareholders** being given in general meeting;

♦   **notified** without delay disclosing the information specified by Schedule Four and insofar as it is with a **related party**, the additional information required by rule 13; and

♦ accompanied by the publication of a circular containing details of the disposal and any proposed change in business together with the information specified above and convening the general meeting.

Where the effect of the proposed disposal is to divest the **AIM company** of all, or substantially all, of its trading business, activities or assets the **AIM company** will, upon completion of the disposal, be treated as an **investing company**. The **notification** and circular containing the information specified by Schedule Four convening the general meeting must also state its **investing policy** to be followed going forward which must also be approved by **shareholders.**

The **AIM company** will then have to make an acquisition or acquisitions which constitute a reverse takeover under rule 14 or otherwise implement the **investing policy** approved at the general meeting to the satisfaction of the **Exchange** within twelve months of becoming an **investing company**.

Where an **AIM company** proposes to take any other action, the effect of which is that it will cease to own, control or conduct all, or substantially all, of its existing trading business, activities or assets (including the cessation of all, or substantially all, of the **AIM company's** business), the above requirements to **notify** the action, publish a circular setting out its **investing policy** going forward, obtain **shareholder** consent for that **investing policy** and implement it within twelve months of taking such action, will apply. **Shareholder** consent for the action itself will not be required.

Aggregation of transactions

16. Transactions completed during the twelve months prior to the date of the latest transaction must be aggregated with that transaction for the purpose of determining whether rules 12, 13, 14 and/or 19 apply where:

♦ they are entered into by the **AIM company** with the same **person** or **persons** or their **families**;

♦ they involve the acquisition or disposal of securities or an interest in one particular business; or

♦ together they lead to a principal involvement in any business activity or activities which did not previously form a part of the AIM company's principal activities.

Disclosure of miscellaneous information

17. An **AIM company** must issue **notification** without delay of:

♦ any **deals** by **directors** disclosing, insofar as it has such information, the information specified by Schedule Five;

♦ any **relevant changes** to any **significant shareholders**, disclosing, insofar as it has such information, the information specified by Schedule Five;

♦ the resignation, dismissal or appointment of any **director**, giving the date of such occurrence and for an appointment, the information specified by Schedule Two paragraph (g) and any shareholding in the company;

♦ any change in its accounting reference date;

♦ any change in its registered office address;

♦ any change in its legal name;

♦ any material change between its actual trading performance or financial condition and any profit forecast, estimate or projection included in the **admission document** or otherwise made public on its behalf;

7

- any decision to make any payment in respect of its **AIM securities** specifying the net amount payable per security, the payment date and the **record date**;

- the reason for the application for **admission** or **cancellation** of any **AIM securities**;

- the occurrence and number of shares taken into and out of treasury, as specified by Schedule Seven;

- the resignation, dismissal or appointment of its **nominated adviser** or **broker**;

- any change in the website address at which the information required by rule 26 is available;

- any subsequent change to the details disclosed pursuant to sub-paragraphs (iii) to (viii) inclusive of paragraph (g) of Schedule Two, whether such details were first disclosed at **admission** or on subsequent appointment;

- the admission to trading (or cancellation from trading) of the **AIM securities** (or any other securities issued by the **AIM company**) on any other exchange or trading platform, where such admission or cancellation is at the application or agreement of the **AIM company**. This information must also be submitted separately to the **Exchange**.

Half-yearly reports

18. An **AIM company** must prepare a half-yearly report in respect of the six month period from the end of the financial period for which financial information has been disclosed in its **admission document** and at least every subsequent six months thereafter (apart from the final period of six months preceding its accounting reference date for its annual audited accounts). All such reports must be **notified** without delay and in any event not later than three months after the end of the relevant period.

The information contained in a half-yearly report must include at least a balance sheet, an income statement, a cash flow statement and must contain comparative figures for the corresponding period in the preceding financial year. Additionally the half-yearly report must be presented and prepared in a form consistent with that which will be adopted in the **AIM company's** annual accounts having regard to the accounting standards applicable to such annual accounts.

Annual accounts

19. An **AIM company** must publish annual audited accounts which must be sent to its **shareholders** without delay and in any event not later than six months after the end of the financial year to which they relate.

An **AIM company** incorporated in an **EEA country** must prepare and present these accounts in accordance with **International Accounting Standards**. Where, at the end of the relevant financial period, such company is not a parent company, it may prepare and present such financial information either in accordance with **International Accounting Standards** or in accordance with the accounting and company legislation and regulations that are applicable to that company due to its country of incorporation.

An **AIM company** incorporated in a **non-EEA country** must prepare and present these accounts in accordance with either:
- **International Accounting Standards**;
- US Generally Accepted Accounting Principles;
- Canadian Generally Accepted Accounting Principles;

- Australian International Financial Reporting Standards (as issued by the Australian Accounting Standards Board); or
- Japanese Generally Accepted Accounting Principles.

The accounts produced in accordance with this rule must provide disclosure of:

- any transaction with a **related party**, whether or not previously disclosed under these rules, where any of the **class tests** exceed 0.25% and must specify the identity of the **related party** and the consideration for the transaction; and
- details of **directors' remuneration** earned in respect of the financial year by each **director** of the **AIM company** acting in such capacity during the financial year.

Publication of documents sent to shareholders

20. Any document provided by an **AIM company** to its **shareholders**, must be made available pursuant to rule 26 and its provision must be **notified**.

    An electronic copy of any such document must be sent to the **Exchange**.

Restriction on deals

21. An **AIM company** must ensure that its **directors** and **applicable employees** do not **deal** in any of its **AIM securities** during a **close period**. In addition, the purchase or early redemption by an **AIM company** of its **AIM securities** or sale of any **AIM securities** held as **treasury shares** must not be made during a **close period**.

    This rule will not apply, however, where such individuals have entered into a binding commitment prior to the **AIM company** being in such a **close period** where it was not reasonably foreseeable at the time such commitment was made that a **close period** was likely and provided that the commitment was **notified** at the time it was made.

    The **Exchange** may permit a **director** or **applicable employee** of an **AIM company** to sell its **AIM securities** during a **close period** to alleviate severe personal hardship.

Provision and disclosure of information

22. The **Exchange** may require an **AIM company** to provide it with such information in such form and within such limit as it considers appropriate. The **Exchange** may also require the **AIM company** to publish such information.

23. The **Exchange** may disclose any information in its possession as follows:

    - to co-operate with any **person** responsible for supervision or regulation of financial services or for law enforcement;
    - to enable it to discharge its legal or regulatory functions, including instituting, carrying on or defending proceedings; or
    - for any other purpose where it has the consent of the **person** from whom the information was obtained and, if different, the **person** to whom it relates.

Corporate action timetables

24. An **AIM company** must inform the **Exchange** in advance of any **notification** of the timetable for any proposed action affecting the rights of its existing **shareholders**.

25. Any amendments to the timetable proposed by the **AIM company**, including amendment to the publication details of a **notification**, must be immediately disclosed to the **Exchange**.

Company information disclosure

26. Each **AIM company** must from **admission** maintain a website on which the following information should be available, free of charge:

   ♦ a description of its business and, where it is an **investing company**, its **investing policy** and details of any **investment manager** and/or key personnel;

   ♦ the names of its **directors** and brief biographical details of each, as would normally be included in an **admission document**;

   ♦ a description of the responsibilities of the members of the board of **directors** and details of any committees of the board of **directors** and their responsibilities;

   ♦ its country of incorporation and main country of operation;

   ♦ where the **AIM company** is not incorporated in the **UK**, a statement that the rights of **shareholders** may be different from the rights of **shareholders** in a **UK** incorporated company;

   ♦ its current constitutional documents (e.g. its articles of association);

   ♦ details of any other exchanges or trading platforms on which the **AIM company** has applied or agreed to have any of its securities (including its **AIM securities**) admitted or traded;

   ♦ the number of **AIM securities** in issue (noting any held as **treasury shares**) and, insofar as it is aware, the percentage of **AIM securities** that is **not in public hands** together with the identity and percentage holdings of its **significant shareholders**. This information should be updated at least every 6 months.

   ♦ details of any restrictions on the transfer of its **AIM securities**;

   ♦ its most recent annual report published pursuant to rule 19 and all half-yearly, quarterly or similar reports published since the last annual report pursuant to rule 18;

   ♦ all **notifications** the **AIM company** has made in the past 12 months;

   ♦ its most recent **admission document** together with any circulars or similar publications sent to **shareholders** within the past 12 months; and

   ♦ details of its **nominated adviser** and other key advisers (as might normally be found in an **admission document**).

Further issues of securities following admission

Further admission documents

27. A further **admission document** will be required for an **AIM company** only when it is:

- required to issue a **Prospectus** under the **Prospectus Rules** for a further issue of **AIM securities**; or

- seeking **admission** for a new class of securities; or

- undertaking a reverse takeover under rule 14.

Omissions from further admission documents

28.   The **Exchange** may authorise the omission of information from further **admission documents** (other than a **Prospectus**) in the same circumstances as for an **applicant** under rule 4.

In addition, an **AIM company** may omit the information required by section 20 of **Annex I** from any further **admission document** (other than a **Prospectus**) provided that the **AIM company** has been complying with the requirements of these rules.

In such circumstances, the **nominated adviser** to an **AIM company** must confirm to the **Exchange** in writing that equivalent information is available publicly by reason of the **AIM company's** compliance with these rules.

Applications for further issues

29.   At least three **business days** before the expected date of **admission** of further **AIM securities** an **AIM company** must submit an **application form** and where required by rule 27, an electronic version of any further **admission document**.

Where an **AIM company** intends to issue **AIM securities** on a regular basis, the **Exchange** may permit **admission** of those securities under a **block admission** arrangement.

Under a **block admission** an **AIM company** must **notify** the information required in Schedule Six every six months.

Language

30.   All **admission documents**, any documents sent to **shareholders** and any information required by these rules must be in English.

AIM company and directors' responsibility for compliance

31.   An **AIM company** must:

- have in place sufficient procedures, resources and controls to enable it to comply with these rules;

- seek advice from its **nominated adviser** regarding its compliance with these rules whenever appropriate and take that advice into account;

- provide its **nominated adviser** with any information it reasonably requests or requires in order for that **nominated adviser** to carry out its responsibilities under these rules and the **AIM Rules for Nominated Advisers**, including any proposed changes to the board of **directors** and provision of draft **notifications** in advance;

- ensure that each of its **directors** accepts full responsibility, collectively and individually, for its compliance with these rules; and

♦ ensure that each **director** discloses to the **AIM company** without delay all information which the **AIM company** needs in order to comply with rule 17 insofar as that information is known to the **director** or could with reasonable diligence be ascertained by the **director**.

Ongoing eligibility requirements

Transferability of shares

32. An **AIM company** must ensure that its **AIM securities** are freely transferable except where:

♦ in any jurisdiction, statute or regulation places restrictions upon transferability; or

♦ the **AIM company** is seeking to limit the number of **shareholders** domiciled in a particular country to ensure that it does not become subject to statute or regulation.

Securities to be admitted

33. Only securities which have been unconditionally allotted can be **admitted** as **AIM securities**.

An **AIM company** must ensure that application is made to **admit** all securities within a class of **AIM securities**.

34. *[Deleted pursuant to AIM Notice 27]*

Retention of a broker

35. An **AIM company** must retain a **broker** at all times.

Settlement

36. An **AIM company** must ensure that appropriate settlement arrangements are in place. In particular, save where the **Exchange** otherwise agrees, **AIM securities** must be eligible for electronic settlement.

General

37. An **AIM company** must pay **AIM fees** set by the **Exchange** as soon as such payment becomes due.

38. Details of an **AIM company** contact, including an e-mail address, must be provided to the **Exchange** at the time of the application for **admission** and the **Exchange** must be immediately informed of any changes thereafter.

Nominated advisers

39. A **nominated adviser** must comply with the **AIM Rules for Nominated Advisers**,

Maintenance of orderly markets

Precautionary Suspension

40.   The **Exchange** may suspend the trading of **AIM securities** where:

♦   trading in those securities is not being conducted in an orderly manner;

♦   it considers that an **AIM company** has failed to comply with these rules;

♦   the protection of investors so requires; or

♦   the integrity and reputation of the market has been or may be impaired by dealings in those securities.

Suspensions are effected by a **dealing notice**.

Cancellation

41.   An **AIM company** which wishes the **Exchange** to **cancel admission** of its **AIM securities** must **notify** such intended **cancellation** and must separately inform the **Exchange** of its preferred **cancellation** date at least twenty **business days** prior to such date and save where the **Exchange** otherwise agrees, the **cancellation** shall be conditional upon the consent of not less than 75% of votes cast by its **shareholders** given in a general meeting.

The **Exchange** will **cancel** the **admission** of **AIM securities** where these have been suspended from trading for six months.

Cancellations are effected by a **dealing notice**.

Sanctions and appeals

Disciplinary action against an AIM company

42.   If the **Exchange** considers that an **AIM company** has contravened these rules, it may take one or more of the following measures in relation to such **AIM company**:

♦   issue a **warning notice**;

♦   fine it;

♦   censure it; or

♦   **cancel** the **admission** of its **AIM securities**; and

♦   publish the fact that it has been fined or censured and the reasons for that action.

43.   *[Deleted pursuant to AIM Notice 27]*

Disciplinary process

44.   Where the **Exchange** proposes to take any of the steps described in rule 42, the **Exchange** will follow the procedures set out in the **Disciplinary Procedures and Appeals Handbook**.

Appeals

45.   Any decision of the **Exchange** in relation to these rules may be appealed in accordance with the procedures set out in the **Disciplinary Procedures and Appeals Handbook**.

Websites

The following websites are referred to in this book:

BBC News	news.bbc.co.uk
BIS	www.bis.gov.uk
City of London Law Society	www.citysolicitors.org
Competition and Markets Authority	www.gov.uk/government/organisations/competition-and-markets-authority
Competition Commission	www.competition-commission.org.uk
Euroclear UK & Ireland	www.euroclear.com
European Commission	www.ec.europa.eu/index_en.htm
European Securities Markets Authority (ESMA)	http://esma.europa.eu
FCA	www.fca.gov.uk
FCA Handbook	www.fshandbook.info/FS/html/FCA
Financial Reporting Council	www.frc.org.uk
Hermes	www.hermes.co.uk
Institute of Chartered Secretaries and Administrators	www.icsaglobal.com
Institutional Investor Committee (IIC)	iicomm.org
Institutional Voting Information Service	www.ivis.co.uk
London Stock Exchange	www.londonstockexchange.com
National Storage Mechanism (NSM)	www.morningstar.co.uk/NSM
OFT	www.oft.gov.uk
Pre-Emption Group	www.pre-emptiongroup.org.uk
Quoted Companies Alliance	www.theqca.com
Sky News	news.sky.com
Takeover Appeal Board	www.thetakeoverappealboard.org.uk
Takeover Panel	www.thetakeoverpanel.org.uk

The following websites may also be of interest:

ABI	www.abi.org.uk
CBI	www.cbi.org.uk
Companies House	www.companieshouse.gov.uk
EEA	www.efta.int
European Union	www.europa.eu
HM Treasury	www.hm-treasury.gov.uk
Institute of Directors	www.iod.com

Investment Management Association	www.investmentfunds.org.uk
NAPF	www.napf.co.uk
NASDAQ	www.nasdaq.com
New York Stock Exchange	www.nyse.nyx.com
PIRC	www.pirc.co.uk
RNS (Regulatory News Service)	www.londonstockexchange.com

Bibliography

The Prospectus Rules, the Listing Rules and the Disclosure and Transparency Rules (Financial Conduct Authority)

The City Code on Takeovers and Mergers (The Panel on Takeovers and Mergers)

Practical Law Company (online)

LexisLibrary (online)

Westlaw (online)

Index